EXODUS

Kabbalah Publishing is a registered DBA of
The Kabbalah Centre International, Inc.

For further information:

The Kabbalah Centre
155 E. 48th St., New York, NY 10017
1062 S. Robertson Blvd., Los Angeles, CA 90035

1.800.Kabbalah
www.kabbalah.com

First Edition
November 2008
ISBN13: 978-1-57189-614-8

Design: HL Design (Hyun Min Lee) www.hldesignco.com

THE KABBALISTIC BIBLE

EXODUS

TECHNOLOGY FOR THE SOUL™

www.kabbalah.com™

EDITED BY **YEHUDA BERG**

TABLE OF CONTENTS

INTRODUCTION

For thousands of years, the sages of Kabbalah have studied the Bible and its teachings. But "study" is not really an adequate word to describe the deep relationship that has existed and will always exist between kabbalists and the biblical textv. Study, for example, typically refers to the intellectual contemplation or understanding of a book or story. This certainly has an important place in Kabbalah, but the kabbalists' deep connection with the infinitely powerful spiritual energy that the Bible embodies is much more than conventional study.

Therefore, it should come as no surprise that scholarly or historical interpretations have not so much as skimmed the surface of what is really available to us through the Bible. The Zohar, for example, states that the Bible, if taken literally, provides no more value to us than the reading of a good story. Instead, we should realize that the Bible is an encrypted document—a code in which not just information but infinite spiritual energy lies in potential, awaiting our connection. Furthermore, this energy resides less in the personalities and events that are depicted in the Bible than in the letters and phrases themselves.

Understanding this concept is very important with respect to the present volume. In English translations, the second book of the Bible is usually referred to as Exodus, and for the sake of familiarity that title is retained here. But the Hebrew word shemot literally means "names," and this term gives us a much greater understanding of the *true* power of this text and the spiritual technology that is encoded within it.

While "Exodus" refers to what happens in the book's narrative—that is, the departure from bondage in Egypt—"Names" points to a long-hidden spiritual treasure that can help us to free ourselves from those things that enslave us in our own lives. Kabbalah refers to this treasure as the 72 Names of God, an encoded technology that has the power to bring about miracles.

These are not names in the ordinary sense. Rather, they are 72 three-letter combinations formed from the text of the Story of Beshalach, which describes the miraculous parting of the Red Sea. Meditating on these 72 combinations of letters—or even just scanning them for a few minutes—connects us to invincible energies of healing, protection, positive transformation, and so much more, from infertility to removal of chaos. Without in any way diminishing the great teachings that are to be found here in the Story of Shemot, the presence of the 72 Names is an extra dimension to this second book of the Bible that can be found nowhere else—nowhere in spiritual literature, nowhere in the world, nowhere in all Creation.

In this brief space, I will not attempt to fully discuss the origin and discovery of the 72 Names or to reveal the energy of transformation they can bring to all who connect with them. For that purpose, I urge you to consult Yehuda Berg's book entitled The 72 Names of God: Technology for the Soul. Many books state that they can revolutionize the lives of their readers, but the

72 Names have been given by God to all humanity for precisely that purpose. We need only make use of these powerful tools that have been provided to us.

Most importantly, the book you now hold in your hands is the means by which these tools were provided. May it bring you the true joy and fulfillment that you deserve and that the Creator desires for you.

Rav Berg

SHEMOT

LESSON OF SHEMOT
(Exodus 1-6:1)

"And a new king arose in Egypt who did not know Joseph."

At the start of this story, the Bible speaks about whether Pharaoh knew Joseph. Is it not more important to first learn that Pharaoh was wicked? Or that Pharaoh says, "Who is God that I should listen to His voice?" Why is it important that he didn't know Joseph, when he didn't know God?

The answer is this: When a person stops appreciating other people, it is the end of his spiritual path. The minute that Pharaoh forgot Joseph—and forgot that Joseph had saved the kingdom—the road could only lead him to failure. The new king had set out to govern Egypt without acknowledging that Joseph and the Israelites had been pivotal to its prosperity and that Joseph indeed had actually saved Egypt from famine. If the new Pharaoh had been informed of this fact, he conveniently forgot it in order to justify enslaving the Children of Israel, in part because he feared that they had grown too powerful. His ingratitude to Joseph and Joseph's people gave rise to the misery that enveloped the Israelites and in the end, the Egyptians as well.

When we forget someone who has done even something small for us, we also begin to forget what the Creator does for us every single day. In our morning prayers, when we recite the blessing that helps to "open the eyes of the blind," how many of us consider the possibility that we could wake up one morning without the blessing of sight? Maybe only one in a million reaches this very high level of awareness, but if we have the desire to achieve such a consciousness, we can do so only when we appreciate the people who have helped us. In this way, we can develop appreciation for what the Creator gives us and does for us.

There is a story that Rav Berg tells about his teacher, Rav Brandwein. In 1967, following the Six Day War between Israel and several surrounding countries, a Muslim man delivered a box of grapefruit to Rav Brandwein. The man said he had waited 25 years for the day he could serve Rav Brandwein with this gift. Then he embraced Rav Brandwein and departed. When Rav asked his teacher what this meant, Rav Brandwein answered that in 1942 there had been a serious depression and this man had come to him to ask for work. At that time, only Jews could get work and there was very little to go around.

But Rav Brandwein helped the man, telling him, "From now on, your name is Isaac. I can help you get a job under that name, but you must disappear during the time of prayer." By helping this Muslim masquerade as a Jew, Rav Brandwein was able to find employment for him. For this, the man wanted to thank him and did so...25 years later. Yet in the course of our lives, how often do we forget those who have helped us, losing all memory of their goodness after even only one day. But in truth, we shouldn't want to remember just because it is the right thing to do; we should want to remember because when we appreciate other people and what they do for us, we are then able to strengthen our connection to the Light by appreciating all that the Creator does for us.

So how is it possible that Pharaoh, having been so close to Jacob and Joseph and the other brothers, suddenly did not even know who Joseph was? The Midrash (biblical commentary) reveals that there has been a long-standing controversy about the phrase "a new king arose," with some saying that there was really a new king and some saying that only the king's decrees were new. Since the Bible does not state that the king of Egypt had died and a new king had come to the throne, it implies that the old king was still alive and that only his policies had changed so that he was acting like a new king. (*Rashi, Sotah 11a*) So the phrase "who did not know" means that Pharaoh only acted as if he did not know about Joseph.

On this question, the *Zohar* explains the inner meaning:

> "And a new king arose over Egypt..." In the book of Rav Hamnuna Saba, it is written thus: "...what lies in what is written" (Exodus 1:8). None of the nations of the world or the kings in the world became secure in their dominion except for the sake of Israel. Egypt did not rule over the whole world until the children of Israel came and entered into exile there. Then they overpowered all the nations of the world only because of Israel, so they should be in exile because of them. Babylon acquired power over all the nations of the world only so that the children of Israel should be in exile because of them. Edom acquired power over all the nations of the world only so that Israel should be exiled by them. For these nations were once humble among the other nations, and were lower than all of them, and [it was] because of Israel that they became strong.

> And all of them received power only on account of Israel; for when the children of Israel were in exile among them, they immediately achieved power over all the nations in the world. When the children of Israel began their exile in Egypt, Egypt immediately experienced an elevation and their rule was strengthened above all the nations, as it is written: "And a new king arose over Egypt." "Arose" means they rose and became strong! And the angel, the minister appointed to the ruler of Egypt was strengthened, and rose up. He was given power and dominion over all who are appointed over the other nations, because dominion is given first to the one who is appointed above and then to the nation below. Therefore the verse says, "And a new king arose over Egypt." This is the one who was appointed over them. He was "new" because until then he had no dominion over the other nations, yet at that time he was raised to rule over all the nations in the world.

> "And a new king arose." Rav Yosi says, Every day God makes angels into messengers to the world, as is written: "Who makes the winds his messengers" (Psalms 104:4). It is not written 'made,' but rather "makes" in the present tense, because the Creator makes every day. At that time, then, an angel was appointed as an overseer of Egypt and this is what is written: "And a new king arose." He was definitely "new," for he was the overseer whom God had just made.
> — The Zohar, Shemot 13:75-77, 16:157

Pharaoh believed that Egypt's success was a result of his own doing, of his own wisdom, strength, and power. He chose to disregard the connection between the end of the famine and the arrival of Jacob and Joseph.

Spiritually, this reduced Pharaoh's relationship from the status of being a "friend" with Jacob and Joseph to someone who did not know them—or, in other words, know God.

It takes only a second for us to forget that everything comes from the Creator. When this happens, it's the beginning of the end for our spiritual development.

In the Torah Compilations of Rav Isaac Luria (*the Ari*), we read:

> *That is the Evil Inclination that is "an old and foolish king" (Ecclesiastes 4:13). "Over Egypt" (Exodus 1:8) means while the person is still in the womb. "Who knew not Joseph" (Ibid.) refers to ignorance of God. "And he said to his people," (Ibid. 9) who are the forces of defilement: "Behold, the people of the children of Israel," (Ibid.) who are the forces of the soul, "are more and mightier than we." What does the Evil Inclination do? "And they built for Pharaoh," who is the Evil Inclination, "treasure cities" (Ibid. 11). Pharaoh is spelled with the same letters as oreph (Eng. 'back of the neck'). The treasure cities (lit. 'cities of affliction') are the body, with which the Evil Inclination could grow stronger. Pitom is the mouth (Heb. peh), where all the desires are, and which strengthens the Evil Inclination by eating and drinking. That is Pitom, the mouth of the abyss (Heb. pi tehom). For it says, 'give, give to eat and drink.' The abyss always swallows. Ramases is the omasum (Heb. meses) that digests the food. It is an evil omasum (Heb. meses ra). "But the more" the forces of defilement and the Evil Inclinations "afflicted them"—the forces of the soul—"the more they multiplied and grew" (Ibid. 12), because as long as the body is growing, the soul enters it further.*
>
> *— Torah Compilations 4, Exodus: 2*

SYNOPSIS OF SHEMOT

The Aramaic word shemot literally means "names." Beginning with the biblical chapter of Shemot and continuing all the way to the story of Mishpatim, the Bible describes the Israelites' process of going forth from Egypt, a process that eventually culminated in the building of the *Mishkan* (the Tabernacle). This process, which takes place through the biblical stories of this and the coming weeks, is known as Shovavim, an acronym for the first letters of the titles of the those stories. At this time, the cosmos is open for teshuvah, which literally means "to return." We can return to the origin of our negative actions and correct them at the seed. According to Rav Isaac Luria, this refers especially to sexual transgressions. Simple awareness of our shortcomings is not enough; the only way to achieve this correction is through the powerful codes of the 72 Names of God.

FIRST READING - ABRAHAM - CHESED

1:1 **T**hese are the names of the sons of Israel who went to Egypt with Jacob, each with his family:

2 Reuben, Simeon, Levi and Judah; 3 Issaschar, Zebulun and Benjamin; 4 Dan and Naphtali; Gad and Asher.

5 And all the souls that were descendants of Jacob numbered seventy souls; Joseph was already in Egypt.

6 Now Joseph and all his brothers and all that generation died,

7 but the Israelites were fruitful and multiplied greatly and became exceedingly numerous, so that the land was filled with them.

FROM THE RAV

The story of Exodus is not really about an exodus, but rather, it deals with the matters leading to the exodus— that of entering into the land of Egypt. The sages have taught us that the word Egypt (Mitzrayim) does not refer to the physical land of Egypt but is instead a code for "exile" (galut). In other words, Mitzrayim refers to our personal "galut"—to the slavery of illness, pain, and suffering that we have to undergo; to those aspects of life that cause us distress and chaos.

So when Jacob enters Egypt, we understand this to mean that when we consciously choose to enter our exile—our chaos—with the understanding that this a process, it is not an end in itself, and the chaos we experience exists because of a correction (tikkun) made necessary from prior choices we have made and actions we have taken. Once we understand this exile—this chaos—for what it is, we can immediately get out of it.

The story of Shemot is about both the freedom that emerges from this chaos and how to eliminate Satan from our lives. The Zohar and Rav Isaac Luria stressed that the word Mitzrayim comes from the word mitzra, which means "to compress," "to close in," "to restrict without freedom of movement." Mitzra covers every aspect of distress and chaos in our lives in one form or another. Mitzra is a totality of chaos.

Exodus 1:5—During the period covered by this verse, Joseph and all the people who went "down" with Jacob into the land of Egypt passed away. These individuals were the true nation of Israel, the ones who were connected with the Light. But the second they entered the land of Egypt, their connection with the Light became weak and was replaced by a connection with the negative, ego-driven energy represented by Egypt. The Zohar says:

"And these are the names of the children of Israel who came into Egypt with Jacob, every man came with his household" (Exodus 1:1). "And they who are wise shall shine as the brightness of the firmament; and they who turn many to

FIRST READING - ABRAHAM - CHESED

וְאֵ֣לֶּה מ״ב שְׁמוֹת֙ בְּנֵ֣י יִשְׂרָאֵ֔ל הַבָּאִ֖ים מִצְ מִצְרָ֑יְמָה אֵ֖ת יַעֲקֹ֔ב 1 1

ד' יהוה, יאהדונהי אידהנויה אִ֣ישׁ ע״ה קנ״א קס״א וּבֵיתֽוֹ בָּֽאוּ׃ 2 רְאוּבֵ֣ן ג״פ אלהים שִׁמְע֔וֹן

לֵוִ֖י דמ״ב, מילוי ע״ב וִֽיהוּדָֽה׃ 3 יִשָּׂשכָ֥ר י״פ אל י״פ בן זְבוּלֻ֖ן וּבִנְיָמִֽן׃ 4 דָּ֥ן וְנַפְתָּלִ֖י

גָּ֥ד וְאָשֵֽׁר׃ 5 וַֽיְהִ֗י אל, יא״י כָּל־ י״ נֶ֖פֶשׁ רמ״ח ז׳ הוויות יֹצְאֵ֣י יֶֽרֶךְ־יַעֲקֹ֑ב

ד' יהוה, יאהדונהי אידהנויה שִׁבְעִ֣ים נָ֑פֶשׁ רמ״ח ז׳ הוויות וְיוֹסֵ֖ף ציון, קנאה, ר' הוויות, ה'פ אל הָיָ֥ה הָיָ֥ה

בְמִצְרָֽיִם מצר ׃ 6 וַיָּ֤מָת יוֹסֵף֙ ציון, קנאה, ר' הוויות, ה'פ אל וְכָל־ ילי אֶחָ֔יו וְכֹ֖ל ילי יהה

הַדּ֥וֹר הַהֽוּא׃ 7 וּבְנֵ֣י יִשְׂרָאֵ֗ל פָּר֧וּ וַיִּשְׁרְצ֛וּ וַיִּרְבּ֥וּ וַיַּֽעַצְמ֖וּ בִּמְאֹ֣ד מ״ה

---

righteousness like the stars for ever and ever" (Daniel 12:3). "And they who are wise," are those who observe the secret of wisdom; "shall shine," means they illuminate and sparkle with the shine of supernal Chochmah; and "as the brightness," MEANS the brightness and sparkle of the river that emanates from Eden. This is the concealed secret that is called 'firmament'" for in it are located the stars and the constellations, the sun, WHICH IS THE ZEIR ANPIN, and moon, WHICH IS THE NUKVA, and all the candles that give light, WHICH ARE ALL THE LIGHTS THAT ARE IN THE WORLDS BRIYAH, YETZIRAH AND ASIYAH. The brightness of this firmament illuminates the garden, WHICH IS MALCHUT, and the Tree of Life, WHICH IS TIFERET, stands in the center of the garden . . . In this tree, there is one radiation, WHICH IS MALCHUT, in which body, all the colors - WHITE, RED, AND GREEN, WHICH ARE THE SECRET OF THE LIGHTS OF CHESED, GEVURAH, AND TIFERET - are found. These colors rise IN OR YASHAR (DIRECT LIGHT) and descend IN OR CHOZER (RETURNING LIGHT), and they do not settle in any place except in this tree BECAUSE IT IS THE SECRET OF THE CENTRAL COLUMN. When THE LIGHTS emanate from it, FROM THE TREE, to appear in the glow that does not illuminate, THESE LIGHTS sometimes settle and SOMETIMES do not settle in it; they are sometimes found and sometimes not found, because they settle in no other place EXCEPT THIS TREE. From this tree emanated twelve tribes whose boundaries are therein contained. They descended in this splendor that does not illuminate, into the exile of Egypt with many supernal camps. This is the meaning of: "And these are the names of the children of Israel. . ."
— The Zohar, Shemot 1:1-5

Humanity's spiritual work is to rise above the temptations of the 1 Percent material World by removing the veils that are a consequence of our negative behavior and that prevent us from recognizing and connecting to the 99 Percent Reality.

In the same way, at the moment we sever our connection with the Light of the Creator, we create a space that Satan is more than happy to fill. This happens immediately. At one instant, there is Light; only an instant later, the Light is replaced by darkness.

8 Then a new king, who did not know Joseph, came to power in Egypt. 9 "Here," he said to his people, "the Israelites have become more numerous than us.

10 Come, we must deal shrewdly with them or they will become even more numerous and, if war breaks out, will join our enemies, fight against us and leave the country.

" 11 So they put slave masters over them to oppress them with forced labor, and they built Pithom and Rameses as store cities for Pharaoh.

12 But the more they were oppressed, the more they multiplied and spread; so the Egyptians came to dread the Israelites.

13 And the Egyptians worked them ruthlessly with labor.

14 They made their lives bitter with hard labor in brick and mortar and with all kinds of work in the field; in all their hard labor they used them ruthlessly.

15 The King of Egypt said to the Hebrew midwives, one whose name was Shifrah and the second whose name was Puah,

16 saying, "When you help the Hebrew women in childbirth and observe them on the delivery stool, if it is a boy, kill him; but if it is a girl, let her live."

17 The midwives, however, feared God and did not do what the King of Egypt had told them to do; they let the boys live.

וַיָּקָם

Exodus 1:8—The "new" Pharaoh, who did not know Joseph.

Another explanation of: "Now there arose a new king..." (Exodus 1:8) Rav Shimon said: On that day, permission was granted to the Minister of Egypt to be SUPERIOR over all the other nations. For we learned that before Joseph died, Egypt was not granted dominion over Israel, but when Joseph died, "Now there arose a new king." "Arose" MEANS as one who was lowly and arose, FOR ON THAT DAY THE MINISTER OF EGYPT AROSE TO BE GREAT, AS MENTIONED EARLIER.
— The Zohar, Shemot 36:281

In what sense was Pharaoh "new?" Physically, he was the same man, but he was a different person in the sense that he had forgotten all that Joseph had done for him.

There are two important messages here. First, Pharaoh can be seen as a mirror of our own nature. There is a Pharaoh present in each of us.

And second, remember that the land of Egypt had been destined for a terrible famine, but Joseph had saved both the land and Pharaoh, in the process making Pharaoh a powerful and successful ruler. Yet Pharaoh forgot about Joseph's deeds. In our own lives, we too, forget the kindness that others have shown us. The moment our benefactors fail to live according to our agenda and our expectations, we lose appreciation for the good they have done us in the past.

Eventually, the Egyptians enslaved the Israelites, forcing them to do hard physical labor. Yet later,

מְאֹד ‎מ״ה‎ וַתִּמָּלֵא הָאָרֶץ ‎אלהים דההין ע״ה‎ אֹתָם: 8 ‎וַיָּקָם‎ מֶלֶךְ־חָדָשׁ ‎ל״ב הוויות‎

עַל־מִצְרָיִם ‎מצר‎ אֲשֶׁר לֹא־יָדַע ‎ב״פ מ״ב‎ אֶת־יוֹסֵף ‎ציון, קנאה, ר הויות, ה״פ אל׳‎:

9 וַיֹּאמֶר אֶל־עַמּוֹ הִנֵּה ‎מ״ה יה‎ עַם בְּנֵי יִשְׂרָאֵל רַב ‎ע״ב ורבוע מ״ה‎ וְעָצוּם

מִמֶּנּוּ: 10 הָבָה נִתְחַכְּמָה לוֹ פֶּן־יִרְבֶּה וְהָיָה ‎יהוה‎ כִּי־תִקְרֶאנָה מִלְחָמָה

וְנוֹסַף גַּם ‎יב״ל‎ הוּא עַל־שֹׂנְאֵינוּ וְנִלְחַם־בָּנוּ וְעָלָה מִן־הָאָרֶץ ‎אלהים דההין ע״ה‎:

11 וַיָּשִׂימוּ עָלָיו שָׂרֵי מִסִּים לְמַעַן עַנֹּתוֹ בְּסִבְלֹתָם וַיִּבֶן ‎וייט‎ עָרֵי ‎ערי‎

מִסְכְּנוֹת לְפַרְעֹה אֶת־פִּתֹם וְאֶת־רַעַמְסֵס: 12 וְכַאֲשֶׁר יְעַנּוּ אֹתוֹ כֵּן

יִרְבֶּה וְכֵן יִפְרֹץ וַיָּקֻצוּ מִפְּנֵי ‎חכמה בינה‎ בְּנֵי יִשְׂרָאֵל: 13 וַיַּעֲבִדוּ מִצְרַיִם ‎מצר‎

אֶת־בְּנֵי יִשְׂרָאֵל בְּפָרֶךְ ‎ר״ת אביב‎: 14 וַיְמָרְרוּ אֶת־חַיֵּיהֶם בַּעֲבֹדָה

קָשָׁה בְּחֹמֶר וּבִלְבֵנִים וּבְכָל ‎ב״ן, לכב, יבם‎ ־עֲבֹדָה בַּשָּׂדֶה אֵת כָּל ‎ילי‎ ־

עֲבֹדָתָם אֲשֶׁר־עָבְדוּ בָהֶם בְּפָרֶךְ: 15 וַיֹּאמֶר מֶלֶךְ מִצְרַיִם ‎מצר‎

לַמְיַלְּדֹת הָעִבְרִיֹּת ‎עסמ״ב נתה ע״ה‎ אֲשֶׁר שֵׁם ‎שדי יהוה ע״ה‎ הָאַחַת שִׁפְרָה וְשֵׁם

הַשֵּׁנִית פּוּעָה ‎קס״א‎: 16 וַיֹּאמֶר בְּיַלֶּדְכֶן אֶת־הָעִבְרִיּוֹת ‎עסמ״ב נתה ע״ה‎

וּרְאִיתֶן עַל־הָאָבְנָיִם אִם ‎ע״ה מ״ב יוהך,‎ ־בֵּן הוּא ‎וַהֲמִתֶּן‎ אֹתוֹ וְאִם ‎יוהך, ע״ה מ״ב‎

־בַּת הִוא וָחָיָה: 17 וַתִּירֶאןָ הַמְיַלְּדֹת אֶת־הָאֱלֹהִים ‎מום, אהיה אדני, ילה‎ וְלֹא

עָשׂוּ כַּאֲשֶׁר דִּבֶּר ‎ראה‎ אֲלֵיהֶן מֶלֶךְ מִצְרַיִם ‎מצר‎ וַתְּחַיֶּיןָ אֶת־

הַיְלָדִים:

---

when they were wandering in the desert, the Israelites yearned for their lives of bondage in Egypt.

Why would anyone want to return to slavery? The answer lies in the challenges that accompany freedom. When the Israelites were in Egypt, they had no choices to make, no responsibilities to fulfill. We may wish for the familiarity and comfort of "spiritual slavery," no matter how physically taxing this may be, rather than looking forward to the difficulties of doing spiritual work. We might be tempted to stay in an abusive relationship or an unfulfilling job simply to avoid the painful process of self-understanding and change.

וַהֲמִתֶּן

Exodus 1:16—Pharaoh ordered the slaughter of all newborn Israelite males. The ruler's desire to control and dominate the Israelites had no limits. His hatred and selfishness allowed him to rationalize even the most despicable of acts. It is in this way that Pharaoh is a mirror for each of us, because his rationalization is a reflection of what often takes place in our own lives when we use any excuse to get what we want.

SECOND READING - ISAAC - GEVURAH

¹⁸ Then the King of Egypt called the midwives and asked them, "Why have you done this? Why have you let the boys live?"

¹⁹ The midwives answered Pharaoh, "Hebrew women are not like Egyptian women; they are vigorous and give birth before the midwives arrive."

²⁰ So God was kind to the midwives and the people increased and became even more numerous.

²¹ And because the midwives feared God, He made for them houses.

²² Then Pharaoh commanded all of his people, saying: "Every boy that is born you must throw into the Nile, but let every girl live."

^{2:1} Now, a man of the house of Levi married a woman of the house of Levi,

² and she became pregnant and gave birth to a son. When she saw that he was a fine child, she hid him for three months.

³ But when she could hide him no longer, she got a papyrus basket for him and coated it with tar and pitch. Then she placed the child in it and put it among the reeds along the bank of the Nile.

⁴ His sister stood at a distance to see what would happen to him.

⁵ Then Pharaoh's daughter went down to the Nile to bathe, and her maids were walking along the river bank. She saw the basket among the reeds and sent her slave girl to get it.

Exodus 2:1—Moses was born.

A man named Amram, grandson of Levi, married Jochebed, his aunt, and Moses was born from that union. Once again, we see an illicit marriage resulting in the birth of a very righteous and important individual. In truth, such a marriage can be a device to fool Satan. Satan's perception of these unions is that no good can come from them. Yet the Light can be concealed within

such a marriage, enabling a very high soul to enter the world without interference from Satan. Commentary says that when Moses was born, the whole room was filled with Light. (*Megillah 14a*) The *Zohar* repeats this same idea:

Rav Yosi said: Jochebed saw the light of the Shechinah that shone in Moses. For at the time that he was born, the entire house was filled with light, as is written: "And when she saw that he was a goodly son." Everything was included in him; HE CONTAINED THE LIGHT OF

SECOND READING - ISAAC - GEVURAH

18 וַיִּקְרָא ב"פ קס"א ± ה' אותיות מֶלֶךְ־מִצְרַיִם מצר לַמְיַלְּדֹת וַיֹּאמֶר לָהֶן עיה אלהים, מום מַדּוּעַ עֲשִׂיתֶן הַדָּבָר ראה הַזֶּה והו וַתְּחַיֶּיןָ אֶת־הַיְלָדִים:

19 וַתֹּאמַרְןָ הַמְיַלְּדֹת אֶל־פַּרְעֹה כִּי לֹא כַנָּשִׁים הַמִּצְרִיֹּת מצר הָעִבְרִיֹּת עסמ"ב נתה עיה כִּי־חָיוֹת הֵנָּה מ"ה יה בְּטֶרֶם רמ"ח עיה תָּבוֹא אֲלֵהֶן הַמְיַלֶּדֶת וְיָלָדוּ:

20 וַיֵּיטֶב אֱלֹהִים מום, אהיה אדני, ילה לַמְיַלְּדֹת וַיִּרֶב הָעָם וַיַּעַצְמוּ מְאֹד מ"ה:

21 וַיְהִי אל, ייא"י כִּי־יָרְאוּ הַמְיַלְּדֹת אֶת־הָאֱלֹהִים מום, אהיה אדני, ילה וַיַּעַשׂ לָהֶם בָּתִּים:

22 וַיְצַו פַּרְעֹה לְכָל־ יה אדני עַמּוֹ לֵאמֹר כָּל־ ילי הַבֵּן הַיִּלּוֹד הַיְאֹרָה תַּשְׁלִיכֻהוּ וְכָל־ ילי הַבַּת תְּחַיּוּן:

1 2 וַיֵּלֶךְ כלי אִישׁ עיה קנ"א קס"א מִבֵּית ב"פ ראה לֵוִי דמב, מלוי עיב וַיִּקַּח וזם אֶת־בַּת־לֵוִי דמב, מלוי עב:

2 וַתַּהַר הָאִשָּׁה וַתֵּלֶד בֵּן וַתֵּרֶא אֹתוֹ והו כִּי־טוֹב הוּא וַתִּצְפְּנֵהוּ שְׁלֹשָׁה יְרָחִים:

3 וְלֹא־יָכְלָה עוֹד הַצְּפִינוֹ וַתִּקַּח רבוע אהיה דאלפין ־לוֹ תֵּבַת גֹּמֶא וַתַּחְמְרָה בַחֵמָר וּבַזָּפֶת וַתָּשֶׂם בָּהּ ב"פ עיע אֶת־הַיֶּלֶד וַתָּשֶׂם ב"פ עיע בַּסּוּף עַל־שְׂפַת הַיְאֹר כף ויו זין ויו:

4 וַתֵּתַצַּב אֲחֹתוֹ מֵרָחֹק לְדֵעָה מ"ה מַה ־יֵּעָשֶׂה לוֹ:

5 וַתֵּרֶד בַּת־פַּרְעֹה לִרְחֹץ עַל־הַיְאֹר כף ויו זין ויו וְנַעֲרֹתֶיהָ הֹלְכֹת עַל־יַד הַיְאֹר כף ויו זין ויו וַתֵּרֶא אֶת־הַתֵּבָה בְּתוֹךְ הַסּוּף וַתִּשְׁלַח אֶת־אֲמָתָהּ

THE SHECHINAH, AND ALSO, AS WAS WRITTEN EARLIER, HE WAS BORN CIRCUMCISED.
— The Zohar, Shemot 19:187

Moses came into the world as the individual chosen to help those of his generation. Yet Moses is also present in every generation as a channel to help each of us overcome our personal bondage.

Pharaoh had ordered the death of every newborn male Israelite. To protect Moses, his mother and the midwife—Miriam, the sister of Moses— placed him in a basket and floated it down the Nile. For us, that basket is the *Zohar*, and it is our protection. We can be surrounded by all types of negativity, but when we clothe ourselves in the Light of the *Zohar*, we have nothing to fear. The *Midrash* says that when Moses was cast into the water, Pharaoh's astrologers said, "Their redeemer has been thrown into the water." Forthwith, the edict that all male infants were to be thrown in the Nile was revoked. (*Sotah* 12b)

6 She opened it and saw the baby. He was crying, and she felt sorry for him. "This is one of the Hebrew babies," she said.

7 Then his sister asked Pharaoh's daughter, "Shall I go and get one of the Hebrew women to nurse the baby for you?"

8 "Yes, go," she answered. And the girl went and got the baby's mother.

9 Pharaoh's daughter said to her, "Take this baby and nurse him for me, and I will pay you." So the woman took the baby and nursed him.

10 When the child grew older, she took him to Pharaoh's daughter and he became her son. She named him Moses, saying, "I drew him out of the water."

THIRD READING - JACOB - TIFERET

11 And it was in those days, after Moses had grown up, he went out to his brethren and saw their labor. He saw an Egyptian beating a Hebrew, one of his brethren.

12 Glancing this way and that and seeing no one, he killed the Egyptian and hid him in the sand.

וַתִּקְרָא

Exodus 2:5—Pharaoh's daughter rescued Moses from the Nile. Although Batya, Pharaoh's daughter, was from a negative family and lived in Pharaoh's house, she was a sharing person. This teaches us that no matter where we come from or what our ancestry might be, we have the potential to be sharing and proactive. In fact, each of us has the responsibility, as well as the potential, to be a sharing human being, to live proactively, and to grow spiritually. Pharaoh's daughter could have found many excuses—her fear of being caught, her social position, even her ancestry—not to rescue Moses. But she made the correct choice, and each of us must do the same. We cannot place responsibility on anyone else. Once we come to this world, our tikkun (spiritual correction) is our own, and we must become completely willing to walk the path of our own spiritual destiny.

Pharaoh's daughter brought Moses to a wet nurse, but Moses rejected her. She tried several other Egyptian wet nurses, but he rejected them all because of their negativity. Finally, Miriam, the sister of Moses, was summoned to find a woman from whom Moses would accept breast milk. She recommended her own mother, Jochebed, who was then able to breast-feed her son and raise him for the first few years of his life.

The child's unwillingness to accept nourishment from none but the most enlightened woman reminds us that we need to seek out wisdom from those who are most qualified to give it. Spiritual wisdom is how the Creator sends us our spiritual nourishment, and the search for our proper companions on this earth is a part of that process.

וַתִּפְתַּח֙ וַתִּרְאֵ֣הוּ אֶת־הַיֶּ֔לֶד וְהִנֵּה־נַ֖עַר בֹּכֶ֑ה 6 : וַתִּקְחֵ֖הוּ

וַתַּחְמֹ֣ל עָלָ֔יו וַתֹּ֕אמֶר מִיַּלְדֵ֥י הָֽעִבְרִ֖ים זֶֽה׃ 7 וַתֹּ֣אמֶר אֲחֹתוֹ֮ אֶל־בַּת־

פַּרְעֹה֒ הַאֵלֵ֗ךְ וְקָרָ֤אתִי לָךְ֙ אִשָּׁ֣ה מֵינֶ֔קֶת מִ֖ן הָֽעִבְרִיֹּ֑ת וְתֵינִ֥ק

לָ֖ךְ אֶת־הַיָּֽלֶד׃ 8 וַתֹּֽאמֶר־לָ֥הּ בַּת־פַּרְעֹ֖ה לֵ֑כִי וַתֵּ֨לֶךְ֙ הָֽעַלְמָ֔ה

וַתִּקְרָ֖א אֶת־אֵ֥ם הַיָּֽלֶד׃ 9 וַתֹּ֧אמֶר לָ֣הּ בַּת־פַּרְעֹ֗ה הֵילִ֜יכִי

אֶת־הַיֶּ֤לֶד הַזֶּה֙ וְהֵינִקִ֣הוּ לִ֔י וַֽאֲנִ֖י אֶתֵּ֣ן אֶת־שְׂכָרֵ֑ךְ וַתִּקַּ֧ח

הָֽאִשָּׁ֛ה הַיֶּ֖לֶד וַתְּנִיקֵֽהוּ׃ 10 וַיִּגְדַּ֣ל הַיֶּ֗לֶד וַתְּבִאֵ֙הוּ֙ לְבַת־

פַּרְעֹ֔ה וַֽיְהִי־לָ֖הּ לְבֵ֑ן וַתִּקְרָ֤א שְׁמוֹ֙ מֹשֶׁ֔ה וַתֹּ֕אמֶר

כִּ֥י מִן־הַמַּ֖יִם מְשִׁיתִֽהוּ׃

THIRD READING - JACOB - TIFERET

11 וַיְהִ֣י בַּיָּמִ֣ים הָהֵ֗ם וַיִּגְדַּ֤ל מֹשֶׁה֙ וַיֵּצֵ֣א אֶל־אֶחָ֔יו

וַיַּ֖רְא בְּסִבְלֹתָ֑ם וַיַּרְא֙ אִ֣ישׁ מִצְרִ֔י

מַכֶּ֥ה אִֽישׁ־עִבְרִ֖י מֵֽאֶחָֽיו׃ 12 וַיִּ֤פֶן כֹּה֙ וָכֹ֔ה וַיַּ֖רְא

מְשִׁיתִֽהוּ

Exodus 2:10—Pharaoh's daughter named the infant Moses (in Aramaic, Moshe, spelled by the letters *Mem, Shin, Hei*). We are told that she actually named him Monios, which means "he was drawn out of the water," and Moshe is the translation of that word. (*Ibn Ezra*) Many names have been given to this great leader by various people, but the only name that has persisted is Moses. This teaches us that we should never dismiss what anyone says just because we don't respect them. If Pharaoh's daughter, who came from a negative family and a negative people, could name this most remarkable soul, we should be aware that positive messages can come to us from anywhere. We should never disregard a message simply because of our perception of the messenger.

וַיִּגְדַּל

Exodus 2:11–Moses grew up in Pharaoh's house, but when he reached maturity, he decided he wanted to feel the pain of the people. When we have abundance, security, and happiness, we should always remain aware that there are people in the world who don't have our blessings. We must always keep in mind that others are suffering. Even if we cannot share with them directly, we can at least feel for them and care about them. This is what Moses achieved by feeling the pain of his people.

¹³ *The next day he went out and saw two Hebrews fighting. He asked the one in the wrong, "Why are you hitting your fellow Hebrew?"*

¹⁴ *The man said, "Who made you ruler and judge over us? Are you thinking of killing me as you killed the Egyptian?" Then Moses was afraid and thought, "What I did must have become known."*

¹⁵ *When Pharaoh heard of this, he asked that Moses be killed, but Moses fled from Pharaoh and went to live in Midian, where he sat down by a well.*

¹⁶ *Now the priest of Midian had seven daughters, and they came to draw water and fill the troughs to water their father's flock.*

¹⁷ *Some shepherds came along and drove them away, but Moses got up and came to their rescue and watered their flock.*

¹⁸ *When the girls returned to Reuel, their father, he asked them, "Why have you returned so quickly today?"*

¹⁹ *They answered, "An Egyptian rescued us from the shepherds. He even drew water for us and watered the flock."*

²⁰ *He asked his daughters, "And where is he? Why did you leave him? Call him so that we may break bread."*

וַיִּרֶךְ

Exodus 2:12—Moses killed the Egyptian who was tormenting an Israelite slave.

After Cain killed Abel, Cain was destined to return to the world in three different lifetimes. Jethro (Moses's father-in-law) was Cain's first reincarnation, the Egyptian in this passage was the second, and Korach was the third. In this verse, the Egyptian represents total negativity: There was no Light in him whatsoever. The *Zohar* says:

> *"And he looked this way [Heb. koh (Kaf-Hei)] and that (koh)" (Exodust 2:12). SINCE he saw in these fifty letters that Israel proclaim twice every day in the prayer: "Shema Israel" (Hear O Israel), that contains Kaf-Hei (=25) and Kaf-Hei LETTERS twice; but he did not see THAT THE EGYPTIAN WOULD BE*

SAYING THEM. "And he looked Koh and Koh." Rav Aba said: THE FIRST Koh IS BECAUSE he looked to see whoever possessed good deeds, and THE SECOND Koh IS BECAUSE he desired to perceive whether a righteous son would emerge from him. Immediately, "he saw that there was no man." He saw by the Holy Spirit that no righteous son would emerge from him.
> — *The Zohar, Shemot 23:207*

Moses was the reincarnation of Abel; therefore, as part of his own cleansing, Cain reincarnated as the Egyptian. By returning to this physical domain and in turn being killed by Moses, Cain was completing his correction.

According to the sages, Moses did not physically kill the Egyptian. Rather, he used the 72 Names of God—specifically, the *Kaf, Hei, Tav* (כ, ה, ת) and the *Yud, Kaf, Shin* (י,כ,ש) (from the *Ana Beko'ach* prayer)—and the awesome Light

אלף למד יהוה **כִּי אֵין אִישׁ** ע"ה קנ"א קס"א **וַיַּ֤ךְ** ע"ה מהש **אֶת־הַמִּצְרִ֔י** מהש **וַֽיִּטְמְנֵ֖הוּ בַּחֽוֹל׃**

רבוע אהיה ע"ה **וַיֵּצֵא֙** ע"ה **בַּיּ֣וֹם** נגד, זן, מזבח **הַשֵּׁנִ֔י וְהִנֵּ֛ה** מ"ה יה **שְׁנֵֽי־אֲנָשִׁ֥ים** 13

עִבְרִ֖ים נִצִּ֑ים **וַיֹּ֙אמֶר֙ לָֽרָשָׁ֔ע** כהת **לָ֥מָּה תַכֶּ֖ה רֵעֶֽךָ׃** 14 **וַיֹּ֗אמֶר מִ֣י** ילי

שָׂמְךָ֞ **לְאִ֣ישׁ** ע"ה קנ"א קס"א; ס"ת יכ"ש **שַׂ֤ר** אלהים דיודין ורבוע אלהים **וְשֹׁפֵט֙ עָלֵ֔ינוּ** ריבוע ס"ג

הַֽלְהָרְגֵ֙נִי֙ אַתָּ֣ה אֹמֵ֔ר כַּֽאֲשֶׁ֥ר הָרַ֖גְתָּ אֶת־הַמִּצְרִ֑י מהש **וַיִּירָ֤א מֹשֶׁה֙**

מהש, אל שדי **וַיֹּאמַ֔ר אָכֵ֖ן** יהוה מ"ה **נוֹדַ֥ע הַדָּבָֽר׃** ראה 15 **וַיִּשְׁמַ֤ע פַּרְעֹה֙ אֶת־**

הַדָּבָ֣ר ראה **הַזֶּ֔ה** והו **וַיְבַקֵּ֖שׁ לַֽהֲרֹ֣ג אֶת־מֹשֶׁ֑ה** מהע, אל שדי **וַיִּבְרַ֤ח מֹשֶׁה֙**

מהע, אל שדי **מִפְּנֵ֣י** חכמה בינה **פַרְעֹ֔ה וַיֵּ֥שֶׁב בְּאֶֽרֶץ** אלהים דאלפין **מִדְיָ֖ן וַיֵּ֥שֶׁב עַל־**

הַבְּאֵֽר׃ קנ"א ב"ן 16 **וּלְכֹהֵ֥ן** מלה **מִדְיָ֖ן** ע"ב ואלהים דיודין **שֶׁ֣בַע** בְּנ֑וֹת **וַתָּבֹ֣אנָה**

וַתִּדְלֶ֗נָה וַתְּמַלֶּ֙אנָה֙ אֶת־הָ֣רְהָטִ֔ים לְהַשְׁק֖וֹת צֹ֥אן מלוי אהיה דיודין ע"ה **אֲבִיהֶֽן׃**

17 **וַיָּבֹ֥אוּ הָֽרֹעִ֖ים וַיְגָֽרְשׁ֑וּם וַיָּ֤קָם מֹשֶׁה֙** מהע, אל שדי **וַיּ֣וֹשִׁעָ֔ן וַיַּ֖שְׁקְ אֶת־**

צֹאנָֽם׃ 18 **וַתָּבֹ֕אנָה אֶל־רְעוּאֵ֖ל אֲבִיהֶ֑ן וַיֹּ֕אמֶר מַדּ֛וּעַ מִֽהַרְתֶּ֥ן בֹּ֖א**

הַיּֽוֹם׃ ע"ה = נגד, זן, מזבח 19 **וַתֹּאמַ֕רְןָ אִ֣ישׁ** ע"ה קנ"א קס"א **מִצְרִ֔י** מצר **הִצִּילָ֖נוּ מִיַּ֥ד**

---

revealed through these Names caused the Egyptian to simply disappear.

The next day, Moses saw two Israelites fighting. Moses called the instigator a wicked person, someone who is filled with hatred for no reason.

וַיִּבְרַח

Exodus 2:15—Moses was forced to leave Egypt. After Moses learned that Pharaoh wanted to kill him—because of what happened to the Egyptian—he went to Midian, where he met his soul mate, Tziporah (whom he would later marry), at her father's well. How do we know that she was his soul mate? She was Jethro's daughter, and the Ari teaches us that Jethro was the first reincarnation of Cain, just as Moses was a reincarnation of Abel.

When Cain was born of Eve, he was born with a "twin sister," a sister who was joined to him. Abel was born with two such twin sisters.

The *Zohar* says:

> As long as the woman [Eve] was adjoined to his side, the man [Adam] was alone. Afterwards two came out AND MATED, and seven emerged, NAMELY, CAIN WITH HIS TWIN SISTER, AND ABEL WITH HIS TWO TWIN SISTERS, WHICH MAKES FIVE. TOGETHER WITH ADAM AND EVE THEY ARE SEVEN.
> — The Zohar, Tazria 11:44

Therefore, Cain was born full of jealousy for his brother because Abel had one more twin sister than he did, and this feeling overwhelmed him in the end. By giving his daughter to Moses, Jethro (as the reincarnated Cain) was correcting the jealousy that Cain had once felt for Abel.

²¹ Moses agreed to stay with the man, who gave his daughter Tziporah to Moses in marriage.

²² Tziporah gave birth to a son, and Moses named him Gershom, saying, "I have become a stranger in a foreign land."

²³ During that long period, the King of Egypt died. The Israelites moaned in their slavery and cried out, and their cry for help went up to God because of their slavery.

²⁴ God heard their moaning and He remembered His Covenant with Abraham, with Isaac and with Jacob.

²⁵ So God looked on the Israelites and knew about them.

FOURTH READING - MOSES - NETZACH

3:¹ Now Moses was tending the flock of Jethro, his father-in-law, the priest of Midian, and he led the flock to the desert and came to the mountain of God in Horeb.

וַיְּמָת

Exodus 2:23—Pharaoh died.
Whenever a ruler dies in the material world, it is because the angel who rules him or her is being replaced. Whenever a change occurs in the Upper Worlds, the change must also manifest itself on Earth. So a change in national leadership, such as an election in our present day, indicates that there has been a change in the relevant ruling angel in the Upper Worlds.

"And it came to pass in the course of those many days" (Exodus 2:23). Rav Yehoshua of Sachnin said it was at the end of their exile that Israel were subjugated with all kinds of labor. "In the course of those many days:" They were many to THE SOJOURN OF Israel in Egypt, MEANING THAT THE END HAD ARRIVED. Since the end of their exile was complete, it is written: "And the king of Egypt died." (Ibid.). What does this mean? IT IS that the Minister of Egypt was lowered from his high position and fell from his glory. THEREFORE, THE TORAH SAYS ABOUT HIM, "AND

THE KING OF EGYPT DIED," SINCE HIS DESCENT WAS CONSIDERED BY HIM AS DEATH. Since the king of Egypt who was their minister fell, the Holy One, blessed be He, remembered Israel and heard their prayers.
    — The *Zohar*, Shemot 48:340

הַסְּנֶה בֹּעֵר

Exodus 3:2—The Burning Bush
When Moses was beginning his spiritual transformation, God used the burning bush to initiate the process of elevating his soul. The nature of Moses was part-angel and part-human. He became the physical channel to draw down the Light, which is why he was able to stand on Mount Sinai. As part-angel, he was capable of surviving forty days and forty nights without eating, and yet still be an active participant in the physical world.

The burning bush reveals this principle. It represents the concept of mind over matter, of the soul rising above the physical realm.

"And the angel of God appeared to him in a flame of fire." (Exodus 3:2). HE ASKS:

הָרֹעִים וַיְגָ֣רְשׁ֔וּם דָּלֹה דָּלָה֙ טל אלהים, מום וַיַּ֖שְׁקְ אֶת־הַצֹּֽאן לָנוּ טל

20 וַיֹּ֥אמֶר אֶל־בְּנֹתָ֖יו וְאַיּ֑וֹ לָ֤מָּה זֶּה֙ עֲזַבְתֶּ֣ן אֶת־הָאִ֔ישׁ מלוי אהיה דיודין ע"ה

21 וַיֹּ֥ואֶל מֹשֶׁ֖ה מהע, אל שדי לָשֶׁ֣בֶת קִרְאֶ֥ן ל֖וֹ וְיֹ֥אכַל לָֽחֶם: ג"פ יהוה י"פ אדם

אֶת־הָאִ֑ישׁ אל שדי ו"פ אדם; ר"ת לאה וַיִּתֵּ֛ן י"פ מלוי ע"ב אֶת־צִפֹּרָ֥ה בִתּ֖וֹ לְמֹשֶֽׁה: מהע, אל שדי

22 וַתֵּ֣לֶד בֵּ֔ן וַיִּקְרָ֥א עם ה' אותיות = ב"פ קס"א אֶת־שְׁמ֖וֹ מהע ע"ה, אל שדי ע"ה גֵּרְשֹׁ֑ם כִּ֣י

אָמַ֔ר גֵּ֣ר בין קנ"א הָיִ֔יתִי אלהים דאלפין בְּאֶ֖רֶץ נָכְרִיָּֽה: 23 וַיְהִי֩ אל, ייא" בַיָּמִ֨ים הָֽרַבִּ֜ים הָהֵ֗ם [וַיָּ֣מָת] מצ מֶ֣לֶךְ מִצְרַ֔יִם וַיֵּאָנְח֧וּ בְנֵֽי־יִשְׂרָאֵ֛ל מִן־הָעֲבֹדָ֖ה

אלהים ע"ה, מום ע"ה וַיִּזְעָ֑קוּ וַתַּ֧עַל שַׁוְעָתָ֛ם אֶל־הָאֱלֹהִ֖ים מום, אהיה אדני ; ילה מִן־

הָעֲבֹדָֽה: אלהים ע"ה, מום ע"ה 24 וַיִּשְׁמַ֥ע אֱלֹהִ֖ים מום, אהיה אדני; ילה אֶת־נַאֲקָתָ֑ם

וַיִּזְכֹּ֤ר אֱלֹהִים֙ מום, אהיה אדני; ילה אֶת־בְּרִית֔וֹ אֶת־אַבְרָהָ֖ם רמזח, ויס אל אֶת־יִצְחָ֥ק

וְֽאֶת־יַעֲקֹֽב: ריו בן י"פ יהוה, יאהדונהי אירהנויה 25 וַיַּ֥רְא אלף למד יהוה אֱלֹהִ֖ים מום, אהיה אדני; ילה אֶת־

בְּנֵ֣י יִשְׂרָאֵ֑ל וַיֵּ֖דַע בי"פ מ"ב אֱלֹהִֽים: מום, אהיה אדני; ילה:

FOURTH READING - MOSES - NETZACH

3 1 וּמֹשֶׁ֗ה מהע, אל שדי הָיָ֥ה יהה רֹעֶ֛ה רהע אֶת־צֹ֥אן מלוי אהיה דיודין ע"ה יִתְר֥וֹ

חֹתְנ֖וֹ כֹּהֵ֣ן מלה מִדְיָ֑ן וַיִּנְהַ֤ג אכדטם אֶת־הַצֹּאן֙ מלוי אהיה דיודין ע"ה קס"א קס"א קנ"א קמ"ג

אַחַ֣ר הַמִּדְבָּ֔ר וַיָּבֹ֛א אֶל־הַ֥ר הָאֱלֹהִ֖ים רבוע אלהים + ה' אותיות מום, אהיה אדני; ילה

חֹרֵֽבָה: ע"ה ריו 2 וַיֵּ֠רָא אלף למד יהוה מַלְאַ֨ךְ יְהֹוָ֥ה יאהדונהי יְהֹוִה־אָֽהֹדֹנֹהִיֵלָ֛יו אֵלָ֛יו בְּלַבַּת־

אֵ֖שׁ אלהים דיודין ע"ה אל אדני מִתּ֣וֹךְ הַסְּנֶ֑ה קן וַיַּ֗רְא אלף למד יהוה וְהִנֵּ֤ה יהוה יהוה מצפץ יה אדני

[הַסְּנֶה֙] קן בֹּעֵ֣ר מ"ה יה בָּאֵ֔שׁ וְהַסְּנֶ֖ה אלהים דיודין ע"ה אֵינֶ֥נּוּ קן אֻכָּֽל: 3 וַיֹּ֣אמֶר

Why did He appear to Moses in a flame of fire, and not to the other prophets? Rav Yehuda said: Moses is not like the other prophets, for we learned that everyone who approaches the fire is burnt by it. Yet Moses approached it and was not burnt,

as it is written: "And Moses drew near to the thick darkness where the Lord was," (Exodus 20:18) and, "And the angel of God appeared to him in a flame of fire out of the midst of a bush."
— The Zohar, Shemot 55:390

2 *There the angel of the Lord appeared to him in flames of fire from within a bush. Moses saw that though the bush was on fire it was not consumed.*

3 *So Moses said, "I will go over and see this great sight—why the bush doesn't burn."*

4 *When the Lord saw that he had gone over to look, God called to him from within the bush, "Moses! Moses!" And he said, "Here I am."*

5 *And He said, "Do not come any closer. Remove your sandals from your feet, for the place where you are standing is holy ground."*

6 *Then He said, "I am the God of your father, the God of Abraham, the God of Isaac and the God of Jacob." And Moses hid his face, because he was afraid to look at God.*

7 *The Lord said, "I have indeed seen the misery of my people in Egypt. I have heard their crying out from their oppressors and I know about their suffering.*

8 *So I have come down to rescue them from the hand of the Egyptians and to bring them up out of that land into a good and spacious land, a land of milk and honey— the home of the Canaanites, Hittites, Amorites, Perizzites, Hivites and Jebusites.*

9 *And now the cry of the Israelites has reached me, and I have seen the way the Egyptians are oppressing them.*

10 *So now, go. I am sending you to Pharaoh to bring my people, the Israelites, out of Egypt."*

11 *But Moses said to God, "Who am I that I should go to Pharaoh and bring the Israelites out of Egypt?"*

12 *And God said, "I will be with you. And this will be the sign to you that it is I who have sent you: When you have brought the people out of Egypt, you will worship God on this mountain."*

13 *Moses said to God, "Suppose I go to the Israelites and say to them, 'The God of your fathers has sent me to you,' and they ask me, 'What is his name?' Then what shall I tell them?"*

14 *God said to Moses, "I am who I am. This is what you are to say to the Israelites: 'I AM has sent me to you.' "*

15 *God also said to Moses, "Say to the Israelites, 'The Lord, the God of your fathers—the God of Abraham, the God of Isaac and the God of Jacob—has sent me to you.' This is My Name forever, by which I am to be remembered from generation to generation.*

מֹשֶׁה אָסֻרָה־נָּא וְאֶרְאֶה אֶת־הַמַּרְאֶה הַגָּדֹל הַזֶּה מַדּוּעַ לֹא־יִבְעַר הַסְּנֶה: 4 וַיַּרְא יְהוָה כִּי סָר לִרְאוֹת וַיִּקְרָא אֵלָיו אֱלֹהִים מִתּוֹךְ הַסְּנֶה וַיֹּאמֶר מֹשֶׁה מֹשֶׁה וַיֹּאמֶר הִנֵּנִי: 5 וַיֹּאמֶר אַל־תִּקְרַב הֲלֹם שַׁל־נְעָלֶיךָ מֵעַל רַגְלֶיךָ כִּי הַמָּקוֹם אֲשֶׁר אַתָּה עוֹמֵד עָלָיו אַדְמַת־קֹדֶשׁ הוּא: 6 וַיֹּאמֶר אָנֹכִי אֱלֹהֵי אָבִיךָ אֱלֹהֵי אַבְרָהָם אֱלֹהֵי יִצְחָק וֵאלֹהֵי יַעֲקֹב וַיַּסְתֵּר מֹשֶׁה פָּנָיו כִּי יָרֵא מֵהַבִּיט אֶל־הָאֱלֹהִים: 7 וַיֹּאמֶר יְהוָה רָאֹה רָאִיתִי אֶת־עֳנִי עַמִּי אֲשֶׁר בְּמִצְרָיִם וְאֶת־צַעֲקָתָם שָׁמַעְתִּי מִפְּנֵי נֹגְשָׂיו כִּי יָדַעְתִּי אֶת־מַכְאֹבָיו: 8 וָאֵרֵד לְהַצִּילוֹ מִיַּד מִצְרַיִם וּלְהַעֲלֹתוֹ מִן־הָאָרֶץ הַהִוא אֶל־אֶרֶץ טוֹבָה וּרְחָבָה אֶל־אֶרֶץ זָבַת חָלָב וּדְבָשׁ אֶל־מְקוֹם הַכְּנַעֲנִי וְהַחִתִּי וְהָאֱמֹרִי וְהַפְּרִזִּי וְהַחִוִּי וְהַיְבוּסִי: 9 וְעַתָּה הִנֵּה צַעֲקַת בְּנֵי־יִשְׂרָאֵל בָּאָה אֵלָי וְגַם־רָאִיתִי אֶת־הַלַּחַץ אֲשֶׁר מִצְרַיִם לֹחֲצִים אֹתָם: 10 וְעַתָּה לְכָה וְאֶשְׁלָחֲךָ אֶל־פַּרְעֹה וְהוֹצֵא אֶת־עַמִּי בְנֵי־יִשְׂרָאֵל מִמִּצְרָיִם: 11 וַיֹּאמֶר מֹשֶׁה אֶל־הָאֱלֹהִים מִי אָנֹכִי כִּי אֵלֵךְ אֶל־פַּרְעֹה וְכִי אוֹצִיא אֶת־בְּנֵי יִשְׂרָאֵל מִמִּצְרָיִם: 12 וַיֹּאמֶר כִּי־אֶהְיֶה עִמָּךְ וְזֶה־לְּךָ הָאוֹת כִּי אָנֹכִי שְׁלַחְתִּיךָ בְּהוֹצִיאֲךָ אֶת־הָעָם מִמִּצְרַיִם תַּעַבְדוּן אֶת־הָאֱלֹהִים עַל הָהָר הַזֶּה: 13 וַיֹּאמֶר מֹשֶׁה אֶל־הָאֱלֹהִים הִנֵּה אָנֹכִי בָא אֶל־בְּנֵי יִשְׂרָאֵל וְאָמַרְתִּי לָהֶם אֱלֹהֵי אֲבוֹתֵיכֶם שְׁלָחַנִי אֲלֵיכֶם וְאָמְרוּ־

FIFTH READING - AARON - HOD

[16] *Go, assemble the elders of Israel and say to them, 'The Lord, the God of your fathers—the God of Abraham, Isaac and Jacob—appeared to me and said: I have watched over you and have seen what has been done to you in Egypt.*

[17] *And I will bring you up out of your misery in Egypt into the land of the Canaanites, Hittites, Amorites, Perizzites, Hivites and Jebusites—a land of milk and honey.'*

[18] *They will listen to you. Then you and the elders are to go to the King of Egypt and say to him, 'The Lord, the God of the Hebrews, has met with us. Let us take a three-day journey into the desert to offer sacrifices to the Lord, our God.'*

[19] *But I know that the King of Egypt will not let you go unless a mighty hand compels him.*

[20] *So I will stretch out My Hand and strike the Egyptians with all the wonders that I will perform among them. After that, he will let you go.*

אֶהְיֶה אֲשֶׁר אֶהְיֶה

Exodus 3:14—I am that I am.

When God told Moses that He was charging him with the task of freeing the Israelites from slavery in Egypt, Moses asked, "If they ask me Your Name, what will I say to them?" And God gave him this Name: *Alef, Hei, Yud*, and *Hei* (א, ה, י, ה). We should note that every situation brings forth a different Name for God; for example, there is one Name for Judgment (אלוקים) and another for Mercy (י, ה, ו, ה). This teaches us that when we seek a connection to the Creator, we must know what connection we're seeking. From the many different connections that we can make to God, we must choose the Name that is most appropriate to our purpose.

זְקְנֵי

Exodus 3:16— God told Moses to gather the elders of Israel.

God instructed Moses to consult with the elders, reassuring him that what he was about to say to them would be believed. To achieve the Israelites' redemption, Moses needed to have both the trust and the corresponding affirmative actions of the Israelites—even a soul as great as Moses could not do all the work for them. Similarly, when Rav Shimon undertook the great work of writing the *Zohar*, this by itself could not bring about the Redemption. Many people must study Kabbalah and the *Zohar* and put it into action to bring about the final transformation of humanity.

In *Pirkei Avot* (The *Ethics of the Fathers*), we read:

> "Ben Hei Hei said:
> Effort is its own reward.
> We are here to do.
> And through doing to learn;and
> through learning to know;
> and through knowing to
> experience wonder;
> and through wonder to attain
> wisdom;
> and through wisdom to find
> simplicity;
> and through simplicity to give
> attention;
> and through attention
> to see what needs to be done..."
> — Pirkei Avot 5:27

לִי מַה־שְּׁמוֹ מ״ה מהטע ע״ה, אל שדי ע״ה מַה־ מ״ה, ס״ת יהוה אָמַר אֲלֵהֶם׃ 14 וַיֹּאמֶר

אֱלֹהִים מום, אהיה אדני; ילה אֶל־מֹשֶׁה מהטע, אל שדי **אֶהְיֶה** בי״ט **אֲשֶׁר אֶהְיֶה** בי״ט

וַיֹּאמֶר כֹּה היי תֹאמַר לִבְנֵי יִשְׂרָאֵל אֶהְיֶה בי״ט שְׁלָחַנִי אֲלֵיכֶם׃ 15 וַיֹּאמֶר

עוֹד אֱלֹהִים מום, אהיה אדני ; ילה אֶל־מֹשֶׁה מהטע, אל שדי כֹּה־תֹאמַר אֶל־בְּנֵי

יִשְׂרָאֵל יְהֹוָהאהדונהיאדני אֱלֹהֵי דמב, ילה אֲבֹתֵיכֶם אֱלֹהֵי דמב, ילה אַבְרָהָם

אֱלֹהֵי אל וח״פ רמ״וז, דמב, ילה יִצְחָק ד״פ ב״ן וֵאלֹהֵי לכב, דמב, ילה יַעֲקֹב ד״פ יהוה, יאהדונהי אידהנויה

שְׁלָחַנִי אֲלֵיכֶם זֶה־שְּׁמִי רביע ע״ב ורביע ס״ג לְעֹלָם ריבוע ס״ג ב ־ י׳ אותיות וְזֶה זִכְרִי

לְדֹר דֹּר׃

FIFTH READING - AARON - HOD

16 לֵךְ וְאָסַפְתָּ אֶת־ זִקְנֵי יִשְׂרָאֵל וְאָמַרְתָּ אֲלֵהֶם יְהֹוָהאהדונהיאדני אֱלֹהֵי

אֲבֹתֵיכֶם נִרְאָה ע״ב ורביע ע״ב אֵלַי אֱלֹהֵי דמב, ילה אַבְרָהָם רמ״וז, וח״פ אל

יִצְחָק ד״פ ב״ן וְיַעֲקֹב ד״פ יהוה, יאהדונהי אידהנויה לֵאמֹר פָּקֹד רביע ע״ב פָּקַדְתִּי אֶתְכֶם

וְאֶת־הֶעָשׂוּי לָכֶם בְּמִצְרָיִם מצר׃ 17 וָאֹמַר אַעֲלֶה אֶתְכֶם מֵעֳנִי ריבוע מ״ה

מִצְרַיִם מצר אֶל־אֶרֶץ אלהים דאלפין הַכְּנַעֲנִי וְהַחִתִּי וְהָאֱמֹרִי וְהַפְּרִזִּי וְהַחִוִּי

וְהַיְבוּסִי אֶל־אֶרֶץ אלהים דאלפין זָבַת חָלָב וּדְבָשׁ׃ 18 וְשָׁמְעוּ לְקֹלֶךָ וּבָאתָ

אַתָּה וְזִקְנֵי יִשְׂרָאֵל אֶל־מֶלֶךְ מִצְרַיִם מצר וַאֲמַרְתֶּם אֵלָיו יְהֹוָהאהדונהיאדני

אֱלֹהֵי דמב, ילה הָעִבְרִיִּים נִקְרָה ריבוע ס״ג עָלֵינוּ וְעַתָּה נֵלֲכָה־נָּא דֶּרֶךְ ב״פ יב״ק

שְׁלֹשֶׁת יָמִים נכך בַּמִּדְבָּר רמ״וז, וח״פ אל וְנִזְבְּחָה לַיהֹוָהאהדונהיאדני אֱלֹהֵינוּ ילה׃

19 וַאֲנִי אני, ב״פ אהיה יהוה יָדַעְתִּי כִּי לֹא־יִתֵּן אֶתְכֶם מֶלֶךְ מִצְרַיִם מצר לַהֲלֹךְ

וְלֹא בְּיָד וָזָקָה׃ 20 וְשָׁלַחְתִּי אֶת־יָדִי וְהִכֵּיתִי אֶת־מִצְרַיִם מצר בְּכֹל

ב״ן, לכב, יבם נִפְלְאֹתַי אֲשֶׁר אֶעֱשֶׂה בְּקִרְבּוֹ וְאַחֲרֵי־כֵן יְשַׁלַּח אֶתְכֶם׃

21 וְנָתַתִּי אֶת־חֵן מוזי הָעָם־הַזֶּה הזו בְּעֵינֵי ריבוע מ״ה מִצְרָיִם מצר וְהָיָה יהוה כִּי

²¹ *And I will make the Egyptians favorably disposed toward this people, so that when you leave you will not go empty-handed.*

²² *Every woman is to ask her neighbor and any woman living in her house for articles of silver and gold, and for clothing, which you will put on your sons and daughters. And so you will take advantage of the Egyptians."*

4:¹ *Moses answered, "What if they do not believe me or listen to me and say, 'The Lord did not appear to you?' "*

² *Then the Lord said to him, "What is that in your hand?" "A staff," he replied.*

³ *The Lord said, "Throw it on the ground." Moses threw it on the ground and it became a snake, and he ran from it.*

⁴ *Then the Lord said to him, "Reach out your hand and take it by the tail." So Moses reached out and took hold of the snake and it turned back into a staff in his hand.*

⁵ *"This," said the Lord, "is so that they may believe that the Lord, the God of their fathers—the God of Abraham, the God of Isaac and the God of Jacob—has appeared to you."*

⁶ *Then the Lord continued saying, "Put your hand on your chest." So Moses put his hand on his chest, and when he took it out, it was leprous, like snow.*

⁷ *"Now put it back on your chest," He said. So Moses put his hand back on his chest, and when he took it out, it returned to flesh.*

⁸ *"If they do not believe you or pay attention to the first miraculous sign, they may believe the latter.*

⁹ *But if they do not believe these two signs or listen to you, take some water from the Nile and pour it on the dry ground. The water you take from the river will become blood on the ground."*

¹⁰ *Moses said to the Lord, "Lord, I have never been an orator, neither yesterday, or the*

וְשָׁאֲלָה

Exodus 3:22—God told the Israelites to borrow silver and gold from the Egyptians. This verse leads us to ask a question: "Since the Israelites had no plans to return to Egypt, why does the Bible say 'borrow'?"

The answer is that everything we "have" is borrowed—nothing is truly ours. When we "lose" what was in our possession, it is because we have failed to appreciate the fact that we never "owned" it in the first place. By sharing continually, we can ignite in our consciousness the realization that nothing comes to us from our own merit and that whatever we have comes to us from the Light.

תֵלְכ֖וּן לֹ֥א תֵלְכ֖וּ רֵיקָֽם: 22 וְשָׁאֲלָ֨ה אִשָּׁ֤ה מִשְּׁכֶנְתָּהּ֙ וּמִגָּרַ֣ת בֵּיתָ֔הּ

כְּלֵי־כֶסֶף֙ וּכְלֵ֣י כלי זהב זָהָ֔ב וּשְׂמָלֹ֑ת וְשַׂמְתֶּ֗ם עַל־בְּנֵיכֶם֙ וְעַל־בְּנֹ֣תֵיכֶ֔ם

וְנִצַּלְתֶּ֖ם אֶת־מִצְרָֽיִם: מצר 1 וַיַּ֤עַן מֹשֶׁה֙ מהעו, אל שדי וַיֹּ֔אמֶר וְהֵן֙ לֹֽא־

יַאֲמִ֣ינוּ לִ֔י וְלֹ֥א יִשְׁמְע֖וּ בְּקֹלִ֑י כִּ֣י יֹֽאמְר֔וּ לֹֽא־נִרְאָ֥ה ע״ב ורבוע ע״ב אֵלֶ֖יךָ אני

יְהוָֽה: אהניאהדונהי 2 וַיֹּ֧אמֶר אֵלָ֛יו יְהוָ֖ה אהניאהדונהי מַ֣ה־זֶּ֑ה (כתיב: מזה) בְיָדֶ֖ךָ בוכו

וַיֹּ֥אמֶר מַטֶּֽה: 3 וַיֹּ֨אמֶר֙ הַשְׁלִיכֵ֣הוּ אַ֔רְצָה אלהים דההן וַיַּשְׁלִיכֵ֖הוּ אַ֑רְצָה

אלהים דההן וַיְהִ֥י אל, ייא״י לְנָחָ֖שׁ שדי ורבוע אהיה מהעו, אל שדי וַיָּ֥נָס מֹשֶׁ֖ה מִפָּנָֽיו:

4 וַיֹּ֤אמֶר יְהוָה֙ אהניאהדונהי אֶל־מֹשֶׁ֔ה מהעו, אל שדי שְׁלַח֙ יָֽדְךָ֔ בוכו וֶֽאֱחֹ֖ז בִּזְנָב֑וֹ

וַיִּשְׁלַ֤ח יָדוֹ֙ וַיַּ֣חֲזֶק בּ֔וֹ וַיְהִ֥י אל, ייא״י לְמַטֶּ֖ה בְּכַפּֽוֹ: 5 לְמַ֣עַן יַאֲמִ֔ינוּ כִּֽי־

נִרְאָ֥ה ע״ב ורבוע ע״ב אֵלֶ֖יךָ אני יְהוָ֣ה אהניאהדונהי אֱלֹהֵ֣י דמב, ילה אֲבֹתָ֑ם אֱלֹהֵ֤י

אַבְרָהָם֙ דמב, ילה רמז, וו״ז, וז״פ אל אֱלֹהֵ֣י דמב, ילה יִצְחָ֔ק ד״פ בן וֵֽאלֹהֵ֖י דמב, ילה יַֽעֲקֹ֑ב

ד״פ יהוה, יאהדונהי אדהנוהי אידהנויה 6 וַיֹּ֩אמֶר֩ יְהוָ֨ה אהניאהדונהי ל֜וֹ ע֣וֹד הָֽבֵא־נָ֤א יָֽדְךָ֙ בוכו

בְּחֵיקֶ֔ךָ וַיָּבֵ֥א יָד֖וֹ בְּחֵיק֑וֹ וַיּ֣וֹצִאָ֔הּ וְהִנֵּ֥ה מ׳ה יה יָד֖וֹ מְצֹרַ֥עַת כַּשָּֽׁלֶג: ג״פ אלף

7 וַיֹּ֗אמֶר הָשֵׁ֤ב יָֽדְךָ֙ בוכו אֶל־חֵיקֶ֔ךָ וַיָּ֥שֶׁב יָד֖וֹ אֶל־חֵיק֑וֹ וַיּֽוֹצִאָהּ֙ מֵֽחֵיק֔וֹ

וְהִנֵּה מ׳ה יה שָׁ֖בָה כִּבְשָׂר֑וֹ: 8 וְהָיָה֙ יהוה יאהדונהי אִם־ יוהך, ע״ה מ״ב לֹ֣א יַאֲמִ֣ינוּ לָ֔ךְ

וְלֹ֣א יִשְׁמְע֔וּ לְקֹ֖ל הָאֹ֣ת הָרִאשׁ֑וֹן וְהֶֽאֱמִ֔ינוּ לְקֹ֖ל הָאֹ֥ת הָאַֽחֲרֽוֹן: 9 וְהָיָ֡ה

יהוה אם יוהך, ע״ה מ״ב אִם־לֹ֣א יַֽאֲמִ֡ינוּ גַּם֩ יג״ל לִשְׁנֵ֨י הָֽאֹת֜וֹת הָאֵ֗לֶּה וְלֹ֤א יִשְׁמְעוּן֙

לְקֹלֶ֔ךָ וְלָֽקַחְתָּ֙ מִמֵּימֵ֣י הַיְאֹ֔ר כף ויו זין ויו וְשָֽׁפַכְתָּ֖ הַיַּבָּשָׁ֑ה וְהָי֤וּ הַמַּ֨יִם֙

מַטֶּה

Exodus 4:2—God told Moses to perform miracles.

Moses asked God, "What if they don't believe me?" And in fact, even after the Israelites had seen the miracles in Egypt, in the desert, and on Mount Sinai, their certainty wavered, not because anything was lacking in the miracles but because of a weakness in the people themselves. To truly take in the Light revealed by a miracle, we must be sincerely committed to growing and sharing. Otherwise, we don't even notice the miracles that are constantly being revealed around us! We need to wake up and appreciate these many miracles in order to achieve spiritual growth.

day before, nor since you have spoken to your servant. I am slow of speech and tongue."

[11] The Lord said to him, "Who gave man his mouth? Who makes him deaf or mute? Who gives him sight or makes him blind? Is it not I, the Lord?

[12] Now go; I will help you speak and will teach you what to say." [13] But Moses said, "Lord, please send someone by your hand."

[14] Then the Lord's anger burned against Moses and he said, "What about your brother, Aaron the Levite? I know he is well spoken. He is already on his way to meet you, and his heart will be glad when he sees you.

[15] You shall speak to him and put words in his mouth; I will help both of you speak and will teach you what to do.

[16] He will speak to the people for you, and it will be as if he were your mouth and as if you were God to him. [17] But take this staff in your hand so you can perform miraculous signs with it."

כָבֵד־פֶּה

Exodus 4:10—Moses was fearful that because of his speech impediment he would be unable to speak with Pharaoh. The *Zohar* explains the following:

> *Come and see: It is written: "Behold, the children of Israel did not listen to me; how than shall Pharaoh hear me, who am of uncircumcised lips" (Exodus 6:12). HE ASKS, What is "who am of uncircumcised lips?" At first it was written: "I am not an eloquent man... but I am slow of speech and of a slow tongue" to which the Holy One, blessed be He, replied, "Who gave man a mouth" and He said, "And I will be with your mouth" (Exodus 4:10-12). Can you imagine that it was not so? Yet now he says, "I am of uncircumcised lips." If so, where is the previous assurance of the Holy One, blessed be He, to him, NAMELY THE ASSURANCE, "AND I WILL BE WITH YOUR MOUTH . . ."*
> — *The Zohar, Va'era 7:66*

God told Moses that only He gives people the ability to speak; however, eventually, He told Moses to let Aaron do the talking for him.

Often, when we begin an important task or assignment, our minds are filled with all sorts of ego-based, self-serving agendas. But Moses displayed no ego when he questioned God; he simply wanted to be sure that the best possible person was entrusted with the critical task of persuading Pharaoh to let the Israelites leave Egypt.

הַמַּטֶה

Exodus 4:17—God gave Moses the staff with which he would achieve the coming miracles. On one side, the staff had the 72 Names of God engraved on it, and on the other side, the 42-letter Name of God (the *Ana Beko'ach*). The *Zohar* says:

> *What is the reason that the staff of Aaron and not the staff of Moses was SELECTED FOR THIS? HE ANSWERS: The staff of Moses was especially holy because the Holy Name was carved into it in the Supernal Garden of EDEN, and God did not want to defile it with these staffs of the sorcerers, BECAUSE IT HAD TO SWALLOW THEM, AS WRITTEN: "AND THE STAFF OF AARON SWALLOWED THEIR STAFFS."*
> — *The Zohar, Va'era 15:17*

אֲשֶׁר תִּקָּח רבוע אהיה דאלפין מִן־הַיְאֹר כף ויו זין ויו וְהָיוּ לְדָם רבוע אהיה בַּיַּבָּשֶׁת:

10 וַיֹּאמֶר מֹשֶׁה מהע, אל שדי אֶל־יְהֹוָהאדני בִּי אֲדֹנָי ללה לֹא אִישׁ דְּבָרִים רבוע קס"א אָנֹכִי ראה גַּם יגל מִתְּמוֹל יגל גַּם מִשִּׁלְשֹׁם יגל גַּם מֵאָז דַּבֶּרְךָ ראה אֶל־עַבְדֶּךָ פוי כִּי כְבַד־פֶּה מילה, ע"ה אלהים, ע"ה מום וּכְבַד

11 לָשׁוֹן אלהים פשוט ודירין ע"ה אָנֹכִי ע"ה: וַיֹּאמֶר יְהֹוָהאדני אֵלָיו מִי יְלי שָׂם פֶּה מילה, ע"ה אלהים ע"ה מום לָאָדָם מ"ה אוֹ מִי יָלי יָשׂוּם אִלֵּם מ"ה כ"ו אוֹ חֵרֵשׁ אוֹ פִקֵּחַ מ"ה קמ"ג אוֹ עִוֵּר הֲלֹא אָנֹכִי יְהֹוָהאדני איע:

12 וְעַתָּה לֵךְ וְאָנֹכִי איע אֶהְיֶה בי"ט עִם־פִּיךָ וְהוֹרֵיתִיךָ אֲשֶׁר תְּדַבֵּר ראה:

13 וַיֹּאמֶר בִּי אֲדֹנָי ללה שְׁלַח־נָא בְּיַד־תִּשְׁלָח:

14 וַיִּחַר־אַף יְהֹוָהאדני בְּמֹשֶׁה מהע, אל שדי וַיֹּאמֶר הֲלֹא אַהֲרֹן ע"ב ורבוע ע"ה אָחִיךָ הַלֵּוִי למב, מלוי ע"ב יָדַעְתִּי כִי־דַבֵּר ראה יְדַבֵּר ראה הוּא וְגַם יגל הִנֵּה מ"ה ה־ הוּא יֹצֵא לִקְרָאתֶךָ וְרָאֲךָ וְשָׂמַח בְּלִבּוֹ:

15 וְדִבַּרְתָּ אֵלָיו וְשַׂמְתָּ אֶת־הַדְּבָרִים ראה בְּפִיו וְאָנֹכִי איע אֶהְיֶה בי"ט עִם־פִּיךָ וְעִם־פִּיהוּ וְהוֹרֵיתִי אֶתְכֶם אֵת אֲשֶׁר תַּעֲשׂוּן:

16 וְדִבֶּר ראה הוּא לְךָ אֶל־הָעָם וְהָיָה יהוה הוּא יִהְיֶה יי לְּךָ לְפֶה מילה, ע"ה אלהים וְאַתָּה תִּהְיֶה־לּוֹ לֵאלֹהִים מום, אהיה אדני ; ילה:

17 וְאֶת־הַמַּטֶּה הֲוָה תִּקָּח רבוע אהיה דאלפין בְּיָדֶךָ אֲשֶׁר תַּעֲשֶׂה־בּוֹ בכו אֶת־הָאֹתֹת:

And it is for them that the staff of Moses was engraved with the Holy Name on both sides, the one of mercy of judgment, THE GRADE OF Israel, and the other judgment of judgment, THE GRADE OF Jacob.
-- The Zohar, Vayechi 1:14

The Midrash tells us that God created the staff after creating absolutely everything else. When Adam was banished from the Garden of Eden, he took the staff and went out to till the land. Eventually, Noah inherited the staff, leaving it to Shem and his descendants, until it finally reached Abraham, who gave it to Isaac. Jacob took it along with him when he fled to Padan-Aram, and when he went to Egypt, he gave it to Joseph. The staff later belonged to Jethro the Midianite. After Jethro left Egypt, he planted the staff in his garden and said that whoever could extract it from the ground would marry his daughter Tziporah. Many men of Canaan tried to pull it out by the roots because they wanted to marry Tziporah, but no one was successful. The staff remained in the garden until Moses came and pulled it out, and so Jethro gave his daughter Tziporah to Moses. Thus we can see that from the time of Creation, this staff had been intended for the purpose of achieving these miracles.

SIXTH READING - JOSEPH - YESOD

18 Then Moses went back to Jethro his father-in-law and said to him, "Let me go back to my brethren in Egypt to see if any of them are still alive." Jethro said, "Go in peace."

19 Now the Lord had said to Moses in Midian, "Go back to Egypt, for all the men who wanted to kill you are dead."

20 So Moses took his wife and sons, put them on a donkey and started back to Egypt. And Moses took the staff of God in his hand.

21 The Lord said to Moses, "When you return to Egypt, see that you perform before Pharaoh all the wonders I have given you the power to do. But I will harden his heart so that he will not let the people go.

22 Then say to Pharaoh, 'This is what the Lord says: Israel is my firstborn son,

23 and I told you, "Let My son go, so he may worship Me." But you refused to let him go; so I will kill your firstborn son.' "

24 At a lodging place on the way, the Lord met [Moses] and desired to kill him.

25 But Tziporah took a flint knife, cut off her son's foreskin and touched (Moses') feet with it. "Surely you are a bridegroom of blood to me," she said.

26 So the Lord let him alone. Then she said "bridegroom of blood," in regard to the circumcision.

27 The Lord said to Aaron, "Go into the desert to meet Moses." So he met Moses at the mountain of God and kissed him.

מִצְרַיִם

Exodus 4:19—Moses was told to return to Egypt. Because he was wanted for the death of the Egyptian, Moses left Egypt for forty years. This period represents the process of transformation and cleansing that Moses achieved at the end of that time, enabling him to return to Egypt. All of us must go through a period of cleansing to allow us to accomplish the great deeds for which we have come into the world.

הֱמִיתוֹ

Exodus 4:24— While Moses was returning to Egypt, the Angel of Death hovered over him with the intention of killing him.

Why did this happen? It was because the newborn son of Moses was eight days old, ready for his circumcision. (For eight days, the Satan is part of a newborn child, but after the eighth day, the Satan is separated from the child, through the act of circumcision.) By briefly postponing

SIXTH READING - JOSEPH - YESOD

וַיֵּ֤לֶךְ כלי מֹשֶׁה֙ מהע, אל שדי וַיָּ֣שָׁב ׀ אֶל־יֶ֣תֶר וְחֹֽתְנ֔וֹ וַיֹּ֤אמֶר לוֹ֙ אֵ֣לְכָה נָּ֗א 18
וְאָשׁ֨וּבָה֙ אֶל־אַחַ֣י אֲשֶׁר־בְּמִצְרַ֔יִם מצר וְאֶרְאֶ֖ה הַעוֹדָ֣ם חַיִּ֑ים בינה עה
וַיֹּ֧אמֶר יִתְר֛וֹ קס״א קס״א קנ״א קמ״ג לְמֹשֶׁ֖ה מהע, אל שדי לֵ֥ךְ לְשָׁלֽוֹם: 19 וַיֹּ֨אמֶר
יְהֹוָ֤האהדונהי אֶל־מֹשֶׁה֙ מהע, אל שדי בְּמִדְיָ֔ן לֵ֖ךְ שֻׁ֣ב מִצְרָ֑יִם מצר כִּי־מֵ֨תוּ֙
כָּל־ יל׳ הָ֣אֲנָשִׁ֔ים הַֽמְבַקְשִׁ֖ים אֶת־נַפְשֶֽׁךָ: 20 וַיִּקַּ֨ח וזאם מֹשֶׁ֜ה מהע, אל שדי
אֶת־אִשְׁתּ֣וֹ וְאֶת־בָּנָ֗יו וַיַּרְכִּבֵם֙ עַל־הַ֣חֲמֹ֔ר וַיָּ֖שָׁב אַ֣רְצָה אלהים דההן
מִצְרָ֑יִם מצר וַיִּקַּ֥ח וזאם מֹשֶׁ֛ה אֶת־מַטֵּ֥ה הָאֱלֹהִ֖ים מום, אהיה אדני ; ילה
בְּיָדֽוֹ: 21 וַיֹּ֣אמֶר יְהֹוָה֮אהדונהי אֶל־מֹשֶׁה֒ מהע, אל שדי בְּלֶכְתְּךָ֙ לָשׁ֣וּב
מִצְרַ֔יְמָה מצר רְאֵ֗ה ראה כָּל־ ילי הַמֹּֽפְתִים֙ אֲשֶׁר־שַׂ֣מְתִּי בְיָדֶ֔ךָ בוכו וַֽעֲשִׂיתָ֖ם
לִפְנֵ֣י וחכמה בינה פַרְעֹ֑ה וַֽאֲנִי֙ אני, ב״פ אהיה יהוה אֲחַזֵּ֣ק פהל אֶת־לִבּ֔וֹ וְלֹ֥א יְשַׁלַּ֖ח
אֶת־הָעָֽם: 22 וְאָֽמַרְתָּ֖ אֶל־פַּרְעֹ֑ה כֹּ֚ה יי אָמַ֣ר יְהֹוָ֔האהדונהי בְּנִ֥י בְכֹרִ֖י
יִשְׂרָאֵֽל: 23 וָֽאֹמַ֣ר אֵלֶ֗יךָ אני שַׁלַּ֤ח אֶת־בְּנִי֙ וְיַֽעַבְדֵ֔נִי וַתְּמָאֵ֖ן לְשַׁלְּח֑וֹ
הִנֵּה֙ מ״ה יה אָֽנֹכִ֣י איע אל, ייא״י הֹרֵ֔ג אֶת־בִּנְךָ֖ בְּכֹרֶֽךָ: 24 וַיְהִ֥י ב״פ יב״ק בַדֶּ֖רֶךְ
בַּמָּל֑וֹן וַיִּפְגְּשֵׁ֣הוּ יְהֹוָ֔האהדונהי וַיְבַקֵּ֖שׁ הֲמִיתֽוֹ: 25 וַתִּקַּ֨ח צִפֹּרָ֜ה צֹ֗ר
וַתִּכְרֹת֙ אֶת־עָרְלַ֣ת בְּנָ֔הּ וַתַּגַּ֖ע לְרַגְלָ֑יו וַתֹּ֕אמֶר כִּ֧י חֲתַן־דָּמִ֛ים אַתָּ֖ה
לִֽי: 26 וַיִּ֖רֶף מִמֶּ֑נּוּ אָ֚ז אָֽמְרָ֔ה חֲתַ֥ן דָּמִ֖ים לַמּוּלֹֽת: 27 וַיֹּ֤אמֶר יְהֹוָה֙אהדונהי

---

the circumcision in order to flee from Pharaoh, Moses allowed the Angel of Death to remain in the child. It was Tziporah, the wife of Moses, who actually performed the circumcision so that the Angel of Death might be expelled. This shows that everyone, even Moses, is capable of making a mistake. We should always be aware of this potential for error within ourselves. The Zohar says:

Under these spirits are those called 'foreskin,' the foreskin of the shoot, the foreskin of the branch. Above them there is a chieftain called 'Gezar Dinaya' (Eng. 'verdict'). He is appointed over those who do not observe these two foreskins of trees, and those who delay the circumcision of their sons. For that the serpent wanted to kill the son of Moses, until Tziporah circumcised him, as it is written, ". . . and cut off the foreskin of her son. . ." (Exodus 4:25).
— The Zohar, Pekudei 58:901

28 And Moses told Aaron everything the Lord had said, about sending him and about all the miraculous signs He had commanded him to perform.

29 Moses and Aaron went and brought together all the elders of the Israelites.

30 And Aaron told them everything the Lord had said to Moses. He also performed the signs before the people.

31 And they believed. And when they heard that the Lord was concerned about them and had seen their misery, they bowed down and worshipped.

SEVENTH READING - DAVID - MALCHUT

5:1 Afterward Moses and Aaron went to Pharaoh and said, "This is what the Lord, the God of Israel, says: 'Let My people go, so that they may hold a festival to Me in the desert.' "

2 Pharaoh said, "Who is the Lord, that I should listen to his voice and let Israel go? I do not know the Lord and I will not let Israel go."

3 Then they said, "The God of the Hebrews has met with us. Now let us take a three-day journey into the desert to offer sacrifices to the Lord, our God, or he may strike us with plagues or with the sword."

4 But the King of Egypt said to them, "Moses and Aaron, why are you taking the people away from their labor? Get back to your work!"

5 Then Pharaoh said, "Look, the people of the land are now numerous, and you are stopping them from working."

וַיִּפְגְּשֵׁהוּ

Exodus 4:27—Aaron, the brother of Moses, came to meet him.

To ensure that the task of freeing the Israelites was completed, it was crucial that neither Aaron nor Moses experience jealousy or ego-driven resentments. The *Midrash* says that *Aaron and Moses were complete equals.* (*Bereishis Rabbah 1:15*) They had to cooperate by remaining constantly aware that their sacred task had been entrusted to them by the Creator. Each of us should remember that, wherever we may be and whoever we are, our position and our tasks are those that the Light of the Creator has chosen for us. No matter how seemingly high or low our work may be, we should remember that we are working not for ourselves but for the Light of the Creator.

פַּרְעֹה

Exodus 5:1—Moses and Aaron came to Pharaoh. While Moses was still in Midian, God had appeared to him at the Burning Bush and had

אֶל־אַהֲרֹן ע״ב רבוע ע״ב לֵךְ לִקְרַאת מֹשֶׁה מהע, אל שדי הַמִּדְבָּרָה וַיֵּלֶךְ כלי

וַיִּפְגְּשֵׁהוּ בְּהַר אור, רז הָאֱלֹהִים מום, אהיה אדני ; ילה וַיִּשַּׁק־לוֹ׃ 28 וַיַּגֵּד מֹשֶׁה

לְאַהֲרֹן מהע, אל שדי ע״ב רבוע ע״ב אֵת כָּל־ יל דִּבְרֵי יְהֹוָהּאדניהאדני ראה אֲשֶׁר

שְׁלָחוֹ וְאֵת כָּל־ יל הָאֹתֹת אֲשֶׁר צִוָּהוּ׃ 29 וַיֵּלֶךְ כלי מֹשֶׁה מהע, אל שדי

וְאַהֲרֹן ע״ב רבוע ע״ב וַיַּאַסְפוּ אֶת־כָּל־ יל זִקְנֵי בְּנֵי יִשְׂרָאֵל׃ 30 וַיְדַבֵּר ראה

אַהֲרֹן ע״ב רבוע ע״ב אֵת כָּל־ יל הַדְּבָרִים אֲשֶׁר־דִּבֶּר ראה יְהֹוָהּאדניהאדני ראה

אֶל־מֹשֶׁה מהע, אל שדי וַיַּעַשׂ הָאֹתֹת לְעֵינֵי ריבוע מ״ה הָעָם׃ 31 וַיַּאֲמֵן הָעָם

וַיִּשְׁמְעוּ כִּי־פָקַד רבוע ע״ב יְהֹוָהּאדניהאדני אֶת־בְּנֵי יִשְׂרָאֵל וְכִי רָאָה ראה

אֶת־עָנְיָם ריבוע מ״ה וַיִּקְּדוּ וַיִּשְׁתַּחֲוּוּ׃

SEVENTH READING - DAVID - MALCHUT

5 וְאַחַר בָּאוּ מֹשֶׁה מהע, אל שדי וְאַהֲרֹן ע״ב רבוע ע״ב וַיַּאמְרוּ אֶל־פַּרְעֹה

כֹּה הי ־אָמַר יְהֹוָהּאדניהאדני אֱלֹהֵי דמב, ילה יִשְׂרָאֵל שַׁלַּח אֶת־עַמִּי וְיָחֹגּוּ

לִי בַּמִּדְבָּר רמ״ח, וז״פ אל׃ 2 וַיֹּאמֶר פַּרְעֹה מִי ילי יְהֹוָהּאדניהאדני אֲשֶׁר אֶשְׁמַע

בְּקֹלוֹ לְשַׁלַּח אֶת־יִשְׂרָאֵל לֹא יָדַעְתִּי אֶת־ יְהֹוָהּאדניהאדני וְגַם יגל אֶת־

יִשְׂרָאֵל לֹא אֲשַׁלֵּחַ׃ 3 וַיֹּאמְרוּ אֱלֹהֵי דמב, ילה הָעִבְרִים נִקְרָא עָלֵינוּ

ריבוע ס״ג נֵלֲכָה נָּא דֶרֶךְ ב״פ יב״ק שְׁלֹשֶׁת יָמִים גלך בַּמִּדְבָּר רמ״ח, וז״פ אל וְנִזְבְּחָה

---

shown him miraculous signs and wonders that he could perform for the Israelites in Egypt to persuade them of the truth of God's message. Moses returned to Egypt and did as he had been commanded. The Israelites were overjoyed and optimistic because of the revelation that God had given Moses. Eagerly, the people made plans for their departure from Egypt. But when Moses and Aaron appeared before Pharaoh and asked him to let the Israelites go, Pharaoh refused. In fact, he increased the workload of the Israelites and even refused to provide them with the materials needed to perform their slave labor.

Whenever we enter a situation that gives us an opportunity to grow and transform, we must first pass through some difficulty or test. This is especially true in our spiritual work. To achieve our next and higher level, we must undergo a rite of passage that causes us to ask, "Do I really want to continue with this?" We must make the conscious choice of saying "yes," and then make the necessary effort to go forward.

6 That same day Pharaoh gave this order to the slave drivers and foremen in charge of the people:

7 "You are no longer to supply the people with straw for making bricks like yesterday and the day before; let them go and gather their own straw.

8 But require them to make the same number of bricks as before; don't reduce the quota. They are lazy; that is why they are crying out, 'Let us go and sacrifice to our God.'

9 Make the work harder for the men so that they keep working and pay no attention to lies."

10 Then the slave drivers and the foremen went out and said to the people, "This is what Pharaoh says: 'I will not give you any more straw.

11 Go and get your own straw wherever you can find it, but your work will not be reduced at all.' "

12 So the people scattered all over Egypt to gather stubble to use for straw.

13 The slave drivers kept pressing them, saying, "Complete the work required of you for each day, just as when you had straw."

14 The Israelite foremen appointed by Pharaoh's slave drivers were beaten and were asked, "Why didn't you meet your quota of bricks yesterday or today, as before?"

15 Then the Israelite foremen went and appealed to Pharaoh: "Why have you treated your servants this way?

16 Your servants are given no straw, yet we are told to make do. Your servants are being beaten, but the fault is with your own people."

17 Pharaoh said, "Lazy, that's what you are—lazy! That is why you keep saying, 'Let us go and sacrifice to the Lord.'

18 Now get to work. You will not be given any straw, yet you must produce your full quota of bricks."

19 The Israelite foremen realized they were in trouble when they were told, "You are not to reduce the number of bricks required of you for each day." 20 They found Moses and Aaron waiting to meet them when they left Pharaoh.

21 And they said, "May the Lord look upon you and judge you! You have made us a stench to Pharaoh and his officials and have put a sword in their hand to kill us."

לַיהֹוֶׄהֹ֒אֱלֹהֵ֫ינוּ אהֹדֹנהי יֶלה פֶּן־יִפְגָּעֵ֫נוּ בַּדֶּ֫בֶר ראה אֹ֣ו בֶחָ֑רֶב רבוע ס"ג ורבוע אהיה:

4 וַיֹּ֨אמֶר אֲלֵהֶ֜ם מֶ֣לֶךְ מִצְרַ֗יִם מצר לָ֤מָּה מֹשֶׁ֣ה מהע, אל שדי וְאַהֲרֹ֔ן ע"ב רבוע ע"ב תַּפְרִ֖יעוּ אֶת־הָעָ֣ם מִֽמַּעֲשָׂ֑יו לְכ֖וּ לְסִבְלֹתֵיכֶֽם: 5 וַיֹּ֣אמֶר פַּרְעֹ֔ה הֵן־רַבִּ֥ים עַתָּ֖ה עַ֣ם הָאָ֑רֶץ אלהים דההין ע"ה וְהִשְׁבַּתֶּ֥ם אֹתָ֖ם מִסִּבְלֹתָֽם: 6 וַיְצַ֥ו פּרֹעֹ֖ה בַּיֹּ֣ום ע"ה = נגד, זן, מזבח הַה֑וּא אֶת־הַנֹּגְשִׂ֣ים בָּעָ֔ם באר, ענן, מן וְאֶת־שֹׁטְרָ֖יו לֵאמֹֽר: 7 לֹ֣א תֹאסִפ֞וּן לָתֵ֨ת תֶּ֧בֶן לָעָ֛ם עלם לִלְבֹּ֥ן הַלְּבֵנִ֖ים כִּתְמ֣וֹל שִׁלְשֹׁ֑ם הֵ֚ם יֵֽלְכ֔וּ וְקֹשְׁשׁ֥וּ לָהֶ֖ם תֶּֽבֶן: 8 וְאֶת־מַתְכֹּ֨נֶת הַלְּבֵנִ֜ים אֲשֶׁ֣ר הֵם֩ עֹשִׂ֨ים תְּמ֤וֹל שִׁלְשֹׁם֙ תָּשִׂ֣ימוּ עֲלֵיהֶ֔ם לֹ֥א תִגְרְע֖וּ מִמֶּ֑נּוּ כִּֽי־נִרְפִּ֣ים הֵ֔ם עַל־כֵּ֗ן הֵ֤ם צֹֽעֲקִים֙ לֵאמֹ֔ר נֵֽלְכָ֖ה נִזְבְּחָ֥ה לֵאלֹהֵֽינוּ: ילה 9 תִּכְבַּ֧ד הָעֲבֹדָ֛ה אלהים, מום עַל־הָאֲנָשִׁ֖ים וְיַֽעֲשׂוּ־בָ֑הּ וְאַל־יִשְׁע֖וּ בְּדִבְרֵי־שָֽׁקֶר: ראה 10 וַיֵּֽצְא֗וּ נֹֽגְשֵׂ֤י הָעָם֙ וְשֹׁ֣טְרָ֔יו וַיֹּֽאמְר֥וּ אֶל־הָעָ֖ם לֵאמֹ֑ר כֹּ֚ה אָמַ֣ר פַּרְעֹ֔ה היי אֵינֶ֥נִּי נֹתֵ֖ן אבג'יתץ, ושר, אהבת חנם לָכֶ֥ם תֶּֽבֶן: 11 אַתֶּ֗ם לְכ֨וּ קְח֤וּ לָכֶם֙ תֶּ֔בֶן מֵֽאֲשֶׁ֖ר תִּמְצָ֑אוּ כִּ֣י אֵ֥ין נִגְרָ֛ע מֵֽעֲבֹֽדַתְכֶ֖ם דָּבָֽר: ראה: 12 וַיָּ֥פֶץ הָעָ֖ם בְּכָל־אֶ֣רֶץ אלהים דאלפין מִצְרָ֑יִם מצר לְקֹשֵׁ֥שׁ קַ֖שׁ לַתֶּֽבֶן: 13 וְהַנֹּגְשִׂ֖ים אָצִ֣ים לֵאמֹ֑ר כַּלּ֤וּ מַֽעֲשֵׂיכֶם֙ דְּבַר ראה ־יֹום֙ ע"ה = נגד, זן, מזבח בְּיֹומֹ֔ו כַּֽאֲשֶׁ֖ר בִּֽהְיֹ֥ות הַתֶּֽבֶן: 14 וַיֻּכּ֗וּ שֹֽׁטְרֵי֙ בְּנֵ֣י יִשְׂרָאֵ֔ל אֲשֶׁר־שָׂ֣מוּ עֲלֵהֶ֔ם נֹֽגְשֵׂ֥י פַרְעֹ֖ה לֵאמֹ֑ר מַדּ֡וּעַ לֹא֩ כִלִּיתֶ֨ם חָקְכֶ֤ם לִלְבֹּן֙ כִּתְמ֣וֹל שִׁלְשֹׁ֔ם גַּם־תְּמ֖וֹל גַּם־הַיּֽוֹם ע"ה = נגד, זן, מזבח: 15 וַיָּבֹ֗אוּ שֹֽׁטְרֵי֙ בְּנֵ֣י יִשְׂרָאֵ֔ל וַיִּצְעֲק֥וּ אֶל־פַּרְעֹ֖ה לֵאמֹ֑ר לָ֧מָּה תַֽעֲשֶׂ֛ה היי כֹ֖ה לַֽעֲבָדֶֽיךָ: 16 תֶּ֗בֶן אֵ֤ין נִתָּן֙ לַֽעֲבָדֶ֔יךָ וּלְבֵנִ֛ים אֹֽמְרִ֥ים לָ֖נוּ מום, אלהים, אהיה אדני עֲשׂ֑וּ וְהִנֵּ֧ה מ"ה יה עֲבָדֶ֛יךָ מֻכִּ֖ים וְחָטָ֥את עַמֶּֽךָ ה הויות, נמב: 17 וַיֹּ֛אמֶר נִרְפִּ֥ים אַתֶּ֖ם נִרְפִּ֑ים עַל־כֵּן֙ אַתֶּ֣ם אֹֽמְרִ֔ים נֵֽלְכָ֖ה נִזְבְּחָ֥ה לַֽיהֹוֶׄהֹ֒ אהֹדֹנהי: 18 וְעַתָּה֙ לְכ֣וּ עִבְד֔וּ וְתֶ֖בֶן לֹא־יִנָּתֵ֣ן לָכֶ֑ם וְתֹ֥כֶן לְבֵנִ֖ים תִּתֵּֽנּוּ: 19 וַיִּרְא֞וּ שֹֽׁטְרֵ֤י בְנֵֽי־יִשְׂרָאֵל֙ אֹתָ֔ם בְּרָ֣ע לֵאמֹ֑ר לֹֽא־תִגְרְע֥וּ מִלִּבְנֵיכֶ֖ם דְּבַר ראה

MAFTIR

²² Moses returned to the Lord and said, "Lord, why have You brought trouble upon this people? Is this why You sent me?

²³ Ever since I went to Pharaoh to speak in Your Name, he has brought trouble upon this people, and You have not rescued Your people at all."

6:1 Then the Lord said to Moses, "Now you will see what I will do to Pharaoh: Because of My Mighty Hand he will let them go; because of My Mighty Hand he will drive them out of his country."

Exodus 5:22—Moses went back to God.
After Pharaoh had increased the burden of work on the Israelites, Moses spoke to God about Pharaoh's refusal to let them go. Moses was not complaining; he was merely expressing the frustration of the people. The Israelites had, unfortunately, already forgotten the miracles that Moses had performed for them. To be successful on our spiritual path, we cannot forget the miracles that the Light of the Creator has already shown us. Rather than focusing on present details and difficulties, we should always maintain the perspective of the big picture of our lives.

יוֹם ע״ה = נגד, זן, מזבח בְּיוֹמְוֹ: 20 וַיִּפְגְּעוּ אֶת־מֹשֶׁה מהע׳, אל עדי וְאֶת־אַהֲרֹן

ע״ב רבוע ע״ב נִצָּבִים לִקְרָאתָם בְּצֵאתָם מֵאֵת פַּרְעֹה: 21 וַיֹּאמְרוּ אֲלֵהֶם

ירא אלף למד יהוה יְהֹוָׁהֽ אֲדֹנֽי-אהדונהי עֲלֵיכֶם וְיִשְׁפֹּט אֲשֶׁר הִבְאַשְׁתֶּם אֶת־

רֵיחֵנוּ בְּעֵינֵי רבוע מ״ה פַרְעֹה וּבְעֵינֵי רבוע מ״ה עֲבָדָיו לָתֶת־חֶרֶב רבוע ס״ג ורבוע אהיה

בְּיָדָם לְהָרְגֵנוּ:

MAFTIR

22 וַיָּשָׁב מֹשֶׁה מהע׳, אל עדי אֶל־יְהֹוָׁהֽ-אֲדֹנֽיֽ-אהדונהי וַיֹּאמַר אֲדֹנָׁי ללה לָמָה

הֲרֵעֹתָה לָעָם עלם הַזֶּה והו לָמָּה זֶּה שְׁלַחְתָּנִי: 23 וּמֵאָז ומב בָּאתִי אֶל־

פַּרְעֹה לְדַבֵּר ראה בִּשְׁמֶךָ הֵרַע לָעָם הַזֶּה והו וְהַצֵּל לֹא־הִצַּלְתָּ אֶת־

עַמֶּךָ ה הויות, גמם : 16 וַיֹּאמֶר יְהֹוָׁהֽ-אֲדֹנֽיֽ-אהדונהי אֶל־מֹשֶׁה מהע׳, אל עדי עַתָּה

תִרְאֶה אֲשֶׁר אֶעֱשֶׂה לְפַרְעֹה כִּי בְיָד חֲזָקָה יְשַׁלְּחֵם וּבְיָד חֲזָקָה

יְגָרְשֵׁם מֵאַרְצוֹ:

HAFTARAH OF SHEMOT

In this Haftarah, Jeremiah speaks about the destruction of the Temple, while the story of Shemot itself is talking about Egypt. "Egypt" represents the first time that we—the "Israelites"—experienced a disconnection or "exile" from the Light of the Creator. When you combine the two (the story of Shemot with this Haftarah), a powerful lesson is revealed. Jeremiah is reminding us that when we have fallen—when we are in a place of destruction, when we are angry or depressed—this is the

Jeremiah 1:1 - 2:3

1:1 The words of Jeremiah son of Hilkiah, one of the priests at Anathoth in the territory of Benjamin.

2 The word of the Lord came to him in the thirteenth year of the reign of Josiah son of Amon, king of Judah,

3 and through the reign of Jehoiakim son of Josiah king of Judah, down to the fifth month of the eleventh year of Zedekiah son of Josiah king of Judah, when the people of Jerusalem went into exile.

4 The word of the Lord came to me, saying,

5 "Before I formed you in the womb I knew you, before you were born I set you apart; I appointed you as a prophet to the nations."

6 "Lord, God," I said, "I do not know how to speak; I am only a child."

7 The Lord said to me, "Do not say, 'I am only a child.' You must go to everyone I send you to and say whatever I command you.

8 Do not be afraid of them, for I am with you and will rescue you," declares the Lord.

9 Then the Lord reached out His hand and touched my mouth and the Lord said to me, "Here, I have put my words in your mouth.

10 See, today I appoint you over nations and kingdoms to uproot and tear down, to destroy and overthrow, to build and to plant."

11 The word of the Lord was to me, saying, "What do you see, Jeremiah?" "I see the branch of an almond tree," I replied.

HAFTARAH OF SHEMOT

most valuable opportunity we can have to increase our connection to the Light of the Creator. It is easy to be connected to the Light when we are in a positive mindset. However, we must remember that the reason we were created—and, therefore, where our authentic spiritual work lies—is to make the effort to achieve connection to the Light of the Creator, even when we are experiencing our darkest moments.

ירמיהו פרק א

1 1 דִּבְרֵי ראה יִרְמְיָהוּ בֶּן־חִלְקִיָּהוּ מִן־הַכֹּהֲנִים מלה אֲשֶׁר בַּעֲנָתוֹת
בְּאֶרֶץ אלהים דאלפין בִּנְיָמִן: 2 אֲשֶׁר הָיָה דְבַר יהה ראה ־יְהֹוָואדניאהדונהי אֵלָיו
בִּימֵי יֹאשִׁיָּהוּ בֶן־אָמוֹן מֶלֶךְ יְהוּדָה בִּשְׁלֹשׁ־עֶשְׂרֵה שָׁנָה לְמָלְכוֹ פוני:
3 וַיְהִי אל, ייאי בִּימֵי יְהוֹיָקִים בֶּן־יֹאשִׁיָּהוּ מֶלֶךְ יְהוּדָה עַד־תֹּם יפ רבוע אהיה
עַשְׁתֵּי עֶשְׂרֵה שָׁנָה לְצִדְקִיָּהוּ בֶן־יֹאשִׁיָּהוּ מֶלֶךְ יְהוּדָה עַד־גְּלוֹת
יְרוּשָׁלָ͏ִם ריו שע בַּחֹדֶשׁ יב הוויות הַחֲמִישִׁי: 4 וַיְהִי אל, ייאי דְּבַר ראה ־
יְהֹוָואדניאהדונהי אֵלַי לֵאמֹר: 5 בְּטֶרֶם רמיח עה אֶצָּרְךָ (כתיב: אצורך) בַּבֶּטֶן
יְדַעְתִּיךָ רמיח עה וּבְטֶרֶם תֵּצֵא מֵרֶחֶם רמיח הִקְדַּשְׁתִּיךָ נָבִיא לַגּוֹיִם
נְתַתִּיךָ: 6 וָאֹמַר אֲהָהּ אֲדֹנָי ללה יֱהֹוִ͏הֵאדניאהדונהי הִנֵּה מה יה לֹא־יָדַעְתִּי
דַבֵּר ראה כִּי־נַעַר שיך אָנֹכִי איע: 7 וַיֹּאמֶר יְהֹוָואדניאהדונהי אֵלַי אַל־תֹּאמַר
נַעַר שיך איע כִּי עַל־כָּל ילי, עמם ־אֲשֶׁר אֶשְׁלָחֲךָ תֵּלֵךְ וְאֵת כָּל ילי
־אֲשֶׁר אֲצַוְּךָ תְּדַבֵּר ראה: 8 אַל־תִּירָא מִפְּנֵיהֶם כִּי־אִתְּךָ אֲנִי אני, טדהד כוזו
לְהַצִּלֶךָ נְאֻם־יְהֹוָואדניאהדונהי: 9 וַיִּשְׁלַח יְהֹוָואדניאהדונהי אֶת־יָדוֹ וַיַּגַּע עַל־פִּי
וַיֹּאמֶר יְהֹוָואדניאהדונהי אֵלַי הִנֵּה מה יה נָתַתִּי דְבָרַי ראה בְּפִיךָ: 10 רְאֵה ראה
הִפְקַדְתִּיךָ | הַיּוֹם עה ־היה = נגד, זן, מזבח הַזֶּה וחו עַל־הַגּוֹיִם וְעַל־הַמַּמְלָכוֹת
לִנְתוֹשׁ וְלִנְתוֹץ וּלְהַאֲבִיד וְלַהֲרוֹס לִבְנוֹת וְלִנְטוֹעַ: 11 וַיְהִי אל, ייאי דְּבַר

¹² The Lord said to me, "You have seen correctly, for I am watching to see that my word is fulfilled."

¹³ The word of the Lord came to me again, saying, "What do you see?" "I see a boiling pot, tilting away from the north," I answered.

¹⁴ The Lord said to me, "From the north disaster will be poured out on all who live in the land.

¹⁵ I am about to summon all the peoples of the northern kingdoms," declares the Lord. "Their kings will come and set up their thrones in the entrance of the gates of Jerusalem; they will come against all her surrounding walls and against all the towns of Judah.

¹⁶ I will pronounce My judgments on My people because of their wickedness in forsaking Me, in burning incense to other gods and in worshiping what their hands have made.

¹⁷ Get yourself ready! Stand up and say to them everything I command you. Do not be terrified by them, or I will terrify you before them.

¹⁸ Today I have made you a fortified city, an iron pillar and a bronze wall to stand against the whole land—against the kings of Judah, its officials, its priests and the people of the land.

¹⁹ They will fight against you but will not overcome you, for I am with you and will rescue you," declares the Lord.

2:¹ The word of the Lord came to me, saying,

² "Go and proclaim in the ears of Jerusalem, saying, 'So declares the Lord: "I remember the devotion of your youth, how as a bride you loved me and followed me through the desert, through a land not sown.

³ Israel was holy to the Lord, the first fruits of his harvest; all who devoured her were held guilty, and disaster overtook them," ' " declares the Lord.

יְהֹוָה אֵלַי לֵאמֹר מָה־אַתָּה רֹאֶה יִרְמְיָהוּ וָאֹמַר

מַקֵּל שָׁקֵד אֲנִי רֹאֶה׃ 12 וַיֹּאמֶר יְהֹוָה אֵלַי

הֵיטַבְתָּ לִרְאוֹת כִּי־שֹׁקֵד אֲנִי עַל־דְּבָרִי לַעֲשֹׂתוֹ׃ 13 וַיְהִי

דְבַר־יְהֹוָה אֵלַי שֵׁנִית לֵאמֹר מָה אַתָּה רֹאֶה

וָאֹמַר סִיר נָפוּחַ אֲנִי רֹאֶה וּפָנָיו מִפְּנֵי צָפוֹנָה׃

14 וַיֹּאמֶר יְהֹוָה אֵלָי מִצָּפוֹן תִּפָּתַח הָרָעָה עַל כָּל־

יֹשְׁבֵי הָאָרֶץ׃ 15 כִּי הִנְנִי קֹרֵא לְכָל־מִשְׁפְּחוֹת

מַמְלְכוֹת צָפוֹנָה נְאֻם־יְהֹוָה וּבָאוּ וְנָתְנוּ אִישׁ

כִּסְאוֹ פֶּתַח שַׁעֲרֵי יְרוּשָׁלַם וְעַל כָּל־חוֹמֹתֶיהָ סָבִיב וְעַל

כָּל־עָרֵי יְהוּדָה׃ 16 וְדִבַּרְתִּי מִשְׁפָּטַי אוֹתָם עַל כָּל־

רָעָתָם אֲשֶׁר עֲזָבוּנִי וַיְקַטְּרוּ לֵאלֹהִים אֲחֵרִים וַיִּשְׁתַּחֲווּ

לְמַעֲשֵׂי יְדֵיהֶם׃ 17 וְאַתָּה תֶּאְזֹר מָתְנֶיךָ וְקַמְתָּ וְדִבַּרְתָּ אֲלֵיהֶם

אֵת כָּל־אֲשֶׁר אָנֹכִי אֲצַוֶּךָּ אַל־תֵּחַת מִפְּנֵיהֶם פֶּן־אֲחִתְּךָ

לִפְנֵיהֶם׃ 18 וַאֲנִי הִנֵּה נְתַתִּיךָ הַיּוֹם לְעִיר

מִבְצָר וּלְעַמּוּד בַּרְזֶל וּלְחֹמוֹת נְחֹשֶׁת

עַל־כָּל־הָאָרֶץ לְמַלְכֵי יְהוּדָה לְשָׂרֶיהָ לְכֹהֲנֶיהָ וּלְעַם

הָאָרֶץ׃ 19 וְנִלְחֲמוּ אֵלֶיךָ וְלֹא־יוּכְלוּ לָךְ כִּי־אִתְּךָ אֲנִי

נְאֻם־יְהֹוָה לְהַצִּילֶךָ׃ 2 1 וַיְהִי דְבַר־יְהֹוָה

אֵלַי לֵאמֹר׃ 2 הָלֹךְ וְקָרָאתָ בְאָזְנֵי יְרוּשָׁלַם לֵאמֹר כֹּה אָמַר

יְהֹוָה זָכַרְתִּי לָךְ חֶסֶד נְעוּרַיִךְ אַהֲבַת כְּלוּלֹתָיִךְ

לֶכְתֵּךְ אַחֲרַי בַּמִּדְבָּר בְּאֶרֶץ לֹא זְרוּעָה׃ 3 קֹדֶשׁ

יִשְׂרָאֵל לַיהֹוָה רֵאשִׁית תְּבוּאָתֹה כָּל־אֹכְלָיו יֶאְשָׁמוּ רָעָה

תָּבֹא אֲלֵיהֶם נְאֻם־יְהֹוָה׃

VA'ERA

LESSON OF VA'ERA
(Exodus 6:2-9:35)

"And God spoke to Moses and said to him, 'I am God.'"

In the Bible, God is sometimes referred to as Elohim, which means "judgment," and also as *Yud*, *Hei*, *Vav*, and *Hei* (the Tetragrammaton, a Name we do not pronounce), which means "mercy." Sometimes, both Names appear in the same sentence. As King Solomon wrote, "To everything there is a season, and a time to every purpose under heaven." (*Ecclesiastes 3:1*) In other words, we are either in a time of judgment, as at the counting of the Omer, or in a time of mercy, as during Sukkot. So how can judgment and mercy both occur at the same time, as might be indicated by the juxtaposition of both Names in the same sentence?

We are conditioned to think of judgment as negative and mercy as positive. But there is no such thing as any aspect of negativity when referring to the Creator. Rather, there is only the supreme wisdom and understanding of how to treat each person exactly in accordance with what that person really needs. To change and transform, some people need judgment, while others need mercy. And strangely, there are even some people from whom the Creator needs to remain concealed completely.

The *Zohar* says:

> *An explanation OF THE PASSAGE: "Trust in God forever," IS THAT a person has to strengthen himself in God throughout his life. No one can harm a person who properly places his trust and strength in God, since one who places his strength in the Holy Name endures forever.*

> *Another explanation of: "And Elohim spoke," THIS IS the decree of Judgment, AS THE NAME ELOHIM IS JUDGMENT, NAMELY MALCHUT. "And said to him, 'I am God.'" This is a different grade, NAMELY, ZEIR ANPIN which is Mercy, and here everything is connected together, Judgment and Mercy TOGETHER, WHICH IS GREAT WHOLENESS. This is the meaning of: "And said to him, 'I am God,'" WHICH IS THE ATTRIBUTE OF MERCY. Rav Shimon said, If it were written: "And Elohim spoke to Moses, 'I am God,'" I would say THAT FOR HIM JUDGMENT AND MERCY WERE LINKED TOGETHER. But it is not written so. Rather, it is first written: "And Elohim spoke to Moses" and then: "And said to him, 'I am God,'" which means they are a grade after another grade INSTEAD OF JUDGMENT AND MERCY LINKED TOGETHER.*
> — *The Zohar, Va'era 1:7, 11*

Most people are somewhere in between. Sometimes, we need mercy, while at other times, we require judgment. The choice is really ours to make, and that choice depends on our actions and our consciousness. If, at the level of our soul, we need and want pressure to be put on us because we are not doing what we are supposed to be doing, then we will choose judgment. But if, after struggling and suffering, we need Divine love and kindness, we can choose to receive mercy from the Creator.

So when we really understand what's happening in our lives, we don't say, "How could the Creator do this to me?" because in the truest sense, we do "this" to ourselves—"this" being the choices we make. The Baal Shem Tov (Rav Israel ben Eliezer, 1698–1760) said that the Creator is always angry at us for the negativity that is in us, but at the same time, the Creator loves us for all the good that we do. Both of those elements—the capacity for negativity and the capacity for good—are present in each of us; it is our consciousness that draws down either the force of judgment from the Creator or the force of mercy. What we receive from the Creator depends on our choices and the actions we take. We determine the connection, so we need to ask ourselves, since we do have free will, why we continue to make the choices we do.

When we read the *Zohar* every day, even if it's only for a few minutes, we are using the tools that Rav Shimon gave us to make a positive connection. The Light that is revealed in even five minutes of *Zohar* study will connect us to the merciful aspect of the Creator. At the same time, we should remember what the Baal Shem Tov said: "If a person who prays leaves the synagogue the same person they were when they came in, it is as if that person had not prayed at all." It is the same with the study of the Zohar. We need to open ourselves to the Light so that it can help us in our transformation, as it is written:

> "Open to Me," (Song of Solomon 5:2) MEANS OPEN TO ME an opening as small as the eye of a needle, and I shall open to you the Celestial Gates.
> — The Zohar, Emor 24:129

"And the people did not listen to Moses because of anguish of spirit and hard work." (Exodus 6:9)

We must wonder why the people, who certainly knew Moses and knew of all the miracles he had performed, did not listen to him. Scripture seems to imply that it was because they were too busy working.

> "And the people did not listen to Moses because of anguish of spirit and hard work." (Exodus 6:9)HE ASKS, What is "anguish of spirit?" Rav Yehuda said, "They did not rest FROM THEIR LABOR and they did not gather into themselves SUFFICIENT breath. Rav Shimon said, Anguish of spirit MEANS the Jubilee was still not released, WHICH IS BINAH, to give them rest AND FREEDOM, and the last spirit, WHICH IS MALCHUT, had not yet ruled IN THE WORLD to institute JUST laws IN THE WORLD. Therefore, there was anguish of spirit. Which spirit is it? It is the last spirit that we mentioned, WHICH IS MALCHUT, WHO WAS TOO HELPLESS TO SAVE ISRAEL, WHICH IS THE MEANING OF "ANGUISH OF SPIRIT."
> — The Zohar, Va'era 6:65

This seems very hard to understand, but actually, we do this all the time. "Work" is so often our excuse for not reading the Zohar, or for not taking part in a connection with the Light of the Creator, or for not "listening to Moses" in the many ways that continue to speak to us at every moment. All the same, given that we know that the real purpose of our work is to strengthen our connection with the Creator, why is it that we don't put aside our mundane work and pay attention?

The answer lies in the following story: There was once a king who was very ill. He said that whoever could heal him would be granted two hours in the royal treasury to amass all the gold, diamonds, and rubies he could gather in that window of time. One of the king's advisors cured the king. Though the king was completely healed, he naturally did not want to part with any of his treasure, so he devised a plan to thwart the advisor. Knowing that this particular advisor was passionate about music, the king hired one hundred of the greatest musicians in his kingdom to play inside the treasury while his advisor was gathering his fortune.

As the advisor began collecting his reward, he became distracted by the beautiful music. He decided to take a few minutes to sit and listen; after all, he had two hours. But each time the advisor realized that his bags were still empty and he had better get started, the music grew louder or a new instrument would be introduced and he was distracted all over again.

Finally with all his might, he tried to tear himself away from the music and start collecting his treasure. But just as his hand closed around the first bar of gold, one of the king's soldiers grabbed his wrist and said, "Your time is up!"

In our lives, we become distracted, just like the king's advisor. Whenever we start to focus on the true purpose of life, Satan—our ultimate Opponent—diverts our attention. The only way to defeat Satan at this game is to give him no space to enter in the first place. It takes constant work and effort: We cannot let a single day pass without reading or scanning the Zohar, and not one day go by without giving and sharing. There is no such thing as a "stop-and-go" connection with the Light of the Creator. Our effort should be diligent and consistent.

Satan is like a houseguest who asks to stay the night. After the host agrees, Satan mentions that he doesn't have a job. So the host gives him a job. Before long, Satan is not only a partner in the business but has also taken over the house! The only way to stop Satan is not to let him in because in the beginning, Satan is a guest, but in the end, he becomes the master of the home.

There is a saying: "If you do not know where you're going, you will never get there," and another that says: "If you don't know where you're going, any road will take you there." This can be applied to our spiritual work. Without direction, we will always be lost. And with every step forward, Satan tries to move us four steps back. The lesson is to focus on the goal of our transformation—connection with the Light of the Creator—every minute of every day.

SYNOPSIS OF VA'ERA

The Ten Plagues of Egypt that occur in this story represent the ten levels of Satan's negativity. When we read about the plagues and hear the phrases in the original Hebrew, we are inoculated with a spiritual antidote to help us overcome those negative forces.

> *And the secret of the matter is that all the ten signs the Holy One, blessed be He, performed originated from the strong hand, WHICH IS GEVURAH, and this hand overpowered all the levels of their dominion in order to confuse them. They did not know what to do TO BE SAVED. When the grades tried to do something, it became apparent to all that they could do nothing TO BE SAVED FROM THE PLAGUES because of the strong hand that rested upon them.*
> *-- The Zohar, Va'era 17:145*

While in Egypt, the state of consciousness of the people had descended to the 49th Gate of Negativity—the 50th Gate is a level from which there is no return. The extent of the people's inner slavery was such that only the Creator Himself could free them. Not angels nor emissaries nor even emanations of the Creator's Light: They needed the totality of the Creator's Light, the spiritual equivalent of an explosion, to release them from their spiritual chains.

FIRST READING - ABRAHAM - CHESED

6:2 Good then said to Moses, "I am the Lord. ³ I appeared to Abraham, to Isaac and to Jacob as God Almighty, but by My Name, the Lord, I did not make myself known to them.

⁴ I also established My Covenant with them to give them the land of Canaan, where they lived as strangers.

⁵ Moreover, I have heard the moaning of the Israelites, whom the Egyptians are enslaving, and I have remembered My Covenant.

⁶ "Therefore, say to the Israelites: 'I am the Lord, and I will bring you out from under the hardship of the Egyptians. I will save you from being slaves to them, and I will redeem you with an outstretched arm and with mighty acts of judgment.

⁷ I will take you as My Own People, and I will be your God. Then you will know that I am the Lord, your God, who brings you out from under the hardship of the Egyptians.

FROM THE RAV

In the Story of Va'era, we have the beginning of the manifestation of this awesome power of the Light that can endow us with control over physical reality—mind over matter. Let me remind you that the chaos that humankind experiences is manifested only in the physical 1 Percent Realm. The metaphysical 99 Percent Realm is not affected by negativity or chaos. The problem has always been how to make a bridge to connect the 99 Percent Reality with the physical 1 Percent Realm.

The kabbalists teach us that the entire Torah is about consciousness—a consciousness that is beyond the 1 Percent rational mind, which we, unfortunately, make so much use of in our daily lives.

The Torah says the staff, the piece of wood of Aaron, swallowed up (bilah) the pieces of wood of the Egyptians. They changed physical matter. Is that magic? No, it was mind over matter.

There is a rule in the physical world that nothing disappears. So then how do you make things disappear? It doesn't say the snake of Aaron swallow up the snakes of the Egyptians; it says that the etz (wood) swallowed up the other etz.

We learned previously that the snake represents an aspect of chaos, and chaos cannot eliminate chaos. So the Torah is telling us that the outside is not our enemy. Etz is our answer. Etz is something that has a sharing nature, and only something with a sharing consciousness can swallow up negativity.

The whole Torah, says Rav Shimon, is a metaphor. This is such a wonderful lesson to instill in our consciousness—that when we have absolute certainty and in doing so connect to the 99 Percent Realm, then we can swallow up chaos. The physical realm can be in our grasp, and we can control it.

FIRST READING - ABRAHAM - CHESED

וַיְדַבֵּ֥ר רְאֵה אֱלֹהִ֖ים מום, אהיה אדני ; ילה אֶל־מֹשֶׁ֑ה מהש, אל שדי וַיֹּ֖אמֶר אֵלָ֥יו 2

אֲנִ֥י אני, טדהד כוזו יְהֹוָ֔ה ואדניאהדונהי: וָאֵרָ֗א אֶל־אַבְרָהָ֛ם דַע רמ"ח, וז"פ אל אֶל־יִצְחָ֥ק 3

וְאֶֽל־יַעֲקֹ֖ב ד"פ בן ז"פ יהוה, יאהדונהי אידהנויה בְּאֵ֣ל יא"י שַׁדָּ֑י רפ"ח יהוה; מהש וּשְׁמִ֣י

יְהֹוָ֔ה ואדניאהדונהי רבוע ע"ב ורבוע ס"ג לֹ֥א נוֹדַ֖עְתִּי לָהֶֽם: וְגַ֨ם יג"ל הֲקִמֹ֤תִי אֶת־ 4

בְּרִיתִי֙ אִתָּ֔ם לָתֵ֥ת לָהֶ֖ם אֶת־אֶ֣רֶץ אלהים דאלפין כְּנָ֑עַן אֵ֛ת אֶ֥רֶץ אלהים דאלפין

מְגֻרֵיהֶ֖ם אֲשֶׁר־גָּ֥רוּ בָֽהּ: וְגַ֣ם | יג"ל אֲנִ֣י אני, טדהד כוזו שָׁמַ֔עְתִּי אֶֽת־נַאֲקַת֙ 5

בְּנֵ֣י יִשְׂרָאֵ֔ל מצר אֲשֶׁ֥ר מִצְרַ֖יִם מַעֲבִדִ֣ים אֹתָ֑ם וָאֶזְכֹּ֖ר אֶת־בְּרִיתִֽי:

לָכֵ֞ן אֱמֹ֥ר לִבְנֵֽי־יִשְׂרָאֵל֮ אֲנִ֣י אני, טדהד כוזו יְהֹוָה֒ ואדניאהדונהי וְהוֹצֵאתִ֣י אֶתְכֶ֗ם 6

וַיֹּאמֶר

Exodus 6:2—God told Moses He would reveal Himself. God spoke to Moses and said that when He revealed Himself to Abraham, Isaac, and Jacob, God had revealed Himself in a lower dimension and not by the Name *Yud, Hei, Vav,* and *Hei.* God then told Moses that Moses would receive Him on a higher and more revealed level:

"And I appeared to Abraham, to Isaac, and to Jacob, by the name of El Shadai" WHICH IS THE NAME OF MALCHUT BEFORE SHE UNITED WITH ZEIR ANPIN FACE TO FACE. THIS MEANS, *I APPEARED TO THE PATRIARCHS BY THE NAME OF EL SHADAI, WHICH IS MALCHUT when she was unmarried in My house. I was not spoken to face to face as I did with you, and you, at the beginning of your speech, said to My daughter in My presence such words. Therefore, IT IS WRITTEN: "And I appeared to Abraham, to Isaac, and to Jacob, by the name of El Shadai, but by My Name, God, I was not known to them,"* THAT IS, *to speak to them in the grade in which I spoke to you.*
— *The Zohar, Va'era 1:18*

This was because Moses was being prepared to lead an entire nation. Commentary says that Moses was Israel and Israel was Moses. (*Bamidbar Rabbah 19:28*) By comparison, Abraham, Isaac, and Jacob were responsible for essentially themselves alone; therefore Moses needed a more complete connection to the Light of the Creator than the patriarchs did in order to accomplish his formidable task. For this reason, the wisdom of Kabbalah is being more openly revealed in our day as multitudes will be using and depending on this revelation of Light.

Moses told the Israelites that they would be leaving Egypt, but they didn't pay attention to his words. We too, often ignore the many messages that are given to us. In dreams and in the circumstances of our lives, we receive messages daily from the Light, but most of the time, we are not spiritually attuned sufficiently to be able to either hear or heed them.

God told Moses to return to Pharaoh to ask for the release of the Israelites. On this occasion, as on many others, Moses tried to refuse the task God set before him, not because he did not want to take responsibility but out of humility and a feeling of unworthiness.

8 And I will bring you to the land I swore with uplifted hand to give to Abraham, to Isaac and to Jacob. I will give it to you as a possession. I am the Lord.' "

9 Moses spoke this to the Israelites, but they did not listen to him because of their discouragement and cruel bondage.

10 Then the Lord said to Moses, 11 "Come, tell Pharaoh, King of Egypt, to let the Israelites go out of his country."

12 But Moses said to the Lord, "If the Israelites will not listen to me, why would Pharaoh listen to me, since I am of uncircumcised lips?"

13 Now the Lord spoke to Moses and Aaron and commanded the Israelites, and Pharaoh, the King of Egypt, to take out the Israelites from the land of Egypt.

SECOND READING - ISAAC - GEVURAH

14 These were the heads of their families. The sons of Reuben: the firstborn son of Israel was Hanoch, and Pallu, Hezron and Carmi. These were the families of Reuben.

15 The sons of Simeon were Jemuel, Jamin, Ohad, Jakin, Tzohar and Saul the son of a Canaanite woman. These were the families of Simeon.

16 These were the names of the sons of Levi according to their records: Gershon, Kohath and Merari. Levi lived 137 years.

17 The sons of Gershon, by families, were Libni and Shimei.

18 The sons of Kohath were Amram, Izhar, Hebron and Uzziel. Kohath lived 133 years.

19 The sons of Merari were Mahli and Mushi. These were the families of Levi according to their records.

אֵלֶּה

Exodus 6:14—The Bible recounts the life and lineage of Moses.

The long list of the forebears of Moses reminds us of the importance of those who came before us. None of us accomplish our spiritual work alone or in a vacuum; we stand on the shoulders of our predecessors. This is why in each generation, we are able to reach higher and higher levels—we have our ancestors' Light and our own Light as well.

מִתַּחַת סִבְלֹת מִצְרַיִם מ"צ וְהִצַּלְתִּי אֶתְכֶם מֵעֲבֹדָתָם וְגָאַלְתִּי אֶתְכֶם

בִּזְרוֹעַ נְטוּיָה וּבִשְׁפָטִים גְּדֹלִים: 7 וְלָקַחְתִּי אֶתְכֶם לִי לְעָם וְהָיִיתִי

לָכֶם לֵאלֹהִים מ"ום, אהיה אדני ; ילה וִידַעְתֶּם כִּי אֲנִי אני, טדה"ד כוז"ו יְהוָֹאֲדֹנָיאהדונהי

אֱלֹהֵיכֶם ילה הַמּוֹצִיא אֶתְכֶם מִתַּחַת סִבְלוֹת מִצְרָיִם מ"צר: 8 וְהֵבֵאתִי

אֶתְכֶם אֶל־הָאָרֶץ אלהים דההין ע"ה אֲשֶׁר נָשָׂאתִי אֶת־יָדִי לָתֵת אֹתָהּ

לְאַבְרָהָם רמ"ח, וז"פ אל לְיִצְחָק ד"פ ב"ן וּלְיַעֲקֹב ז"פ יהוה, יאהדונהי אידהנויה וְנָתַתִּי אֹתָהּ

לָכֶם מוֹרָשָׁה אֲנִי אני, טדה"ד כוז"ו יְהוָֹאֲדֹנָיאהדונהי 9 וַיְדַבֵּר רָאה מֹשֶׁה מהש, אל שדי

כֵּן אֶל־בְּנֵי יִשְׂרָאֵל וְלֹא שָׁמְעוּ אֶל־מֹשֶׁה מהש, אל שדי מִקֹּצֶר רוּחַ

מלוי אלהים דיודין וּמֵעֲבֹדָה קָשָׁה: 10 וַיְדַבֵּר רָאה יְהוָֹאֲדֹנָיאהדונהי אֶל־מֹשֶׁה

מהש, אל שדי לֵּאמֹר: 11 בֹּא דַבֵּר רָאה אֶל־פַּרְעֹה מֶלֶךְ מִצְרָיִם מ"צר וִישַׁלַּח

אֶת־בְּנֵי־יִשְׂרָאֵל מֵאַרְצוֹ: 12 וַיְדַבֵּר רָאה מֹשֶׁה מהש, אל שדי לִפְנֵי וחכמה בינה

יְהוָֹאֲדֹנָיאהדונהי לֵאמֹר הֵן בְּנֵי־יִשְׂרָאֵל לֹא־שָׁמְעוּ אֵלַי וְאֵיךְ אל יִשְׁמָעֵנִי

פַרְעֹה וַאֲנִי אני, ב"פ אהיה יהוה עָרֵל אלהים דיודין שְׂפָתָיִם: 13 וַיְדַבֵּר רָאה

יְהוָֹאֲדֹנָיאהדונהי אֶל־מֹשֶׁה מהש, אל שדי וְאֶל־אַהֲרֹן ע"ב ורבוע ע"ב וַיְצַוֵּם אֶל־בְּנֵי

יִשְׂרָאֵל וְאֶל־פַּרְעֹה מֶלֶךְ מִצְרָיִם מ"צר לְהוֹצִיא אֶת־בְּנֵי־יִשְׂרָאֵל מֵאֶרֶץ

אלהים דאלפין מִצְרָיִם מ"צר:

SECOND READING - ISAAC - GEVURAH

14 אֵלֶּה רָאשֵׁי בֵית ב"פ ראה ־אֲבֹתָם רָאה בְּנֵי רְאוּבֵן ג"פ אלהים בְּכֹר יִשְׂרָאֵל ג"פ אלהים

חֲנוֹךְ וּפַלּוּא חֶצְרֹן וְכַרְמִי אֵלֶּה מִשְׁפְּחֹת רְאוּבֵן ג"פ אלהים: 15 וּבְנֵי שִׁמְעוֹן

יְמוּאֵל וְיָמִין וְאֹהַד וְיָכִין וְצֹחַר וְשָׁאוּל בֶּן־הַכְּנַעֲנִית אֵלֶּה מִשְׁפְּחֹת

שִׁמְעוֹן: 16 וְאֵלֶּה מ"ב שְׁמוֹת בְּנֵי־לֵוִי דמב, מלוי ע"ב לְתֹלְדֹתָם גֵּרְשׁוֹן

ע"ה ב"פ סז"ח"ך וּקְהָת וּמְרָרִי ה"פ מים וּשְׁנֵי וַזֵּי לֵוִי דמב, מלוי ע"ב שֶׁבַע ואלהים דיודין

20 *Amram married his father's sister Jochebed, who bore him Aaron and Moses. Amram lived 137 years.*

21 *The sons of Izhar were Korah, Nepheg and Zicri.*

22 *The sons of Uzziel were Mishael, Elzaphan and Sithri.*

23 *Aaron married Elisheba, daughter of Amminadab and sister of Nahshon, and she bore him Nadab and Abihu, Eleazar and Itamar.*

24 *The sons of Korah were Assir, Elkanah and Abiasaph. These were the Korahite families.*

25 *Eleazar son of Aaron married one of the daughters of Putiel, and she bore him Phinehas. These were the heads of the Levite families.*

26 *It was Aaron and Moses to whom the Lord said, "Bring the Israelites out of Egypt by their divisions."*

27 *The ones who spoke to Pharaoh, King of Egypt, about bringing the Israelites out of Egypt were Moses and Aaron.*

28 *And it was on the day that the Lord spoke to Moses in Egypt,*

וַיִּקַּח

Exodus 6:23—Aaron married Elisheva. In an apparent non sequitur, the verse mentions that Elisheva was Nahshon's sister. This is important because later, Nahshon, who will be one of the foremost of the tribal princes, will also be the first person to enter the Red Sea when it parts. But there is also a relevant lesson here for us today. Whenever we are considering entering into a relationship, we must take into account the other person's family because they are the people who have shaped our partner's concept of the world.

אַהֲרֹן וּמֹשֶׁה

Exodus 6:26—Moses and Aaron were equals in serving God. In two successive verses, Moses and Aaron are mentioned first in one order and then in reverse order. From this, we learn that the two brothers were equal servants of the Light. They never felt jealousy or the tensions of an inflated

ego towards one another—each was busy doing his best for the Light. In our own lives, we must adopt this attitude as well. Rather than looking at what others have or do, we must concentrate our energies on determining the goals that the Light wants each of us, uniquely and personally, to achieve in our lifetime.

> *"And you shall lay on your heart" (Heb. levavecha, spelled with two Bet's) is to include them together, the left and the right, and then you will know that "God He is the Elohim." Rav Aba said, "definitely it is so." And now it is understandable, WHAT IS SAID, "He is Aaron and Moses" (Exodus 6:26), "he is Moses and Aaron." (Ibid. 27). IT IS TO TEACH THAT air, WHICH IS TIFERET, COMBINED with water, WHICH IS CHESED, and water, WHICH IS CHESED, COMBINED with air, WHICH IS TIFERET, to be one. Therefore, it is written "he."*
> — The Zohar, Va'era 10:97

וּשְׁלֹשִׁים וּמְאַת שָׁנָה: 17 בְּנֵי גֵרְשׁוֹן ע״ה ב״פ סזדר״ך לִבְנִי וְשִׁמְעִי לְמִשְׁפְּחֹתָם:

18 וּבְנֵי קְהָת עַמְרָם וְיִצְהָר וְחֶבְרוֹן וְעֻזִּיאֵל וּשְׁנֵי וַחַיֵּי קְהָת שָׁלֹשׁ

וּשְׁלֹשִׁים וּמְאַת שָׁנָה: 19 וּבְנֵי מְרָרִי ה״פ מיים מַחְלִי וּמוּשִׁי אֵלֶּה מִשְׁפְּחֹת

הַלֵּוִי דמב, מלוי ע״ב לְתֹלְדֹתָם: 20 וַיִּקַּח וחעם עַמְרָם אֶת־יוֹכֶבֶד מ״ב דֹּדָתוֹ לוֹ

לְאִשָּׁה וַתֵּלֶד לוֹ אֶת־אַהֲרֹן ע״ב ורבוע ע״ב וְאֶת־מֹשֶׁה מהע, אל שדי וּשְׁנֵי וַחַיֵּי

עַמְרָם שֶׁבַע ע״ב ואלהים דיודין וּשְׁלֹשִׁים וּמְאַת שָׁנָה: 21 וּבְנֵי יִצְהָר קֹרַח

וָנֶפֶג וְזִכְרִי: 22 וּבְנֵי עֻזִּיאֵל מִישָׁאֵל וְאֶלְצָפָן וְסִתְרִי: 23 וַיִּקַּח וחעם אַהֲרֹן

ע״ב ורבוע ע״ב אֶת־אֱלִישֶׁבַע בַּת־עַמִּינָדָב אֲחוֹת נַחְשׁוֹן לוֹ לְאִשָּׁה וַתֵּלֶד

לוֹ אֶת־נָדָב ע״ה אהיה בוכ״ו וְאֶת־אֲבִיהוּא אֶת־אֶלְעָזָר וְאֶת־אִיתָמָר: 24 וּבְנֵי

קֹרַח אַסִּיר וְאֶלְקָנָה וַאֲבִיאָסָף ר״פ אל, יהוה ברבוע אֵלֶּה מִשְׁפְּחֹת הַקָּרְחִי:

25 וְאֶלְעָזָר בֶּן־אַהֲרֹן ב״פ יהוה אדני אהיה לָקַח ע״ב ורבוע ע״ב לוֹ מִבְּנוֹת פּוּטִיאֵל

לוֹ לְאִשָּׁה וַתֵּלֶד לוֹ אֶת־פִּינְחָס אֵלֶּה רָאשֵׁי אֲבוֹת הַלְוִיִּם לְמִשְׁפְּחֹתָם:

26 הוּא אַהֲרֹן ע״ב ורבוע ע״ב וּמֹשֶׁה מהע, אל שדי אֲשֶׁר אָמַר יְהוֹ‍ַאֲדֹנָיאהדונהי

לָהֶם הוֹצִיאוּ אֶת־בְּנֵי יִשְׂרָאֵל מֵאֶרֶץ מִצְרַיִם אלהים דאלפין עַל־

צִבְאֹתָם: 27 הֵם הַמְדַבְּרִים ראה אֶל־פַּרְעֹה מֶלֶךְ־מִצְרַיִם מצר לְהוֹצִיא

אֶת־בְּנֵי־יִשְׂרָאֵל מִמִּצְרָיִם מצר הוּא מֹשֶׁה מהע, אל שדי וְאַהֲרֹן ע״ב ורבוע ע״ב:

28 וַיְהִי אל, ייא״י בְּיוֹם ע״ה = נגד, זן, מזבח דִּבֶּר ראה יְהוֹ‍ָהאֲדֹנָיאהדונהי אֶל־מֹשֶׁה

מהע, אל שדי בְּאֶרֶץ אלהים דאלפין מִצְרָיִם מצר:

THIRD READING - JACOB - TIFERET

29 and the Lord spoke to Moses, saying, "I am the Lord. Tell Pharaoh, King of Egypt, everything I tell you."

30 But Moses said to the Lord, "Since I am of uncircumcised lips, why would Pharaoh listen to me?"

7:1 Then the Lord said to Moses, "See, I have made you like God to Pharaoh, and your brother Aaron will be your prophet.

2 You are to say everything I command you, and your brother Aaron will speak to Pharaoh and he will send the Israelites out of his country.

3 But I will harden Pharaoh's heart, and though I multiply My miraculous signs and wonders in Egypt,

4 he will not listen to you. Then I will lay My hand on Egypt and I will bring out My legions, My people, the Israelites, from Egypt, with mighty acts of judgment.

5 And the Egyptians will know that I am the Lord when I stretch out My hand against Egypt and bring the Israelites out of it."

6 Moses and Aaron did so; just as the Lord commanded them they did. 7 Moses was eighty years old and Aaron eighty-three when they spoke to Pharaoh.

Exodus 6:29—God again told Moses to speak to Pharaoh one more time, and Moses again protested that he could not speak. When God told Moses to have Aaron speak to Pharaoh, it is because the energy that Moses could reveal would be so powerful that Pharaoh would have difficulty connecting with it. Aaron, in a sense, would make the energy "digestible" for Pharaoh. The Zohar says:

AND HE ANSWERS: It is a secret. Moses IS voice, NAMELY ZEIR ANPIN THAT IS CALLED VOICE, and speech, which is his words, NAMELY MALCHUT, was in exile. THEREFORE, Moses was impeded IN MOUTH from explaining things, and therefore he said, "How then shall

Pharaoh hear me when my speech, WHICH IS MALCHUT, is still in exile, and I am speechless, a speechless voice, for it is in exile." Therefore the Holy One, blessed be He, made Aaron a partner to him, INSTEAD OF MALCHUT, AS HE IS THE QUEEN'S BEST MAN.
— The Zohar, Va'era 7:67

From this, we learn that a prophet's voice is given to him to speak what the Creator will have him speak. Prophets and wise teachers are so rare and precious that we must always be on the lookout for our appropriate spiritual teacher. Although many may be available, we can maximize our understanding by finding the teacher who is most compatible with us and who can speak to us on our level.

THIRD READING - JACOB - TIFERET

29 וַיְדַבֵּ֥ר יְהֹוָ֖הֱאֲדֹנָ֑יֱאֱלֹהִ֑ים אֶל־מֹשֶׁ֥ה לֵאמֹ֖ר אֲנִ֣י

יְהֹוָ֑הֱאֲדֹנָ֑יֱאֱלֹהִ֑ים דַּבֵּ֕ר אֶל־פַּרְעֹ֖ה מֶ֣לֶךְ מִצְרַ֑יִם אֵ֚ת כָּל־ אֲשֶׁ֣ר

אֲנִ֖י דֹּבֵ֥ר אֵלֶ֑יךָ 30 וַיֹּ֥אמֶר מֹשֶׁ֖ה לִפְנֵ֣י

יְהֹוָ֑הֱאֲדֹנָ֑יֱאֱלֹהִ֑ים הֵ֣ן אֲנִ֖י עֲרַ֣ל שְׂפָתָ֑יִם וְאֵ֕יךְ

יִשְׁמַ֥ע אֵלַ֖י פַּרְעֹֽה׃ 7 1 וַיֹּ֤אמֶר יְהֹוָה֙ אֶל־מֹשֶׁ֔ה רְאֵ֛ה

נְתַתִּ֥יךָ אֱלֹהִ֖ים לְפַרְעֹ֑ה וְאַהֲרֹ֥ן אָחִ֖יךָ יִהְיֶ֥ה

נְבִיאֶֽךָ׃ 2 אַתָּ֣ה תְדַבֵּ֔ר אֵ֖ת כָּל־אֲשֶׁ֣ר אֲצַוֶּ֑ךָּ וְאַהֲרֹ֤ן

אָחִ֙יךָ֙ יְדַבֵּ֣ר אֶל־פַּרְעֹ֔ה וְשִׁלַּ֥ח אֶת־בְּנֵֽי־יִשְׂרָאֵ֖ל מֵאַרְצֽוֹ׃ 3 וַאֲנִ֥י

אַקְשֶׁ֖ה אֶת־לֵ֣ב פַּרְעֹ֑ה וְהִרְבֵּיתִ֧י אֶת־אֹתֹתַ֛י וְאֶת־מוֹפְתַ֖י

בְּאֶ֥רֶץ מִצְרָֽיִם׃ 4 וְלֹֽא־יִשְׁמַ֤ע אֲלֵכֶם֙ פַּרְעֹ֔ה וְנָתַתִּ֥י אֶת־

יָדִ֖י בְּמִצְרָ֑יִם וְהוֹצֵאתִ֨י אֶת־צִבְאֹתַ֜י אֶת־עַמִּ֤י בְנֵֽי־יִשְׂרָאֵל֙ מֵאֶ֣רֶץ

מִצְרַ֔יִם בִּשְׁפָטִ֖ים גְּדֹלִֽים׃ 5 וְיָדְע֤וּ מִצְרַ֙יִם֙ כִּי־אֲנִ֣י

יְהֹוָ֑הֱאֲדֹנָ֑יֱאֲהֹוָ֑ה בִּנְטֹתִ֥י אֶת־יָדִ֖י עַל־מִצְרָ֑יִם וְהוֹצֵאתִ֥י אֶת־

בְּנֵֽי־יִשְׂרָאֵ֖ל מִתּוֹכָֽם׃ 6 וַיַּ֥עַשׂ מֹשֶׁ֖ה וְאַהֲרֹ֑ן כַּאֲשֶׁ֨ר

אַקְשֶׁה

Exodus 7:3—God told Moses that He would harden Pharaoh's heart. It does not seem reasonable that God would harden Pharaoh's heart, and yet, if we think about why this might have been so, we realize that even Pharaoh deserved to be able to exercise free will. When God caused Pharaoh to forget the suffering caused by the plagues, He was giving him free will to choose. After each plague was over, Pharaoh forgot the suffering of his people; therefore, he did not feel a sense of urgency to release the Israelites.

By reading about Pharaoh's process, we are reminded about the experience of our own lives. We make the same mistakes over and over again because we are either unaware or have forgotten the consequences of our earlier actions. Without this understanding, we will not make different choices that will bring us closer to the Light of the Creator. But when we start to see the pattern that causes us to make the same errors again and again, we can address the seed level of our actions and have the strength and insight to gain control.

FOURTH READING - MOSES - NETZACH

8 The Lord said to Moses and Aaron, 9 "When Pharaoh says to you, 'Perform a miracle,' then say to Aaron, 'Take your staff and throw it down before Pharaoh,' and it will become a serpent." 10 So Moses and Aaron went to Pharaoh and did just as the Lord commanded. Aaron threw his staff down in front of Pharaoh and his servants, and it became a serpent.

11 Pharaoh then summoned wise men and sorcerers, and the Egyptian magicians also did the same things by their secret arts: 12 Each one threw down his staff and they became serpents. But Aaron's staff swallowed up their staffs. 13 Yet Pharaoh's heart became hard and he would not listen to them, just as the Lord had said.

14 Then the Lord said to Moses, "Pharaoh's heart is heavy; he refuses to let the people go. 15 Go to Pharaoh in the morning as he goes out to the water. Wait on the bank of the Nile to meet him, and take in your hand the staff that was changed into a serpent.

16 Then say to him, 'The Lord, the God of the Hebrews, has sent me to say to you: "Let My people go, so that they may worship Me in the desert." But until now you have not listened.

וַיָּבֹא

Exodus 7:10—Moses and Aaron appeared before Pharaoh.

When Pharaoh commanded Moses and Aaron to show him a miracle, Aaron threw his staff to the ground and it became a snake. However, Pharaoh's priests were able to do the same thing. The Zohar speaks about this as follows:

Rav Chiya asked Rav Yosi, "It was revealed before God that these sorcerers would make serpents AND, IF SO, what is the significance of making serpents in front of Pharaoh"? He said to him," It is because the origin of the punishments is in there," MEANING THE PRIMORDIAL SERPENT THAT CAUSED ADAM AND EVE TO FALL. The reign OF PHARAOH starts at the origin of the serpent, NAMELY FROM THE LEFT SIDE. Then WHEN THEY SAW THE TRANSITION OF AARON'S ROD TO A SERPENT, all the sorcerers rejoiced, because the beginning of the wisdom of their serpent

was such. Immediately Aaron's rod turned back into a dry piece of wood and swallowed them.
— The Zohar, Va'era 15:118

We must never underestimate the power of Satan. Although we may believe that our connection to the Light is strong and protected like Moses, we must be cautious and aware that Satan is an ever-present formidable and wily Opponent.

The Plagues

The Ten Plagues correspond to the *Ten Sefirot* or Emanations, ascending from *Malchut* to *Keter*.

Exodus 7:17—The first plague, the Plague of Blood, is the level of Malchut.

Rav Abin the Levite said that even if the Egyptians and Israelites drank from the same vessel, the Egyptians encountered blood, while the

צִוָּ֣ה פ"י יְהֹוָ֨ה֙אֲדֹנָי֤ אֹתָ֔ם כֵּ֖ן עָשֽׂוּ׃ 7 וּמֹשֶׁ֣ה מהע, אל שדי בֶּן־שְׁמֹנִ֣ים שָׁנָ֔ה

וְאַהֲרֹ֕ן ע"ב ורבוע ע"ב בֶּן־שָׁלֹ֥שׁ וּשְׁמֹנִ֖ים שָׁנָ֑ה בְּדַבְּרָ֖ם ראה אֶל־פַּרְעֹֽה׃

FOURTH READING - MOSES - NETZACH

8 וַיֹּ֣אמֶר יְהֹוָ֔ה֙אֲדֹנָי֤ אֶל־מֹשֶׁ֥ה מהע, אל שדי וְאֶֽל־אַהֲרֹ֖ן ע"ב ורבוע ע"ב לֵאמֹֽר׃

9 כִּי֩ יְדַבֵּ֨ר ראה אֲלֵכֶ֤ם פַּרְעֹה֙ לֵאמֹ֔ר תְּנ֥וּ לָכֶ֖ם מוֹפֵ֑ת וְאָמַרְתָּ֣ אֶֽל־

אַהֲרֹ֗ן ע"ב ורבוע ע"ב קַ֧ח אֶֽת־מַטְּךָ֛ וְהַשְׁלֵ֥ךְ דצ לִפְנֵֽי־פַרְעֹ֖ה יְהִ֥י לְתַנִּֽין׃ חכמה בינה

10 וַיָּבֹ֨א מֹשֶׁ֤ה מהע, אל שדי וְאַהֲרֹן֙ ע"ב ורבוע ע"ב אֶל־פַּרְעֹ֔ה וַיַּ֣עֲשׂוּ כֵ֔ן כַּאֲשֶׁ֖ר

צִוָּ֣ה פ"י יְהֹוָ֔ה֙אֲדֹנָי֤ וַיַּשְׁלֵ֤ךְ אַהֲרֹן֙ ע"ב ורבוע ע"ב אֶֽת־מַטֵּ֔הוּ לִפְנֵ֥י חכמה בינה

פַרְעֹ֖ה וְלִפְנֵ֣י חכמה בינה עֲבָדָ֑יו וַיְהִ֖י יאא"י לְתַנִּֽין׃ 11 וַיִּקְרָא֙ ב"פ קס"א + ה' אותיות אל, אל,

גַּם֙ יג"ל ־פַּרְעֹ֔ה לַֽחֲכָמִ֖ים וְלַֽמְכַשְּׁפִ֑ים וַיַּֽעֲשׂ֨וּ גַם־ יג"ל הֵ֜ם וְחַרְטֻמֵּ֥י מִצְרַ֛יִם

מצר בְּלַהֲטֵיהֶ֖ם כֵּֽן׃ 12 וַיַּשְׁלִ֙יכוּ֙ אִ֣ישׁ ע"ה קנ"א קס"א מַטֵּ֔הוּ וַיִּֽהְי֖וּ מלוי ס"ג לְתַנִּינִ֑ם

וַיִּבְלַ֥ע מַטֵּֽה־אַהֲרֹ֖ן ע"ב ורבוע ע"ב אֶת־מַטֹּתָֽם׃ 13 וַיֶּחֱזַק֙ לֵ֣ב פַּרְעֹ֔ה וְלֹ֥א

שָׁמַ֖ע אֲלֵהֶ֑ם כַּאֲשֶׁ֖ר דִּבֶּ֥ר ראה יְהֹוָֽה֙אֲדֹנָֽי֤׃ 14 וַיֹּ֤אמֶר יְהֹוָ֔ה֙אֲדֹנָי֤

אֶל־מֹשֶׁ֔ה מהע, אל שדי כָּבֵ֖ד לֵ֣ב פַּרְעֹ֑ה מֵאֵ֖ן לְשַׁלַּ֥ח הָעָֽם׃ 15 לֵ֣ךְ אֶל־

פַּרְעֹ֞ה בַּבֹּ֗קֶר הִנֵּה֙ מ"ה יה יֹצֵ֣א הַמַּ֔יְמָה וְנִצַּבְתָּ֥ לִקְרָאת֖וֹ עַל־שְׂפַ֣ת

הַיְאֹ֑ר כף ויו זין ויו וְהַמַּטֶּ֛ה אֲשֶׁר־נֶהְפַּ֥ךְ לְנָחָ֖שׁ שדי ורבוע אהיה תִּקַּ֥ח בְּיָדֶֽךָ׃ בוכ"ו

16 וְאָמַרְתָּ֣ אֵלָ֗יו יְהֹוָ֞ה֙אֲדֹנָי֤ אֱלֹהֵ֤י דמב, ילה הָֽעִבְרִים֙ שְׁלָחַ֣נִי אֵלֶ֔יךָ

אֲנִי, טדהד כוו"ו לֵאמֹ֔ר שַׁלַּח֙ אֶת־עַמִּ֔י וְיַֽעַבְדֻ֖נִי בַּמִּדְבָּ֑ר רמ"ח, וז"פ אל וְהִנֵּ֥ה

מ"ה ־ יה לֹא־שָׁמַ֖עְתָּ עַד־כֹּֽה׃ היי 17 כֹּ֚ה היי אָמַ֣ר יְהֹוָ֔ה֙אֲדֹנָֽי֤ בְּזֹ֣את תֵּדַ֔ע

כִּ֖י אֲנִ֑י אני, טדהד כוו"ו יְהֹוָ֑ה֙אֲדֹנָֽי֤ מ"ה יה הִנֵּ֨ה מ"ה יה אָֽנֹכִ֜י איע מַכֶּ֣ה היי | בַּמַּטֶּ֣ה

אֲשֶׁר־בְּיָדִ֗י עַל־הַמַּ֛יִם אֲשֶׁ֥ר בַּיְאֹ֖ר כף ויו זין ויו וְנֶהֶפְכ֥וּ לְדָֽם׃ רבוע אהיה

18 וְהַדָּגָ֧ה אֲשֶׁר־בַּיְאֹ֛ר כף ויו זין ויו תָּמ֖וּת וּבָאַ֣שׁ הַיְאֹ֑ר כף ויו זין ויו וְנִלְא֣וּ

17 This is what the Lord says: By this you will know that I am the LORD: With the staff that is in my hand I will strike the water of the Nile, and it will be changed into blood. 18 And the fish in the Nile will die, and the river will stink; the Egyptians will not be able to drink its water.' "

19 The Lord said to Moses, "Tell Aaron, 'Take your staff and stretch out your hand over the waters of Egypt—over the streams and canals, over the ponds and all the reservoirs—and they will turn to blood. Blood will be everywhere in Egypt, even in the wood and the stone."

20 Moses and Aaron did just as the Lord had commanded. He raised his staff in the presence of Pharaoh and his servants and struck the water of the Nile, and all the water in the Nile turned into blood.

21 The fish in the Nile died, and the river smelled so bad that the Egyptians could not drink its water. Blood was everywhere in Egypt.

22 But the Egyptian magicians did the same things by their secret arts, and Pharaoh's heart became hard; he would not listen to Moses and Aaron, just as the Lord had said.

23 Instead, he turned and went into his palace, and did not take even this to heart.

24 And all the Egyptians dug along the Nile to get drinking water, because they could not drink the water of the river.

25 Seven days passed after the Lord struck the Nile.

Israelites experienced water. (*Midrash Rabbah*) Throughout history until today, humanity yearns for an existence free of negativity—pain, illness, and even death, as well as the destruction of our physical environment—as symbolized by the bloody water.

It was Aaron who actually activated the Plague of Blood by striking his staff against the waters of the Nile. Rav Tanhum said that Moses did not activate the plague because it was upon those very waters that he had been floated to safety as an infant. (*Midrash Rabbah*) Therefore, Moses could not act as the channel for this plague. This act of restriction reminds us that we must always have appreciation for all things and people, even for forces of nature that have helped us in the past. All too often, we receive assistance in our times of need, but later, we forget the good that was done for us.

The Zohar talks about the higher waters that nurture our world:

In the time that judgment reigns, the Lower World, which is Malchut, does not nurture from that firmament, but nurtures from the Left Side that is not included in the Right. Then Malchut is called, "The sword of God is full of blood" (Isaiah 34:6). Woe to those who then nurture from it and are sustained by it, because at that time the sea, which is Malchut, was nurturing from two sides, from Yesod of Zeir Anpin, and [also] from the Left Side. Therefore, it is divided into two parts, white from the side of Yesod, and red from the Left Side. Then it throws into the river the portion of Egypt, namely the red, and smites their source above, and smites below. Therefore, the

מִצְרַ֫יִם מצר לְשָׁתּ֖וֹת מַ֣יִם מִן־הַיְאֹ֑ר כף ויי זון ויו 19 וַיֹּ֣אמֶר יְהֹוָָ֘֘ה֘אדנ֘י֘אהדונהי

אֶל־מֹשֶׁ֗ה מהע, אל שדי אֱמֹ֣ר אֶֽל־אַהֲרֹ֞ן ע"ב ורבוע ע"ב קַ֣ח מַטְּךָ֣ וּנְטֵֽה־יָדְךָ֗ בוכ"ו

עַל־מֵימֵ֣י מִצְרַ֗יִם מצר עַֽל־נַהֲרֹתָ֣ם ׀ עַל־יְאֹרֵיהֶ֣ם וְעַל־אַגְמֵיהֶ֗ם וְעַ֛ל כָּל־

יל״י מִקְוֵ֥ה קנ"א, אלהים אדני מֵימֵיהֶ֖ם וְיִֽהְיוּ־דָ֑ם אל רבוע אהיה וְהָ֤יָה דָם֙ יהוה

רבוע אהיה בְּכָל־ ב"ן, לכב, יבמ אֶ֣רֶץ אלהים דאלפין מִצְרַ֔יִם מצר וּבָעֵצִ֖ים וּבָאֲבָנִֽים׃

20 וַיַּֽעֲשׂוּ־כֵ֨ן מֹשֶׁ֜ה מהע, אל שדי וְאַהֲרֹ֗ן ע"ב ורבוע ע"ב כַּֽאֲשֶׁ֣ר ׀ צִוָּ֣ה פוי

יְהֹוָָ֘֘ה֘אדנ֘י֘אהדונהי וַיָּ֤רֶם בַּמַּטֶּה֙ וַיַּ֤ךְ אֶת־הַמַּ֨יִם֙ אֲשֶׁ֣ר בַּיְאֹ֔ר כף ויי זון ויו לְעֵינֵ֣י

רִבּוע מ"ה פַרְעֹ֔ה מ"ה וּלְעֵינֵ֖י רִבּוע מ"ה עֲבָדָ֑יו וַיֵּהָֽפְכ֛וּ כָּל־ יל"י הַמַּ֥יִם אֲשֶׁר־בַּיְאֹ֖ר

כף ויי זון ויו לְדָ֑ם רבוע אהיה 21 וְהַדָּגָ֨ה אֲשֶׁר־בַּיְאֹ֤ר כף ויי זון ויו מֵ֨תָה֙ וַיִּבְאַ֣שׁ

הַיְאֹ֔ר כף ויי זון ויו וְלֹֽא־יָכְל֣וּ מִצְרַ֔יִם מצר לִשְׁתּ֥וֹת מַ֖יִם מִן־הַיְאֹ֑ר כף ויי זון ויו

וַיְהִ֥י אל, ייא"י הַדָּ֖ם רבוע אהיה בְּכָל־ ב"ן, לכב, יבמ אֶ֥רֶץ אלהים דאלפין מִצְרָֽיִם׃ מצר

22 וַיַּֽעֲשׂוּ־כֵ֛ן וְחַרְטֻמֵּ֥י מִצְרַ֖יִם מצר בְּלָטֵיהֶ֑ם וַיֶּֽחֱזַ֤ק לֵב־פַּרְעֹה֙ וְלֹֽא־שָׁמַ֣ע

אֲלֵהֶ֔ם כַּֽאֲשֶׁ֖ר דִּבֶּ֥ר ראה יְהֹוָָ֘֘ה֘אדנ֘י֘אהדונהי׃ 23 וַיִּ֣פֶן פַּרְעֹ֔ה וַיָּבֹ֖א אֶל־בֵּית֑וֹ

ב"פ ראה וְלֹא־שָׁ֥ת לִבּ֖וֹ גַּם־ יג"ל לָזֹֽאת׃ 24 וַיַּחְפְּר֧וּ כָל־ יל"י מִצְרַ֛יִם מצר

סְבִיבֹ֥ת הַיְאֹ֖ר כף ויי זון ויו מַ֣יִם לִשְׁתּ֑וֹת כִּ֣י לֹ֤א יָֽכְלוּ֙ לִשְׁתֹּ֔ת מִמֵּימֵ֖י הַיְאֹֽר

כף ויי זון ויו 25 וַיִּמָּלֵ֖א שִׁבְעַ֣ת יָמִ֑ים נלך אַֽחֲרֵ֥י הַכּֽוֹת־יְהֹוָָ֘֘ה֘אדנ֘י֘אהדונהי אֶת־

הַיְאֹֽר כף ויי זון ויו׃ 26 וַיֹּ֤אמֶר יְהֹוָָ֘֘ה֘אדנ֘י֘אהדונהי אֶל־מֹשֶׁ֔ה מהע, אל שדי בֹּ֖א אֶל־

---

children of Israel drink water because they are attached in Yesod of Zeir Anpin, which is the white part of Malchut, and Egyptians drink blood, which is the red part of Malchut. So if you say that the Plague of Blood was only to repel them, come and see. They drank the blood, which entered their intestines and split and rose until the children of Israel sold them water for money. Then they drank water. Therefore, the first plague that smote them was blood.

— *The Zohar, Va'era 16:131-132*

From this, we learn that the source to which we cling determines the quality of our nourishment. If we cling to the things of this world, our knowledge will be of this limited 1 Percent Illusion only. If we cling to the Upper Worlds, our connection will include the 99 Percent Reality of the Light of the Creator.

26 Then the Lord said to Moses, "Come to Pharaoh and say to him, 'This is what the Lord says: "Let My people go, so that they may worship Me."

27 If you refuse to let them go, I will plague your whole country with frogs.

28 The Nile will teem with frogs. They will come up into your palace and your bedroom and onto your bed, into the houses of your servants and on your people, and into your ovens and kneading troughs.

29 The frogs will go up on you and your people and all your servants.' "

8:1 Then the Lord said to Moses, "Tell Aaron, 'Stretch out your hand with your staff over the streams and canals and ponds, and make frogs come up on the land of Egypt.' "

2 So Aaron stretched out his hand over the waters of Egypt, and the frog came up and covered the land of Egypt.

3 But the magicians did the same things by their secret arts; they also made frogs come up on the land of Egypt.

4 Pharaoh summoned Moses and Aaron and said, "Pray to the Lord to take the frogs away from me and my people, and I will let your people go and offer sacrifices to the Lord."

5 Moses said to Pharaoh, "I leave to you the honor of setting the time for me to pray for you and your officials and your people that you and your houses may be rid of the frogs, except for those that remain in the Nile."

6 "Tomorrow," Pharaoh said. Moses replied, "It will be as you say, so that you may know there is no one like the Lord, our God.

צְפַרְדְּעִים

Exodus 7:27—The second plague, the Plague of Frogs, is the level of *Yesod*.

After Aaron had again stretched out his hand, great swarms of frogs appeared everywhere. This plague was so extreme that if by chance any frogs were cooked in the food of the Egyptians, they came to life as the Egyptians ate their meal.

The Zohar says:

> "And the frog came up." (Exodus 8:2) IT SHOULD HAVE SAID 'FROGS' IN THE PLURAL. HE ANSWERS, "It was one frog, but it bred and the land became filled with them. And they all gave themselves over to the fire, as written: 'And into your ovens and into your kneading troughs.'" (Exodus 7:28). What did they say: "We went through fire and through water; but You did bring us out into abundance." (Psalms 66:12) And if you ask, how does this concern the Egyptians that all these frogs went into the fire? HE ANSWERS, "they all came into the fire and went into the ovens yet did not die." Those that did die, what did they do? There was bread in the oven, and they came into the bread and burst, and others came out of them and were swallowed in the bread. And

פַּרְעֹה וְאָמַרְתָּ אֵלָיו כֹּה אָמַר יְהֹוָאדְנִיאהדונהי שַׁלַּח אֶת־עַמִּי וְיַעַבְדֻנִי:

27 וְאִם־מָאֵן אַתָּה לְשַׁלֵּחַ הִנֵּה אָנֹכִי נֹגֵף אֶת־כָּל־גְּבוּלְךָ בַּצְפַרְדְּעִים: 28 וְשָׁרַץ הַיְאֹר צְפַרְדְּעִים וְעָלוּ וּבָאוּ בְּבֵיתֶךָ וּבַחֲדַר מִשְׁכָּבְךָ וְעַל־מִטָּתֶךָ וּבְבֵית עֲבָדֶיךָ וּבְעַמֶּךָ וּבְתַנּוּרֶיךָ וּבְמִשְׁאֲרוֹתֶיךָ: 29 וּבְכָה וּבְעַמְּךָ וּבְכָל־עֲבָדֶיךָ יַעֲלוּ הַצְפַרְדְּעִים:

8 1 וַיֹּאמֶר יְהֹוָאדְנִיאהדונהי אֶל־מֹשֶׁה אֱמֹר אֶל־אַהֲרֹן נְטֵה אֶת־יָדְךָ בְּמַטֶּךָ עַל־הַנְּהָרֹת עַל־הַיְאֹרִים וְעַל־הָאֲגַמִּים וְהַעַל אֶת־הַצְפַרְדְּעִים עַל־אֶרֶץ מִצְרָיִם: 2 וַיֵּט אַהֲרֹן אֶת־יָדוֹ עַל מֵימֵי מִצְרָיִם וַתַּעַל הַצְּפַרְדֵּעַ וַתְּכַס אֶת־אֶרֶץ מִצְרָיִם: 3 וַיַּעֲשׂוּ כֵן הַחַרְטֻמִּים בְּלָטֵיהֶם וַיַּעֲלוּ אֶת־הַצְפַרְדְּעִים עַל־אֶרֶץ מִצְרָיִם: 4 וַיִּקְרָא פַרְעֹה לְמֹשֶׁה וּלְאַהֲרֹן וַיֹּאמֶר הַעְתִּירוּ אֶל־יְהֹוָאדְנִיאהדונהי וְיָסֵר הַצְפַרְדְּעִים מִמֶּנִּי וּמֵעַמִּי וַאֲשַׁלְּחָה אֶת־הָעָם וְיִזְבְּחוּ לַיהֹוָאדְנִיאהדונהי: 5 וַיֹּאמֶר מֹשֶׁה לְפַרְעֹה הִתְפָּאֵר עָלַי לְמָתַי אַעְתִּיר לְךָ וְלַעֲבָדֶיךָ וּלְעַמְּךָ לְהַכְרִית הַצְפַרְדְּעִים מִמְּךָ וּמִבָּתֶּיךָ רַק בַּיְאֹר תִּשָּׁאַרְנָה: 6 וַיֹּאמֶר לְמָחָר וַיֹּאמֶר כִּדְבָרְךָ לְמַעַן תֵּדַע כִּי־אֵין כַּיהֹוָאדְנִיאהדונהי אֱלֹהֵינוּ:

---

when they wanted to eat of the bread, the bread in their bowels turned back into frogs that danced and raised their voices until THE EGYPTIANS died. This PLAGUE was harder on them than all the others. Come and see, it is written: "And the River shall bring forth frogs in swarms, and these will go up and come into your house, and on your bedchamber...AND THE FROGS SHALL COME UP BOTH ON (LIT. 'IN') YOU, AND ON (IN) YOUR PEOPLE, AND ON (IN) ALL YOUR SERVANTS" (Exodus 7:28-29) SO THEY CAME INSIDE THEIR BODIES. Pharaoh was smitten first and more than everyone else, FOR IT SAYS, "ON YOU, AND ON YOUR PEOPLE, AND ON ALL YOUR SERVANTS." May the Name of God be blessed from everlasting to everlasting, for He examines the actions of people in everything they do.
— The Zohar, Va'era 17:153

Just as the frogs were resurrected because they were willing to be sacrificed in the cooking fire for the sake of the Light, we too, will be restored from death in all of its manifestations—end of life, end of sustenance, end of relationships, end of health—if we are willing to do whatever it takes to connect to the Light.

FIFTH READING - AARON - HOD

7 The frogs will leave you and your houses, your servants and your people; they will remain only in the Nile."

8 After Moses and Aaron left Pharaoh, Moses cried out to the Lord about the frogs he had brought on Pharaoh.

9 And the Lord did what Moses asked. The frogs died in the houses, in the courtyards and in the fields.

10 They were piled into heaps, and the land reeked of them. 11 But when Pharaoh saw that there was relief, he hardened his heart and would not listen to them, just as the Lord had said.

12 Then the Lord said to Moses, "Tell Aaron, 'Stretch out your staff and strike the dust of the ground,' and throughout the land of Egypt it will become lice."

13 They did this, and when Aaron stretched out his hand with the staff and struck the dust of the ground, lice came upon men and animals. All the dust throughout the land of Egypt became lice.

14 But when the magicians tried to produce lice by their secret arts, they could not. And the lice were on men and animals.

15 The magicians said to Pharaoh, "This is the Finger of God." But Pharaoh's heart was hard and he would not listen to them, just as the Lord had said.

16 The Lord said to Moses, "Get up early in the morning and confront Pharaoh as he goes to the water and say to him, 'This is what the Lord says: "Let My people go, so that they may worship Me."

לְכִנָּם	הָעָרֹב
Exodus 8:12—The third plague, the Plague of Lice, is the level of *Hod*.	Exodus 8:17—The fourth plague, the Plague of Wild Beasts, is the level of *Netzach*.
During the third plague, the very dust of the earth became lice. This plague was the first that Pharaoh's magicians were unable to duplicate, and they had to concede that the plague came from the Hand of God. This particular plague, occasioned by such tiny creatures—the smallest aspect of physical reality, reveals to us that we will have dominion over both the largest and smallest dimensions of reality.	Rashi said that "wild beasts" referred to a mixture of all kinds of wild beasts, snakes, and scorpions, which caused devastation among the Egyptians. When we read about this plague, we receive protection from diseases like bird flu and mad cow disease that begin in the animal kingdom.

FIFTH READING - AARON - HOD

וְסָרוּ הַצְפַרְדְּעִים מִמְּךָ וּמִבָּתֶּיךָ וּמֵעֲבָדֶיךָ וּמֵעַמֶּךָ רַק בַּיְאֹר 7

תִּשָּׁאַרְנָה: 8 וַיֵּצֵא מֹשֶׁה וְאַהֲרֹן מֵעִם פַּרְעֹה

וַיִּצְעַק מֹשֶׁה אֶל־יְהֹוָה עַל־דְּבַר הַצְפַרְדְּעִים

אֲשֶׁר־שָׂם לְפַרְעֹה: 9 וַיַּעַשׂ יְהֹוָה כִּדְבַר מֹשֶׁה

וַיָּמֻתוּ הַצְפַרְדְּעִים מִן־הַבָּתִּים מִן־הַחֲצֵרֹת וּמִן־הַשָּׂדֹת:

10 וַיִּצְבְּרוּ אֹתָם חֳמָרִם חֳמָרִם וַתִּבְאַשׁ הָאָרֶץ 11 וַיַּרְא

פַּרְעֹה כִּי הָיְתָה הָרְוָחָה וְהַכְבֵּד אֶת־לִבּוֹ וְלֹא שָׁמַע אֲלֵהֶם

כַּאֲשֶׁר דִּבֶּר יְהֹוָה: 12 וַיֹּאמֶר יְהֹוָה אֶל־מֹשֶׁה

אֱמֹר אֶל־אַהֲרֹן נְטֵה אֶת־מַטְּךָ וְהַךְ אֶת־עֲפַר

הָאָרֶץ וְהָיָה לְכִנִּם בְּכָל־אֶרֶץ

מִצְרָיִם: 13 וַיַּעֲשׂוּ־כֵן וַיֵּט אַהֲרֹן אֶת־יָדוֹ בְמַטֵּהוּ וַיַּךְ

אֶת־עֲפַר הָאָרֶץ וַתְּהִי הַכִּנָּם בָּאָדָם וּבַבְּהֵמָה

כָּל־עֲפַר הָאָרֶץ הָיָה כִנִּים בְּכָל־אֶרֶץ

מִצְרָיִם: 14 וַיַּעֲשׂוּ־כֵן הַחַרְטֻמִּים בְּלָטֵיהֶם לְהוֹצִיא אֶת־

הַכִּנִּים וְלֹא יָכֹלוּ וַתְּהִי הַכִּנָּם בָּאָדָם וּבַבְּהֵמָה:

15 וַיֹּאמְרוּ הַחַרְטֻמִּם אֶל־פַּרְעֹה אֶצְבַּע אֱלֹהִים הִוא

וַיֶּחֱזַק לֵב־פַּרְעֹה וְלֹא־שָׁמַע אֲלֵהֶם כַּאֲשֶׁר דִּבֶּר יְהֹוָה:

16 וַיֹּאמֶר יְהֹוָה אֶל־מֹשֶׁה הַשְׁכֵּם בַּבֹּקֶר וְהִתְיַצֵּב

לִפְנֵי פַרְעֹה הִנֵּה יוֹצֵא הַמָּיְמָה וְאָמַרְתָּ אֵלָיו כֹּה אָמַר

יְהֹוָה שַׁלַּח עַמִּי וְיַעַבְדֻנִי: 17 כִּי אִם־אֵינְךָ מְשַׁלֵּחַ

אֶת־עַמִּי הִנְנִי מַשְׁלִיחַ בְּךָ וּבַעֲבָדֶיךָ וּבְעַמְּךָ וּבְבָתֶּיךָ אֶת־

הֶעָרֹב וּמָלְאוּ בָּתֵּי מִצְרַיִם אֶת־הֶעָרֹב

17 If you do not let My people go, I will send wild animals on you and your servants, on your people and into your houses. The houses of the Egyptians will be full of wild animals, and even the ground where they are.

18 But on that day I will deal differently with the land of Goshen, where My people live; no wild animals will be there, so that you will know that I, the Lord, am in this land.

SIXTH READING - JOSEPH - YESOD

19 I will make a distinction between My people and your people. This miraculous sign will occur tomorrow.' "

20 And the Lord did this, and a heavy swarm of wild animals poured into Pharaoh's palace and into the houses of his servants, and throughout Egypt the land was ruined by the wild animals.

21 Then Pharaoh summoned Moses and Aaron and said, "Go, sacrifice to your God here in the land."

22 But Moses said, "That would not be right. The sacrifices we offer the Lord, our God, would be detestable to the Egyptians. And if we offer sacrifices that are detestable in their eyes, will they not stone us?

23 We must take a three-day journey into the desert and offer sacrifices to the Lord, our God, as He tells us."

24 Pharaoh said, "I will let you go to offer sacrifices to the Lord, your God, in the desert, but you must not go very far. Now pray for me."

25 Moses answered, "As soon as I leave you, I will pray to the Lord, and tomorrow the wild animals will leave Pharaoh and his servants and his people. Only be sure that Pharaoh does not act deceitfully again by not letting the people go to offer sacrifices to the Lord."

26 Then Moses left Pharaoh and prayed to the Lord,

27 and the Lord did what Moses asked: The wild animals were removed from Pharaoh and his servants and his people; not one remained.

28 But this time also Pharaoh hardened his heart and would not let the people go.

רבוע יהוה ורבוע אלהים יְּגַּ וְּגַם הָאֲדָמָה אֲשֶׁר־הֵם עָלֶיהָ פ״הלל 18 וְהִפְלֵיתִי בַיּוֹם

ע״ה = נגד, זן, מזבח הַהוּא אֶת־אֶרֶץ אלהים דאלפין גֹּשֶׁן אֲשֶׁר עַמִּי עֹמֵד עָלֶיהָ פ״הל

לְבִלְתִּי הֱיוֹת־שָׁם יהוה שדי עָרֹב רבוע יהוה ורבוע אלהים לְמַעַן תֵּדַע כִּי אֲנִי

אני, טדה״ד כוז״ו יְהוָֹואדנֹיאהדונהי בְּקֶרֶב קמ״ג קס״א הָאָרֶץ אלהים דההין ע״ה:

SIXTH READING - JOSEPH - YESOD

19 וְשַׂמְתִּי פְדֻת בֵּין עַמִּי וּבֵין עַמֶּךָ ה' הויות, נמם לְמָחָר רמ״ח יִהְיֶה ייי הָאֹת

הַזֶּה וה״ו: 20 וַיַּעַשׂ יְהוָֹואדנֹיאהדונהי כֵּן וַיָּבֹא עָרֹב רבוע יהוה ורבוע אלהים כָּבֵד

בֵּיתָה ב״פ ראה פַרְעֹה וּבֵית ב״פ ראה עֲבָדָיו וּבְכָל ב״ן, לכב, יבמ ־אֶרֶץ אלהים דאלפין

מִצְרַיִם מצר תִּשָּׁחֵת הָאָרֶץ אלהים דההין ע״ה מִפְּנֵי הֶעָרֹב רבוע יהוה ורבוע אלהים:

21 וַיִּקְרָא עם ה' אותיות = ב״פ קס״א פַרְעֹה אֶל־מֹשֶׁה מהש, אל שדי וְלְאַהֲרֹן ע״ב ורבוע ע״ב

וַיֹּאמֶר לְכוּ זִבְחוּ לֵאלֹהֵיכֶם יל״ה בָּאָרֶץ אלהים דאלפין: 22 וַיֹּאמֶר מֹשֶׁה

מהש, אל שדי לֹא נָכוֹן לַעֲשׂוֹת כֵּן כִּי תּוֹעֲבַת מִצְרַיִם מצר נִזְבַּח לַיהוָֹואדנֹיאהדונהי

אֱלֹהֵינוּ יל״ה הֵן נִזְבַּח אֶת־תּוֹעֲבַת מִצְרַיִם מצר לְעֵינֵיהֶם ריבוע מ״ה וְלֹא

יִסְקְלֻנוּ: 23 דֶּרֶךְ ב״פ יב״ק שְׁלֹשֶׁת יָמִים נלך נֵלֵךְ נלך בַּמִּדְבָּר רמ״ח, וז״ח אל

וְזָבַחְנוּ לַיהוָֹואדנֹיאהדונהי אֱלֹהֵינוּ יל״ה כַּאֲשֶׁר יֹאמַר אֵלֵינוּ: 24 וַיֹּאמֶר פַּרְעֹה

אָנֹכִי איע אֲשַׁלַּח אֶתְכֶם וּזְבַחְתֶּם לַיהוָֹואדנֹיאהדונהי אֱלֹהֵיכֶם יל״ה בַּמִּדְבָּר

רמ״ח, וז״ח אל רַק הַרְחֵק שדי לֹא־תַרְחִיקוּ לָלֶכֶת הַעְתִּירוּ בַּעֲדִי: 25 וַיֹּאמֶר

מֹשֶׁה מהש, אל שדי הִנֵּה מ״ה יה אָנֹכִי איע יוֹצֵא מֵעִמָּךְ ה' הויות, נמם וְהַעְתַּרְתִּי

אֶל־יְהוָֹואדנֹיאהדונהי וְסָר י' הויות רבוע יהוה ורבוע אלהים הֶעָרֹב מִפַּרְעֹה מֵעֲבָדָיו

וּמֵעַמּוֹ מָחָר רמ״ח רַק אַל־יֹסֵף פַרְעֹה הָתֵל לְבִלְתִּי שַׁלַּח אֶת־הָעָם

לִזְבֹּחַ לַיהוָֹואדנֹיאהדונהי: 26 וַיֵּצֵא מֹשֶׁה מהש, אל שדי מֵעִם פַּרְעֹה וַיֶּעְתַּר אֶל־

יְהוָֹואדנֹיאהדונהי: 27 וַיַּעַשׂ יְהוָֹואדנֹיאהדונהי כִּדְבַר ראה מֹשֶׁה מהש, אל שדי וַיָּסַר

9:1 The Lord said to Moses, "Come to Pharaoh and say to him, 'This is what the Lord, the God of the Hebrews, says: "Let My people go, so that they may worship Me."

2 If you refuse to let them go and continue to hold them back, 3 the Hand of the Lord will bring a heavy pestilence on your livestock in the field—on your horses and donkeys and camels and on your cattle and sheep and goats.

4 But the Lord will make a distinction between the livestock of Israel and that of Egypt, so that no animal belonging to the Israelites will die.' "

5 The Lord set a time and said, "Tomorrow the Lord will do this in the land."

6 And the next day the Lord did it: All the livestock of the Egyptians died, but not one animal belonging to the Israelites died.

7 Pharaoh sent men and found that not even one of the animals of the Israelites had died. Yet his heart was unyielding and he would not let the people go.

8 Then the Lord said to Moses and Aaron, "Take handfuls of soot from a furnace and have Moses toss it toward the skies in the presence of Pharaoh.

9 It will become fine dust over the whole land of Egypt, and bubbling boils will break out on men and animals throughout the land of Egypt."

10 So they took soot from a furnace and stood before Pharaoh. Moses tossed it toward the skies, and bubbling boils broke out on men and animals.

11 The magicians could not stand before Moses because of the boils that were on them and on all the Egyptians.

12 But the Lord hardened Pharaoh's heart and he would not listen to them, just as the Lord had said to Moses.

Exodus 9:3—The fifth plague, the Plague of Pestilence, is the level of *Tiferet*.

During the fifth plague, all the livestock of Egypt died, yet all the livestock of the Children of Israel were spared. The discussion of this plague in the Bible provides protection from ailments that affect large numbers of people. When we see disease that affects either individuals or a small number of people, we understand that Satan has been permitted to unleash negativity on a small scale. But when we see widespread illnesses such as AIDS and cancer, we know that Satan

has been granted greater scope to wreak havoc. By connecting to this reading, we can help to thwart Satan.

Exodus 9:9—The sixth plague, the Plague of Boils, is the level of *Gevurah*.

The sixth plague represents all diseases that affect all parts of the body. From reading about this plague, we receive protection from those ailments.

הֶעָרֹב ‏רבוע יהוה ורבוע אלהים‎ מִפַּרְעֹה מֵעֲבָדָיו וּמֵעַמּוֹ לֹא נִשְׁאַר אֶחָד

‏אהבה, דאגה‎ 28 וַיַּכְבֵּד פַּרְעֹה אֶת־לִבּוֹ ‏יג‎ גַּם בַּפַּעַם הַזֹּאת וְלֹא שִׁלַּח

אֶת־הָעָם: 1 9 וַיֹּאמֶר יְהֹוָה ‏ואדני‎ אֶל־מֹשֶׁה ‏מהע, אל שדי‎ בֹּא אֶל־פַּרְעֹה

וְדִבַּרְתָּ ‏ראה‎ אֵלָיו כֹּה ‏היי‎ אָמַר יְהֹוָה ‏ואדני‎ אֱלֹהֵי ‏דמב, ילה‎ הָעִבְרִים

שַׁלַּח אֶת־עַמִּי וְיַעַבְדֻנִי: 2 כִּי אִם ‏יוהך, ע"ב מ"ב‎ מָאֵן אַתָּה לְשַׁלֵּחַ וְעוֹדְךָ

מַחֲזִיק בָּם ‏מ"ה יה‎ 3 הִנֵּה יַד־יְהֹוָה ‏ואדני‎ הוֹיָה ‏יהוה‎ בְּמִקְנְךָ אֲשֶׁר

בַּשָּׂדֶה בַּסּוּסִים בַּחֲמֹרִים בַּגְּמַלִּים בַּבָּקָר וּבַצֹּאן ‏מלוי אהיה דיודין ע"ה‎ דֶּבֶר

‏ראה‎ כָּבֵד מְאֹד ‏מ"ה‎ 4 וְהִפְלָה יְהֹוָה ‏ואדני‎ בֵּין מִקְנֵה יִשְׂרָאֵל וּבֵין

מִקְנֵה מִצְרָיִם ‏מצר‎ וְלֹא יָמוּת מִכָּל ‏ילי‎ לִבְנֵי יִשְׂרָאֵל דָּבָר ‏ראה‎ 5 וַיָּשֶׂם

יְהֹוָה ‏ואדני‎ מוֹעֵד לֵאמֹר מָחָר ‏רמ"ח‎ יַעֲשֶׂה יְהֹוָה ‏ואדני‎ הַדָּבָר ‏ראה‎

הַזֶּה ‏והו‎ בָּאָרֶץ ‏אלהים דאלפין‎ 6 וַיַּעַשׂ יְהֹוָה ‏ואדני‎ אֶת־הַדָּבָר ‏ראה‎ הַזֶּה ‏והו‎

מִמָּחֳרָת וַיָּמָת כֹּל ‏ילי‎ מִקְנֵה מִצְרָיִם ‏מצר‎ וּמִמִּקְנֵה בְנֵי־יִשְׂרָאֵל לֹא־מֵת

אֶחָד ‏י"פ רבוע אהיה‎ ‏אהבה, דאגה‎ 7 וַיִּשְׁלַח פַּרְעֹה וְהִנֵּה ‏מ"ה יה‎ לֹא־מֵת ‏י"פ רבוע אהיה‎

מִמִּקְנֵה יִשְׂרָאֵל עַד־אֶחָד ‏אהבה, דאגה‎ וַיִּכְבַּד לֵב פַּרְעֹה וְלֹא שִׁלַּח אֶת־

הָעָם: 8 וַיֹּאמֶר יְהֹוָה ‏ואדני‎ אֶל־מֹשֶׁה ‏מהע, אל שדי‎ וְאֶל־אַהֲרֹן ‏ע"ב ורבוע ע"ב‎

קְחוּ לָכֶם מְלֹא חָפְנֵיכֶם פִּיחַ כִּבְשָׁן וּזְרָקוֹ מֹשֶׁה ‏מהע, אל שדי‎ הַשָּׁמַיְמָה

לְעֵינֵי ‏ריבוע מ"ה‎ פַּרְעֹה: 9 וְהָיָה ‏יהוה‎ לְאָבָק עַל כָּל ‏ילי‎ אֶרֶץ ‏אלהים דאלפין‎

מִצְרָיִם ‏מצר‎ וְהָיָה ‏יהוה‎ עַל־הָאָדָם ‏מ"ה‎ וְעַל־הַבְּהֵמָה ‏ב"ן, לכב, יבמ‎ לִשְׁחִין

פֹּרֵחַ ‏רפ"ח‎ אֲבַעְבֻּעֹת בְּכָל ‏ב"ן, לכב, יבמ‎ אֶרֶץ ‏אלהים דאלפין‎ מִצְרָיִם ‏מצר‎ 10 וַיִּקְחוּ

אֶת־פִּיחַ הַכִּבְשָׁן וַיַּעַמְדוּ לִפְנֵי פַרְעֹה וַיִּזְרֹק אֹתוֹ מֹשֶׁה ‏מהע, אל שדי‎

הַשָּׁמַיְמָה וַיְהִי ‏אל, ייא"י‎ שְׁחִין אֲבַעְבֻּעֹת פֹּרֵחַ ‏רפ"ח‎ בָּאָדָם ‏מ"ה‎ וּבַבְּהֵמָה

‏ב"ן, לכב, יבמ‎ 11 וְלֹא־יָכְלוּ הַחַרְטֻמִּים לַעֲמֹד לִפְנֵי מֹשֶׁה ‏מהע, אל שדי‎ ‏וחכמה בינה‎

מִפְּנֵי ‏וחכמה בינה‎ הַשְּׁחִין כִּי־הָיָה ‏יהה‎ הַשְּׁחִין בַּחַרְטֻמִּם וּבְכָל ‏ב"ן, לכב, יבמ‎

מִצְרָיִם ‏מצר‎ 12 וַיְחַזֵּק יְהֹוָה ‏ואדני‎ אֶת־לֵב פַּרְעֹה וְלֹא שָׁמַע אֲלֵהֶם

¹³ Then the Lord said to Moses, "Get up early in the morning, confront Pharaoh and say to him, 'This is what the Lord, the God of the Hebrews, says: "Let My people go, so that they may worship Me,"

¹⁴ or this time I will send the full force of My plagues against your heart and against your servants and your people, so you may know that there is no one like Me in all the Earth.

¹⁵ For by now I could have stretched out My Hand and struck you and your people with a plague that would have wiped you off the Earth.

¹⁶ But I have raised you up for this very purpose, that I might show you My power and that My Name might be proclaimed in all the Earth.

SEVENTH READING - DAVID - MALCHUT

¹⁷ You still set yourself against My people and will not let them go.

¹⁸ Therefore, at this time tomorrow I will send the worst hailstorm that has ever fallen on Egypt, from the day it was founded till now.

¹⁹ Give an order now to bring your livestock and everything you have in the field inside, because the hail will fall on every man and animal that has not been brought in and is still out in the field, and they will die.' "

²⁰ Those of Pharaoh's officials who feared the word of the Lord hurried to bring their slaves and their livestock inside.

²¹ But those who ignored the word of the Lord left their slaves and livestock in the field.

Exodus 9:18—The seventh plague, the Plague of Hail, is the level of *Chesed*.

The seventh plague concerns the environment and the atmosphere. By having the awareness of what this reading gives us, we acquire protection against airborne diseases. The Zohar says:

> *Since Egypt did not return IN REPENTANCE, the very letters OF 'PESTILENCE' (Heb: dever — Dalet, Bet, Reish) returned and killed all those who*

survived, AND THE LETTERS Dalet, Bet, Reish turned into hail (Heb. BARAD, Bet, Reish, Dalet). What is the difference between them? PESTILENCE is affected quietly while HAIL is affected with the strength of anger. Both of these were in one place, namely in five fingers.

Pestilence (Dalet, Bet, Reish): These are letters that are quiet, a quiet death, for they died of themselves. [Then] there was hail (Bet, Reish, Dalet) since the letters changed to be infused with the strength of anger, and killed everything.
> *— The Zohar, Va'era 20:192-3*

13 וַיֹּאמֶר יְהֹוָה אֶל־מֹשֶׁה כַּאֲשֶׁר דִּבֶּר

יְהֹוָה אֶל־מֹשֶׁה הַשְׁכֵּם בַּבֹּקֶר וְהִתְיַצֵּב לִפְנֵי

פַרְעֹה וְאָמַרְתָּ אֵלָיו כֹּה אָמַר יְהֹוָה אֱלֹהֵי הָעִבְרִים

שַׁלַּח אֶת־עַמִּי וְיַעַבְדֻנִי: 14 כִּי בַּפַּעַם הַזֹּאת אֲנִי שֹׁלֵחַ

אֶת־כָּל־מַגֵּפֹתַי אֶל־לִבְּךָ וּבַעֲבָדֶיךָ וּבְעַמֶּךָ בַּעֲבוּר תֵּדַע

כִּי אֵין כָּמֹנִי בְּכָל־הָאָרֶץ: 15 כִּי עַתָּה שָׁלַחְתִּי

אֶת־יָדִי וָאַךְ אוֹתְךָ וְאֶת־עַמְּךָ בַּדָּבֶר וַתִּכָּחֵד מִן־

הָאָרֶץ: 16 וְאוּלָם בַּעֲבוּר זֹאת הֶעֱמַדְתִּיךָ בַּעֲבוּר הַרְאֹתְךָ

אֶת־כֹּחִי וּלְמַעַן סַפֵּר שְׁמִי בְּכָל־הָאָרֶץ:

SEVENTH READING - DAVID - MALCHUT

17 עוֹדְךָ מִסְתּוֹלֵל בְּעַמִּי לְבִלְתִּי שַׁלְּחָם: 18 הִנְנִי מַמְטִיר כָּעֵת

מָחָר בָּרָד כָּבֵד מְאֹד אֲשֶׁר לֹא־הָיָה כָמֹהוּ בְּמִצְרַיִם

לְמִן־הַיּוֹם הִוָּסְדָה וְעַד־עָתָּה: 19 וְעַתָּה שְׁלַח הָעֵז אֶת־

מִקְנְךָ וְאֵת כָּל־אֲשֶׁר לְךָ בַּשָּׂדֶה כָּל־הָאָדָם וְהַבְּהֵמָה

אֲשֶׁר־יִמָּצֵא בַשָּׂדֶה וְלֹא יֵאָסֵף הַבַּיְתָה וְיָרַד עֲלֵהֶם הַבָּרָד

וָמֵתוּ: 20 הַיָּרֵא אֶת־דְּבַר יְהֹוָה מֵעַבְדֵי פַּרְעֹה

הֵנִיס אֶת־עֲבָדָיו וְאֶת־מִקְנֵהוּ אֶל־הַבָּתִּים: 21 וַאֲשֶׁר לֹא־שָׂם

לִבּוֹ אֶל־דְּבַר יְהֹוָה וַיַּעֲזֹב אֶת־עֲבָדָיו וְאֶת־מִקְנֵהוּ בַּשָּׂדֶה:

22 וַיֹּאמֶר יְהֹוָה אֶל־מֹשֶׁה נְטֵה אֶת־יָדְךָ עַל־

הַשָּׁמַיִם וִיהִי בָרָד בְּכָל־אֶרֶץ

מִצְרָיִם עַל־הָאָדָם וְעַל־הַבְּהֵמָה וְעַל כָּל־עֵשֶׂב

22 Then the Lord said to Moses, "Stretch out your hand toward the sky so that hail will fall all over Egypt—on men and animals and on everything growing in the fields of Egypt."

23 When Moses stretched out his staff toward the sky, the Lord sent thunder and hail, and lightning flashed down to the ground. So the Lord rained hail on the land of Egypt.

24 There was a heavy hail, and within the hail burning fire fell, none like Egypt had ever seen, since it had first become a nation.

25 Throughout Egypt hail struck everything in the fields—both men and animals; it beat down everything growing in the fields and stripped every tree.

26 Only in the land of Goshen, where the Israelites were, did there fall no hail.

27 Then Pharaoh summoned Moses and Aaron. "This time I have sinned," he said to them. "The Lord is in the right, and I and my people are in the wrong.

28 Pray to the Lord, for we have had enough of the thunder and hail of God. I will let you go; you don't have to stay any longer."

29 Moses replied, "When I have gone out of the city, I will spread out my hands to the Lord. The thunder will stop and there will be no more hail, so you may know that the Earth is the Lord's.

30 But I know that you and your servants still do not fear the Lord, God."

31 The flax and barley were destroyed, since the barley had headed and the flax was in bloom.

32 The wheat and spelt, however, were not destroyed, because they ripen later.

הַעְתִּירוּ

Exodus 9:28—Pharaoh asked Moses to stop the hail, and Moses agreed, but only after the Israelites were safely out of Egypt. Moses did not want to pray in the supremely negative Egyptian environment. Egypt was so negative that even after the land and people had been devastated by the plagues, no one repented. We too, must avoid praying in a negative place. As much as possible, we should pray in a positive setting. If a positive place is not available, we should at least try to find a neutral environment. When we pray, our intention is to connect with the Upper Realms, to achieve closeness with the Light of the Creator. If we choose to pray in a negative place, we are blocking the connection to the Upper Worlds.

‏23 וַיֵּט מֹשֶׁה אֶת־מַטֵּהוּ עַל־הַשָּׁמַיִם וַיהוָה נָתַן קֹלֹת וּבָרָד וַתִּהֲלַךְ אֵשׁ אַרְצָה וַיַּמְטֵר יְהוָה בָּרָד עַל־אֶרֶץ מִצְרָיִם:

‏24 וַיְהִי בָרָד וְאֵשׁ מִתְלַקַּחַת בְּתוֹךְ הַבָּרָד כָּבֵד מְאֹד אֲשֶׁר לֹא־הָיָה כָמֹהוּ בְּכָל־אֶרֶץ מִצְרַיִם מֵאָז הָיְתָה לְגוֹי:

‏25 וַיַּךְ הַבָּרָד בְּכָל־אֶרֶץ מִצְרַיִם אֵת כָּל־אֲשֶׁר בַּשָּׂדֶה מֵאָדָם וְעַד־בְּהֵמָה וְאֵת כָּל־עֵשֶׂב הַשָּׂדֶה הִכָּה הַבָּרָד וְאֶת־כָּל־עֵץ הַשָּׂדֶה שִׁבֵּר:

‏26 רַק בְּאֶרֶץ גֹּשֶׁן אֲשֶׁר־שָׁם בְּנֵי יִשְׂרָאֵל לֹא הָיָה בָּרָד:

‏27 וַיִּשְׁלַח פַּרְעֹה וַיִּקְרָא לְמֹשֶׁה וּלְאַהֲרֹן וַיֹּאמֶר אֲלֵהֶם חָטָאתִי הַפָּעַם יְהוָה הַצַּדִּיק וַאֲנִי וְעַמִּי הָרְשָׁעִים:

‏28 הַעְתִּירוּ אֶל־יְהוָה וְרַב מִהְיֹת קֹלֹת אֱלֹהִים וּבָרָד וַאֲשַׁלְּחָה אֶתְכֶם וְלֹא תֹסִפוּן לַעֲמֹד:

‏29 וַיֹּאמֶר אֵלָיו מֹשֶׁה כְּצֵאתִי אֶת־הָעִיר אֶפְרֹשׂ אֶת־כַּפַּי אֶל־יְהוָה הַקֹּלוֹת יֶחְדָּלוּן וְהַבָּרָד לֹא יִהְיֶה־עוֹד לְמַעַן תֵּדַע כִּי לַיהוָה הָאָרֶץ:

‏30 וְאַתָּה וַעֲבָדֶיךָ יָדַעְתִּי כִּי טֶרֶם תִּירְאוּן מִפְּנֵי יְהוָה אֱלֹהִים:

‏31 וְהַפִּשְׁתָּה וְהַשְּׂעֹרָה נֻכָּתָה כִּי הַשְּׂעֹרָה אָבִיב וְהַפִּשְׁתָּה גִּבְעֹל:

‏32 וְהַחִטָּה וְהַכֻּסֶּמֶת לֹא נֻכּוּ כִּי אֲפִילֹת הֵנָּה:

MAFTIR

33 Then Moses left Pharaoh and went out of the city. He spread out his hands toward the Lord; the thunder and hail stopped, and the rain no longer poured down on the land.

34 When Pharaoh saw that the rain and hail and thunder had stopped, he sinned again: He and his servants' hearts became hardened.

35 So Pharaoh's heart was hard and he would not let the Israelites go, just as the Lord had said through Moses.

HAFTARAH OF VA'ERA

In this Haftarah, Ezekiel the prophet foresaw the downfall of Egypt and the return of the Israelites to their homeland. Egypt was a place where tremendous negativity was concentrated. There are certain places in the world where negativity is so deeply rooted that it is very difficult to dislodge. In the 20th century, Germany was certainly such a place, and both World Wars originated there.

Fortunately, places also exist with a high concentration of positive energy. Once we are aware of a setting in which positive energy is particularly strong, we can always go there to connect to its energy.

Ezekiel 28:25 - 29:21

28:25 This is what the Lord, God, says: "When I gather the people of Israel from the nations where they have been scattered, I will show Myself holy among them in the sight of the nations. Then they will live in their own land, which I gave to My servant, Jacob.

26 They will live there in safety and will build houses and plant vineyards; they will live in safety when I inflict punishment on all their neighbors who maligned them. Then they will know that I am the Lord, their God."

29:1 In the tenth year, in the tenth month on the twelfth day, the word of the Lord came to me, saying,

MAFTIR

33 וַיֵּצֵ֨א מֹשֶׁ֜ה מהע, אל שדי מֵעִ֤ם פַּרְעֹה֙ אֶת־הָעִ֔יר וַיִּפְרֹ֥שׂ בוזהר, ערי, סנדלפון
כַּפָּ֖יו אֶל־יְהוֹוּאדניליאהדונהי וַיַּחְדְּל֣וּ הַקֹּל֔וֹת וְהַבָּרָ֖ד ראה וּמָטָ֥ר רמ"ח ע"ה לֹא־
נִתַּ֣ךְ אָ֑רְצָה אלהים דההין: 34 וַיַּ֣רְא אלף למד יהוה פַּרְעֹ֗ה כִּֽי־חָדַ֤ל הַמָּטָ֨ר רמ"ח ע"ה
וְהַבָּרָד֙ ראה וְהַקֹּלֹ֔ת וַיֹּ֣סֶף לַחֲטֹ֑א וַיַּכְבֵּ֥ד לִבּ֖וֹ ה֥וּא וַעֲבָדָֽיו: 35 וַֽיֶּחֱזַק֙
לֵ֣ב פַּרְעֹ֔ה וְלֹ֥א שִׁלַּ֖ח אֶת־בְּנֵ֣י יִשְׂרָאֵ֑ל כַּאֲשֶׁ֛ר דִּבֶּ֥ר ראה יְהוֹוּאדניליאהדונהי
בְּיַד־מֹשֶֽׁה מהע, אל שדי :

HAFTARAH OF VA'ERA

Similarly, if there is a place where people have experienced miracles, we can go there to connect to that power.

If we live in a negative location or if we are required to go to a negative place, it is important to strengthen ourselves and fortify beforehand with prayer and meditation. The Negative Side has been successful in these places and will strive to succeed again.

יוֹחֶזְקֵאל פרק כוז

28 כה היי אָמַ֣ר אֲדֹנָ֣י ללה יְהוֹוּאדניליאהדונהי בְּקַבְּצִ֣י | אֶת־בֵּ֣ית ב"פ ראה
יִשְׂרָאֵ֗ל ע"ה קס"א מִן־הָ֣עַמִּים֮ אֲשֶׁ֣ר נָפֹ֣צוּ בָם֒ מ"ב וְנִקְדַּ֥שְׁתִּי בָ֖ם מ"ב לְעֵינֵ֣י
ריבוע מ"ה הַגּוֹיִ֑ם וְיָֽשְׁב֣וּ עַל־אַדְמָתָ֔ם אֲשֶׁ֥ר נָתַ֖תִּי לְעַבְדִּ֥י לְיַֽעֲקֹֽב
ז"פ יהוה, יאהדונהי אידהנויה: 26 וְיָשְׁב֣וּ עָלֶיהָ֮ פהל לָבֶטַח֒ וּבָנ֣וּ בָתִּ֗ים וְנָֽטְע֣וּ כְרָמִ֔ים
וְיָֽשְׁב֖וּ לָבֶ֑טַח בַּֽעֲשׂוֹתִ֣י שְׁפָטִ֗ים ב"ן, לכב, יבמ בְּכֹ֠ל הַשָּׁאטִ֨ים אֹתָ֤ם
מִסְּבִֽיבוֹתָ֔ם וְיָֽדְע֕וּ כִּ֣י אֲנִ֖י אני, טרה"ד כוז"ו יְהוֹוּאדניליאהדונהי אֱלֹֽהֵיהֶֽם ילה:
29 1 בַּשָּׁנָ֣ה הָעֲשִׂרִ֗ית בָּֽעֲשִׂרִ֛י בִּשְׁנֵ֥ים עָשָׂ֖ר לַחֹ֑דֶשׁ י"ב הוויות הָיָ֤ה יהה

2 *"Son of man, set your face against Pharaoh king of Egypt and prophesy against him and against all Egypt.*

3 *Speak to him and say: 'This is what the Lord, God says: I am against you, Pharaoh king of Egypt, you great monster lying among your streams. You say, "The Nile is mine; I made it for myself."*

4 *But I will put hooks in your jaws and make the fish of your streams stick to your scales. I will pull you out from among your streams, with all the fish sticking to your scales.*

5 *I will leave you in the desert, you and all the fish of your streams. You will fall on the open field and not be gathered or picked up. I will give you as food to the beasts of the earth and the birds of the air.*

6 *Then all who live in Egypt will know that I am the Lord.' You have been a staff of reed for the house of Israel.*

7 *When they grasped you with their hands, you splintered and you tore open their shoulders; when they leaned on you, you broke and their backs were wrenched.*

8 *Therefore this is what the Lord, God, says: 'I will bring a sword against you and kill your men and their animals.*

9 *Egypt will become a desolate wasteland. Then they will know that I am the Lord.' Because you said, "The Nile is mine; I made it,"*

10 *therefore I am against you and against your streams, and I will make the land of Egypt a ruin and a desolate waste from Migdol to Aswan, as far as the border of Cush.*

11 *No foot of man will pass through it; no foot of an animal will pass through it; no one will live there for forty years.*

12 *I will make the land of Egypt desolate among devastated lands, and her cities will lie desolate forty years among ruined cities. And I will disperse the Egyptians among the nations and scatter them through the countries.'*

13 *Yet this is what the Lord, God, says: 'At the end of forty years I will gather the Egyptians from the nations where they were scattered.*

דְּבַר ‏רַאַה‎ ‏־יְהֹוָה‎אדניאהדונהי אֵלַ֥י לֵאמֹֽר׃ 2 בֶּן־אָדָ֗ם סמ״ב שִׂ֤ים פָּנֶ֙יךָ֙ עַל־

פַּרְעֹה֙ מֶ֣לֶךְ מִצְרַ֔יִם וְהִנָּבֵ֣א עָלָ֔יו וְעַל־מִצְרַ֖יִם כֻּלָּֽהּ׃ 3 דַּבֵּ֨ר

‏וְאָמַרְתָּ֜‎ ‏רַאַה‎ ‏כֹּה‎־אָמַ֣ר ‏‏‎ ‏אֲדֹנָ֣י‎ ׀ ‏‏‎ ‏‎יֱהֹוִה‎אדניאהדונהי הִנְנִ֤י עָלֶ֙יךָ֙ רבוע מ״ה

פַּרְעֹה֙ מֶֽלֶךְ־מִצְרַ֔יִם מצר הַתַּנִּים֙ הַגָּדוֹל֙ אֲשֶׁ֥ר אָמַ֛ר לִ֥י יְאֹרִ֖י וַאֲנִ֥י עֲשִׂיתִֽנִי׃ 4 וְנָתַתִּ֤י חַחִיִּים֙

(כתיב: וחחיים) בִּלְחָיֶ֔יךָ וְהִדְבַּקְתִּ֥י דְגַת־יְאֹרֶ֖יךָ בְּקַשְׂקְשֹׂתֶ֑יךָ וְהַעֲלִיתִ֙יךָ֙

מִתּ֣וֹךְ יְאֹרֶ֔יךָ וְאֵת֙ כָּל־דְּגַ֣ת יְאֹרֶ֔יךָ בְּקַשְׂקְשֹׂתֶ֖יךָ תִּדְבָּֽק׃

5 וּנְטַשְׁתִּ֣יךָ הַמִּדְבָּ֗רָה אוֹתְךָ֙ וְאֵת֙ כָּל־דְּגַ֣ת יְאֹרֶ֔יךָ עַל־פְּנֵ֤י

הַשָּׂדֶה֙ תִּפּ֔וֹל לֹ֥א תֵאָסֵ֖ף וְלֹ֣א תִקָּבֵ֑ץ לְחַיַּ֥ת הָאָ֛רֶץ

וּלְע֥וֹף הַשָּׁמַ֖יִם נְתַתִּ֣יךָ לְאׇכְלָֽה׃ 6 וְֽיָדְע֞וּ כׇּל־יֹשְׁבֵ֣י

מִצְרַ֗יִם מצר כִּ֣י אֲנִ֣י יְהֹוָ֑האדניאהדונהי יַ֧עַן הֱיוֹתָ֛ם מִשְׁעֶ֥נֶת קָנֶ֖ה

לְבֵ֥ית יִשְׂרָאֵֽל׃ 7 בְּתׇפְשָׂ֨ם בְּךָ֤ בַכַּף֙ (כתיב: בכפך)

תֵּר֔וֹץ וּבָקַעְתָּ֥ לָהֶ֖ם כׇּל־כָּתֵ֑ף וּבְהִשָּׁעֲנָ֤ם עָלֶ֙יךָ֙ תִּשָּׁבֵ֔ר

וְהַעֲמַדְתָּ֥ לָהֶ֖ם כׇּל־מׇתְנָֽיִם׃ 8 לָכֵ֗ן כֹּ֤ה אָמַר֙ אֲדֹנָ֣י

יֱהֹוִה֒אדניאהדונהי הִנְנִ֛י מֵבִ֥יא עָלַ֖יִךְ חָ֑רֶב וְהִכְרַתִּ֥י

מִמֵּ֖ךְ אָדָ֥ם וּבְהֵמָֽה׃ 9 וְהָיְתָ֤ה אֶֽרֶץ־מִצְרַ֙יִם֙ מצר

לִשְׁמָמָ֣ה וְחׇרְבָּ֔ה וְיָדְע֖וּ כִּֽי־אֲנִ֣י יְהֹוָ֑האדניאהדונהי יַ֧עַן אָמַ֛ר יְאֹ֥ר

לִ֖י וַאֲנִ֥י עָשִֽׂיתִי׃ 10 לָכֵ֛ן הִנְנִ֥י אֵלֶ֖יךָ וְאֶל־יְאֹרֶ֑יךָ

וְנָתַתִּ֞י אֶת־אֶ֣רֶץ מִצְרַ֗יִם מצר לְחׇרְבוֹת֙ חֹ֣רֶב שְׁמָמָ֔ה

מִמִּגְדֹּ֥ל סְוֵנֵ֖ה וְעַד־גְּב֥וּל כּֽוּשׁ׃ 11 לֹ֤א תַעֲבׇר־בָּהּ֙ רֶ֣גֶל

אָדָ֔ם וְרֶ֥גֶל בְּהֵמָ֖ה לֹ֣א תַעֲבׇר־

בָּ֑הּ וְלֹ֥א תֵשֵׁ֖ב אַרְבָּעִ֥ים שָׁנָֽה׃ 12 וְנָתַתִּ֣י אֶת־אֶ֣רֶץ מִצְרַ֗יִם מצר

שְׁמָמָ֞ה בְּת֣וֹךְ ׀ אֲרָצ֣וֹת נְשַׁמּ֗וֹת וְעָרֶ֙יהָ֙ בְּת֣וֹךְ עָרִ֣ים מׇחֳרָב֔וֹת

תִּהְיֶ֥יןָ שְׁמָמָ֖ה אַרְבָּעִ֣ים שָׁנָ֑ה וַהֲפִצֹתִ֤י אֶת־מִצְרַ֙יִם֙ מצר בַּגּוֹיִ֔ם

14 I will bring them back from captivity and return them to Upper Egypt, the land of their ancestry. There they will be a lowly kingdom.

15 It will be the lowliest of kingdoms and will never again exalt itself above the other nations. I will make it so weak that it will never again rule over the nations.

16 Egypt will no longer be a source of confidence for the people of Israel but will be a reminder of their sin in turning to her for help. Then they will know that I am the Lord, God.'

"17 In the twenty-seventh year, in the first month on the first day, the word of the Lord came to me, saying,

18 "Son of man, Nebuchadnezzar, king of Babylon drove his army in a hard campaign against Tyre; every head was rubbed bare and every shoulder made raw. Yet he and his army got no reward from the campaign he led against Tyre".

19 Therefore this is what the Lord, God, says: "I am going to give Egypt to Nebuchadnezzar, king of Babylon, and he will carry off its wealth. He will loot and plunder the land as pay for his army.

20 I have given him Egypt as a reward for his efforts because he and his army did it for me," declares the Lord, God.

21 "On that day I will make a horn grow for the house of Israel, and I will open your mouth among them. Then they will know that I am the Lord."

וְזֵרִיתִים בָּאֲרָצֽוֹת: 13 כִּי כֹּה אָמַר אֲדֹנָי יֱהֹוִאדֹנָיֵאֱלֹהִים מִקֵּץ

אַרְבָּעִים שָׁנָה אֲקַבֵּץ אֶת־מִצְרַיִם מִן־הָעַמִּים אֲשֶׁר־נָפֹצוּ

שָׁמָּה: 14 וְשַׁבְתִּי אֶת־שְׁבוּת מִצְרַיִם וַהֲשִׁבֹתִי אֹתָם

אֶרֶץ פַּתְרוֹס עַל־אֶרֶץ מְכוּרָתָם וְהָיוּ שָׁם

מַמְלָכָה שְׁפָלָה: 15 מִן־הַמַּמְלָכוֹת תִּהְיֶה שְׁפָלָה וְלֹא־תִתְנַשֵּׂא עוֹד

עַל־הַגּוֹיִם וְהִמְעַטְתִּים לְבִלְתִּי רְדוֹת בַּגּוֹיִם: 16 וְלֹא יִהְיֶה־עוֹד

לְבֵית יִשְׂרָאֵל לְמִבְטָח מַזְכִּיר עָוֹן בִּפְנוֹתָם אַחֲרֵיהֶם

וְיָדְעוּ כִּי אֲנִי אֲדֹנָי יֱהֹוִאדֹנָיֵאֱלֹהִים: 17 וַיְהִי בְּעֶשְׂרִים

וָשֶׁבַע שָׁנָה בָּרִאשׁוֹן בְּאֶחָד לַחֹדֶשׁ הָיָה

דְבַר־יְהֹוִאדֹנָיֵאֱלֹהִים אֵלַי לֵאמֹר: 18 בֶּן־אָדָם נְבוּכַדְרֶאצַּר

מֶלֶךְ־בָּבֶל הֶעֱבִיד אֶת־חֵילוֹ עֲבֹדָה גְדוֹלָה אֶל־צֹר כָּל־רֹאשׁ

מֻקְרָח וְכָל־כָּתֵף מְרוּטָה וְשָׂכָר לֹא־הָיָה

לוֹ וּלְחֵילוֹ מִצֹּר עַל־הָעֲבֹדָה אֲשֶׁר־עָבַד עָלֶיהָ:

19 לָכֵן כֹּה אָמַר אֲדֹנָי יֱהֹוִאדֹנָיֵאֱלֹהִים הִנְנִי נֹתֵן

לִנְבוּכַדְרֶאצַּר מֶלֶךְ־בָּבֶל אֶת־אֶרֶץ מִצְרָיִם וְנָשָׂא

הֲמֹנָהּ וְשָׁלַל שְׁלָלָהּ וּבָזַז בִּזָּהּ וְהָיְתָה שָׂכָר לְחֵילוֹ:

20 פְּעֻלָּתוֹ אֲשֶׁר־עָבַד בָּהּ נָתַתִּי לוֹ אֶת־אֶרֶץ מִצְרָיִם

אֲשֶׁר עָשׂוּ לִי נְאֻם אֲדֹנָי יֱהֹוִאדֹנָיֵאֱלֹהִים: 21 בַּיּוֹם הַהוּא

אַצְמִיחַ קֶרֶן לְבֵית יִשְׂרָאֵל וּלְךָ אֶתֵּן פִּתְחוֹן־פֶּה

בְּתוֹכָם וְיָדְעוּ כִּי־אֲנִי יְהֹוִאדֹנָיֵאֱלֹהִים:

BO

LESSON OF BO
(Exodus 10-13:16)

Regarding the Ten Plagues

What is the significance of the Ten Plagues?

The conventional interpretation is that the plagues were intended to punish or intimidate Pharaoh so that he would release the Israelites from their long bondage. But the plagues have a much greater significance.

The deeper meaning of the Ten Plagues is related to nothing less than the Creation of the world itself.

> Come and behold: we have learned that the Ten Plagues that the Holy One, blessed be He, caused in Egypt were all by One Hand, because the Left Hand was included in the Right. And ten fingers were included in each other, corresponding to the ten sayings with which the Holy One, blessed be He, was afterwards named. Corresponding to them all, the one of the sea was strong and great and dominating, as is said: "And afterward (lit. 'the last one') He afflicted her more" (Hosea 8:23). This is what is meant by: "The chariots of Pharaoh and his host has he thrown into the sea." In the time to come, the Holy One, blessed be He, shall slay multitudes, and different officers, and leaders of Edom. This is what is said: "Who is this, who comes from Edom, with crimsoned garments from Batzrah?" (Hosea 63:1).
> — The Zohar, Beshalach 19:266

In this physical dimension, Light is encased in a shell or covering (klipah). It is our job to reveal and elevate that Light from within the shell. In the Book of Genesis, the phrase "and God said..." appears ten times. Each of these appearances is a concealed reference to one of the *Ten Sefirot*, or Emanations, of the Light of the Creator. Each of the plagues described in the Book of Exodus removed a *klipah*, or covering, from one of these phrases or Emanations. Through this purification process, the ten instances of "and God said…" in the Book of Genesis were revealed as the Ten Utterances that Moses received on Mount Sinai. So in effect, Creation was the seed and the Ten Utterances were the manifestation. But there had been so much negativity since the seed was sown—the Flood, the Tower of Babel, Sodom and Gomorrah, and more—that a cleansing had to happen at the seed level before the manifestation could take place.

> Come and behold: all the time that the Holy One, blessed be He, arouses war in the world, those Above and those Below, NAMELY, THE NATION BELOW AND THEIR PATRONS ABOVE, are dislodged from their places, as we have established. This is the meaning of the verse: "The chariots of Pharaoh and his hosts has He thrown into the sea" (Exodus 15:4). And in the time to come,

the Holy One, blessed be He, shall wage a great and powerful war against the
nations in order to glorify His Name, as it is written: "Then God shall go forth and
fight against those nations, as when He fights in the day of battle" (Zachariah
14:3), and: "Thus will I magnify Myself and sanctify Myself; and I will make
Myself known..." (Ezekiel 38:23).
        — The Zohar, Beshalach 19:259

What can the revelation of the hidden meaning of the Ten Plagues do for us right now? Can we use this knowledge in some way to solve our problems and seize the opportunities we're being offered at this exact moment? Often, when people start on a spiritual path, they want change to happen instantly, and they wonder what is holding them back. But change is not just a matter of insights and understanding. Change is not just about thinking—it is a battle! At every moment, we have to put all our strength into the war against the Negative Side—and the word "war" has been chosen very deliberately because that's exactly what it is!

From this lesson, we gain the strength to fight this war without any reservation— and to win it. It is not enough to make spirituality just another part of our personality. The war cannot be won if we're also devoting energy to a lot of other things as well. We can only win if we fight with everything we have.

The strength we get from reading about the Ten Plagues will remove the negativity that blocks us. Once it is removed, nothing can manifest within us except the Light of the Creator. This is the most positive change that can possibly happen. But it won't be a permanent change unless we give it all our energy. Once the plagues have performed the necessary cleansing, we must commit to spiritual transformation.

We can't give one hundred percent of ourselves until we really know in our hearts that this is a war. It is not a physical war, but something much harder. It is a war of consciousness, a war that tests how much we really want to be a better person. It is not easy, but then it is not supposed to be easy. Satan doesn't want us to see this, but rather wants us to lose focus on what our spiritual work is. Once that work becomes of less than primary importance in our life, we have lost the war.

Regarding the Exodus from Egypt

During Shabbat when this story of Bo is read, we have a chance to finally emerge from Egypt. We are not speaking here about the nation of Egypt that existed three thousand years ago, but rather about the symbolic Egypt that is the collective negativity of the world manifesting itself in our lives today. Our spiritual work is to learn how to emerge from our own personal "Egypt"—our own negativity.

In one of his letters, Rav Ashlag explained that the Negative Side will try to convince us that we are not in "Egypt" at all. The Negative Side will cause us to think, "I like the way I am. I don't want to change anything." But if we don't know we are in "Egypt," how can we escape from it? We must learn that we are always in exile, even if things seem to be going well for us at a specific moment. Life is full of ups and downs, and when an "up" happens, it's easy to forget the pain we feel during a "down" period.

There is another extremely important reason for perceiving the reality of our own exile in "Egypt." If we deny our negativity, we will lose an opportunity to sincerely ask for the Creator's help. It is written that when the Creator cursed the serpent after the sin of Adam, the serpent was condemned to "eat dirt all the days of his life." But what kind of a curse is that?

This is precisely the point. The serpent will never get the chance to ask for help from the Creator. This means the serpent will never have the opportunity to change and grow because the only way transformation can occur is with the Creator's help. God wants us to give one hundred percent to everything we do, but it is impossible to succeed on our own without help from Above. We must strengthen ourselves to ask for God's assistance, and we can do this only when we realize that we are in exile.

SYNOPSIS OF BO

The story of Bo includes the final three plagues. The *Ten Sefirot* can be divided into the lower seven, which represent the human body, and the upper three, which represent the head. In this schema, the body represents the manifestation of our thoughts, while the head is the seed level— our thoughts, our consciousness—the potential rather than the manifestation. As the plagues represent the ascending order of the *Sefirot*, it is the seed level that Bo addresses; it is the most basic level of our consciousness and helps us to focus our thoughts in a proactive and positive direction.

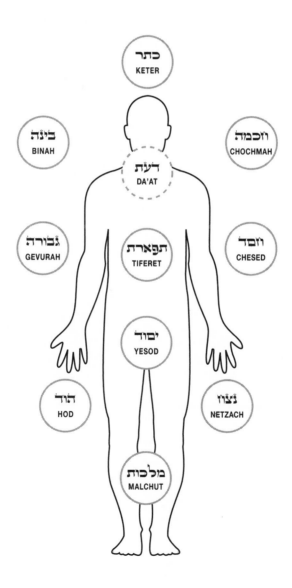

FIRST READING - ABRAHAM - CHESED

10:1 Then the Lord said to Moses, "Come to Pharaoh, for I have hardened his heart and the hearts of his servants so that I may perform these miraculous signs of Mine among him;

² that you may tell your children and grandchildren how I dealt harshly with the Egyptians and how I performed My signs among them, and that you may know that I am the Lord."

³ So Moses and Aaron went to Pharaoh and said to him, "This is what the Lord, the God of the Hebrews, says: 'How long will you refuse to humble yourself before Me? Let My people go, so that they may worship Me.

⁴ If you refuse to let them go, tomorrow I will bring locusts into your borders.

⁵ They will cover the face of the ground so that it cannot be seen. They will devour what you have left after the hail, including every tree that is growing in your fields.

FROM THE RAV

When we connect with this story, we are fortunate to be able to prevent the Angel of Death from entering our lives. The *Zohar* says the plague of the Slaying of the First-Born took place for one reason only: the slaying of Satan and the removal of the Angel of Death. Literally removing Satan at the root level where he exists. It is crucial to attack the root cause of the problem, to go deeper than just attacking the symptoms, even if the symptom is a cancerous tumor, because that's not where the Opponent resides. The symptoms are merely an extension and an expression of the fundamental source of chaos in the universe.

The *Zohar* clearly states that nobody dies from a heart attack; nobody dies from cirrhosis of the liver; nobody dies from a brain tumor; nobody dies from anything that is written on a medical death certificate. None of those things are the true cause of death. Death is always caused by the negative energy of the Adversary (Satan), to which we have made

ourselves vulnerable. When we are vulnerable we provide entry for the Angel of Death, into our lives, into our families, into our world. Once that entry-way has been opened, then and only then can the Angel of Death choose the means to execute his victim.

He may choose the heart; he may choose the brain; he may choose the liver; he may choose dying in an accident or a military action. But that's simply the means by which the Angel of Death causes death in the human body. The way was opened long before that.

Exodus 10:1—God sent Moses to Pharaoh. God told Moses to "come to Pharaoh," a phrase that seems strangely expressed. Moreover, the text does not reveal what Moses was supposed to do or say once he reached the Egyptian ruler. On this point, the *Zohar* says that God took Moses into the Upper Worlds to battle with the forces of evil. In confronting the most powerfully negative forces, Moses was afraid to come close to that

FIRST READING - ABRAHAM - CHESED

10 1 וַיֹּאמֶר יְהֹוָה אֶל־מֹשֶׁה מהע, אל שדי בֹּא אֶל־פַּרְעֹה כִּי־אֲנִי

אני, טדהד כוזו הִכְבַּדְתִּי אֶת־לִבּוֹ וְאֶת־לֵב עֲבָדָיו לְמַעַן שִׁתִי אֹתֹתַי אֵלֶּה

בְּקִרְבּוֹ: 2 וּלְמַעַן תְּסַפֵּר בְּאָזְנֵי בִנְךָ וּבֶן־בִּנְךָ אֵת אֲשֶׁר הִתְעַלַּלְתִּי

בְּמִצְרַיִם מצר וְאֶת־אֹתֹתַי אֲשֶׁר־שַׂמְתִּי בָם מב וִידַעְתֶּם כִּי־אֲנִי

אני, טדהד כוזו יְהֹוָה: 3 וַיָּבֹא מֹשֶׁה מהע, אל שדי וְאַהֲרֹן עב ורבוע עב אֶל־

פַּרְעֹה וַיֹּאמְרוּ אֵלָיו הי אָמַר יְהֹוָה אֱלֹהֵי דמב, ילה הָעִבְרִים

עַד־מָתַי מֵאַנְתָּ לֵעָנֹת מִפָּנָי חכמה בינה שַׁלַּח עַמִּי וְיַעַבְדֻנִי: 4 כִּי אִם

יוהך, עה מב מָאֵן אַתָּה לְשַׁלֵּחַ אֶת־עַמִּי הִנְנִי מֵבִיא מָחָר רמזו אַרְבֶּה

יצחק, דפ בן בִּגְבֻלֶךָ: 5 וְכִסָּה אֶת־עֵין ריבוע מה הָאָרֶץ אלהים דההין עה וְלֹא יוּכַל

לִרְאֹת אֶת־הָאָרֶץ אלהים דההין עה וְאָכַל | אֶת־יֶתֶר הַפְּלֵטָה הַנִּשְׁאֶרֶת

---

negativity. Therefore, God told Moses to "come to Pharaoh" to force Moses to overcome his fear of defeating the final level of evil. God assured Moses that He would be with him, and together they would overcome. The *Zohar* says:

> *Rav Shimon said: "Now it is proper to reveal secrets that are attached Above and Below. It is written: 'Come to Pharaoh,' but it should have said 'Go to Pharaoh.'" What is the meaning of "Come?" HE ANSWERS: "He brought MOSES in to the innermost rooms, to a very powerful crocodile, from which many levels evolve and come down. And what was it? It was the secret of the great serpent. Moses was afraid and approached only the rivers that were at his grade. But he feared THE SERPENT itself, and did not approach because he saw that it was rooted in high sources. When the Holy One, blessed be He, saw that Moses was afraid and that other appointed messengers above could not approach him, the Holy One, blessed be He, said: 'Behold, I am against you, Pharaoh, king of Egypt, the great crocodile that couches in the midst of his streams' (Ezekiel 29:3). The Holy One,*

blessed be He, had to wage war with him and no other."
— *The Zohar, Bo 3:36-38*

אַרְבֶּה

Exodus 10:4—Moses warned Pharaoh of the Plague of Locusts. Pharaoh's advisors told him to release the Israelites after the destruction caused by the first seven plagues. Pharaoh asked Moses who should be released, and Moses replied that all the Israelites must be set free.

According to Rashi, Pharaoh had seen, with the help of his astrologers, that the planet Ra'ah was against the Israelites, and therefore, he felt empowered to tell Moses he could not take all the Israelites. Moses still insisted on freedom for all the people. Although he was aware that the Israelites would face challenges in the desert, Moses was demonstrating that they could and would rise above the effects of the cosmos. If we truly wish to grow spiritually, we must have certainty beyond all doubt that we are able to rise above whatever negative influences are upon us.

6 They will fill your houses and those of all your servants and all the Egyptians—something neither your fathers nor your forefathers have ever seen from the day they settled in this land till now.' " Then Moses turned and left Pharaoh.

7 Pharaoh's servants said to him, "How long will this man be a snare to us? Let the people go, so that they may worship the Lord, their God. Do you not yet realize that Egypt is lost?"

8 Then Moses and Aaron were brought back to Pharaoh. "Go, worship the Lord, your God," he said. "But just who will be going?"

9 Moses answered, "We will go with our young and old, with our sons and daughters, and with our flocks and herds, because we are to celebrate a festival to the Lord."

10 Pharaoh said, "The Lord be with you—if I let you go, along with your women and children! Clearly you are bent on evil.

11 No! Have only the men go; and worship the Lord, since that's what you have been asking for." Then they were driven out of Pharaoh's presence.

SECOND READING - ISAAC - GEVURAH

12 And the Lord said to Moses, "Stretch out your hand over Egypt so that locusts will swarm over the land of Egypt and devour everything growing in the land, everything left by the hail."

13 So Moses stretched out his staff over Egypt, and the Lord made a mighty wind blow across the land all that day and all that night. By morning the wind had brought the locusts.

אַרְבֶּה

Exodus 10:12—The Eighth Plague, the Plague of Locusts, is the level of *Binah*.

Binah is also known as our Supernal Mother. In the physical world, a mother draws her energy from *Binah* to have the right consciousness and to complete all the duties of motherhood. The *Zohar* speaks about the locusts this way:

However, when God brought upon Egypt the locusts, it is written: "For they covered the surface of the whole Earth,

so that the land was darkened." (Exodus 10:15) Why? Because all magicians and sorcerers in the world can only do their sorcery and witchcraft, in one thing, in one level, at one time. And for this nation he brought about a blend of locusts, with many kinds mixed each with the other, to the point where all the magicians and sorcerers, could not prevail against them. And that is the meaning of "behold, they cover the face of the Earth," THAT IS, THEY COULD NOT RISE FROM BEFORE IT.
— The Zohar, Balak 4:27

לָכֶם מִן־הַבָּרָד רְאֵה וְאָכַל אֶת־כָּל יִלִי ־הָעֵץ יִלִי הַצֹּמֵחַ עֵ"ה קס"א לָכֶם מִן־
הַשָּׂדֶה שׁדִי: 6 וּמָלְאוּ בָתֶּיךָ וּבָתֵּי כָל יִלִי ־עֲבָדֶיךָ יִלִי וּבָתֵּי כָל יִלִי ־מִצְרַיִם
מצר אֲשֶׁר לֹא־רָאוּ אֲבֹתֶיךָ וַאֲבוֹת אֲבֹתֶיךָ מִיּוֹם עֵ"ה = נגד, זן, מזבח הֱיוֹתָם
עַל־הָאֲדָמָה עַד הַיּוֹם עֵ"ה = נגד, זן, מזבח הַזֶּה וְהוּ וַיִּפֶן וַיֵּצֵא מֵעִם פַּרְעֹה:
7 וַיֹּאמְרוּ עַבְדֵי פַרְעֹה אֵלָיו עַד־מָתַי יִהְיֶה יי"י זֶה לָנוּ מום, אלהים, אהיה אדני
לְמוֹקֵשׁ שַׁלַּח אֶת־הָאֲנָשִׁים וְיַעַבְדוּ אֶת־יְהֹוָ‌ה‌אדנ‌יאהדונ‌הי אֱלֹהֵיהֶם ילה
הֲטֶרֶם רמ"ח עֵ"ה תֵּדַע כִּי אָבְדָה מִצְרָיִם מצר: 8 וַיּוּשַׁב אֶת־מֹשֶׁה מהש, אל שדי
וְאֶת־אַהֲרֹן עֵ"ב ורבוע עֵ"ב אֶל־פַּרְעֹה וַיֹּאמֶר אֲלֵהֶם לְכוּ עִבְדוּ אֶת־
יְהֹוָ‌ה‌אדנ‌יאהדונ‌הי אֱלֹהֵיכֶם ילה מִי יִלִי וָמִי יִלִי הַהֹלְכִים: 9 וַיֹּאמֶר מֹשֶׁה
מהש, אל שדי בִּנְעָרֵינוּ וּבִזְקֵנֵינוּ נֵלֵךְ נלך בְּבָנֵינוּ וּבִבְנוֹתֵנוּ בְּצֹאנֵנוּ וּבִבְקָרֵנוּ
נֵלֵךְ נלך כִּי חַג־יְהֹוָ‌ה‌אדנ‌יאהדונ‌הי לָנוּ מום, אלהים, אהיה אדני: 10 וַיֹּאמֶר אֲלֵהֶם יְהִי
כֵן יְהֹוָ‌ה‌אדנ‌יאהדונ‌הי עִמָּכֶם כַּאֲשֶׁר אֲשַׁלַּח אֶתְכֶם וְאֶת־טַפְּכֶם רְאוּ כִּי
רָעָה רהע נֶגֶד זן, נגד מזבח פְּנֵיכֶם: 11 לֹא כֵן לְכוּ־נָא הַגְּבָרִים וְעִבְדוּ אֶת־
יְהֹוָ‌ה‌אדנ‌יאהדונ‌הי כִּי אֹתָהּ אַתֶּם מְבַקְשִׁים וַיְגָרֶשׁ אֹתָם מֵאֵת פְּנֵי וחכמה בינה
פַּרְעֹה:

SECOND READING - ISAAC - GEVURAH

12 וַיֹּאמֶר יְהֹוָ‌ה‌אדנ‌יאהדונ‌הי אֶל־מֹשֶׁה מהש, אל שדי נְטֵה יָדְךָ בוכ"ו עַל־אֶרֶץ
מִצְרַיִם אלהים דאלפין מצר בָּאַרְבֶּה יצחק, ד"פ ב"ן וְיַעַל עַל־אֶרֶץ אלהים דאלפין
מִצְרָיִם מצר וְיֹאכַל אֶת־כָּל יִלִי ־עֵשֶׂב יִלִי הָאָרֶץ עֵ"ב שמות אלהים דההין עֵ"ה אֵת כָּל
יִלִי ־אֲשֶׁר הִשְׁאִיר הַבָּרָד רְאֵה וַיֵּט מֹשֶׁה מהש, אל שדי אֶת־מַטֵּהוּ עַל־
אֶרֶץ אלהים דאלפין מִצְרַיִם מצר וַיהֹוָ‌ה‌אדנ‌יאהדונ‌הי נִהַג רוּחַ מלוי אלהים דיודין ־קָדִים
בָּאָרֶץ אלהים דאלפין כָּל יִלִי ־הַיּוֹם עֵ"ה = נגד, זן, מזבח הַהוּא וְכָל יִלִי ־הַלָּיְלָה מלה

¹⁴ They invaded all Egypt and settled down in every area of the country in great numbers. Never before had there been such a heavy plague of locusts nor will there ever be again.

¹⁵ The land became dark as they devoured everything growing in the fields and the fruit on the trees – all that was left after the hail. Nothing green remained on tree or plant in all the land of Egypt.

¹⁶ Pharaoh quickly summoned Moses and Aaron and said, "I have sinned against the Lord, your God and against you.

¹⁷ Now forgive my sin once more and pray to the Lord, your God, to just take this death from me." ¹⁸ Moses then left Pharaoh and prayed to the Lord.

¹⁹ And the Lord changed the wind to a very strong seaward wind, which caught up the locusts and carried them into the Red Sea. Not a locust was left anywhere in Egypt.

²⁰ But the Lord hardened Pharaoh's heart, and he would not let the Israelites go.

²¹ Then the Lord said to Moses, "Stretch out your hand toward the sky so that darkness will spread over Egypt—darkness that can be felt."

²² So Moses stretched out his hand toward the sky, and total darkness covered all Egypt for three days.

²³ No one could see anyone else or leave his place for three days. Yet all the Israelites had light in the places where they lived.

וּשֶׁךְ

Exodus 10:21—The Ninth Plague, the Plague of Darkness, is the level of Chochmah.

Chochmah represents the level of our Spiritual Father. In addition to this, it is important to know that during the Plague of Darkness, all the people who had reached the 50th Gate of Negativity were completely overcome by the darkness. The only hope for them to accomplish their correction was to exit completely from this world—to die.

After the Plague of Darkness, Pharaoh released the Israelites but told them that they must leave without their cattle. Moses refused this offer, in part because animals have a spark of the Light—a soul—within them and Pharaoh wanted to retain some of the physical possessions of the Israelites. If we truly want to grow spiritually, we have to be willing to completely sever our connection with those things that keep us from growing. At times, we try to retain a small connection because we get some energy from it. But we need to dig deep and discover the courage and discipline to let go completely so that we may reach the next level of our spiritual growth.

Moses warned the Israelites that the last plague was coming and that it was now time to borrow what they would need in the desert. The Israelites were to borrow silver and gold from the Egyptians. Everything they took into the desert with them was borrowed. There is, to be sure, no difference between that and our present day where we seem to have so many possessions. But in truth, everything we have in this world—our talents, our fortune, our health, our intellect, our spirituality, all of our gifts—is on loan to us for the period of our lifetime to use for the benefit of others.

הַבֹּקֶר הָיָה יהה וְרוּחַ מלוי אלהים דיורין הַקָּדִים נָשָׂא אֶת־הָאַרְבֶּה יצוחק, ד״פ ב״ן:

14 וַיַּעַל הָאַרְבֶּה יצוחק, ד״פ ב״ן עַל כָּל יל ־אֶרֶץ אלהים דאלפין מצרים מצר וַיָּנַח

בְּכֹל ב״ן, לכב, יבם גְּבוּל מִצְרָיִם מצר כָּבֵד מְאֹד מ״ה לְפָנָיו לֹא־הָיָה יהה כֵן

אַרְבֶּה יצוחק, ד״פ ב״ן כָּמֹהוּ וְאַחֲרָיו לֹא יִהְיֶה יי ־כֵּן: 15 וַיְכַס אֶת־עֵין רביעו מ״ה

כָּל יל ־הָאָרֶץ אלהים דההין ע״ה וַתֶּחְשַׁךְ הָאָרֶץ אלהים דההין ע״ה וַיֹּאכַל אֶת־כָּל

־עֵשֶׂב יל ע״ב שמות הָאָרֶץ אלהים דההין ע״ה וְאֵת כָּל ־פְּרִי ע״ה יל אלהים דאלפין הָעֵץ

ע״ה קס״א אֲשֶׁר הוֹתִיר הַבָּרָד ראה וְלֹא־נוֹתַר כָּל יל ־יֶרֶק בָּעֵץ ע״ה קס״א

וּבְעֵשֶׂב הַשָּׂדֶה שדי בְּכָל ב״ן, לכב, יבם ־אֶרֶץ אלהים דאלפין מִצְרָיִם מצר: 16 וַיְמַהֵר

פַּרְעֹה לִקְרֹא לְמֹשֶׁה מהש, אל שדי וּלְאַהֲרֹן ע״ב ורבוע ע״ב וַיֹּאמֶר חָטָאתִי

לַיהוה אהדונהי אֱלֹהֵיכֶם ילה וְלָכֶם: 17 וְעַתָּה שָׂא נָא חַטָּאתִי אַךְ אהיה

הַפַּעַם וְהַעְתִּירוּ לַיהוה אהדונהי אֱלֹהֵיכֶם ילה וְיָסֵר מֵעָלַי רַק אֶת־

הַמָּוֶת הַזֶּה והו: 18 וַיֵּצֵא מֵעִם פַּרְעֹה וַיֶּעְתַּר אֶל־יהוה אהדונהי: 19 וַיַּהֲפֹךְ

יהוה אהדונהי רוּחַ מלוי אלהים דיורין ־יָם ילי וְחָזָק פהל מְאֹד מ״ה וַיִּשָּׂא אֶת־

הָאַרְבֶּה יצוחק, ד״פ ב״ן וַיִּתְקָעֵהוּ יָמָּה סּוּף לֹא נִשְׁאַר אַרְבֶּה יצוחק, ד״פ ב״ן אֶחָד

אהבה, דאגה בְּכֹל ב״ן, לכב, יבם גְּבוּל מִצְרָיִם מצר: 20 וַיְחַזֵּק יהוה אהדונהי אֶת־

לֵב פַּרְעֹה וְלֹא שִׁלַּח אֶת־בְּנֵי יִשְׂרָאֵל: 21 וַיֹּאמֶר יהוה אהדונהי אֶל־

מֹשֶׁה מהש, אל שדי נְטֵה יָדְךָ בוכ״ו עַל־הַשָּׁמַיִם י״פ ט״ל י״פ כוז״ו **וַיְהִי** ש״פ טל אל, ייא״י   וְ|שֶׁךְ|

עַל־אֶרֶץ אלהים דאלפין מלכים מִצְרָיִם מצר וְיָמֵשׁ וְ|שֶׁךְ| ע״ך ניצוצות של ו׳ מלכים

22 וַיֵּט מֹשֶׁה מהש, אל שדי אֶת־יָדוֹ עַל־הַשָּׁמַיִם י״פ טל י״פ כוז״ו ע״ך ניצוצות של ו׳ מלכים

וַיְהִי וְ|שֶׁךְ| אל ־ ע״ך ניצוצות של ו׳ מלכים ־אֲפֵלָה בְּכָל ב״ן, לכב, יבם ־אֶרֶץ אלהים דאלפין

מִצְרָיִם מצר שְׁלֹשֶׁת יָמִים נלך: 23 לֹא־רָאוּ אִישׁ ע״ה קנ״א קס״א אֶת־אָחִיו

וְלֹא־קָמוּ אִישׁ ע״ה קנ״א קס״א מִתַּחְתָּיו שְׁלֹשֶׁת יָמִים נלך וּלְכָל אדני יה ־בְּנֵי

יִשְׂרָאֵל הָיָה יהה אוֹר רז, אין־סוף בְּמוֹשְׁבֹתָם:

THIRD READING - JACOB - TIFERET

24 Then Pharaoh summoned Moses and said, "Go, worship the Lord; only leave your flocks and herds behind – your families may join you." 25 But Moses said, "You must allow us to have sacrifices and burnt offerings to present to the Lord our God.

26 Our livestock too must go with us; not a hoof is to be left behind. We have to use some of them in worshiping the Lord our God, and until we get there we will not know what we are to use to worship the Lord." 27 But the Lord hardened Pharaoh's heart, and he was not willing to let them go.

28 Pharaoh said to Moses, "Get out of my sight! Make sure you do not appear before me again! The day you see my face you will die." 29 "Just as you say," Moses replied, "I will never appear before you again."

11:1 The Lord said to Moses, "I will bring one more plague on Pharaoh and on Egypt. After that, he will let you go from here, and when he does, he will drive you out completely.

2 Tell the people that the men should ask their neighbors and the women should ask their neighbors for articles of silver and gold."

3 The Lord made the Egyptians favorably disposed toward the people, and Moses himself was highly regarded in Egypt by Pharaoh's servants and by the people.

FOURTH READING - MOSES - NETZACH

4 So Moses said, "This is what the Lord says: 'About midnight I will go throughout Egypt 5 and every firstborn son in Egypt will die, from the firstborn son of Pharaoh, who sits on the throne, to the firstborn son of the slave girl, who is at her hand mill, and all the firstborn of the cattle.

בְּכוֹר

Exodus 11:5—The Tenth Plague, the Plague of the Slaying of the First-Born, is the level of *Keter*.

Moses told Pharaoh that as midnight approached, all the first-born males of Egypt—both human and animal—would be killed. This is the plague of *Keter*, the closest level to the Creator and the level at which all negativity is washed away.

IT IS WRITTEN: "all the first-born." "FIRST-BORN" IS THE ASPECT CHOCHMAH, AND "ALL THE FIRST-BORN" DENOTES THAT even Upper and Lower Levels were broken in power - MEANING all those levels

THIRD READING - JACOB - TIFERET

24 וַיִּקְרָא עם ה אותיות = ב״פ קס״א פַּרְעֹה אֶל־מֹשֶׁה מהע, אל שדי, וַיֹּאמֶר לְכוּ עִבְדוּ
אֶת־יְהוָֹואהדי׳אהדונהי רַק צֹאנְכֶם וּבְקַרְכֶם יֻצָּג גַּם יג״ל ־טַפְּכֶם יֵלֵךְ כלי עִמָּכֶם:

25 וַיֹּאמֶר מֹשֶׁה מהע, אל שדי יג״ל גַּם ־אַתָּה תִּתֵּן ב״פ כהת בְּיָדֵנוּ זְבָחִים וְעֹלֹת
וְעָשִׂינוּ לַיהוָֹואהדי׳אהדונהי אֱלֹהֵינוּ ילה: 26 וְגַם ־מִקְנֵנוּ יֵלֵךְ כלי עִמָּנוּ רבוע ס״ג לֹא
תִשָּׁאֵר פַּרְסָה בזֵוֹדֶךְ אדני כִּי מִמֶּנּוּ נִקַּח לַעֲבֹד אֶת־יְהוָֹואהדי׳אהדונהי אֱלֹהֵינוּ ילה
וַאֲנַחְנוּ לֹא־נֵדַע מַה מ״ה ־נַעֲבֹד אֶת־יְהוָֹואהדי׳אהדונהי עַד־בֹּאֵנוּ שָׁמָּה
מהע, משה, אל שדי: 27 וַיְחַזֵּק יְהוָֹואהדי׳אהדונהי אֶת־לֵב פַּרְעֹה וְלֹא אָבָה לְשַׁלְּחָם:

28 וַיֹּאמֶר־לוֹ פַרְעֹה לֵךְ מֵעָלָי הִשָּׁמֶר לְךָ אַל־תֹּסֶף רְאוֹת פָּנַי וחכמה בינה כִּי
בְּיוֹם ע״ה = נגד, זן, מזבח רְאֹתְךָ פָנַי וחכמה בינה תָּמוּת: 29 וַיֹּאמֶר מֹשֶׁה מהע, אל שדי כֵּן
דִּבַּרְתָּ לֹא־אֹסִף עוֹד רְאוֹת פָּנֶיךָ סמ״ב: 11 1 וַיֹּאמֶר יְהוָֹואהדי׳אהדונהי אֶל־מֹשֶׁה
מהע, אל שדי עוֹד נֶגַע מלוי אהיה דאלפין אֶחָד אהבה, דאגה אָבִיא עַל־פַּרְעֹה וְעַל־מִצְרַיִם
מצר אַחֲרֵי־כֵן יְשַׁלַּח אֶתְכֶם מִזֶּה כְּשַׁלְּחוֹ כָּלָה גָּרֵשׁ יְגָרֵשׁ אֶתְכֶם מִזֶּה:

2 דַּבֶּר רֵאה ־נָא בְּאָזְנֵי הָעָם וְיִשְׁאֲלוּ אִישׁ ע״ה קס״א קס״א | מֵאֵת רֵעֵהוּ וְאִשָּׁה
מֵאֵת רְעוּתָהּ כְּלֵי ־כֶסֶף וּכְלֵי זָהָב כלי: 3 וַיִּתֵּן ע״ב מלוי ע״ב יְהוָֹואהדי׳אהדונהי אֶת־
חֵן מווי הָעָם בְּעֵינֵי מִצְרַיִם ריבוע מ״ה גַּם יג״ל | הָאִישׁ ד״פ אדם מֹשֶׁה מהע, אל שדי
גָּדוֹל להוו, מבה, יול, אום מְאֹד מ״ה בְּאֶרֶץ אלהים דאלפין מִצְרַיִם מצר בְּעֵינֵי ריבוע מ״ה
עַבְדֵי־פַרְעֹה וּבְעֵינֵי ריבוע מ״ה הָעָם:

FOURTH READING - MOSES - NETZACH

4 וַיֹּאמֶר מֹשֶׁה מהע, אל שדי כֹּה היי אָמַר יְהוָֹואהדי׳אהדונהי כַּחֲצֹת הַלַּיְלָה מלה
אֲנִי אני, טדהד כו״ו יוֹצֵא בְּתוֹךְ מִצְרָיִם מצר: 5 וּמֵת ד״פ ריבוע אהיה כָּל ילי ־בְּכוֹר

⁶ There will be loud cry throughout Egypt—worse than there has ever been or ever will be again.

⁷ But among the Israelites not a dog will bark at any man or animal. Then you will know that the Lord makes a distinction between Egypt and Israel.

⁸ All these officials of yours will come to me, bowing down before me and saying, "Go, you and all the people who follow you!" After that I will leave.' " Then Moses, hot with anger, left Pharaoh.

⁹ The Lord had said to Moses, "Pharaoh will refuse to listen to you—so that my wonders may be multiplied in Egypt."

¹⁰ Moses and Aaron performed all these wonders before Pharaoh, but the Lord hardened Pharaoh's heart, and he would not let the Israelites go out of his country. 12:¹ The Lord said to Moses and Aaron in Egypt,

² "This month is to be for you the first month, the first of the months of the year.

³ Speak to the entire Congregation of Israel, saying that on the tenth day of this month each man is to take a lamb for his family, one for each household.

⁴ If any household is too small for a whole lamb, they must share one with their nearest neighbor, accounting for each person according to how much of the lamb he would consume.

---

that rule by THE POWER OF their wisdom, WHICH IS THE WISDOM OF EGYPT as it is written: "ALL THE FIRST-BORN in the land of Egypt." All the Upper and Lower Levels that were broken in power are all alluded to in the verse, "From the first-born of Pharaoh that sits on his throne, even to the first-born of the maidservant that is behind the mill; and all the first-born of cattle." (Exodus 11:5) So we see that they are all alluded to in the passage.
— The Zohar, Bo 5:118

We may ask why these plagues were brought to bear upon the Egyptians. There are many questions surrounding the significance of the plagues, including which of the plagues took place on a spiritual level and which on a physical level. But this much is certain: The plagues served to end the Israelites' connection to negativity. The plagues released them—and therefore us—from the negative force that was present in Egypt. Although we cannot hope to understand all that is concealed within the secrets of the plagues, the

most important lesson lies in the fact that they were sent by God to help overcome negativity.

Even after the Tenth Plague—and although the progression of the plagues proved to Pharaoh that he had lost control over the Israelites—Pharaoh still refused to surrender. He still believed that because the Israelites had reached the 49th Gate of Negativity, they could be forced into the 50th Gate.

Pharaoh's stubbornness brought pain to himself and to his entire nation. In the same way, Satan uses the powerful tool of our own obstinacy to hold us back from positive change.

Exodus 12:2—We know that there are 613 connections or precepts described in the Bible: 248 are positive and represent the bones and joints of the human body, while 365 are negative and represent the sinews.

בָּאָרֶץ אלהים דאלפין מִצְרַיִם מצר מִבְּכוֹר פַּרְעֹה הַיֹּשֵׁב עַל־כִּסְאוֹ עַד

בְּכוֹר הַשִּׁפְחָה עה ג מלויי אהיה אֲשֶׁר אַחַר הָרֵחָיִם דזן וְכֹל ילי בְּכוֹר בְּהֵמָה

בן, לכב, יבמ 6 וְהָיְתָה צְעָקָה גְדֹלָה בְּכָל בן, לכב, יבמ אֶרֶץ אלהים דאלפין מִצְרַיִם

מצר אֲשֶׁר כָּמֹהוּ לֹא נִהְיָתָה וְכָמֹהוּ לֹא תֹסִף 7 וּלְכֹל יה אדני בְּנֵי |

יִשְׂרָאֵל לֹא יֶחֱרַץ־כֶּלֶב לְשֹׁנוֹ לְמֵאִישׁ עה קנא קסא וְעַד־בְּהֵמָה בן, לכב, יבמ

לְמַעַן תֵּדְעוּן אֲשֶׁר יַפְלֶה יהוה/אדני בֵּין מִצְרַיִם מצר וּבֵין יִשְׂרָאֵל:

8 וְיָרְדוּ כָל ילי עֲבָדֶיךָ אֵלֶּה אֵלַי וְהִשְׁתַּחֲווּ־לִי לֵאמֹר צֵא אַתָּה וְכָל

ילי הָעָם אֲשֶׁר־בְּרַגְלֶיךָ וְאַחֲרֵי־כֵן אֵצֵא וַיֵּצֵא מֵעִם־פַּרְעֹה בָּחֳרִי־

אָף: 9 וַיֹּאמֶר יהוה/אדני אֶל־מֹשֶׁה מהש, אל שדי לֹא־יִשְׁמַע אֲלֵיכֶם

פַּרְעֹה לְמַעַן רְבוֹת מוֹפְתַי בְּאֶרֶץ אלהים דאלפין מִצְרַיִם מצר: 10 וּמֹשֶׁה

מהש, אל שדי וְאַהֲרֹן עב ורבוע עב עָשׂוּ אֶת־כָּל ילי הַמֹּפְתִים הָאֵלֶּה לִפְנֵי

חכמה בינה פַּרְעֹה וַיְחַזֵּק יהוה/אדני אֶת־לֵב פַּרְעֹה וְלֹא־שִׁלַּח אֶת־בְּנֵי

יִשְׂרָאֵל מֵאַרְצוֹ: 12 1 וַיֹּאמֶר יהוה/אדני אֶל־מֹשֶׁה מהש, אל שדי וְאֶל־

אַהֲרֹן עב ורבוע עב בְּאֶרֶץ אלהים דאלפין מִצְרַיִם מצר לֵאמֹר: 2 הַ‎חֹדֶשׁ יב הויות

הַזֶּה והו לָכֶם רֹאשׁ ריבוע אלהים ואלהים דיודין עה חֳדָשִׁים רִאשׁוֹן הוּא לָכֶם

לְחָדְשֵׁי הַשָּׁנָה: 3 דַּבְּרוּ ראה אֶל־כָּל ילי עֲדַת יִשְׂרָאֵל לֵאמֹר בֶּעָשֹׂר

לַחֹדֶשׁ יב הויות הַזֶּה וְיִקְחוּ והו לָהֶם חֹעם אִישׁ עה קנא קסא שֶׂה לְבֵית

אָבֹת שֶׂה לַבָּיִת בפ ראה: 4 וְאִם־יוֹהך יִמְעַט הַבַּיִת בפ ראה מִהְיוֹת

מִשֶּׂה וְלָקַח בפ ראה הוּא וּשְׁכֵנוֹ הַקָּרֹב אֶל־בֵּיתוֹ בְּמִכְסַת נְפָשֹׁת

The first positive connection comes from the process of blessing the new moon. We do this during the Shabbat that precedes Rosh Chodesh (the appearance of the new moon that heralds the beginning of a new astrological month) as well as during the seven days following the first week after Rosh Chodesh.

Rav Yitzchak said: "The Torah should have started with, 'This month shall be to you the beginning of months.' (Exodus 12:2)" Why is that? It is the beginning OF THE RULE of the blessing of the new moon. Therefore, the Torah should have STARTED with these words, for the subject is connected with the Holy One, blessed be He. THE MOON IS THE SECRET OF MALCHUT, WHICH, WHEN FULL, UNITES WITH THE HOLY ONE, BLESSED BE HE. THEREFORE, THE TORAH SHOULD HAVE STARTED AT

⁵ The lamb must be a pure, year-old male lamb, from the lambs and the goats you shall take.   ⁶ You will guard them until the fourteenth day of the month, and slaughter it – the entire assembly of the Congregation of Israel – at twilight.

⁷ And you shall take from the blood and put it on the two doorposts and on the frame of the houses where the lambs are eaten.

⁸ And you shall eat the meat on that night roasted over fire, and unleavened bread with bitter herbs you shall eat.

⁹ Do not eat the meat raw or cooked in water, but roast it over the fire—head, legs and inner parts. ¹⁰ Do not leave any of it till morning; if some is left till morning, you must burn it.

¹¹ This is how you are to eat it: with your cloak tucked into your belt, your sandals on your feet and your staff in your hand. Eat it in haste; it is the Lord's Passover.

¹² I will pass through Egypt on that same night and strike every firstborn in Egypt—both men and animals—and I will bring judgment on all the gods of Egypt. I am the Lord.

THE BEGINNING OF THE FULLNESS OF THE MOON, WHICH IS: "THIS MONTH SHALL BE TO YOU THE BEGINNING OF MONTHS."
— The Zohar, Bo 7:158

These connections are the tools that give us the opportunity to rise above the influence of the zodiac and the physical world. If we fail to make these connections, we remain under the control of our inborn tendencies: A person born under the sign of Libra retains his Libra tendencies, a Scorpio her Scorpio tendencies, and so on—and no one is able to transcend his or her astrological destiny.

וְשָׁוֲזֹטוּ

Exodus 12:6—The Israelites were told to sacrifice the lamb on the14th day of *Nissan*. Before they could do this, however, they had to "take" the lamb on the 10th day of *Nissan*. "Taking" the lamb represents an acknowledgment of the *Desire to Receive for the Self Alone*. Unless we acknowledge that we have this desire and unless we identify it in its many manifestations, we cannot hope to overcome it and move forward in spiritual growth.

And so, why is the paschal sacrifice a lamb? The answer is because a lamb was the idol and deity of the Egyptians. Said the Holy One, blessed be He: "From the tenth of the month, take the fear of the Egyptians, capture and bind it and let it be imprisoned and hold it in your keeping one day, and two, and three days, and on the fourth day carry out its sentence, and assemble over it."

And when Egypt heard the voice of their idol which was being held by Israel, and they were unable to rescue it, they cried and it was as difficult for them as though they themselves had been tied up for the kill. Said the Holy One, blessed be He: "Let it be in your possession day after day for four days, so that THE EGYPTIANS may see it when it is bound and imprisoned, and on the fourth day, bring it out to be killed and let the Egyptians see how you enact judgment on it." And this, NAMELY, THESE JUDGMENTS THAT THEY PERFORMED ON THEIR IDOL, was harder for them to bear than all the plagues that the Holy One, blessed be He, brought on them.
— The Zohar, Pinchas 105:725, 726

אִישׁ ע"ה קנ"א קס"א לְפִי אָכְלוֹ תָּכֹסּוּ עַל־הַשֶּׂה: 5 שֶׂה תָמִים זָכָר בֶּן־שָׁנָה

יִהְיֶה יי לָכֶם מִן־הַכְּבָשִׂים וּמִן־הָעִזִּים תִּקָּחוּ: 6 וְהָיָה יהוה לָכֶם

לְמִשְׁמֶרֶת עַד אַרְבָּעָה עָשָׂר יוֹם ע"ה = נגד, זך, מזבח לַחֹדֶשׁ י"ב הויות הַזֶּה והו

וְשָׁחֲטוּ אֹתוֹ כֹּל יל' קְהַל ע"ב ס"ג עֲדַת־יִשְׂרָאֵל בֵּין הָעַרְבָּיִם: 7 וְלָקְחוּ

מִן־הַדָּם רבוע אהיה וְנָתְנוּ עַל־שְׁתֵּי הַמְּזוּזֹת ניֵת, זך מות וְעַל־הַמַּשְׁקוֹף עַל

הַבָּתִּים אֲשֶׁר־יֹאכְלוּ אֹתוֹ בָּהֶם: 8 וְאָכְלוּ אֶת־הַבָּשָׂר בַּלַּיְלָה מלה הַזֶּה

צְלִי־אֵשׁ וּמַצּוֹת עַל־מְרֹרִים דיודין ע"ה אלהים יֹאכְלֻהוּ: 9 אַל־תֹּאכְלוּ

מִמֶּנּוּ נָא וּבָשֵׁל מְבֻשָּׁל בַּמָּיִם כִּי אִם יוהך, ע"ב מ"ב צְלִי־אֵשׁ דיודין ע"ה אלהים

רֹאשׁוֹ עַל־כְּרָעָיו וְעַל־קִרְבּוֹ: 10 וְלֹא־תוֹתִירוּ מִמֶּנּוּ עַד־בֹּקֶר וְהַנֹּתָר

מִמֶּנּוּ עַד־בֹּקֶר בָּאֵשׁ דיודין ע"ה אלהים תִּשְׂרֹפוּ: 11 וְכָכָה תֹּאכְלוּ אֹתוֹ

מָתְנֵיכֶם חֲגֻרִים נַעֲלֵיכֶם בְּרַגְלֵיכֶם וּמַקֶּלְכֶם בְּיֶדְכֶם וַאֲכַלְתֶּם אֹתוֹ

בְּחִפָּזוֹן פֶּסַח הוּא לַיהֹוָ‌ואדנהיאהדונהי: 12 וְעָבַרְתִּי בְאֶרֶץ אלהים דאלפין

הַמְּזוּזֹת

Exodus 12:7—They were then told to take the blood from the lamb and smear it on their doorposts to protect them from the Plague of the Slaying of the First-Born. To fully understand the protection that the blood on the doorposts provided them, we can examine the words used to describe it. In Aramaic, the word for doorposts is *mezuzot*. The numerical value of *mezuzot* (460) has the same value as Nun, Yud, Tav—the 72 Name of God that expresses the energy of the "death of death." And if we rearrange the Hebrew letters of the word *mezuzot*, we create the words *zaz mavet,* which means "to remove death." In the *Zohar*, we read:

> *Rav Aba said: "The Holy One, blessed be He, had compassion for His children on many occasions. A man made a house and the Holy One, blessed be He, said to him: 'Write My Name and place it on your door so when you sit in your house, I will sit outside by your door to guard you.' Here AT PASSOVER, He said: 'Mark on*

your entrance the secret of Faith in Me,' NAMELY THE THREE COLUMNS ON THE TWO SIDE POSTS AND ON THE LINTEL, AS MENTIONED. 'Sit in your house and I will guard you from outside,' as it is written: "And none of you shall go out at the door entrance of his house until the morning...and when He sees the blood on the lintel, and on the two side posts, God will pass over the door, and will not allow the Destroyer to come into your house to smite you" (Exodus 12:22-23). SO WE SEE THAT THE HOLY ONE, BLESSED BE HE, GUARDED THEM FROM OUTSIDE.
> — *The Zohar, Bo 4:81*

פֶּסַח הוּא לַיהֹוָ‌ואדנהי

Exodus 12:11—The verse "*pesach hu lashem*," (it is a *pesach*-offering to God), corresponds to *Pei, Hei, Lamed* (פ,ה,ל) from the 72 Names of God and has the same numerical value (115) as the word *chazak* (strength). *Pei, Hei, Lamed* gives us the strength to combat Satan.

¹³ *The blood will be a sign for you on the houses where you are; and when I see the blood, I will pass over you. No deadly plague will touch you when I strike Egypt.*

¹⁴ *This is a day you are to commemorate; for the generations to come you shall celebrate it as a festival to the Lord—a lasting ordinance.*

¹⁵ *For seven days you are to eat unleavened bread, but on the first day you shall remove grain from your houses, for whoever eats anything leavened must be cut off from Israel, from the first day through the seventh day.*

¹⁶ *On the first day hold a sacred assembly, and another one on the seventh day. You shall do no work at all on these days, except to prepare food for everyone to eat— that is all you may do.*

¹⁷ *And you shall guard the unleavened bread, because it was on this very day that I brought your legions out of Egypt. You shall keep this day as a lasting ordinance for the generations to come.*

¹⁸ *From the beginning of the fourteenth day, in the evening, you shall eat unleavened bread until the twenty-first day of the month in the evening.*

¹⁹ *For seven days no grain shall be found in your houses, because anyone who eats that which is leavened shall be cut off from the Congregation of Israel, whether he is a stranger or native-born.* ²⁰ *Eat nothing that is leavened; in all of your habitations, you shall eat unleavened bread."*

Satan is very strong, and he has countless years more experience than we do! We must use the power of this Name to gain the strength to fight him.

פְּסַחְתִּי

Exodus 12:13—God said that the Angel of Death would "pass over" (Passover) the houses of the Israelites. The sign of the blood on the doorposts was to protect the sons of the Israelites from the judgment of the Plague of the Slaying of the First-Born. It is from this that we derive both the Aramaic and English names of this holiday—*Pesach* and Passover. *Pesach* has two other Aramaic words included in it: pe[h], meaning "*mouth*," and sach, meaning "*speak*." For example, by using our mouth to speak the 42-Letter Name of God (*Ana Beko'ach*), we gain the energy we need to fight the war against negativity.

וְזִמֵץ

Exodus 12:15—The Bible notes that during *Pesach*, we are not to eat leavened products made with flour and yeast (*chametz* in Hebrew). We should be aware that *chametz* is a code word for the Desire to Receive for the Self Alone. For each of us to escape our own personal "Egypt," we have to restrict ourselves from eating *chametz*. By accepting and living with this restriction, we gain the strength to stop feeding our ego, our anger, or whatever other manifestation of the Desire to Receive we have in ourselves, for the coming year. As the Rav has explained, the only reason we experience chaos of any kind is due to the Desire to Receive for the Self Alone; therefore, the work that we do during *Pesach* has the potential to shield us in the coming year from any kind of chaos. The nature of bread is to draw unto itself—to expand and to absorb, much like our ego. From a spiritual point of view, we should avoid giving in to this self-absorbed nature. The *Zohar* explains:

מִצְרַיִם בַּלַּיְלָה הָיָה וְהִכֵּיתִי כָל־בְּכוֹר בְּאֶרֶץ

מִצְרַיִם מֵאָדָם וְעַד־בְּהֵמָה וּבְכָל־אֱלֹהֵי

מִצְרַיִם אֶעֱשֶׂה שְׁפָטִים אֲנִי יְהוָה׃ 13 וְהָיָה

הַדָּם לָכֶם לְאֹת עַל הַבָּתִּים אֲשֶׁר אַתֶּם שָׁם וְרָאִיתִי

אֶת־הַדָּם וּפָסַחְתִּי עֲלֵכֶם וְלֹא־יִהְיֶה בָכֶם נֶגֶף לְמַשְׁחִית

בְּהַכֹּתִי בְּאֶרֶץ מִצְרָיִם׃ 14 וְהָיָה הַיּוֹם

הַזֶּה לָכֶם לְזִכָּרוֹן וְחַגֹּתֶם אֹתוֹ חַג לַיהוָה לְדֹרֹתֵיכֶם

חֻקַּת עוֹלָם תְּחָגֻּהוּ׃ 15 שִׁבְעַת יָמִים מַצּוֹת תֹּאכֵלוּ אַךְ בַּיּוֹם

הָרִאשׁוֹן תַּשְׁבִּיתוּ שְּׂאֹר מִבָּתֵּיכֶם כִּי כָּל

אֹכֵל חָמֵץ וְנִכְרְתָה הַנֶּפֶשׁ הַהִוא מִיִּשְׂרָאֵל מִיּוֹם

הָרִאשֹׁן עַד־יוֹם הַשְּׁבִעִי׃ 16 וּבַיּוֹם

הָרִאשׁוֹן מִקְרָא־קֹדֶשׁ וּבַיּוֹם הַשְּׁבִיעִי מִקְרָא

קֹדֶשׁ יִהְיֶה לָכֶם כָּל־מְלָאכָה לֹא־יֵעָשֶׂה בָהֶם

אַךְ אֲשֶׁר יֵאָכֵל לְכָל־נֶפֶשׁ הוּא לְבַדּוֹ יֵעָשֶׂה לָכֶם׃

17 וּשְׁמַרְתֶּם אֶת־הַמַּצּוֹת כִּי בְּעֶצֶם הַיּוֹם הַזֶּה הוֹצֵאתִי אֶת־

צִבְאוֹתֵיכֶם מֵאֶרֶץ מִצְרָיִם וּשְׁמַרְתֶּם אֶת־הַיּוֹם

הַזֶּה לְדֹרֹתֵיכֶם חֻקַּת עוֹלָם׃ 18 בָּרִאשֹׁן בְּאַרְבָּעָה עָשָׂר יוֹם

לַחֹדֶשׁ בָּעֶרֶב תֹּאכְלוּ מַצֹּת עַד יוֹם

הָאֶחָד וְעֶשְׂרִים לַחֹדֶשׁ בָּעָרֶב׃ 19 שִׁבְעַת

This is what Rav Shimon said: "It is written, 'But on the first day you shall remove leaven out of your houses' and 'For whoever eats that which is leavened.' It has been explained that this leaven and leavened fermentation are one level, and they are all the same. Another dominion is the princes called 'Evil Inclination,' who are appointed over the other nations, and another dominion is Strange El, other gods. Here also, leaven, leavened fermentation, and leavened bread are all one. God said: 'All these years, you were under the authority of others and you served another nation. From now and further, you are free men. "But on the first day, you shall remove leaven out of your houses…you shall eat nothing leavened" and "no leavened bread shall be seen with you".' "

— The Zohar, Bo 9:166

FIFTH READING - AARON - HOD

²¹ Then Moses summoned all the elders of Israel and said to them, "Go at once and select a flock for your families and slaughter the Passover lamb.

²² And you shall take a bunch of hyssop, dip it into the blood in the basin and touch it to both sides and the top of the doorframe, with the blood from the basin; and not one of you shall go out the door of his house until morning.

²³ When the Lord goes through the land to strike down the Egyptians, He will see the blood on the top and sides of the doorframe. And the Lord will pass over that doorway, and He will not permit the destroyer to enter your houses and strike you down.

²⁴ Obey these instructions as a lasting ordinance for you and your descendants.

²⁵ When you enter the land that the Lord will give you as He promised, observe this ceremony.

²⁶ And when your children ask you, 'What does this ceremony mean to you?'

²⁷ tell them, 'It is the Passover sacrifice to the Lord, who passed over the houses of the Israelites in Egypt and spared our homes when He struck down the Egyptians.' " Then the people bowed down and worshiped.

²⁸ The Israelites did just what the Lord commanded Moses and Aaron.

וַיִּקְרָא

Exodus 12:21—Moses told the Israelites that they must perform the sacrifice. The final stage in the process of restriction from *chametz* at *Pesach* is the actual sacrifice of the lamb. This is to remind us that we must be willing to go the distance with our spiritual work—well beyond the first steps of personal sacrifice. Rav Ashlag tells us that we can only answer the questions: "What is my personal tikkun?" and "When and with whom is it difficult for us to share?" by observing which actions are difficult for us. Once we identify the difficulty—knowing when and with whom we find it difficult to share—our individual correction reveals itself in the answers to these questions.

יָמִ֑ים נלך שְׂאֹ֗ר ג מוזון דאלהים דקטנות לֹ֣א יִמָּצֵ֣א בְּבָתֵּיכֶ֔ם כִּ֣י | כָּל־ ילי ־אֹכֵ֣ל מַחְמֶ֗צֶת

וְנִכְרְתָ֞ה הַנֶּ֤פֶשׁ רמ"ח ־ ז הויות הַהִוא֙ מֵעֲדַ֣ת יִשְׂרָאֵ֔ל בַּגֵּ֖ר בין קס"א וּבְאֶזְרַ֥ח הָאָֽרֶץ

אלהים דההין ע"ה: 20 כָּל־ ילי ־מַחְמֶ֖צֶת לֹ֣א תֹאכֵ֑לוּ בְּכֹל֙ בין, לכב, יבמ מֽוֹשְׁבֹ֣תֵיכֶ֔ם

תֹּאכְל֖וּ מַצּֽוֹת:

FIFTH READING - AARON - HOD

21 וַיִּקְרָ֥א עם ה' אותיות = ב"פ קס"א מֹשֶׁ֛ה מהע, אל שדי לְכָל־ ילי ־זִקְנֵ֥י יִשְׂרָאֵ֖ל

וַיֹּ֣אמֶר אֲלֵהֶ֑ם מִֽשְׁכ֗וּ וּקְח֨וּ לָכֶ֥ם צֹ֛אן מלוי אהיה דיודין ע"ה לְמִשְׁפְּחֹתֵיכֶ֖ם

וְשַׁחֲט֥וּ הַפָּֽסַח: 22 וּלְקַחְתֶּ֞ם אֲגֻדַּ֣ת אֵז֗וֹב וּטְבַלְתֶּם֮ בַּדָּ֣ם רבוע אהיה אֲשֶׁר־

בַּסַּף֒ וְהִגַּעְתֶּ֤ם אֶל־הַמַּשְׁקוֹף֙ וְאֶל־שְׁתֵּ֣י הַמְּזוּזֹ֔ת נית, זז מות מִן־הַדָּ֖ם רבוע אהיה

אֲשֶׁ֣ר בַּסָּ֑ף וְאַתֶּ֗ם לֹ֥א תֵצְא֛וּ אִ֖ישׁ ע"ה קנ"א קס"א מִפֶּֽתַח־בֵּית֖וֹ עַד־בֹּֽקֶר:

23 וְעָבַ֣ר רבוע יהוה ורבוע אלהים יְהֹוָה֮אדניאהדונהי לִנְגֹּ֣ף אֶת־מִצְרַיִם֒ מצר וְרָאָ֤ה ראה

אֶת־הַדָּם֙ רבוע אהיה עַל־הַמַּשְׁק֔וֹף וְעַ֖ל שְׁתֵּ֣י הַמְּזוּזֹ֑ת נית, זז מות וּפָסַ֤ח

יְהֹוָה֙אדניאהדונהי עַל־הַפֶּ֔תַח וְלֹ֤א יִתֵּן֙ הַמַּשְׁחִ֔ית לָבֹ֥א אֶל־בָּתֵּיכֶ֖ם לִנְגֹּֽף:

24 וּשְׁמַרְתֶּ֖ם אֶת־הַדָּבָ֣ר ראה הַזֶּ֑ה והו לְחָק־לְךָ֥ וּלְבָנֶ֖יךָ עַד־עוֹלָֽם:

25 וְהָיָ֞ה יהוה כִּֽי־תָבֹ֣אוּ אֶל־הָאָ֗רֶץ אלהים דההין ע"ה אֲשֶׁ֨ר יִתֵּ֧ן יְהֹוָ֛האדניאהדונהי

לָכֶ֖ם כַּאֲשֶׁ֣ר דִּבֵּ֑ר ראה וּשְׁמַרְתֶּ֖ם אֶת־הָעֲבֹדָ֥ה הַזֹּֽאת: 26 וְהָיָ֕ה יהוה כִּֽי־

יֹאמְר֥וּ אֲלֵיכֶ֖ם בְּנֵיכֶ֑ם מָ֛ה מ"ה הָעֲבֹדָ֥ה הַזֹּ֖את לָכֶֽם: 27 וַאֲמַרְתֶּ֡ם

זֶֽבַח־פֶּ֨סַח ה֜וּא לַֽיהֹוָ֗האדניאהדונהי אֲשֶׁ֣ר פָּ֠סַח עַל־בָּתֵּ֤י בְּנֵֽי־יִשְׂרָאֵל֙

בְּמִצְרַ֔יִם מצר בְּנָגְפּ֥וֹ אֶת־מִצְרַ֖יִם מצר וְאֶת־בָּתֵּ֣ינוּ הִצִּ֑יל וַיִּקֹּ֥ד הָעָ֖ם

וַיִּֽשְׁתַּחֲוֽוּ: 28 וַיֵּלְכ֥וּ וַיַּֽעֲשׂ֖וּ בְּנֵ֣י יִשְׂרָאֵ֑ל כַּאֲשֶׁ֨ר צִוָּ֧ה פוי יְהֹוָ֛האדניאהדונהי

אֶת־מֹשֶׁ֥ה מהע, אל שדי וְאַהֲרֹ֖ן ע"ב ורבוע ע"ב כֵּ֥ן עָשֽׂוּ:

SIXTH READING - JOSEPH - YESOD

²⁹ At midnight the Lord struck down all the firstborn in Egypt, from the firstborn of Pharaoh, who sat on the throne, to the firstborn of the prisoner, who was in the dungeon, and the firstborn of all the livestock.

³⁰ Pharaoh and all his officials and all the Egyptians got up during the night, and there was a great cry in Egypt, for there was not a house without someone dead.

³¹ He summoned Moses and Aaron that night and said, "Get up and leave my people, you and the Israelites, and go worship the Lord as you have requested.

³² Take your flocks and herds, as you have said, and go. And also bless me."

³³ The Egyptians urged the people to hurry and leave the country. "For otherwise," they said, "we will all die!"

³⁴ So the people took their dough before it had risen, and carried it on their shoulders in kneading troughs wrapped in clothing.

³⁵ The Israelites did as Moses instructed and borrowed from the Egyptians articles of silver and gold and clothing.

³⁶ The Lord had made the Egyptians favorably disposed toward the people, and they gave them what they asked for; so they took advantage of the Egyptians.

בְּחֲצִי הַלַּיְלָה

Exodus 12:29—The Plague of the Slaying of the First-Born occurred at midnight. The plague occurred at midnight because that is always the moment when God goes into the Garden of Eden to study and converse with the *tzaddikim* (righteous people). There is so much Light revealed at this moment that all levels of negativity are destroyed, just as the Ten Plagues removed negativity from the world. For this reason, many of the kabbalists would—and still do—awaken at midnight to make that connection with the Creator and receive the wisdom that is dispensed to them at this special time in the Garden of Eden. During certain holidays, we also stay up all night so that we, too, may make this connection with the Creator and, together with the *tzaddikim*, remove negativity.

Because of this, *BECAUSE THE SOULS ARE THE FRUIT OF THE HANDIWORK*

OF THE HOLY ONE, BLESSED BE HE, on each and every night, the souls of the righteous rise up TO THE GARDEN OF EDEN. And at midnight, the Holy One, blessed be He, comes to the Garden of Eden to delight Himself with them. With whom DOES HE DELIGHT HIMSELF? IS IT WITH THE SOULS OF THE LIVING OR THE DECEASED? Rav Yosi answers: "With them all! With those who dwell in that World OF TRUTH, and with those who dwell in this world. Together, with them all, the Holy One, blessed be He, finds delight at midnight in the Garden of Eden." . . . Rav Yesa said: "YOU SAY THAT HE even delights himself with those SOULS of this world. How can that be?" He replied, "Because at midnight, all the truly righteous people awaken to study Torah and recite all the praises of Torah." And we have learned that the Holy One, blessed be He, together with all the righteous who are in the Garden of

SIXTH READING - JOSEPH - YESOD

29 וַיְהִי | בַּחֲצִי הַלַּיְלָה וַיהוה הִכָּה כָל־בְּכוֹר
בְּאֶרֶץ מִצְרַיִם מִבְּכֹר פַּרְעֹה הַיֹּשֵׁב עַל־כִּסְאוֹ עַד
בְּכוֹר הַשְּׁבִי אֲשֶׁר בְּבֵית הַבּוֹר וְכֹל בְּכוֹר בְּהֵמָה:
30 וַיָּקָם פַּרְעֹה לַיְלָה הוּא וְכָל־עֲבָדָיו וְכָל־
מִצְרַיִם וַתְּהִי צְעָקָה גְדֹלָה בְּמִצְרָיִם כִּי־אֵין בַּיִת אֲשֶׁר
אֵין־שָׁם מֵת: 31 וַיִּקְרָא לְמֹשֶׁה
וּלְאַהֲרֹן לַיְלָה וַיֹּאמֶר קוּמוּ צְּאוּ מִתּוֹךְ עַמִּי
גַּם־אַתֶּם גַּם־בְּנֵי יִשְׂרָאֵל וּלְכוּ עִבְדוּ אֶת־יהוה
כְּדַבֶּרְכֶם: 32 גַּם־צֹאנְכֶם גַּם־בְּקַרְכֶם קְחוּ כַּאֲשֶׁר דִּבַּרְתֶּם
וָלֵכוּ וּבֵרַכְתֶּם גַּם־אֹתִי: 33 וַתֶּחֱזַק מִצְרַיִם עַל־הָעָם לְמַהֵר
לְשַׁלְּחָם מִן־הָאָרֶץ כִּי אָמְרוּ כֻּלָּנוּ מֵתִים: 34 וַיִּשָּׂא הָעָם
אֶת־בְּצֵקוֹ טֶרֶם יֶחְמָץ מִשְׁאֲרֹתָם צְרֻרֹת בְּשִׂמְלֹתָם עַל־
שִׁכְמָם: 35 וּבְנֵי־יִשְׂרָאֵל עָשׂוּ כִּדְבַר מֹשֶׁה וַיִּשְׁאֲלוּ
מִמִּצְרַיִם כְּלֵי־כֶסֶף וּכְלֵי זָהָב וּשְׂמָלֹת: 36 וַיהוה נָתַן

Eden, all listen attentively to their voices. And during the day, a thread of grace is woven around them. As it is written: "Yet God will command His loving kindness in the daytime, and in the night, His song shall be with me...." (Psalms 42:9) BECAUSE OF THE SONG AT NIGHT, THEY MERIT HIS LOVING KINDNESS DURING THE DAY. Therefore, the praises that rise up before the Holy One, blessed be He, at night, are the most complete. Come and behold: When Israel were shut in their houses, while the Holy One, blessed be He, was slaying the first-born of the Egyptians, they were reciting these praises and Psalms before the Holy One, blessed be He.
— The Zohar, Lech Lecha 15:130, 132-133

צְאוּ

Exodus 12:31—Pharaoh finally released the Israelites. Often, when we are doing our spiritual work, we have to fully release our negative tendencies and habits, which we may have been suppressing from long habit, but not really overcoming. During our early spiritual work, for instance, if we have a tendency to get angry or jealous, we try to suppress our usual behavior, but the negative thoughts still remain. When we really want to reach the next level, we have to let go of even these negative thoughts, just as Pharaoh fully and finally released all the Israelites.

[37] *The Israelites journeyed from Rameses to Succoth. There were about six hundred thousand men on foot, besides women and children.*

[38] *A Mixed Multitude went up with them, as well as large droves of livestock, both flocks and herds.*

[39] *With the dough they had brought from Egypt, they baked cakes of unleavened bread. The dough had not risen because they had been driven out of Egypt and did not have time to prepare food for themselves.*

[40] *Now the length of time the Israelite people lived in Egypt was 430 years.* [41] *At the end of the 430 years, to the very day, all the Lord's divisions left Egypt.*

[42] *Because the Lord kept vigil that night to bring them out of Egypt, on this night all the Israelites are to keep vigil to honor the Lord for the generations to come.*

[43] *The Lord said to Moses and Aaron, "These are the regulations for the Passover: 'No foreigner is to eat of it.*

[44] *Any slave you have bought may eat of it after you have circumcised him,* [45] *but a temporary resident and a hired worker may not eat of it.*

וַיִּסְעוּ

Exodus 12:37—The Israelites left Egypt. With the Israelites came the *erev rav*, "the mixed multitude." The *erev rav* represents people who hate—those who continually manifest a tremendous amount of negativity. We can have a little ego, a little anger, and still improve ourselves. But when people harbor real hatred, they take themselves out of the spiritual game. We must guard against descending to that point.

The Ari wrote:

> This is the meaning of, "And a mixed multitude went up also with them," (Exodus 12:38) for these are what is meant by mixed multitude—sparks of holiness mixed in Egypt—so Moses wanted to bring them up. But God saw that they were not yet corrected and worthy, and did not want to bring them out yet. There were two kinds. There were those called 'mixed multitude' (lit. 'great mixture') and a 'small mixture,' as mentioned in section Tisa of the Zohar. There it says that there is a great mixture

> and a small mixture, as mentioned in the Zohar in relation to the inner meaning of arbayim (Eng. 'evening', also: 'two mixtures'). These are the great mixture that comes from supernal Da'at called 'great', rather than from Yesod that is called 'small'. So erev rav (Eng. 'mixed multitude') equals Da'at, they being those who sinned and caused separation above, according to the inner meaning of "a stiff-necked people" (Deuteronomy 9:13) in section Ekev—the meaning of Dalet of echad (Eng. 'one').
> — *Writings of the Ari, Torah Compilations 4:8*

And from the *Zohar*:

> THEY ARE CALLED 'erev rav' (mixed multitudes) because Lilit, the wicked one of them, who is called 'the mother of the mixed multitudes, IS CONSIDERED IMMORAL BECAUSE THE DOMINION OF THE SHECHINAH AND HER SUSTENANCE BEING THE MOUTH OF ISRAEL WENT OVER TO HER DURING THE EXILE, AND THEREFORE they caused Israel to sin, and destroyed their flesh of the Sign of the Covenant.
> — *Tikkuna Tresar, Tikkun 21:300*

אֶת־חֵן הָעָם בְּעֵינֵי מִצְרַיִם וַיַּשְׁאִלוּם וַיְנַצְּלוּ אֶת־מִצְרָיִם

37 וַיִּסְעוּ בְנֵי־יִשְׂרָאֵל מֵרַעְמְסֵס סֻכֹּתָה כְּשֵׁשׁ־מֵאוֹת אֶלֶף

רַגְלִי הַגְּבָרִים לְבַד מִטָּף: 38 וְגַם־

עֵרֶב רַב עָלָה אִתָּם וְצֹאן

וּבָקָר מִקְנֶה כָּבֵד מְאֹד: 39 וַיֹּאפוּ אֶת־הַבָּצֵק אֲשֶׁר הוֹצִיאוּ

מִמִּצְרַיִם עֻגֹת מַצּוֹת כִּי לֹא חָמֵץ כִּי־גֹרְשׁוּ מִמִּצְרַיִם וְלֹא יָכְלוּ

לְהִתְמַהְמֵהַּ וְגַם־צֵדָה לֹא־עָשׂוּ לָהֶם: 40 וּמוֹשַׁב בְּנֵי יִשְׂרָאֵל אֲשֶׁר

יָשְׁבוּ בְּמִצְרָיִם שְׁלֹשִׁים שָׁנָה וְאַרְבַּע מֵאוֹת שָׁנָה: 41 וַיְהִי

מִקֵּץ שְׁלֹשִׁים שָׁנָה וְאַרְבַּע מֵאוֹת שָׁנָה וַיְהִי בְּעֶצֶם הַיּוֹם

הַזֶּה יָצְאוּ כָּל־צִבְאוֹת יְהוָה מֵאֶרֶץ

מִצְרָיִם: 42 לֵיל שִׁמֻּרִים הוּא לַיהוָה לְהוֹצִיאָם

מֵאֶרֶץ מִצְרָיִם הוּא־הַלַּיְלָה הַזֶּה לַיהוָה

שִׁמֻּרִים לְכָל־בְּנֵי יִשְׂרָאֵל לְדֹרֹתָם: 43 וַיֹּאמֶר יְהוָה אֶל־

מֹשֶׁה וְאַהֲרֹן זֹאת חֻקַּת הַפָּסַח כָּל־בֶּן־נֵכָר לֹא־

יֹאכַל בּוֹ: 44 וְכָל־עֶבֶד אִישׁ מִקְנַת־כָּסֶף וּמַלְתָּה אֹתוֹ אָז

יֹאכַל בּוֹ: 45 תּוֹשָׁב וְשָׂכִיר לֹא־יֹאכַל בּוֹ: 46 בְּבַיִת אֶחָד

יֵאָכֵל לֹא־תוֹצִיא מִן־הַבַּיִת מִן־הַבָּשָׂר חוּצָה וְעֶצֶם לֹא תִשְׁבְּרוּ־

בוֹ: 47 כָּל־עֲדַת יִשְׂרָאֵל יַעֲשׂוּ אֹתוֹ: 48 וְכִי־יָגוּר אִתְּךָ גֵּר

וְעָשָׂה פֶסַח לַיהוָה הִמּוֹל לוֹ כָל־זָכָר וְאָז יִקְרַב לַעֲשֹׂתוֹ

עֵרֶב רַב

Exodus 12:38—This verse is about those who can and cannot connect to the escape from bondage. Whoever is connected to the Creator—in other words, whoever believes in the higher power of the Light—can escape from any spiritual bondage. But we must first realize that there is a higher power and that we cannot free ourselves without the help of the Creator. Anyone who believes solely in himself or herself and does not acknowledge the Creator's role in his or her growth will not move forward. Therefore, we must use the Light and become partners with the Light.

⁴⁶ *It must be eaten inside one house; take none of the meat outside the house. Do not break any of the bones.*

⁴⁷ *The whole community of Israel must do this.*

⁴⁸ *A foreigner living among you who wants to celebrate the Lord's Passover must have all the males in his household circumcised; then he may take part like one born in the land. No uncircumcised male may eat of it.*

⁴⁹ *The same law applies to the native-born and to the foreigner living among you.' "*

⁵⁰ *All the Israelites did just what the Lord had commanded Moses and Aaron.*

⁵¹ *And on that very day the Lord brought the Israelites out of Egypt by their divisions.*

SEVENTH READING - DAVID - MALCHUT

13: ¹ *The Lord said to Moses,* ² *"Consecrate to Me every firstborn male. The first offspring of every womb among the Israelites belongs to Me, whether man or animal."*

³ *Then Moses said to the people, "Remember this day, the day you came out of Egypt, out of the land of slavery, because the Lord brought you out of it with a mighty hand. Eat nothing containing yeast.* ⁴ *Today, in the month of Aviv, you are leaving.*

⁵ *When the Lord brings you into the land of the Canaanites, Hittites, Amorites, Hivites and Jebusites—the land He swore to your forefathers to give you, a land flowing with milk and honey—you are to perform this ceremony in this month:*

⁶ *For seven days eat unleavened bread and on the seventh day hold a festival to the Lord.*

⁷ *Eat unleavened bread during those seven days; nothing with yeast in it is to be seen among you, nor shall any grain be seen anywhere within your borders.*

⁸ *On that day tell your son, 'I do this because of what the Lord did for me when I came out of Egypt.'*

⁹ *This observance will be for you like a sign on your hand and a reminder on your forehead that the law of the Lord is to be on your lips. For the Lord brought you out of Egypt with His Mighty Hand.*

וְהָיָה יהוה כְּאֶזְרַח הָאָרֶץ אלהים דההין ע״ה וְכָל יל״י ־עָרֵל אלהים דיורן לֹא־יֹאכַל

בּוֹ: 49 תּוֹרָה אַחַת יִהְיֶה יי׳ לָאֶזְרָח וְלַגֵּר בין קנ״א הַגָּר בין קנ״א בְּתוֹכְכֶם:

50 וַיַּעֲשׂוּ כָּל יל״י ־בְּנֵי יִשְׂרָאֵל כַּאֲשֶׁר צִוָּה פוי יְהֹוָהַאדני אֶת־מֹשֶׁה

מהע׳, אל שדי וְאֶת־אַהֲרֹן ע״ב ורבוע ע״ב כֵּן עָשׂוּ: 51 וַיְהִי יא״י אל, ייא״י בְּעֶצֶם הַיּוֹם

ע״ה = נגד, זן, מזבח הַזֶּה והו הוֹצִיא יְהֹוָהַאדנ יאהדונהי אֶת־בְּנֵי יִשְׂרָאֵל מֵאֶרֶץ

אלהים דאלפין מצר מִצְרָיִם עַל־צִבְאֹתָם:

SEVENTH READING - DAVID - MALCHUT

13 1 וַיְדַבֵּר ראה יְהֹוָהַאדנ יאהדונהי אֶל־מֹשֶׁה מהע׳, אל שדי לֵּאמֹר: 2 קַדֶּשׁ־לִי כָּל

יל״י ־בְּכוֹר ר״ת לכבב פֶּטֶר רפ״ח ע״ה כָּל יל״י ־רֶחֶם אברהם, וז״פ אל, רמ״ח בִּבְנֵי יִשְׂרָאֵל

בָּאָדָם מ״ה וּבַבְּהֵמָה בין, לכבב, יבמ לִי הוּא: 3 וַיֹּאמֶר מֹשֶׁה מהע׳, אל שדי אֶל־

הָעָם זָכוֹר ע״ב = קס״א אֶת־הַיּוֹם ע״ה = נגד, זן, מזבח הַזֶּה והו אֲשֶׁר יְצָאתֶם מִמִּצְרַיִם

מצר מִבֵּית ב״פ ראה עֲבָדִים כִּי בְּחֹזֶק פהל יָד הוֹצִיא יְהֹוָהַאדנ יאהדונהי אֶתְכֶם

מִזֶּה וְלֹא יֵאָכֵל חָמֵץ ע״ה = נגד, זן, מזבח: 4 הַיּוֹם אַתֶּם יֹצְאִים בְּחֹדֶשׁ י״ב הויות

הָאָבִיב: 5 וְהָיָה יהוה כִי־יְבִיאֲךָ יְהֹוָהַאדנ יאהדונהי אֶל־אֶרֶץ אלהים דאלפין הַכְּנַעֲנִי

וְהַחִתִּי וְהָאֱמֹרִי וְהַחִוִּי וְהַיְבוּסִי אֲשֶׁר נִשְׁבַּע לַאֲבֹתֶיךָ לָתֶת לָךְ אֶרֶץ

אלהים דאלפין זָבַת חָלָב וּדְבָשׁ וְעָבַדְתָּ אֶת־הָעֲבֹדָה הַזֹּאת בַּחֹדֶשׁ י״ב הויות

הַזֶּה והו: 6 שִׁבְעַת יָמִים נלך תֹּאכַל מַצֹּת וּבַיּוֹם ע״ה = נגד, זן, מזבח הַשְּׁבִיעִי חַג

לַיהֹוָהַאדנ יאהדונהי: 7 מַצּוֹת יֵאָכֵל אֵת שִׁבְעַת הַיָּמִים נלך וְלֹא־יֵרָאֶה רי״ו, גבורה

לְךָ חָמֵץ וְלֹא־יֵרָאֶה רי״ו, גבורה לְךָ שְׂאֹר ג: מוזחין דאלהים דקטנות בְּכָל בין, לכבב, יבמ -

גְּבֻלֶךָ: 8 וְהִגַּדְתָּ לְבִנְךָ בַּיּוֹם ע״ה = נגד, זן, מזבח הַהוּא לֵאמֹר בַּעֲבוּר זֶה

עָשָׂה יְהֹוָהַאדנ יאהדונהי לִי בְּצֵאתִי מִמִּצְרָיִם מצר: 9 וְהָיָה יהוה לְךָ לְאוֹת עַל־

יָדְךָ בוכו׳ וּלְזִכָּרוֹן ע״ב קס״א נע״ב בֵּין עֵינֶיךָ ע״ב קס״א לְמַעַן תִּהְיֶה תּוֹרַת

10 You must keep this ordinance at the appointed time year after year. 11 After the Lord brings you into the land of the Canaanites and gives it to you, as He promised on oath to you and your forefathers,

12 you are to give over to the Lord the first offspring of every womb. All the firstborn males of your livestock belong to the Lord. 13 Redeem with a lamb every firstborn donkey, but if you do not redeem it, break its neck. Redeem every firstborn among your sons.

MAFTIR

14 In days to come, when your son asks you, 'What does this mean?' say to him, 'With a mighty hand the Lord brought us out of Egypt, out of the land of slavery. 15 When Pharaoh stubbornly refused to let us go, the Lord killed every firstborn in Egypt, from the firstborn human to the firstborn animal. This is why I sacrifice to the Lord the first male offspring of every womb and redeem each of my firstborn sons.' 16 And it will be like a sign on your hand and a symbol on your forehead that the Lord brought us out of Egypt with His Mighty Hand."

לְאֹת

Exodus 13:9—The power of the *Tefillin* (phylacteries: two black leather boxes containing specific meditations; the boxes have leather straps and are worn, one on the forehead and the other on the left arm, during the morning connection).

Each part of the body is an antenna for a different energy. The left side connects with the Desire to Receive. The head is the seed level, where we receive the thoughts that will transform themselves into actions—possibly negative ones. The Tefillin are a tool to help us to control our desires and our thoughts. If we didn't have negative and selfish tendencies, we wouldn't need the tools. But the fact is that we do need them to shore up our spiritual intentions.

"And it shall be for a token upon your hand, and for frontlets between your eyes." (Exodus 13:16) This precept is considered in a different category, since it is not considered a precept but rather a matter of holiness. And these are the Tefillin, the Hand Tefillin and the Head

Tefillin, for they are a manifestation of glorification and beauty of supernal visions. Therefore they are called "frontlets," as it is written: "Israel, in whom I will be glorified." (Isaiah 49:3)
— The Zohar, Bo 15:231

בְּכוֹר

Exodus 13:13—**The Redemption of the First-Born (***Pidyon haBen***).** The sages teach that when a first-born son comes into the world, he has a tremendous amount of energy. Unless we perform the necessary action of redeeming the first-born son, that energy can be transformed into negativity—or "death-energy," as the *Zohar* says.

"Sanctify to Me all the first-born, whatever opens the womb...." (Exodus 13:2) A common person needs two things. He should be redeemed from under the power of the Evil Inclination, which is his master. As Jacob said to Esau, "Let my master, I pray you, pass over before his servant," (Genesis 33:14) MEANING in this world HE IS the master because

יְהֹוָאדֹנָיאהדֹנֹהי בְּפִיךָ כִּי בְּיָד חֲזָקָה הוֹצִאֲךָ יְהֹוָאדֹנָיאהדֹנֹהי מִמִּצְרָיִם

מצר, ר"ת מי"ה 10 וְשָׁמַרְתָּ אֶת־הַחֻקָּה הַזֹּאת לְמוֹעֲדָהּ מִיָּמִים יָמִימָה:

11 וְהָיָה כִּי־יְבִאֲךָ יְהֹוָאדֹנָיאהדֹנֹהי אֱלֹהִים דאלפין אֶל־אֶרֶץ הַכְּנַעֲנִי כַּאֲשֶׁר

נִשְׁבַּע לְךָ וְלַאֲבֹתֶיךָ וּנְתָנָהּ לָךְ: 12 וְהַעֲבַרְתָּ כָל־פֶּטֶר יְלִי רֶחֶם

רמ"ח, וח"פ אל לַיהֹוָאדֹנָיאהדֹנֹהי וְכָל־פֶּטֶר יְלִי | שֶׁגֶר בְּהֵמָה ב"ן, לכב, יבמ

אֲשֶׁר יִהְיֶה לְךָ הַזְּכָרִים לַיהֹוָאדֹנָיאהדֹנֹהי: 13 וְכָל־פֶּטֶר יְלִי חֲמֹר וְזָבַר

תִּפְדֶּה בְשֶׂה וְאִם יוהך, ע"ה מ"ב ־לֹא תִפְדֶּה וַעֲרַפְתּוֹ וְכֹל יְלִי בְּכוֹר אָדָם

מ"ה בְּבָנֶיךָ תִּפְדֶּה:

MAFTIR

14 וְהָיָה כִּי־יִשְׁאָלְךָ בִנְךָ מָחָר לֵאמֹר מַה מ"ה ־זֹּאת וְאָמַרְתָּ

אֵלָיו בְּחֹזֶק פֿהל יָד הוֹצִיאָנוּ יְהֹוָאדֹנָיאהדֹנֹהי מִמִּצְרָיִם מצר מִבֵּית ב"פ ראה

עֲבָדִים: 15 וַיְהִי אל, ייא"י כִּי־הִקְשָׁה פַרְעֹה לְשַׁלְּחֵנוּ וַיַּהֲרֹג יְהֹוָאדֹנָיאהדֹנֹהי

כָּל־בְּכוֹר בְּאֶרֶץ אֱלֹהִים דאלפין מִצְרַיִם מצר מִבְּכֹר אָדָם מ"ה וְעַד־בְּכוֹר

בְּהֵמָה ב"ן, לכב, יבמ עַל־כֵּן אֲנִי זֹבֵחַ לַיהֹוָאדֹנָיאהדֹנֹהי כָּל־פֶּטֶר יְלִי

רֶחֶם ע"ה רמ"ח, וח"פ אל הַזְּכָרִים וְכָל־בְּכוֹר יְלִי בָּנַי אֶפְדֶּה: 16 וְהָיָה

לְאוֹת עַל־יָדְכָה וּלְטוֹטָפֹת בֵּין עֵינֶיךָ ע"ה קס"א כִּי בְּחֹזֶק פֿהל יָד הוֹצִיאָנוּ

יְהֹוָאדֹנָיאהדֹנֹהי מִמִּצְרָיִם מצר:

---

of the many sins upon the body. As we explained, the Evil Inclination judges the wicked, and the Good Inclination judges the righteous. The average man is judged by both; an average man is a brother of the Evil Inclination and a brother of the Good Inclination, AS IT IS WRITTEN: "My brother; keep what you have to yourself." (Ibid. 9)

— The Zohar, Bo 13:197

This verse is a connection, not only to redeem the first-born but also to support all of us.

When we perform negative acts, we create negative angels. The more negative actions we do, the more negative angels we bring into being. Connecting to this story helps us disperse and destroy all the negative angels we have accumulated, as well as any death-energy that is around us.

HAFTARAH OF BO

In this Haftarah, the prophet Jeremiah told of the coming of King Nebuchadnezzar of Babylon who would attack Egypt. In essence, though, Jeremiah was telling us not to be afraid as long as we are connected to the Light of the Creator. But we should also remember that the Light is the only

Jeremiah 46:13-28

46:13 This is the message the Lord spoke to Jeremiah the Prophet about the coming of Nebuchadnezzar king of Babylon to attack Egypt:

14 "Announce this in Egypt, and proclaim it in Migdol; proclaim it also in Memphis and Tahpanhes: 'Take your positions and get ready, for the sword devours those around you.'

15 Why will your warriors be laid low? They cannot stand, for the Lord will push them down.

16 They will stumble repeatedly; they will fall over each other. They will say, 'Get up, let us go back to our own people and our native lands, away from the sword of the oppressor.'

17 There they will exclaim, 'Pharaoh, king of Egypt is only a loud noise; he has missed his opportunity.'

18 As surely as I live," declares the King, whose Name is the Lord of Hosts, "one will come who is like Tabor among the mountains, like Carmel by the sea.

19 Pack your belongings for exile, you who live in Egypt, for Memphis will be laid waste and lie in ruins without inhabitant.

20 Egypt is a beautiful heifer, but a gadfly is coming against her from the north.

21 The mercenaries in her ranks are like fattened calves. They too will turn and flee together; they will not stand their ground, for the day of disaster is coming upon them, the time for them to be punished.

22 She will hiss like a fleeing serpent as the enemy advances in force; they will come against her with axes, like men who cut down trees.

23 They will chop down her forest," declares the Lord, "dense though it be. They are more numerous than locusts, they cannot be counted.

HAFTARAH OF BO

weapon we have against the Negative Side. Without it, we are totally vulnerable and can do nothing.
If we try to rely on the power of ego against the Negative Side, all our vulnerabilities will come into
play. At that point, we will certainly feel afraid, and our fears will be very much justified.

ירמיהו פרק מו

46 13 הַדָּבָר רַאה אֲשֶׁר דִּבֶּר רַאה יְהֹוָאהדניאהדניהי אֶל־יִרְמְיָהוּ הַנָּבִיא לָבוֹא
נְבוּכַדְרֶאצַּר מֶלֶךְ בָּבֶל לְהַכּוֹת אֶת־אֶרֶץ אלהים דאלפין מִצְרָיִם מצר:

14 הַגִּידוּ בְמִצְרַיִם מצר וְהַשְׁמִיעוּ בְמִגְדּוֹל וְהַשְׁמִיעוּ בְנֹף וּבְתַחְפַּנְחֵס
אִמְרוּ הִתְיַצֵּב וְהָכֵן לָךְ כִּי־אָכְלָה חֶרֶב רבוע ס"ג ורבוע אהיה סְבִיבֶיךָ:

15 מַדּוּעַ נִסְחַף אַבִּירֶיךָ לֹא עָמַד כִּי יְהֹוָאהדניאהדניהי הֲדָפוֹ: 16 הִרְבָּה
כּוֹשֵׁל גַּם יָכ"ל ־נָפַל אִישׁ ע"ה קנ"א קס"א אֶל־רֵעֵהוּ וַיֹּאמְרוּ קוּמָה קנ"א, מקוה |
וְנָשֻׁבָה אֶל־עַמֵּנוּ רבוע ס"ג וְאֶל־אֶרֶץ אלהים דאלפין מוֹלַדְתֵּנוּ מִפְּנֵי חֶרֶב
הַיּוֹנָה רבוע ס"ג ורבוע אהיה כ"ו מ"ה: 17 קָרְאוּ שָׁם יהוה שדי פַּרְעֹה מֶלֶךְ־מִצְרַיִם מצר
שָׁאוֹן הֶעֱבִיר הַמּוֹעֵד: 18 חַי־אָנִי אני, טדה"ד כוזו נְאֻם־הַמֶּלֶךְ יְהֹוָאהדניאהדניהי
צְבָאוֹת נתה ורבוע אהיה, פני שכינה שְׁמוֹ מהש ע"ה, אל שדי ע"ה כִּי כְּתָבוֹר בֶּהָרִים
וּכְכַרְמֶל בַּיָּם יָבוֹא: 19 כְּלֵי כלי גוֹלָה עֲשִׂי לָךְ יוֹשֶׁבֶת בַּת־מִצְרָיִם
מצר כִּי־נֹף לְשַׁמָּה תִהְיֶה וְנִצְּתָה מֵאֵין יוֹשֵׁב: 20 עֶגְלָה יְפֵה־פִיָּה מִצְרָיִם
מצר קֶרֶץ מִצָּפוֹן בָּא בָא: 21 גַּם יָכ"ל ־שְׂכִרֶיהָ בְקִרְבָּהּ כְּעֶגְלֵי מַרְבֵּק
כִּי־גַם יָכ"ל הֵמָּה הִפְנוּ נָסוּ יַחְדָּיו לֹא עָמָדוּ כִּי יוֹם ע"ה = נגד, זן, מזבח אֵידָם
בָּא עֲלֵיהֶם עֵת י"פ אהיה י' הויות פְּקֻדָּתָם: 22 קוֹלָהּ כַּנָּחָשׁ שדי ורבוע אהיה יֵלֵךְ
כְּלי כִּי־בְחַיִל ומב יֵלֵכוּ וּבְקַרְדֻּמּוֹת בָּאוּ לָהּ כְּחֹטְבֵי עֵצִים: 23 כָּרְתוּ
יַעְרָהּ נְאֻם־יְהֹוָאהדניאהדניהי כִּי לֹא יֵחָקֵר כִּי רַבּוּ מֵאַרְבֶּה יצחק, ד"פ ב"ן וְאֵין

24 The Daughter of Egypt will be put to shame, handed over to the people of the north." 25 The Lord of Hosts, the God of Israel, says: "I am about to bring punishment on Amon god of Thebes, on Pharaoh, on Egypt and her gods and her kings, and on those who rely on Pharaoh.

26 I will hand them over to those who seek their lives, to Nebuchadnezzar king of Babylon and his officers. Later, Egypt will be inhabited as in times past," declares the Lord.

27 "Do not fear, Jacob My servant; do not be dismayed, Israel. I will surely save you out of a distant place, your descendants from the land of their exile. Jacob will again have peace and security, and no one will make him afraid.

28 Do not fear, Jacob, My servant" declares the Lord, "for I am with you. Though I completely destroy all the nations among which I scatter you, I will not completely destroy you. I will discipline you but only with justice; I will not let you go entirely unpunished."

לָהֶם בְּמִסְפָּר: 24 הֹבִישָׁה בַּת־מִצְרָיִם מצר נִתְּנָה בְּיַד עַם־צָפוֹן: 25 אָמַר

יְהֹוָה אַדנָי צְבָאוֹת נתה ורבוע אהיה; פני שכינה אֱלֹהֵי יְלה דמב, יִשְׂרָאֵל הִנְנִי פוֹקֵד

אֶל־אָמוֹן מִנֹּא וְעַל־פַּרְעֹה וְעַל־מִצְרַיִם מצר וְעַל־אֱלֹהֶיהָ ילה וְעַל־

מְלָכֶיהָ וְעַל־פַּרְעֹה וְעַל־הַבֹּטְחִים בּוֹ: 26 וּנְתַתִּים בְּיַד מְבַקְשֵׁי נַפְשָׁם

וּבְיַד נְבוּכַדְרֶאצַּר מֶלֶךְ־בָּבֶל וּבְיַד־עֲבָדָיו וְאַחֲרֵי־כֵן תִּשְׁכֹּן כִּימֵי־

קֶדֶם רבוע ב"ן נְאֻם־יְהֹוָה אַדני ואהנהי: 27 וְאַתָּה אַל־תִּירָא עַבְדִּי יַעֲקֹב

וְאַל־תֵּחַת יִשְׂרָאֵל ז"פ יהוה, יאהדונהי אידהנויה כִּי הִנְנִי מוֹשִׁעֲךָ מֵרָחוֹק שדי

וְאֶת־זַרְעֲךָ מֵאֶרֶץ אלהים דאלפין שִׁבְיָם וְשָׁב יַעֲקֹב וְשָׁקַט וְשַׁאֲנַן וְאֵין

מַחֲרִיד: 28 אַתָּה אַל־תִּירָא עַבְדִּי יַעֲקֹב ז"פ יהוה, יאהדונהי אידהנויה נְאֻם־

יְהֹוָה אדני כִּי אִתְּךָ אָנִי אני, טדהד כוו"ו כִּי אֶעֱשֶׂה כָלָה בְּכָל־ב"ן, לכב, יבמ

הַגּוֹיִם | אֲשֶׁר הִדַּחְתִּיךָ שָׁמָּה מהש, מ"ה, אל שדי וְאֹתְךָ לֹא־אֶעֱשֶׂה כָלָה

וְיִסַּרְתִּיךָ לַמִּשְׁפָּט ע"ה ה"פ אלהים וְנַקֵּה קס"א לֹא אֲנַקֶּךָּ:

BESHALACH

LESSON OF BESHALACH
(Exodus 13:17-17)

"Why should we die in the desert?"

How is it possible that only a short time after their escape from bondage in Egypt, the people of Israel were longing to go back? Instead of embracing the challenges that freedom always brings, they were already missing the security of slavery. All this is expressed in their self-pitying lament, "Why should we die in the desert?"

Rav Isaac Luria (the Ari) teaches us that the exile in Egypt was an exile of consciousness. In Egypt, the people of Israel were enslaved to the Desire to Receive for the Self Alone. As long as this selfish consciousness was in force, no spiritual work could take place—their consciousness was enslaved to darkness. The Ari wrote:

> *Let us now explain the differences between a sin and iniquity and rebellion. It is considered a rebellion when a man knows his Rav, yet intentionally and purposely acts against him. He then causes the klipot to receive all the plenty (shefa: Shin, Pei, Ayin) for that rebellion (pesha: Pei, Shin, Ayin). The klipot do not bestow any of it on the lower beings, Israel. An iniquity is when a man does as he pleases, not on purpose but sinning for his own enjoyment. He also causes the klipot to receive the descending plenty, but after they receive it, they lower some of it and give it to us, which is the meaning of exile. By this you will understand the two sayings of the sages in the last chapter of the Tractate Yoma. The one says that the greatest repentance is when willful misdeeds have become for the sinner like misdeeds that were done by mistake, since it refers to a willful misdeed that is considered a rebellion. At first, the man caused the klipot to receive all the plenty for themselves, and now by repentance, he has caused the klipot to receive all of it, but still they bring us down some of it of their own accord after taking it for themselves. The other saying is that willful misdeeds turn to merits for a man. This is because an iniquity involves only sinning for one's own enjoyment. Then, when the man repents, he causes the klipot to take nothing of the descending plenty for themselves, and withholds from them even the plenty they used to take to themselves.*
> — *Writings of the Ari, Gate of Reincarnation, 21st Introduction, 14*

This slavery still exists today and expresses itself in many ways, some of which even seem intensely positive. The temporary excitement that comes from gratifying selfish desires can be alluring. If we never look beyond it, this excitement can feel like true joy. We accept the endless pursuit for the next source of gratification without realizing that this is actually slavery. When this consciousness has really taken hold of our minds and souls, liberation can seem frightening. We may plead to be put back in our prison, as this lesson shows.

There are people today who literally can't understand the true meaning of connection with the Light. They are like those Israelites who thought, "For this I was taken out of Egypt? So I can give instead of take? So I can share with others instead of keeping for myself?" Those were people who did not experience the bondage in Egypt as suffering because their Desire to Receive for the Self Alone had become the essence and the foundation of their being. Going out from Egypt brought them a kind of pain that they were not prepared to accept, even though ultimate transformation lay just beyond it.

Consider this example. A man has always lived in a tiny apartment. He's used to it, so the cramped quarters don't cause him any pain. He never looks for a bigger living space because he's not uncomfortable where he is and because looking for something else would require some effort. A different kind of person, on the other hand, would find the small apartment intolerable. The man contented in his small apartment may be motivated primarily by inertia and a familiar level of misery, while the other person sets his sights on something better, even if it means working through some adjustments. For one person, necessity means keeping everything exactly as it is; for the other, necessity means creating positive change.

Therefore, we can see that "slavery in Egypt"—that is, the Desire to Receive for the Self Alone—can take many forms. The most powerful and pervasive of these is the unbreakable habit of being reactive. A negative person does not want to change because it is so much easier to react. "Going out from Egypt" is proactive. It means that we must open up new territory within ourselves and escape from our worn-out hang-ups and habitual ways of doing things. That proactive behavior is the greatest thing about our escape from slavery, but also the most difficult. For some people, this change is just too difficult and frightening, but for others, it is a challenge that reinvigorates them in their search for connection.

Regardless of what we do, if our action is based on servitude to an idea, a person, an object, or a situation, then we are still "enslaved in Egypt." Conversely, if we do something because it is right and not because it is attached to some material reward or compensation, this means we are "going out from Egypt." By undertaking those positive actions and by nurturing the consciousness that underlies them, we make ourselves ready to receive the Light at Mount Sinai.

The Splitting of the Red Sea

The miracle of the Splitting of the Red Sea is one of the best-known episodes in the Bible, but why was it necessary? True, it was at the Red Sea that God gave us the 72 Names, but couldn't this have happened without the sea having to be split?

There is no doubt that God could have found another route for the Israelites' escape, a route that wouldn't have put them in this extremely dangerous predicament. The miracle of the Red Sea was, however, a fundamental necessity for the spiritual development of the Israelites. The splitting of the sea elevated the consciousness of the people to the level of the 50th Gate of Binah. This elevated consciousness was a precondition for the giving of the Torah—not just for that generation but for all the generations to come. The 50th Gate supersedes all the previous gates, removing any and all connections to the klipah (the veil or shell of negativity that keeps us from seeing the Light) that we hold onto. The dry path through the waters that were held back on either side of the Israelites in the Red Sea opened a pathway or conduit on a spiritual level to the 50th Gate so that other generations to come would not have to go through the process of experiencing the previous 49 Gates to get to the highest level of consciousness.

The Light is always here to assist us in our transformation, but making this journey step by step can take a lot of time. Reaching the 50th Gate allows us to bypass the slowest and most painful part of the journey.

The consciousness of the 50th Gate can be explained by an analogy to the human body. There are nerves in the hands and feet and other parts of the body that are very sensitive to pain. If you place your finger next to the flame of a candle, you immediately pull back. Your finger is connected to the realities of the everyday world. But paradoxically, despite the fact that it is the nerve center of the body, the brain itself feels no pain. For this reason, anesthetics are not required during brain surgery. The brain is the center of consciousness and is beyond pain. It is like the eye of a hurricane, where perfect calm prevails.

The Red Sea served as a massive mikveh, or spiritual cleansing bath, for all the people of Israel. The Zohar tells us that when a soul leaves this world for the higher reality, it must immerse itself in the river of Dinur to forget its connections with the physical realm. We also read:

> And in this very same River Dinur, the souls immerse to cleanse themselves from their defiling blemishes that they had become soiled with in the lower world.
> — The Zohar, Hakdam 10:79

The splitting of the Red Sea enabled the people to forget their connection to Egypt and all that it represented. Often, even if we want to disconnect ourselves from a particular negative experience, the connection is hard to break. Deep in our souls, we are not completely able to say that we really want to be free. The splitting of the Red Sea removes that difficult barrier.

A man came to his spiritual teacher and said, "I've heard that when a person runs away from power and respect, then power and respect run after him. Well, I've been running away, but power and respect have not been pursuing me." The teacher answered, "Well, then I guess you are always looking behind you to make sure you are not too far ahead."

For us to really get out of our personal Egypt, there has to be a complete break in our connection to the Desire to Receive for the Self Alone. The splitting of the Red Sea creates a torrent that carries away all the negativity of bondage. We connect directly with that energy at the time of Passover, while during the rest of the year, we rely on the mikveh.

The 72 Names of God

There are many secrets hidden in the 72 Names of God, the most important of which is the fact that the Aramaic letter Gimel never appears in any of them. This was explained by a kabbalist who lived more than 400 years ago, Rav Nathan Nata Shapiro (1585–1633, author of Megaleh Amukot), who was known as "the revealer of deep things." The Megaleh Amukot (as he was known) taught that anyone afflicted with pride (ge'avah in Hebrew), which begins with the letter Gimel, cannot use the 72 Names of God. As many times as he tries, his pride will inevitably interfere with the power that resides in this great tool.

By themselves, the Names have little power. It's like without a Vessel the Light cannot be revealed. Only through the Vessel can we see that there is Light. In the same way, the Names have to pass through the consciousness of a human being. If that consciousness is dominated by ego-based energy, the Light will ask, "Whom are you serving? Is it yourself or Me? If you want to remain in bondage, I will leave you here. But if you let Me, I will set you free. The choice is yours." Thus, the absence of the letter Gimel gives us insight into the secret of the danger of pride.

SYNOPSIS OF BESHALACH

This story describes the Splitting of the Red Sea, and it also introduces the 72 Names of God. Contrary to conventional descriptions of this event, God did not part the Red Sea. Rather, it was Moses and the Israelites who performed this act, which overturned physical nature. It was the first time that humanity had been given the tools to bring about a miracle. The miracle was made possible by means of the 72 Names of God, while every other miracle up to this point in biblical history had been brought about directly by God. Through this story, we learn about and are connected to the potential reality of mind over matter—consciousness controlling physicality. The Zohar writes about the Splitting of the Red Sea by speaking about the Supernal Laws that were being fulfilled:

> Then it is written: "And God said to Moses, 'Why do you cry to Me?'" (Exodus 14:15). We learned in the Hidden Book that "to Me" is exact, FOR IT IS THE ATTRIBUTE OF ZEIR ANPIN, because it all depends upon Atika. At that moment, Atika Kadisha was revealed, goodwill was present in all the worlds Above, and then the collective Light shone.

> Rav Yitzchak said: Then, when everything shone together, the sea executed the Supernal Laws—NAMELY, TO DROWN THE EGYPTIANS AND SAVE THE CHILDREN OF ISRAEL— because those Above and those Below were given over to it.
> — The Zohar, Beshalach 14:180-181

FIRST READING - ABRAHAM - CHESED

13:17 **A**nd it was when Pharaoh let the people go, God did not lead them toward the sea on the road through the Philistine country, though that was shorter. For God said, "If they face war, they might change their minds and return to Egypt."

18 So God led the people around by the desert road toward the Red Sea. The Israelites went up out of Egypt armed for battle.

19 Moses took the bones of Joseph with him because Joseph had made the sons of Israel swear an oath. He had said, "God will surely come to your aid, and then you must carry my bones up with you from this place."

20 After leaving Succoth they camped at Etham on the edge of the desert.

FROM THE RAV

Right now, in the Age of Aquarius, we are as close to the removal of chaos in our universe as we have ever been since Moses ascended Mount Sinai. We are ready to enact miracles that are every bit as great as the Splitting of the Red Sea.

However, as this story reveals, it is still up to you and me to eliminate chaos from our personal lives. The real problem is our nature as human beings, which is something that we have so far been unable to change.

We have been given the tools. But we also came here with the Evil Inclination, and we should be aware that it does exist within us. Once we are aware, we know there is a war we need to fight every day.

This is an incredible reading. We have to know that in the grand scheme of things, we are in control. We can achieve mastery over the physical universe, and even if some discomfort appears in our lives for a period of time, we are still in control. Who cares if there are problems for these few moments or even these few days? We know the final outcome—and we know it will be good.

With an appreciation for our ability to know about and to understand the technology of the 72 Names of God presented in Beshalach, we can, indeed, control our environment; control all of the chaos that we experience, and bring together so many of our lifetimes to create the tikkunim (corrections) and speed up that process.

These tools, however, are only effective for those of us who, by being proactive, are following the path of the Lightforce of God. But we can never achieve a proactive state of consciousness if we do not exercise restriction every step of the way. Some of us are weak at times and succumb to the game of Satan, as is so clearly demonstrated in this story.

We live in a game of Satan. We are armchair detectives. Had I only not done this and that, everything would have been perfect. We are always brilliant later. This is Satan's way. He will provide us with all the material we need to continue our chaos. He will validate everything for us, no matter how stupid it might be. But because we are not stupid, Satan tells us how brilliant we are. He tells us how the last mistake, which was a disaster, was really missing

FIRST READING - ABRAHAM - CHESED

17 וַיְהִי אֵל, יֵאָ"י בְּשַׁלַּח פַּרְעֹה אֶת־הָעָם וְלֹא־נָחָם אֱלֹהִים מום, אהיה אדני ; ילה

דֶּרֶךְ ב"פ יב"ק אֶרֶץ אלהים דאלפין פְּלִשְׁתִּים י"פ אלהים כִּי קָרוֹב הוּא כִּי | אָמַר

אֱלֹהִים מום, אהיה אדני ; ילה פֶּן־יִנָּחֵם הָעָם בִּרְאֹתָם מִלְחָמָה וְשָׁבוּ מִצְרָיְמָה

מצר: 18 וַיַּסֵּב אֱלֹהִים מום, אהיה אדני ; ילה אֶת־הָעָם | דֶּרֶךְ ב"פ יב"ק הַמִּדְבָּר יַם

ילי ־סוּף וַחֲמֻשִׁים עָלוּ בְנֵי־יִשְׂרָאֵל מֵאֶרֶץ אלהים דאלפין מִצְרָיִם מצר:

19 וַיִּקַּח חֹעם מֹשֶׁה מהע, אל שדי אֶת־עַצְמוֹת יוֹסֵף ציון, קנאה, רי"פ יהוה, ה"פ אל ע"ה עִמּוֹ

כִּי הַשְׁבֵּעַ ע"ב ואלהים דיודין הִשְׁבִּיעַ אֶת־בְּנֵי יִשְׂרָאֵל לֵאמֹר פָּקֹד רבוע ע"ב

יִפְקֹד רבוע ע"ב אֱלֹהִים מום, אהיה אדני ; ילה אֶתְכֶם וְהַעֲלִיתֶם אֶת־עַצְמֹתַי מִזֶּה

אִתְּכֶם: 20 וַיִּסְעוּ מִסֻּכֹּת וַיַּחֲנוּ בְאֵתָם בִּקְצֵה ה"פ טל, ג"פ אדני הַמִּדְבָּר:

---

just that "one little thing"—that had we not done it a certain way, everything would have worked out.

This was Pharaoh. Suddenly, he became brilliant. The story of Beshalach says that Pharaoh woke up the day after the Israelites left Egypt and said, "Oh, what did I do? Why did I let them go? Let's bring them back; they cannot sustain themselves outside." His advisors told him that this would be a mistake, but he pursued them anyway. Was Pharaoh stupid? No, he was only acting out the game of Satan.

How many times are we told by our inner voice or by others around us: "Don't do it," but we know better? Because we live Satan's reactive game, we do not exercise a connection with the only game that can beat Satan at his own game— restriction. Restriction is the only game we have left. Every other game, where we figure out and manipulate, plays right into Satan's hands. Without restriction,

there is no way that these tools, the 72 Names of God, which are the bridge between the non-physical reality and the physical reality, can be actualized. We can talk and be convinced about mind over matter, but we will never achieve that kind of result without the employment of the 72 Names of God.

בְּשַׁלַּח

Exodus 13:17—Beshalach means "sent away."

This verse, where Pharaoh sent the Israelites away and God turned them toward the Red Sea, is meant to give us the power to banish and cleanse any and all negativity as long as we sincerely let go of our own negative energy. But we must actively expel our own negativity, not passively wait for it to disappear.

21 By day the Lord went ahead of them in a pillar of cloud to guide them on their way and by night in a pillar of fire to give them light, so that they could travel by day and night.

22 Neither the pillar of cloud by day nor the pillar of fire by night left its place in front of the people.

14:1 Then the Lord said to Moses, 2 "Tell the Israelites to turn back and encamp near Pi Hahiroth, between Migdol and the sea. They are to encamp by the sea, directly opposite Baal Zephon.

3 Pharaoh will think, 'The Israelites are wandering around the land in confusion, hemmed in by the desert.'

4 And I will strengthen Pharaoh's heart, and he will pursue them. But I will gain glory for myself through Pharaoh and all his army, and the Egyptians will know that I am the Lord." So the Israelites did this.

5 When the King of Egypt was told that the people had fled, Pharaoh and his officials changed their minds about them and said, "What have we done? We have sent away the Israelites from serving us!"

6 So he had his chariot made ready and took his people with him.

7 He took six hundred of the best chariots, along with all the other chariots of Egypt, with officers over all of them.

8 The Lord hardened the heart of Pharaoh king of Egypt, so that he pursued the Israelites, who were marching out with a strong hand.

בְּעַמּוּד עָנָן, בְּעַמּוּד אֵשׁ

Exodus 13:21—The protective cloud and the pillar of fire.

As the Israelites traveled through the desert, they were guided by a protective cloud during the day and a pillar of fire at night. The cloud and the pillar of fire offered protection on both the physical and metaphysical levels. The Israelites were unaffected by all the limitations of living in the material world. We're told that their clothes did not wear out, for example, and their bodies produced no waste. The *Zohar* says:

> "And God went before them by day." "And God" means God and His court of law, which is Malchut, because the

Vav (Eng. 'and') of Vav, Yud, Hei, Vav, and Hei ('and God') includes Malchut. Rav Yitzchak said: We learned that the Shechinah travels with the Patriarchs, because "went before them by day" is Abraham, "in a pillar of a cloud" is Isaac, and "to lead them the way" is Jacob, of whom it is written: "And Jacob went on his way" (Genesis 32:2). "By night in a pillar of fire, to give them light" is King David. They are all the holy Chariot of Above. Abraham, Isaac and Jacob are Chesed, Gevurah and Tiferet, the three legs of the Throne, and King David is the fourth leg. In order that the children of Israel should be perfect in everything and that the Patriarchs should see their redemption, it is written: "And I will also surely bring you up" (Genesis 46:4) with

21 וַיהֹוָאֲדֹנָיאהֹדֹנֹהי הֹלֵךְ מיה לִפְנֵיהֶם יוֹמָם בְּעַמּוּד עָנָן לַנְחֹתָם הַדֶּרֶךְ

ב״פ יב״ק וְלַיְלָה מלה בְּעַמּוּד אֵשׁ אלהים דיודין ע״ה לְהָאִיר לָהֶם לָלֶכֶת יוֹמָם

וָלָיְלָה מלה: 22 לֹא־יָמִישׁ עַמּוּד הֶעָנָן יוֹמָם וְעַמּוּד הָאֵשׁ אלהים דיודין ע״ה

לָיְלָה מלה לִפְנֵי וחכמה בינה הָעָם: 14 1 וַיְדַבֵּר ראה יְהֹוָאֲדֹנָיאהֹדֹנֹהי אֶל־מֹשֶׁה

מהוע, אל שדי לֵאמֹר: 2 דַּבֵּר ראה אֶל־בְּנֵי יִשְׂרָאֵל וְיָשֻׁבוּ וְיַחֲנוּ לִפְנֵי וחכמה בינה

פִּי הַחִירֹת בֵּין מִגְדֹּל עו וּבֵין הַיָּם וחכמה בינה לִפְנֵי ילי בַּעַל צְפֹן נִכְחוֹ תַחֲנוּ

עַל־הַיָּם: 3 וְאָמַר פַּרְעֹה לִבְנֵי יִשְׂרָאֵל נְבֻכִים הֵם בָּאָרֶץ אלהים דאלפין

סָגַר עֲלֵיהֶם הַמִּדְבָּר: 4 וְחִזַּקְתִּי אֶת־לֵב־פַּרְעֹה וְרָדַף אַחֲרֵיהֶם

וְאִכָּבְדָה בְּפַרְעֹה וּבְכָל בין, לכב, יבם חֵילוֹ וְיָדְעוּ מִצְרַיִם מצר כִּי־אֲנִי

אני, טדהד כוזו יְהֹוָאֲדֹנָיאהֹדֹנֹהי וַיַּעֲשׂוּ־כֵן: 5 וַיֻּגַּד לְמֶלֶךְ מִצְרַיִם מצר כִּי בָרַח

הָעָם וַיֵּהָפֵךְ לְבַב בכו פַּרְעֹה וַעֲבָדָיו אֶל־הָעָם וַיֹּאמְרוּ מַה־מֹּה זֹּאת

עָשִׂינוּ כִּי־שִׁלַּחְנוּ אֶת־יִשְׂרָאֵל מֵעָבְדֵנוּ: 6 וַיֶּאְסֹר אֶת־רִכְבּוֹ וְאֶת־עַמּוֹ

לָקָח ב״פ יהוה אדני אהיה עִמּוֹ: 7 וַיִּקַּח שֵׁשׁ־מֵאוֹת רֶכֶב בָּחוּר וְכֹל ילי

רֶכֶב מִצְרַיִם מצר וְשָׁלִשִׁם עַל־כֻּלּוֹ: 8 וַיְחַזֵּק יְהֹוָאֲדֹנָיאהֹדֹנֹהי אֶת־לֵב

פַּרְעֹה מֶלֶךְ מִצְרַיִם מצר וַיִּרְדֹּף אַחֲרֵי בְּנֵי יִשְׂרָאֵל וּבְנֵי יִשְׂרָאֵל יֹצְאִים

בְּיָד רָמָה:

---

the Chariot. It is also written: "And God went... that they might go by day and by night." He questions: Why did they travel day and night, like people who are fleeing? God was guarding them, so they were not afraid. He answers: In order that they should be complete with everything, because there is no completeness unless day is with night, as day is the aspect of Zeir Anpin and night is the aspect of Nukva. All perfection prevails when they are joined together in the secret of: "And there was evening and there was morning, one day." (Genesis 1:5)
— The Zohar, Beshalach 4:52-53

וַיֵּהָפֵךְ

Exodus 14:5—Pharaoh had a change of heart. Pharaoh suddenly regretted letting the Israelites go. Despite the suffering caused by the plagues and the difficulties the Israelites had brought upon Egypt in those last days, Pharaoh still felt attached to them. This is meant to reveal to us our own behavior. In spite of the chaos and pain that our negative actions and thoughts bring to us, we repeat them again and again, returning to the same inevitable dead end.

SECOND READING - ISAAC - GEVURAH

⁹ The Egyptians pursued the Israelites and overtook them as they camped by the sea—all Pharaoh's horses and chariots, horsemen and troops—near Pi Hahiroth, opposite Baal Zephon.

¹⁰ As Pharaoh approached, the Israelites raised their eyes upwards, and there were the Egyptians, marching after them. They were terrified and cried out to the Lord.

¹¹ They said to Moses, "Was it because there were no graves in Egypt that you brought us to the desert to die? What have you done to us by bringing us out of Egypt?

¹² Didn't we say to you in Egypt, 'Leave us alone; let us serve the Egyptians?' It would have been better for us to serve the Egyptians than to die in the desert!"

¹³ Moses answered the people, "Do not be afraid. Stand firm and see the deliverance the Lord will bring you today. The Egyptians you see today you will never see again.

¹⁴ The Lord will fight for you; you need only to be quiet."

וַיִּרְדְּפוּ

Exodus 14:9—Pharaoh pursued the Israelites, and they panicked.

In spite of all the miracles done on their behalf that they had witnessed in Egypt, the Israelites were panic-stricken when Pharaoh chased them through the desert. They began to complain and even to long for slavery once again.

We need to have certainty to be able to appreciate the miracles the Light does for us every day. When we lack that certainty that today and tomorrow will be good, we will lose appreciation and fall back to slave-consciousness, no matter how many miracles we have experienced. On the other hand, when we have that certainty, we do not need to depend on miracles to know God. Our certainty sustains us, and miracles come freely and constantly.

> Israel were approaching the sea and saw the sea before them, raging and storming. Its waves were towering above, and they feared. They raised their eyes and saw Pharaoh and his army and flying stones and arrows, and they feared greatly. What did they do? "And the children of Israel cried out." So, who caused the children of Israel to come closer to their Father in heaven? Pharaoh. "And Moses said to the people, 'Fear not, stand still and see the salvation of God.' " (Exodus 14:13) Rav Shimon said: Fortunate is the portion of Israel that a shepherd like Moses goes among them, because Moses was equal to all of Israel. We learned from this that the shepherd of the people is really the whole people.
> — The Zohar, Beshalach 6:67

In a letter to Rav Berg, Rav Brandwein wrote about miracles:

> "But sometimes one needs to attract a miracle, which is outside of nature. The only way one attracts miracles—to rearrange nature from the way God has arranged it to be—is through self-sacrifice. For in man, the force and desire to receive is built into his very existence, along with the desire to own and rule over everything. If he overcomes himself, learning to sacrifice himself for

SECOND READING - ISAAC - GEVURAH

9 וַיִּרְדְּפוּ מִצְרַיִם אַחֲרֵיהֶם וַיַּשִּׂיגוּ אוֹתָם חֹנִים עַל־הַיָּם כָּל־

סוּס רֶכֶב פַּרְעֹה וּפָרָשָׁיו וְחֵילוֹ עַל־פִּי הַחִירֹת לִפְנֵי

בַּעַל צְפֹן: 10 וּפַרְעֹה הִקְרִיב וַיִּשְׂאוּ בְנֵי־יִשְׂרָאֵל אֶת־עֵינֵיהֶם

וְהִנֵּה מִצְרַיִם | נֹסֵעַ אַחֲרֵיהֶם וַיִּירְאוּ מְאֹד וַיִּצְעֲקוּ

בְנֵי־יִשְׂרָאֵל אֶל־יְהֹוָה: 11 וַיֹּאמְרוּ אֶל־מֹשֶׁה הֲמִבְּלִי

אֵין־קְבָרִים בְּמִצְרַיִם לְקַחְתָּנוּ לָמוּת בַּמִּדְבָּר מַה־

זֹּאת עָשִׂיתָ לָּנוּ לְהוֹצִיאָנוּ מִמִּצְרָיִם: 12 הֲלֹא־

זֶה הַדָּבָר אֲשֶׁר דִּבַּרְנוּ אֵלֶיךָ בְמִצְרַיִם לֵאמֹר

חֲדַל מִמֶּנּוּ וְנַעַבְדָה אֶת־מִצְרָיִם כִּי טוֹב לָנוּ

עֲבֹד אֶת־מִצְרַיִם מִמֻּתֵנוּ בַּמִּדְבָּר: 13 וַיֹּאמֶר מֹשֶׁה

אֶל־הָעָם אַל־תִּירָאוּ הִתְיַצְּבוּ וּרְאוּ אֶת־יְשׁוּעַת יְהֹוָה

אֲשֶׁר־יַעֲשֶׂה לָכֶם הַיּוֹם כִּי אֲשֶׁר רְאִיתֶם אֶת־מִצְרַיִם

הַיּוֹם לֹא תֹסִפוּ לִרְאֹתָם עוֹד עַד־עוֹלָם: 14 יְהֹוָה

יִלָּחֵם לָכֶם וְאַתֶּם תַּחֲרִישׁוּן:

---

the sake of the honour of God, then this force rises and tears all the veils—and no power among the higher or lower beings is able to stop him or block anything he asks for, and his prayer will be answered in full. Added to this is the interpretation of the holy Baal Shem Tov of the verse, "God is your shade." (Psalms 121:5) Just as one's shadow imitates every movement of a person, God does the same. If a man is willing to sacrifice himself for the sanctity of God, then God voids all the rules of nature that He established, and turns toward that self-sacrificing man. And even if the man is neither honest nor deserving, according to the standards laid down, and should wait until "its time" (Isaiah 60:22), he can still, through self-sacrifice, hasten his own salvation through the scriptural promise of 'I will hasten it.'"

THIRD READING - JACOB - TIFERET

15 Then the Lord said to Moses, "Why are you crying out to me? Tell the Israelites and move on. 16 Raise your staff and stretch out your hand over the sea to divide the water so that the Israelites can go through the sea on dry ground.

17 I will harden the hearts of the Egyptians so that they will go in after them. And I will gain glory through Pharaoh and all his army, through his chariots and his horsemen.

18 The Egyptians will know that I am the Lord when I gain glory through Pharaoh, his chariots and his horsemen." 19 Then the Angel of God, who had been traveling in front of Israel's army, went behind them. The pillar of cloud moved from in front and stood behind them, 20 coming between the armies of Egypt and Israel. Throughout the night the cloud brought darkness to the one side and light to the other side; so neither went near the other all night long.

מַה יִּתְצַעַק אֵלָי

Exodus 14:15—God told Moses to order the Israelites forward.

Moses called out to God, and God replied, "Why are you crying out to Me? Tell them to jump into the sea!" We often call out to God when we are in trouble. But it is our destiny to take an active role, to become like God; it is through our positive actions and through our willingness to move forward in certainty with the Light that we are able to bring miracles into our lives. We cannot expect everything to be done for us. We are in this world to become partners in Creation.

Rav Brandwein wrote:

"But for a miracle, beyond the natural path, one needs self-sacrifice. This is what God said to Moses: "Why do you cry to Me?" Now that I wish to perform miracles for them that are not according to nature's way, God is telling him, this depends on Atika. For there is a grade called Zeir Anpin, which ordinarily accepts the prayers of Israel and answers them. This is "to Me." But here it depends upon Me, since a miracle outside the boundaries of nature should be revealed to the children of Israel. Therefore, "Speak to the children of Israel, that they go forward," so that they will show self-sacrifice below—and thus the supernal

grade will awaken, which reforms all natural ways and makes the seas into dry land. The scripture, "He turned the wilderness into a pool of water, and dry ground into springs of water" [Psalms 107:35] shows that He hastens salvation to His people in a way that is contrary to what is natural."

And from the Ari:

They said in the Zohar that the issue originates in Atika, and in the Idra that this originates in Atika, in the two apples. Hence the initials of, "why do you cry to me" form 'truth' (Heb. emet) in Hebrew.

— Torah Compilations 4, Story of Beshalach, 5

The three verses with 72 letters

The *Zohar* reveals that the letters of three biblical verses (Exodus 14:19-21) can be rearranged in a sequence of 72 triads of letters to form the 72 Names of God. To bring miracles into our lives, we must unite with these 72 Names and with God. By so doing, we can create miracles.

Come and behold: at that moment, the moon became full, WHICH IS MALCHUT of all THE ASPECTS, and she inherited

THIRD READING - JACOB - TIFERET

15 וַיֹּאמֶר יְהֹוָה אֶל־מֹשֶׁה מַה־ תִּצְעַק אֵלָי דַּבֵּר אֶל־בְּנֵי־יִשְׂרָאֵל וְיִסָּעוּ: 16 וְאַתָּה הָרֵם אֶת־מַטְּךָ וּנְטֵה אֶת־יָדְךָ עַל־הַיָּם וּבְקָעֵהוּ וְיָבֹאוּ בְנֵי־יִשְׂרָאֵל בְּתוֹךְ הַיָּם בַּיַּבָּשָׁה: 17 וַאֲנִי הִנְנִי מְחַזֵּק אֶת־לֵב מִצְרַיִם וְיָבֹאוּ אַחֲרֵיהֶם וְאִכָּבְדָה בְּפַרְעֹה וּבְכָל־חֵילוֹ בְּרִכְבּוֹ וּבְפָרָשָׁיו: 18 וְיָדְעוּ מִצְרַיִם כִּי־אֲנִי יְהֹוָה בְּהִכָּבְדִי בְּפַרְעֹה בְּרִכְבּוֹ וּבְפָרָשָׁיו:

19 וַיִּסַּע מַלְאַךְ הָאֱלֹהִים הַהֹלֵךְ לִפְנֵי מַחֲנֵה יִשְׂרָאֵל וַיֵּלֶךְ מֵאַחֲרֵיהֶם וַיִּסַּע עַמּוּד הֶעָנָן מִפְּנֵיהֶם וַיַּעֲמֹד מֵאַחֲרֵיהֶם:

כהת	אכא	ללה	מהש	עלם	סיט	ילי	והו
הקם	הרי	מבה	יזל	ההע	לאו	אלד	הזי
והו	מלה	ייי	נלך	פהל	לוו	כלי	לאו
ושר	לכב	אום	ריי	שאה	ירת	האא	נתה
ייי	רהע	ועם	אני	מנד	כוק	להו	יוו
מיה	עשל	ערי	סאל	ילה	ולו	מיכ	ההה
פוי	מבה	נית	עמם	הוע	דני		והו
מוי	ענו	יהה	ומב	מצר	הרח	ייל	נמם
מום	היי	יבמ	ראה	חבו	איע	מנק	דמב

72 Holy Names on three sides, NAMELY THREE COLUMNS. On one side, MALCHUT was attired with the crowns of the supernal Chesed, with seventy engravings of the light of supernal Aba illuminating Her, WHICH IS THE SECRET OF "MOVED." On the second side, MALCHUT was attired with the spears of Gevurah, MEANING THE JUDGMENTS IN HER, by sixty lashes of fire and ten lashes of Her own that descended from the side of Supernal Ima in set Judgments. AND THIS IS THE SECRET OF THE LEFT COLUMN AND THE PASSAGE: "AND IT CAME..." On the third side, MALCHUT was attired in a purple garment that the supernal King, called "Tiferet," wore and which the Holy

²¹ Then Moses stretched out his hand over the sea, and all that night the Lord drove the sea back with a strong east wind and turned it into dry land. The waters were divided, ²² and the Israelites went through the sea on dry ground, with a wall of water on their right and on their left.

Son, WHO IS TIFERET, inherited with the seventy supernal crowns from the side of Aba and Ima. He includes both sides, NAMELY THE RIGHT, WHICH IS CHESED, AND THE LEFT, WHICH IS GVURAH, WHICH IS THE SECRET OF "STRETCHED OUT." There are two crowns from the side of Aba and Ima, which are the Ayin-Bet (72) Names. We learned that there are seventy from the side of Chesed plus two witnesses. From the side of Gevurah, there are seventy plus two scribes. From the side of Tiferet, there are seventy plus two colors for glorification.

In this place, NAMELY MALCHUT, they are engraved one in the other, SO THAT THE 72 CROWNS IN EVERY COLUMN ARE COMBINED WITH EACH OTHER. And the Holy Name emerges from them, which is the secret of the Chariot, FOR THEY BECOME AYIN-BET (72) NAMES, EACH ONE CONSISTING OF THREE LETTERS. Here the Patriarchs are engraved, WHICH ARE CHESED, GEVURAH, AND TIFERET, THE THREE COLUMNS to be joined together. Thus is the Holy Name, AYIN-BET, engraved with its letters. The combination of these letters is as follows: the first set of letters, NAMELY THE 72 LETTERS IN THE PASSAGE, "AND THE ANGEL... MOVED," are written in their order in a straightforward manner - BECAUSE STRAIGHT IS AN INDICATION OF CHESED - and all the original letters are in Chesed, NAMELY, IN THE RIGHT COLUMN, to follow a straightforward manner, in a proper order. The second set of letters, NAMELY THE 72 LETTERS IN THE PASSAGE, "AND IT CAME," are written backwards, MEANING THEY ARE WRITTEN FROM BELOW UPWARDS, AS WRITTEN FURTHER IN THE SECOND DIAGRAM. All the second 72 letters pertain to Gevurah so as to reveal

Judgments and weapons that come from the left side. AND WHEN THEY ARE IN REVERSE ORDER, THEY ALLUDE TO JUDGMENTS. The third set of letters, NAMELY THE 72 LETTERS IN THE PASSAGE, "AND MOSES STRETCHED OUT," are letters that are written so as to expose the colors, WHICH ARE THE JUDGMENTS, with which to adorn the Holy King, WHICH IS THE SECRET OF THE 72 COLORS OF GLORIFICATION. They all join and are bound to Him BECAUSE HE IS THE CENTRAL COLUMN. And He glorifies in His crowns in a straight forward manner and makes an imprint on this side and the other side— NAMELY, TO THE RIGHT COLUMN AND TO THE LEFT COLUMN— AS HE ESTABLISHES THE ILLUMINATION OF BOTH OF THEM as a King who is adorned with everything. Here is marked the Holy Name, engraved with 72 letters. THAT IS, THREE TIMES 72 LETTERS IN EACH OF THE THREE COLUMNS COMBINE AND JOIN TOGETHER, AND THEY FORM 72 WORDS. EACH WORD CONTAINS THREE LETTERS FROM THE THREE COLUMNS that are adorned with the Patriarchs, NAMELY CHESED, GEVURAH, AND TIFERET, which are the supernal Holy Chariot. HE ASKS: Why is the third group of letters not written IN 2 WAYS, part of them straightforward and part of them in reverse, in order to be equal to both sides - MEANING TO THE RIGHT COLUMN AND TO THE LEFT COLUMN, SINCE IT SUSTAINS THE ILLUMINATION OF BOTH. Because we learned that, "You have established equity," (Psalms 99:4) means that the Holy One, blessed be He, establishes equity AND SUSTAINS on both sides. It is written: "And the middle bar in the midst of the boards," (Exodus 26:28), which is the Holy One, blessed be He, NAMELY THE CENTRAL COLUMN THAT

20 וַיָּבֹא בֵּין | מַחֲנֵה מִצְרַיִם מצר וּבֵין מַחֲנֵה יִשְׂרָאֵל וַיְהִי אל, ייא״י הֶעָנָן
וְהַחֹשֶׁךְ שׁין ניצוצות של וי מלכים וַיָּאֶר אלף למד יהוה אֶת־הַלָּיְלָה מלה וְלֹא־קָרַב זֶה
אֶל־זֶה כָּל ילי הַלָּיְלָה מלה:

21 וַיֵּט מֹשֶׁה מהע, אל שדי אֶת־יָדוֹ עַל־הַיָּם ילי וַיּוֹלֶךְ יְהֹוָהאהדונהי | אֶת־
הַיָּם ילי בְּרוּחַ מלוי אלהים דיודין קָדִים עַזָּה כָּל ילי הַלָּיְלָה מלה וַיָּשֶׂם אֶת־
הַיָּם ילי לֶחָרָבָה וַיִּבָּקְעוּ הַמָּיִם:

SUSTAINS THE TWO SIDES. IF SO, IT SHOULD HAVE BEEN WRITTEN 'HALF STRAIGHT,' LIKE THE RIGHT COLUMN, AND 'HALF IN REVERSE ORDER,' LIKE THE LEFT COLUMN. Rav Yitzchak said: This is Jacob, and it is all one, BECAUSE JACOB ALSO INDICATES THE CENTRAL COLUMN.

-- The Zohar, Beshalach 14:160-168

23 The Egyptians pursued them, and all Pharaoh's horses and chariots and horsemen followed them into the sea.

24 During the last watch of the night the Lord looked down from the pillar of fire and cloud and confused the Egyptian army.

25 He made the wheels of their chariots come off so that they had difficulty driving. And the Egyptians said, "Let's get away from the Israelites! The Lord is fighting for them against Egypt."

FOURTH READING - MOSES - NETZACH

26 Then the Lord said to Moses, "Stretch out your hand over the sea so that the waters may flow back over the Egyptians and their chariots and horsemen."

27 Moses stretched out his hand over the sea, and at daybreak the sea went back to its place. The Egyptians were fleeing toward it, and the Lord tossed them in the sea.

28 The water flowed back and covered the chariots and horsemen—the entire army of Pharaoh that had followed the Israelites into the sea. Not one of them survived.

29 But the Israelites went through the sea on dry ground, with a wall of water on their right and on their left.

30 That day the Lord saved Israel from the hands of the Egyptians, and Israel saw the Egyptians lying dead on the shore. 31 And when the Israelites saw the Great Hand of the Lord displayed against the Egyptians, the people feared the Lord and put their trust in him and in Moses his servant.

לְאִיתָנוֹ

Exodus 14:27—The water crashed down upon the pursuing Egyptians after the Israelites had passed through the Red Sea.

The Aramaic word used to express this idea of crashing back is *leitano*. This means "to return" or "go back to." These same Aramaic letters, if rearranged, spell the word *letna'av*, which means "condition." From the time of Creation, water was formed with this "provision"—that it could go against its nature; that it could "split." If this "specification" had not been present in water since the beginning

of time, the miracle of the Red Sea could not have occurred.

This teaches us that some things can be changed and others cannot. We cannot always bend the universe to our wishes because the Light may have a different plan for us; a plan that is beyond our grasp. For example, we may try to change some people to help them become more "spiritual." Although this is a positive act, we must balance our efforts with the awareness that we cannot see the whole picture. The water of the Red Sea already had a built-in capacity to change its nature, but not everything or everyone has this inherent provision. We must accept the

22 וַיָּבֹאוּ בְנֵי־יִשְׂרָאֵל בְּתוֹךְ הַיָּם יּלי בַּיַּבָּשָׁה וְהַמַּיִם לָהֶם חוֹמָה מִימִינָם וּמִשְּׂמֹאלָם: 23 וַיִּרְדְּפוּ מִצְרַיִם מצר וַיָּבֹאוּ אַחֲרֵיהֶם כֹּל יּלי סוּס פַּרְעֹה רִכְבּוֹ וּפָרָשָׁיו אֶל־תּוֹךְ הַיָּם יּלי: 24 וַיְהִי אל, ייא"י בְּאַשְׁמֹרֶת הַבֹּקֶר וַיַּשְׁקֵף יְהוָֹהאדנילאהדונהי אֶל־מַחֲנֵה מִצְרַיִם מצר בְּעַמּוּד אֵשׁ וְעָנָן וַיָּהָם אֵת מַחֲנֵה מִצְרָיִם מצר: 25 וַיָּסַר אֵת אֹפַן מַרְכְּבֹתָיו וַיְנַהֲגֵהוּ בִּכְבֵדֻת וַיֹּאמֶר מִצְרַיִם מצר אָנוּסָה מִפְּנֵי יִשְׂרָאֵל כִּי יְהוָֹהאדנילאהדונהי נִלְחָם לָהֶם בְּמִצְרָיִם מצר:

FOURTH READING - MOSES - NETZACH

26 וַיֹּאמֶר יְהוָֹהאדנילאהדונהי אֶל־מֹשֶׁה נְטֵה אֶת־יָדְךָ עַל־הַיָּם יּלי וְיָשֻׁבוּ הַמַּיִם עַל־מִצְרַיִם מצר עַל־רִכְבּוֹ וְעַל־פָּרָשָׁיו: 27 וַיֵּט מֹשֶׁה אֶת־יָדוֹ עַל־הַיָּם יּלי וַיָּשָׁב הַיָּם יּלי לִפְנוֹת בֹּקֶר לְאֵיתָנוֹ וּמִצְרַיִם מצר נָסִים לִקְרָאתוֹ וַיְנַעֵר יְהוָֹהאדנילאהדונהי אֶת־מִצְרַיִם מצר בְּתוֹךְ הַיָּם יּלי: 28 וַיָּשֻׁבוּ הַמַּיִם וַיְכַסּוּ אֶת־הָרֶכֶב וְאֶת־הַפָּרָשִׁים לְכֹל וְחֵיל ומב פַּרְעֹה הַבָּאִים אַחֲרֵיהֶם בַּיָּם יּלי לֹא־נִשְׁאַר בָּהֶם עַד־אֶחָד

---

fact that sometimes we cannot (and sometimes should not) try to bring about change.

הַבָּאִים

Exodus 14:28—The Aramaic letter *Hei* at the top of the page. The letter *Vav* usually appears at the top of each column of the Torah scroll, but there are six locations where an exception has been made. This is one of them: Here the letter *Hei* in the word *habayim* is at the top of the column. The six locations represent the six levels of *Zeir Anpin*. The *Zohar* states that at the moment of Creation, six of the

Ten Sefirot of the Tree of Life compressed into one dimension known as *Zeir Anpin*.

"Haleluyah, praise God from the heavens" refers to the beginning from where the six directions, CHESED, GEVURAH, TIFERET, NETZACH, HOD AND YESOD, emanate downward, for this secret may be examined, OR COMPREHENDED, NAMELY, ZEIR ANPIN, according to the verse, "For ask now of the days that are past, which were before you...." (Deuteronomy 4:32) THEY ARE THE SEVEN DAYS: CHESED, GEVURAH, TIFERET, NETZACH, HOD, YESOD AND MALCHUT OF ZEIR ANPIN,

15:¹ Then Moses and the Israelites will sing this song to the Lord: "I will sing to the Lord, for He is highly exalted. The horse and its rider He has hurled into the sea.

² The Lord is my strength and my song; He has become my salvation. He is my God, and I will praise Him, my father's God, and I will exalt Him. ³ The Lord is a warrior; the Lord is His name. ⁴ Pharaoh's chariots and his army He has hurled into the sea. The best of Pharaoh's officers are drowned in the Red Sea.

⁵ The deep waters have covered them; they sank to the depths like a stone.⁶ Your Right Hand, Lord, was majestic in power. Your Right Hand, Lord, shattered the enemy. ⁷ In the greatness of Your Majesty You threw down those who opposed You. You unleashed Your burning anger; it consumed them like stubble.

⁸ By the blast of Your Nostrils the waters piled up. The surging waters stood firm like a wall; the deep waters congealed in the heart of the sea. ⁹ The enemy boasted, 'I will pursue, I will overtake them. I will divide the spoils; I will gorge myself on them. I will draw my sword and my hand will destroy them.'

¹⁰ But You blew with Your Breath, and the sea covered them. They sank like lead in the mighty waters. ¹¹ Who among the gods is like You, Lord? Who is like You— majestic in holiness, awesome in glory, working wonders?

---

up to which one may investigate, "From the day of Creation until the end of heaven" (Ibid.), CHESED OF ZEIR ANPIN. From here and further, WHICH ARE KETER, CHOCHMAH AND BINAH OF ZEIR ANPIN, one may not inquire there, because that place is hidden and concealed.
— The Zohar, Pekudei 23:218

This left four dimensions: our three-dimensional physical world plus the fourth dimension—the time-space continuum.

וַיּוֹשַׁע

Exodus 14:30—God saved the Israelites from the hand of the Egyptians and left the enemy dead on the shore.

This verse has the power to minimize our negativity and thus shorten and lighten our tikkun process by sweetening the judgment against us. When we are judged, the positive actions we have done in this world are weighed against the baggage we were born with, along with the negative actions we have done in our lives thus far.

The Holy One, blessed be He, performs miracles for Israel in this LOWER world, and marvels occur for them. When this world aroused to do miracles, all the Egyptians sank in the sea through the actions of this world, and a miracle occurred to Israel in this world. Therefore, it is written: "You shall not see them again any more for ever (lit. 'until the world')," MEANING until that world is aroused and they are given over to its Judgments. As soon as they were given over to it to be judged, it is written: "And Israel saw Egypt dead upon the sea shore." This is the meaning of the verse: "from the world and until the world"—until the world precisely, MEANING UNTIL THE WORLD OF BELOW IS AROUSED. Then it is written, "And believed in God and in Moses his servant."
— The Zohar, Beshalach 15:206

אהבה, דאגה: 29 וּבְנֵי יִשְׂרָאֵל הָלְכוּ בַיַּבָּשָׁה בְּתוֹךְ הַיָּם יל״ וְהַמַּיִם לָהֶם

וֹמָה מִימִינָם וּמִשְּׂמֹאלָם: 30 וַיּוֹשַׁע יְהֹוָֽאדנֹיאהדונֹהי בַּיּוֹם ע״ה = נגד, זך, מזבח

הַהוּא אֶת־יִשְׂרָאֵל מִיַּד מִצְרָיִם מצר וַיַּרְא אלף למד יהוה יִשְׂרָאֵל אֶת־

מִצְרַיִם מצר מֵת י״פ רבוע אהיה עַל־שְׂפַת הַיָּם: 31 וַיַּרְא יל״י אלף למד יהוה יִשְׂרָאֵל

אֶת־הַיָּד הַגְּדֹלָה ר״ת אהיה אֲשֶׁר עָשָׂה יְהֹוָֽאדנֹיאהדונֹהי בְּמִצְרַיִם מצר וַיִּֽירְאוּ

הָעָם אֶת־יְהֹוָֽאדנֹיאהדונֹהי וַיַּאֲמִינוּ בַּיהֹוָֽאדנֹיאהדונֹהי ר״ת אויב וּבְמֹשֶׁה משה, אל עדי עַבְדּוֹ:

15 1 אָז יָשִׁיר־מֹשֶׁה משה, אל עדי וּבְנֵי יִשְׂרָאֵל אֶת־הַשִּׁירָה הַזֹּאת

לַֽיהֹוָֽאדנֹיאהדונֹהי וַיֹּאמְרוּ לֵאמֹר אָשִׁירָה לַֽיהֹוָֽאדנֹיאהדונֹהי כִּי־גָאֹה גָּאָה

סוּס רבוע אדני, כוזו וְרֹכְבוֹ רָמָה בַיָּם: 2 עָזִּי יל״י אלהים ע״ה, מום ע״ה וְזִמְרָת יָהּ וַיְהִי

אל, יא״י ־לִי לִישׁוּעָה זֶה אֵלִי וְאַנְוֵהוּ אֱלֹהֵי דמב, ילה אָבִי וַאֲרֹמְמֶנְהוּ:

3 יְהֹוָֽאדנֹיאהדונֹהי אִישׁ ע״ה קנ״א קס״א מִלְחָמָה יְהֹוָֽאדנֹיאהדונֹהי שְׁמוֹ מהע ע״ה, אל עדי ע״ה:

4 מַרְכְּבֹת פַּרְעֹה וְחֵילוֹ ומב יָרָה בַיָּם יל״י וּמִבְחַר שָׁלִשָׁיו טֻבְּעוּ בְיַם־ יל״י

סוּף: 5 תְּהֹמֹת יְכַסְיֻמוּ יָרְדוּ בִמְצוֹלֹת כְּמוֹ־אָבֶן יוד הה ואו הה: 6 יְמִינְךָ

אָז

Exodus 15:1—Moses and all the Israelites sang the Song of the Sea to praise God. It is here that we are able to tap into the energy of the 72 Names of God in their completed form. The actual song begins using the future tense, although past or present tense might have been expected. Use of the future tense signifies that it is important for us in our day to use the 72 Names to deal with any difficulty we may encounter. The power behind the Song of the Sea is the 72 Names of God, and these Names give us the power to overcome any crisis.

Az Yashir (Ibid.) means "will sing." The formation of these letters in the Bible is similar to a genetic code. Our DNA is originally intact and without blemish, but because of the negative actions from our past and present lives, the DNA code becomes flawed. By using the Song of the Sea, which, in essence, is the code of the 72 Names, we have the power to heal any flaw or damage in our genetic makeup.

In one of Rav Brandwein's letters to Rav Berg, we read:

"...there is no connection between the reading on Noah and this. The situation in the days of the Flood is very different from the situation at the Splitting of the Red Sea and the Revelation at Mount Sinai, about which it was written that a handmaid saw upon the sea what the prophet Ezekiel had not beheld, and the children of Israel merited the hidden Light that will shine upon us at the end of all Corrections. Hence, it was written: "Then Moses sang." (Exodus 15:1) [In Aramaic], it does not say "sang," but literally "will sing." They were all as one, with one heart, and even the children recited the song because the holy Shechinah dwelt upon them, and was embraced within them, and sang from within their throats."

¹² You stretched out Your Right Hand and the earth swallowed them. ¹³ In Your unfailing love You will lead the people You have redeemed. In Your Strength You will guide them to Your Holy Dwelling.

¹⁴ The nations will hear and tremble; anguish will grip the people of Philistia. ¹⁵ The chiefs of Edom will be terrified, the leaders of Moab will be seized with trembling, the people of Canaan will melt away; ¹⁶ terror and dread will fall upon them. By the power of Your Arm they will be as still as a stone—until Your people pass by, Lord, until the people You acquired pass by. ¹⁷ You will bring them in and plant them on the mountain of Your inheritance—the place, Lord, You made for Your Dwelling, the Sanctuary, Lord, Your Hands established.

¹⁸ The Lord will reign for ever and ever." ¹⁹ When Pharaoh's horses, chariots and horsemen went into the sea, the Lord brought the waters of the sea back over them, but the Israelites walked through the sea on dry ground. ²⁰ Then Miriam the prophetess, Aaron's sister, took a tambourine in her hand, and all the women followed her, with tambourines and dancing. ²¹ Miriam sang to them: "Sing to the Lord, for He is highly exalted. The horse and its rider He has hurled into the sea." ²² Then Moses led Israel from the Red Sea and they went into the Desert of Shur. For three days they traveled in the desert without finding water.

And in the *Zohar*, we find the following:

Therefore, we learned Moses will sing the song in the future to come. What is the reason? Because it is written: "As in the days of your coming out of the land of Egypt, I will show him marvelous things." (Micah 7:15) HE ASKS: Should "I will show him" have been said "I will show you?" HE ANSWERS: Rather, I will show the very one who saw originally, NAMELY MOSES, for he will see a second time, and this is the meaning of "I will show him." It is written: "I will show him the salvation of Elohim," (Psalms 50:23) and, "show him My salvation." (Psalms 91:16) And "Then shall sing Moses and the children of Israel to God." It is the song of the Queen, WHICH IS MALCHUT, to the Holy One, blessed be He. We learned that every person who says this song daily and has the proper intention merits to say it in the time to come. It contains the world that has passed, and it contains the World to Come, and it contains the bonds of Faith, and it contains the days of King Messiah. And

all the other praises of those above and those below stir from it.
— The Zohar, Beshalach 16:219-220

שִׁירוּ

Exodus 15:21—The women sang. At the completion of the Song of the Sea, Miriam, the sister of Moses and Aaron, led the women in song. Kabbalah teaches that men represent *Zeir Anpin*, a point of Light that contains six of the upper dimensions (*Sefirot*) of the Tree of Life, while women represent the spiritual level of *Malchut*, the physical dimension in which we live (Earth) and that has no Light of its own. Here, the women sang because according to the sages, women are the channels to bring Divine energy down to *Malchut*, this physical world. The virtuous action they performed was not only for themselves, but for all humankind and for all generations. The *Talmud* says, "In the merit of righteous women of that generation were the Children of Israel redeemed from Egypt." (*Sotah 11b*) Likewise, we are reminded that all of our actions have an impact on literally everyone. Every positive, every negative act, word, or thought has an effect, which is greater than we can even imagine.

רבוע מ״ה יְהֹוָואדניאהדונהי נֶאְדָּרִי בַּכֹּחַ ר״ת ע״ב יְמִינְךָ רבוע מ״ה יְהֹוָואדניאהדונהי

תִּרְעַץ אוֹיֵב: 7 וּבְרֹב יפ אהיה גְּאוֹנְךָ תַּהֲרֹס קָמֶיךָ תְּשַׁלַּח חֲרֹנְךָ יֹאכְלֵמוֹ

כַּקַּשׁ: 8 וּבְרוּחַ מלוי אלהים דיודין אַפֶּיךָ נֶעֶרְמוּ מַיִם ר״ת אמן נִצְּבוּ כְמוֹ־נֵד

נֹזְלִים קָפְאוּ תְהֹמֹת בְּלֶב־יָם: 9 אָמַר אוֹיֵב אֶרְדֹּף אַשִּׂיג אֲחַלֵּק

שָׁלָל ב״פ עס״מ תִּמְלָאֵמוֹ נַפְשִׁי אָרִיק חַרְבִּי תּוֹרִישֵׁמוֹ יָדִי: 10 נָשַׁפְתָּ

בְרוּחֲךָ ר״ת ב״ן כִּסָּמוֹ יָם צָלְלוּ כַּעוֹפֶרֶת בְּמַיִם אַדִּירִים הרי 11 מִי

־כָמֹכָה בָּאֵלִם יְהֹוָואדניאהדונהי ר״ת ע״ב מִי כָּמֹכָה נֶאְדָּר בַּקֹּדֶשׁ ר״ת יב״ק

נוֹרָא ע״ה ג״פ אלהים תְהִלֹּת עֹשֵׂה פֶלֶא: 12 נָטִיתָ יְמִינְךָ רבוע מ״ה תִּבְלָעֵמוֹ

אָרֶץ אלהים דאלפין ר״ת נית, זו מות 13 נָחִיתָ בְחַסְדְּךָ ר״ת ב״ן עַם־זוּ גָּאָלְתָּ נֵהַלְתָּ

בְעָזְּךָ ר״ת ב״ן אֶל־נְוֵה קָדְשֶׁךָ ר״ת קנ״א 14 שָׁמְעוּ עַמִּים ע״ה קס״א יִרְגָּזוּן חִיל

אָחַז יֹשְׁבֵי פְּלָשֶׁת: 15 אָז נִבְהֲלוּ אַלּוּפֵי אֱדוֹם אֵילֵי מוֹאָב יוד הא ואו הה

יֹאחֲזֵמוֹ רָעַד נָמֹגוּ כֹּל יֹשְׁבֵי כְנָעַן: 16 תִּפֹּל עֲלֵיהֶם אֵימָתָה וָפַחַד

בִּגְדֹל זְרוֹעֲךָ יִדְּמוּ כָּאָבֶן יוד הה וא וה עַד־יַעֲבֹר עַמְּךָ ה הויות, גמם יְהֹוָואדניאהדונהי

עַד־יַעֲבֹר עַם־זוּ קָנִיתָ: 17 תְּבִאֵמוֹ וְתִטָּעֵמוֹ בְּהַר אור, רו נַחֲלָתְךָ ר״ת ב״ן

מָכוֹן לְשִׁבְתְּךָ פָּעַלְתָּ יְהֹוָואדניאהדונהי מִקְּדָשׁ אֲדֹנָי כֹּנְנוּ יָדֶיךָ: לבה

18 יְהֹוָואדניאהדונהי | יִמְלֹךְ לְעֹלָם ר״ת ייל וָעֶד: 19 כִּי בָא סוּס ריבוע אדני, כוך

פַּרְעֹה בְּרִכְבּוֹ וּבְפָרָשָׁיו בַּיָּם וַיָּשֶׁב יְהֹוָואדניאהדונהי עֲלֵהֶם אֶת־מֵי

הַיָּם וּבְנֵי יִשְׂרָאֵל הָלְכוּ בַיַּבָּשָׁה בְּתוֹךְ הַיָּם: 20 וַתִּקַּח רבוע אהיה דאלפין

מִרְיָם הַנְּבִיאָה אֲחוֹת אַהֲרֹן ע״ב ורבוע ע״ב אֶת־הַתֹּף בְּיָדָהּ וַתֵּצֶאןָ כָל

הַנָּשִׁים אַחֲרֶיהָ בְּתֻפִּים וּבִמְחֹלֹת: 21 וַתַּעַן לָהֶם מִרְיָם ⟦שָׁירוּ⟧

לַיהֹוָואדניאהדונהי כִּי־גָאֹה גָּאָה ריבוע אדני, כוך סוּס וְרֹכְבוֹ רָמָה בַיָּם:

22 וַיַּסַּע מֹשֶׁה מהע, אל שדי אֶת־יִשְׂרָאֵל מִיַּם־סוּף וַיֵּצְאוּ אֶל־מִדְבַּר־

שׁוּר אבגיתצ, ושר, אהבת חנם וַיֵּלְכוּ שְׁלֹשֶׁת־יָמִים נלך בַּמִּדְבָּר רמ״ווז, אברהם, וו״פ אל

²³ When they came to Marah, they could not drink its water because it was bitter. That is why its name is Marah. ²⁴ So the people complained against Moses, saying, "What are we to drink?" ²⁵ Then Moses cried out to the Lord, and the Lord showed him a piece of wood. He threw it into the water, and the water became sweet. There the Lord made a decree and a law for them, and there he tested them. ²⁶ He said, "If you listen carefully to the voice of the Lord, your God, and do what is right in His Eyes, if you pay attention to His commands and keep all His decrees, I will not bring on you any of the diseases I brought on the Egyptians, for I am the Lord, who heals you."

FIFTH READING - AARON - HOD

²⁷ Then they came to Elim, where there were twelve springs and seventy palm trees, and they camped there near the water.

16:¹ The whole Israelite community set out from Elim and came to the Desert of Zin, which is between Elim and Sinai, on the fifteenth day of the second month after they had come out of Egypt. ² In the desert the whole community complained against Moses and Aaron.

וְלֹא־מָצְאוּ מַיִם

Exodus 15:22—**The Israelites could not find water.** At that time, the Israelites had spent three days in the desert without water. The *Zohar* says that water symbolizes both the Torah (Bible) and Kabbalah. The Torah is necessary for life, and the Kabbalah signifies study and understanding. The lesson here is that spiritual study is just as necessary for survival as water is. More specifically, we learn that it is important for us to have some connection to spiritual growth or learning at least every three days.

"And they marched three days in the wilderness, and found no water." (Exodus 15:22) Water means nothing if not the Torah, as is written, "Ho, everyone that thirsts, come to the water." (Isaiah 55:1) Rav Yisa said: And who gave them Torah here? For until now the Torah was not yet given to them. Rav Elazar said: They went out into the wilderness to gaze and perceive, but the Holy One, blessed be He, removed His precious splendor from there. They went in order to conceive

Him, but did not find Him. We have learned that the Holy One, blessed be He, is called 'Torah.' Therefore, water is Torah, and Torah is the Holy One, blessed be He. Rav Shimon said: While they were still traveling in the wilderness, a different government appeared to them, namely, that one which dominates the wilderness, and it met them there. Then Israel saw that it was not the precious splendor of their King. This is what is meant by, "And when they came to Marah, they could not drink the waters of Marah." (Exodus 15:28) Why? "For they were bitter." Their souls were not gratified, as before. And even more, he had come to accuse them.

— The Zohar, Beshalach 27:345-347

עָלֶיךָ כִּי אֲנִי יְהוָ״ה

Exodus 15:26—**The four Aramaic letter** *Yuds* **of Healing.** This verse activates the power of healing. The original name, *Yud, Hei, Vav,* and *Hei,* adds up to 26. However, there are

וְלֹא־מָצְאוּ מַיִם 23 וַיָּבֹאוּ מָרָתָה ב״פ ע״ר וְלֹא יָכְלוּ לִשְׁתֹּת מַיִם

מִמָּרָה כִּי מָרִים הֵם עַל־כֵּן קָרָא־שְׁמָהּ מָרָה: 24 וַיִּלֹּנוּ הָעָם עַל־

מֹשֶׁה מהע, אל עדי לֵאמֹר מ״ה מַה־נִּשְׁתֶּה: 25 וַיִּצְעַק אֶל־יְהֹוָהּ אהיהאהדונהי

וַיּוֹרֵהוּ יְהֹוָהּ אהדי—אהדונהי עֵץ ע״ה קס״א וַיַּשְׁלֵךְ אֶל־הַמַּיִם וַיִּמְתְּקוּ הַמָּיִם שָׁם

שָׁם יהוה עדי לוֹ וָזָק וּמִשְׁפָּט ע״ה ה״פ אלהים וְשָׁם יהוה עדי נִסָּהוּ: 26 וַיֹּאמֶר

אִם יוהך, ע״ה מ״ב שָׁמוֹעַ תִּשְׁמַע לְקוֹל ע״ב ס״ג ע״ה | יְהֹוָהּ אהדני—אהדונהי אֱלֹהֶיךָ ילה

וְהַיָּשָׁר בְּעֵינָיו רִיבוע מ״ה תַּעֲשֶׂה וְהַאֲזַנְתָּ לְמִצְוֺתָיו וְשָׁמַרְתָּ כָּל־ ילי חֻקָּיו

כָּל־ ילי הַמַּחֲלָה אֲשֶׁר־שַׂמְתִּי בְמִצְרַיִם מצר לֹא־אָשִׂים

עָלֶיךָ רביע מ״ה יי כִּי אֲנִי אני, טדהד כוז״ו יְהֹוָהּ אהדני—אהדונהי רֹפְאֶךָ ד יודין (שבעים ע״ב)

רת איר:

FIFTH READING - AARON - HOD

27 וַיָּבֹאוּ אֵילִמָה וְשָׁם יהוה עדי שְׁתֵּים עֶשְׂרֵה עֵינֹת מַיִם וְשִׁבְעִים תְּמָרִים

וַיַּחֲנוּ־שָׁם יהוה עדי עַל־הַמָּיִם: 16 1 וַיִּסְעוּ מֵאֵילִם וַיָּבֹאוּ כָּל־ ילי עֲדַת

בְּנֵי־יִשְׂרָאֵל אֶל־מִדְבַּר־סִין נמם, ה״פ יהוה אֲשֶׁר בֵּין־אֵילִם וּבֵין סִינָי

בַּחֲמִשָּׁה עָשָׂר יוֹם ע״ה = נגד, זן, מזבח לַחֹדֶשׁ יב הויות הַשֵּׁנִי לְצֵאתָם מֵאֶרֶץ

---

other combinations of the Tetragrammaton that are further divided into the four worlds of *Asiyah* (*Malchut*), *Yetzirah* (*Zeir Anpin*), *Briyah* (*Binah*), and *Atzilut* (*Chochmah*). Each world has its own numerical value as to the way the Tetragrammaton is spelled out. The one in question concerns the world of *Atzilut* (*Chochmah*), where the Tetragrammaton is spelled out as follows:

Yud	י	ד	ו	י	20
Hei	ה			י	ה	15
Vav	ו	ו	י	ו	22
Hei	ה			י	ה	15
				TOTAL	72

Yud spelled out as *Yud, Vav, Dalet*
Hei spelled out as *Hei, Yud*
Vav spelled out as *Vav, Yud, Vav*
Hei spelled out as *Hei, Yud*

³ The Israelites said to them, "If only we had died by the Lord's hand in Egypt! There we sat around pots of meat and ate all the bread we wanted, but you have brought us out into this desert to starve this entire assembly to death."

⁴ Then the Lord said to Moses, "I will rain down bread from heaven for you. The people are to go out each day and gather enough for that day. In this way I will test them and see whether they will follow my instructions or not.

⁵ On the sixth day they are to prepare what they bring in, and that is to be twice as much as they gather daily."

⁶ So Moses and Aaron said to all the Israelites, "In the evening you will know that it was the Lord who brought you out of Egypt, ⁷ and in the morning you will see the glory of the Lord, because He has heard your complaining against Him. Who are we, that you should complain about us?"

⁸ Moses also said, "You will know that it was the Lord when he gives you meat to eat in the evening and all the bread you want in the morning, because He has heard your complaining against Him. Who are we? You are not complaining against us, but against the Lord."

When you add the numerical values of these letters together, the sum is 72. This numerical value of the Tetragrammaton (72), is the power of Chesed or Mercy, and it ignites the healing energy of the letter Yud in the Tetragrammaton. There is a lesson in this: When we behave with mercy towards other people, we ignite the power of healing in ourselves. But if we do not show mercy, we become vulnerable to disease. This applies equally to physical disease and spiritual disease.

וַיִּלּוֹנוּ

Exodus 16:2—The Israelites complained to Moses that they had nothing to eat. This section awakens our consciousness to our own complaining. When we complain, we instantly forfeit whatever Light we would have gained from the process we are going through. When we complain about not having something, not only do we lose the energy of our present experience, but we cannot hope to gain what we lack, either.

לֶחֶם

Exodus 16:4—Manna from Heaven Manna has the ability to become whatever food the eater

desires. Whatever the needs of an individual happen to be, both spiritual and physical, manna was designed to fulfill them. Manna is custom designed, in a sense, to fortify each person in the specific way that he or she requires.

The more spiritual a person was, the closer to his tent the manna would fall. Less spiritual people had to walk farther. And if individuals were very negative, the manna would fall a very long distance from their tents. The most magnificent thing about the manna is this intelligence, this Divine Spark. Spiritually speaking, our food today is dead. By injecting Light into our food through our spiritual meditations, we make it possible for food to elevate us spiritually. The *Zohar* says:

> . . .all the food of the inhabitants of the world comes from Above. That food that comes from the Heaven and the Earth is the food of the whole world. It is the food of all, and it is coarse, thick nourishment. The food that comes from a higher source and is a finer food comes from the place where judgment is prevalent, namely Malchut, and this is the food that the Children of Israel ate when they left Egypt, namely, unleavened bread. The

אלהים דאלפין מִצְרַיִם מצר: 2 וַיִלּוֹנוּ (כתיב: וילינו) כָּל ־יְלִ ־עֲדַת בְּנֵי־יִשְׂרָאֵל

עַל־מֹשֶׁה מהש, אל שדי וְעַל־אַהֲרֹן ע"ב ורבוע ע"ב בַּמִּדְבָּר רמ"ח, אברהם, וז"פ אל:

3 וַיֹּאמְרוּ אֲלֵהֶם בְּנֵי יִשְׂרָאֵל מִי ־יְלִ ־יִתֵּן מוּתֵנוּ בְיַד־יְהוָֹאדְנִיאהדונהי בְּאֶרֶץ

מִצְרַיִם אלהים דאלפין מצר־ בְּשִׁבְתֵּנוּ עַל־סִיר הַבָּשָׂר בְּאָכְלֵנוּ לֶחֶם ג"פ יהוה

לָשֹׂבַע ע"ב ואלהים דיודין כִּי ־הוֹצֵאתֶם אֹתָנוּ אֶל־הַמִּדְבָּר הַזֶּה והו לְהָמִית אֶת־

כָּל ־יְלִ ־הַקָּהָל הַזֶּה ע"ב סג בָּרָעָב והו ע"ב ורבוע אלהים: 4 וַיֹּאמֶר יְהוָֹאדְנִיאהדונהי אֶל־

מֹשֶׁה מהש, אל שדי הִנְנִי מַמְטִיר לָכֶם לֶחֶם ג"פ יהוה מִן־הַשָּׁמַיִם י"פ טל, י"פ כוזו וַיָּצָא

הָעָם וְלָקְטוּ דְּבַר ראה ־יוֹם עה = נגד, זן, מזבח בְּיוֹמוֹ לְמַעַן אֲנַסֶּנּוּ הֲיֵלֵךְ רית לאה

בְּתוֹרָתִי אִם יותר, עה ־לֹא: 5 וְהָיָה יהוה מ"ב בַּיּוֹם יהוה עה = נגד, זן, מזבח הַשִּׁשִּׁי וְהֵכִינוּ

אֶת אֲשֶׁר־יָבִיאוּ וְהָיָה יהוה עַל אֲשֶׁר־יִלְקְטוּ יוֹם עה = נגד, זן, מזבח מִשְׁנֶה | יוֹם

עה = נגד, זן, מזבח: 6 וַיֹּאמֶר מֹשֶׁה מהש, אל שדי וְאַהֲרֹן ע"ב ורבוע ע"ב אֶל־כָּל יה אדני ־בְּנֵי

יִשְׂרָאֵל עֶרֶב רבוע יהוה ורבוע אלהים וִידַעְתֶּם כִּי יְהוָֹאדְנִיאהדונהי הוֹצִיא אֶתְכֶם

מֵאֶרֶץ אלהים דאלפין מִצְרַיִם מצר: 7 וּבֹקֶר וּרְאִיתֶם אֶת־כְּבוֹד לב יְהוָֹאדְנִיאהדונהי

בְּשָׁמְעוֹ אֶת־תְּלֻנֹּתֵיכֶם עַל ־יְהוָֹאדְנִיאהדונהי וְנַחְנוּ מָה מה כִּי תַלִּינוּ (כתיב:

תלונו) עָלֵינוּ רבוע סג: 8 וַיֹּאמֶר מֹשֶׁה מהש, אל שדי בְּתֵת יְהוָֹאדְנִיאהדונהי לָכֶם

בָּעֶרֶב רבוע יהוה ורבוע אלהים בָּשָׂר לֶאֱכֹל וְלֶחֶם ג"פ יהוה בַּבֹּקֶר לִשְׂבֹּעַ ע"ב ואלהים דיודין

בִּשְׁמֹעַ יְהוָֹאדְנִיאהדונהי אֶת־תְּלֻנֹּתֵיכֶם אֲשֶׁר־אַתֶּם מַלִּינִם עָלָיו וְנַחְנוּ מָה

מה לֹא־עָלֵינוּ תְלֻנֹּתֵיכֶם כִּי עַל ־יְהוָֹאדְנִיאהדונהי: 9 וַיֹּאמֶר מֹשֶׁה ריבוע סג

מִשְׁנֶה

food that was provided to the Children of Israel during their time in the wilderness was from a higher place, called 'heavens', which is Zeir Anpin. It is an [even] finer food, and it enters into the soul more than any other food. It is more separate from the body and is called 'the food of the angels,' namely MANNA.

— The Zohar, Beshalach 29:376

Exodus 16:5—On Friday, the Israelites received a double portion of manna for Shabbat. To tap into the Light that comes on Shabbat, we too, can make some spiritual and physical preparation in the days before. This can take the form of meditating, either on a positive action we could be doing or on transforming a behavior we want to change. By meditating, we prepare our Vessel to truly connect with and receive the Light that is available in such abundance on Shabbat.

⁹ Then Moses told Aaron, "Say to the entire Israelite community, 'Come before the Lord, for He has heard your complaining.' "

¹⁰ While Aaron was speaking to the whole Israelite community, they looked toward the desert, and there was the glory of the Lord appearing in the cloud.

SIXTH READING - JOSEPH - YESOD

¹¹ The Lord said to Moses, ¹² "I have heard the complaining of the Israelites. Tell them, 'At twilight you will eat meat, and in the morning you will be filled with bread. Then you will know that I am the Lord your God.' "

¹³ That evening quail came and covered the camp, and in the morning there was a layer of dew around the camp.

¹⁴ When the dew was gone, thin flakes, thin like frost, on the ground appeared on the desert floor. ¹⁵ When the Israelites saw it, they said to each other, "What is it?" For they did not know what it was. Moses said to them, "It is the bread the Lord has given you to eat.

¹⁶ This is what the Lord has commanded: 'Each one is to gather as much as he needs. Take an omer for each person you have in your tent.' " ¹⁷ The Israelites did as they were told; some gathered much, some little.

¹⁸ And when they measured it by the omer, he who gathered much did not have too much, and he who gathered little did not have too little. Each one gathered as much as he needed.

¹⁹ Then Moses said to them, "No one is to keep any of it until morning." ²⁰ However, some of them didn't listen to Moses; they kept part of it until morning, but it was full of worms and began to smell. So Moses was angry with them.

Exodus 16:13—In addition to manna, the Israelites were given quail each evening.

This was due to the animalistic desire that is an inherent part of each one of us. It is that very

nature that motivates us to act without thinking and to do those things that later makes us say, "I don't know what came over me." We hear about people who suddenly lose all control or act completely unlike themselves. The purpose of the quail was to combat that animalistic nature, and by reading this section, we are aided in mastering that side of ourselves.

אֶל־אַהֲרֹן מהע, אל שדי עֵ"ב ורבוע עֵ"ב אֱמֹר אֶל־כָּל־ ילי עֲדַת בְּנֵי יִשְׂרָאֵל קִרְבוּ

לִפְנֵי וחכמה בינה יְהוֹוֵאדִנְיאהדונהי כִּי שָׁמַע אֵת תְּלֻנֹּתֵיכֶם: 10 וַיְהִי אל, ייא כְּדַבֵּר

רֵאה אַהֲרֹן עֵ"ב ורבוע עֵ"ב אֶל־כָּל־ ילי עֲדַת בְּנֵי־יִשְׂרָאֵל וַיִּפְנוּ אֶל־הַמִּדְבָּר וְהִנֵּה

מה יה כְּבוֹד ל"ב יְהוֹוֵאדִנְיאהדונהי נִרְאָה עֵ"ב ורבוע עֵ"ב ק, יאו בֶּעָנָן:

SIXTH READING - JOSEPH - YESOD

11 וַיְדַבֵּר רֵאה יְהוֹוֵאדִנְיאהדונהי אֶל־מֹשֶׁה מהע, אל שדי לֵאמֹר: 12 שָׁמַעְתִּי אֶת־

תְּלוּנֹּת בְּנֵי יִשְׂרָאֵל דַּבֵּר רֵאה אֲלֵהֶם לֵאמֹר בֵּין הָעַרְבַּיִם תֹּאכְלוּ

בָשָׂר וּבַבֹּקֶר תִּשְׂבְּעוּ־לָחֶם ג"פ יהוה וִידַעְתֶּם כִּי אֲנִי אני, טדהד כווו

יְהוֹוֵאדִנְיאהדונהי אֱלֹהֵיכֶם ילה: 13 וַיְהִי אל, ייא בָעֶרֶב רבוע יהוה ורבוע אלהים וַתַּעַל

הַשְּׂלָו וַתְּכַס אֶת־הַמַּחֲנֶה וּבַבֹּקֶר הָיְתָה שִׁכְבַת הַטַּל כווו סָבִיב

לַמַּחֲנֶה: 14 וַתַּעַל שִׁכְבַת הַטָּל כווו וְהִנֵּה מה יה עַל־פְּנֵי וחכמה בינה הַמִּדְבָּר

דַּק מְחֻסְפָּס דַּק כַּכְּפֹר עַל־הָאָרֶץ אלהים דההין עֵ"ה: 15 וַיִּרְאוּ בְנֵי־יִשְׂרָאֵל

וַיֹּאמְרוּ אִישׁ עֵ"ה קנ"א קס"א אֶל־אָחִיו מָן הוּא כִּי לֹא יָדְעוּ מַה מה הוּא

וַיֹּאמֶר מֹשֶׁה מהע, אל שדי אֲלֵהֶם הוּא הַלֶּחֶם ג"פ יהוה אֲשֶׁר נָתַן יְהוֹוֵאדִנְיאהדונהי

לָכֶם לְאָכְלָה: 16 זֶה הַדָּבָר רֵאה אֲשֶׁר צִוָּה פוי יְהוֹוֵאדִנְיאהדונהי לִקְטוּ מִמֶּנּוּ

אִישׁ עֵ"ה קנ"א קס"א לְפִי אָכְלוֹ עֹמֶר ייט (עולמות) לַגֻּלְגֹּלֶת מִסְפַּר נַפְשֹׁתֵיכֶם

אִישׁ עֵ"ה קנ"א קס"א לַאֲשֶׁר בְּאָהֳלוֹ תִּקָּחוּ: 17 וַיַּעֲשׂוּ־כֵן בְּנֵי יִשְׂרָאֵל וַיִּלְקְטוּ

הַמַּרְבֶּה וְהַמַּמְעִיט: 18 וַיָּמֹדּוּ בָעֹמֶר ייט (עולמות) וְלֹא הֶעְדִּיף הַמַּרְבֶּה

וְהַמַּמְעִיט לֹא הֶחְסִיר אִישׁ עֵ"ה קנ"א קס"א לְפִי־אָכְלוֹ לָקָטוּ: 19 וַיֹּאמֶר

מֹשֶׁה מהע, אל שדי אֲלֵהֶם אִישׁ עֵ"ה קנ"א קס"א אַל־יוֹתֵר מִמֶּנּוּ עַד־בֹּקֶר:

20 וְלֹא־שָׁמְעוּ אֶל־מֹשֶׁה מהע, אל שדי וַיּוֹתִרוּ אֲנָשִׁים מִמֶּנּוּ עַד־בֹּקֶר

וַיָּרֻם תּוֹלָעִים וַיִּבְאַשׁ וַיִּקְצֹף עֲלֵהֶם מֹשֶׁה מהע, אל שדי: 21 וַיִּלְקְטוּ אֹתוֹ

21 Each morning everyone gathered as much as he needed, and when the sun grew hot, it melted. 22 On the sixth day, they gathered twice as much—two omers for each person—and the leaders of the community came and reported this to Moses.

23 He said to them, "This is what the Lord said: 'Tomorrow is to be a day of rest, a holy Sabbath to the Lord. So bake what you want to bake and cook what you want to cook. Save whatever is left and keep it until morning.' "

24 So they saved it until morning, as Moses commanded, and it did not spoil or stink. 25 "Eat it today," Moses said, "because today is a Sabbath to the Lord. You will not find any of it in the field today. 26 Six days you are to gather it, but on the seventh day, the Sabbath, there will not be any." 27 Nevertheless, some of the people went out on the seventh day to gather it, but they found none.

28 Then the Lord said to Moses, "How long will you refuse to keep My commands and My instructions? 29 See how the Lord has given you the Sabbath; that is why on the sixth day He gives you bread for two days. Everyone is to stay where he is; no one is to go out on the seventh day."

30 So the people rested on the seventh day. 31 The people of Israel called the bread manna. It was white like coriander seed and tasted like wafers in honey.

32 Moses said, "This is what the Lord has commanded: 'Take an omer of manna and keep it for the generations to come, so they can see the bread I gave you to eat in the desert when I brought you out of Egypt.' "

33 So Moses said to Aaron, "Take a jar and put a full omer of manna in it. Then place it before the Lord to be kept for the generations to come."

שַׁבָּת־קֹדֶשׁ

Exodus 16:23—Moses gave the Israelites a glimpse of the meaning of Shabbat. The seventh day of the week is the day of *Malchut*. Because *Malchut* represents the Vessel, it has the potential to be a place of "the self." But the Light that comes on Shabbat is meant to fill the Vessel. This is why the seventh day was chosen to be the time where our souls connect to the Light directly. If Shabbat energy did not enter on the seventh day, we would think only of our physical needs, and our spiritual needs would not be fulfilled.

It is written: "Let no man go out of his place on the seventh day...." We learned that *ITS MEANING IS* from the place that is proper to go, *MEANING OUT OF THE CITY. And the secret of the matter is, "Blessed be the glory of God from His place," (Ezekiel 3:12) WHICH IS MALCHUT, and this is 'the place.' This is the secret of what is written: "For the place on which you stand is Holy ground." (Exodus 3:5) It is the known area that is called "place," which is known by the supernal glory, NAMELY MALCHUT. "Let no man go out of his place." This is the precious place of Holiness, because outside of it, there are other Elohim. "Blessed be the glory of God," is the glory of Above, NAMELY MALCHUT FROM THE CHEST AND ABOVE. "From*

בַּבֹּקֶר בַּבֹּקֶר אִישׁ ע״ה קנ״א קס״א כְּפִי אָכְלוֹ וְחַם הַשֶּׁמֶשׁ ב״פ ש״ך וְנָמָס:

22 וַיְהִי אל, ייא״י | בַּיּוֹם ע״ה = נגד, זן, מזבח הַשִּׁשִּׁי לָקְטוּ לֶחֶם ג״פ יהוה מִשְׁנֶה

שדי יה אדני הָעֹמֶר י״ע (עולמות) לָאֶחָד אהבה, דאגה אהבה וַיָּבֹאוּ יל כָּל ־נְשִׂיאֵי

הָעֵדָה וַיַּגִּידוּ לְמֹשֶׁה מהע, אל שדי: 23 וַיֹּאמֶר אֲלֵהֶם הוּא אֲשֶׁר דִּבֶּר ראה

יְהֹוָה אדני יאהדונהי שַׁבָּתוֹן שַׁבַּת־קֹדֶשׁ לַיהֹוָה אדני יאהדונהי מָחָר רמ״ז אֶת אֲשֶׁר־

תֹּאפוּ אֵפוּ וְאֵת אֲשֶׁר־תְּבַשְּׁלוּ בַּשֵּׁלוּ וְאֵת כָּל־ יל ־הָעֹדֵף הַנִּיחוּ לָכֶם

לְמִשְׁמֶרֶת עַד־הַבֹּקֶר: 24 וַיַּנִּיחוּ אֹתוֹ עַד־הַבֹּקֶר כַּאֲשֶׁר צִוָּה פֵי מֹשֶׁה

מהע, אל שדי וְלֹא הִבְאִישׁ וְרִמָּה לֹא־הָיְתָה בּוֹ: 25 וַיֹּאמֶר מֹשֶׁה מהע, אל שדי

אִכְלֻהוּ הַיּוֹם ע״ה = נגד, זן, מזבח כִּי־שַׁבָּת הַיּוֹם ע״ה = נגד, זן, מזבח לַיהֹוָה אדני יאהדונהי

הַיּוֹם ע״ה = נגד, זן, מזבח לֹא תִמְצָאֻהוּ בַּשָּׂדֶה: 26 שֵׁשֶׁת יָמִים נלך תִּלְקְטֻהוּ

וּבַיּוֹם ע״ה = נגד, זן, מזבח הַשְּׁבִיעִי שַׁבָּת לֹא יִהְיֶה יי ־בּוֹ: 27 וַיְהִי אל, ייא״י בַּיּוֹם

ע״ה = נגד, זן, מזבח הַשְּׁבִיעִי יָצְאוּ מִן־הָעָם לִלְקֹט וְלֹא מָצָאוּ: 28 וַיֹּאמֶר

יְהֹוָה אדני יאהדונהי אֶל־מֹשֶׁה מהע, אל שדי עַד־אָנָה מֵאַנְתֶּם לִשְׁמֹר מִצְוֺתַי

וְתוֹרֹתָי: 29 רְאוּ כִּי־יְהֹוָה אדני יאהדונהי נָתַן לָכֶם הַשַּׁבָּת עַל־כֵּן הוּא נֹתֵן

אבגיתצ, ועד, אהבת חנם לָכֶם בַּיּוֹם ע״ה = נגד, זן, מזבח הַשִּׁשִּׁי לֶחֶם ג״פ יהוה יוֹמָיִם שְׁבוּ |

אִישׁ ע״ה קנ״א קס״א תַּחְתָּיו אַל־יֵצֵא אִישׁ ע״ה קנ״א קס״א מִמְּקֹמוֹ בַּיּוֹם ע״ה = נגד, זן, מזבח

הַשְּׁבִיעִי: 30 וַיִּשְׁבְּתוּ הָעָם בַּיּוֹם ע״ה = נגד, זן, מזבח הַשְּׁבִעִי: 31 וַיִּקְרְאוּ בֵית

ב״פ ראה ־יִשְׂרָאֵל אֶת־שְׁמוֹ מהע אל שדי ע״ה מָן וְהוּא כְּזֶרַע י״פ ז״ך גַּד לָבָן

וְטַעְמוֹ כְּצַפִּיחִת בִּדְבָשׁ: 32 וַיֹּאמֶר מֹשֶׁה מהע, אל שדי זֶה הַדָּבָר ראה

אֲשֶׁר צִוָּה פֵי יְהֹוָה אדני יאהדונהי מְלֹא הָעֹמֶר י״ע (עולמות) מִמֶּנּוּ לְמִשְׁמֶרֶת

לְדֹרֹתֵיכֶם לְמַעַן | יִרְאוּ אֶת־הַלֶּחֶם ג״פ יהוה אֲשֶׁר הֶאֱכַלְתִּי אֶתְכֶם

בַּמִּדְבָּר רמ״ח, אל אברהם, וד״פ אל בְּהוֹצִיאִי אֶתְכֶם מֵאֶרֶץ אלהים דאלפין מִצְרָיִם מצר:

33 וַיֹּאמֶר מֹשֶׁה מהע, אל שדי אֶל־אַהֲרֹן ע״ב ורבוע ע״ב קַח צִנְצֶנֶת אַחַת וְתֶן־

שָׁמָּה מהע, אל שדי מְלֹא־הָעֹמֶר שי״י (עולמות) מָן וְהַנַּח אֹתוֹ לִפְנֵי חכמה בינה

34 As the Lord commanded Moses, Aaron put the manna in front of the community, to be kept. 35 The Israelites ate manna forty years, until they came to a land that was settled; they ate manna until they reached the border of Canaan.

36 And the omer is one tenth of an ephah.

SEVENTH READING - DAVID - MALCHUT

17:1 The whole Israelite community set out from the Desert of Zin, traveling from place to place as the Lord commanded. They camped at Rephidim, but there was no water for the people to drink. 2 So they quarreled with Moses and said, "Give us water to drink." Moses replied, "Why do you quarrel with me? Why do you test the Lord?"

3 But the people were thirsty for water there, and they grumbled against Moses. They said, "Why did you bring us up out of Egypt to make us and our children and livestock die of thirst?" 4 Then Moses cried out to the Lord, "What am I to do with these people? They are about to stone me!"

5 The Lord answered Moses, "Walk on ahead of the people. Take with you some of the elders of Israel and take in your hand the staff with which you struck the Nile, and go.

6 I will stand there before you by the rock at Horeb. Strike the rock, and water will come out of it for the people to drink." So Moses did this in the sight of the elders of Israel.

---

his place," is the glory of Below, NAMELY MALCHUT FROM THE CHEST AND BELOW. This is the secret of the Crown of the Shabbat, WHICH IS CALLED 'PLACE.' Therefore, a person should not go out from his place, BECAUSE OUTSIDE OF IT ARE OTHER ELOHIM. Blessed is the portion of one who has merited the splendors of the Shabbat.
— The Zohar, Beshalach 29:417-419

Exodus 17:3—When they camped in Rephidim, the Israelites again complained about the lack of water. In response to their complaints, Moses struck his staff on the rock in Horeb, and water

gushed forth. Again, this event demonstrated the power of mind over matter.

"And your rod, with which you smote the river, take in your hand, and go." (Exodus 17:5) Why was this? Because it [the rod] was engraved with miracles, and the Supernal Holy Name was imprinted on it. At first, THE ROD WAS TURNED INTO a snake, WHICH IS THE SECRET OF YESOD OF ZEIR ANPIN OF SMALLNESS. As we have learned: "The way of a snake upon a rock." (Proverbs 30:19) The snake, it is known, arouses the rock, WHICH IS MALCHUT. In which area was THE HOLY ONE, BLESSED BE HE, revealed? Here He became revealed, as is written: "Behold, I will stand before you

יְהֹוֹאֲדֹנִיאהדונהי לְמִשְׁמֶרֶת לְדֹרֹתֵיכֶם: 34 כַּאֲשֶׁר צִוָּה פּי יְהֹוֹאֲדֹנִיאהדונהי

אֶל־מֹשֶׁה מהע, אל שדי וַיַּנִּיחֵהוּ אַהֲרֹן ע״ב ורבוע ע״ב לִפְנֵי וחכמה בינה הָעֵדֻת

לְמִשְׁמָרֶת: 35 וּבְנֵי יִשְׂרָאֵל אָכְלוּ אֶת־הַמָּן אַרְבָּעִים שָׁנָה עַד־בֹּאָם

אֶל־אֶרֶץ אלהים דאלפין נוֹשָׁבֶת אֶת־הַמָּן אָכְלוּ עַד־בֹּאָם אֶל־קְצֵה

אֶרֶץ ה״פ טל, ג״פ אדני אלהים דאלפין כְּנָעַן: 36 וְהָעֹמֶר שׁ״י (עולמות) עֲשִׂרִית הָאֵיפָה

הוּא:

SEVENTH READING - DAVID - MALCHUT

17 1 וַיִּסְעוּ כָּל יוי ־עֲדַת בְּנֵי־יִשְׂרָאֵל מִמִּדְבַּר־סִין לְמַסְעֵיהֶם עַל־פִּי

יְהֹוֹאֲדֹנִיאהדונהי וַיַּחֲנוּ בִּרְפִידִים וְאֵין מַיִם לִשְׁתֹּת הָעָם: 2 וַיָּרֶב הָעָם

עִם־מֹשֶׁה מהע, אל שדי וַיֹּאמְרוּ תְּנוּ־לָנוּ מום, אלהים, אהיה אדני מַיִם וְנִשְׁתֶּה

וַיֹּאמֶר לָהֶם מֹשֶׁה מהע, אל שדי מַה־מ״ה תְּרִיבוּן עִמָּדִי מַה־מ״ה תְּנַסּוּן

אֶת־יְהֹוֹאֲדֹנִיאהדונהי: 3 וַיִּצְמָא שָׁם הָעָם לַמַּיִם [וַיִּלֶן דצ״נ] הָעָם עַל־מֹשֶׁה

מהע, אל שדי וַיֹּאמֶר לָמָּה זֶּה הֶעֱלִיתָנוּ מִמִּצְרַיִם מצר לְהָמִית אֹתִי וְאֶת־

בָּנַי וְאֶת־מִקְנַי בַּצָּמָא: 4 וַיִּצְעַק מֹשֶׁה מהע, אל שדי אֶל־יְהֹוֹאֲדֹנִיאהדונהי

לֵאמֹר מָה מ״ה אֶעֱשֶׂה לָעָם הַזֶּה והו עוֹד מְעַט וּסְקָלֻנִי: 5 וַיֹּאמֶר

יְהֹוֹאֲדֹנִיאהדונהי אֶל־מֹשֶׁה מהע, אל שדי עֲבֹר רבוע יהוה ורבוע אלהים לִפְנֵי וחכמה בינה

הָעָם וְקַח אִתְּךָ מִזִּקְנֵי יִשְׂרָאֵל וּמַטְּךָ אֲשֶׁר הִכִּיתָ בּוֹ אֶת־הַיְאֹר

---

there upon the rock." (Exodus 17:6) And who is the rock? It is as written, "He is the rock, His work is perfect," (Deuteronomy 32:4) WHICH IS MALCHUT. Rav Yehuda said: If the Torah had remained silent and had not said more, it would be good. But rather, it is written, "And you shall smite the rock, and there shall come water out of it." (Exodus 17:6) IS THIS

THE CUSTOM OF THE HOLY NAME? He said to him: "Certainly, it is so. For there is no single Name of all the Holy Names of the Holy One, blessed be He, that does not perform miracles and mighty acts, and does not bring forth whatever is necessary for the world, especially to bring forth water here."
— The Zohar, Beshalach 31:424-425

7 And he called the place Massah uMeribah because the Israelites quarreled and because they tested the Lord saying, "Is the Lord among us or not?" 8 Amalek came and attacked the Israelites at Rephidim. 9 Moses said to Joshua, "Choose some of our men and go out to fight Amalek. Tomorrow I will stand on top of the hill with the staff of God in my hands."

10 So Joshua did what Moses told him, to fight the Amalek, and Moses, Aaron and Hur went to the top of the hill. 11 As long as Moses held up his hands, the Israelites triumphed, but whenever he lowered his hands, Amalek triumphed.

12 When Moses' hands became heavy, they took a stone and put it under him and he sat on it. Aaron and Hur held his hands up—one on one side, one on the other—so that his hands remained steady till sunset. 13 So Joshua overcame Amalek and its people by sword.

MAFTIR

14 Then the Lord said to Moses, "Write this on a scroll as something to be remembered and make sure that Joshua hears it, because I will completely blot out the memory of Amalek from under the heavens." 15 Moses built an altar and called it Adonai Nisi.

עֲמָלֵק

Exodus 17:8—The war with Amalek.

The numerical value of the Aramaic letters that spell *Amalek* is equal to the numerical value (240) of the Aramaic word *safek*, which means "doubt." Doubt can potentially permeate any area of our lives—in relationships, career, or sense of self-worth—creating immediate separation between us and the Light of the Creator. Doubt is Satan's greatest weapon against us, and it is for this reason that doubt and its opposite, certainty, are such important spiritual concepts.

> *"Write this (Heb. zot) for a memorial." Zot is precise, WHICH IS A NAME OF MALCHUT; "and rehearse it in the ears of Joshua," because he is destined to slay other kings, NAMELY 31 KINGS. "That I will utterly blot out (lit. 'I will blot a blotting')." "Blotting" refers to Above; "I will blot" refers to Below. "The*

memory," means the memory above and the memory below. Rav Yitzchak said: It is written, "I will utterly blot out" WHICH INDICATES THAT THE HOLY ONE, BLESSED BE HE, WILL BLOT OUT, and: "You shall blot out the remembrance of Amalek," (Deuteronomy 25:19) WHICH INDICATES THAT WE ARE OBLIGATED TO ERASE REMEMBRANCE OF AMALEK. HE ANSWERS: But the Holy One, blessed be He, said: "You will blot out the memory OF AMALEK of Below, and I shall blot out the memory OF AMALEK of Above." Rav Yosi said: Other allied nations accompanied Amalek. They were all afraid to approach Israel, except it (Amalek). Therefore, Joshua ruled over them. Rav Yisa said: "And Joshua harried," for he broke their power from Above.
> *— The Zohar, Beshalach 33:470-472*

כֵּף וָיו זַיִן וָיו קֹ֖ו בְּיָדֶ֑ךָ בּוכ"ו וְהָלָ֑כְתָּ וְהִנְנִ֣י עֹמֵד֩ לְפָנֶ֨יךָ סמ"ב שָּׁ֥ם יהוה שדי | עַל־

הַצּוּר֙ אלהים ההין ע"ה בְחֹרֵב֒ אלהים קס"ו ורבוע אהיה וְהִכִּ֣יתָ בַצּ֗וּר אלהים ההין ע"ה וְיָֽצְא֤וּ

מִמֶּ֨נּוּ֙ מַ֔יִם וְשָׁתָ֣ה הָעָ֑ם וַיַּ֤עַשׂ כֵּן֙ מֹשֶׁ֔ה מהע, אל שדי לְעֵינֵ֖י ריבוע מ"ה זִקְנֵ֥י

יִשְׂרָאֵֽל׃ 7 וַיִּקְרָא֙ ב"פ קס"א - ה אותיות שֵׁ֣ם יהוה שדי הַמָּק֔וֹם יהוה ברבוע, ר"פ אל מַסָּ֖ה

וּמְרִיבָ֑ה עַל־רִ֣יב | בְּנֵ֣י יִשְׂרָאֵ֗ל וְעַ֨ל נַסֹּתָ֤ם אֶת־יְהֹוָה֙אלהיאהדונהי לֵאמֹ֔ר

הֲיֵ֧שׁ יי"פ אל יְהֹוָ֛ה֙אלהיאהדונהי בְּקִרְבֵּ֖נוּ אִם־אָֽיִן׃ יוהך, ע"ה מ"ב 8 וַיָּבֹ֖א עֲמָלֵ֑ק

ב"פ ק"ך וַיִּלָּ֥חֶם עִם־יִשְׂרָאֵ֖ל בִּרְפִידִֽם׃ 9 וַיֹּ֨אמֶר מֹשֶׁ֤ה מהע, אל שדי אֶל־

יְהוֹשֻׁ֨עַ בְּחַר־לָ֣נוּ אֲנָשִׁ֔ים וְצֵ֖א הִלָּחֵ֣ם בַּעֲמָלֵ֑ק ב"פ ק"ך מָחָ֗ר רמ"ח אָֽנֹכִי֙

אי"ע נִצָּ֤ב עַל־רֹ֨אשׁ ריבוע אלהים ואלהים דיודין ע"ה הַגִּבְעָ֔ה וּמַטֵּ֥ה הָאֱלֹהִ֖ים

מום, אהיה אדני ; ילה בְּיָדִֽי׃ 10 וַיַּ֣עַשׂ יְהוֹשֻׁ֗עַ כַּאֲשֶׁ֤ר אָֽמַר־לוֹ֙ מֹשֶׁ֔ה מהע, אל שדי

לְהִלָּחֵ֖ם בַּעֲמָלֵ֑ק ב"פ ק"ך וּמֹשֶׁ֤ה מהע, אל שדי וְאַהֲרֹ֣ן ע"ב ורבוע ע"ב חֻ֔ר וְחוּר֙ עָל֖וּ

רֹ֥אשׁ ריבוע אלהים ואלהים דיודין ע"ה הַגִּבְעָֽה׃ 11 וְהָיָ֗ה יהוה כַּאֲשֶׁ֨ר יָרִ֥ים מֹשֶׁ֛ה

מהע, אל שדי יָד֖וֹ וְגָבַ֣ר יִשְׂרָאֵ֑ל וְכַֽאֲשֶׁ֥ר יָנִ֛יחַ דכ"ע יָד֖וֹ וְגָבַ֥ר עֲמָלֵֽק׃ ב"פ ק"ך

12 וִידֵ֤י מֹשֶׁה֙ מהע, אל שדי כְּבֵדִ֔ים וַיִּקְחוּ־אֶ֛בֶן ולעם יוד הה ואו הה וַיָּשִׂ֥ימוּ

תַחְתָּ֖יו וַיֵּ֣שֶׁב עָלֶ֑יהָ פהל וְאַהֲרֹ֨ן ע"ב ורבוע ע"ב וְח֜וּר תָּֽמְכ֣וּ בְיָדָ֗יו מִזֶּ֤ה אֶחָד֙

אהבה, דאגה וּמִזֶּ֣ה אֶחָ֔ד אהבה, דאגה וַיְהִ֥י ויהי אהיה אל, יא"י יָדָ֛יו אֱמוּנָ֖ה עַד־בֹּ֥א הַשָּֽׁמֶשׁ

ב"פ ש"ך׃ 13 וַיַּחֲלֹ֧שׁ יְהוֹשֻׁ֛עַ אֶת־עֲמָלֵ֖ק ב"פ ק"ך וְאֶת־עַמּ֑וֹ לְפִי־חָֽרֶב׃

רבוע ס"ג ורבוע אהיה׃

MAFTIR

14 וַיֹּ֨אמֶר יְהֹוָ֜ה֙אלהיאהדונהי אֶל־מֹשֶׁ֗ה מהע, אל שדי כְּתֹ֨ב זֹ֤את זִכָּרוֹן֙ ע"ב קס"א נ"גע"ב

בַּסֵּ֔פֶר וְשִׂ֖ים בְּאָזְנֵ֣י יְהוֹשֻׁ֑עַ כִּֽי־מָחֹ֤ה אֶמְחֶה֙ אֶת־זֵ֣כֶר עֲמָלֵ֔ק ב"פ ק"ך

מִתַּ֖חַת הַשָּׁמָֽיִם׃ י"פ טל, י"פ כוזו 15 וַיִּ֥בֶן וֹ חיים, בינה ע"ה מֹשֶׁ֖ה מהע, אל שדי מִזְבֵּ֑חַ זן, נגד

[16] He said, "For hands were lifted up to the throne of the Lord. The Lord will be at war against Amalek from generation to generation."

HAFTARAH OF BESHALACH

In this Haftarah, Deborah, the judge of Israel, sings a song after a victory in battle. This can be likened to Miriam and the song that she and the women sang as they crossed the Red Sea. Rav Isaac Luria (the Ari), tells us that redemption takes place through women. The following excerpt of the Ari's writings reveals the immense responsibility and power that women have. With such a responsibility, it is critical that women study Kabbalah.

Judges 5:1-5:31

5:[1] On that day Deborah and Barak son of Abinoam sang this song: [2] "When the princes in Israel take the lead, when the people willingly offer themselves—praise the Lord!

[3] Hear this, you kings! Listen, you rulers! I will sing to the Lord, I will sing; I will make music to the Lord, the God of Israel.

[4] Lord, when you went out from Seir, when you marched from the land of Edom, the earth shook, the heavens poured, the clouds also poured down water.

[5] The mountains quaked before the Lord, the One of Sinai, before the Lord, the God of Israel.

מִדְּר דְּר

Exodus 17:16— Moses said that the battle with Amalek was eternal.

Moses taught us that our war with doubt is never-ending. We must never grow complacent and think that this struggle is over.

> Rav Yehuda said: In every single generation and in all the subsequent generations to come to the world, there

is no generation that does not contain that evil seed OF AMALEK. The Holy One, blessed be He, wages war against them. About them, it is written: "The sinners (sins) will be consumed out of the earth...." (Psalms 104:35)—"Out of the earth," MEANING in this world and in the World to Come. About that same time is written: "Bless you God, my soul. Halleluyah" (Ibid.).
— The Zohar, Beshalach 35:486

וַיִּקְרָא ב״פ קס״א - ה אותיות שֵׁמוֹ מהשע ע״ה, אל שדי ע״ה יְהֹוָאֲדֹנִיאֲהִדֹוֶנֹהִי | נָסִי: 16 וַיֹּאמֶר

כִּי־יָד עַל־כֵּס יָהּ מִלְחָמָה לַיהֹוָאֲדֹנִיאֲהִדֹוֶנֹהִי בַּעֲמָלֵק ב״פ ק״ך מִדֹּר דֹּר :

HAFTARAH OF BESHALACH

In Egypt, the woman was Batya, during the wanderings in the wilderness it was Miriam,
here it was Deborah, at Hanukkah it was Judith, and at Purim it was Esther—and the final
removal of chaos will also be through a woman.
 — Writings of the Ari

שׁוֹפְטִים פֶּרֶק ה

5 1 וַתָּשַׁר שקוצ״ת דְּבוֹרָה וּבָרָק בֶּן־אֲבִינֹעַם בַּיּוֹם ע״ה = נגד, זן, מזבח הַהוּא

לֵאמֹר: 2 בִּפְרֹעַ פְּרָעוֹת בְּיִשְׂרָאֵל בְּהִתְנַדֵּב עָם בָּרְכוּ יהוה ע״ב ורבוע מ״ה

יְהֹוָאֲדֹנִיאֲהִדֹוֶנֹהִי: 3 שִׁמְעוּ מְלָכִים הַאֲזִינוּ רֹזְנִים אָנֹכִי איע לַיהֹוָאֲדֹנִיאֲהִדֹוֶנֹהִי

אָנֹכִי איע אָשִׁירָה אָמַר לַיהֹוָאֲדֹנִיאֲהִדֹוֶנֹהִי אֱלֹהֵי דמב, ילה יִשְׂרָאֵל:

4 יְהֹוָאֲדֹנִיאֲהִדֹוֶנֹהִי בְּצֵאתְךָ מִשֵּׂעִיר בְּצַעְדְּךָ מִשְּׂדֵה אֱדוֹם אֶרֶץ אלהים דאלפין

רָעָשָׁה גַם שָׁמַיִם י״פ טל, י״פ כוזו נָטָפוּ גַם י״ב עָבִים נָטְפוּ מָיִם: 5 הָרִים

נָזְלוּ מִפְּנֵי חכמה בינה יְהֹוָאֲדֹנִיאֲהִדֹוֶנֹהִי זֶה סִינַי נמם, ה״פ יהוה מִפְּנֵי חכמה בינה

יְהֹוָאֲדֹנִיאֲהִדֹוֶנֹהִי אֱלֹהֵי דמב, ילה יִשְׂרָאֵל: 6 בִּימֵי שַׁמְגַּר בֶּן־עֲנָת בִּימֵי יָעֵל

חָדְלוּ אֳרָחוֹת וְהֹלְכֵי נְתִיבוֹת יֵלְכוּ כלי אֳרָחוֹת עֲקַלְקַלּוֹת: 7 וְחָדְלוּ

פְרָזוֹן בְּיִשְׂרָאֵל חָדֵלּוּ עַד שַׁקַּמְתִּי דְּבוֹרָה שַׁקַּמְתִּי אֵם יוהך, ע״ה מ״ב

בְּיִשְׂרָאֵל: 8 יִבְחַר אֱלֹהִים מום, אהיה אדני ; ילה חֲדָשִׁים אָז לָחֶם ג״פ יהוה

עָרִים כתר מָגֵן ר״ת מיכאל, גבריאל, נוריאל אִם יוהך, ע״ה מ״ב יֵרָאֶה רי״ו, גבורה וָרֹמַח

בְּאַרְבָּעִים אֶלֶף אלף למד - עין דלת יוד ע״ה בְּיִשְׂרָאֵל: 9 לִבִּי לְחוֹקְקֵי

⁶ *In the days of Shamgar son of Anath, in the days of Jael, the roads were abandoned; travelers took to winding paths.*

⁷ *Village life in Israel ceased, ceased until I, Deborah, arose, arose a mother in Israel.*

⁸ *When they chose new gods, war came to the city gates, and not a shield or spear was seen among forty thousand in Israel.*

⁹ *My heart is with Israel's princes, with the willing volunteers among the people. Praise the Lord!*

¹⁰ *You who ride on white donkeys, sitting on your saddle blankets, and you who walk along the road, consider*

¹¹ *the voice of the singers at the watering places. They recite the righteous acts of the Lord, the righteous acts of his warriors in Israel. Then the people of the Lord went down to the city gates.*

¹² *'Wake up, wake up, Deborah! Wake up, wake up, break out in song! Arise, Barak! Take captive your captives, son of Abinoam.'*

¹³ *Then the men who were left came down to the nobles; the people of the Lord came to me with the mighty.*

¹⁴ *Some came from Ephraim, whose roots were in Amalek; Benjamin was with the people who followed you. From Makir captains came down, from Zebulun those who bear a commander's staff.*

¹⁵ *The princes of Issachar were with Deborah; yes, Issachar was with Barak, rushing after him into the valley. In the districts of Reuben there was much searching of heart.*

¹⁶ *Why did you stay among the campfires to hear the whistling for the flocks? In the districts of Reuben there was much searching of heart.*

¹⁷ *Gilead stayed beyond the Jordan. And Dan, why did he linger by the ships? Asher remained on the coast and stayed in his coves.*

¹⁸ *The people of Zebulun risked their very lives; so did Naphtali on the heights of the field.*

¹⁹ *Kings came, they fought; the kings of Canaan fought at Taanach by the waters of Megiddo, but they carried off no silver, no plunder.*

יִשְׂרָאֵל הַמִּתְנַדְּבִים בָּעָם ר״ת באר ענן מן דָּן יהוה יהוה ע״ב ורבוע מ״ה בָּרְכוּ יְהֹוָהאדניאהדונהי:

10 רֹכְבֵי אֲתֹנוֹת צְחֹרוֹת יֹשְׁבֵי עַל־מִדִּין וְהֹלְכֵי עַל־דֶּרֶךְ ב״פ יב״ק שִׂיחוּ:

11 מִקּוֹל ע״ב ס״ג עה מְחַצְצִים בֵּין מַשְׁאַבִּים שָׁם יְתַנּוּ צִדְקוֹת יְהֹוָהאדניאהדונהי

צִדְקֹת פִּרְזוֹנוֹ בְּיִשְׂרָאֵל אָז יָרְדוּ לַשְּׁעָרִים כתר עַם־יְהֹוָהאדניאהדונהי:

12 עוּרִי עוּרִי דְּבוֹרָה עוּרִי עוּרִי דַּבְּרִי רֹאה ־שִׁיר קוּם בָּרָק וּשֲׁבֵה שֶׁבְיְךָ בֶּן־אֲבִינֹעַם:

13 אָז יְרַד שָׂרִיד לְאַדִּירִים הרי עָם יְהֹוָהאדניאהדונהי יְרַד־לִי בַּגִּבּוֹרִים:

14 מִנִּי אֶפְרַיִם אל מצפצ שָׁרְשָׁם בַּעֲמָלֵק ב״פ קך אַחֲרֶיךָ בִנְיָמִין בַּעֲמָמֶיךָ מִנִּי מָכִיר יָרְדוּ מְחֹקְקִים וּמִזְּבוּלֻן מֹשְׁכִים בְּשֵׁבֶט סֹפֵר:

15 וְשָׂרַי בְּיִשָּׂשכָר י״פ אל י״פ ב״ן עִם־דְּבֹרָה וְיִשָּׂשכָר י״פ אל י״פ ב״ן כֵּן בָּרָק בָּעֵמֶק שֻׁלַּח בְּרַגְלָיו בִּפְלַגּוֹת רְאוּבֵן ג״פ אלהים גְּדֹלִים חִקְקֵי־לֵב:

16 לָמָּה יָשַׁבְתָּ בֵּין הַמִּשְׁפְּתַיִם לִשְׁמֹעַ שְׁרִקוֹת עֲדָרִים לִפְלַגּוֹת רְאוּבֵן גְּדוֹלִים ג״פ אלהים חִקְרֵי־לֵב: ג״פ אל

17 גִּלְעָד בְּעֵבֶר רבוע יהוה ורבוע אלהים הַיַּרְדֵּן י״פ יהוה ור׳ אותיות שָׁכֵן ע״ע וְדָן לָמָּה יָגוּר אֳנִיּוֹת וְאָשֵׁר יָשַׁב לְחוֹף יַמִּים נצח

וְעַל מִפְרָצָיו יִשְׁכּוֹן: 18 זְבֻלוּן עַם חֵרֵף נַפְשׁוֹ לָמוּת וְנַפְתָּלִי עַל מְרוֹמֵי שָׂדֶה:

19 בָּאוּ מְלָכִים נִלְחָמוּ אָז נִלְחֲמוּ מַלְכֵי כְנַעַן בְּתַעְנַךְ עַל־מֵי י׳ מְגִדּוֹ בֶּצַע כֶּסֶף לֹא לָקָחוּ: 20 מִן־שָׁמַיִם י״פ טל, י״פ כוז נִלְחָמוּ הַכּוֹכָבִים מִמְּסִלּוֹתָם ר״ת הבטן נִלְחֲמוּ עִם־סִיסְרָא:

21 נַחַל קִישׁוֹן גְּרָפָם נַחַל קְדוּמִים נַחַל קִישׁוֹן תִּדְרְכִי נַפְשִׁי עֹז אני יהוה: 22 אָז הָלְמוּ עִקְּבֵי־סוּס רבוע אדני, כוך מִדַּהֲרוֹת דַּהֲרוֹת אַבִּירָיו: אהדונהי 23 אוֹרוּ מֵרוֹז אָמַר מַלְאַךְ יְהֹוָהאדניאהדונהי

אֹרוּ אָרוֹר יֹשְׁבֶיהָ כִּי לֹא־בָאוּ לְעֶזְרַת יְהֹוָהאדניאהדונהי לְעֶזְרַת יְהֹוָהאדניאהדונהי בַּגִּבּוֹרִים: 24 תְּבֹרַךְ מִנָּשִׁים יָעֵל אֵשֶׁת חֶבֶר רבוע ס״ג ורבוע אהיה הַקֵּינִי מִנָּשִׁים בָּאֹהֶל לאה תְּבֹרָךְ:

25 מַיִם שָׁאַל חָלָב נָתָנָה בְּסֵפֶל אַדִּירִים הקְרִיבָה חֶמְאָה: 26 יָדָהּ הרי לַיָּתֵד תִּשְׁלַחְנָה וִימִינָהּ לְהַלְמוּת

[20] *From the heavens the stars fought, from their courses the stars fought against Sisera.* [21] *The river Kishon swept them away, the age-old river, the river Kishon. March on, my soul; be strong!*

[22] *Then thundered the horses' hoofs—galloping, galloping go his mighty steeds.*

[23] *'Curse Meroz,' said the angel of the Lord. 'Curse its people bitterly, because they did not come to help the Lord, to help the Lord against the mighty.'*

[24] *Most blessed of women be Yael, the wife of Heber the Kenite, most blessed of tent-dwelling women.*

[25] *He asked for water, and she gave him milk; in a bowl fit for nobles she brought him curdled milk.*

[26] *Her hand reached for the tent peg, her right hand for the workman's hammer. She struck Sisera, she crushed his head, she shattered and pierced his temple.*

[27] *At her feet he sank, he fell; there he lay. At her feet he sank, he fell; where he sank, there he fell dead.*

[28] *Through the window peered Sisera's mother; behind the lattice she cried out, 'Why is his chariot so long in coming? Why is the clatter of his chariots delayed?'* [29] *The wisest of her ladies answer her; indeed, she keeps saying to herself,*

[30] *'Are they not finding and dividing the spoils: a girl or two for each man, colorful garments as plunder for Sisera, colorful garments embroidered, highly embroidered garments for my neck— all this as plunder?'*

[31] *So may all Your enemies perish, Lord! But may they who love You be like the sun when it rises in its strength." Then the land had peace forty years.*

עֲמֵלִים וְהָלְמָה סִיסְרָא מֶחֲקָה רֹאשׁוֹ וּמֶחֲצָה וְחָלְפָה רַקָּתוֹ: 27 בֵּין

רַגְלֶיהָ כָּרַע נָפַל שָׁכָב בֵּין רַגְלֶיהָ כָּרַע נָפַל בַּאֲשֶׁר כָּרַע שָׁם יהוה שדי

נָפַל שָׁדוּד: 28 בְּעַד הַחַלּוֹן מּנּד נִשְׁקְפָה וַתְּיַבֵּב אֵם יוהך, ע״ה מ״ב סִיסְרָא

בְּעַד הָאֶשְׁנָב מַדּוּעַ בֹּשֵׁשׁ רִכְבּוֹ לָבוֹא ר״ת רל״ב = עסמ״ב מַדּוּעַ אֶחֱרוּ

פַּעֲמֵי מַרְכְּבוֹתָיו ר״ת גימ קס״א: 29 וַחַכְמוֹת שָׂרוֹתֶיהָ תַּעֲנֶינָה אַף־הִיא

תָּשִׁיב אֲמָרֶיהָ לָהּ: 30 הֲלֹא יִמְצְאוּ יְחַלְּקוּ שָׁלָל ב״פ עס״מ רַחַם רמ״ח, וו״פ אל

רַחֲמָתַיִם לְרֹאשׁ ריבוע אלהים ואלהים דיודין ע״ה גֶּבֶר שָׁלָל ב״פ עס״מ צְבָעִים לְסִיסְרָא

שָׁלָל ב״פ עס״מ צְבָעִים רִקְמָה צֶבַע רִקְמָתַיִם לְצַוְּארֵי שָׁלָל ב״פ עס״מ: 31 כֵּן

יֹאבְדוּ כָל־אוֹיְבֶיךָ יהֹוָ֫ה ילי אהדנהי וְאֹהֲבָיו כְּצֵאת הַשֶּׁמֶשׁ ב״פ ש״ך

בִּגְבֻרָתוֹ וַתִּשְׁקֹט הָאָרֶץ אלהים ההין ע״ה אַרְבָּעִים שָׁנָה:

YITRO

LESSON OF YITRO
Exodus 18:1-20:23

"And Jethro heard…" (Exodus 18:1)

Every person comes into this world with a specific purpose that is unique to that individual as well as a general purpose that we all share—that of our spiritual correction, or *tikkun*—the negative effects from previous lifetimes. Transforming and clearing out this "baggage" is how we achieve our correction and ultimately our perfection.

There are two ways that we can complete our spiritual correction. The first begins with a realization. When we look at ourselves and say, "This is not the person I want to be. I cannot be someone who lives merely to take from others; I will be someone who gives." As a result of this understanding, we begin our spiritual work.

This is in itself an accomplishment. Just to see ourselves clearly and to make a decision to change represents a huge step forward. It is our nature as physical beings to be dominated by the *Desire to Receive for the Self Alone*. We come into the world with our hands clenched into little fists, as if to grab on to whatever we can. To depart from this mindset and commit to spirituality is actually quite amazing—and it does not happen to everybody.

Many people never discover this inner clarity that allows them to differentiate between who they are as compared to the person they want to be. Nevertheless, the purpose of life remains the same: We are all in this world to complete our tikkun. However, there is another way to finish our correction. For those who are unaware, the process of tikkun will still take place, albeit through external events and their effects. If we do not willingly come to see our need for change, we will eventually see it and be required to change by the pain and suffering the universe will bear down on us as an effect of our own actions.

One wouldn't want to give the impression that these two paths to achieving our tikkun are of equal value in a spiritual sense. A person who has consciously chosen to do the spiritual work of transformation reveals more Light for him or herself and for the world than does the person who is merely reacting to outside forces. In making the choice to move proactively toward transformation, one not only corrects his or her own tikkun, but also has a positive impact on the global collective tikkun.

One way or the other, we will all eventually get there and finish the job, if not in this life, then in a future one. The choice is simply which path we will choose: the path of our spiritual transformation or the path of suffering. Even if we choose the second path, we will, nevertheless, some day complete our own tikkun, just as the tikkun of the world will also be achieved in spite of us. But when we choose the path of spiritual work, then all our efforts serve the world as well as ourselves.

This brings us to the story of Yitro (Jethro). The sin of worshipping the Golden Calf caused a great rift between the people of Israel and *Mashiach* (Messiah) consciousness, immortality, and the Final Redemption. Immortality should have been achieved by the people when they stood before Moses at Mount Sinai, but because of the incident of the Golden Calf, immortality was lost. The Zohar teaches us that nothing spiritual ever disappears, the potential of immortality still remains, even though it has not yet been actualized in our physical dimension. Therefore, each time we read this story, the power of the Revelation at Mount Sinai empowers our consciousness toward immortality.

The *Zohar* further tells us that whoever remains awake throughout the night of Shavuot will live through the coming year. This is because on the day of Shavuot, a connection is established with the power of immortality that was originally revealed at Mount Sinai.

> *This is why this day OF SHAVUOT, THE CENTRAL COLUMN THAT CORRESPONDS TO ZEIR ANPIN THAT IS CALLED ISRAEL, is the bond of faith that bonds everything. Also, it is written, "She is a Tree of Life to those who lay hold on her," (Proverbs 3:18) SINCE THE TREE OF LIFE, ZEIR ANPIN, is a tree called 'One.' Hence, since ISRAEL BELOW are attached AND HOLD onto to this place, THE TREE OF LIFE, ZEIR ANPIN, they are called ONE. For the Tree of Life is called 'One,' since everything is attached to it, and its day, SHAVUOT, is assuredly one, bonding everything and being the center of everything, SINCE IT IS THE CENTRAL COLUMN.*
> — The Zohar, Emor 25:142

Just as a seed embodies the full-grown tree, the first words of this chapter embody the power of the whole story. The first words are: "And Jethro heard." The Bible says he heard everything that God had done for Moses and his people. In addition, Rashi explains that Jethro heard the Splitting of the Red Sea and he heard the war with Amalek.

What did he hear from the Splitting of the Red Sea? He heard all the waters of the world parting. But why did he also hear the war of Amalek? It was because he needed another reason to come to the desert to meet Moses. Although the Splitting of the Red Sea was a miracle, it was not enough for Jethro.

With each miracle, Jethro saw that there was a Creator, a higher Spiritual Power in this physical world. He saw that power in Nachshon (Aaron's brother-in-law-to-be). It was Nachshon's connection to the Creator and his certainty in the system that empowered him to enter water that was neck-deep, and it was his conviction that parted the sea. The second miracle that Jethro needed to hear was in the war of Amalek, the victory rested completely in Moses's hands. When he raised his hands, the Israelites were victorious; as he lowered them, they were defeated. Moses kept his hands raised.

Jethro was the high priest of Pharaoh and was a master of the occult. Magic was not new to him. It was not until the second miracle, the war with Amalek, that Jethro became convinced that these feats were not simply magic, that they were coming from a higher Spiritual Power that was guiding the Israelites.

To connect to this Power, Jethro knew that he must become one with the Creator's essence. In other words, he had to transform his Desire to Receive for the Self Alone into the Desire to Share. He chose the path of spiritual work, and because of his desire for transformation and connection, Jethro merited to have the energy of the Ten Utterances in the chapter of the Bible that bears his name.

What was different about Jethro?

How could a person like Jethro, who started as an extremely negative individual, transform himself so completely? He became not just an observant follower of the precepts laid down in the Bible, but also someone whose advice and vision were sought after by Moses himself. In the biblical chapter of Beha'alotcha, Moses begged Jethro to stay with the people of Israel and "be their eyes."

What was different and unique about Jethro? To illustrate, we can refer to a story of Rav Mordechai Sharabi (1908–1983). A man came to Rav Mordechai and said, "I am searching for my spiritual path and I can't find it." The rabbi answered, "If you are seeking the right path, you are already on the right path." When Jethro was a priest of Midian, he was never complacent, never satisfied. He continuously looked for a higher truth. Jethro was open to hearing and listening.

The only thing the Creator wants from us is to be open. As it is written:

> "Open for Me an opening the size of the eye of a needle and I will open for you the Eternal Gates."
> — Song of Songs 5:2

Often, we ask something of the Creator and then complain we do not get an answer, when the truth is that we are not open to hear the Creator's reply. We are only receptive to listen if it is the answer we want to hear.

Being open to the Creator begins with being open to other people. We don't have to defend ourselves, and we don't have to argue every point. We don't have to fight every battle just to prove we are right.

Jethro heard the Creator because Jethro's heart was open to listen to others. We can all merit the connection that Jethro had, simply by awakening our desire to be open to the Creator. Where we are spiritually at the moment is not important. If we want to hear the Creator, all we need to do is open our hearts and ears to hear the Creator's voice.

"I was a stranger in a strange land..."

Why did Moses name his first son Gershom—*ger* meaning "stranger" and *shom* meaning "there,""away from here "or "stranger in a strange land?" By giving his son this name, Moses wanted to remind him—and by extension, us—that every day that we live in this world, it is as if we are in exile. Only when the soul returns to the Upper World do we really feel at home.

A student of Rav Eliyahu Dessler (1891–1954) was about to depart for a distant country. Rav Eliyahu gave him a blessing for a safe trip. But strangely, the student felt hurt. He couldn't understand why his teacher did not bless him to stay in his native country all his life, to marry a good woman, and to fulfill other conventional aspirations. So he asked his teacher why he blessed him only with a safe trip? The teacher answered, "This blessing is for your whole life, wherever you are." He wanted his student to understand that our lives are always a journey, even if we remain in one place.

By naming his son Gershom, Moses taught us that we are all like nomads, moving from one place to another in a physical world that changes and disappears, and that the real world is spiritual, never-changing, and eternal. If we understand this, we will we have a better passage in this physical and temporary existence because we know that the spiritual world is our authentic home.

SYNOPSIS OF YITRO

This chapter deals with the Giving of the Ten Utterances on Mount Sinai—the revelation of immortality in this world. This is the most important section of the Bible because the essence of everything is here for us in the Ten Utterances.

FIRST READING - ABRAHAM - CHESED

18:1 **N**ow Jethro, the priest of Midian and father-in-law of Moses, heard of everything God had done for Moses and for his people Israel, that the Lord had brought Israel out of Egypt.

² After Moses had sent away his wife Tziporah, his father-in-law Jethro received her

³ and her two sons. One son was named Gershom, for Moses said, "I have become a stranger in a foreign land;"

⁴ and one was named Eliezer, for he said, "My father's God was my helper; he saved me from the sword of Pharaoh."

FROM THE RAV

There are three pillars to health and wholeness, and thereby, to immortality. These are: first, the Left Column—the egg, representing the *Desire to Receive*; second, the Right Column—the *mikveh* (ritual bath) or water, representing healing, mercy, and the Desire to Share; and third, the Central Column, representing the *Desire to Receive for the Sake of Sharing*, which acts as a filament between the other two.

As you know, the *Desire to Receive* can be either positive or negative, depending upon whether you wish to *Receive for the Sake of Sharing* or whether you wish to Receive for the Self Alone. Because we can't negate our Desire to Receive, we need to bring about a balance.

As long as these three pillars are in place, our immune system will stay well and will protect us both physically and spiritually. The ritual bathing in the mikveh purifies us of negativity both symbolically and physically. This, in effect, is what is happening when we read and connect with the story of Yitro. We can remove the energy of death with this story, but human nature demands that we need proof that it has been removed.

However, demanding proof makes us vulnerable to the force of death. We are present for the miracle, but this isn't good enough for us. We can become vulnerable again to that energy-force known as the Angel of Death. What proof do we have now? What kind of proof do we need?

The idea that today, we are able to raise our consciousness and become more aware is difficult. It is difficult because we need to recognize the power of the Light to create immortality—not the power of Tylenol, not the power of antibiotics, but the higher force of the Endless and of the 72 Names of God, the higher force that tells us that when we complete the reading of this chapter, our bodies are cleansed of that energy-force known as death.

Can you imagine that even the people who witnessed the Ten Plagues still wanted proof? Then they saw the bodies. That's when they believed. Then after three days, they stopped believing again.

As a prerequisite to receiving the connection that is available to us through this story, we have to believe and we have to understand that there is a little creature inside us. It has bored its way into our bodies and into our consciousness. It very convincingly tells us, "You're going to

FIRST READING - ABRAHAM - CHESED

18 1 וַיִּשְׁמַע ‏יִתְרוֹ‏ כֹהֵן מִדְיָן וֹתֵן מֹשֶׁה
אֵת כָּל־אֲשֶׁר עָשָׂה אֱלֹהִים לְמֹשֶׁה
וּלְיִשְׂרָאֵל עַמּוֹ כִּי־הוֹצִיא יְהוָֹה אֶת־יִשְׂרָאֵל מִמִּצְרָיִם:
2 וַיִּקַּח יִתְרוֹ וֹתֵן מֹשֶׁה אֶת־צִפֹּרָה אֵשֶׁת
מֹשֶׁה אַחַר שִׁלּוּחֶיהָ: 3 וְאֵת שְׁנֵי בָנֶיהָ אֲשֶׁר שֵׁם
הָאֶחָד גֵּרְשֹׁם כִּי אָמַר גֵּר הָיִיתִי בְּאֶרֶץ
נָכְרִיָּה: 4 וְשֵׁם הָאֶחָד אֱלִיעֶזֶר כִּי־אֱלֹהֵי
אָבִי בְּעֶזְרִי וַיַּצִּלֵנִי מֵחֶרֶב פַּרְעֹה: 5 וַיָּבֹא יִתְרוֹ
וֹתֵן מֹשֶׁה וּבָנָיו וְאִשְׁתּוֹ אֶל־מֹשֶׁה

---

become a victim of death." But the creature will be removed by this reading because that is the power of the Ten Utterances. I don't just believe that, I know it. I know that the *Zohar* works and I know that the Torah works on the most practical level. We just need to make the connection and take advantage of it.

יִתְרוֹ

Exodus 18:1—Why Jethro?

Why does Jethro (in Hebrew, Yitro), the father-in-law of Moses, receive the honor of having this story named after him? Jethro was a high priest of occult arts and black magic. As he grew closer to Moses, he changed his life and became righteous. Jethro was open and receptive to a better understanding of this world. For this reason, he was able to transform his nature from that of extreme negativity to the other extreme of great positive energy.

This chapter is named for Jethro to show us that our effort toward spiritual transformation is the criterion by which we are judged. Moses had spiritual parents, so spiritually speaking, he had a head start. Jethro, on the other hand, came from a thoroughly negative environment and was himself a source of negativity. It is said in *Mechilta Yisro 1:1* that there was not a deity in the world that Jethro had not worshipped. The leap he made from one end of the spiritual spectrum to the other earns him the blessing of having this chapter named after him. Rashi said that Jethro lived in the company of the greatest power and honor of the time, but his heart prompted him to go forth to the desert wasteland to seek out and to hear words of the Torah.

The *Zohar* says:

Jethro, the great and supreme priest, appointed ruler over the whole pagan world, came and acknowledged God, saying: "Now I know that [your] God is greater than all the other gods." Then God was exalted in His glory from Above and Below, and afterwards He gave the Torah in the completeness of His dominion.
— *The Zohar, Yitro 1:20*

5 Jethro, Moses' father-in-law, together with Moses' sons and wife, came to him in the desert, where he was camped near the mountain of God.

6 Jethro had sent word to him, "I, your father-in-law Jethro, am coming to you with your wife and her two sons that are with her."

7 So Moses went out to meet his father-in-law and bowed down and kissed him. They greeted each other in peace and then went into the tent.

8 Moses told his father-in-law about everything the Lord had done to Pharaoh and the Egyptians for Israel's sake and about all the hardships they had met along the way and how the Lord had saved them.

9 Jethro was delighted to hear about all the good things the Lord had done for Israel in rescuing them from the hand of the Egyptians.

10 He said, "Praise be to the Lord, who rescued you from the hand of the Egyptians and of Pharaoh, and who rescued the people from under the hand of the Egyptians.

11 Now I know that the Lord is greater than all other gods, for He did this to those who had treated Israel arrogantly."

12 Then Jethro, Moses' father-in-law, brought a burnt offering and other sacrifices to God, and Aaron came with all the elders of Israel to eat bread with Moses' father-in-law in the presence of God.

SECOND READING - ISAAC - GEVURAH

13 The next day Moses took his seat to serve as judge for the people, and they stood around him from morning till evening.

14 When his father-in-law saw all that he was doing for the people, he said, "What is this you are doing for the people? Why do you sit alone, while the nation stands around you from morning till evening?"

וַיִּרְא

Exodus 18:14—Jethro was in the camp of the Israelites where he witnessed Moses's devotion to caring for his people, answering all their questions and dealing with their many concerns.

He advised Moses to introduce a system for answering questions. If a question was extremely important, it would go to Moses. If not, it would go to an appropriate person in the hierarchy.

We should also introduce a type of hierarchy into our prayers. On Shabbat, our prayers should focus on loftier and more important ideas than during the rest of the week. Likewise, on *Rosh Hashanah* and *Yom Kippur*, we should pray about matters that are truly life-defining.

הָאֱלֹהִים ה ־ רבוע אלהים יהוה שדי עַם וְהִנֵּה הִוּא אֲשֶׁר הַמִּדְבָּר אֶל־

וְחֹתְנֶךָ יִתְרוֹ אֲנִי אל שדי מהע, 6 וַיֹּאמֶר אֶל־מֹשֶׁה מום, אהיה אדני ; יכה:

וַיֵּצֵא 7 עִמָּהּ בָנֶיהָ וּשְׁנֵי וְאִשְׁתְּךָ אני בָּא אֵלֶיךָ ר"ת אוזי קס"א קנ"א קמ"ג קס"א

אִישׁ קס"א קנ"א עה וַיִּשְׁאֲלוּ וַיִּשַּׁק־לוֹ וַיִּשְׁתַּחוּ לִקְרַאת וְחֹתְנוֹ אל שדי מהע מֹשֶׁה

אֶת לְחֹתְנוֹ מֹשֶׁה אל שדי מהע 8 וַיְסַפֵּר הָאֹהֱלָה וַיָּבֹאוּ לְשָׁלוֹם לְרֵעֵהוּ

עַל מצר לְפַרְעֹה וּלְמִצְרַיִם יְהֹוָאדֹנָיאהדונהי עָשָׂה אֲשֶׁר ר"ת מלאך יכו: כָּל

ב"פ יב"ק בַּדֶּרֶךְ מְצָאָתַם אֲשֶׁר כָּל אֵת ־הַתְּלָאָה יכו יִשְׂרָאֵל אוֹדֹת

עַל כָּל ־ יכו קס"א קס"א קנ"א קמ"ג כ"ב אתוון יִתְרוֹ 9 וַיִּחַדְּ יְהֹוָאדֹנָיאהדונהי וַיַּצִּלֵם

מִיַּד הִצִּילוֹ אֲשֶׁר לְיִשְׂרָאֵל יְהֹוָאדֹנָיאהדונהי עָשָׂה אֲשֶׁר אכא הַטּוֹבָה

יְהֹוָאדֹנָיאהדונהי מ"ה ורבוע ע"ב יהוה בָּרוּךְ קס"א קס"א קנ"א קמ"ג יִתְרוֹ 10 וַיֹּאמֶר מצר: מִצְרָיִם

אֶת ־הִצִּיל אֲשֶׁר פַּרְעֹה וּמִיַּד מצר מִצְרַיִם מִיַּד אֶתְכֶם הִצִּיל אֲשֶׁר

גָּדוֹל כִּי־ יָדַעְתִּי עַתָּה 11 מצר: מִצְרָיִם יַד־ מִתַּחַת הָעָם

זָדוּ אֲשֶׁר רָאה בַּדָּבָר כִּי יכה ; אדני אהיה מום, הָאֱלֹהִים ־ יכו מִכָּל יְהֹוָאדֹנָיאהדונהי

עֹלָה אל שדי מהע מֹשֶׁה וַיִּקַּח קס"א קס"א קנ"א קמ"ג יִתְרוֹ וחֹעם 12 וַיִּקַּח עֲלֵיהֶם:

זִקְנֵי | יכו וְכֹל ע"ב ורבוע ע"ב אַהֲרֹן וַיָּבֹא אדני אהיה ; יכה הָאֱלֹהִים לֵאלֹהִים וּזְבָחִים

וחכמה בינה לִפְנֵי אל שדי מהע מֹשֶׁה עִם־וֹחֹתֵן ג"פ יהוה לֶחֶם לֶאֱכָל־ יִשְׂרָאֵל

הָאֱלֹהִים מום, אהיה אדני ; יכה:

SECOND READING - ISAAC - GEVURAH

ר"ת לאה לִשְׁפֹּט אֶת־הָעָם אל שדי מהע מֹשֶׁה וַיֵּשֶׁב מִמָּחֳרָת אל, ייא"י 13 וַיְהִי

רבוע יהוה ורבוע אלהים מִן־הַבֹּקֶר עַד־הָעָרֶב אל שדי מהע הָעָם עַל־מֹשֶׁה וַיַּעֲמֹד

עָשָׂה אֲשֶׁר־הוּא־ יכו כָּל אֵת אל שדי מהע מֹשֶׁה וֹחֹתֵן אלף למד יהוה 14 וַיַּרְא

מַדּוּעַ לָעָם עֹשֶׂה אַתָּה אֲשֶׁר והו הַהֲוֶה רָאה הַדָּבָר מ"ה מָה וַיֹּאמֶר לָעָם

¹⁵ *Moses answered his father-in-law, "Because the people come to me to seek God.*

¹⁶ *Whenever they have a dispute, it is brought to me, and I decide between a man and his neighbor and inform them of God's decrees and laws."*

¹⁷ *Moses' father-in-law replied, "What you are doing is not good.*

¹⁸ *You and these people who come to you will only wear yourselves out. The work is too heavy for you; you cannot handle it alone.*

¹⁹ *Listen now to me and I will give you some advice, and may God be with you. You must be the people's representative before God and bring their disputes to him.*

²⁰ *Teach them the decrees and laws, and show them the way to live and the things they are to do.*

²¹ *But select valorous men from all the people—men who fear God, trustworthy men, who hate dishonest gain—and appoint them as officials over thousands, officials over hundreds, officials over fifties and officials over tens.*

²² *They will judge the people at all times, but have them bring every difficult case to you; the simple cases they can decide themselves. That will make your load lighter, because they will carry it with you.*

²³ *If you do this and God so commands, you will be able to stand the strain, and all these people will go home peacefully."*

תֶחֱזֶה

Exodus 18:21—Jethro advised Moses to choose his deputies from among all the people, according to their talents. The secrets of how to make these choices are embodied in the gifts of palm-and-face reading that were given to Moses. The word *techezeh* (to see), refers to these secrets.

The Ari tells us this:

If a man's Nefesh is completely whole and restored, all the sparks of the heel will appear in him and shine in his body. In order for him to be corrected, they have to appear on his forehead, where he will be recognized by one whom God has graced with the knowledge of face reading; the presence of all 613 sparks of that root, either of the Nefesh, Ruach or Neshamah, [the three levels of the soul] has to be revealed on his

forehead…. Everything is in accordance with man's actions; when he sins, they will again leave him, heaven forbid, and the number of sparks to leave him will be in proportion to the magnitude of the sin.

— Writings of the Ari, Gate of Reincarnation 34:225

Rav Avraham Azulai (1570–1644) has extensive commentary in the *Zohar* on palm-and-face reading:

"And you shall behold," THAT IS, in the hair, the creases on the brow, and the eyebrows. "…out of all the people…" IS TO BE INTERPRETED AS with eyes, in the membranes in the eyes, and in the folds under the eyes; "…able men…," REFERS TO those who have the strength to stand in the palace of the King. They are recognized by the brightness on their faces, by their face, by the wrinkles

אַתָּה יוֹשֵׁב לְבַדֶּךָ וְכָל־הָעָם נִצָּב עָלֶיךָ יְלי רבוע מ״ה מִן־בֹּקֶר עַד־עָרֶב

רבוע יהוה ורבוע אלהים: 15 וַיֹּאמֶר מֹשֶׁה מהש, אל שדי לְחֹתְנוֹ כִּי־יָבֹא אֵלַי הָעָם

לִדְרֹשׁ אֱלֹהִים מום, אהיה אדני ; יאהדונהי 16 כִּי־יִהְיֶה יְיִ לָהֶם דָּבָר ראה בָּא אֵלַי

וְשָׁפַטְתִּי בֵּין אִישׁ ע״ה קנ״א קס״א וּבֵין רֵעֵהוּ וְהוֹדַעְתִּי אֶת־חֻקֵּי הָאֱלֹהִים במוכן

מום, אהיה אדני ; יאהדונהי וְאֶת־תּוֹרֹתָיו: 17 וַיֹּאמֶר חֹתֵן מֹשֶׁה מהש, אל שדי אֵלָיו לֹא־

טוֹב וה הַדָּבָר ראה אֲשֶׁר אַתָּה עֹשֶׂה: 18 נָבֹל תִּבֹּל גַּם־אַתָּה גַּם

יא״ל הָעָם הַזֶּה וה אֲשֶׁר עִמָּךְ ה הויות, נגמ כִּי־כָבֵד מִמְּךָ הַדָּבָר ראה לֹא־

תוּכַל עֲשֹׂהוּ לְבַדֶּךָ: 19 עַתָּה שְׁמַע בְּקֹלִי אִיעָצְךָ וִיהִי אל, ייא״י אֱלֹהִים

מום, אהיה אדני ; יאהדונהי עִמָּךְ ה הויות, נגמ הֱיֵה יהוה אַתָּה לָעָם ר״ת לאה מוּל הָאֱלֹהִים

מום, אהיה אדני ; יאהדונהי וְהֵבֵאתָ אַתָּה אֶת־הַדְּבָרִים ראה אֶל־הָאֱלֹהִים

מום, אהיה אדני ; יאהדונהי 20 וְהִזְהַרְתָּה אֶתְהֶם אֶת־הַחֻקִּים וְאֶת־הַתּוֹרֹת וְהוֹדַעְתָּ

לָהֶם אֶת־הַדֶּרֶךְ ב״פ יב״ק יֵלְכוּ בָהּ וְאֶת־הַמַּעֲשֶׂה אֲשֶׁר יַעֲשׂוּן: 21 וְאַתָּה

תֶחֱזֶה מִכָּל־הָעָם יְלי אַנְשֵׁי־חַיִל וּמב יִרְאֵי אֱלֹהִים מום, אהיה אדני ; יאהדונהי אַנְשֵׁי

אֱמֶת אהיה פעמים אהיה, ז״פ ס״ג שֹׂנְאֵי בָצַע וְשַׂמְתָּ עֲלֵהֶם שָׂרֵי אֲלָפִים קס״א שָׂרֵי

מֵאוֹת שָׂרֵי חֲמִשִּׁים וְשָׂרֵי עֲשָׂרֹת: 22 וְשָׁפְטוּ אֶת־הָעָם בְּכָל־עֵת ב״ן, לכב, יבמ

עֵ״ת י״פ אהיה י הויות וְהָיָה יהוה כָּל־הַדָּבָר ראה יְלי הַגָּדֹל לתהו, מבה, יזל, אום יָבִיאוּ

אֵלֶיךָ אני וְכָל־הַדָּבָר ראה יְלי הַקָּטֹן יִשְׁפְּטוּ־הֵם וְהָקֵל מֵעָלֶיךָ רבוע מ״ה

וְנָשְׂאוּ אִתָּךְ: 23 אִם יוהך, ע״ה מ״ב אֶת־הַדָּבָר ראה הַזֶּה וה תַּעֲשֶׂה וְצִוְּךָ

אֱלֹהִים מום, אהיה אדני ; יאהדונהי וְיָכָלְתָּ עֲמֹד וְגַם יא״ל כָּל־הָעָם הַזֶּה וה עַל־

מְקֹמוֹ יָבֹא בְשָׁלוֹם:

---

on their faces, and by the marks in their beards. "...hating unjust gain...," REFERS TO the hands, and the lines in the hands, and the marks in them. All these six aspects implied here, IN THE SCRIPTURAL VERSE, were transmitted to Moses to contemplate and from which to learn concealed wisdom. This wisdom is inherited by those who are properly righteous and truthful. Happy is their lot.
—The Zohar, Yitro 12:181

THIRD READING - JACOB - TIFERET

24 Moses listened to his father-in-law and did everything he said. 25 He chose valorous men from all Israel and made them heads of the people, officials over thousands, officials over hundreds, officials over fifties and officials over tens.

26 They judged the people at all times. The difficult cases they brought to Moses, but the simple cases they decided themselves.

27 Then Moses sent his father-in-law on his way, and Jethro returned to his own country.

FOURTH READING - MOSES - NETZACH

19:1 In the third month after the Israelites left Egypt—on the very day—they came to the Desert of Sinai.

2 After they set out from Rephidim, they entered the Desert of Sinai, and Israel camped there in the desert in front of the mountain.

3 Then Moses went up to God, and the Lord called to him from the mountain and said, "This is what you are to say to the house of Jacob and what you are to tell the sons of Israel:

4 'You have seen what I did to Egypt, and how I carried you on eagles' wings and brought you to Myself.

5 Now if you listen to My voice and keep My Covenant, then you will be My treasured possession out of all nations, for the whole Earth is Mine, 6 you will be for Me a kingdom of priests and a holy nation.' These are the words you are to speak to the Israelites."

Exodus 19:2—The Israelites reached Mount Sinai.

Before the Revelation of Light on Mount Sinai, all the mountains came to God and asked for the privilege of being the place where the Revelation would take place. Mount Sinai was chosen because it was the smallest and least lofty of all the mountains. This teaches us that for our prayers to be heard, we require humility and absence of ego. Certain qualities are necessary on our spiritual path, and humility is one of these essentials. Without it, we have no hope of moving forward.

In the *Zohar* (*Yitro* 14:247-252), Rav Yosi gives a discourse on the journey of Moses to Mount Sinai. We learn that both Moses and the mountain had been prepared for each other from the time of Creation. As soon as Moses saw Mount Sinai, he knew that this was the mountain of God and he was drawn to it. He saw birds flying from the mountain and falling at his feet, and interpreting this as a sign, he led the Israelites "far away into the desert," and ascended the mountain alone.

THIRD READING - JACOB - TIFERET

24 וַיִּשְׁמַ֥ע מֹשֶׁ֖ה מהע, אל שדי לְק֣וֹל ע"ב ס"ג עה חֹתְנ֑וֹ וַיַּ֕עַשׂ יּלי כֹּ֖ל אֲשֶׁ֥ר אָמָֽר׃

25 וַיִּבְחַ֨ר מֹשֶׁ֤ה מהע, אל שדי אַנְשֵׁי־חַ֙יִל֙ ומב מִכָּל־יּלי יִשְׂרָאֵ֔ל וַיִּתֵּ֥ן יּ"פ מלוי ע"ב

אֹתָ֛ם רָאשִׁ֖ים עַל־הָעָ֑ם שָׂרֵ֣י אֲלָפִ֗ים קס"א שָׂרֵ֤י מֵאוֹת֙ שָׂרֵ֣י חֲמִשִּׁ֔ים

וְשָׂרֵ֖י עֲשָׂרֹֽת׃ 26 וְשָׁפְט֥וּ אֶת־הָעָ֖ם בְּכָל־ב"ן, לכב, יבמ עֵ֑ת יּ"פ אהיה י' הוויות אֶת־

הַדָּבָ֤ר ראה הַקָּשֶׁה֙ יְבִיא֣וּן אֶל־מֹשֶׁ֔ה מהע, אל שדי וְכָל־יּלי הַדָּבָ֥ר ראה הַקָּטֹ֖ן

יִשְׁפּוּט֥וּ הֵֽם׃ 27 וַיְשַׁלַּ֥ח מֹשֶׁ֖ה מהע, אל שדי אֶת־חֹתְנ֑וֹ וַיֵּ֥לֶךְ כּלי ל֖וֹ אֶל־

אַרְצֽוֹ׃

FOURTH READING - MOSES - NETZACH

19 1 בַּחֹ֙דֶשׁ֙ יּ"ב הוויות הַשְּׁלִישִׁ֔י לְצֵ֥את ר"ת הבל בְּנֵֽי־יִשְׂרָאֵ֖ל מֵאֶ֣רֶץ אלהים דאלפין

מִצְרָ֑יִם מצר בַּיּ֣וֹם ע"ה = נגד, זן, מזבח הַזֶּ֔ה והו בָּ֖אוּ מִדְבַּ֥ר סִינָֽי נגמם, ה"פ יהוה׃

2 וַיִּסְע֣וּ מֵרְפִידִ֗ים וַיָּבֹ֙אוּ֙ מִדְבַּ֣ר סִינַ֔י נגמם, ה"פ יהוה וַיַּחֲנ֖וּ בַּמִּדְבָּ֑ר

רמ"ח, אברהם וו"פ אל וַיִּֽחַן־שָׁ֥ם יהוה שדי יִשְׂרָאֵ֖ל נֶ֣גֶד זן, נגד, מזבח | הָהָֽר׃ 3 וּמֹשֶׁ֥ה

מהע, אל שדי עָלָ֖ה אֶל־הָאֱלֹהִ֑ים מום, אהיה אדני ; ילה וַיִּקְרָ֨א ב"פ קס"א + ה' אותיות אֵלָ֤יו

יְהֹוָה֙ אלדיאהדונהי מִן־הָהָ֣ר לֵאמֹ֔ר כֹּ֤ה היי תֹאמַר֙ לְבֵ֣ית ב"פ ראה יַעֲקֹ֔ב

ד"פ יהוה, יאהדונהי אידהנויה וְתַגֵּ֖יד לִבְנֵ֥י יִשְׂרָאֵֽל׃ 4 אַתֶּ֣ם רְאִיתֶ֔ם אֲשֶׁ֥ר עָשִׂ֖יתִי

לְמִצְרָ֑יִם מצר וָאֶשָּׂ֤א אֶתְכֶם֙ עַל־כַּנְפֵ֣י נְשָׁרִ֔ים וָאָבִ֥א אֶתְכֶ֖ם אֵלָֽי׃

5 וְעַתָּ֗ה אִם־יוהך, ע"ה מ"ב שָׁמ֤וֹעַ תִּשְׁמְעוּ֙ בְּקֹלִ֔י וּשְׁמַרְתֶּ֖ם אֶת־בְּרִיתִ֑י

וִהְיִ֨יתֶם לִ֤י סְגֻלָּה֙ מִכָּל־יּלי הָ֣עַמִּ֔ים ע"ה קס"א כִּי־לִ֖י כָּל־יּלי הָאָֽרֶץ׃

אלהים דההן ע"ה 6 וְאַתֶּ֧ם תִּהְיוּ־לִ֛י מַמְלֶ֥כֶת כֹּהֲנִ֖ים מלה וְג֣וֹי קָד֑וֹשׁ אֵ֚לֶּה

הַדְּבָרִ֔ים ראה אֲשֶׁ֥ר תְּדַבֵּ֖ר ראה אֶל־בְּנֵ֥י יִשְׂרָאֵֽל׃

FIFTH READING - AARON - HOD

⁷ So Moses went back and summoned the elders of the people and set before them all the words the Lord had commanded him to speak.

⁸ The people all responded together, saying, "We will do everything the Lord has said." So Moses brought their answer back to the Lord.

⁹ The Lord said to Moses, "I am going to come to you in a dense cloud, so that the people will hear Me speaking with you and will always put their trust in you." Then Moses told the Lord what the people had said.

¹⁰ And the Lord said to Moses, "Go to the people and consecrate them today and tomorrow. Have them wash their clothes

¹¹ and be ready by the third day, because on that day the Lord will come down in the sight of all the people on Mount Sinai.

¹² Put limits for the people around and tell them, 'Be careful that you do not go up the mountain or touch the foot of it. Whoever touches the mountain shall surely die.

¹³ Not a hand shall be laid on it, lest he be stoned or shot with arrows; whether man or animal, he shall not be permitted to live.' Only when the ram's horn sounds a long blast may they go up to the mountain."

¹⁴ After Moses had gone down the mountain to the people, he consecrated them, and they washed their clothes.

וְקִדַּשְׁתָּם

Exodus 19:10—The Israelites were "chosen" to receive the Torah.

When the Bible states that the Israelites were "chosen" to receive it, this means that the Israelites were given the technology of the Universal Three Column System to connect to the Light of the Creator. They learned the method of creating circuitry and connection by balancing the Left Column of Receiving and the Right Column of Sharing with Central Column of Resistance. The Israelites were the fiduciaries of this technology, which is the wisdom of Kabbalah. Because they possessed this element and awareness, they were called the "chosen people." "Chosen people" is not, however, a reference to a group designated by religion or nationality. Nor does it imply preferential treatment on the part of the Creator. "Israelite" is simply the term used to describe those people who understood and accepted the spiritual system of transforming the *Desire to Receive for the Self Alone* into the *Desire to Share* as the method of connecting to the Light of the Creator

וַיֵּרֶד

Exodus 19:14—Moses returned from Mount Sinai after speaking to God. Moses told the Israelites that God wanted them to spend three days preparing to receive the Bible. Every person who connected to the Revelation of Light at Mount Sinai did so in a distinct way, with the difference partly determined by how much the

FIFTH READING - AARON - HOD

7 וַיָּבֹא מֹשֶׁה וַיִּקְרָא לְזִקְנֵי הָעָם וַיָּשֶׂם לִפְנֵיהֶם

אֵת כָּל־הַדְּבָרִים הָאֵלֶּה אֲשֶׁר צִוָּהוּ יְהוָה: 8 וַיַּעֲנוּ כָל

הָעָם יַחְדָּו וַיֹּאמְרוּ כֹּל אֲשֶׁר־דִּבֶּר יְהוָה נַעֲשֶׂה

וַיָּשֶׁב מֹשֶׁה אֶת־דִּבְרֵי הָעָם אֶל־יְהוָה: 9 וַיֹּאמֶר

יְהוָה אֶל־מֹשֶׁה הִנֵּה אָנֹכִי בָּא אֵלֶיךָ בְּעַב

הֶעָנָן בַּעֲבוּר יִשְׁמַע הָעָם בְּדַבְּרִי עִמָּךְ וְגַם־בְּךָ

יַאֲמִינוּ לְעוֹלָם וַיַּגֵּד מֹשֶׁה אֶת־דִּבְרֵי הָעָם אֶל־

יְהוָה: 10 וַיֹּאמֶר יְהוָה אֶל־מֹשֶׁה לֵךְ אֶל־הָעָם

וְקִדַּשְׁתָּם הַיּוֹם וּמָחָר וְכִבְּסוּ שִׂמְלֹתָם: 11 וְהָיוּ נְכֹנִים

לַיּוֹם הַשְּׁלִישִׁי כִּי בַּיּוֹם הַשְּׁלִישִׁי יֵרֵד

יְהוָה לְעֵינֵי כָל־הָעָם עַל־הַר סִינָי

12 וְהִגְבַּלְתָּ אֶת־הָעָם סָבִיב לֵאמֹר הִשָּׁמְרוּ לָכֶם עֲלוֹת

בָּהָר וּנְגֹעַ בְּקָצֵהוּ כָּל־הַנֹּגֵעַ בָּהָר

מוֹת יוּמָת: 13 לֹא־תִגַּע בּוֹ יָד כִּי־סָקוֹל יִסָּקֵל אוֹ־יָרֹה יִיָּרֶה אִם

בְּהֵמָה אִם־אִישׁ לֹא יִחְיֶה

בִּמְשֹׁךְ הַיֹּבֵל הֵמָּה יַעֲלוּ בָהָר: 14 וַיֵּרֶד מֹשֶׁה מִן

הָהָר אֶל־הָעָם וַיְקַדֵּשׁ אֶת־הָעָם וַיְכַבְּסוּ שִׂמְלֹתָם: 15 וַיֹּאמֶר אֶל־

---

individual had prepared to receive the Light and partly by the spiritual level the person had already achieved.

It is written: "Be ready by the third day, come not near a woman," (Exodus 19:15) and "And it came to pass, on the third day." Rav Shimon said that at the time that the Holy One, blessed be He, desired to be revealed on Mount Sinai, He gathered all His retinue and told them: 'Now Israel are like children who do not know My Commandments, and I desire to be revealed before them with Mercy, and they will accept My Law.' Therefore it is written: "And it came to pass on the third day." Indeed, the manifestation took place on the third day, FOR IT IS THE DAY OF TIFERET, which is Mercy. And how do we know all that? It is written: "He bowed the heavens also, and came down," (II Samuel 22:10) AND "HEAVENS" ARE TIFERET, WHICH

15 Then he said to the people, "Prepare yourselves for the third day. Do not approach a woman."

16 On the morning of the third day there was thunder and lightning, with a thick cloud over the mountain, and a very loud trumpet blast. Everyone in the camp trembled.

17 Then Moses led the people out of the camp to meet with God, and they stood at the foot of the mountain.

18 Mount Sinai was covered with smoke, because the Lord descended on it in fire. The smoke billowed up from it like smoke from a furnace, the whole mountain trembled violently,

19 and the sound of the trumpet grew louder and louder. Then Moses spoke and the voice of God answered him.

SIXTH READING - JOSEPH - YESOD

20 The Lord descended to the top of Mount Sinai and the Lord called Moses to the top of the mountain. So Moses went up

21 and the Lord said to him, "Go down and warn the people so they do not force their way through to see the Lord and many of them perish.

IS MERCY, AS IS EXPLAINED ABOVE.
— The Zohar, Yitro 17:286

To connect to the greatest possible measure of Light, we must prepare ourselves by trying to reach our next spiritual level. For instance, any time before a great revelation of Light, as on Rosh Hashanah or Pesach, we could promise to work diligently over the next year to transform some aspect of our Desire to Receive. In this way, we can take out a "spiritual loan": We can borrow some extra Light as long as we work on fulfilling the spiritual promise that we have made.

The Israelites were camped at the foot of Mount Sinai. They cried out because Moses was coming to give them messages from God and they feared they did not have the consciousness to hear. They spent three days without interruption preparing for this opportunity. But when the actual moment came that Moses returned with the messages, everyone was asleep!

And Moses went forth and came to the camp of the Israelites, and he aroused the Israelites from their sleep, saying to them, "Arise you from your sleep, for behold, your God desires to give the Torah to you. Already the bridegroom wishes to lead the bride and to enter the bridal chamber." ... And the Holy One, blessed be He, also went forth to meet them; like a bridegroom who goes forth to meet the bride, so the Holy One, blessed be He, went forth to meet them, to give them the Torah.
— Pirkei de Rebbi Eliezer 41

It is incomprehensible that the Israelites would be so cavalier about an event of such magnitude. This is how our Adversary captures us: He can weaken our resolve about important spiritual matters so that we lack perseverance and consciousness and become lackadaisical and careless. And conversely, he can also inspire great tenacity in us to give exaggerated importance to concerns that are less than spiritual.

הָעָם הָיוּ נְכֹנִים לִשְׁלֹשֶׁת יָמִים נלך אֶל־תִּגְּשׁוּ אֶל־אִשָּׁה: 16 וַיְהִי אל, ייא׳

בַיּוֹם ע״ה = נגד, זן, מזבח הַשְּׁלִישִׁי בִּהְיֹת הַבֹּקֶר וַיְהִי אל, ייא׳ קֹלֹת וּבְרָקִים

וְעָנָן כָּבֵד עַל־הָהָר וְקֹל נמם, רבוע מ״ה שֹׁפָר וְחָזָק מְאֹד פהל מ״ה וַיֶּחֱרַד כָּל־

הָעָם אֲשֶׁר בַּמַּחֲנֶה: 17 וַיּוֹצֵא מֹשֶׁה מהע, אל שדי אֶת־הָעָם לִקְרַאת ילי

הָאֱלֹהִים מום, אהיה אדני ר״ת לאה ; ילה מִן־הַמַּחֲנֶה וַיִּתְיַצְּבוּ בְּתַחְתִּית הָהָר:

18 וְהַר רבוע אלהים - ה סִינַי נמם, ה״פ יהוה עָשַׁן כֻּלּוֹ מִפְּנֵי וחכמה בינה אֲשֶׁר יָרַד

עָלָיו יְהוָֹהדנילאהדנ״י בָּאֵשׁ אלהים דיודין ע״ה וַיַּעַל עֲשָׁנוֹ כְּעֶשֶׁן הַכִּבְשָׁן וַיֶּחֱרַד

כָּל־הָהָר ילי מְאֹד מ״ה: 19 וַיְהִי אל, ייא׳ קוֹל ע״ב ס״ג ע״ה הַשֹּׁפָר הוֹלֵךְ וְחָזֵק

מְאֹד פהל מ״ה מֹשֶׁה מהע, אל שדי יְדַבֵּר ראה וְהָאֱלֹהִים מום, אהיה אדני ; ילה יַעֲנֶנּוּ

בְקוֹל ע״ב ס״ג ע״ה:

SIXTH READING - JOSEPH - YESOD

20 וַיֵּרֶד ריי יְהוָֹהדנילאהדנ״י עַל־הַר רבוע אלהים - ה סִינַי נמם, ה״פ יהוה אֶל־רֹאשׁ

הָהָר ריבוע אלהים ואלהים דיודין ע״ה וַיִּקְרָא ב״פ קס״א - ה אותיות יְהוָֹהדנילאהדנ״י לְמֹשֶׁה

אֶל־רֹאשׁ מהע, אל שדי הָהָר ריבוע אלהים ואלהים דיודין ע״ה וַיַּעַל מֹשֶׁה מהע, אל שדי:

21 וַיֹּאמֶר יְהוָֹהדנילאהדנ״י אֶל־מֹשֶׁה מהע, אל שדי רֵד הָעֵד בָּעָם פֶּן־יֶהֶרְסוּ אֶל־

יְהוָֹהדנילאהדנ״י לִרְאוֹת וְנָפַל מִמֶּנּוּ רָב ע״ב ורבוע מ״ה: 22 וְגַם יגל הַכֹּהֲנִים מלה

The Ten Utterances (Exodus 20:1-14)

Rav Elazar explained that in the Ten Utterances were engraved all the laws of the Torah, all the decrees and punishments, all the laws concerning purity and impurity, all the branches and the roots, trees and plants, heavens and Earth, seas and depths, for the Torah is the Name of the Holy One, blessed be He. As the Name of the Holy One, blessed be He, is engraved in the Ten Utterances, the Ten Utterances are the

Name of the Holy One, blessed be He. So is the whole Torah engraved in them, and the whole Torah is thus One Name, the Holy Name of the Holy One, blessed be He, indeed. Blessed is the one who is worthy of the Torah, for he will be worthy of the Holy Name. Rav Yosi said that he will be worthy of the Holy One, blessed be He, Himself, as He and His Name are one. Blessed be His Name, for ever and ever. Amen.
     — The Zohar, Yitro 28:497-498

22 Even the priests, who approach the Lord must consecrate themselves, or the Lord will break out against them."

23 Moses said to the Lord, "The people cannot come up Mount Sinai, because You Yourself warned us, 'Put limits around the mountain and set it apart as holy.' "

24 The Lord replied, "Go down and bring Aaron up with you. But the priests and the people must not force their way through to come up to the Lord, or He will break out against them."

25 So Moses went down to the people and told them. 20:1 And God spoke all these words, saying: 2 "I am the Lord, your God, who brought you out of Egypt, the land of slavery. You shall have no other gods before me.

3 You shall not make for yourself an idol in the form of anything in heaven above or on the earth beneath or in the waters below.

4 You shall not bow down to them or worship them; for I, the Lord, your God, am a jealous God, punishing the children for the sin of the fathers to the third and fourth generation of those who hate Me, 5 but showing love to thousands of those who love Me and keep My Precepts.

אָנֹכִי יְהֹוָ(אֱדֹנָי)

Exodus 20:2—First Utterance (*Sefira* of *Keter*)

"I am the Lord your God, Who has brought you out of the land of Egypt, out of the house of bondage."

This really means that on our spiritual path, we must have certainty in the existence of the Creator. The only way to avoid the endless cycle of successes and failures in life is to continually bring the Creator into our consciousness. Sometimes, we think that we are spiritual, yet we still experience a succession of ups and downs. We need to realize that the reason for any chaos is that we are not yet connecting to the Light of the Creator at an optimal level. Real certainty in the Creator means finding the Light in every aspect of life's journey. The *Zohar* tells us more about how God delivered the Israelites from Egypt:

> "...who (asher) has brought you out of the land of Egypt." (Exodus 20:2) Asher means a place which everyone calls happy (osher), which is Binah. "...brought you out of Egypt..." designates Yovel (Jubilee) which is Binah, called 'asher,' "who have brought you out of the land of Egypt," for as we have learned, the aspect of Jubilee which is Binah was the cause of Israel's exodus from Egypt. Therefore, this event is mentioned fifty times in the Torah. Fifty days passed from the exodus to the receiving of the Torah, and fifty years had to pass for the liberation of the slaves, for all these events correspond to the Fifty Gates of Binah.
> — The Zohar, Yitro 22:389

The Jubilee was also the 50th year (following seven sabbatical cycles) during which certain important land regulations were observed by the Israelites.

לֹא־יִהְיֶה

Exodus 20:2—Second Utterance (*Sefira* of *Chochmah*)

"You shall have no other gods before me."

We must not believe in other gods. People have always been tempted to worship false gods: money, fame, or social standing. These are not

הַנִּגָּשִׁים אֶל־יְהוָֹהאדנים־אהדונהי יִתְקַדָּ֑שׁוּ פֶּן־יִפְרֹ֥ץ בָּהֶ֖ם יְהוָֹהאדניאאהדונהי׃ 23 וַיֹּ֤אמֶר

מֹשֶׁה מהע, אל שדי אֶל־יְהוָֹהאדניאאהדונהי לֹא־יוּכַ֣ל הָעָ֔ם לַעֲלֹ֖ת אֶל־הַ֑ר רבוע אלהים ־ ה

סִינָ֑י נמם, ה"פ יהוה כִּֽי־אַתָּ֞ה הַעֵדֹ֤תָה בָּ֨נוּ֙ ר"ת הבל לֵאמֹ֔ר הַגְבֵּ֥ל אֶת־הָהָ֖ר

וְקִדַּשְׁתּֽוֹ׃ 24 וַיֹּ֨אמֶר אֵלָ֤יו יְהוָֹהאדניאאהדונהי לֶךְ־רֵ֔ד וְעָלִ֥יתָ אַתָּ֖ה וְאַהֲרֹ֣ן

עִמָּ֑ךְ ע"ב ורבוע ע"ב וְהַכֹּהֲנִ֣ים ה הויות, נמם מלה וְהָעָ֗ם אַל־יֶֽהֶרְס֛וּ לַעֲלֹ֥ת אֶל־

יְהוָֹהאדניאאהדונהי פֶּן־יִפְרׇץ־בָּֽם׃ מ"ב 25 וַיֵּ֥רֶד רי"ו מֹשֶׁ֖ה מהע, אל שדי אֶל־הָעָ֑ם

וַיֹּ֖אמֶר אֲלֵהֶֽם׃ ס 20 1 וַיְדַבֵּ֣ר ראה אֱלֹהִ֔ים מום, אהיה אדני ; ילה אֵ֥ת כׇּל־ יל"י

הַדְּבָרִ֥ים ראה הָאֵ֖לֶּה לֵאמֹֽר׃ 2 כתר אָֽנֹכִ֖י איע יְהוָֹהאדניאאהדונהי אֱלֹהֶ֑יךָ ילה

אֲשֶׁ֧ר הֽוֹצֵאתִ֛יךָ מֵאֶ֥רֶץ מִצְרַ֖יִם מצר אלהים דאלפין מִבֵּ֣ית ב"פ ראה עֲבָדִֽים עֲבָדִֽים

וכחמה לֹא־יִֽהְיֶֽה יל"י לְךָ֣ אֱלֹהִ֥ים מום, אהיה אדני ; ילה אֲחֵרִ֖ים עַל־פָּנָֽיֽ׃ וחכמה בינה

3 לֹֽא־תַֽעֲשֶׂ֨ה לְךָ֥ פֶ֨סֶל֙ וְכׇל־ יל"י תְּמוּנָ֔ה אֲשֶׁ֤ר בַּשָּׁמַ֨יִם֙ י"פ טל, י"פ כוז מִמַּ֔עַל

עלם וַֽאֲשֶׁ֥ר בָּאָ֖רֶץ אלהים דאלפין מִתָּ֑חַת וַֽאֲשֶׁ֥ר בַּמַּ֖יִם מִתַּ֥חַת לָאָֽרֶץ אלהים דאלפין׃

4 לֹֽא־תִשְׁתַּֽחֲוֶ֥ה לָהֶ֖ם וְלֹ֣א תָעׇבְדֵ֑ם כִּ֣י אָֽנֹכִ֞י איע יְהוָֹהאדניאאהדונהי אֱלֹהֶ֨יךָ֙ ילה

אֵ֣ל יא"י קַנָּ֔א קנ"א, מקוה פֹּקֵ֞ד רבוע ע"ב עֲוֺ֤ן גי'ם מ"ב אָבֹ֨ת עַל־בָּנִ֜ים עַל־שִׁלֵּשִׁ֣ים

---

the same as the physical god-idols that existed during the time of Moses, but they are just as powerful and dangerous to our spiritual well-being. About idolatry the Ari wrote:

"And they said, Come, let us build us a city and a tower," (Genesis 11:4) the idol they wished to make; "whose top may reach to heaven," (Ibid.) so the idol would have power from supernal holiness by the use of His Names, because they already knew that an idol is powerless unless some holiness comes over it. Their intention was that it would, perforce, bestow goodness upon them—by means of the use of His Names, even if they were not good—because they wanted to walk in the stubbornness of their evil hearts, and did not want to be subdued under holiness, since it requires much toil in renouncing the lust for material things. They

wanted to have pleasure in the lusts of this world, and idolatry would bestow goodness upon them by means of the usage of the Names.

— Writings of the Ari, Torah Compilations 2 , Noah 12.

6 You shall not use the name of the Lord, your God, in vain, for the Lord will not hold anyone guiltless who uses His name in vain.

7 Remember the Sabbath day by sanctifying it.

8 Six days you shall labor and do all your work, 9 but the seventh day is a Sabbath to the Lord, your God. On it you shall not do any work, neither you, nor your son or daughter, nor your manservant or maidservant, nor your animals, nor the stranger within your gates.

10 For in six days the Lord made the heavens and the earth, the sea, and all that is in them, but He rested on the seventh day. Therefore, the Lord blessed the Sabbath day and made it holy.

11 Honor your father and your mother, so that you may live long in the land the Lord, your God, is giving you.

לֹא תִשָּׂא

Exodus 20:6—Third Utterance (*Sefira* of *Binah*)

"You shall not take the Name of the Lord your God in vain, for God will not hold him guiltless that takes His Name in vain."

Whenever we use one of the Names of God or the names of angels, we draw down a force of energy, and if we do so for reasons other than our spiritual work (for example, for unimportant reasons or in anger), we debase the power of that Name, thereby depriving ourselves of the true energy and connection with the Name when we really do need it. The *Zohar* tells us:

> *Rav Shimon said: "The Holy Name is mentioned only in connection with a completed world, namely, Yud, Hei, Vav and Hei, as it is written: 'In the day that the Lord, God made the Earth and the heavens.' (Genesis 2:4). From this it follows that one should not mention the Holy Name in vain, as it is written: 'You shall not take the Name of the Lord your God in vain.' " (Exodus 20:7) Rav Yosi said: "What is the blessing? It is the Holy Name, being the source of blessing for the whole Universe. A blessing does not*

dwell in an empty place, nor does it rest upon it, and therefore it is written: 'You shall not take the Name of the Lord your God in vain.' "
> — *The Zohar, Yitro 26:442-443*

זָכוֹר

Exodus 20:7—Fourth Utterance (*Sefira* of *Chesed*)

"Remember the Sabbath Day by keeping it holy."

Shabbat is not just a time for physical ritual; it is a gift given to us by the Creator that allows us, once a week, to connect to our perfected state of consciousness. We don't have to wait a whole year until next Rosh Hashanah to make teshuvah (repentance) to truly transform on a DNA level. Each Shabbat gives us this powerful opportunity. This is why before each Shabbat, we should take a few minutes to quietly reflect on our lives—about where we are spiritually and what we need to work on to grow. During the 24 hours from sundown on Friday to sundown on Saturday, we can simply use the physical requirements of Shabbat to disconnect us from the rest of the week. But to truly connect with the energy of Shabbat, our consciousness needs to aligned with the greater opportunity that is available to help us with our spiritual growth.

וְעַל־רִבֵּעִים לְשֹׂנְאָי׃ 5 וְעֹשֶׂה חֶסֶד ע״ב, ריבוע יהוה לַאֲלָפִים קס״א לְאֹהֲבַי
וּלְשֹׁמְרֵי מִצְוֺתָי׃ 6 בינה **לֹא תִשָּׂא** אֶת־שֵׁם יהוה שדי יְהֹוָה אדני אהדונהי אֱלֹהֶיךָ ילה
לַשָּׁוְא כִּי לֹא יְנַקֶּה יְהֹוָה אדני אהדונהי אֵת אֲשֶׁר־יִשָּׂא אֶת־שְׁמוֹ מהש ע״ה, אל שדי ע״ה
לַשָּׁוְא׃ 7 חסד **זָכוֹר** ע״ב קס״א אֶת־יוֹם ע״ה = נגד, זן, מזבח הַשַּׁבָּת ר״ת איה לְקַדְּשׁוֹ׃
8 שֵׁשֶׁת יָמִים נלך תַּעֲבֹד וְעָשִׂיתָ כָּל ילי ־מְלַאכְתֶּךָ׃ 9 וְיוֹם ע״ה = נגד, זן, מזבח
הַשְּׁבִיעִי שַׁבָּת לַיהֹוָה אדני אהדונהי אֱלֹהֶיךָ ילה לֹא־תַעֲשֶׂה כָל ילי ־מְלָאכָה אל אדני
אַתָּה | וּבִנְךָ וּבִתֶּךָ עַבְדְּךָ פוי וַאֲמָתְךָ וּבְהֶמְתֶּךָ וְגֵרְךָ אֲשֶׁר בִּשְׁעָרֶיךָ׃ 10 כִּי
שֵׁשֶׁת־יָמִים נלך עָשָׂה יְהֹוָה אדני אהדונהי אֶת־הַשָּׁמַיִם י״פ טל, י״פ כוזו וְאֶת־הָאָרֶץ
אלהים דההין ע״ה אֶת־הַיָּם ילי וְאֶת־כָּל ילי ־אֲשֶׁר־בָּם מ״ב וַיָּנַח בַּיּוֹם ע״ה = נגד, זן, מזבח
הַשְּׁבִיעִי עַל־כֵּן בֵּרַךְ יְהֹוָה אדני אהדונהי אֶת־יוֹם ע״ה = נגד, זן, מזבח הַשַּׁבָּת וַיְקַדְּשֵׁהוּ׃
11 גבורה **כַּבֵּד** אֶת־אָבִיךָ וְאֶת־אִמֶּךָ לְמַעַן יַאֲרִכוּן יָמֶיךָ עַל הָאֲדָמָה
אֲשֶׁר־יְהֹוָה אדני אהדונהי אֱלֹהֶיךָ ילה נֹתֵן אבגיתץ, ושר, אהבת חנם לָךְ׃

כַּבֵּד

Exodus 20:11—Fifth Utterance (*Sefira* of *Gevurah*)

"Honor your father and your mother so that you may live long in the land that the Lord, your God, has given you."

There are certain people whose gifts to us we can never repay, and first and foremost among these are our parents who brought us into this world. We can never hope to repay them, but we can do our best to show our deep appreciation and respect. This inner appreciation is more important than any physical action we could undertake on their behalf.

12 You shall not murder. You shall not commit adultery. You shall not steal. You shall not give false testimony against your neighbor. 13 You shall not covet your neighbor's house. You shall not covet your neighbor's wife, or his manservant or maidservant, his ox or donkey, or anything that belongs to your neighbor."

לֹא תִּרְצַח

Exodus 20:12—Sixth Utterance (*Sefira* of *Tiferet*)

"You shall not murder."

This Utterance refers to more than just the physical act of killing, something few of us take part in. But for most of us, this Utterance refers to the assassination of another's character through our words or through any other form of humiliation or embarrassment.

> We have learned that the first Five Utterances IN THE RIGHT SIDE are all inclusive. In these Five Utterances the second Five OF THE LEFT are engraved, Five within Five. How? The First Utterance, "I am the Lord your God," (Exodus 20:2) corresponds to, "You shall not murder," for as we learned, these two are under one principle. For one who murders diminishes the image and likeness of his Master, because according to the scripture, "in the image of God made He man," (Genesis 9:6) and, "And upon the likeness of the throne was the likeness as the appearance of a man." (Ezekiel 1:26) Rav Chiya said: It is written, "Whoever sheds the blood of man, by man shall his blood be shed." (Genesis 9:6) He who sheds blood is considered as if he diminishes the Supernal Image and likeness Above, meaning that he does not diminish the image of the man BELOW, but another image, and this is the interpretation of the verse: "Whoever sheds the blood of man, by man shall his blood be shed." The damage he does by shedding blood reaches the Supernal Man. Why? ". . . for in the image of Elohim made He man." Therefore, they are interdependent, THE FIRST UTTERANCE DEPENDS ON "YOU SHALL NOT MURDER."
> — The Zohar, Yitro 28:490-491

לֹא תִּנְאָף

Exodus 20:12—Seventh Utterance (*Sefira* of *Netzach*)

"You shall not commit adultery."

This Utterance is very important because it refers to and includes all forms of trust. Trust must exist not just between a husband and wife, but also among friends and between us and God.

> "You shall have no other God beside Me," corresponds to, "You shall not commit adultery." THE ADULTERER is false to the Name of the Holy One, blessed be He, which is impressed upon man, a sin including many other sins and entailing corresponding punishments. He, who is unfaithful in this, is unfaithful towards the King, as it is written: "They have dealt treacherously against God, for they have begotten strange children," (Hosea 5:7) and, "You shall not bow down to them, nor serve them." One is the result of the other. THUS, "YOU SHALL HAVE NO OTHER GOD" IS CONNECTED WITH, "YOU SHALL NOT COMMIT ADULTERY."
> — The Zohar, Yitro 28:492

לֹא תִּגְנֹב

Exodus 20:12—Eighth Utterance (*Sefira* of *Hod*)

"You shall not steal."

Stealing can refer to the physical action of removing and secreting away something that rightfully belongs to another. But we also "steal" whenever we behave with entitlement, as if we deserve something that we do not in fact deserve.

If we take a physical object from another person, the Light of that object (which is what fulfills us), remains with the original possessor.

לֹא תַעֲנֶה בְרֵעֲךָ ^{יסוד} לֹא תִגְנֹב ^{הוד} לֹא תִנְאָף ^{נצח} לֹא תִרְצָח ^{תפארת} 12

רֵעֶךָ וְעַבְדּוֹ וַאֲמָתוֹ וְשׁוֹרוֹ וַחֲמֹרוֹ וְכֹל ^{יסי} אֲשֶׁר לְרֵעֶךָ:   לֹא תַחְמֹד ^{מלכות} בֵּית ^{בופ ראה} רֵעֶךָ לֹא־תַחְמֹד אֵשֶׁת 13   עֵד שָׁקֶר:

All we take is the physical item, not the energy that we desire of it. Moreover, a person who steals incurs a powerful judgment. Every year, the amount of sustenance and goods that will come to us is determined in the Upper Worlds. When we steal, we are forfeiting—through our own negativity—that which would have come to us anyway. We are also forfeiting the spiritual Light that would have come to us along with the material sustenance.

> "You shall not take the Name of the Lord your God in vain," corresponds to, "You shall not steal." A thief is inclined to swear falsely, because he who steals also lies, as it is written: "Whoever is partner with a thief is his own enemy, he hears the adjuration of witnesses, but discloses nothing." (Proverbs 29:24)
> — The Zohar, Yitro 28:493

לֹא־תַעֲנֶה

Exodus 20:12—Ninth Utterance (*Sefira* of *Yesod*)

"You shall not bear false witness against your neighbor."

Bearing false witness includes *lashon hara* (evil speech), that is, gossip and slander. The *Zohar* teaches that it is almost impossible to make adequate repentance for evil speech.

> "Remember the Sabbath day to keep it holy," corresponds to, "You shall not bear false witness against your neighbor," for as Rav Yosi said, "The Sabbath day is called 'a witness,' and man should bear testimony to the verse: 'in six days God made Heaven and Earth.'" And Shabbat comprises everything. Rav Yosi said that whoever bears false witness against his neighbor lies against the Shabbat, which is the true witness, and the verse, "You will show truth to Jacob," (Micah 7:20) refers

to the same motive which is expressed in the verse: "Wherefore the children of Israel shall keep the Shabbat." (Exodus 31:16) Therefore, whoever lies against the Shabbat lies against the whole Torah. Hence, they are interdependent. THUS, "REMEMBER" IS CONNECTED TO "YOU SHALL NOT BEAR FALSE WITNESS AGAINST YOUR NEIGHBOR."
> — The Zohar, Yitro 28:494

The *Zohar* also says:

> It is written, "You shall not bear false witness against your neighbor," (Exodus 20:13) and in the works of Creation, "And God said, 'Let us make man in our image,'" (Genesis 1:26) WHICH MEANS THAT you shall not bear false witness against whomever exists in the form of the King. When anyone bears false witness against his neighbor, it is as if he has given false witness against that which is Above.
> — The Zohar, Vayikra 25:188

לֹא תַחְמֹד

Exodus 20:13—Tenth Utterance (*Sefira* of *Malchut*)

"You shall not covet your neighbor's house."

When we covet what someone else has, we are in effect saying that God is acting wrongly toward us; that He is not giving us what we need or deserve. When we have this consciousness of lack, we ignore the fact that a precise balance exists in each person's particular spiritual situation. For example, someone with a perfect house may actually have an illness or problems with relationships. Each of us has advantages and disadvantages, and each of us has a particular path of our *tikkun*, or spiritual correction. When we leave our own path to pick and choose from others, we are going completely against God's desires.

SEVENTH READING - DAVID - MALCHUT

14 When the people saw the noises and lightning and the noise of the shofar and the mountain in smoke, they saw and trembled with fear and they stood at a distance.

15 They said to Moses, "Speak to us yourself and we will listen. But do not have God speak to us or we will die."

16 Moses said to the people, "Do not be afraid. God has come to test you, so that the fear of God will be with you to keep you from sinning."

17 The people remained at a distance, while Moses approached the thick darkness where God was.

MAFTIR

18 Then the Lord said to Moses, "Tell the Israelites this: 'You have seen that I have spoken to you from heaven: 19 Do not make any gods to be alongside Me; do not make for yourselves gods of silver or gods of gold.

20 Make an altar of earth for Me and sacrifice on it your burnt offerings and fellowship offerings, your sheep and goats and your cattle. Wherever I cause My Name to be mentioned, I will come to you and bless you.

The *Zohar* explains:

"Honor your father and your mother," corresponds to, "You shall not covet your neighbor's wife." According to the explanation of Rav Yitzchak, "Honor your father," refers to one's own father; for when a man who covets a woman and begets a child, the child will honor another who is not his own father. It is written: "Honor your father and your mother," and "You shall not covet your neighbor's wife." The second part OF THE FORMER is, "so that you may live long in the land the Lord, your God is giving you," MEANING that whatever is given to you shall be yours, and you shall not covet another. Assuredly, they are interdependent. THUS, "HONOR YOUR FATHER AND MOTHER" IS CONNECTED WITH "YOU SHALL NOT COVET."
— The Zohar, Yitro 28:495

רֹאִים אֶת־הַקּוֹלֹת

Exodus 20:14—All the people saw the voices.

We all know that we cannot "see" voices. The message here is that our five senses are limited. Our ears should see and our eyes should hear; we should have total and unlimited perception. But instead, our senses deceive us.

Rav Aba said: It is written, "And all the people perceived the thunderings (lit. 'saw the voices')." (Exodus 20:18) HE ASKS: WHY IS IT WRITTEN "see," rather than "hear?" AND HE ANSWERS that we have already learned that those voices were carved out upon the darkness, cloud and the fog, as visible as a body is. And they saw whatever it was they saw, and heard what they heard from within the darkness, cloud and fog.

SEVENTH READING - DAVID - MALCHUT

14 וְכָל־ יִלִי הָעָם֩ רֹאִים֙ אֶת־הַקּוֹלֹת֙ וְאֶת־הַלַּפִּידִ֔ם וְאֵת֙ קוֹל֙ ע"ב ס"ג ע"ה
הַשֹּׁפָ֔ר וְאֶת־הָהָ֖ר עָשֵׁ֑ן וַיַּ֣רְא אלף למד יהוה הָעָ֔ם וַיָּנֻ֕עוּ וַיַּֽעַמְד֖וּ מֵֽרָחֹֽק: שדי
15 וַיֹּֽאמְרוּ֙ אֶל־מֹשֶׁ֔ה מהע, אל שדי רָאה דַּבֵּר־ אַתָּ֥ה עִמָּ֖נוּ וְנִשְׁמָ֑עָה וְאַל־יְדַבֵּ֥ר
רָאה עִמָּ֛נוּ אֱלֹהִ֖ים מום, אהיה אדני ; ילה פֶּן־נָמֽוּת: 16 וַיֹּ֨אמֶר מֹשֶׁ֜ה מהע, אל שדי אֶל־
הָעָם֮ אַל־תִּירָאוּ֒ כִּ֗י לְבַֽעֲבוּר֙ נַסּ֣וֹת אֶתְכֶ֔ם בָּ֖א הָאֱלֹהִ֑ים מום, אהיה אדני ; ילה
וּבַֽעֲב֗וּר תִּֽהְיֶ֧ה יִרְאָת֛וֹ עַל־פְּנֵיכֶ֖ם לְבִלְתִּ֥י תֶחֱטָֽאוּ: 17 וַיַּֽעֲמֹ֥ד הָעָ֖ם מֵֽרָחֹ֑ק
שדי וּמֹשֶׁה֙ מהע, אל שדי נִגַּ֣שׁ אֶל־הָֽעֲרָפֶ֔ל אֲשֶׁר־שָׁ֖ם יהוה שדי הָֽאֱלֹהִֽים מום, אהיה אדני ; ילה:

MAFTIR

18 וַיֹּ֤אמֶר יְהֹוָה֙ ואדני ואהדונהי אֶל־מֹשֶׁ֔ה מהע, אל שדי כֹּ֥ה היי תֹאמַ֖ר אֶל־בְּנֵ֣י יִשְׂרָאֵ֑ל
אַתֶּ֣ם רְאִיתֶ֔ם כִּ֚י מִן־הַשָּׁמַ֔יִם יפ טל, יפ כוזו דִּבַּ֖רְתִּי רָאה עִמָּכֶֽם: 19 לֹ֥א תַֽעֲשׂ֖וּן
אִתִּ֑י אֱלֹ֤הֵי דמב, ילה כֶסֶף֙ וֵֽאלֹהֵ֣י דמב, ילה זָהָ֔ב לֹ֥א תַֽעֲשׂ֖וּ לָכֶֽם: 20 מִזְבַּ֣ח ח, נגד

And because they saw that sight they were illuminated with a Supernal Illumination and knew things beyond the understanding of all other generations to come.

Rav Elazar said: "And all the people see" means, as we have said that they saw all those wonderful things that no generation after will ever see, by means of the illumination of those voices. "... the voices..." has the same meaning as in the verse: "I saw God." (Isaiah 6:1) It is written: "God" preceded by the particle "ET," WHICH MEANS THAT HE SAW THE SHECHINAH WHICH IS CALLED 'ET.' In this verse too it is written: "And all the people see the voices," with the particle Et (lit. 'the'), TO INDICATE THAT THEY SAW THE SHECHINAH.
— The Zohar, Yitro 19:296, 298

מִזְבַּח

Exodus 20:20—We should create an altar for God.

We need a place inside us for the Light of the Creator. This is not a physical place, but rather a period of time that we devote to our spiritual connection. Whether it takes only half an hour each week or five minutes each day, it is important for us to create an inner space where we can connect with the Light of the Creator. This private time of connection with God is a place of refuge and peace to which we are always able to return.

21 If you make an altar of stones for Me, do not build it with dressed stones, for you will defile it if you use a tool on it.

22 And do not go up to my altar on steps, lest your nakedness be exposed on it.' "

HAFTARAH OF YITRO

Isaiah spoke about the Upper World. He was a prophet who could see only the spiritual dimension. His entire being was present in the 99 Percent Realm. In fact, for him there was no 1 Percent Illusionary Reality because his whole being was connected to the Upper World.   Through the

Isaiah 6:1 -6:13

6:1 In the year that King Uzziah died, I saw the Lord seated on a throne, high and exalted, and the train of his robe filled the temple.

2 Above Him were seraphs, each one with six wings: With two wings they covered their faces, with two wings they covered their feet, and with two wings they were flying.

3 And they were calling to one another: "Holy, holy, holy is the Lord of Hosts; the whole earth is full of His glory." 4 At the sound of their voices the doorposts and thresholds shook and the temple was filled with smoke.

5 "Woe to me!" I cried. "I am ruined! For I am a man of unclean lips, and I live among a people of unclean lips, and my eyes have seen the King, the Lord Almighty."

6 Then one of the seraphs flew to me with a live coal in his hand, which he had taken with tongs from the altar.

7 With it he touched my mouth and said, "See, this has touched your lips; your guilt is taken away and your sin atoned for."

8 Then I heard the voice of the Lord saying, "Whom shall I send? And who will go for us?" And I said, "Here am I. Send me!"

אֲדָמָה תַּעֲשֶׂה־לִּי וְזָבַחְתָּ עָלָיו אֶת־עֹלֹתֶיךָ וְאֶת־שְׁלָמֶיךָ אֶת־צֹאנְךָ

וְאֶת־בְּקָרֶךָ בְּכָל־הַמָּקוֹם אֲשֶׁר אַזְכִּיר אֶת־שְׁמִי

אָבוֹא אֵלֶיךָ וּבֵרַכְתִּיךָ: 21 וְאִם־מִזְבַּח אֲבָנִים

תַּעֲשֶׂה־לִּי לֹא־תִבְנֶה אֶתְהֶן גָּזִית כִּי חַרְבְּךָ הֵנַפְתָּ עָלֶיהָ וַתְּחַלְלֶהָ:

22 וְלֹא־תַעֲלֶה בְמַעֲלֹת עַל־מִזְבְּחִי אֲשֶׁר לֹא־תִגָּלֶה עֶרְוָתְךָ עָלָיו:

HAFTARAH OF YITRO

example of Isaiah, we realize that it is possible for each and every one of us to gain that total and complete connection to the Upper World as he did.

ישעיהו פרק ו

1 6 בִּשְׁנַת־מוֹת הַמֶּלֶךְ עֻזִּיָּהוּ וָאֶרְאֶה אֶת־אֲדֹנָי יֹשֵׁב עַל־כִּסֵּא

רָם וְנִשָּׂא וְשׁוּלָיו מְלֵאִים אֶת־הַהֵיכָל: 2 שְׂרָפִים

עֹמְדִים | מִמַּעַל לוֹ שֵׁשׁ כְּנָפַיִם שֵׁשׁ כְּנָפַיִם לְאֶחָד

בִּשְׁתַּיִם | יְכַסֶּה פָנָיו וּבִשְׁתַּיִם יְכַסֶּה רַגְלָיו וּבִשְׁתַּיִם יְעוֹפֵף: 3 וְקָרָא

זֶה אֶל־זֶה וְאָמַר קָדוֹשׁ | קָדוֹשׁ קָדוֹשׁ יְהֹוָה צְבָאוֹת

מְלֹא כָל־הָאָרֶץ כְּבוֹדוֹ: 4 וַיָּנֻעוּ אַמּוֹת הַסִּפִּים מִקּוֹל

הַקּוֹרֵא וְהַבַּיִת יִמָּלֵא עָשָׁן: 5 וָאֹמַר אוֹי־לִי כִי־נִדְמֵיתִי

כִּי אִישׁ טְמֵא־שְׂפָתַיִם אָנֹכִי וּבְתוֹךְ עַם־טְמֵא שְׂפָתַיִם

אָנֹכִי יוֹשֵׁב כִּי אֶת־הַמֶּלֶךְ יְהֹוָה צְבָאוֹת רָאוּ עֵינָי

6 וַיָּעָף אֵלַי אֶחָד מִן־הַשְּׂרָפִים וּבְיָדוֹ רִצְפָּה בְּמֶלְקַחַיִם

לָקַח מֵעַל הַמִּזְבֵּחַ: 7 וַיַּגַּע עַל־פִּי וַיֹּאמֶר הִנֵּה

⁹ He said, "Go and tell this people: 'Be ever hearing, but never understanding; be ever seeing, but never perceiving.'

¹⁰ Make the heart of this people calloused; make their ears dull and close their eyes. Otherwise they might see with their eyes, hear with their ears, understand with their hearts, and turn and be healed."

¹¹ Then I said, "For how long, Lord?" And He answered: "Until the cities lie ruined and without inhabitant, until the houses are left deserted and the fields ruined and ravaged, ¹² until the Lord has sent everyone far away and the land is utterly forsaken.

¹³ And though a tenth remains in the land, it will again be laid waste. But as the terebinth and oak leave stumps when they are cut down, so the holy seed will be the stump in the land."

זֶה עַל־שְׂפָתֶיךָ וְסָר עֲוֹנֶךָ וְחַטָּאתְךָ תְּכֻפָּר: נָגַע

8 וָאֶשְׁמַע אֶת־קוֹל אֲדֹנָי אֹמֵר אֶת־מִי אֶשְׁלַח וּמִי

יֵלֶךְ־לָנוּ וָאֹמַר הִנְנִי שְׁלָחֵנִי: 9 וַיֹּאמֶר לֵךְ וְאָמַרְתָּ

לָעָם הַזֶּה שִׁמְעוּ שָׁמוֹעַ וְאַל־תָּבִינוּ וּרְאוּ רָאוֹ וְאַל־תֵּדָעוּ: 10 הַשְׁמֵן

לֵב־הָעָם הַזֶּה וְאָזְנָיו הַכְבֵּד וְעֵינָיו הָשַׁע פֶּן־יִרְאֶה

בְעֵינָיו וּבְאָזְנָיו יִשְׁמָע וּלְבָבוֹ יָבִין וָשָׁב וְרָפָא לוֹ: 11 וָאֹמַר עַד־

מָתַי אֲדֹנָי וַיֹּאמֶר עַד אֲשֶׁר אִם־שָׁאוּ עָרִים מֵאֵין יוֹשֵׁב

וּבָתִּים מֵאֵין אָדָם וְהָאֲדָמָה תִּשָּׁאֶה שְׁמָמָה: 12 וְרִחַק

יְהוָה אֶת־הָאָדָם וְרַבָּה הָעֲזוּבָה בְּקֶרֶב הָאָרֶץ: 13 וְעוֹד בָּהּ עֲשִׂרִיָּה וְשָׁבָה וְהָיְתָה לְבָעֵר כָּאֵלָה וְכָאַלּוֹן אֲשֶׁר בְּשַׁלֶּכֶת מַצֶּבֶת בָּם זֶרַע קֹדֶשׁ מַצַּבְתָּהּ:

MISHPATIM

LESSON OF MISHPATIM
(Exodus 21:1-24:18)

Mishpatim and Shabbat Shekalim

The chapter of Mishpatim (which means "ordinances") teaches us about the laws of this world. We know that each story in the Bible reveals a deeper meaning than what is simply read and observable. In the chapter of Mishpatim, we see that there are laws that govern interactions between people. Moreover, each and every one of us has a personal law that governs our interactions with the Light of the Creator. Under this law, we know that there is a reason for everything. This helps us to understand that whatever happens to us at any given time is exactly what needs to happen at that moment. The Light of the Creator is only good and thereby can only do good. Though the reasons may not be apparent to us at the time, the events of our lives occur only because we deserve them and because they are designed to help us in our transformation, a transformation that results in a closer connection with the Light of the Creator, which is only good.

Instead of meeting every seemingly negative situation with the question: "How could God allow this to happen to me?" we can try to find in that circumstance the lesson that can take us to a higher spiritual level. In moments of distress, it is very hard to see the reason for our hardships, but we must always find within ourselves the strength to say, "For now I will accept this hardship, not knowing the reason for it, but trusting that God has sent it to me for my own good and that someday I will fully understand."

We learn here that our purpose in this world is to learn how to connect ourselves completely to the Holiness of God. Unfortunately, our Desire to Receive for the Self Alone distracts us from this goal. But in the Endless World, the Creator gave the Vessel His Light, along with the ability to be one with His Light—so each and every one of us has that the ability within us.

Rav Ashlag teaches that we all have "a Godly nature from Above." But inside of us is also a reactive side. Only by resisting this reactive part of our nature can we reveal the Light within and become like the Creator—the Cause rather than the Effect. This is what it means to connect ourselves to the Holiness of God—connecting to the proactive part of ourselves.

Rav Berg explains it with this example: IBM developed a chess-playing computer that defeated world champion Garry Kasparov in 1997. Deep Blue, as it was called, could review 200 million chess moves in a second.

Anything that is created receives its potential from its creator; therefore, it stands to reason that the creator must possess at least the same capacity and ability as the creation. Yet the programmers of Deep Blue could not see the millions of moves their creation could see. How can it be that the effect could be greater than the cause?

As Rav Berg explains, the computer works on what's called a binary numeral system, a base-2 number system that represents numeric values using two symbols, usually 0 and 1. Owing to its straightforward implementation in digital electronic circuitry using logic gates, the binary system is used internally by all modern computers. The Rav explains that if the human mind were always in a similar state, it would perform faster and greater than any computer because it is always in a state of restriction—switching back and forth between being 0 and being 1. But when we react, Satan puts a curtain over approximately 96 percent of our brain, leaving us to use only about 4 percent of our brain capacity.

Fulfillment in every sense depends on resisting the Desire to Receive for the Self Alone, the force that prevents us from receiving everything we need in our lives.

Participating in this reading and connecting with the essence of chapter of Mishpatim gives us the strength to break free of that desire. By ceasing to do those things that limit our access to the infinite intelligence of the Lightforce of God, we are able to allow more Light to enter our consciousness. Resistance allows us unrestricted access to the Light.

"If you lend money to any of My people..." (*Exodus 22:24*)

The precept of lending money originates from "Love your neighbor as you would yourself." The Midrash says that "if we lend and charge no interest, it is as though we have performed all the teaching of the Bible." Of this Midrash, Rav Chaim Ben Atar the (Ohr HaChaim 1696–1743) asked, "Why is it written as a question [using the word] 'if,' and not stated with certainty?"

When we see a man who is blessed with money and property, so much so that his life seems overabundant, we might ask why he has so much when others have nothing. Why does he deserve more than what Jacob the Patriarch asked for: "bread to eat and clothes to wear," (Genesis 28:20)?

The answer to this question is hinted at here. A man is not given riches so he can indulge in pleasure and waste. If he has more than he needs, then it does not really belong to him. It has been given to him to hold in escrow and is intended to be shared with other people. This is why it is said: "If you see that God has blessed you with more money than you need for yourself, know that this is not what you deserve, but rather what someone else needs."

A story that is told in the name of the Chafetz Chaim (Rav Israel Meir "HaCohen" Kagan, 1838–1933) tells of a wealthy man whose sons had died. In his grief, he went to a kabbalist for advice and enlightenment. The wise man said to him, "Create a charitable fund. Perhaps through your generosity toward other people, God will give you more children."

The man took this advice to heart, lending money to every needy person in the city. At the end of three years, he was given a son on the Shabbat of Mishpatim because of the goodness and generosity he had bestowed upon others. The man continued to be generous to the needy, and throughout the years, he had more sons. But then he grew weary. He came before his teacher and asked if he could appoint someone else to do this work. The sage listened and then agreed.

The next day, the man reappeared before the teacher. He said that something terrible had happened: In the middle of the night, one of his sons had choked to death. With all his might, he begged to again assume the responsibility of giving charity.

We see here that by sharing, we can remove the judgments that are set upon us. By failing to share, however, we have no power against the decrees that we have brought upon ourselves. The precept of "Love your neighbor" is not meant to be a nice and moral idea, but rather a concealed formula for living a fulfilled and chaos-free life. Living by this ideal to its fullest is what it means to live the whole Bible.

This story shows us how shortsighted we can be and how quickly we forget. The rich man felt the need to be generous as long as he was experiencing a lack. But when he received the blessing of children, he no longer felt the urgency to share. This Haftarah of Mishpatim emphasizes the same message. Jeremiah told the Israelites of Jerusalem that if they would only release all their slaves, the king of Babylon would not destroy them. And indeed, once they had released the slaves, the king of Babylon chose to wage war against Egypt instead.

So what did the Israelites do? They took back their slaves! This is the way we behave: It is our nature to "wake up" only when the sharp edge of the blade is piercing our flesh. A minute later— not a year or a month or even a week later—when things are set "right," we go back to our old ways as if nothing had happened. The lesson that we take away from this is that we don't really have the luxury to forget because it is we ourselves who bear responsibility for whatever happens to us next.

SYNOPSIS OF MISHPATIM

The word mishpatim literally means "laws and judgments." This chapter looks at actions and their effects in this physical world. The *Zohar* tells us that this chapter also refers to the process of reincarnation—making us aware that the insights here teach us not only about the law of Cause and Effect in the physical world but also about the impact of our actions in the spiritual dimension.

> *Rav Shimon opened with the words, "And these are the judgments which you shall set before them." (Exodus 21:1) ALSO IN THE ARAMAIC TRANSLATION, IT SPEAKS OF JUDGMENTS. These are the rules concerning reincarnation, NAMELY, the judgments of souls that INCARNATE AGAIN IN THIS WORLD to be sentenced each according to its punishable acts.*
> — The Zohar, Mishpatim 1:1

FIRST READING - ABRAHAM - CHESED

21:1 **T**"hese are the laws you are to set before them: ² 'If you buy a Hebrew servant, he is to serve you for six years. But in the seventh year, he shall be released free of charge. ³ If he comes alone, he is to go free alone; but if he has a wife, she is to go with him. ⁴ If his master gives him a wife and she bears him sons or daughters, the woman and her children shall belong to her master, and only the man shall go free.

⁵ But if the servant declares, "I love my master and my wife and children and do not want to go free," ⁶ then his master must present him before the Lord. He shall take him to the door or the doorpost and pierce his ear with an awl. Then he will be his servant forever.

⁷ If a man sells his daughter as a maidservant, she is not to go free as menservants do. ⁸ If she is bad in the eyes of her master who has selected her for himself, he must let her be redeemed. He has no right to sell her to foreigners, because he has broken faith with her.

FROM THE RAV

We are all born into the playing field of Satan, and as long as we are in his game, we have to play by his rules. Rav Ashlag tells us that God, in His infinite compassion for His creatures, understood that we would have no chance to get out of this playing field of Satan, so He provided us with a tool—our soul.

The chapter of Mishpatim (with all its different abstruse segments about slaves and oxen) is usually thought to concern slavery. However, it's really about reincarnation. It is about moving from one lifetime to the next, about all the baggage that we accumulate from each lifetime, and about what we must do to free ourselves from that baggage.

There are rules as to how to defeat Satan at his game. Rav Isaac Luria (the Ari) says that these rules embrace one basic principal: If you cannot connect with at least one prior lifetime, you are not connected to the Light of the Creator. Many of us have gone through hundreds

of lifetimes, but if we cannot connect back to at least one prior lifetime, or get it—we will be forever imprisoned in Satan's game plan, with no hope of getting out.

Once we can identify with a prior lifetime or lifetimes, all our idiosyncrasies in this lifetime will start to make sense, and we then can choose to hold onto them or release them.

Exodus 21:2—Male slaves.

Slavery in its literal physical form exists today in only a few countries, yet slavery of consciousness—slavery to chaos, to our egos, to our lifestyles, to our fears, to our limited thinking—exists in each and every one of us. We are enslaved by anything that prevents growth and positive change. "Male slave" is a code that brings awareness to whatever is blocking us from being a channel of Light. The *Zohar* gives a deeper explanation:

"If you buy a Hebrew servant, six years he shall serve, and in the seventh he shall go

FIRST READING - ABRAHAM - CHESED

21 1 וְאֵ֗לֶּה מ״ב הַמִּשְׁפָּטִ֔ים אֲשֶׁ֥ר תָּשִׂ֖ים לִפְנֵיהֶֽם: 2 כִּ֤י תִקְנֶה֙ ג״פ אלף למד

עֶ֣בֶד עִבְרִ֔י עֵ֚שׁ שָׁנִ֣ים יַעֲבֹ֔ד וּבַ֨שְּׁבִעִ֔ת יֵצֵ֥א לַֽחָפְשִׁ֖י חִנָּֽם: 3 אִם־

בְּגַפּ֥וֹ יָבֹ֖א בְּגַפּ֣וֹ יֵצֵ֑א אִם־ יוהך, ע״ה מ״ב, ע״ה ר״ת אביב בַּ֤עַל אִשָּׁה֙ ה֔וּא

וְיָצְאָ֥ה אִשְׁתּ֖וֹ עִמּֽוֹ: 4 אִם־ יוהך, ע״ה מ״ב אֲדֹנָיו֙ יִתֶּן־ ל֣וֹ אִשָּׁ֔ה וְיָֽלְדָה־ לּ֤וֹ

בָנִים֙ א֣וֹ בָנ֔וֹת הָֽאִשָּׁ֣ה וִֽילָדֶ֔יהָ תִּֽהְיֶה֙ לַֽאדֹנֶ֔יהָ וְה֖וּא יֵצֵ֥א בְגַפּֽוֹ: 5 וְאִם־

יוהך, ע״ה מ״ב אָמֹ֤ר יֹאמַר֙ הָעֶ֔בֶד אָהַ֨בְתִּי֙ אֶת־ אֲדֹנִ֔י אֶת־ אִשְׁתִּ֖י וְאֶת־ בָּנָ֑י

לֹ֥א אֵצֵ֖א חָפְשִֽׁי: 6 וְהִגִּישׁ֤וֹ אֲדֹנָיו֙ אֶל־ הָ֣אֱלֹהִ֔ים מום, אהיה אדני; ילה וְהִגִּישׁוֹ֙

אֶל־ הַדֶּ֔לֶת א֖וֹ אֶל־ הַמְּזוּזָ֑ה אדני, ללה וְרָצַ֨ע אֲדֹנָ֤יו אֶת־ אָזְנוֹ֙ בַּמַּרְצֵ֔עַ

וַעֲבָד֖וֹ לְעֹלָֽם: 7 וְכִֽי־ יִמְכֹּ֥ר אִ֛ישׁ ע״ה קנ״א קס״א אֶת־ בִּתּ֖וֹ ריבוע ס״ג + י׳ אותיות

לְאָמָ֑ה דמב, מלוי ע״ב לֹ֥א תֵצֵ֖א כְּצֵ֥את הָעֲבָדִֽים: 8 אִם־ יוהך, ע״ה מ״ב רָעָ֞ה

לְאָמָה

Exodus 21:7—Female slaves.

The verse concerns the female slave. Unlike the male energy of channeling Light, female energy is receiving. This verse refers to the nature of the Vessel. "Female slave" is a code for the mindset that blocks us from receiving Light. A small Vessel is content and desires nothing more. However, our desire for more Light allows us to receive more from the Creator. For this, we need a large Vessel. If we don't desire growth, then we are slaves to complacency. We should always want more from life, but we also need to make very sure that our Vessel is large enough and strong enough to receive more. This verse helps us to remove the limitations on our desires so we can expand our Vessel and receive infinite Light.

Rav Brandwein writes:

Concerning Vessels and Lights; these are two distinct matters and one cannot ever interfere with the borders of the other. This is like the soul and the body where the soul is the Light and the body is the Vessel. Desire is the name given to the Vessel and not to the Light, be it the Desire to Share which is the Vessel for sharing or the Desire to Receive which is the Vessel for receiving. And it is forbidden to touch upon the Light without fear and to play around with Light and to determine that the essence of expanding Light is to be a Desire to Share.

— Letters of Rav Brandwein

⁹ If he selects her for his son, he must grant her the rights of a daughter. ¹⁰ If he marries another woman, he must not deprive the first one of her food, clothing and marital rights.

¹¹ If he does not provide her with these three things, she is to go free, without money. ¹² Anyone who strikes a man and kills him shall surely be put to death.

¹³ However, if he does not do it intentionally, but God lets it happen, I will designate a place for him to flee there.

¹⁴ But if a man schemes and kills another man deliberately, take him away from my altar and put him to death. ¹⁵ Anyone who strikes his father or his mother must surely be put to death.

¹⁶ Anyone who kidnaps another and either sells him or still has him when he is caught must surely be put to death. ¹⁷ Anyone who curses his father or mother must surely be put to death.

¹⁸ If men quarrel and one hits the other with a stone or with his fist and he does not die but is confined to bed, ¹⁹ the one who struck the blow will not be held responsible if the other gets up and walks around outside with his staff; however, he must pay the injured man for the loss of his time and see that he is completely healed.

מַכֵּה אִישׁ וָמֵת

Exodus 21:12—Killing someone by accident.

This section discusses an accidental killing. But according to the *Zohar* there are no accidents, a person who dies seemingly by accident was a murderer in a past life. We are responsible for all of our actions, even those from past incarnations. Every action has a consequence that transcends space and time. The Ari speaks about this concept:

Let us now examine the subject of the negative precepts. There are negative precepts that simple repentance and Yom Kippur atone for, while others require suffering in addition to atonement. But there are also serious transgressions, such as those for which one's soul is cut off from the Light, and those that warrant the four forms of capital punishment—the kind of sins that are atoned for until death. They have different categories. There is the kind of transgression that causes the body to disintegrate, so that it cannot rise

at the Resurrection of the Dead—referred to by the sages as, 'those who do not have a share in the World to Come, the apostates and heretics, and so on.' Such a soul will incarnate to correct the sin, while the first body disintegrates and perishes. If it does not belong to this category then the first body is not lost, but still the soul incarnates in another body, joined by a spark from the root which entered it. The incarnated soul being corrected there is considered a guest rather than the landlord.

—Writngs of the Ari, Gate of Reincarnation, 11ᵗʰ Introduction, 19

וּמַכֵּה אָבִיו וְאִמּוֹ

Exodus 21:15—Hitting one's parents

This verse describes a person who physically hits his parents. Our parents are the seed that brought us into this world, and we must have an appreciation for them, no matter what our story and regardless of what kind of people they might

רהע בְּעֵינֵי רִבוּעַ מ״ה אֲדֹנֶיהָ אֲשֶׁר־לֹא (כתיב: לֹא) יְעָדָהּ וְהֶפְדָּהּ לְעַם נָכְרִי

לֹא־יִמְשֹׁל לְמָכְרָהּ בְּבִגְדוֹ־בָהּ: 9 וְאִם יוהך, ע״ה מ״ב ־לִבְנוֹ יִיעָדֶנָּה

כְּמִשְׁפַּט ע״ה ה״פ אלהים הַבָּנוֹת יַעֲשֶׂה־לָּהּ: 10 אִם יוהך, ע״ה מ״ב ־אַחֶרֶת

יִקַּח וחם ־לוֹ שְׁאֵרָהּ כְּסוּתָהּ וְעֹנָתָהּ לֹא יִגְרָע: 11 וְאִם יוהך, ע״ה מ״ב ־

שְׁלָשׁ־אֵלֶּה לֹא יַעֲשֶׂה לָהּ וְיָצְאָה חִנָּם אֵין כָּסֶף: 12

מַכֵּה אִישׁ | י״פ רבוע אהיה ע״ה קנ״א קס״א וָמֵת מוֹת יוּמָת: 13 וַאֲשֶׁר לֹא

צָדָה וְהָאֱלֹהִים מום, אהיה אדני ; ילה אִנָּה לְיָדוֹ וְשַׂמְתִּי לְךָ ר״ת אלול מָקוֹם

יהוה ברבוע, ו״פ אל אֲשֶׁר יָנוּס שָׁמָּה מהע, משה, אל עדי: 14 וְכִי־יָזִד אִישׁ

ע״ה קנ״א קס״א עַל־רֵעֵהוּ לְהָרְגוֹ בְעָרְמָה מֵעִם עּמם מִזְבְּחִי תִּקָּחֶנּוּ לָמוּת:

15 וּמַכֵּה אָבִיו וְאִמּוֹ מוֹת יוּמָת: 16 | וְגֹנֵב אִישׁ | ע״ה קנ״א קס״א וּמְכָרוֹ

וְנִמְצָא בְיָדוֹ מוֹת יוּמָת: 17 וּמְקַלֵּל אָבִיו וְאִמּוֹ מוֹת יוּמָת: 18 וְכִי־

יְרִיבֻן אֲנָשִׁים | וְהִכָּה אִישׁ־ ע״ה קנ״א קס״א אֶת־רֵעֵהוּ בְּאֶבֶן יוד הה ואו הה אוֹ

---

be. It is not necessary that we have a perfect relationship with them, but at the very least, we need to be at peace with them and show our respect for the fact that they created us.

וְגֹנֵב אִישׁ

Exodus 21:16—Kidnapping.

Abducting a person is not the only form of kidnapping. Any time we take over or try to control someone else's life, we are taking a hostage. We must always remember that the stories of the Bible require more than a literal interpretation. The *Zohar* teaches that there is always a larger lesson to be learned.

וּמְקַלֵּל אָבִיו וְאִמּוֹ

Exodus 21:17—Cursing one's parents.

"And he that curses his father, or his mother, shall surely be put to death." Strangely, we often cause

pain to those who have given us more than we deserve. This concept describes the kabbalistic principle of Bread of Shame. We reincarnate to correct Bread of Shame. Fulfillment and shame cannot co-exist; therefore, we cannot achieve our birthright of complete joy if we are experiencing, or have caused someone else shame. There are many people in our lives for whom we may feel hatred despite—or perhaps because of—the fact that they have done something helpful for us. This reading helps to balance this condition so that we will know when to receive but not be greedy and when to share but not enable.

וְהִכָּה

Exodus 21:18—Physically hurting others for no reason.

Here baseless hatred is addressed. By discussing people who physically strike one another, this section reveals that all the chaos in this world begins with people who feel hatred for each other.

SECOND READING - ISAAC - GEVURAH

[20] *If a man beats his male or female slave with a rod and the slave dies as a direct result, he must be punished,* [21] *but he is not to be punished if the slave gets up after a day or two, since the slave is his property.*

[22] *If men who are fighting hit a pregnant woman and she gives birth prematurely but there is no serious injury, the offender must be fined whatever the woman's husband demands and the court allows.*

[23] *But if there is serious injury, you are to take life for life,* [24] *an eye for eye, tooth for tooth, hand for hand, foot for foot,* [25] *burn for burn, wound for wound, bruise for bruise.*

The *Zohar* shows how hatred has existed since the earliest days of humanity:

> Rav Loytes Choza'ah opened with "And I will bring enmity between you and the woman; and between your seed and her seed...." (Genesis 3:15) There has been a great deal of hatred ever since the world was created, from the time when it was cursed due to the enticement of the Serpent. He, THE SERPENT, was cast out, away from the gate of the King, and he always sneaks between the 'fences of the world.' IN OTHER WORDS finding a breach in these 'fences' (or 'restrictions') of the Torah. For all those who 'step over these fences with their heels,' MEANING THAT THEY DO NOT TAKE PRECAUTIONS WITH THEM, the Serpent shall bite them!
> — The Zohar, Eichah 13

וְרַפֹּא יְרַפֵּא

Exodus 21:19—"...and shall cause him to be thoroughly healed."

Doctors assist the Light of the Creator in the healing process, but doctors are simply channels and messengers of God. The *Talmud* teaches that doctors who believe that they are the source of the healing may experience the process of hell. A doctor who understands that he or she cannot heal but can only channel healing from the Source of the healing, which is the Lightforce

of the Creator, is a true doctor. The *Zohar* speaks about the way that healing is granted to the whole world:

> And so it is that all mortals are parts of the one body. When God wishes to grant healing to the world, He inflicts diseases and pestilence on one righteous man from among them, and, for his sake, gives healing to everyone. Where do we learn this from? From the verse: "But he was wounded because of our transgressions... and by his injury we are healed" (Isaiah 53:5). "And by his injury" refers to the letting of blood, as one who lets blood from the arm, for in that injury "we are healed," that is to say, we, the parts of the whole body, find healing.
> ---The Zohar, Pinchas 15:110, 32:178

And from the *Zohar* section on the *Book of the Physician Kartana* we read:

> THIS IS WHAT HE WROTE IN THAT BOOK (THE WORDS OF THE PHYSICIAN KARTANA): when a wise physician visited a sick man, "He found him in a desert land, and in the waste howling wilderness," that is, since illnesses rest on him, he is placed in the King's jail, IN A WASTE WILDERNESS. You may say that since the Holy One, blessed be He, ordered to detain him in jail, one must not try for his sake TO CAUSE HIM TO REPENT. This is not so, as King David

בְּאֶגְרֹף וְלֹא יָמוּת וְנָפַל לְמִשְׁכָּב: 19 אִם יוהך, ע״ה מ״ב יָקוּם וְהִתְהַלֵּךְ

בַּחוּץ עַל־מִשְׁעַנְתּוֹ וְנִקָּה קס״א הַמַּכֶּה רַק שִׁבְתּוֹ יִתֵּן וְרַפֹּא יְרַפֵּא :

SECOND READING - ISAAC - GEVURAH

20 וְכִי־יַכֶּה אִישׁ ע״ה קנ״א קס״א אֶת־עַבְדּוֹ אוֹ אֶת־אֲמָתוֹ בַּשֵּׁבֶט וּמֵת

תַּחַת יָדוֹ נָקֹם יִנָּקֵם מנק: 21 אַךְ אהיה אִם יוהך, ע״ה מ״ב יוֹם י״פ רבוע אהיה

אוֹ יוֹמַיִם יַעֲמֹד לֹא יֻקַּם ר״ת יתרו, קין, מצרי כִּי כַסְפּוֹ הוּא: ע״ה = נגד, זן, מזבח

22 וְכִי־יִנָּצוּ אֲנָשִׁים וְנָגְפוּ אִשָּׁה הָרָה וְיָצְאוּ יְלָדֶיהָ וְלֹא יִהְיֶה יי אָסוֹן

עָנוֹשׁ יֵעָנֵשׁ כַּאֲשֶׁר יָשִׁית עָלָיו בַּעַל הָאִשָּׁה וְנָתַן אב״ג ית״ץ, ושר, אהבת חינם

---

said, "Blessed is he who considers the poor...." (Psalms 41:2) That SICK MAN who lies on his bed is poor. If HIS NEIGHBOR is a wise physician, the Holy One, blessed be He, blessed whoever strives for His sake. HE EXPLAINS HIS WORDS, that physician "found him in a desert land," namely lying on his sickbed; "and in the waste howling wilderness," beset by illnesses. What should he do? "he led him about" (Deuteronomy 32:10), to bring about reasons AND EXCUSES to withhold from him what is harmful to him, to let HIS BLOOD, and take out of him the evil blood; "he instructed him" - he should observe and understand the origin of the disease, and make sure the disease will not spread but diminish. Then, "he kept him as the apple of his eye" (Ibid.), so that he will be properly kept in regard to the drinks and the medicines he needs, and not get confused between them. For if he confuses even one thing AND DIES, the Holy One, blessed be He, considers that doctor as if he shed blood and killed him. For the Holy One, blessed be He, wishes it that though that person is in the King's prison and is imprisoned there, UNABLE TO FREE HIMSELF, someone will make an effort for him and help him get out of jail. And he used to say: The Holy

One, blessed be He above sentences the people in the world either to death, to be uprooted from the root BOTH ONE AND ONE'S CHILDREN, to be punished in property, or to be put in jail.

Whoever is sentenced to a punishment regarding his property falls ill and is not healed until he pays whatever he was sentenced to. After being punished in his money and having given whatever he was sentenced to, he is healed and leaves prison. This is why one must persuade him to serve his penalty and leave prison. Whoever is sentenced to uprooting, he is seized and put in prison until he is uprooted in every sense, THAT IS, UNTIL HE AND HIS CHILDREN DIE. Sometimes he is uprooted in limbs or in one of them. Whoever is sentenced to death, it so happens THAT HE DIES. And even if he gives as ransom all the money in the world, he cannot be saved. A wise physician is therefore needed to make efforts for him. If he can administer bodily medicine, it is well. Otherwise, he should give him healing for his soul, and strive for healing for the soul. The Holy One, blessed be He, will strive TO BLESS such a physician in this world and in the World to Come.
-- The Zohar, Ha'azinu 60:249-253

²⁶ *If a man hits a manservant or maidservant in the eye and destroys it, he must let the servant go free to compensate for the eye.* ²⁷ *And if he knocks out the tooth of a manservant or maidservant, he must let the servant go free to compensate for the tooth.*²⁸ *If a bull gores a man or a woman to death, the bull must surely be stoned to death, and its meat must not be eaten. But the owner of the bull will not be held responsible.*

²⁹ *If, however, the bull has gored before and the owner has been warned but has not kept it penned up and it kills a man or woman, the bull must be stoned and the owner also must be put to death.*

³⁰ *However, if payment is demanded of him, he may redeem his life by paying whatever is demanded.* ³¹ *This law also applies if the bull gores a son or daughter.* ³² *If the bull gores a male or female slave, the owner must pay thirty shekels of silver to the master of the slave, and the bull must be stoned.*

³³ *If a man uncovers a pit or digs a pit and fails to cover it and an ox or a donkey falls into it,* ³⁴ *the owner of the pit must pay for the loss; he must pay its owner, and the dead animal will be his.*

שׁוֹר

Exodus 21:28—Oxen.

This section speaks about the restitution that is made when someone's ox gores another person or another ox. Today, many of us don't own livestock. So what can we possibly learn from this? The Bible was never intended to be accepted at face value. The *Zohar* decodes the reading and reveals its true meaning. This is a lesson about the battle between good and evil. Circumcision—a technology for removing negativity and death, which is not just a tradition followed by those of the Jewish faith—is mentioned here as a clue to the deeper message. The ox that gores another ox teaches us about the layers of our negativity that we need to shed. Some layers are more difficult to peel away than others, but the greater the difficulty the greater the reward.

An ox indicates Gevurah, and there are many Gevurot, as in, "Who can utter the mighty acts (Heb. Gevurot) of God." (Psalms 106:2) They are included in three—Gevurah, Hod and Malchut—from which all the Gevurot are drawn. There are three primary causes of injury in the ox: the horn, the tooth and the foot, the initial letters of which are 'lie,' (in Hebrew) *because they are below in the Klipot.*
— *Writings of the Ari, Torah Compilations 5*

And the *Zohar* says:

Arise, Faithful Shepherd, to arrange the Judgments regarding the laws of damage in the order of the name Yud, Hei, Vav and Hei, being: "The chariot of Elohim are twice ten thousand, thousands upon thousands (lit. "shin'an'")," (Psalms 68:18) that is, the ox, eagle, lion and man. From the right side where there is Yud, Hei, Vav and Hei, such is the order of the four living creatures: man, lion, eagle, ox, MEANING THAT OX, BEING GEVURAH, IS LISTED LAST, and according to the changes that take place in them, so is their movement and order. The animals on the Other Side are the caves of injuries on the left, "shin'an" ("thousand," also: "angel"), MEANING THE INITIALS OF OX, EAGLE, LION, MAN. Hence it starts with ox, which is connected with the four primary causes of injury: the ox, the pit, crop destroying beast, and fire. Their last one is man, WHO IS ALWAYS prone to harm.
—*The Zohar, Mishpatim 15:445*

בִּפְלִלִֽים: 23 וְאִם אָסֽוֹן יִהְיֶ֑ה וְנָתַתָּ֥ה נֶ֖פֶשׁ תַּ֥חַת נָֽפֶשׁ:

24 עַ֚יִן תַּ֣חַת עַ֔יִן שֵׁ֖ן תַּ֣חַת שֵׁ֑ן יָ֚ד תַּ֣חַת יָ֔ד רֶ֖גֶל תַּ֥חַת רָֽגֶל: 25 כְּוִיָּה֙ תַּ֣חַת כְּוִיָּ֔ה פֶּ֖צַע תַּ֣חַת פָּ֑צַע חַבּוּרָ֕ה תַּ֖חַת חַבּוּרָֽה: 26 וְכִֽי־יַכֶּ֨ה אִ֜ישׁ אֶת־עֵ֥ין עַבְדּ֛וֹ אֽוֹ־אֶת־עֵ֥ין אֲמָת֖וֹ וְשִֽׁחֲתָ֑הּ לַֽחָפְשִׁ֥י יְשַׁלְּחֶ֖נּוּ תַּ֥חַת עֵינֽוֹ: 27 וְאִם־שֵׁ֥ן עַבְדּ֛וֹ אֽוֹ־שֵׁ֥ן אֲמָת֖וֹ יַפִּ֑יל לַֽחָפְשִׁ֥י יְשַׁלְּחֶ֖נּוּ תַּ֥חַת שִׁנּֽוֹ:

28 וְכִֽי־יִגַּ֨ח שׁ֜וֹר אֶת־אִ֣ישׁ א֤וֹ אֶת־אִשָּׁה֙ וָמֵ֔ת סָק֤וֹל יִסָּקֵל֙ הַשּׁ֔וֹר וְלֹ֥א יֵֽאָכֵל֙ אֶת־בְּשָׂר֔וֹ וּבַ֥עַל הַשּׁ֖וֹר נָקִֽי: 29 וְאִ֡ם שׁוֹר֩ נַגָּ֨ח ה֜וּא מִתְּמֹ֣ל שִׁלְשֹׁ֗ם וְהוּעַ֤ד בִּבְעָלָיו֙ וְלֹ֣א יִשְׁמְרֶ֔נּוּ וְהֵמִ֥ית אִ֖ישׁ א֣וֹ אִשָּׁ֑ה הַשּׁוֹר֙ יִסָּקֵ֔ל וְגַם־בְּעָלָ֖יו יוּמָֽת: 30 אִם־כֹּ֖פֶר יוּשַׁ֣ת עָלָ֑יו וְנָתַן֙ פִּדְיֹ֣ן נַפְשׁ֔וֹ כְּכֹ֥ל אֲשֶׁר־יוּשַׁ֖ת עָלָֽיו: 31 אוֹ־בֵ֥ן יִגָּ֖ח אוֹ־בַ֣ת יִגָּ֑ח כַּמִּשְׁפָּ֥ט הַזֶּ֖ה יֵעָ֥שֶׂה לּֽוֹ: 32 אִם־עֶ֛בֶד יִגַּ֥ח הַשּׁ֖וֹר א֣וֹ אָמָ֑ה כֶּ֣סֶף ׀ שְׁלֹשִׁ֣ים שְׁקָלִ֗ים יִתֵּן֙ לַֽאדֹנָ֔יו וְהַשּׁ֖וֹר יִסָּקֵֽל: 33 וְכִֽי־יִפְתַּ֨ח אִ֜ישׁ בּ֗וֹר א֠וֹ כִּֽי־יִכְרֶ֥ה אִ֛ישׁ בֹּ֖ר וְלֹ֣א יְכַסֶּ֑נּוּ וְנָֽפַל־שָׁ֥מָּה שּׁ֖וֹר א֥וֹ חֲמֽוֹר: 34 בַּ֤עַל הַבּוֹר֙ יְשַׁלֵּ֔ם כֶּ֖סֶף יָשִׁ֣יב לִבְעָלָ֑יו וְהַמֵּ֖ת יִֽהְיֶה־לּֽוֹ: 35 וְכִֽי־יִגֹּ֧ף שֽׁוֹר־אִ֛ישׁ אֶת־שׁ֥וֹר רֵעֵ֖הוּ וָמֵ֑ת וּמָ֨כְרוּ אֶת־הַשּׁ֤וֹר הַחַי֙ וְחָצ֣וּ אֶת־כַּסְפּ֔וֹ וְגַ֥ם אֶת־הַמֵּ֖ת יֶֽחֱצֽוּן: 36 א֣וֹ נוֹדַ֗ע כִּ֠י שׁ֥וֹר

35 If a man's bull injures the bull of another and it dies, they are to sell the live one and divide both the money and the dead animal equally.

36 However, if it was known that the bull had gored yesterday or the day before, yet the owner did not keep it penned up, the owner must pay, ox for ox, and the dead animal will be his. 37 If a man steals an ox or a sheep and slaughters it or sells it, he must pay back five head of cattle for the ox and four sheep for the sheep.

22:1 If a thief is caught breaking in and is struck so that he dies, the defender is not guilty of bloodshed; 2 but if it happens after sunrise, he is guilty of bloodshed. A thief must certainly make restitution, but if he has nothing, he must be sold to pay for his theft. 3 If the stolen animal is found alive in his possession—whether ox or donkey or sheep—he must pay back double.

THIRD READING - JACOB - TIFERET

4 If a man grazes his livestock in a field or vineyard and lets them stray and they graze in another man's field, he must make restitution from the best of his own field or the best of his own vineyard. 5 If a fire breaks out and spreads into thorn bushes so that it burns shocks of grain or standing grain or the whole field, the one who started the fire must make restitution.

6 If a man gives his neighbor silver or goods for safekeeping and they are stolen from the neighbor's house, if the thief is caught, he must pay back double.

Exodus 21:37—Stealing.

This section talks about various kinds of thievery. Every year at the time of Rosh Hashanah, we are judged. It is then determined and sealed how much money we will earn in the coming year. This quantity is a manifestation of the law of Cause and Effect. When a man steals, he is challenging the Laws of the Universe, in effect saying to the Creator, "Take me out of your system." Imagine a person who decides that the law of gravity does not apply to him and jumps from a tenth floor window! The system does require us to believe in it. Simply speaking, we benefit when we live by the rules, and we subject ourselves to chaos if we don't.

The *Zohar* tells how Moses, as the good shepherd of his flock, led his people away from thievery.

"And Moses kept the flock of Jethro, his father in law, the priest of Midian." (Exodus 3:1) Rav Chiya opened the discussion saying, "A Psalm of David, the Lord is my shepherd; I shall not want." (Psalms 23:1) "The Lord is my shepherd" means "the shepherd of mine." In the same way, a shepherd leads his sheep and brings them to a good pasture, to a fertile pasture, to a place where a stream of water [flows]. He makes straight their path with righteousness and justice; also, of God it is written: "He makes me to lie down in green pastures, He leads me beside the still waters. He restores

נֶגְחֹ הוּא מִתְּמוֹל שִׁלְשֹׁם וְלֹא יִשְׁמְרֶנּוּ בְּעָלָיו שַׁלֵּם בּ״פ רבוע ע״ב יְשַׁלֵּם

שׁוֹר אבגית׳, ועיר, אהבת חנם תַּחַת הַשּׁוֹר אבגית׳, ועיר, אהבת חנם וְהַמֵּת י״פ רבוע אהיה יִהְיֶה

י׳ לּוֹ: 37 כִּי יִגְנֹב ־אִישׁ ע״ה קנ״א קס״א שׁוֹר אבגית׳, ועיר, אהבת חנם אוֹ־שֶׂה

וּטְבָחוֹ אוֹ מְכָרוֹ וַחֲמִשָּׁה בָקָר יְשַׁלֵּם תַּחַת הַשּׁוֹר אבגית׳, ועיר, אהבת חנם

וְאַרְבַּע־צֹאן מלוי אהיה דיודין ע״ה תַּחַת הַשֶּׂה: 22 1 אִם יוהך, ע״ה מ״ב ־בַּמַּחְתֶּרֶת

יִמָּצֵא הַגַּנָּב וְהֻכָּה וָמֵת י״פ רבוע אהיה אֵין לוֹ דָּמִים: 2 אִם יוהך, ע״ה מ״ב ־זָרְחָה

הַשֶּׁמֶשׁ ב״פ שׂד עָלָיו דָּמִים לוֹ שַׁלֵּם ב״פ רבוע ע״ב יְשַׁלֵּם אִם יוהך, ע״ה מ״ב ־אֵין

לוֹ וְנִמְכַּר בִּגְנֵבָתוֹ: 3 אִם יוהך, ע״ה מ״ב ־הִמָּצֵא תִמָּצֵא בְיָדוֹ הַגְּנֵבָה מִשּׁוֹר

אבגית׳, ועיר, אהבת חנם עַד־חֲמוֹר עַד־שֶׂה חַיִּים בינה ע״ה שְׁנַיִם יְשַׁלֵּם:

THIRD READING - JACOB - TIFERET

4 כִּי יַבְעֶר ־אִישׁ ע״ה קנ״א קס״א שָׂדֶה אוֹ־כֶרֶם הויות ׳ וְשִׁלַּח אֶת־בְּעִירֹה

וּבִעֵר בִּשְׂדֵה אַחֵר מֵיטַב שָׂדֵהוּ וּמֵיטַב כַּרְמוֹ יְשַׁלֵּם: 5 כִּי־תֵצֵא אֵשׁ

אלהים דיודין ע״ה וּמָצְאָה קֹצִים וְנֶאֱכַל גָּדִישׁ אוֹ הַקָּמָה אוֹ הַשָּׂדֶה שׂד׳ שַׁלֵּם

ב״פ רבוע ע״ב יְשַׁלֵּם הַמַּבְעִר אֶת־הַבְּעֵרָה: 6 כִּי־יִתֵּן אִישׁ ע״ה קנ״א קס״א אֶל־

רֵעֵהוּ כֶּסֶף אוֹ־כֵלִים כלי לִשְׁמֹר וְגֻנַּב מִבֵּית ב״פ ראה הָאִישׁ ז״פ אדם אִם

---

my soul." Rav Yosi said, "The way of the shepherd is to lead his flock with righteousness, to distance them from stealing, to lead them in the pasture. And at all times the rod is in his hand so that they do not turn off, [neither] to the right nor the left."

— The Zohar, Shemot 54:371-372

יַבְעֶר

Exodus 22:4—Here we read about a fire that consumes grain and the judgment against the one who started the fire.

Once again, the Bible reinforces the lesson that there is a consequence to everything we do. If we start a fire and it burns someone else's property or hurts another person in any way, we are responsible, and the effect is inevitable. The next few sections all deal with actions and their consequences as well as with the concept of responsibility.

Acts that Manipulate the Laws of the Universe

The following sections discuss other acts that manipulate the Laws of the Universe and are therefore not permissible or recommended.

⁷ But if the thief is not found, the owner of the house must appear before the Lord to determine whether he has laid his hands on the other man's property.

⁸ In all cases of illegal possession of an ox, a donkey, a sheep, a garment, or any other lost property about which somebody says, 'This is mine,' both parties are to bring their cases before the Lord. The one whom the Lord declares guilty must pay back double to his neighbor.

⁹ If a man gives a donkey, an ox, a sheep or any other animal to his neighbor for safekeeping and it dies or is injured or is taken away while no one is looking, ¹⁰ an oath before the Lord shall be taken between them that the neighbor did not lay hands on the other person's property. The owner is to accept this, without restitution.

¹¹ But if the animal was stolen from the neighbor, he must make restitution to the owner. ¹² If it was torn to pieces, he shall bring it before a witness and he will not be required to pay for the torn animal.

¹³ If a man borrows from his neighbor and it breaks or dies while the owner is not present, he must make restitution. ¹⁴ But if the owner is with it, the borrower will not have to pay. If it was hired, the money paid for the hire covers the loss.

¹⁵ If a man seduces a virgin who is not pledged to be married and sleeps with her, he must pay the bride-price, and she shall be his wife. ¹⁶ If her father absolutely refuses to give her to him, he must still pay the bride-price for virgins. ¹⁷ Do not allow a sorceress to live. ¹⁸ Anyone who has sexual relations with an animal must be put to death.

¹⁹ Whoever sacrifices to any god other than the Lord must be destroyed.

מְכַשֵּׁפָה

Exodus 22:17—Witchcraft and bestiality.

Here the practice of witchcraft is discussed. Witchcraft (or black magic) manipulates the Laws of the Universe for selfish reasons and alters the flow of energy in the spiritual system. This creates a mutation that sets off a force of destruction and devastation. The 72 Names of God and other kabbalistic tools are part of the Laws of the Universe and are only effective if they are used for the sake of sharing and removing ego—so they are permitted. This section also talks about fornicating with animals

as something that alters the Laws of the Universe and is therefore not allowed.

The *Zohar* explains:

Bilaam took his witchcraft from there (from the mountains of darkness), and he learned from them, from Uza and Azael, in these mountains, as it is written: "Balak, the King of Moab, has brought me from Aram, out of the mountains of the East," (Numbers 23:7) and from there all those who know witchcraft in the world were crowned. And because they came in complaint to their Master at first, when man was created, and

יוהך, ע"ה מ"ב ־יִמָּצֵא הַגַּנָּב יְשַׁלֵּם שְׁנָיִם: 7 אִם יוהך, ע"ה מ"ב ־לֹא יִמָּצֵא הַגַּנָּב

וְנִקְרַב בַּעַל־הַבַּיִת ב"פ ראה אֶל־הָאֱלֹהִים מום, אהיה אדני ; ילה אִם יוהך, ע"ה מ"ב ־

לֹא שָׁלַח יָדֹו בִּמְלֶאכֶת רֵעֵהוּ: 8 עַל־כָּל־ ילי, עמם ־דְּבַר ראה ־פֶּשַׁע עַל־

שֹׁור אבג"יתצ, ושר, אהבת חנם עַל־חֲמֹור עַל־שֶׂה עַל־שַׂלְמָה עַל־כָּל־ ילי; עמם

אֲבֵדָה אֲשֶׁר יֹאמַר כִּי־הוּא זֶה עַד הָאֱלֹהִים מום, אהיה אדני ; ילה יָבֹא דְּבַר

ראה ־שְׁנֵיהֶם אֲשֶׁר יַרְשִׁיעֻן אֱלֹהִים מום, אהיה אדני ; ילה יְשַׁלֵּם שְׁנַיִם לְרֵעֵהוּ:

9 כִּי־יִתֵּן אִישׁ ע"ה קנ"א קס"א אֶל־רֵעֵהוּ חֲמֹור אֹו־שֹׁור אבג"יתצ, ושר, אהבת חנם אֹו־

שֶׂה וְכָל־ ילי ־בְּהֵמָה ב"ן, לכב, יבמ לִשְׁמֹר וּמֵת ־י"פ רבוע אהיה אֹו־נִשְׁבַּר אֹו־

נִשְׁבָּה אֵין רֹאֶה ראה: 10 שְׁבֻעַת יְהֹוָ‍ֱ‍ אֲדֹנָי אהיה אדני יאהדונהי תִּהְיֶה בֵּין שְׁנֵיהֶם אִם

יוהך, ע"ה מ"ב ־לֹא שָׁלַח יָדֹו בִּמְלֶאכֶת רֵעֵהוּ וְלָקַח ב"פ יהוה אדני אהיה בְּעָלָיו

וְלֹא יְשַׁלֵּם: 11 וְאִם יוהך, ע"ה מ"ב ־גָּנֹב יִגָּנֵב מֵעִמֹּו יְשַׁלֵּם לִבְעָלָיו: 12 אִם

יוהך, ע"ה מ"ב ־טָרֹף רפ"ח ע"ה יִטָּרֵף יְבִאֵהוּ עֵד הַטְּרֵפָה לֹא יְשַׁלֵּם: 13 וְכִי־

יִשְׁאַל אִישׁ ע"ה קנ"א קס"א מֵעִם רֵעֵהוּ וְנִשְׁבַּר אֹו־מֵת י"פ רבוע אהיה בְּעָלָיו

אֵין־עִמֹּו שַׁלֵּם ב"פ רבוע ע"ב יְשַׁלֵּם: 14 אִם יוהך, ע"ה מ"ב ־בְּעָלָיו עִמֹּו לֹא יְשַׁלֵּם

אִם יוהך, ע"ה מ"ב ־שָׂכִיר הוּא בָּא בִּשְׂכָרֹו: 15 וְכִי־יְפַתֶּה אִישׁ ע"ה קנ"א קס"א

בְּתוּלָה אֲשֶׁר לֹא־אֹרָשָׂה וְשָׁכַב עִמָּהּ מָהֹר יִמְהָרֶנָּה לֹּו לְאִשָּׁה:

16 אִם יוהך, ע"ה מ"ב ־מָאֵן יְמָאֵן אָבִיהָ לְתִתָּהּ לֹו כֶּסֶף יִשְׁקֹל כְּמֹהַר

הַבְּתוּלֹת: 17 מְכַשֵּׁפָה לֹא תְחַיֶּה: 18 כָּל־ ילי ־שֹׁכֵב עִם־בְּהֵמָה ב"ן, לכב, יבמ

מֹות יוּמָת: 19 זֹבֵחַ לָאֱלֹהִים מום, אהיה אדני ; ילה יָחֳרָם בִּלְתִּי לַיהֹוָ‍ֱ‍ אֲדֹנָייאהדונהי

לְבַדֹּו מ"ב:

---

until this day they plague their Master very much with this witchcraft that weakens the groups of above; therefore they were tied in chains of iron. And had it not been for those chains which are sunk deep inside

the Great Abyss, and which hold them with great strength, they would have destroyed the world, and the world would not have been able to survive.
— The Zohar, Ruth 34:290-291

20 Do not mistreat a stranger or oppress him, for you were strangers in Egypt. 21 Do not take advantage of a widow or an orphan. 22 If you take advantage and he cries out to Me, I will certainly hear his cry.

23 My anger will be aroused, and I will kill you with the sword; your wives will become widows and your children orphans. 24 If you lend money to one of my people among you who is needy, do not be like a moneylender; charge him no interest.

25 If you take your neighbor's garment as a pledge, return it to him by sunset, 26 because his garment is the only covering he has for his body. What else will he sleep in? When he cries out to Me, I will hear, for I am compassionate.

FOURTH READING - MOSES - NETZACH

27 Do not blaspheme God or curse the ruler of your people. 28 Do not hold back offerings from your granaries or your vats. You must give me the firstborn of your sons.

תִּכְוֶה

Exodus 22:24—Usury or lending money at exorbitant rates of interest.

This section addresses the lending of money, which is a responsibility that cannot be taken lightly. When we lend money, we need to know to whom we are lending and all the circumstances and ramifications pertaining to the loan. We need to bear in mind the bigger picture and whether the loan should be made in conjunction with other means of helping in a non-material way. It is important to always remember human side in everything, even in business. The Laws of the Universe apply in financial matters as well as in our personal lives.

אֱלֹהִים לֹא תְקַלֵּל

Exodus 22:27—Cursing God.

This verse tells us not to curse God. The *Zohar* once again reveals a deeper meaning that is relevant to our own fulfillment. The lesson here is not about the Creator at all. God neither requires our blessings nor repels our curses. Because we all have a spark of God within, when we do something harmful to another or to ourselves, we are cursing and disconnecting from the Source of the Light within.

Therefore, it is ill advised for a person to curse himself when he is angry, since many ADVERSARIES are standing by to accept such speeches, MEANING THAT HIS CURSE WILL COME TRUE. At another time, WHEN MOSES requested death AT THE EPISODE OF THE GOLDEN CALF, SAYING, "BLOT ME, I PRAY YOU, OUT OF YOUR BOOK WHICH YOU HAVE WRITTEN," (EXODUS 32:32), they did not accept it from him because it was all for the benefit of the children of Israel. This time, he said it out of pressure and anger, and therefore they accepted. Therefore, Eldad and Meidad remained IN THE CAMP and said that Moses would be gathered to his people and Joshua would usher the children of Israel into the land.
*   --The Zohar, Beha'alotcha 24:138*

20 וְגֵ֥ר בֶּן קֹלֹ"א לֹֽא־תוֹנֶ֖ה וְלֹ֣א תִלְחָצֶ֑נּוּ כִּֽי־גֵרִ֥ים הֱיִיתֶ֖ם בְּאֶ֥רֶץ אלהים דאלפין

מִצְרָֽיִם: מצר" 21 כָּל יל" ־אַלְמָנָ֥ה כוק, רבוע אדני וְיָת֖וֹם יוסף לֹ֥א תְעַנּֽוּן: 22 אִם

יוהך, ע"ה מ"ב ־עַנֵּ֥ה תְעַנֶּ֖ה אֹת֑וֹ כִּ֣י אִם יוהך, ע"ה מ"ב ־צָעֹ֤ק יִצְעַק֙ אֵלַ֔י שָׁמֹ֥עַ

אֶשְׁמַ֖ע צַעֲקָתֽוֹ: 23 וְחָרָ֣ה אַפִּ֔י וְהָרַגְתִּ֥י אֶתְכֶ֖ם בֶּחָ֑רֶב רבוע ס"ג ורבוע אהיה

וְהָי֤וּ נְשֵׁיכֶם֙ אַלְמָנ֔וֹת וּבְנֵיכֶ֖ם יְתֹמִֽים: 24 אִם יוהך, ע"ה מ"ב ־כֶּ֣סֶף תלוה

אֶת־עַמִּ֗י אֶת־הֶֽעָנִי֙ רבוע מ"ה עִמָּ֔ךְ ה הויות, גמם לֹא־תִהְיֶ֥ה ל֖וֹ כְּנֹשֶׁ֑ה לֹֽא־

תְשִׂימ֥וּן עָלָ֖יו נֶֽשֶׁךְ: 25 אִם יוהך, ע"ה מ"ב ־חָבֹ֥ל תַּחְבֹּ֖ל שַׂלְמַ֣ת רֵעֶ֑ךָ עַד־

בֹּ֥א הַשֶּׁ֖מֶשׁ ב"פ שׁיך תְּשִׁיבֶ֥נּוּ לֽוֹ: 26 כִּ֣י הִ֤וא כְסוּתֹה֙ לְבַדָּ֔הּ הִ֥וא שִׂמְלָת֖וֹ

לְעֹר֑וֹ בַּמֶּ֣ה יִשְׁכָּ֑ב וְהָיָה֙ יהוה כִּֽי־יִצְעַ֣ק אֵלַ֔י וְשָׁמַעְתִּ֖י כִּֽי־חַנּ֥וּן

אֽנִי֮ אני, טרדה"ד כוו"ו: יהוה ע"ה ואלהים ע"ה

FOURTH READING - MOSES - NETZACH

27 אֱלֹהִ֖ים מום, אהיה אדני ; ילה לֹ֣א תְקַלֵּ֑ל וְנָשִׂ֥יא בְעַמְּךָ֖ ה הויות, גמם לֹ֥א תָאֹֽר:

28 מְלֵאָתְךָ֥ וְדִמְעֲךָ֖ לֹ֣א תְאַחֵ֑ר בְּכ֥וֹר בָּנֶ֖יךָ תִּתֶּן ב"פ כהת ־לִּֽי: 29 כֵּֽן־תַּעֲשֶׂ֥ה

And in the compilation of the first part, HE SAYS: There are three who cause harm to themselves, two of whom are in this world, and one in another world. And these are: The one who curses himself, as we have learnt; one official is appointed before man, and when a man curses himself this official together with his seventy appointed subordinates take that word and respond "amen," and they raise it up on high and judge it. And THE OFFICIAL follows him until he does something and then he puts into effect for him THE CURSE OF that word THAT HE UTTERED.

Who do we have that is greater than Moses, who said: "and if not, blot me, I pray you, out of Your Book which You have written." (Exodus 32:32). This he said for the sake of Israel, and although the Holy One, blessed be He, did his wish AND FORGAVE ISRAEL, nevertheless Moses was not spared punishment, for it has already been noted that HIS NAME is not mentioned in the portion of Tetzaveh, but has been blotted out from there. And this has already been taught. And who do we have that is greater than King David, who said: "I said: I will take heed to my ways that I sin not with my tongue: I will keep a curb on my mouth, while the wicked is before me." (Psalm 39:2). What is the meaning of "while the wicked is before me?" This refers to that official who was appointed over the one WHO CURSES HIMSELF, and takes that word to harm a man, AS ABOVE.

-- The Zohar, Pinchas 93:642, 643

29 Do the same with your cattle and your sheep. Let them stay with their mothers for seven days, but give them to me on the eighth day.

30 You are to be My holy people. The meat of an animal found in the fields is an abomination; do not eat it, throw it to the dogs.

23:1 Do not spread false reports. Do not help a wicked man by being a malicious witness. 2 Do not follow the crowd in doing wrong and when you give Covenant in a dispute, do not pervert justice by siding with the crowd,

3 and do not show favoritism to a poor man in his dispute. 4 If you come across your enemy's ox or donkey wandering off, return it to him.

5 If you see the donkey of someone who hates you fallen down under its load, do not leave it there; be sure you help him with it.

FIFTH READING - AARON - HOD

6 Do not deny justice to your poor people in their disputes. 7 Distance yourself from lies and do not put an innocent or righteous person to death, for I will not acquit the wicked.

8 Do not accept a bribe, for a bribe blinds those who see and twists the words of the righteous.

9 Do not oppress a stranger; you yourselves know how it feels to be a stranger, because you were strangers in Egypt.

10 For six years you are to sow your fields and harvest its crops, 11 but during the seventh year let the land lie unplowed and unused. Then the poor among your people may get food from it, and the wild animals may eat what they leave. Do the same with your vineyard and your olive grove.

עֵד וְזֹמֵם

Exodus 23:1—Bearing false witness.

To say that someone did something that they did not do, by bearing false witness—we bring onto ourselves an effect (consequence) of the lie, and we compound that effect by also causing a "judge" to rule against an innocent party.

While traveling, Rav Aba said, We have already learned that, due to eleven causes, plagues come about to human beings. They are due to idol worship, cursing the Holy Name, incest, theft, the evil tongue, bearing false witness, a judge who is crooked in a trial, swearing falsely, one who encroaches on his friend's boundary rights, one who contemplates evil thoughts and ideas, and one who instigates quarrels between brothers. Some say also due to the evil eye, and we were taught all this in the Mishnah.
-- The Zohar, Balak 38:385

לְשֹׁרְךָ לְצֹאנְךָ שִׁבְעַת יָמִים גֵּוּ יִהְיֶה … עִם־אִמּוֹ בַּיּוֹם עה = נגד, ח, מזלות הַשְּׁמִינִי

תִּתְּנוֹ־לִי: 30 וְאַנְשֵׁי־קֹדֶשׁ תִּהְיוּן לִי וּבָשָׂר בַּשָּׂדֶה טְרֵפָה לֹא תֹאכֵלוּ

לְכֶלֶב תַּשְׁלִכוּן אֹתוֹ: 23 1 לֹא תִשָּׂא שֵׁמַע שָׁוְא אַל־תָּשֶׁת יָדְךָ בוכי עִם־

רָשָׁע לִהְיֹת ‎עֵד וחמס‎ : 2 לֹא־תִהְיֶה אַחֲרֵי־רַבִּים לְרָעֹת וְלֹא־תַעֲנֶה עַל־

רִב לִנְטֹת אַחֲרֵי רַבִּים לְהַטֹּת: 3 וְדָל לֹא תֶהְדַּר בְּרִיבוֹ: 4 כִּי תִפְגַּע שׁוֹר

אֹיִבְךָ אבוותצ, ועוד, אהבת וחם אוֹ חֲמֹרוֹ תֹּעֶה הָשֵׁב תְּשִׁיבֶנּוּ לוֹ: 5 כִּי־תִרְאֶה חֲמוֹר

שֹׂנַאֲךָ ‎רבן‎ רֹבֵץ תַּחַת מַשָּׂאוֹ וְחָדַלְתָּ מֵעֲזֹב לוֹ עָזֹב תַּעֲזֹב עִמּוֹ:

FIFTH READING - AARON - HOD

6 לֹא תַטֶּה מִשְׁפַּט עה הּפ אלהים אֶבְיֹנְךָ בְּרִיבוֹ: 7 מִדְּבַר ראה ‎שֶׁקֶר‎ תִּרְחָק

וְנָקִי וְצַדִּיק אַל־תַּהֲרֹג כִּי לֹא־אַצְדִּיק רָשָׁע: 8 וְשֹׁחַד לֹא תִקָּח

רבוע אהיה דאלפין כִּי הַשֹּׁחַד יְעַוֵּר פִּקְחִים וִיסַלֵּף דִּבְרֵי ראה צַדִּיקִים: 9 וְגֵר

בן קנא לֹא תִלְחָץ וְאַתֶּם יְדַעְתֶּם אֶת־נֶפֶשׁ רמ"ח + ז הויות הַגֵּר בן קנא כִּי־גֵרִים

הֱיִיתֶם בְּאֶרֶץ אלהים דאלפין מִצְרָיִם מצר: 10 וְשֵׁשׁ שָׁנִים תִּזְרַע אֶת־אַרְצֶךָ

וְאָסַפְתָּ אֶת־תְּבוּאָתָהּ: 11 וְהַשְּׁבִיעִת תִּשְׁמְטֶנָּה וּנְטַשְׁתָּהּ וְאָכְלוּ אֶבְיֹנֵי

רבן

Exodus 23:5—Compassion for animals.

There is Light in all creatures of the Earth and even in all inanimate things. It is our duty to ensure that we do everything we can to protect animals from pain or harm and to assist them if they are hurt.

שֶׁקֶר

Exodus 23:7—Lying.

We are told to distance ourselves from false words. Rav Bunam of Pschyscha says that God abhors falsehood to the extent that we are commanded to stay far away from even the appearance of a lie. When Rav Ashlag was a young boy, he used to tell white lies until he realized he could not become a leader unless he embraced the truth wholeheartedly.

When people lie, they cannot attain a high spiritual level. This is not only because they deceive others, but just as importantly, because they lie to themselves. White lies are by definition small, but small lies can sometimes be a marker to something big, as they can indicate that we think that the small things don't matter. But everything matters in the universe, and every action is significant.

12 Six days do your work, but on the seventh day do not work, so that your ox and your donkey may rest and the children of your handmaids and the stranger as well, may be refreshed.

13 Observe everything I have said to you. Do not invoke the names of other gods; do not let them be heard on your lips.

14 Three festivals you shall celebrate for Me a year.

15 Celebrate the Feast of Unleavened Bread; for seven days eat unleavened bread, as I commanded you. Do this at the appointed time in the month of Aviv, for in that month you came out of Egypt. No one is to appear before me empty.

16 Celebrate the Feast of Harvest with the first fruits of the crops you sow in your field. Celebrate the Feast of Ingathering at the end of the year, when you gather in your crops from the field.

17 Three times a year all the men are to appear before the Sovereign Lord.

18 Do not offer the blood of a sacrifice to Me along with anything containing yeast. The fat of My festival offerings must not be kept until morning.

הַשְּׁבִיעִי

Exodus 23:12—The Sabbath.

This verse describes Shabbat as a flame that sparks the energy for the entire week. It is so valuable to bring some quality of spirituality into the week, and connecting in some way to Shabbat achieves this. No matter how small the participation, it's helpful to take even a few moments on Friday night or Saturday morning to reflect and take stock of where we are spiritually—to look at our actions of the past week and see where we are heading.

> *"Remember the Shabbat day, to keep it holy." We have explained the secret of Shabbat in many places. It is to be remembered as the day of the world's rest, and it includes the whole Torah, and he who keeps the Shabbat is considered as one who keeps the whole Torah. We have already learned that a man who remembers the Shabbat has to sanctify it in all manners of sanctifications ... "Remember" applies to the Male, WHICH IS ZEIR ANPIN, and "keep" applies to the Female, WHICH IS MALCHUT. The Shabbat day is the secret*

of the whole Faith which is suspended from the Supernal Head, WHICH IS KETER, to the bottom of all the grades. Shabbat is everything.

— *The Zohar, Yitro, 32:528-529*

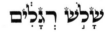

Exodus 23:14—*Pesach, Shavuot,* and *Sukkot.*

Here we are given the opportunity to bring in the energy of three holidays: *Pesach, Shavuot,* and *Sukkot.*

The *Zohar* says this about *Pesach, Shavuot* and *Sukkot:*

> *This is why this day of Shavuot, the Central Column that corresponds to Zeir Anpin that is called Israel, is the bond of faith that bonds everything. Also, it is written, "She is a Tree of Life to those who lay hold on her," (Proverbs 3:18) since the Tree of Life, Zeir Anpin, is a tree called 'One.' Hence, since Israel below are attached and hold to this place, the Tree of Life, Zeir Anpin, they are called 'One.' For the Tree*

עַמֶּךָ ה הויות, נמם וְיִתְרָם תֹּאכַל חַיַּת הַשָּׂדֶה שׁדי כֵּן־תַּעֲשֶׂה לְכַרְמְךָ

לְזֵיתֶךָ: 12 שֵׁשֶׁת יָמִים גלך תַּעֲשֶׂה מַעֲשֶׂיךָ וּבַיּוֹם עה = נגד, זן, מזמו **הַשְּׁבִיעִי**

תִּשְׁבֹּת לְמַעַן יָנוּחַ שׁוֹרְךָ וַחֲמֹרֶךָ וְיִנָּפֵשׁ בֶּן־אֲמָתְךָ וְהַגֵּר דים בן: 13 וּבְכֹל

בין, לכב, יבם אֲשֶׁר־אָמַרְתִּי יפ אדני עה אֲלֵיכֶם תִּשָּׁמֵרוּ וְשֵׁם יהוה שׁדי אֱלֹהִים

מום, אהיה אדני ; ילה אֲחֵרִים לֹא תַזְכִּירוּ לֹא יִשָּׁמַע עַל־פִּיךָ: 14 **שָׁלֹשׁ רְגָלִים**

תָּחֹג לִי בַּשָּׁנָה: 15 אֶת־חַג הַמַּצּוֹת תִּשְׁמֹר שִׁבְעַת יָמִים גלך תֹּאכַל

מצר מַצּוֹת כַּאֲשֶׁר צִוִּיתִךָ לְמוֹעֵד חֹדֶשׁ יב הויות הָאָבִיב כִּי־בוֹ יָצָאתָ מִמִּצְרַיִם

מצר וְלֹא־יֵרָאוּ פָנַי חכמה בינה רֵיקָם: 16 וְחַג הַקָּצִיר בִּכּוּרֵי מַעֲשֶׂיךָ אֲשֶׁר

תִּזְרַע בַּשָּׂדֶה וְחַג הָאָסִף בְּצֵאת הַשָּׁנָה בְּאָסְפְּךָ אֶת־מַעֲשֶׂיךָ מִן־

הַשָּׂדֶה שׁדי: 17 שָׁלֹשׁ פְּעָמִים בַּשָּׁנָה יֵרָאֶה ריו, גבורה כָּל יל זְכוּרְךָ אֶל־

פְּנֵי חכמה בינה **הָאָדֹן** | יהוה אדני ואהדנהי: 18 לֹא־תִזְבַּח עַל־חָמֵץ דַּם רבוע אהיה

---

of Life is called 'One,' since everything is attached to it, and its day, Shavuot, is assuredly one, bonding everything and being the center of everything, since it is the Central Column. This is the meaning of, "the Tree of Life also in the midst of the Garden," (Genesis 2:9) as Zeir Anpin called the Tree of Life is actually inside, in the center and includes all directions, namely, the Right and Left Columns, and is attached to them—hence, Passover and Sukkot, and it, Shavuot, between them, since Passover is the Right Column, Sukkot the Left Column, and Shavuot the Central Column. For it is central to everything, which is why that day is to the praise of the Torah, because this is the time of the giving of our Torah, and no more. For Torah is the secret of Zeir Anpin, the Central Column, and it is the praise of faith, Malchut, and the bonding of everything, namely the first three Sefirot, for all those are connected to the Central Column.

— The Zohar, Emor 23:142-143

Pesach (Passover) is a powerful holiday during which we challenge and free ourselves from all that enslaves us. "Enslaves," of course, does not refer to physical slavery, but to the spiritual slavery caused by those ego-driven qualities that bind our free will—anger, lack of self-control, even the need for approval and praise.

In An Introduction to the Tikkunim of the Zohar, Rav Brandwein wrote:

> Therefore, you people of valor, you Holy Nation, may you find the strength in your hands to form holy groups, to raise the banner of the Torah, to hold on to this holy study by means of which we can now depart from slavery and come to freedom, from bondage to redemption, and from darkness to the great light till it can come true in us that "the Earth shall be full of the knowledge of God . . ." speedily and in our days, Amen.
> — Yedid Nafshi, Part 3, Essay 3

The holiday of Shavuot gives us the ability to achieve immortality by reconnecting to Mount Sinai where we received immortality for the first time.

Sukkot provides the technology to draw in our Surrounding Light (our potential), which sustains us, protects us, and drives us throughout the year.

¹⁹ Bring the best of the first fruits of your soil to the house of the Lord your God. Do not cook a goat in its mother's milk.

SIXTH READING - JOSEPH - YESOD

²⁰ Here I am sending an angel ahead of you to guard you along the way and to bring you to the place I have prepared.

²¹ Pay attention to him and listen to what he says. Do not rebel against him; he will not forgive your rebellion, since My Name is in him.

²² If you listen carefully to what he says and do all that I say, I will be an enemy to your enemies and will oppose those who oppose you.

²³ My angel will go ahead of you and bring you to the Amorites, Hittites, Perizzites, Canaanites, Hivites and Jebusites, and I will wipe them out.

²⁴ Do not bow down before their gods or worship them or follow their practices. You must surely demolish them and surely break their sacred stones to pieces.

²⁵ Worship the Lord, your God, and His blessing will be on your food and water. I will take away sickness from among you.

SEVENTH READING - DAVID – MALCHUT

²⁶ There will be no obstacle or barrenness in your land. I will fill the number of your days.

²⁷ I will send My terror ahead of you and throw into confusion every nation you encounter. I will make all your enemies turn from you.

מַלְאָךְ

Exodus 23:20—"Here I am sending an angel ahead of you. . ." Guardian Angels are sent by God to protect us. Once we learn to recognize their presence and the signs they send our way, we realize how supported we are. We are not alone.

Here is written, "Behold, I send My Angel before you," SO ISRAEL WHO ARE THE

INNERMOST AND ARE CLINGING TO GOD, ARE GIVEN OVER TO THE ANGEL, REPRESENTING THE OUTER ASPECT. Moses said, 'I received a promise from You, that You would never part from us,' FOR AS A RESULT OF THE PRECEPT OF THE FIRST-FRUITS, THE OUTER WORLD SHOULD NOT INTERMINGLE WITH THE INNER, AS EXPLAINED. Surely, "If Your presence go not with me, carry us not up

וְזִבְחִי וְלֹא־יָלִין חֵלֶב־חַגִּי עַד־בְּקֶר: 19 רֵאשִׁית בִּכּוּרֵי אַדְמָתְךָ תָּבִיא
בֵּית בּ״פ ראה יְהֹוָאדִּנִיאהדונהי אֱלֹהֶיךָ ילה לֹא־תְבַשֵּׁל גְּדִי והו בַּחֲלֵב אִמּוֹ:

SIXTH READING - JOSEPH - YESOD

20 הִנֵּה מ״ה יה אָנֹכִי איע שֹׁלֵחַ מַלְאָךְ יאהדונהי לְפָנֶיךָ סמ״ב לִשְׁמָרְךָ בַּדָּרֶךְ
בּ״פ יב״ק וְלַהֲבִיאֲךָ אֶל־הַמָּקוֹם יהוה אל רִפ אל אֲשֶׁר הֲכִנֹתִי: 21 הִשָּׁמֶר
מִפָּנָיו וּשְׁמַע בְּקֹלוֹ אַל־תַּמֵּר בּוֹ כִּי לֹא יִשָּׂא לְפִשְׁעֲכֶם כִּי שְׁמִי
בְּקִרְבּוֹ: רבוע ע״ב ורבוע ס״ג 22 כִּי אִם־שָׁמוֹעַ תִּשְׁמַע בְּקֹלוֹ וְעָשִׂיתָ יוהך, ע״ה מ״ה
כֹּל ילי אֲשֶׁר אֲדַבֵּר ראה וְאָיַבְתִּי אֶת־אֹיְבֶיךָ וְצַרְתִּי אֶת־צֹרְרֶיךָ: 23 כִּי־
יֵלֵךְ מַלְאָכִי לְפָנֶיךָ סמ״ב וֶהֱבִיאֲךָ אֶל־הָאֱמֹרִי וְהַחִתִּי וְהַפְּרִזִּי וְהַכְּנַעֲנִי
הַחִוִּי וְהַיְבוּסִי וְהִכְחַדְתִּיו: 24 לֹא־תִשְׁתַּחֲוֶה לֵאלֹהֵיהֶם ילה וְלֹא תָעָבְדֵם
וְלֹא תַעֲשֶׂה כְּמַעֲשֵׂיהֶם כִּי הָרֵס תְּהָרְסֵם וְשַׁבֵּר תְּשַׁבֵּר מַצֵּבֹתֵיהֶם:
25 וַעֲבַדְתֶּם אֵת יְהֹוָאדִּנִיאהדונהי אֱלֹהֵיכֶם ילה וּבֵרַךְ אֶת־לַחְמְךָ וְאֶת־
מֵימֶיךָ וַהֲסִרֹתִי מַחֲלָה מִקִּרְבֶּךָ:

SEVENTH READING - DAVID – MALCHUT

26 לֹא תִהְיֶה מְשַׁכֵּלָה וַעֲקָרָה בְּאַרְצֶךָ אֶת־מִסְפַּר יָמֶיךָ אֲמַלֵּא:
27 אֶת־אֵימָתִי אֲשַׁלַּח לְפָנֶיךָ סמ״ב וְהַמֹּתִי אֶת־כָּל ילי ־הָעָם אֲשֶׁר תָּבֹא
בָּהֶם וְנָתַתִּי אֶת־כָּל ילי ־אֹיְבֶיךָ אֵלֶיךָ אני עֹרֶף: 28 וְשָׁלַחְתִּי אֶת־

---

from here. For in what shall it be known?"
— The Zohar, Mishpatim 28:557

To benefit from the presence of our angel, we have to be open. Rav Ashlag tells us that not heeding our angel's messages is like walking blindfolded in a room full of obstacles. The

Zohar is the guide that gets us through the obstacle course of life; it is our ultimate and truest angel. There are things we can do, like scanning and studying the *Zohar* and reciting the *Ana Beko'ach* meditation, to help us connect with our angelic guides so that we can receive their messages clearly.

28 I will send the hornet ahead of you to drive the Hivites, Canaanites and Hittites out of your way.

29 But I will not drive them out in a single year, because the land would become desolate and the wild animals too numerous for you.

30 Little by little I will drive them out before you, until you have increased enough to take possession of the land.

31 I will establish your borders from the Red Sea to the Sea of the Philistines, and from the desert to the river. When I will hand over to you the inhabitants of the land and you will drive them out before you,

32 do not make a covenant with them or with their gods.

33 Do not let them live in your land, or they will cause you to sin against Me because the worship of their gods will certainly be a hindrance to you.' "

24:1 Then He said to Moses, "Come up to the Lord, you and Aaron, Nadab and Abihu, and seventy of the elders of Israel. You are to worship at a distance,

2 but Moses alone is to approach the Lord; the others must not come near." And the people may not come up with him.

3 When Moses went and told the people all the Lord's words and all of the laws, they responded with one voice, "Everything the Lord has said we will do."

4 Moses then wrote down everything the Lord had said. He got up early the next morning and built an altar at the foot of the mountain and set up twelve stone pillars representing the twelve tribes of Israel.

5 Then he sent young Israelite men, and they offered burnt offerings and sacrificed young bulls as fellowship offerings to the Lord.

6 Moses took half of the blood and put it in bowls, and the other half he sprinkled on the altar.

Exodus 23:30—The land of Israel.

Here we read about the land of Israel and how important it is for us to view Israel as an energy source, just as our heart is an energy source for our body.

> *... surely we are closer to the Divine King than any of the other peoples. This must*

be so, for the Holy One, blessed be He, made Israel the heart of the whole world, and the relationship of Israel to the other nations is as that of the heart to other parts of the body. And just as the other parts of the body have no existence, even for a moment, without the heart, so it is that none of the other peoples can exist in the world without Israel. Jerusalem, too, has the same relationship with the other countries, being as the heart to the

הַצִּרְעָה לְפָנֶיךָ סמ״ב וְגֵרְשָׁה אֶת־הַחִוִּי אֶת־הַכְּנַעֲנִי וְאֶת־הַחִתִּי מִלְּפָנֶיךָ

סמ״ב 29 לֹא אֲגָרְשֶׁנּוּ מִפָּנֶיךָ סמ״ב בְּשָׁנָה אֶחָת פֶּן־תִּהְיֶה הָאָרֶץ אלהים דההן ע״ה

שְׁמָמָה וְרַבָּה עָלֶיךָ רבוע מ״ה חַיַּת הַשָּׂדֶה: 30 מְעַט מְעַט אֲגָרְשֶׁנּוּ שדי

מִפָּנֶיךָ סמ״ב עַד אֲשֶׁר תִּפְרֶה וְנָחַלְתָּ אֶת־ הָאָרֶץ אלהים דההן ע״ה 31 וְשַׁתִּי

אֶת־גְּבֻלְךָ מִיַּם ילי ־סוּף וְעַד־יָם ילי פְּלִשְׁתִּים ילי אלהים י״פ וּמִמִּדְבָּר עַד־

הַנָּהָר כִּי | אֶתֵּן בְּיֶדְכֶם אֵת יֹשְׁבֵי הָאָרֶץ אלהים דההן ע״ה וְגֵרַשְׁתָּמוֹ

מִפָּנֶיךָ סמ״ב 32 לֹא־תִכְרֹת לָהֶם וְלֵאלֹהֵיהֶם ילה בְּרִית: 33 לֹא יֵשְׁבוּ

בְּאַרְצְךָ פֶּן־יַחֲטִיאוּ אֹתְךָ לִי כִּי תַעֲבֹד אֶת־אֱלֹהֵיהֶם ילה כִּי־יִהְיֶה ייי

לְךָ לְמוֹקֵשׁ: 24 1 וְאֶל־מֹשֶׁה מהש, אל שדי אָמַר עֲלֵה אֶל־יְהֹוָ֕אֱדנילאהדונהי

אַתָּה וְאַהֲרֹן ע״ב ורבוע ע״ב נָדָב ע״ה בוכו וַאֲבִיהוּא וְשִׁבְעִים מִזִּקְנֵי יִשְׂרָאֵל

וְהִשְׁתַּחֲוִיתֶם מֵרָחֹק שדי: 2 וְנִגַּשׁ מֹשֶׁה מהש, אל שדי לְבַדּוֹ מ״ב אֶל־

יְהֹוָ֕אֱדנילאהדונהי וְהֵם לֹא יִגָּשׁוּ וְהָעָם לֹא יַעֲלוּ עִמּוֹ: 3 וַיָּבֹא מֹשֶׁה מהש, אל שדי

וַיְסַפֵּר לָעָם אֵת כָּל ילי ־דִּבְרֵי ילי יְהֹוָ֕אֱדנילאהדונהי ראה וְאֵת כָּל ילי ־הַמִּשְׁפָּטִים

וַיַּעַן כָּל ילי ־הָעָם קוֹל ע״ב ס״ג ע״ה אֶחָד אהבה, דאגה וַיֹּאמְרוּ כָּל ילי ־הַדְּבָרִים

אֲשֶׁר־דִּבֶּר ראה יְהֹוָ֕אֱדנילאהדונהי נַעֲשֶׂה: 4 וַיִּכְתֹּב מֹשֶׁה מהש, אל שדי אֵת

כָּל ילי ־דִּבְרֵי ראה יְהֹוָ֕אֱדנילאהדונהי וַיַּשְׁכֵּם בַּבֹּקֶר וחיים, בינה ע״ה וַיִּבֶן מִזְבֵּחַ

ןגד תַּחַת הָהָר וּשְׁתֵּים עֶשְׂרֵה מַצֵּבָה לִשְׁנֵים עָשָׂר שִׁבְטֵי יִשְׂרָאֵל:

5 וַיִּשְׁלַח אֶת־נַעֲרֵי בְּנֵי יִשְׂרָאֵל וַיַּעֲלוּ עֹלֹת וַיִּזְבְּחוּ זְבָחִים שְׁלָמִים

לַיהֹו֕אֱדנילאהדונהי פָּרִים: 6 וַיִּקַּח וחעם מֹשֶׁה מהש, אל שדי חֲצִי הַדָּם רבוע אהיה

וַיָּשֶׂם בָּאַגָּנֹת וַחֲצִי הַדָּם רבוע אהיה זָרַק עַל־הַמִּזְבֵּחַ ןגד: 7 וַיִּקַּח וחעם

---

parts of the body, which is why it is in the center of the whole world just as the heart is in the center of the limbs.
— The Zohar, Pinchas 25:152

wellspring of energy that we receive from Israel, the greater our connection during meditation and prayer—and the more Light we receive.

When we pray, we spiritually transport ourselves to Israel, the source of all energy, so we can receive more Light. The greater our appreciation is of the

7 Then he took the Book of the Covenant and read it to the people. They responded, "Everything the Lord has said; we will do and we will listen."

8 Moses then took the blood, sprinkled it on the people and said, "This is the blood of the covenant that the Lord has made with you in accordance with all these words." 9 Moses and Aaron, Nadab and Abihu, and the seventy elders of Israel went up

10 and saw the God of Israel. Under His feet was something made of sapphire, clear as the sky itself. 11 But God did not raise His hand against these leaders of the Israelites; they saw God, and they ate and drank.

12 The Lord said to Moses, "Come up to Me on the mountain and stay here, and I will give you the Tablets of stone, with the Torah and precepts that I have written for their instruction."

13 Then Moses set out with Joshua, his aide, and Moses went up on the mountain of God. 14 He said to the elders, "Wait here for us until we come back to you. Aaron and Hur are with you, and anyone involved in a dispute can go to them."

MAFTIR

15 Moses went up on the mountain, and the cloud covered the mountain,

16 and the glory of the Lord settled on Mount Sinai. For six days the cloud covered the mountain, and on the seventh day He called to Moses from within the cloud.

סֵפֶר הַבְּרִית

Exodus 24:7—A Covenant with God.

After hearing Moses read the Book of the Covenant, all the people said, "Everything that God has said, we will do, we will obey." When people are on a high spiritual level, they make the right choices because their connection to the Light will not allow them to do otherwise.

In the *Zohar*, we read:

> When God was ready and present on Mount Sinai to give the Torah to the children of Israel, "My nard sent forth its fragrance," as Israel emitted a wonderful fragrance that has shielded them for countless generations. This was what they said then: "All that God has said will we do, and obey."
> — The Zohar, Acharei Mot 15:100

Rav Elazar said, Even Israel at that time were all proper and the Shechinah was bound to them. This Covenant and the entire Torah took place at one time, *MEANING THEY THEN HAD THE LIGHT FROM THE ENTIRE TORAH. Israel never did experience a time like that. In the future days, the Holy One, blessed be He, will reveal Himself to His children and all will see visually His glory, as the verse writes, "for they shall see eye to eye, God returning to Zion," (Isaiah 52:8) and, "and the glory of God shall be revealed, and all flesh shall see it together ...." (Isaiah 40:5)*
> — The Zohar, Mishpatim 31:581

סֵפֶר הַבְּרִית בְּאׇזְנֵי הָעָם וַיֹּאמְרוּ כֹּל אֲשֶׁר־

דִּבֶּר יְהֹוָה נַעֲשֶׂה וְנִשְׁמָע: 8 וַיִּקַּח מֹשֶׁה אֶת־

הַדָּם וַיִּזְרֹק עַל־הָעָם וַיֹּאמֶר הִנֵּה דַם־הַבְּרִית

אֲשֶׁר כָּרַת יְהֹוָה עִמָּכֶם עַל כׇּל־הַדְּבָרִים הָאֵלֶּה:

9 וַיַּעַל מֹשֶׁה וְאַהֲרֹן נָדָב וַאֲבִיהוּא

וְשִׁבְעִים מִזִּקְנֵי יִשְׂרָאֵל: 10 וַיִּרְאוּ אֵת אֱלֹהֵי יִשְׂרָאֵל וְתַחַת

רַגְלָיו כְּמַעֲשֵׂה לִבְנַת הַסַּפִּיר וּכְעֶצֶם הַשָּׁמַיִם לָטֹהַר:

11 וְאֶל־אֲצִילֵי בְּנֵי יִשְׂרָאֵל לֹא שָׁלַח יָדוֹ וַיֶּחֱזוּ אֶת־הָאֱלֹהִים

וַיֹּאכְלוּ וַיִּשְׁתּוּ: 12 וַיֹּאמֶר יְהֹוָה אֶל־מֹשֶׁה

עֲלֵה אֵלַי הָהָרָה וֶהְיֵה־שָׁם וְאֶתְּנָה לְךָ אֶת־לֻחֹת

הָאֶבֶן וְהַתּוֹרָה וְהַמִּצְוָה אֲשֶׁר כָּתַבְתִּי לְהוֹרֹתָם: 13 וַיָּקׇם

מֹשֶׁה וִיהוֹשֻׁעַ מְשָׁרְתוֹ וַיַּעַל מֹשֶׁה אֶל־הַר

הָאֱלֹהִים: 14 וְאֶל־הַזְּקֵנִים אָמַר שְׁבוּ־לָנוּ

בׇזֶה עַד אֲשֶׁר־נָשׁוּב אֲלֵיכֶם וְהִנֵּה אַהֲרֹן וְחוּר עִמָּכֶם

מִי־בַעַל דְּבָרִים יִגַּשׁ אֲלֵהֶם:

MAFTIR

15 וַיַּעַל מֹשֶׁה אֶל־הָהָר וַיְכַס הֶעָנָן אֶת־הָהָר: 16 וַיִּשְׁכֹּן

כְּבוֹד־יְהֹוָה עַל־הַר סִינַי וַיְכַסֵּהוּ הֶעָנָן

וַיַּעַל

Exodus 24:15—Moses re-ascended Mount Sinai. After Moses revealed the Tablets of the Ten Utterances, God instructed him to go back to the mountain to build a Vessel for the Light that had just been revealed. Even when we connect to the Light through our spiritual work, we still have to manifest it in our lives by performing actions that will draw the Light down to us.

¹⁷ To the Israelites the glory of the Lord looked like a consuming fire on top of the mountain.

¹⁸ Then Moses entered the cloud as he went on up the mountain. And Moses stayed on the mountain forty days and forty nights.

HAFTARAH OF MISHPATIM

During the time of Jeremiah, the Babylonians had Jerusalem under siege. Jeremiah had a vision that if the people freed their slaves, the Babylonians would retreat. So the Israelites freed their slaves, and the Babylonians retreated, waging war against Egypt instead. But after the Babylonians withdrew, the Israelites took back their slaves, and as a result and in accord with God's promise

Jeremiah 34:8-22; 33:25-26

34:⁸ The word came to Jeremiah from the Lord after King Zedekiah had made a covenant with all the people in Jerusalem to proclaim freedom for the slaves.

⁹ Everyone was to free his Hebrew slaves, both male and female; no one was to hold a fellow Jew in bondage.

¹⁰ So all the officials and people who entered into this covenant agreed that they would free their male and female slaves and no longer hold them in bondage. They agreed, and set them free.

¹¹ But afterward they changed their minds and took back the slaves they had freed and enslaved them again.

¹² Then the word of the Lord came to Jeremiah:

שֵׁשֶׁת יָמִים גלך וַיִּקְרָא ב״פ קס״א ← ה׳ אותיות אֶל־מֹשֶׁה מהע, אל שדי בַּיּוֹם

הַשְּׁבִיעִי מִתּוֹךְ הֶעָנָן: 17 וּמַרְאֵה כְּבוֹד ל״ב יְהֹוָה עה = נגד, זן, מזבח

כְּאֵשׁ אלהים דיודין ע״ה אֹכֶלֶת בְּרֹאשׁ ריבוע אלהים ואלהים דיודין ע״ה הָהָר לְעֵינֵי

בְּנֵי יִשְׂרָאֵל: 18 וַיָּבֹא מֹשֶׁה מהע, אל שדי בְּתוֹךְ הֶעָנָן וַיַּעַל אֶל־ ריבוע מ״ה

הָהָר וַיְהִי אל, ייא״י מֹשֶׁה מהע, אל שדי בָּהָר אור, רז אַרְבָּעִים יוֹם עה = נגד, זן, מזבח

וְאַרְבָּעִים לַיְלָה מלה:

HAFTARAH OF MISHPATIM

in Jeremiah's vision, the Temple was destroyed. When we feel a noose tightening around our necks, we'll try anything to get out of our predicament. But once the danger has passed, we have to remember what we did or said and why we did or said it. We must always remain true to our commitment and not revert back to the original behavior that caused the judgment in the first place.

ירמיהו פרק ל״ד (ול״ג)

34 8 הַדָּבָר ראה אֲשֶׁר־הָיָה יהה אֶל־יִרְמְיָהוּ מֵאֵת יְהֹוָה אַחֲרֵי

כְּרֹת הַמֶּלֶךְ צִדְקִיָּהוּ בְּרִית אֶת־כָּל־ יל׳ הָעָם אֲשֶׁר בִּירוּשָׁלַ͏ִם ריו ע״ע

לִקְרֹא לָהֶם דְּרוֹר ב״פ (רבוע אלהים ← ה׳) 9: לְשַׁלַּח אִישׁ ע״ה קנ״א קס״א אֶת־עַבְדּוֹ

וְאִישׁ ע״ה קנ״א קס״א אֶת־שִׁפְחָתוֹ הָעִבְרִי וְהָעִבְרִיָּה חָפְשִׁים לְבִלְתִּי עֲבָד־

בָּם מ״ב בִּיהוּדִי אָחִיהוּ אִישׁ ע״ה קנ״א קס״א: 10 וַיִּשְׁמְעוּ כָל־ יל׳ הַשָּׂרִים וְכָל־

הָעָם אֲשֶׁר־בָּאוּ בַבְּרִית אִישׁ ע״ה קנ״א קס״א לְשַׁלַּח אִישׁ ע״ה קנ״א קס״א אֶת־עַבְדּוֹ וְאִישׁ

אֶת־שִׁפְחָתוֹ חָפְשִׁים לְבִלְתִּי עֲבָד־בָּם מ״ב וַיִּשְׁמְעוּ ע״ה קנ״א קס״א

וַיְשַׁלֵּחוּ: 11 וַיָּשׁוּבוּ אַחֲרֵי־כֵן וַיָּשִׁבוּ אֶת־הָעֲבָדִים וְאֶת־הַשְּׁפָחוֹת

אֲשֶׁר שִׁלְּחוּ חָפְשִׁים וַיִּכְבְּשׁוּם (כתיב: ויכבישום) לַעֲבָדִים וְלִשְׁפָחוֹת:

12 וַיְהִי אל, ייא״י דְּבַר ראה יְהֹוָה אֶל־יִרְמְיָהוּ מֵאֵת יְהֹוָה

לֵאמֹר: 13 כֹּה הי׳ אָמַר יְהֹוָה אֱלֹהֵי דמב, ילה יִשְׂרָאֵל אָנֹכִי איע

[13] "This is what the Lord, the God of Israel, says: 'I made a Covenant with your forefathers when I brought them out of Egypt, out of the land of slavery. I said,

[14] "Every seventh year each of you must free any fellow Hebrew who has sold himself to you. After he has served you six years, you must let him go free." Your fathers, however, did not listen to me or pay attention to me.

[15] Recently you repented and did what is right in my sight: Each of you proclaimed freedom to his countrymen. You even made a covenant before Me in the house that bears My Name.

[16] But now you have turned around and profaned My Name; each of you has taken back the male and female slaves you had set free to go where they wished. You have forced them to become your slaves again.

[17] Therefore, this is what the Lord says: 'You have not obeyed Me; you have not proclaimed freedom for your fellow brothers and fellow countrymen. So I now proclaim "freedom" for you,' declares the Lord –"freedom" to fall by the sword, plague and famine. I will make you abhorrent to all the kingdoms of the Earth.

[18] The men who have violated My Covenant and have not fulfilled the terms of the Covenant they made before Me, I will treat like the calf they cut in two and then walked between its pieces.

[19] The leaders of Judah and the leaders of Jerusalem, the court officials, the priests and all the people of the land who walked between the pieces of the calf,

[20] I will hand over to their enemies who seek their lives. Their dead bodies will become food for the birds of the air and the beasts of the earth.

[21] I will hand Zedekiah King of Judah and his officials over to their enemies who seek their lives, to the army of the king of Babylon, which has withdrawn from you.

[22] I am going to give the order," declares the Lord, "and I will bring them back to this city. They will fight against it, take it and burn it down. And I will lay waste the towns of Judah so no one can live there."

כָּרַ֙תִּי֙ בְּרִ֣ית אֶת־אֲבֽוֹתֵיכֶ֗ם בְּי֙וֹם ע"ה = נגד, זן, מזבח הֽוֹצִיאִ֤י אוֹתָם֙ מֵאֶ֣רֶץ
אלהים דאלפין מִצְרַ֙יִם֙ מֵצר מִבֵּ֣ית ב"פ ראה עֲבָדִ֔ים לֵאמֹֽר׃ 14 מִקֵּ֣ץ מזק שֶׁ֣בַע
שָׁנִ֗ים תְּשַׁלְּחוּ֙ אִ֣ישׁ ע"ה קנ"א קס"א אֶת־אָחִ֣יו הָעִבְרִ֗י אֲשֶֽׁר־יִמָּכֵ֣ר לְךָ֙
וַעֲבָֽדְךָ֙ פרי שֵׁ֣שׁ שָׁנִ֔ים וְשִׁלַּחְתּ֥וֹ חָפְשִׁ֖י מֵעִמָּ֑ךְ ה הויות, נמב וְלֹֽא־שָׁמְע֤וּ
אֲבֽוֹתֵיכֶם֙ אֵלַ֔י וְלֹ֥א הִטּ֖וּ אֶת־אָזְנָֽם׃ 15 וַתָּשֻׁ֙בוּ אַתֶּ֜ם הַיּ֗וֹם ע"ה = נגד, זן, מזבח
וַתַּעֲשׂ֤וּ אֶת־הַיָּשָׁר֙ בְּעֵינַ֔י ריבוע מ"ה לִקְרֹ֥א דְר֖וֹר ב"פ (רבוע אלהים - ה) אִ֥ישׁ
ע"ה קנ"א קס"א לְרֵעֵ֑הוּ וַתִּכְרְת֤וּ בְרִית֙ לְפָנַ֔י חכמה בינה בַּבַּ֕יִת ב"פ ראה אֲשֶׁר־נִקְרָ֥א
שְׁמִ֖י רבוע ע"ב ורבוע ס"ג עָלָ֑יו׃ 16 וַתָּשֻׁ֙בוּ֙ וַתְּחַלְּל֣וּ אֶת־שְׁמִ֔י רבוע ע"ב ורבוע ס"ג וַתָּשִׁ֤בוּ
אִ֣ישׁ ע"ה קנ"א קס"א אֶת־עַבְדּ֗וֹ וְאִ֣ישׁ ע"ה קנ"א קס"א אֶת־שִׁפְחָת֔וֹ אֲשֶׁר־שִׁלַּחְתֶּ֥ם
חָפְשִׁ֖ים לְנַפְשָׁ֑ם וַתִּכְבְּשׁ֣וּ אֹתָ֔ם לִֽהְי֣וֹת לָכֶ֔ם לַעֲבָדִ֖ים וְלִשְׁפָחֽוֹת׃ 17 לָכֵן֮
כֹּה־אָמַ֣ר הי יְהֹוָה֒אלה אַתֶּ֙ם לֹֽא־שְׁמַעְתֶּ֣ם אֵלַ֔י לִקְרֹ֣א דְר֔וֹר
ב"פ (רבוע אלהים - ה) אִ֖ישׁ ע"ה קנ"א קס"א לְאָחִ֣יו ע"ה קנ"א קס"א וְאִ֣ישׁ לְרֵעֵ֑הוּ הִנְנִ֙י קֹרֵ֙א
לָכֶ֤ם דְּרוֹר֙ ב"פ (רבוע אלהים - ה) נְאֻם־ יְהֹוָה֒אלה רבוע ס"ג ורבוע אהיה אֶל־הַחֶ֙רֶב֙
אֶל־הַדֶּ֙בֶר֙ ראה וְאֶל־הָ֣רָעָ֔ב ע"ב ורבוע אלהים ורבוע דההין ע"ה וְנָתַתִּ֤י אֶתְכֶם֙ לְזַעֲוָ֔ה (כתיב: לזועה)
לְכֹ֖ל אדני יה מַמְלְכ֥וֹת הָאָֽרֶץ אלהים דההין ע"ה׃ 18 וְנָֽתַתִּ֞י אֶת־הָאֲנָשִׁ֗ים הָעֹֽבְרִים֙
אֶת־בְּרִתִ֔י אֲשֶׁ֤ר לֹֽא־הֵקִ֙ימוּ֙ אֶת־דִּבְרֵ֣י ראה הַבְּרִ֔ית אֲשֶׁ֥ר כָּרְת֖וּ לְפָנָ֑י
חכמה בינה הָעֵ֕גֶל אֲשֶׁ֤ר כָּרְתוּ֙ לִשְׁנַ֔יִם וַיַּעַבְר֖וּ בֵּ֥ין בְּתָרָֽיו׃ 19 שָׂרֵ֣י יְהוּדָ֣ה
וְשָׂרֵ֣י יְרוּשָׁלַ֗ם ריו ש"ע הַסָּֽרִסִים֙ וְהַכֹּ֣הֲנִ֔ים וְכֹ֖ל ילי עַ֣ם הָאָ֑רֶץ אלהים דההין ע"ה
הָעֹ֣בְרִ֔ים בֵּ֖ין בִּתְרֵ֥י הָעֵֽגֶל׃ 20 וְנָתַתִּ֤י אוֹתָם֙ בְּיַ֣ד אֹֽיְבֵיהֶ֔ם וּבְיַ֖ד מְבַקְשֵׁ֣י
נַפְשָׁ֑ם וְהָיְתָ֤ה נִבְלָתָם֙ לְמַֽאֲכָ֔ל לְע֥וֹף ג"פ ב"ן, יוסף, ציון הַשָּׁמַ֖יִם י"פ טל, ל"פ כוזו אדני יהוה
וּלְבֶהֱמַ֥ת הָאָֽרֶץ אלהים דההין ע"ה׃ 21 וְאֶת־צִדְקִיָּ֤הוּ מֶֽלֶךְ־יְהוּדָה֙ וְאֶת־שָׂרָ֔יו
אֶתֵּ֕ן בְּיַ֣ד אֹֽיְבֵיהֶ֔ם וּבְיַ֖ד מְבַקְשֵׁ֣י נַפְשָׁ֑ם וּבְיַ֗ד וחיל מב"מ ח֚יל מֶ֣לֶךְ בָּבֶ֔ל
הָעֹלִ֖ים מֵעֲלֵיכֶֽם׃ 22 הִנְנִ֙י מְצַוֶּ֜ה נְאֻם־יְהֹוָה֒אלה וַהֲשִׁבֹתִ֤ים אֶל־הָעִיר֙
סוד זכר, ערי, סנדלפון הַזֹּ֔את וְנִלְחֲמ֣וּ עָלֶ֔יהָ פהל וּלְכָד֖וּהָ וּשְׂרָפֻ֣הָ בָאֵ֑שׁ אלהים דיודין ע"ה
וְאֶת־עָרֵ֤י ערי יְהוּדָה֙ אֶתֵּ֥ן שְׁמָמָ֖ה מֵאֵ֣ין יֹשֵֽׁב׃ 25 33 כֹּ֖ה הי אָמַ֣ר

33:²⁵ This is what the Lord says: "If I have not established My Covenant with day and night and the fixed laws of heaven and Earth,

²⁶ then I will reject the descendants of Jacob and David My servant and will not choose one of his sons to rule over the descendants of Abraham, Isaac and Jacob. For I will restore their fortunes and have compassion on them.' "

יְֽהֹוָ֔ה אָ֛ם ־לֹ֥א בְרִיתִ֖י יוֹמָ֣ם וָלָ֑יְלָה וְחֻקּ֖וֹת שָׁמַ֥יִם

וָאָ֔רֶץ לֹ֖א־שָֽׂמְתִּי׃ 26 גַּ֣ם ־זֶ֧רַע יַעֲקֹ֣וב וְדָוִ֣ד עַבְדִּ֗י

אֶמְאַ֞ס מִקַּ֣חַת מִזַּרְע֗וֹ מֹֽשְׁלִ֔ים אֶל־זֶ֖רַע אַבְרָהָ֑ם יִשְׂחָ֣ק וְֽיַעֲקֹ֑ב

כִּֽי־אָשִׁ֣יב (כתיב: אשוב) אֶת־שְׁבוּתָ֖ם וְרִֽחַמְתִּֽים׃

TERUMAH

LESSON OF TERUMAH
(Exodus 25:1-27:19)

"And I will sanctify the Tabernacle of the congregation . . . And I will dwell among the children of Israel and will be their God." (*Exodus 29:44-45*)

The Tabernacle was built to give the people of Israel a physical location where they could connect with the Creator. So why is it written: "And I will dwell among the children of Israel" and not "I dwelled within it," meaning in the Tabernacle (*Mishkan*)?

> *Rav Yosi opened the discussion saying: "The Song of Songs, which is Solomon's" [Shir haShirim] (Song of Songs 1:1). King Solomon was inspired to this song when the Temple was built, and all the worlds Above and Below were completed in one completion. Even though the friends disagree AS TO WHEN IT WAS SAID, THE MAIN OPINION IS THAT IT WAS SAID WHEN THE TEMPLE WAS BUILT. But this song was recited whole only when the moon, WHICH IS MALCHUT, was fully completed, and the Temple was built in the likeness of Above. When the Temple was built below, there was no joy before the Holy One, blessed be He, from the day that the world was created, like [there was] that day.*
> — The Zohar, Terumah 31:313

The Tabernacle—and later, the Holy Temple—were not brought into being so that the Light could be revealed there. They are actually manifestations of the Light that is revealed in each and every one of us. Each person must build a Tabernacle within themselves so that the Light of the Creator can "dwell" within. When a critical mass of people has built this internal edifice, only then will the Holy Temple be revealed to us.

But how do we build a Tabernacle within ourselves? We have learned that the first object created in the Tabernacle was the Ark, which was covered with gold both inside and out. This is a secret to our personal Tabernacle within. Why was it necessary to use gold on both the inside and the outside of the Ark? The lesson here reveals why and how many people fall in their spiritual work. They try to show how good they are on the outside, but on the inside, they are really not what they appear. In the end, however, the truth about a person's character and motivations always comes out. Developing the Light ("gold") within is a process of transforming the negativity that no one sees buried within us.

The important thing is not to lie—to others or to ourselves—in an attempt to cover up that negativity. If we think that we can lie to another person while still holding onto the truth inside ourselves, we are making a serious mistake. Before long, we will believe the lie that was intended for others and will forget the need to remove the negativity that was the source of that lie. This lesson about the lies we tell ourselves is made clear in a story that Rav Brandwein shared with Rav Berg.

There was a king who used to go away on vacation for one month every year. One time, while the king was away, the people of the kingdom gathered together and decided to play a prank on a local innkeeper. They seduced him with alcohol and then put him in the king's bed. When the innkeeper woke up in the morning, he was shocked to find himself in the king's bed. He thought he was dreaming, but he pinched himself and saw that he was not. "How can I know if I am really the King?" he thought. "I know. If I ring the bell for breakfast and nothing happens, then I will know I'm not the king." But when he rang, he was served breakfast immediately. And this is how the day continued: Everything that was customary to do for the king was done for the innkeeper until finally he thought to himself, "I really must be the ruler of the kingdom."

Later that day, the innkeeper discovered a private chamber of the king—a library full of books. "But I don't know how to read," he thought. "How can a ruler who does not know how to read have so many books? I can't be the real king." He felt very disappointed because he was enjoying the experience. Then he reconsidered. "Wait a minute! I know that I can't read, but then neither can anyone else. So I must be the king after all!"

This story may sound ridiculous, but it is exactly how many of us think and manage our lives. We lie to ourselves and then believe our own tales. Being truthful with ourselves is the first criterion we need to build our inner Tabernacle.

A second criterion can be gleaned from this lesson with regards to our ego. Today our culture glorifies self-promotion, but trying to seem "greater" than we are does not "fit in" with the work of building our personal Tabernacle. Our work is first to learn to "shrink" our ego. We learn from the *Gemara* that the Ark of the Covenant was the same size as the door of the Holy Temple itself. Therefore, the Ark could in no way physically pass through the door. But when the time came to bring the Ark inside, it became small enough to fit through the door. This teaches us that if we want a connection to the Holy Temple, we need to make ourselves smaller. The oversized "I" inside each of us must become undersized.

"That they bring me an offering..." (*Exodus 25:2*)

In a discussion on this verse, Rav Moshe asked the question: "Why is it written 'And they will bring me a donation, should it not have been written, 'And they will give me a donation'?" This question identifies the true nature of our spiritual work in this world—transforming our *Desire to Receive for the Self Alone* into the *Desire to Receive for the Sake of Sharing*. When we give from the place of the Desire to Receive for the Self Alone, everything that we "give" is given with a selfish motivation. When we include ourselves in the giving, our ego becomes the recipient. On the other hand, when we "bring" something to someone, we are merely a messenger. Our soul's birthright is to receive endless Light from the Creator. Thus, this simple question that Rav Moshe asked helps us to understand a giant lesson about how to truly receive all that the Light wants to give us.

When we "give," we are like a cup. But this means that unfortunately, the Light can only give us what fits inside our little Vessel. The *Zohar* says:

> *Rav Shimon opened the discussion saying: "That they bring Me an offering,*
> *of every man whose heart prompts him to give." (Exodus 25:2) "That they*
> *bring Me" POINTS OUT that if one wishes to undertake a precept and to aspire*
> *towards the Holy One, blessed be He, it is necessary that the person not strive*
> *in vain and empty handed, but rather that he makes efforts as befitting, and*
> *according to, his strengths. We have established this in many places, AND SO it*
> *is good for a person to strive after the Holy One, blessed be He, as it is written:*
> *"Every man shall give as he is able, according to the blessing of the Lord your*
> *God which He has given you." (Deuteronomy 16:17)*
> *--The Zohar, Terumah 6:34*

When we are a channel; when we "bring" instead of "give," we can receive infinitely because as a channel the endless Light can pass through us.

"...of every man whose heart prompts him to give." (*Exodus 25:2*)

Spiritual work must be done from the heart. This is essential! As we discussed earlier, the instructions for building the Tabernacle did not refer to its physical construction limited by time and place. When we build the Tabernacle in our hearts, it is for everyone through all generations.

My mother, Karen Berg, likes to tell a beautiful story that took place on Yom Kippur. The Gates of Heaven were locked, and even the prayers of the Baal Shem Tov and his students could not pry them open. One little boy wanted to help, but he did not know how to pray. But he had a whistle in his pocket, and he took it out and started to blow it as loud and as hard as he could. Everyone in the temple ran to quiet him down, but just as they were about to throw him out, the Baal Shem Tov announced, "By his merit, the Gates of Heaven have opened!"

Certainly, it's important to know the prayers and meditations. There's no question that the students of the Baal Shem Tov were familiar with all the technology of Kabbalah. Yet, sometimes, too much knowledge in our minds can cause us to lose the simplicity of the heart. According to the *Zohar*, "The Creator desires the heart." Without the simplicity and sincerity of the heart, all of the meditations, prayers, and Sacred Names are powerless.

> *"Of every man whose heart prompts him to give you shall take My offering."*
> *(Exodus 25:2) HE QUESTIONS: This passage should have said, "Every man*
> *whose heart prompts him," instead of "of every man?" HE ANSWERS: Here is*
> *the secret for those who understand measurements. Happy are those righteous*
> *ones who know how to place the desire of their heart before the supernal Holy*
> *King. The entire desire of their heart is not for this world and its vain desire, but*

rather they know and endeavor to place their desire and to cleave unto Above, in order to draw to them the desire of their Master from Above to Below.
The Zohar, Terumah 13:151

In the *Zohar* (*Terumah, Introduction to Chapter 6*), Rav Shimon explains to us that when each of us aspires for a connection with the Creator, we must strive with a pure heart and pay whatever price necessary to make that connection. Rav Shimon says that we are prompted to do this by the heart of God that exists within us. It is our heart and our longing for the Creator that drives our desire to overcome our Evil Inclination and embark on a more spiritual path.

There are people who are so knowledgeable, who have become so learned, that they begin to believe themselves to be *tzadikim* (wise and righteous people). True tzadikim, however, are more like small children in the purity and innocence of their hearts. When we believe that we "know," it will not be long before we believe that we know more than others. But if we observe the behavior of a righteous person, we see that they seek the words and thoughts of others. We never know where or through what source the Light will reveal itself. Righteous people are always listening for that source. This doesn't mean that we should not study and cultivate learning. We should—not for the lure of gathering more information, but rather in a search for spiritual enlightenment. We have to exercise restriction and control so that our hearts will be clean. It is written in the Gemara: "Some do more and some do less, but they should only give their hearts to the One Above."

SYNOPSIS OF TERUMAH

The chapter of Terumah, concerns the Tabernacle, which was the precursor of the Temple. Because we don't have the physical Temple in our time, we must build a spiritual Temple inside ourselves. Rav Berg teaches that according to the sages, the physical Temple does exist but we do not perceive it because we have not yet created our own Temple within. This is our life's work. Every action that we take, however significant or insignificant, helps us to either build or destroy this inner Temple.

Terumah describes the Tabernacle in its entirety. The word terumah means "charity." One way for a person to create our own Temple within and thus access this highest level of the Vessel and its energy is through charity and sharing.

FIRST READING - ABRAHAM - CHESED

25:1 The Lord said to Moses, saying, [2] Tell the Israelites to bring Me a contribution. You are to take the contribution for Me from each man whose heart prompts him to give.

[3] This is the contribution you are to take from them: gold, silver and bronze; [4] blue, purple and scarlet yarn and fine linen; goat hair; [5] ram skins dyed red and seal skins, acacia wood; [6] olive oil for the light; spices for the anointing oil and for the fragrant incense;[7] and onyx stones and other gems for the ephod and breastplate.

[8] Make for Me a sanctuary, and I will dwell among them.

[9] Make this Tabernacle and all its furnishings exactly like the design I will show you.

[10] Have them make a chest of acacia wood—two and a half cubits long, a cubit and a half wide, and a cubit and a half high.

[11] Overlay it with pure gold, both inside and out, and make a gold molding around it.

FROM THE RAV

The *Zohar* says that acquiring information requires nothing because Satan permits everybody to become his "partner" without investment. Satan offers you a free ride—everything you want you can have—but he will not guarantee this ride to last forever. Satan is permitted to let us take this free ride for forty or even of fifty years, until one day, he says, "Sorry, fellow, the trip is over; this is where you get off." Then he drops you and the "free ride" is over.

According to the *Zohar*, "…bring for Me an offering…you will take My Offering" means there is no fee for acquiring this kind of information. But if we want to implement this information—if we want this information to work for us, if we want to "take My Offering"—then we cannot receive it for nothing. Getting it in the first place is no problem, but if we want the security, if we want a guarantee that what we get, we can retain, then we cannot be Satan's partner. As the *Zohar* says:

Information is for everyone, whether you pay for it or not, as long as it remains just information. But if you want to internalize this information as knowledge; to make it an integral part of our life, it cannot be had for free. And removing this "partner" called Satan from our daily life can only be done with terumah (an effort, a personal contribution).

Exodus 25:10—The Ark of the Covenant

The Ark of the Covenant stored the Tablets, the physical manifestation of the Light that Moses received at Mount Sinai. During the time of both the First and Second Temples, the High Priest, once a year, would enter the Holy of Holies, which housed the Ark of the Covenant. The Ark contained all the answers to every question—all possible knowledge and information about yesterday, today, and tomorrow. If we could tap into that power, we would never waste time in bad relationships or unfulfilling careers. Instead, we would know immediately when a person or situation was wrong for us. Although the Ark of

FIRST READING - ABRAHAM - CHESED

וַיְדַבֵּר רָאה יְהוָֹוֹאֲדֹנָיֶאֱהֹדָהִי אֶל־מֹשֶׁה מהש, אל עדי לֵאמֹר: 2 דַּבֵּר רָאה 25 1

אֶל־בְּנֵי יִשְׂרָאֵל וְיִקְחוּ וֹעם ־לִי תְרוּמָה מֵאֵת כָּל ־אִישׁ ילי עֵ"ה קִנ"א קֵס"א

אֲשֶׁר יִדְּבֶנּוּ לִבּוֹ תִּקְחוּ אֶת־תְּרוּמָתִי: 3 וְזֹאת הַתְּרוּמָה אֲשֶׁר תִּקְחוּ

מֵאִתָּם זָהָב וָכֶסֶף וּנְחֹשֶׁת: 4 וּתְכֵלֶת וְאַרְגָּמָן קנ"א קמג וְתוֹלַעַת שׁקוצי"ת שָׁנִי

וְשֵׁשׁ וְעִזִּים: 5 וְעֹרֹת אֵילִם מְאָדָּמִים וְעֹרֹת תְּחָשִׁים וַעֲצֵי שִׁטִּים:

שֶׁמֶן י"פ טל, ביט י"פ כוז"ו, ל מ לְמָאֹר בְּשָׂמִים עצצ"ב, ג' מלוי אהיה לְשֶׁמֶן י"פ טל, ביט י"פ כוז"ו, ביט 6

הַמִּשְׁחָה וְלִקְטֹרֶת הַסַּמִּים י"א אדני הסמים אלהים ארני עֵ"ה קנ"א, אלהים ארני 7 אַבְנֵי־שֹׁהַם מהש, אל עדי

וְאַבְנֵי מִלֻּאִים לָאֵפֹד עֵ"ה אלהים וְלַחֹשֶׁן שׂדי ורבוע אהיה: 8 וְעָשׂוּ לִי מִקְדָּשׁ

וְשָׁכַנְתִּי בְּתוֹכָם: 9 כְּכֹל ילי אֲשֶׁר אֲנִי אני, טרהד כוז"ו מַרְאֶה אוֹתְךָ אֵת

תַּבְנִית הַמִּשְׁכָּן ב"פ (רבוע אלהים + ה) וְאֵת תַּבְנִית כָּל ־כֵּלָיו ילי וְכֵן תַּעֲשׂוּ:

10 וְעָשׂוּ עֵ"ה ג"פ אלהים ‖אֲרוֹן‖ עֲצֵי שִׁטִּים אַמָּתַיִם וָחֵצִי אָרְכּוֹ וְאַמָּה

וָחֵצִי רָחְבּוֹ מלוי ע"ב וְאַמָּה וָחֵצִי קֹמָתוֹ דמב, מלוי ע"ב: 11 וְצִפִּיתָ אֹתוֹ זָהָב

טָהוֹר י"פ אכא ‖מִבַּיִת‖ ב"פ ראה וּמִחוּץ תְּצַפֶּנּוּ וְעָשִׂיתָ עָלָיו זֵר אור, אין סוף זָהָב

---

the Covenant has disappeared, today the Light and wisdom of the Ark is stored in the *Zohar*, our compendium of wisdom and our source of Light—and it's there for all of humanity to use. The Creator's Light never disappears; it just changed form.

"But the wise shall understand." (Daniel 12:10) These are the scholars of Kabbalah. It says about them: "...and they who are wise shall shine like the brightness of the firmaments." (Ibid. 3). This refers to those who place their effort in the splendor called the Zohar, that is like Noah's Ark, to which are gathered two from a city, seven from a kingdom and, occasionally, one from a city and two from a family... This is the Light of this

book OF ZOHAR, and all is due to you.
— The Zohar, Beha'alotcha 16:88

מִבַּיִת וּמִחוּץ

Exodus 25:11—The Ark of the Covenant was covered inside and out with gold.

The lesson we can learn from this verse is that there is only one requirement for accessing the Light and wisdom within the Ark: We must be of the same essence both inside and out. We have to be truthful and honest both with ourselves and with others. We cannot behave one way, while feeling something entirely different in our hearts.

[12] *Cast four gold rings for it and fasten them to its four feet, with two rings on one side and two rings on the other side.*

[13] *Then make pillars of acacia wood and overlay them with gold.*

[14] *Insert the pillars into the rings on the sides of the chest to carry the Ark with them.*

[15] *The pillars are to remain in the rings of this ark; they are not to be removed.*

[16] *Then put in the Ark of the Covenant, which I will give you.*

SECOND READING - ISAAC - GEVURAH

[17] *Make a cover of pure gold—two and a half cubits long and a cubit and a half wide.*

[18] *And make two cherubim out of hammered gold at the ends of the cover.*

[19] *Make one cherub on one end and the second cherub on the other end; make the cherubim of one piece with the cover, at the two ends.*

[20] *The cherubim are to have their wings spread upward, overshadowing the cover with them. The cherubim are to face each other, looking toward the cover.*

[21] *Place the cover on top of the Ark and put in the Ark the Covenant, which I will give you.*

[22] *I will meet with you there and speak to you above the cover between the two cherubim that are over the Ark of the Covenant, everything that I command for the Israelites.*

כְּרֻבִים

Exodus 25:18—At the crown of the Ark was a golden sculpture of two cherubs.

This reminds us that whenever our prayers cannot reach the Heavens by our own merit, angels help us by carrying our prayers to the Upper Worlds. Rashi said that when God spoke to Moses, the Voice would come from Heaven to the top of the Ark, and from between the cherubs it would emanate to where Moses stood in the outer chamber of the Tabernacle.

Rav Aba said: What does THE VERSE wish to say with the statement, "I appear in the cloud upon the ark cover," WHICH MEANS THAT PRIEST SEES THE SHECHINAH? ALSO, in the verse, "Thus (with "zot") shall Aaron come," WHICH IS THE SHECHINAH REFERRED TO AS ZOT. Behold, the priest did not see the Shechinah when he entered THE HOLY OF HOLIES. HE ANSWERS: The cloud, WHICH IS THE SHECHINAH, would come down. In coming down, it reached the covering of the Ark, the wings of

סָבִיב: 12 וְיָצַקְתָּ לּוֹ אַרְבַּע טַבְּעֹת זָהָב וְנָתַתָּה עַל אַרְבַּע פַּעֲמֹתָיו

וּשְׁתֵּי טַבָּעֹת עַל־צַלְעוֹ הָאֶחָת וּשְׁתֵּי טַבָּעֹת עַל־צַלְעוֹ הַשֵּׁנִית:

13 וְעָשִׂיתָ בַדֵּי עֲצֵי שִׁטִּים וְצִפִּיתָ אֹתָם זָהָב: 14 וְהֵבֵאתָ אֶת־הַבַּדִּים

בַּטַּבָּעֹת עַל צַלְעֹת הָאָרֹן ע"ב ורבוע ע"ב לָשֵׂאת אֶת־הָאָרֹן ע"ב ורבוע ע"ב בָּהֶם:

15 בְּטַבְּעֹת הָאָרֹן ע"ב ורבוע ע"ב יִהְיוּ הַבַּדִּים לֹא יָסֻרוּ מִמֶּנּוּ: 16 וְנָתַתָּ

אֶל־הָאָרֹן ע"ב ורבוע ע"ב אֵת הָעֵדֻת אֲשֶׁר אֶתֵּן אֵלֶיךָ אני:

SECOND READING - ISAAC - GEVURAH

17 וְעָשִׂיתָ כַפֹּרֶת זָהָב טָהוֹר י"פ אכא אַמָּתַיִם וָחֵצִי אָרְכָּהּ וְאַמָּה דמב, מלוי ע"ב

וָחֵצִי רָחְבָּהּ: 18 וְעָשִׂיתָ שְׁנַיִם [כְּרֻבִים] זָהָב מִקְשָׁה תַּעֲשֶׂה אֹתָם

מִשְּׁנֵי קְצוֹת הַכַּפֹּרֶת: 19 וַעֲשֵׂה כְּרוּב אֶחָד אהבה, דאגה מִקָּצָה ה"פ טל, ג"פ אדני

מִזֶּה וּכְרוּב־אֶחָד אהבה, דאגה מִקָּצָה ה"פ טל, ג"פ אדני מִזֶּה מִן־הַכַּפֹּרֶת תַּעֲשׂוּ

אֶת־ הַכְּרֻבִים עַל־שְׁנֵי קְצוֹתָיו: 20 וְהָיוּ הַכְּרֻבִים פֹּרְשֵׂי כְנָפַיִם

לְמַעְלָה סֹכְכִים בְּכַנְפֵיהֶם עַל־הַכַּפֹּרֶת וּפְנֵיהֶם אִישׁ ע"ה קנ"א קס"א אֶל־

אָחִיו אֶל־הַכַּפֹּרֶת יִהְיוּ חכמה בינה פְּנֵי הַכְּרֻבִים: 21 וְנָתַתָּ אֶת־הַכַּפֹּרֶת

עַל־הָאָרֹן ע"ב ורבוע ע"ב מִלְמָעְלָה וְאֶל־הָאָרֹן ע"ב ורבוע ע"ב תִּתֵּן ב"פ כהת אֶת־

הָעֵדֻת אֲשֶׁר אֶתֵּן אֵלֶיךָ אני: 22 וְנוֹעַדְתִּי לְךָ שָׁם יהוה שדי וְדִבַּרְתִּי ראה

אִתְּךָ מֵעַל הַכַּפֹּרֶת מִבֵּין עלם שְׁנֵי הַכְּרֻבִים אֲשֶׁר עַל־אֲרֹן ע"ה ג"פ אלהים

הָעֵדֻת אֵת כָּל ילי ־אֲשֶׁר אֲצַוֶּה אוֹתְךָ אֶל־בְּנֵי יִשְׂרָאֵל: 23 וְעָשִׂיתָ

---

the cherubs would stir and the cherubs would strike with their wings and sing a song. FROM THIS, THE PRIEST WOULD REALIZE THAT THE SHECHINAH WAS NOW APPEARING. THIS IS WHAT IS MEANT BY, "I APPEAR IN THE CLOUD UPON THE ARK COVER."
— The Zohar, Acherei Mot 7:53

Angels are the essential link between our world and the Upper World, and so it is valuable to know how to connect with them and gain their assistance. We need to make sure our actions stem from the right intentions so we can access the right angels, both in our prayers and in our dreams.

23 Make a table of acacia wood—two cubits long, a cubit wide and a cubit and a half high. 24 Overlay it with pure gold and make a gold molding around it.

25 Also make around it a rim a handbreadth wide and put a gold molding on the rim.

26 Make four gold rings for it and fasten them to the four corners, where the four legs are. 27 The rings are to be close to the rim to house the poles used in carrying the table.

28 Make the poles of acacia wood, overlay them with gold and carry the table with them.

29 And make its plates and dishes, as well as its pitchers and bowls for the pouring out of offerings, of pure gold you shall make them. 30 Put on the table the showbread to be before Me at all times.

THIRD READING - JACOB - TIFERET

31 Make a candelabra of pure gold and hammer it out, base and shaft; its cups, its knops, and its flowers, shall be of one piece with it. 32 Six branches are to extend from its sides—three branches of the candelabra on one side and three branches of the candelabra on the other.

הַשֻּׁלְחָן

Exodus 25:30—The Tabernacle furnishings: "showbread."

Inside the Tabernacle was a table on which 12 loaves of bread for Shabbat—known as the "showbread"—were placed.

> *Rav Yesa opened the discussion saying: "You shall make a table of acacia wood ...." (Exodus 25:23) This table stands inside the Tabernacle and a supernal blessing dwells upon it. From it emerges food for the whole world, and this table should not be empty for even one moment. There should be food on it because the blessing is not present in an empty place. Therefore, bread must constantly be on it, in order that the Supernal Blessing shall always be present in it. And from that table, blessing*

> *and food come out to all the other tables of the world that are blessed due to it.*
> *— The Zohar, Terumah 47:503*

These twelve loaves represent the twelve signs of the zodiac, while the table was a vehicle for each person to rise above the celestial influences of this physical world and their astrological designation. If a person who is governed by a fire sign rises above the limitations of his or her sign, he or she can share a perfect relationship with a water sign, although the two signs are not traditionally compatible. There are so many more possibilities in life than our astrological destiny offers us. This reading acts as a spiritual support so that we can rise above the influence of our sign and the limitations of this physical world.

מְנֹרַת

Exodus 25:31—A candelabrum (Menorah) was also present on the table in the Tabernacle.

שֻׁלְחָן עֲצֵי שִׁטִּים אַמָּתַיִם אָרְכּוֹ וְאַמָּה רׇחְבּוֹ דמב, מלוי ע"ב וְאַמָּה דמב, מלוי ע"ב

וָחֵצִי קֹמָתוֹ: 24 וְצִפִּיתָ אֹתוֹ זָהָב טָהוֹר י"פ אכא וְעָשִׂיתָ לּוֹ זֵר אור, אין סוף

זָהָב סָבִיב: 25 וְעָשִׂיתָ לּוֹ מִסְגֶּרֶת טֹפַח סָבִיב וְעָשִׂיתָ זֵר אור, אין סוף

זָהָב לְמִסְגַּרְתּוֹ סָבִיב: 26 וְעָשִׂיתָ לּוֹ אַרְבַּע טַבְּעֹת זָהָב וְנָתַתָּ אֶת־

הַטַּבָּעֹת עַל אַרְבַּע הַפֵּאֹת אֲשֶׁר לְאַרְבַּע רַגְלָיו: 27 לְעֻמַּת הַמִּסְגֶּרֶת

תִּהְיֶיןָ הַטַּבָּעֹת לְבָתִּים לְבַדִּים לָשֵׂאת אֶת־הַשֻּׁלְחָן: 28 וְעָשִׂיתָ אֶת־

הַבַּדִּים עֲצֵי שִׁטִּים וְצִפִּיתָ אֹתָם זָהָב וְנִשָּׂא־בָם מ"ב אֶת־הַשֻּׁלְחָן:

29 וְעָשִׂיתָ קְּעָרֹתָיו וְכַפֹּתָיו וּקְשׂוֹתָיו וּמְנַקִּיֹּתָיו אֲשֶׁר יֻסַּךְ בָּהֵן זָהָב

טָהוֹר י"פ אכא תַּעֲשֶׂה אֹתָם: 30 וְנָתַתָּ עַל־הַשֻּׁלְחָן לֶחֶם ג"פ יהוה פָּנִים

לְפָנַי ע"ב ס"ג מ"ה וחכמה בינה תָּמִיד קס"א קנ"א קמ"ג, ע"ה נתה:

THIRD READING - JACOB - TIFERET

31 וְעָשִׂיתָ מְנֹרַת זָהָב טָהוֹר י"פ אכא מִקְשָׁה תֵּעָשֶׂה הַמְּנוֹרָה יְרֵכָהּ

וְקָנָהּ קס"א גְּבִיעֶיהָ כַּפְתֹּרֶיהָ וּפְרָחֶיהָ מִמֶּנָּה יִהְיוּ אל"ד: 32 וְשִׁשָּׁה קָנִים

יֹצְאִים מִצִּדֶּיהָ שְׁלֹשָׁה אהבה, דאגה קְנֵי מְנֹרָה מִצִּדָּהּ הָאֶחָד וּשְׁלֹשָׁה

As long as we have a strong desire to do our spiritual work and we constantly look for opportunities to relinquish our Desire to Receive for the Self Alone, we will always get help. Surrendering this desire is not something we can accomplish alone. The twelve loaves and the Menorah, all present on the table in the Tabernacle, help us to rise above the nature of the Desire to Receive for the Self Alone. The Creator wants to give us more than we could ever hope for—but we need to turn on the Light. It is our actions that give us access to the Light; lighting the Menorah on the table represents those actions.

"When you light the lamps, the seven lamps shall give light towards the body of the candlestick." (Numbers 8:2) Here, the Congregation of Israel, THAT IS MALCHUT, received Light, as Supernal Ima, THAT IS BINAH, is adorned, and all the candles, THAT ARE THE SEFIROT OF MALCHUT, illuminate within and from her. THEY SAID ABOUT THEMSELVES: Two refined souls soar from her; THAT IS, THEY UPLIFT MAYIN NUKVIN (ENG. 'FEMALE WATERS') WITH THEIR TORAH STUDY. All the best men—MEANING ALL WHO UPLIFT FEMALE WATERS THROUGH THEIR TORAH THAT ARE REFERRED TO AS 'GROOMSMEN'—connect MALCHUT to the Upper One, WHICH IS BINAH. From there, THEY DRAW HER LIGHT downwards.
The Zohar, Beha'alotcha 4:20

33 Three cups shaped like almond flowers with buds and blossoms are to be on one branch, and three cups shaped like almond flowers with buds and blossoms are to be on one branch, the same for all six branches extending from the candelabra.

34 And on the candelabra stand there are to be four cups shaped like almond flowers with buds and blossoms.

35 One bud shall be under the first pair of branches extending from it, a second bud under the second pair, and a third bud under the third pair—to be done to all six branches extending from the candelabra.

36 The buds and branches shall all be of one piece with it, hammered out of pure gold. 37 Then make its seven lamps and set them up on it so that they light the space in front of it. 38 Its wick trimmers and trays are to be of pure gold.

39 A talent of pure gold is to be used for the candelabra and all these accessories.

40 See that you make them according to the pattern shown to you on the mountain.

26:1 Make the Tabernacle with ten curtains of finely twisted linen and blue, purple and scarlet yarn, with cherubim worked into them by a skilled craftsman.

2 The length of one curtain is to be twenty-eight cubits long and four cubits wide; this same measure is to be used for all the curtains.

3 Join five of the curtains together, to one another, and join the remaining five curtains together, to one another. 4 Make loops of blue material along the edge of the end curtain in one set, and do the same with the outermost curtain in the second set.

5 Make fifty loops on one curtain and fifty loops on the outermost curtain of the second set, with the loops opposite each other.

עַשְׁתֵּי־עֶשְׂרֵה

Exodus 26:7—The eleven outer coverings of the Tabernacle.

There are ten levels or dimensions in this universe, corresponding to the *Ten Sefirot,* or the Tree of Life. The ten curtains made of fine linen within the Tabernacle point to this truth.

> He opened the discussion saying: "Moreover you shall make the tabernacle with ten curtains...." (Exodus 26:1) Here is the mystery of unison, BECAUSE THE TEN CURTAINS CORRESPOND TO THE TEN SEFIROT. The perfection of the

Tabernacle is made of numerous grades, as it is written: "That the Tabernacle shall be one," (Ibid. 6) in order to show that all the limbs of the body of the Tabernacle are the secret of one body.
> — The Zohar, Terumah 65:664

The eleventh outer covering represents the eleventh dimension, which is the domain of Satan. Although we, in the dimension of *Malchut,* have no Light of our own, *Malchut* has the potential and is, in fact, destined to reveal Light. But in the eleventh dimension of Satan, no Light ever will or ever can be revealed. Satan only receives his Light from us, through our actions. Satan exists in order to challenge us to overcome our ego-driven desires so that we can

קְנֵי מְנֹרָה מִצִּדָּהּ הַשֵּׁנִי: 33 שְׁלֹשָׁה גְבִעִים מְשֻׁקָּדִים בַּקָּנֶה הִ"פ אל
הָאֶחָד אהבה, דאגה כַּפְתֹּר וָפֶרַח רפ"ח וּשְׁלֹשָׁה גְבִעִים מְשֻׁקָּדִים בַּקָּנֶה
הָאֶחָד אהבה, דאגה הִ"פ אל כַּפְתֹּר וָפֶרַח רפ"ח כֵּן לְשֵׁשֶׁת הַקָּנִים הַיֹּצְאִים מִן־
הַמְּנֹרָה: 34 וּבַמְּנֹרָה אַרְבָּעָה גְבִעִים מְשֻׁקָּדִים כַּפְתֹּרֶיהָ וּפְרָחֶיהָ:
35 וְכַפְתֹּר תַּחַת שְׁנֵי הַקָּנִים מִמֶּנָּה וְכַפְתֹּר תַּחַת שְׁנֵי הַקָּנִים מִמֶּנָּה
וְכַפְתֹּר תַּחַת־שְׁנֵי הַקָּנִים מִמֶּנָּה לְשֵׁשֶׁת הַקָּנִים הַיֹּצְאִים מִן־הַמְּנֹרָה:
36 כַּפְתֹּרֵיהֶם וּקְנֹתָם מִמֶּנָּה יִהְיוּ אל כֻּלָּהּ מִקְשָׁה אַחַת זָהָב טָהוֹר
יי"פ אכא 37 וְעָשִׂיתָ אֶת־נֵרֹתֶיהָ שִׁבְעָה וְהֶעֱלָה אֶת־נֵרֹתֶיהָ וְהֵאִיר עַל־
עֵבֶר רבוע יהוה ורבוע אלהים פָּנֶיהָ: 38 וּמַלְקָחֶיהָ וּמַחְתֹּתֶיהָ זָהָב טָהוֹר יי"פ אכא
39 כִּכָּר זָהָב טָהוֹר יי"פ אכא יַעֲשֶׂה אֹתָהּ אֵת כָּל־ יל-י הַכֵּלִים הָאֵלֶּה:
40 וּרְאֵה ראה וַעֲשֵׂה בְּתַבְנִיתָם אֲשֶׁר־אַתָּה מָרְאֶה בָּהָר אור, רֹ: 26 1 וְאֶת־
הַמִּשְׁכָּן ב"פ (רבוע אלהים ÷ ה) תַּעֲשֶׂה עֶשֶׂר יְרִיעֹת שֵׁשׁ מָשְׁזָר וּתְכֵלֶת
וְאַרְגָּמָן קנ"א קמג וְתֹלַעַת שָׁנִי קוצרי"ת כְּרֻבִים מַעֲשֵׂה חֹשֵׁב תַּעֲשֶׂה אֹתָם:
2 אֹרֶךְ | הַיְרִיעָה הָאַחַת שְׁמֹנֶה וְעֶשְׂרִים בָּאַמָּה דמב, מלוי ע"ב וְרֹחַב
אַרְבַּע בָּאַמָּה דמב, מלוי ע"ב הַיְרִיעָה הָאֶחָת אהיה ע"ה יהוה ע"ה מִדָּה אַחַת לְכָל
יה אדני הַיְרִיעֹת: 3 חֲמֵשׁ הַיְרִיעֹת תִּהְיֶיןָ חֹבְרֹת אִשָּׁה אֶל־אֲחֹתָהּ
וְחָמֵשׁ יְרִיעֹת חֹבְרֹת אִשָּׁה אֶל־אֲחֹתָהּ: 4 וְעָשִׂיתָ לֻלְאֹת תְּכֵלֶת עַל
שְׂפַת הַיְרִיעָה הָאֶחָת מִקָּצָה הִ"פ טל, ג"פ אדני בַּחֹבָרֶת וְכֵן תַּעֲשֶׂה בִּשְׂפַת
הַיְרִיעָה הַקִּיצוֹנָה בַּמַּחְבֶּרֶת הַשֵּׁנִית: 5 חֲמִשִּׁים לֻלָאֹת תַּעֲשֶׂה בַּיְרִיעָה
הָאֶחָת וַחֲמִשִּׁים לֻלָאֹת תַּעֲשֶׂה בִּקְצֵה הִ"פ טל, ג"פ אדני הַיְרִיעָה אֲשֶׁר
בַּמַּחְבֶּרֶת הַשֵּׁנִית מַקְבִּילֹת הַלֻּלָאֹת אִשָּׁה אֶל־אֲחֹתָהּ: 6 וְעָשִׂיתָ
חֲמִשִּׁים קַרְסֵי זָהָב וְחִבַּרְתָּ אֶת־הַיְרִיעֹת אִשָּׁה אֶל־אֲחֹתָהּ בַּקְּרָסִים
וְהָיָה יהוה; יהה הַמִּשְׁכָּן ב"פ (רבוע אלהים ÷ ה) אֶחָד אהבה, דאגה 7 וְעָשִׂיתָ יְרִיעֹת
עִזִּים לְאֹהֶל לאה עַל־הַמִּשְׁכָּן ב"פ (רבוע אלהים ÷ ה) עַשְׁתֵּי־עֶשְׂרֵה יְרִיעֹת

6 Then make fifty gold clasps and use them to fasten the curtains together so that the Tabernacle is one.

7 Make curtains of goat hair for the tent over the Tabernacle—eleven curtains altogether you shall make.

8 The first curtain is to be thirty cubits long and four cubits wide—this is to be done to each of the eleven curtains. 9 Join five of the curtains together into one set and the other six into another set. Fold the sixth curtain double at the front of the tent.

10 Make fifty loops along the edge of the external curtain in one set and fifty loops along the edge of the end curtain in the other set. 11 Then make fifty bronze clasps and put them in the loops to fasten the tent together as one.

12 For the remainder of the tent curtains, the half curtain that remains is to hang down at the rear of the Tabernacle.

13 The tent curtains will be a cubit longer on both sides; what is left will hang over the sides of the Tabernacle so as to cover it.

14 Make a covering for the tent of ram skins dyed red, and over that a covering of seal skins.

FOURTH READING - MOSES - NETZACH

15 Make upright boards of acacia wood for the Tabernacle.

16 Each board is to be ten cubits long and a cubit and a half wide,

---

achieve our potential of revealing Light in this physical dimension. Without Satan, we cannot do what we came here to do. However, Satan needs only minimal nourishment, but our negative actions empower him with much more fuel than he requires. The eleventh outer covering of the Tabernacle teaches us that we should throw Satan a bone, but we don't need to feed him a six-course meal.

HE EXPLAINS: Since the former measurement is sacred, with the sacred colors "of fine twined linen, and blue, and purple, and scarlet." (Exodus 26:1). These are sacred colors, ALLUDING TO CHESED, GEVURAH, TIFERET AND MALCHUT; LINEN BEING CHESED; SCARLET, GEVURAH; PURPLE, TIFERET; AND BLUE, MALCHUT. ... To this alludes the verse, "Blessed is he who considers the poor (Heb. dal), God will deliver him in the day of evil," (Psalms 41:2) MEANING THAT in the day of evil, OF JUDGMENT, God will deliver him. FOR THE CURTAINS OF GOATS' HAIR ALLUDE TO POVERTY AND JUDGMENT, COVERING AND PROTECTING HOLINESS, WHICH IS CURTAINS OF FINE TWINED LINEN ... SO THAT THE EXTERNAL FORCES WOULD NOT NOURISH FROM THEM.
— The Zohar, Pekudei 26:247

תַּעֲשֶׂה אֹתָם: 8 אֹרֶךְ | הַיְרִיעָה הָאַחַת שְׁלֹשִׁים בָּאַמָּה רמב, מלוי ע״ב

וְרֹחַב אַרְבַּע בָּאַמָּה רמב, מלוי ע״ב הַיְרִיעָה הָאֶחָת מִדָּה אהיה ע״ה יהוה ע״ה אַחַת

לְעַשְׁתֵּי עֶשְׂרֵה יְרִיעֹת: 9 וְחִבַּרְתָּ֙ אֶת־חֲמֵשׁ הַיְרִיעֹת לְבָד וְאֶת־שֵׁשׁ

הַיְרִיעֹת לְבָד וְכָפַלְתָּ֙ אֶת־הַיְרִיעָה הַשִּׁשִּׁית אֶל־מוּל פְּנֵי חכמה בינה

הָאֹהֶל לאה: 10 וְעָשִׂיתָ לֻלְאֹת חֲמִשִּׁים עַל שְׂפַת הַיְרִיעָה הָאֶחָת

הַקִּיצֹנָה בַּחֹבָרֶת וַחֲמִשִּׁים לֻלָאֹת עַל שְׂפַת הַיְרִיעָה הַחֹבֶרֶת הַשֵּׁנִית:

11 וְעָשִׂיתָ קַרְסֵי נְחֹשֶׁת חֲמִשִּׁים וְהֵבֵאתָ֙ אֶת־הַקְּרָסִים בַּלֻּלָאֹת

וְחִבַּרְתָּ֙ אֶת־הָאֹהֶל לאה וְהָיָה אֶחָד יהוה, יהה אהבה, דאגה 12 וְסֶרַח הָעֹדֵף

בִּירִיעֹת הָאֹהֶל לאה וְחֲצִי הַיְרִיעָה הָעֹדֶפֶת תִּסְרַח עַל אֲחֹרֵי הַמִּשְׁכָּן

ב״פ (רבוע אלהים ־ ה): 13 וְהָאַמָּה רמב, מלוי ע״ב מִזֶּה וְהָאַמָּה רמב, מלוי ע״ב מִזֶּה בָּעֹדֵף

בְּאֹרֶךְ יְרִיעֹת הָאֹהֶל לאה יִהְיֶה סָרוּחַ עַל־צִדֵּי הַמִּשְׁכָּן ב״פ (רבוע אלהים ־ ה)

מִזֶּה וּמִזֶּה לְכַסֹּתוֹ: 14 וְעָשִׂיתָ מִכְסֶה לָאֹהֶל לאה עֹרֹת אֵילִם מְאָדָּמִים

וּמִכְסֵה עֹרֹת תְּחָשִׁים מִלְמָעְלָה:

FOURTH READING - MOSES - NETZACH

15 | וְעָשִׂיתָ אֶת־הַקְּרָשִׁים לַמִּשְׁכָּן ב״פ (רבוע אלהים ־ ה) עֲצֵי שִׁטִּים עֹמְדִים:

16 עֶשֶׂר אַמּוֹת אֹרֶךְ הַקָּרֶשׁ וְאַמָּה רמב, מלוי ע״ב וַחֲצִי הָאַמָּה רמב, מלוי ע״ב

רֹחַב הַקֶּרֶשׁ הָאֶחָד אהבה, דאגה: 17 שְׁתֵּי יָדוֹת לַקֶּרֶשׁ הָאֶחָד אהבה, דאגה

וְעָשִׂיתָ

Exodus 26:15—The Tabernacle walls.

Here we read a detailed description of God's
instructions for the walls of the Tabernacle,
which were to be made of enormous planks of
acacia wood. *Midrash Tanchuma* says that many
generations before the building of the Tabernacle,
Jacob anticipated the future and had planted the
acacia trees in Egypt. Jacob told his children to
take this wood when they fled from their exile.

Life rarely offers a clear distinction between black
and white; so instead, we choose from shades of
gray. It is always better to make a choice, even to
choose black, rather than making no choice at all. If
we discover later that that it was the wrong choice, we
can learn from our mistake, cleanse ourselves, and
move to white. The walls of the Tabernacle provide
us with a clear line between black and white.

17 with two projections set parallel to each other. Make all the boards of the Tabernacle in this way.

18 Make twenty boards for the south side of the Tabernacle

19 and make forty silver sockets to go under them—two boards for each frame, one under each of the twenty sockets.

20 For the other side, the north side of the Tabernacle, make twenty boards

21 and forty silver sockets—two under one board and two on the other.

22 Make six boards for the far end, that is, the west end of the Tabernacle, 23 and make two boards for the corners at the far end.

24 At these two corners they must be double from the bottom all the way to the top, and fitted into a single ring; both shall be like that.

25 So there will be eight boards and sixteen silver sockets—two under one frame, and two under the other frame.

26 Also make crossbars of acacia wood: five for the boards on one side of the Tabernacle,

27 five for those on the second side of the Tabernacle, and five for the boards on the west, at the far end of the Tabernacle.

28 The center crossbar is to extend from end to end at the middle of the boards.

29 Overlay the boards with gold and make gold rings to house the crossbars. Also overlay the crossbars with gold.

30 Erect the Tabernacle according to the plan shown to you on the mountain.

מְשֻׁלָּבֹת אִשָּׁה אֶל־אֲחֹתָהּ כֵּן תַּעֲשֶׂה לְכֹל יה אדני קַרְשֵׁי הַמִּשְׁכָּן

ב"פ (רבוע אלהים ∔ ה): 18 וְעָשִׂיתָ אֶת־הַקְּרָשִׁים לַמִּשְׁכָּן ב"פ (רבוע אלהים ∔ ה) עֶשְׂרִים

קֶרֶשׁ לִפְאַת נֶגְבָּה תֵימָנָה: 19 וְאַרְבָּעִים אַדְנֵי־כֶסֶף תַּעֲשֶׂה תַּחַת

עֶשְׂרִים הַקֶּרֶשׁ שְׁנֵי אֲדָנִים תַּחַת־הַקֶּרֶשׁ הָאֶחָד אהבה, דאגה לִשְׁתֵּי

יְדֹתָיו וּשְׁנֵי אֲדָנִים תַּחַת־הַקֶּרֶשׁ הָאֶחָד אהבה, דאגה לִשְׁתֵּי יְדֹתָיו:

20 וּלְצֶלַע הַמִּשְׁכָּן ב"פ (רבוע אלהים ∔ ה) הַשֵּׁנִית לִפְאַת צָפוֹן עֶשְׂרִים קָרֶשׁ:

21 וְאַרְבָּעִים אַדְנֵיהֶם כָּסֶף שְׁנֵי אֲדָנִים תַּחַת הַקֶּרֶשׁ הָאֶחָד אהבה, דאגה

וּשְׁנֵי אֲדָנִים תַּחַת הַקֶּרֶשׁ הָאֶחָד אהבה, דאגה: 22 וּלְיַרְכְּתֵי הַמִּשְׁכָּן

ב"פ (רבוע אלהים ∔ ה) יָמָּה תַּעֲשֶׂה שִׁשָּׁה קְרָשִׁים: 23 וּשְׁנֵי קְרָשִׁים תַּעֲשֶׂה

לִמְקֻצְעֹת הַמִּשְׁכָּן ב"פ (רבוע אלהים ∔ ה) בַּיַּרְכָתָיִם: 24 וְיִהְיוּ מלוי ס"ג תֹאֲמִם

מִלְּמַטָּה וְיַחְדָּו יִהְיוּ אל תַמִּים עַל־רֹאשׁוֹ אֶל־הַטַּבַּעַת הָאֶחָת כֵּן יִהְיֶה

לִשְׁנֵיהֶם לִשְׁנֵי הַמִּקְצֹעֹת יִהְיוּ אל: 25 וְהָיוּ שְׁמֹנָה קְרָשִׁים וְאַדְנֵיהֶם יי

כֶּסֶף שִׁשָּׁה עָשָׂר אֲדָנִים שְׁנֵי אֲדָנִים תַּחַת הַקֶּרֶשׁ הָאֶחָד אהבה, דאגה

וּשְׁנֵי אֲדָנִים תַּחַת הַקֶּרֶשׁ הָאֶחָד אהבה, דאגה: 26 וְעָשִׂיתָ בְרִיחִם עֲצֵי

שִׁטִּים חֲמִשָּׁה לְקַרְשֵׁי צֶלַע־הַמִּשְׁכָּן ב"פ (רבוע אלהים ∔ ה) הָאֶחָד אהבה, דאגה:

27 וַחֲמִשָּׁה בְרִיחִם לְקַרְשֵׁי צֶלַע־הַמִּשְׁכָּן ב"פ (רבוע אלהים ∔ ה) הַשֵּׁנִית

וַחֲמִשָּׁה בְרִיחִם לְקַרְשֵׁי צֶלַע הַמִּשְׁכָּן ב"פ (רבוע אלהים ∔ ה) לַיַּרְכָתַיִם יָמָּה:

28 וְהַבְּרִיחַ הַתִּיכֹן בְּתוֹךְ הַקְּרָשִׁים מַבְרִחַ מִן־הַקָּצֶה ה"פ טל, ג"פ אדני אֶל־

הַקָּצֶה ה"פ טל, ג"פ אדני: 29 וְאֶת־הַקְּרָשִׁים תְּצַפֶּה זָהָב וְאֶת־טַבְּעֹתֵיהֶם

תַּעֲשֶׂה זָהָב בָּתִּים לַבְּרִיחִם וְצִפִּיתָ אֶת־הַבְּרִיחִם זָהָב: 30 וַהֲקֵמֹתָ

אֶת־הַמִּשְׁכָּן ב"פ (רבוע אלהים ∔ ה) כְּמִשְׁפָּטוֹ אֲשֶׁר הָרְאֵיתָ בָּהָר אור, רו:

FIFTH READING - AARON - HOD

31 Make a curtain of blue, purple and scarlet yarn and finely twisted linen, with cherubim worked into it by a skilled craftsman.

32 Hang it with gold hooks on four pillars of acacia wood overlaid with gold and standing on four silver bases.

33 Hang the curtain from the clasps and place the Ark of the Covenant behind the curtain. The curtain will separate the Holy Place from the Holy of Holies.

34 Put the atonement cover on the Ark of the Covenant in the Holy of Holies. 35 Place the table outside the curtain and put the candelabra opposite it on the south side; the table put on the north side of the Tabernacle.

36 For the entrance to the tent make a curtain of blue, purple and scarlet yarn and finely twisted linen—the work of an embroiderer. 37 Make gold hooks for this curtain and five posts of acacia wood overlaid with gold. And cast five bronze bases for them.

SIXTH READING - JOSEPH - YESOD

27:1 Build an altar of acacia wood, five cubits long and five cubits wide; it is to be square, three cubits high.

2 Make its horns at each of the four corners, so that the horns and the altar are of one piece, and overlay the altar with bronze.

וְהִבְדִּילָה

Exodus 26:33—Separating the Holy of Holies from the rest of the Tabernacle.

A partition separated the Holy of Holies, where the Ark of the Covenant rested, from the rest of the Tabernacle. This reminds us of the importance of being able to distinguish what is ordinary from what is significant. Specifically, there are powerful cosmic openings to connect to the Light, and it's important to be aware of these opportunities so that we don't miss them. In these brief windows of time, we should invest more of ourselves— more effort and more energy. *Shabbat*, holidays, and New Moon (*Rosh Chodesh*) connections are examples of these occasions.

הַמִּזְבֵּחַ

Exodus 27:1—The Altar.

The Altar in the Tabernacle is where sacrifices were performed, but this section is not referring to sacrificing animals. Instead, it describes the sacrifices we need to make in our own lives. When we challenge ourselves, when we forgo our own desires in order to care for someone else, when we reduce our ego for the sake of growing—each time we sacrifice our *Desire to Receive for the Self Alone*, we exchange our destiny for a better one, with measurably less chaos.

FIFTH READING - AARON - HOD

31 וְעָשִׂיתָ פָרֹכֶת תְּכֵלֶת וְאַרְגָּמָן קנ״א קמ״ג וְתוֹלַעַת שקוצי״ת שָׁנִי וְשֵׁשׁ מָשְׁזָר מַעֲשֵׂה חֹשֵׁב יַעֲשֶׂה אֹתָהּ כְּרֻבִים: 32 וְנָתַתָּה אֹתָהּ עַל־אַרְבָּעָה עַמּוּדֵי שִׁטִּים מְצֻפִּים זָהָב וָוֵיהֶם זָהָב עַל־אַרְבָּעָה אַדְנֵי־כָסֶף: 33 וְנָתַתָּה אֶת־הַפָּרֹכֶת תַּחַת הַקְּרָסִים וְהֵבֵאתָ שָׁמָּה מהע, משה, אל שדי מִבֵּית ב״פ ראה לַפָּרֹכֶת אֵת אֲרוֹן ע״ה ג״פ אלהים הָעֵדוּת וְהִבְדִּילָה הַפָּרֹכֶת לָכֶם בֵּין הַקֹּדֶשׁ וּבֵין קֹדֶשׁ הַקֳּדָשִׁים: 34 וְנָתַתָּ אֶת־הַכַּפֹּרֶת עַל אֲרוֹן הָעֵדֻת בְּקֹדֶשׁ הַקֳּדָשִׁים: ע״ה ג״פ אלהים 35 וְשַׂמְתָּ אֶת־הַשֻּׁלְחָן מִחוּץ לַפָּרֹכֶת וְאֶת־הַמְּנֹרָה נֹכַח ג״פ יהוה הַשֻּׁלְחָן עַל צֶלַע הַמִּשְׁכָּן ב״פ (רבוע אלהים + ה) תֵּימָנָה וְהַשֻּׁלְחָן תִּתֵּן עַל־צֶלַע ב״פ כהת צָפוֹן: 36 וְעָשִׂיתָ מָסָךְ לְפֶתַח הָאֹהֶל לאה תְּכֵלֶת וְאַרְגָּמָן קנ״א קמ״ג וְתוֹלַעַת שקוצי״ת שָׁנִי וְשֵׁשׁ מָשְׁזָר מַעֲשֵׂה רֹקֵם: 37 וְעָשִׂיתָ לַמָּסָךְ חֲמִשָּׁה עַמּוּדֵי שִׁטִּים וְצִפִּיתָ אֹתָם זָהָב וָוֵיהֶם זָהָב וְיָצַקְתָּ לָהֶם חֲמִשָּׁה אַדְנֵי נְחֹשֶׁת:

SIXTH READING - JOSEPH - YESOD

1 27 וְעָשִׂיתָ אֶת־הַמִּזְבֵּחַ זן, נגד עֲצֵי שִׁטִּים חָמֵשׁ אַמּוֹת אֹרֶךְ וְחָמֵשׁ אַמּוֹת רֹחַב רָבוּעַ יִהְיֶה יייי הַמִּזְבֵּחַ זן, נגד וְשָׁלֹשׁ אַמּוֹת קֹמָתוֹ: 2 וְעָשִׂיתָ קַרְנֹתָיו עַל אַרְבַּע פִּנֹּתָיו מִמֶּנּוּ תִּהְיֶיןָ קַרְנֹתָיו וְצִפִּיתָ אֹתוֹ נְחֹשֶׁת: 3 וְעָשִׂיתָ סִּירֹתָיו לְדַשְּׁנוֹ וְיָעָיו וּמִזְרְקֹתָיו וּמִזְלְגֹתָיו וּמַחְתֹּתָיו לְכָל־כֵּלָיו תַּעֲשֶׂה יה אדני נְחֹשֶׁת: 4 וְעָשִׂיתָ לּוֹ מִכְבָּר מַעֲשֵׂה רֶשֶׁת נְחֹשֶׁת וְעָשִׂיתָ עַל־הָרֶשֶׁת אַרְבַּע טַבְּעֹת נְחֹשֶׁת עַל אַרְבַּע קְצוֹתָיו: 5 וְנָתַתָּה אֹתָהּ תַּחַת כַּרְכֹּב הַמִּזְבֵּחַ זן, נגד מִלְּמָטָּה וְהָיְתָה הָרֶשֶׁת עַד וָצִי

³ Make all its utensils—its pots to remove the ashes, and its shovels, sprinkling bowls, forks and firepans—of bronze.

⁴ Make a grating for it, a bronze network, and make four bronze rings at each of the four corners of the network. ⁵ Put it under the ledge of the altar, on the bottom, so that it is halfway up the altar.

⁶ Make poles of acacia wood for the altar and overlay them with bronze.

⁷ Bring the poles into the rings so they will be on two sides of the altar when it is carried. ⁸ Make the altar hollow, out of boards. It is to be made just as you were shown on the mountain.

SEVENTH READING - DAVID - MALCHUT

⁹ Make a courtyard for the Tabernacle. The south side shall be a hundred cubits long and is to have curtains of finely twisted linen, ¹⁰ with twenty pillars and twenty bronze sockets and with silver hooks and bands on the posts.

¹¹ The north side shall also be a hundred cubits long and is to have curtains, with twenty pillars and twenty bronze sockets and with silver hooks and bands on the pillars.

¹² The west end of the courtyard shall be fifty cubits wide and have curtains, with ten pillars and ten sockets. ¹³ On the east end, toward the sunrise, the courtyard shall be fifty cubits wide.

¹⁴ Curtains fifteen cubits long are to be on one side of the entrance, with three pillars and three sockets, ¹⁵ and curtains fifteen cubits long are to be on the other side, with three pillars and three sockets.

¹⁶ For the entrance to the courtyard, provide a curtain twenty cubits long, of blue, purple and scarlet yarn and finely twisted linen—the work of an embroiderer—with four pillars and four sockets.

Exodus 27:9—The perimeter of the Tabernacle.

Just as there was a courtyard around the Tabernacle, every person is surrounded by an energy field that is about eight feet in diameter.

Energies can be transferred to other people when we interact with them, so we should be mindful that the people in our energy field are positive. At the same time, we need to be cautious to steer clear of those who do not wish us well and not cause others to give us evil eye. Negative people can disturb our positive energy field.

הַמִּזְבֵּחַ יִי, נגד: 6 וְעָשִׂיתָ בַדִּים לַמִּזְבֵּחַ יִי, נגד בַּדֵּי עֲצֵי שִׁטִּים וְצִפִּיתָ אֹתָם נְחֹשֶׁת: 7 וְהוּבָא אֶת־בַּדָּיו בַּטַּבָּעֹת וְהָיוּ הַבַּדִּים עַל־שְׁתֵּי צַלְעֹת הַמִּזְבֵּחַ יִי, נגד בִּשְׂאֵת אֹתוֹ: 8 נְבוּב לֻחֹת תַּעֲשֶׂה אֹתוֹ כַּאֲשֶׁר הֶרְאָה אֹתְךָ בָּהָר אור, רז, אין-סוף כֵּן יַעֲשׂוּ:

SEVENTH READING - DAVID - MALCHUT

9 וְעָשִׂיתָ אֵת חֲצַר הַמִּשְׁכָּן ב״פ (רבוע אלהים = ה׳) לִפְאַת נֶגֶב־תֵּימָנָה קְלָעִים לֶחָצֵר שֵׁשׁ מָשְׁזָר מֵאָה קלט בָּאַמָּה דמב, מלוי ע״ב אֹרֶךְ לַפֵּאָה הָאֶחָת: 10 וְעַמֻּדָיו עֶשְׂרִים וְאַדְנֵיהֶם עֶשְׂרִים נְחֹשֶׁת וָוֵי הָעַמֻּדִים וַחֲשֻׁקֵיהֶם כָּסֶף: 11 וְכֵן לִפְאַת צָפוֹן בָּאֹרֶךְ קְלָעִים מֵאָה אֹרֶךְ וְעַמֻּדָיו עֶשְׂרִים וְאַדְנֵיהֶם עֶשְׂרִים נְחֹשֶׁת וָוֵי הָעַמֻּדִים וַחֲשֻׁקֵיהֶם כָּסֶף: 12 וְרֹחַב הֶחָצֵר לִפְאַת־יָם קְלָעִים חֲמִשִּׁים אַמָּה דמב, מלוי ע״ב עַמֻּדֵיהֶם עֲשָׂרָה וְאַדְנֵיהֶם עֲשָׂרָה: 13 וְרֹחַב הֶחָצֵר לִפְאַת קֵדְמָה מִזְרָחָה חֲמִשִּׁים אַמָּה דמב, מלוי ע״ב: 14 וַחֲמֵשׁ עֶשְׂרֵה אַמָּה דמב, מלוי ע״ב קְלָעִים לַכָּתֵף עַמֻּדֵיהֶם שְׁלֹשָׁה וְאַדְנֵיהֶם שְׁלֹשָׁה: 15 וְלַכָּתֵף הַשֵּׁנִית חֲמֵשׁ עֶשְׂרֵה קְלָעִים עַמֻּדֵיהֶם שְׁלֹשָׁה וְאַדְנֵיהֶם שְׁלֹשָׁה: 16 וּלְשַׁעַר הֶחָצֵר מָסָךְ | עֶשְׂרִים אַמָּה דמב, מלוי ע״ב תְּכֵלֶת וְאַרְגָּמָן קנ״א קמ״ג וְתוֹלַעַת שָׁנִי שקוצי״ת וְשֵׁשׁ מָשְׁזָר מַעֲשֵׂה רֹקֵם עַמֻּדֵיהֶם אַרְבָּעָה וְאַדְנֵיהֶם אַרְבָּעָה:

MAFTIR

17 All the pillars around the courtyard are to have silver bands and hooks, and bronze bases.

18 The courtyard shall be a hundred cubits long and fifty cubits wide, with curtains of finely twisted linen five cubits high, and with bronze sockets.

19 All the other articles used in the service of the Tabernacle, whatever their function, including all the tent pegs for it and those for the courtyard, are to be of bronze.

HAFTARAH OF TERUMAH

In this Haftarah, we read about King Solomon's construction of the Temple. Just as God gave wisdom to King Solomon, the Light gives each of us a unique quality. We need to ask ourselves continuously what that quality really is.

This way, we can discover our true mission in life and carry it out. After all, if Gandhi had decided to be a hockey player, he would have deprived the world of his gift of peace! A good way to know whether we are in touch with our true purpose is the sense of fulfillment we have at the end of a day. If we do not feel fulfilled, we are not aligned with what God sent us here to do.

> *He opened the discussion saying: "And God gave Solomon wisdom, as He promised him. And there was peace between Hiram and Solomon; and they two made a league together." (I Kings 5:26) We have learned this passage in many places, but "And God" POINTS OUT the approval of Above, ZEIR ANPIN, and Below, MALCHUT, as one because "And God"*

Kings 1 5:26-6:13

5:26 And the Lord gave Solomon wisdom, as He promised him; and there was peace between Hiram and Solomon; and they two made a league together.

27 And King Solomon raised a levy out of all Israel; and the levy was thirty thousand men.

28 And he sent them to Lebanon, ten thousand a month by courses: a month they were in Lebanon, and two months at home; and Adoniram was over the levy.

MAFTIR

17 כָּל ־עַמּוּדֵי הֶחָצֵר סָבִיב מְחֻשָּׁקִים כֶּסֶף וָוֵיהֶם כֶּסֶף וְאַדְנֵיהֶם
נְחֹשֶׁת: 18 אֹרֶךְ הֶחָצֵר מֵאָה בָאַמָּה וְרֹחַב
חֲמִשִּׁים בַּחֲמִשִּׁים וְקֹמָה חָמֵשׁ אַמּוֹת שֵׁשׁ מָשְׁזָר וְאַדְנֵיהֶם נְחֹשֶׁת:
19 לְכֹל כְּלֵי הַמִּשְׁכָּן בְּכֹל עֲבֹדָתוֹ
וְכָל ־יְתֵדֹתָיו וְכָל ־יִתְדֹת הֶחָצֵר נְחֹשֶׁת:

HAFTARAH OF TERUMAH

INDICATES Him, ZEIR ANPIN, and His court, MALCHUT. "Gave Solomon wisdom," like one who gives a present and gift to his friend. "As he promised Him": This is the perfection of wisdom in riches and peace and domination, as it is written: "...as He promised him."

King Solomon looked and saw that even though that generation was more perfect than all the other generations, it was not the desire of the Supernal King that so much wisdom should be revealed through it, and that the Torah that was concealed before it would be revealed. AND HE CAME and opened doors. Even though he opened [them], they are obstructed except for those sages who had merit. They stammer [when trying to speak about] them and cannot speak about them. But it is the desire of the Holy One, blessed be He, that for the sake of Rav Shimon, through the generation in which he lives, concealed things should be revealed.
— The Zohar, Terumah 38:419, 421

מלכים א פרק ה–ו

5 26 וַיהֹוָה נָתַן חָכְמָה לִשְׁלֹמֹה כַּאֲשֶׁר דִּבֶּר
ראה ־לוֹ וַיְהִי שָׁלֹם בֵּין וְחִירָם וּבֵין שְׁלֹמֹה וַיִּכְרְתוּ
בְרִית שְׁנֵיהֶם: 27 וַיַּעַל הַמֶּלֶךְ שְׁלֹמֹה מַס מִכָּל ־יִשְׂרָאֵל וַיְהִי
הַמַּס שְׁלֹשִׁים אָלֶף אִישׁ 28 וַיִּשְׁלָחֵם

[29] *And Solomon had threescore and ten thousand that bore burdens, and fourscore thousand that were hewers in the mountains;*

[30] *besides Solomon's chief officers that were over the work, three thousand and three hundred, who bore rule over the people that wrought in the work.*

[31] *And the king commanded, and they quarried great stones, costly stones, to lay the foundation of the house with hewn stone.*

[32] *And Solomon's builders and Hiram's builders and the Gebalites did fashion them, and prepared the timber and the stones to build the house.*

[6:1] *In the four hundred and eightieth year after the Israelites had come out of Egypt, in the fourth year of Solomon's reign over Israel, in the month of Ziv, the second month, he built the Temple for the Lord.*

[2] *The Temple that King Solomon built for the Lord was sixty cubits long, twenty cubits wide and thirty cubits high.*

[3] *The portico at the front of the main hall of the Temple extended the width of the Temple, that is twenty cubits, and projected ten cubits from the front of the Temple.*

[4] *He made narrow clerestory windows in the Temple.*

[5] *Against the walls of the main hall and inner sanctuary he built a structure around the building, in which there were side rooms.*

[6] *The lowest floor was five cubits wide, the middle floor six cubits wide and the third floor seven cubits wide. He made offset ledges around the outside of the Temple so that nothing would be inserted into the Temple walls.*

[7] *In building the Temple, only blocks dressed at the quarry were used, and no hammer, chisel or any other iron tool was heard at the Temple site while it was being built.*

[8] *The entrance to the lowest floor was on the south side of the Temple; a stairway led up to the middle level and from there to the third level.*

[9] *So he built the Temple and completed it, roofing it with beams and cedar planks.*

[10] *And he built the side rooms all along the Temple. The height of each was five cubits, and they were attached to the Temple by beams of cedar.*

לִבְנֹנָה עֲשֶׂרֶת אֲלָפִים קס״א בַּחֹדֶשׁ י״ב הוויות וַחֲלִיפוֹת וָחֹדֶשׁ י״ב הוויות יִהְיוּ

בַּלְּבָנוֹן שְׁנַיִם חֳדָשִׁים בְּבֵיתוֹ וַאֲדֹנִירָם עַל־הַמַּס: 29 וַיְהִי אל, ייא״י אל, ייא״י

לִשְׁלֹמֹה שִׁבְעִים אָלֶף אלף למד עין דלת יוד ע״ה נֹשֵׂא סַבָּל וּשְׁמֹנִים אֶלֶף

אלף למד עין דלת יוד ע״ה וְחֹצֵב בָּהָר אור, רז, אין סוף: 30 לְבַד מִשָּׂרֵי הַנִּצָּבִים לִשְׁלֹמֹה

אֲשֶׁר עַל־הַמְּלָאכָה אל אדני שְׁלֹשֶׁת אֲלָפִים קס״א וּשְׁלֹשׁ מֵאוֹת הָרֹדִים

בָּעָם ר״ת באר ענן מן הָעֹשִׂים בַּמְּלָאכָה אל אדני: 31 וַיְצַו פיו הַמֶּלֶךְ וַיַּסִּעוּ

אֲבָנִים גְּדֹלוֹת אֲבָנִים יְקָרוֹת לְיַסֵּד הַבָּיִת ב״פ ראה אַבְנֵי גָזִית: 32 וַיִּפְסְלוּ

בֹּנֵי שְׁלֹמֹה וּבֹנֵי חִירוֹם וְהַגִּבְלִים וַיָּכִינוּ הָעֵצִים וְהָאֲבָנִים לִבְנוֹת

הַבָּיִת ב״פ ראה: 16 וַיְהִי אל, ייא״י בִּשְׁמוֹנִים שָׁנָה וְאַרְבַּע מֵאוֹת שָׁנָה לְצֵאת

בְּנֵי־יִשְׂרָאֵל מֵאֶרֶץ אלהים דאלפין מִצְ מִצְרַיִם בַּשָּׁנָה הָרְבִיעִית בְּחֹדֶשׁ

זִו הוא הַחֹדֶשׁ י״ב הוויות הַשֵּׁנִי לִמְלֹךְ שְׁלֹמֹה עַל־יִשְׂרָאֵל וַיִּבֶן

וזיים, בינה ע״ה הַבָּיִת ב״פ ראה לַיהוָֹואדני״לאהדונהי 2 וְהַבַּיִת ב״פ ראה אֲשֶׁר בָּנָה הַמֶּלֶךְ

שְׁלֹמֹה לַיהוָֹואדני״לאהדונהי שִׁשִּׁים־אַמָּה דמב, מלוי ע״ב אָרְכּוֹ וְעֶשְׂרִים רָחְבּוֹ

וּשְׁלֹשִׁים אַמָּה דמב, מלוי ע״ב קוֹמָתוֹ: 3 וְהָאוּלָם עַל־פְּנֵי וחכמה בינה הֵיכַל

אדני, ללה הַבַּיִת ב״פ ראה עֶשְׂרִים אַמָּה דמב, מלוי ע״ב אָרְכּוֹ עַל־פְּנֵי וחכמה בינה רֹחַב

הַבָּיִת ב״פ ראה עֶשֶׂר בָּאַמָּה דמב, מלוי ע״ב רָחְבּוֹ עַל־פְּנֵי וחכמה בינה הַבָּיִת ב״פ ראה:

4 וַיַּעַשׂ לַבָּיִת ב״פ ראה וְחַלּוֹנֵי שְׁקֻפִים אֲטוּמִים: 5 וַיִּבֶן וזיים, בינה ע״ה עַל־קִיר

הַבַּיִת ב״פ ראה יָצִיעַ (כתיב: יצוע) סָבִיב אֶת־קִירוֹת הַבַּיִת ב״פ ראה סָבִיב

לַהֵיכָל אדני, ללה וְלַדְּבִיר ר״יי וַיַּעַשׂ צְלָעוֹת סָבִיב: 6 הַיָּצִיעַ (כתיב: היצוע)

הַתַּחְתֹּנָה וְזִו חָמֵשׁ בָּאַמָּה דמב, מלוי ע״ב רָחְבָּהּ וְהַתִּיכֹנָה שֵׁשׁ בָּאַמָּה

דמב, מלוי ע״ב רָחְבָּהּ וְהַשְּׁלִישִׁית שֶׁבַע ע״ב ואלהים דיודין בָּאַמָּה דמב, מלוי ע״ב רָחְבָּהּ

כִּי מִגְרָעוֹת נָתַן לַבַּיִת ב״פ ראה סָבִיב חוּצָה לְבִלְתִּי אֲחֹז בְּקִירוֹת־הַבָּיִת

ב״פ ראה: 7 וְהַבַּיִת ב״פ ראה בְּהִבָּנֹתוֹ יוד הה ואו הה אֶבֶן שְׁלֹמֹה מַסָּע נִבְנָה

וּמַקָּבוֹת וְהַגַּרְזֶן כָּל יל״י כְּלִי ר״ת בלהה רחל זלפה לאה בַרְזֶל כלי לֹא־נִשְׁמַע בַּבַּיִת

[11] *The word of the Lord came to Solomon, saying,* [12] *"As for this Temple you are building, if you follow my decrees, carry out my regulations and keep all my precepts and obey them, I will fulfill through you the promise I gave to David your father.*

[13] *And I will live among the Israelites and will not abandon my people Israel."*

בּ״פ ראה בְּהִבָּנֹתוֹ 8 פֶּתַח הַצֵּלָע הַתִּיכֹנָה אֶל־כֶּתֶף הַבַּיִת בּ״פ ראה הַיְמָנִית

וּבְלוּלִים יַעֲלוּ עַל־הַתִּיכֹנָה וּמִן־הַתִּיכֹנָה אֶל־הַשְּׁלִשִׁים: 9 וַיִּבֶן

וזיים, בינה ע״ה אֶת־הַבַּיִת בּ״פ ראה וַיְכַלֵּהוּ וַיִּסְפֹּן אֶת־הַבַּיִת בּ״פ ראה גֵּבִים

וּשְׂדֵרֹת בָּאֲרָזִים: 10 וַיִּבֶן וזיים, בינה ע״ה אֶת־הַיָּצִיעַ (כתיב: היצוע) עַל־כָּל

ילי, עמם ־הַבַּיִת בּ״פ ראה וְחָמֵשׁ אַמּוֹת קוֹמָתוֹ וַיֶּאֱחֹז אֶת־הַבַּיִת בּ״פ ראה בַּעֲצֵי

אֲרָזִים: 11 וַיְהִי אל יי״י דְּבַר ראה ־יְהֹוָאדִיאהדונהי אֶל־שְׁלֹמֹה לֵאמֹר:

12 הַבַּיִת בּ״פ ראה הַזֶּה וַהו אֲשֶׁר־אַתָּה בֹנֶה אִם ־תֵּלֵךְ מ״ב, עה״ה יוֹה״ך בְּחֻקֹּתַי

וְאֶת־מִשְׁפָּטַי תַּעֲשֶׂה וְשָׁמַרְתָּ אֶת־כָּל ילי ־מִצְוֹתַי לָלֶכֶת בָּהֶם וַהֲקִמֹתִי

אֶת־דְּבָרִי ראה אִתָּךְ אֲשֶׁר דִּבַּרְתִּי ראה אֶל־דָּוִד אָבִיךָ: 13 וְשָׁכַנְתִּי

בְּתוֹךְ בְּנֵי יִשְׂרָאֵל וְלֹא אֶעֱזֹב אֶת־עַמִּי יִשְׂרָאֵל:

TETZAVEH

LESSON OF TETZAVEH
(Exodus 27:20-30:10)

The chapter of Tetzaveh is traditionally read before Purim (except when there is an additional month of Adar), and it gives us strength and support to assist us during the holiday. This Shabbat is set apart from all others and titled Shabbat Zachor. In Tetzaveh, the Israelites are told to destroy all the Amalekites, with whom they were at war. The sages teach that the word "amalek" is code word for doubt. The call for war against the Amalekites is really a call to blot out our doubt wherever it is found. This is the only reading in the whole Torah that the entire congregation—men, women, and children—must hear. In a letter from Rav Brandwein to the Rav we learn the following:

> *May there be abundant blessings and much joy to the honor of the beloved among men. A man of life and of many enterprises, beloved Above and cherished Below. The glorious name, our teacher, Rabbi Shraga Feivel, may HaShem's Light bring life upon him.*
>
> *I shall write to you concerning the portion Zachor. It is written, "Remember what Amalek has done unto you." (Deuteronomy 25;17) The words "unto you" seem to be superfluous, because it would have been enough to say, "Remember what Amalek has done." The words "unto you" hint to the klipa (negative blocking consciousness) of Amalek which is what drove the Desire to Receive for the Self Alone into the body of the general public without a spark of sharing. This is the other side and the opposite of holiness, which is sharing and causing tranquility to his Maker.*

Pure olive oil

Why did the oil of the Menorah need to be pure olive oil? The Menorah is a tool for our connection to the Light, and for our connection to be complete, we need a pure heart. The Rav once told a story about the great Rav Yitzchak Caduri (d. 2006):

There was man who lived in a city in Syria. He was divinely inspired and had the gift of prophecy. Whatever he foretold came to pass. His vision was so clear that people came from all over to consult with him.

In the same city lived a wise and righteous rabbi who wanted to know the source of the seer's power. After some time, the rabbi and the seer became good friends and the rabbi offered to share his wisdom. After several months passed, the wise teacher asked the seer to reveal his source of power.

The seer was quite confused. On one hand, he loved to study with the teacher; on the other hand, he could not share his secret. Finally, however, he agreed to the rabbi's request but insisted that before he divulged his source, both men needed to fast for three days.

The rabbi agreed. Soon after, the seer added that they must also immerse themselves in the river seven times to purify their bodies. After both men fasted for three days and purified their bodies in the river, the seer added that they must also meditate to remove their ego and purify their hearts and souls.

After all this preparation, the seer took the teacher into a room, where they found a box. The seer said, "My secret is inside this box. I only enter this room to access this treasure. Otherwise, I do not enter." Then he bowed down to the box and directed the rabbi to do the same. The rabbi was worried that all this might be connected to some form of witchcraft, but he assured himself that in his heart, he was connecting to the Creator, not to a demon in a box.

Trembling with great adoration, the seer opened the box and revealed his secret. It was the Sacred Name of God—*Yud, Hei, Vav, and Hei*—written on parchment. The seer said that if the Name shone with Light, the answer to a question was "Yes," and if it didn't shine, the answer was "No." "This is my whole secret," the man concluded.

The rabbi returned home and said to himself, "How many times a day do we speak the Name of God without consciousness, without even thinking about what we are saying? Yet all this man's strength comes from the reverence and fervor with which he approaches the Sacred Name."

The seer went to great lengths to purify himself—preparing his body, his mind, and his heart. He was so pure in every sense when he approached the Light that he could receive the Light's pure energy. Whoever approaches the Light of the Creator with ego or hatred in their hearts cannot receive the Light. This parable reveals the purpose and intention of the pure clean olive oil in the Menorah.

Moses's name is not in this chapter.

Moses is not mentioned anywhere in the chapter of Tetzaveh. After the sin of the Golden Calf, God wanted to destroy the people of Israel. Moses challenged God and said, "If you bring destruction on the people, then erase my name from Your Book." God did not destroy the people, but the name Moses was "erased" from the chapter of Tetzaveh nonetheless.

The Zohar says:

> Who do we have that is greater than Moses, who said: "and if not, blot me, I pray you, out of Your book which You have written" (Exodus 32:32). This he said for the sake of Israel, and although the Holy One, blessed be He, did his wish AND FORGAVE ISRAEL, nevertheless he was not spared punishment, for it has already been noted that HIS NAME is not mentioned in the portion of Tetzaveh, but has been blotted out from there. And this has already been taught. And who do we have that is greater than King David, who said: "I said: I will take heed to my ways that I sin not with my tongue: I will keep a curb on my mouth, while the

wicked is before me." (Psalms 39:2). What is the meaning of "while the wicked
is before me?" This refers to that official who was appointed over the one WHO
CURSES HIMSELF, and takes that word to harm a man, AS ABOVE.
The Zohar, Pinchas 93:643

Was the absence of the name of Moses some kind of punishment? What could Moses possibly be punished for? Moses only wanted God to spare the people. He protested in the way that Noah did not. Did Moses not do what we are all taught to do to connect to the Light—to think of others before ourselves? Are we not taught that God does not punish, that there are only effects of our actions? The Zohar says that Moses's request for God's mercy upon the Israelites could hardly be considered a negative action that would bring about a negative consequence.

Therefore, it is ill advised for a person to curse himself when he is angry, since
many ADVERSARIES are standing by to accept such speeches, MEANING THAT
HIS CURSE WILL COME TRUE. At another time, WHEN MOSES requested
death AT THE EPISODE OF THE GOLDEN CALF, SAYING, "BLOT ME, I PRAY
YOU, OUT OF YOUR BOOK WHICH YOU HAVE WRITTEN" (EXODUS 32:32),
they did not accept it from him because it was all for the benefit of the children
of Israel.
The Zohar, Beha'alotcha 24:138

The most important, albeit difficult, part of our spiritual work is the restriction of our ego. There is a funny story about a sage who loved to play golf that demonstrates the manner in which the ego's need for approval limits our fulfillment.

One Yom Kippur, a spiritual teacher was on his way to his place of worship when he heard a voice within: It was the voice of the Desire to Receive for the Self Alone. The voice said, "Why are you going to pray? What do you really get from that? You don't really enjoy it. Why don't you go play golf?"

So the sage did, and just as he began to play, he aced a hole-in-one. Amazing! What's more, he scored a hole-in-one on every single tee. He completed all eighteen holes in eighteen shots. He was elated at his brilliant performance—until he realized that he couldn't tell anyone about his day because, after all, how could he play golf on Yom Kippur?"

Our ego nature requires other people to admire what we do. We want to be respected and accepted by others all the time, mostly because we don't accept and respect ourselves. In contrast, we see the greatness of Moses, who chose to wipe out the needs of his ego.

Moses worked all his life to reveal and serve the Torah, but in a single moment, he was prepared to give it all up and erase himself and all his work from the consciousness of the generations to come.

As Rav Berg teaches us, the one who wants to be nobody is really the one who is somebody, and the person who wants to be somebody is really nobody. Moses did not want to be anybody—which is why he was able to create a means for us to be able connect to the Light of the Creator by our own efforts.

In one of his letters, Rav Brandwein wrote:

> In the Talmud, Tractate Nedarim 38, it is written: "Rav Yochanan said,' God only sets His Shechinah upon one who is mighty, wise, rich, and humble, and all those befit Moses.' Yet in Tractate Shabbat it is written, why Moses?" It is different from what our Master has said about the holy Shechinah only settling upon one who is mighty, wise, rich, and of high stature. One who is humble and one who is of a high stature are two contradictory things, and it appears that the two sayings contradict each other. It is written in the Zohar that one who is least, is great. He proves it from the verse, "And Sarah lived a hundred year and twenty years and seven years." (Genesis 23:1) When a hundred, which is the most numerous, is mentioned, it is written 'a year,' in the singular. And when it comes to seven, which is the least, it is written 'years,' in the plural. (Rev. Zohar, Shlach Lecha, paragraph 210) So we see from this that there is no contradiction, because great also means one with a high stature; similarly, least means humble, and it is all the same. Therefore, one who has a high standing is humble.

We have a greater connection to Moses and to our own humility in this chapter then in any other.

Rav Isaac Luria (the Ari) teaches us that every generation has its own Moses, who can be any person.

> Surely Moses is equal to all of Israel, as the sages said that Moses merited and transferred his merit to many, so the communal merit depends on him. "And he shall divide the spoil with the strong," (Isaiah 53:12) because he actually received his own share from God, and the rest of the righteous will receive their share "because he has poured out his soul to death" (Ibid.) in every generation. That is the sense why "Moses, Moses" (Exodus 3:4) is without an interruptive accent, to indicate that he comes again in every generation. "...and was numbered with transgressors; but he bore the sin of many," (Isaiah 53:12) because, through him, the sin of generations was completely atoned for, along with the sin of Adam and Eve, who are great masters.
> — Writings of the Ari, Torah Compilations 6, Va'etchanan, 9

We have the opportunities to be like Moses every day, but don't see them or act on them. The seer in Rav Yitzchak Caduri's story acquired tremendous powers from the Name of God that we see every day in our prayer books. If we could experience the same awe for the Light that is given to us freely, we would really connect to the Light of the Creator. We wouldn't need money or status or possessions. We would know everything and be able to do anything. What is holding us back? As we understand from this reading, nothing—except our ego-based desires.

Moses is known to have ascended to a level of half-angel, half-man. (*Midrash Rabba, Leviticus 30:13*) Many would honor the half that was angelic. Yet the greatness of Moses was in Moses the man. He was a real person who lived through and overcame the challenges of a real life. A tzaddik (righteous person) achieves a more elevated level of consciousness than an angel. For angelic beings, there is no curtain separating them from the Light. For this reason, angels have no free will. There is no Satan to challenge their view of reality. They see only Light. A righteous person, on the other hand, does experience the limitations and obstructions that Satan places in front of him or her, but they rise above them—an infinitely more challenging task.

The greatest level we can reach in our spiritual work is to be an authentic human being. This is more important then studying or understanding. Often, we can lose sight of this as our knowledge deepens. We can become overly pious and lose sight of who we really are and what we came here to do. If increased knowledge causes the loss of our essential humanity, it might have been better if we had not begun to study.

Moses is a channel for humility—the total removal of ego for all generations to come. Abraham, through his acts of kindness, created the spiritual wiring for *Chesed* (Mercy), or Right-Column energy. These great masters were the cables that connect our physical world to the Creator. Their lives and experiences gave birth to the spiritual architecture through which the Light of the Creator travels to reach this physical dimension. They are not "holy" figures in biblical history; rather, they are co-creators of the wiring system of the universe. When we do our own spiritual work, we also co-create the spiritual infrastructure that helps others to connect.

SYNOPSIS OF TETZAVEH

As we have just learned, the name of Moses is not mentioned anywhere in this entire chapter. This may seem like a punishment, but the truth is that we have more of Moses in this chapter than in any other. The more physicality there is in something, the less Light there is there. In this chapter, we have no aspect of physicality of Moses, so we are receiving all of his Light.

FIRST READING - ABRAHAM - CHESED

27:20 **A**nd you will command the Israelites to take to you clear oil of pressed olives to ignite and elevate the Eternal Flame.

21 *In the Tent of Meeting, outside the curtain that is in front of the Testimony, Aaron and his sons are to keep the lamps burning before the Lord from evening till morning. This is to be a lasting ordinance among the Israelites for the generations to come.*

28:1 *Have Aaron your brother brought to you, along with his sons from among the Israelites so they may serve Me as priests: Aaron; Nadab and Abihu, Eleazar and Itamar, the sons of Aaron.*

2 *Make sacred garments for your brother Aaron, to give him dignity and honor.*

FROM THE RAV

Kabbalistically, every element of the body has not only a practical function but also a spiritual meaning. Bone, for example, is connected to the *Sefira* of *Chochmah*. The veins and arteries represent the dimension of *Binah*. The flesh of the human body represents *Zeir Anpin*. And clothing, which is the outermost aspect of the tangible human being, presents itself to the world (as *Malchut*).

What does clothing mean? The answer varies from person to person. For some, it means high fashion. For others, it is simply a way of keeping warm. But for everyone, clothing is a way of concealing the naked body. In order to reveal ourselves to the world, in order to go out into the street without getting arrested for indecent exposure, we've got to conceal our naked physical selves.

In the biblical chapter of Tetzaveh, albeit on a very mundane level, we see the paradox of concealment and revelation. It provides an introduction to the kabbalistic interpretation of clothing. In his treatise on the *Ten Luminous Emanations*, Rav Ashlag

states that all forms of clothing have the potential to act as a channel for the last dimension of *Malchut*—the ultimate channel by which the Light becomes manifest. This is where anti-matter begins to operate.

According to Rav Isaac Luria (the Ari), if we don't know the structure of something, we cannot influence it at its most basic physical level. And this is where the story of Tetzeve is so powerful for us. It begins with the words "*Ve'atah tetzaveh*," which means "And you, you will command." The Zohar asks: Why is "*ve'atah*" (and you) necessary if "*tetzaveh*" means "you will command?" Many commentators have raised the same question: The word "*ve'atah*" is redundant. There is no need, no necessity, for this word to be there.

Kabbalah teaches that the letter Vav is *Zeir Anpin* and the word "*atah*" is *Malchut*. Thus, when we connect to letter Vav with the word "*atah*" to create "*ve'atah*," it empowers us to control physical matter by assisting us to bring the consciousness of *Zeir Anpin*, the Flawless Universe, into the realm of *Malchut*. This was the power of the clothing of the High Priest—the

FIRST READING - ABRAHAM - CHESED

20 וְאַתָּה א־ת לה' מלכות תְּצַוֶּה | אֶת־בְּנֵי יִשְׂרָאֵל וְיִקְחוּ אֵלֶיךָ אני

שֶׁמֶן י"פ טל, י"פ כוזו"ו; ביט זַיִת אלהים אל מצפ"ץ זָךְ כָּתִית לַמָּאוֹר לְהַעֲלֹת נֵר

תָּמִיד קס"א קנ"א קמ"ג, ע"ה נתה2 21 בְּאֹהֶל לאה מוֹעֵד מְחוּץ

לַפָּרֹכֶת אֲשֶׁר עַל־הָעֵדֻת ע"ב ורבוע ע"ב יַעֲרֹךְ אֹתוֹ אַהֲרֹן וּבָנָיו מֵעֶרֶב

עַד־בֹּקֶר לִפְנֵי וחכמה בינה יְהֹוָה וְזָקָת עוֹלָם לְדֹרֹתָם

מֵאֵת בְּנֵי יִשְׂרָאֵל׃ 1 28 וְאַתָּה אני הַקְרֵב אֵלֶיךָ ע"ב ורבוע ע"ב אֶת־אַהֲרֹן אָחִיךָ

וְאֶת־בָּנָיו אִתּוֹ מִתּוֹךְ בְּנֵי יִשְׂרָאֵל לְכַהֲנוֹ־לִי אַהֲרֹן ע"ב ורבוע ע"ב נָדָב עדה אהיה בוכו

וַאֲבִיהוּא אֶלְעָזָר וְאִיתָמָר בְּנֵי אַהֲרֹן ע"ב ורבוע ע"ב 2 וְעָשִׂיתָ בִגְדֵי־קֹדֶשׁ

> bonding of the physical reality with the spiritual reality, which is a tremendous step forward in the work of removing chaos from our lives.

שֶׁמֶן זַיִת זָךְ כָּתִית

Exodus 27:20—Purifying the oil for the Tabernacle.

Only the first six drops of oil extracted from an olive were to be used for the Tabernacle. Oil, especially olive oil, is connected to the dimension of *Binah*. The High Priest wanted to connect with the spiritual aspect of the oil, not to its physical aspect. Like the oil, there are physical and spiritual aspects to everything in our world, including humanity: Our bodily desires are physical, but they can connect to our spiritual side and to our soul through our efforts at our spiritual work.

בִּגְדֵי־קֹדֶשׁ

Exodus 28:2—The High Priest's vestments were tools for cleansing negativity.

With what shall he ready it? With garments resembling what is above, LIKE ZEIR ANPIN, as explained. These garments are all in the secret of six (Heb. shesh), CHESED, GEVURAH, TIFERET, NETZACH, HOD AND YESOD INCLUDED IN CHESED, THE SECRET OF THE HIGH PRIEST. THIS IS THE INNER MEANING OF "AND THEY MADE THE TUNICS OF FINE LINEN (HEB. SHESH)...AND THE MITRE OF FINE LINEN (HEB. SHESH), AND GOODLY TURBANS OF FINE LINEN (HEB. SHESH)." And when the house is built on the top of the mountains, the High Priest, CHESED OF ZEIR ANPIN, it will be elevated into the high existence, BINAH, and the world will be illuminated by that Supernal Light WITHIN BINAH. And "shall be exalted above the hills" (Isaiah 2:22) MEANS above the rest of the supernal armies and legions. Then "all the nations shall flow to it." (Ibid. 2)
— The Zohar, Pekudei 24:226

Each piece of the High Priest's clothing served as a technology for cleansing a different aspect of negativity. The Vest (*Ephod*), worn over his robe and tunic, was meant to cleanse the people from any form of idol-worship.

³ Tell all the skilled men to whom I have given wisdom in such matters that they are to make garments for Aaron, for his consecration, so he may serve Me as priest.

⁴ These are the garments they are to make: a breastplate, an ephod, a robe, a woven tunic, a turban and a sash. They are to make these sacred garments for your brother Aaron and his sons, so they may serve me as priests.

⁵ Have them use gold, and blue, purple and scarlet yarn, and fine linen.

⁶ Make the ephod of gold, and of blue, purple and scarlet yarn, and of finely twisted linen—the work of a skilled craftsman.

⁷ It is to have two shoulder pieces attached to two of its corners, so it can be fastened.

⁸ Its skillfully woven waistband is to be like it—of one piece with the ephod and made with gold, and with blue, purple and scarlet yarn, and with finely twisted linen.

⁹ Take two onyx stones and engrave on them the names of the sons of Israel, ¹⁰ six names on one stone and the remaining six on the other according to their birth.

"Idol-worship" here doesn't refer to bowing to images made of stone or gold. "Idol-worship" here is a code used to describe the forces in our lives that demand worship and thus distract us from seeking the Light. When we give power to anger or ego, we are worshipping idols. We can't get real fulfillment until we break the bonds of the influence of these false gods.

> *. . . One concealed key, NAMELY, DA'AT, ordained and opened one gate on the south side, WHICH IS THE SECRET OF THE RIGHT COLUMN. "Then the High Priest, WHICH IS CHESED, enters into that opening and hurries with his girdle, WHICH IS THE SECRET OF MALCHUT, and his corrections, NAMELY, THE FOUR GARMENTS OF AN ORDINARY PRIEST, NAMELY, MITRE, TUNIC, GIRDLE, AND BREECHES, WHICH CORRESPOND TO THE FOUR LETTERS OF ADONAI, WHICH IS MALCHUT. SUBSEQUENTLY, he is adorned with a diadem of holiness, and puts on a Breastplate and Ephod and a robe of seventy bells and pomegranates, which are "a golden bell and pomegranate" (Exodus 28:34)*

> *THESE BEING THE SECRET OF THE MOCHIN OF THE ILLUMINATION OF CHOCHMAH THAT ARE DRAWN DOWN FROM THE FIRST HEI OF THE YUD, HEI, VAV, and HEI, AS ABOVE. And the plate of the holy crown on his forehead is called 'the plate of the Holy Crown,' NAMELY, THE YUD OF THE YUD, HEI, VAV, and HEI. And he was embellished with the four garments of gold and with the four garments of white, WHICH CORRESPOND TO THE EIGHT LETTERS IN THE NAMES OF THE YUD, HEI, VAV, and HEI AND ADONAI, and on that plate 42 letters sparkle, NAMELY, THE 42-LETTER NAME, and the whole of that palace shines with Upper Lights.*
> *— The Zohar, Pinchas 105:712*

Since we don't have a High Priest today, we must be our own high priest and guide our own lives.

Exodus 28:4—The High Priest's Breastplate (Choshen) was a tool for cleansing judgment.

לְאַהֲרֹן ע״ב ורבוע ע״ב אָחִיךָ לְכָבוֹד ל״ב וּלְתִפְאָרֶת: 3 וְאַתָּה תְּדַבֵּר ראה אֶל־
כָּל־ יוי ־חַכְמֵי־לֵב אֲשֶׁר מִלֵּאתִיו רוּחַ מלוי אלהים דיודין חָכְמָה וְעָשׂוּ אֶת־
בִּגְדֵי אַהֲרֹן ע״ב ורבוע ע״ב לְקַדְּשׁוֹ לְכַהֲנוֹ־לִי: 4 וְאֵלֶּה מ״ב הַבְּגָדִים אֲשֶׁר
יַעֲשׂוּ חֹשֶׁן שדי ורבוע אהיה וְאֵפוֹד יהוה אדני וּמְעִיל ע״ה קנ״א ע״ה וּכְתֹנֶת תַּשְׁבֵּץ
מִצְנֶפֶת וְאַבְנֵט וְעָשׂוּ בִגְדֵי־קֹדֶשׁ לְאַהֲרֹן ע״ב ורבוע ע״ב אָחִיךָ וּלְבָנָיו
לְכַהֲנוֹ־לִי: 5 וְהֵם יִקְחוּ וום אֶת־הַזָּהָב וי וְאֶת־הַתְּכֵלֶת וְאֶת־הָאַרְגָּמָן
קנ״א קמ״ג וְאֶת־תּוֹלַעַת שקוצית הַשָּׁנִי וְאֶת־הַשֵּׁשׁ: 6 וְעָשׂוּ אֶת־הָאֵפֹד ע״ה אלהים
זָהָב תְּכֵלֶת וְאַרְגָּמָן קנ״א קמ״ג תּוֹלַעַת שקוצית שָׁנִי וְשֵׁשׁ מָשְׁזָר מַעֲשֵׂה חֹשֵׁב:
7 שְׁתֵּי כְתֵפֹת חֹבְרֹת יִהְיֶה־ יהוה ־לּוֹ אֶל־שְׁנֵי קְצוֹתָיו וְחֻבָּר: ריבוע ס״ג ורבוע אהיה
8 וְחֵשֶׁב אֲפֻדָּתוֹ אֲשֶׁר עָלָיו כְּמַעֲשֵׂהוּ מִמֶּנּוּ יִהְיֶה יהוה זָהָב תְּכֵלֶת וְאַרְגָּמָן
קנ״א קמ״ג וְתוֹלַעַת שקוצית שָׁנִי וְשֵׁשׁ מָשְׁזָר: 9 וְלָקַחְתָּ אֶת־שְׁתֵּי אַבְנֵי־שֹׁהַם
מהע אל שדי וּפִתַּחְתָּ עֲלֵיהֶם שְׁמוֹת בְּנֵי יִשְׂרָאֵל: 10 שִׁשָּׁה מִשְּׁמֹתָם עַל
הָאֶבֶן יוד הה ואו הה הָאֶחָת וְאֶת־שְׁמוֹת הַשִּׁשָּׁה הַנּוֹתָרִים עַל־הָאֶבֶן

The cosmos works like a mirror, with all the actions and emotions we project being reflected back on us. If we judge others, the universe judges us in return. We have to learn to relate to every human being with love and compassion, from a place of Light and without a personal agenda—not because it is a nice and honorable thing to do, but because it does not pay to have it any other way.

There were twelve stones on the Breastplate—one for each of the twelve tribes—and these stones contained the answers to every possible question.

Here the Zohar discusses the Hebrew letters—the first letter of every tribe of the Children of Israel—that were engraved on the twelve stones of the Breastplate and the ephod, and that spelled out the answers to the High Priest's questions:

Come and see: When the High Priest wore these twelve stones on the Breastplate and on the Ephod, the Shechinah dwelt upon him. The names of all the tribes were engraved upon the twelve stones. Each tribe was engraved upon one stone, and the letters were set in the stones. When the stones shone, the letters stood out and illuminated whatever was to be illuminated.
— The Zohar, Pekudei 21:179

The Ephod and the BREASTPLATE were behind and before, THE BREASTPLATE BEFORE AND THE EPHOD BEHIND. And when the priest wore them, he had the likeness of the higher image, ZEIR ANPIN AND MALCHUT, THE SECRET OF BEHIND AND BEFORE. And we have learned that his face shone and the letters stood out, illuminating and rising up. Then he knew that WHICH WAS NEEDED.
— The Zohar, Pekudei 21:209

11 Engrave the names of the sons of Israel on the two stones the way a gem cutter engraves a seal. Then mount the stones in gold settings

12 and fasten them on the shoulder pieces of the ephod as memorial stones for the sons of Israel. Aaron is to bear the names on his shoulders as a memorial before the Lord.

SECOND READING - ISAAC - GEVURAH

13 Make gold settings.

14 and two braided chains of pure gold, thick, and attach the thick chains to the settings.

15 Fashion a breastplate for making decisions—the work of a skilled craftsman. Make it like the ephod: of gold, and of blue, purple and scarlet yarn, and of finely twisted linen.

16 It is to be square and folded double—a span long and a span wide.

17 Then mount four rows of precious stones on it. In the first row there shall be a ruby, a topaz and a beryl;

18 in the second row a turquoise, a sapphire and an emerald; 19 in the third row a jacinth, an agate and an amethyst; 20 in the fourth row a chrysolite, an onyx and a jasper. Mount them in gold settings.

21 There are to be twelve stones, one for each of the names of the sons of Israel, each engraved like a seal with the name of one of the twelve tribes.

22 For the breastplate make braided chains, thick, of pure gold.

23 Make on the breastplate two gold rings and fasten them to two corners of the breastplate.

24 Fasten the two gold chains to the rings at the corners of the breastplate, 25 and the other ends of the chains to the two settings, attaching them to the shoulder pieces of the ephod at the front.

הַשֵּׁנִית כְּתוֹלְדֹתָם: 11 מַעֲשֵׂה חָרַשׁ אֶבֶן יוד הה ואו הה   יוד הה ואו הה פִּתּוּחֵי

חֹתָם תְּפַתַּח אֶת־שְׁתֵּי הָאֲבָנִים עַל־שְׁמֹת בְּנֵי יִשְׂרָאֵל מְסַבֹּת

מִשְׁבְּצוֹת זָהָב תַּעֲשֶׂה אֹתָם: 12 וְשַׂמְתָּ אֶת־שְׁתֵּי הָאֲבָנִים עַל כִּתְפֹת

הָאֵפֹד ע״ה אלהים אַבְנֵי זִכָּרֹן לִבְנֵי יִשְׂרָאֵל וְנָשָׂא אַהֲרֹן ע״ב ורבוע ע״ב אֶת־

שְׁמוֹתָם לִפְנֵי חכמה בינה יְהֹוָ‬ה‬אֱ‬דֹנָ‬י‬יאהדונהי דעת עַל־שְׁתֵּי כְתֵפָיו לְזִכָּרֹן:

SECOND READING - ISAAC - GEVURAH

13 וְעָשִׂיתָ מִשְׁבְּצֹת זָהָב: 14 וּשְׁתֵּי שַׁרְשְׁרֹת זָהָב טָהוֹר י״פ אכא מִגְבָּלֹת

תַּעֲשֶׂה אֹתָם מַעֲשֵׂה עֲבֹת וְנָתַתָּה אֶת־שַׁרְשְׁרֹת הָעֲבֹתֹת עַל־

הַמִּשְׁבְּצֹת: 15 וְעָשִׂיתָ חֹשֶׁן שדי ורבוע אהיה ע״ה ה״פ אלהים מִשְׁפָּט מַעֲשֵׂה חֹשֵׁב

כְּמַעֲשֵׂה אֵפֹד ע״ה אלהים תַּעֲשֶׂנּוּ זָהָב תְּכֵלֶת וְאַרְגָּמָן וְתוֹלַעַת שָׁנִי שקוצי״ת

וְשֵׁשׁ מָשְׁזָר תַּעֲשֶׂה אֹתוֹ: 16 רָבוּעַ יִהְיֶה ייי כָּפוּל זֶרֶת אׇרְכּוֹ וְזֶרֶת

רׇחְבּוֹ: 17 וּמִלֵּאתָ בוֹ מִלֻּאַת אֶבֶן יוד הה ואו הה אַרְבָּעָה טוּרִים אָבֶן

טוּר אָדֶם מ״ה פִּטְדָה וּבָרֶקֶת הַטּוּר הָאֶחָד אהבה, דאגה אהבה, דאגה יוד הה ואו הה 18 וְהַטּוּר

הַשֵּׁנִי נֹפֶךְ סַפִּיר וְיָהֲלֹם: 19 וְהַטּוּר הַשְּׁלִישִׁי לֶשֶׁם שְׁבוֹ וְאַחְלָמָה:

20 וְהַטּוּר הָרְבִיעִי תַּרְשִׁישׁ וְשֹׁהַם מהש, אל שדי וְיָשְׁפֵה מְשֻׁבָּצִים זָהָב

יִהְיוּ אל בְּמִלּוּאֹתָם: 21 וְהָאֲבָנִים תִּהְיֶיןָ אל עַל־שְׁמֹת בְּנֵי־יִשְׂרָאֵל שְׁתֵּים

עֶשְׂרֵה עַל־שְׁמֹתָם פִּתּוּחֵי חוֹתָם ע״ה נתה, ע״ה קס״א ע״ה קס״א קמ״ג אִישׁ ע״ה קנ״א קס״א

עַל־שְׁמוֹ מהש ע״ה, אל שדי ע״ה תִּהְיֶיןָ לִשְׁנֵי עָשָׂר שָׁבֶט: 22 וְעָשִׂיתָ עַל־

הַחֹשֶׁן שדי ורבוע אהיה שַׁרְשֹׁת גַּבְלֻת מַעֲשֵׂה עֲבֹת זָהָב טָהוֹר י״פ אכא:

23 וְעָשִׂיתָ עַל־הַחֹשֶׁן שדי ורבוע אהיה שְׁתֵּי טַבְּעוֹת זָהָב וְנָתַתָּ אֶת־שְׁתֵּי

הַטַּבָּעוֹת עַל־שְׁנֵי קְצוֹת הַחֹשֶׁן שדי ורבוע אהיה: 24 וְנָתַתָּה אֶת־שְׁתֵּי עֲבֹתֹת

הַזָּהָב וזה עַל־שְׁתֵּי הַטַּבָּעֹת אֶל־קְצוֹת הַחֹשֶׁן שדי ורבוע אהיה: 25 וְאֵת שְׁתֵּי

26 *Make two gold rings and attach them to the other two corners of the breastplate on the inside edge next to the ephod.*

27 *Make two more gold rings and attach them to the bottom of the shoulder pieces on the front of the ephod, close to the seam just above the waistband of the ephod.*

28 *The rings of the breastplate are to be tied to the rings of the ephod with blue cord, connecting it to the waistband, so that the breastplate will not swing out from the ephod.*

29 *Aaron will bear the names of the sons of Israel over his heart on the breastplate of decision when he enters the sanctum as a continuing memorial before the Lord.*

30 *Also put the Urim and the Tumim in the breastplate, so they may be over Aaron's heart whenever he enters the presence of the Lord. Thus Aaron will always bear the means of making decisions for the Israelites over his heart before the Lord.*

THIRD READING - JACOB - TIFERET

31 *Make the robe of the ephod entirely of blue cloth,* 32 *with an opening for the head in its center. There shall be a woven edge like a collar around this opening, so that it will not tear.*

אֶת־הָאוּרִים וְאֶת־הַתֻּמִּים

Exodus 28:30—The Rav refers to this Breastplate as a master computer.

The breastplate was made up of two parts, called the *Urim* and *Tumin*. *Urim* are the 72 Names of God, and the Tumin are the 42 letters of the *Ana Beko'ach*. We can access this "computer" by using these kabbalistic tools.

> It is written, "And you shall put in the breastplate of judgment the Urim and the Tumim." (Exodus 28:30) It was explained that the MEANING OF Urim (Eng. 'lights') is that they illuminate, in the secret of the shining mirror, NAMELY, ZEIR ANPIN, and this is the engravings of the letters of the Holy Name in the secret of 42, with which the worlds were

> created. The letters were sunken into it. The Tumim refer to the secret of the letters contained in the mirror which does not shine, WHICH IS MALCHUT, shining with the 72 engraved letters, in the secret of the Holy Name. THE NAME OF 72 IS THE SECRET OF REVEALING THE LIGHT OF CHOCHMAH THAT IS WITHIN MALCHUT. Together they are called 'Urim and Tumim.'
> — The Zohar, Pekudei 27:268

מְעִיל

Exodus 28:31—The Tunic of the High Priest cleansed evil speech.

Evil speech, or gossiping, is one of the worst sins anyone can commit. It brings negativity to the person who is doing the gossiping, to the person

קְצוֹת שְׁתֵּי הָעֲבֹתֹת תִּתֵּן בּ״פ כהת עַל־שְׁתֵּי הַמִּשְׁבְּצוֹת וְנָתַתָּה עַל־

כִּתְפוֹת הָאֵפֹד ע״ה אלהים אֶל־מוּל פָּנָיו: 26 וְעָשִׂיתָ שְׁתֵּי טַבְּעוֹת זָהָב

וְשַׂמְתָּ אֹתָם עַל־שְׁנֵי קְצוֹת הַחֹשֶׁן שדי ורבוע אהיה עַל־שְׂפָתוֹ אֲשֶׁר אֶל־

עֵבֶר רבוע יהוה ורבוע אלהים הָאֵפֹד ע״ה אלהים בֵּיתָה זָן: 27 וְעָשִׂיתָ שְׁתֵּי טַבְּעוֹת ראה

זָהָב וְנָתַתָּה אֹתָם עַל־שְׁתֵּי כִּתְפוֹת הָאֵפוֹד יהוה אדני מִלְּמַטָּה מִמּוּל פָּנָיו

לְעֻמַּת מַחְבַּרְתּוֹ מִמַּעַל עלם לְחֵשֶׁב הָאֵפוֹד יהוה אדני: 28 וְיִרְכְּסוּ אֶת־

הַחֹשֶׁן שדי ורבוע אהיה מִטַּבְּעֹתָו אֶל־טַבְּעֹת הָאֵפֹד יהוה אדני בִּפְתִיל י״פ בן

תְּכֵלֶת לִהְיוֹת עַל־חֵשֶׁב הָאֵפוֹד יהוה אדני וְלֹא־יִזַּח הַחֹשֶׁן שדי ורבוע אהיה

מֵעַל עלם הָאֵפוֹד יהוה אדני: 29 וְנָשָׂא אַהֲרֹן ע״ב ורבוע ע״ב אֶת־שְׁמוֹת בְּנֵי־

יִשְׂרָאֵל בַּחֹשֶׁן שדי ורבוע אהיה הַמִּשְׁפָּט ע״ה ה״פ אלהים עַל־לִבּוֹ בְּבֹאוֹ אֶל־

הַקֹּדֶשׁ לְזִכָּרֹן לִפְנֵי חכמה בינה יְהֹוָָ֑֬אֱ֒דֹנֹ֒אֵ֒ה֒דֹנ֒י תָּמִיד קס״א קנ״א קמ״ג, ע״ה נתה:

30 וְנָתַתָּ אֶל־חֹשֶׁן שדי ורבוע אהיה הַמִּשְׁפָּט ע״ה ה״פ אלהים אֶת־הָאוּרִים וְאֶת־הַתֻּמִּים

וְהָיוּ עַל־לֵב אַהֲרֹן ע״ב ורבוע ע״ב בְּבֹאוֹ לִפְנֵי חכמה בינה יְהֹוָָ֑֬אֱ֒דֹנֹ֒אֵ֒ה֒דֹנ֒י וְנָשָׂא

אַהֲרֹן ע״ב ורבוע ע״ב אֶת־מִשְׁפַּט ע״ה ה״פ אלהים בְּנֵי־יִשְׂרָאֵל עַל־לִבּוֹ לִפְנֵי

חכמה בינה יְהֹוָָ֑֬אֱ֒דֹנֹ֒אֵ֒ה֒דֹנ֒י תָּמִיד ע״ה קס״א קנ״א קמ״ג, ע״ה נתה:

THIRD READING - JACOB - TIFERET

31 וְעָשִׂיתָ אֶת־מְעִיל הָאֵפוֹד ע״ה קנ״א יהוה אדני כְּלִיל תְּכֵלֶת: 32 וְהָיָה

פִי־רֹאשׁוֹ בְּתוֹכוֹ שָׂפָה ע״ה אלהים פשוט ויודין יִהְיֶה יְהֹוָ֑ה יהוה; יהה ייי לְפִיו סָבִיב

---

who is being gossiped about, and to the person who is listening to the gossip. Every time we say something negative, we create a negative entity, and this entity now exists for the sole purpose of causing chaos in our lives. According to the *Zohar*, *lashon hara* (evil tongue) is one of the strongest negativities we can invoke—and therefore one of the hardest to cleanse—so it's important that we avoid it as much as possible.

33 Make pomegranates of blue, purple and scarlet yarn around the hem of the robe—with gold bells between them. 34 The gold bells and the pomegranates are to alternate around the hem of the robe. 35 Aaron must wear it when he ministers. The sound of the bells will be heard when he enters the sanctum before the Lord and when he comes out; he will not die.

36 Make a plate of pure gold and engrave on it as on a seal: HOLY TO THE LORD.

37 Fasten a blue cord to it to attach it to the turban; it is to be on the front of the turban.

38 It will be on Aaron's forehead, and Aaron will bear the sin involved in the sacred gifts the Israelites consecrate, whatever their gifts may be. It will be on Aaron's forehead continually so that they will be acceptable to the Lord.

39 Weave the tunic of fine linen and make the turban of fine linen. The sash is to be the work of an embroiderer.

40 And for Aaron's sons make tunics, sashes and headbands, to give them dignity and honor. 41 After you put these clothes on your brother Aaron and his sons, anoint them and ordain them. Consecrate them so they may serve Me as priests.

צִיץ

Exodus 28:36—The Forehead Plate.

The Forehead Plate (*Tzitz* in Hebrew) was a gold plate engraved with the words "*Kodesh la haShem,*" or "Sacred to God." It was attached to the *Mitre*. It rested on the High Priest's forehead. This item of garb was designed to remove the traits of audacity and insolence, which essentially arise from the absence of boundaries.

> *He opened and said, "And they made the Head Plate (Heb. Tzitz) of the holy crown of pure gold . . ." (Exodus 39:30). HE ASKS: Why is it called 'Tzitz' (lit. 'to peep')? AND ANSWERS: IT WAS meant to be looked at. And since it was there for men to see, it is called 'Tzitz.' And whoever glanced at that gleam [of Light], it was reflected at once on him WHETHER HE WAS RIGHTEOUS OR NOT. HE EXPLAINS HIS WORDS. In the Head Plate were the letters of the Holy Name, ornamentally engraved in it. If a*

> *righteous man stood before it, the letters engraved in gold would shine in relief and their Lights would go from Below upward protruding from the engraving, and shine in the face of that person. And if a person stood before that Head Plate and his face did not show, NOT EVEN for a short time, the holy reflective sight, then the priest knew that he was brazen, and in need of atonement and mercy.*
> *— The Zohar, Vayak'hel, 37:446-447, 449*

Often, anger and a sense of entitlement allow us to believe that we can do whatever we want and that there should be no limits to our actions. We should try to avoid reaching a point where we have no self-control.

הַמִּצְנֶפֶת

Exodus 28:37—The *Mitre*

The *Mitre* was a turban-like headdress that cleansed the ego, which is the most powerful of all negative influences. Ego triggers our reactive behavior, which is the root of all chaos.

מַעֲשֵׂה אֹרֵג כְּפִי תַחְרָא יִהְיֶה־לּוֹ לֹא יִקָּרֵעַ: 33 וְעָשִׂיתָ עַל־שׁוּלָיו רִמֹּנֵי תְּכֵלֶת וְאַרְגָּמָן וְתוֹלַעַת שָׁנִי עַל־שׁוּלָיו סָבִיב וּפַעֲמֹנֵי זָהָב בְּתוֹכָם סָבִיב: 34 פַּעֲמֹן זָהָב וְרִמּוֹן פַּעֲמֹן זָהָב וְרִמּוֹן עַל־שׁוּלֵי הַמְּעִיל סָבִיב: 35 וְהָיָה עַל־אַהֲרֹן לְשָׁרֵת וְנִשְׁמַע קוֹלוֹ בְּבֹאוֹ אֶל־הַקֹּדֶשׁ לִפְנֵי יְהוָה וּבְצֵאתוֹ וְלֹא יָמוּת: 36 וְעָשִׂיתָ צִּיץ זָהָב טָהוֹר וּפִתַּחְתָּ עָלָיו פִּתּוּחֵי חֹתָם קֹדֶשׁ לַיהוָה: 37 וְשַׂמְתָּ אֹתוֹ עַל־פְּתִיל תְּכֵלֶת וְהָיָה עַל־הַמִּצְנָפֶת אֶל־מוּל פְּנֵי־הַמִּצְנֶפֶת יִהְיֶה: 38 וְהָיָה עַל־מֵצַח אַהֲרֹן וְנָשָׂא אַהֲרֹן אֶת־עֲוֹן הַקֳּדָשִׁים אֲשֶׁר יַקְדִּישׁוּ בְּנֵי יִשְׂרָאֵל לְכָל־מַתְּנֹת קָדְשֵׁיהֶם וְהָיָה עַל־מִצְחוֹ תָּמִיד לְרָצוֹן לָהֶם לִפְנֵי יְהוָה: 39 וְשִׁבַּצְתָּ הַכְּתֹנֶת שֵׁשׁ וְעָשִׂיתָ מִצְנֶפֶת שֵׁשׁ וְאַבְנֵט תַּעֲשֶׂה מַעֲשֵׂה רֹקֵם: 40 וְלִבְנֵי אַהֲרֹן תַּעֲשֶׂה כֻתֳּנֹת וְעָשִׂיתָ לָהֶם אַבְנֵטִים וּמִגְבָּעוֹת תַּעֲשֶׂה לָהֶם לְכָבוֹד וּלְתִפְאָרֶת: 41 וְהִלְבַּשְׁתָּ אֹתָם אֶת־אַהֲרֹן אָחִיךָ וְאֶת־בָּנָיו אִתּוֹ וּמָשַׁחְתָּ אֹתָם וּמִלֵּאתָ אֶת־יָדָם וְקִדַּשְׁתָּ אֹתָם וְכִהֲנוּ לִי: 42 וַעֲשֵׂה לָהֶם מִכְנְסֵי־בָד לְכַסּוֹת בְּשַׂר עֶרְוָה מִמָּתְנַיִם וְעַד־יְרֵכַיִם יִהְיוּ:

הַכְּתֹנֶת

Exodus 28:39—The High Priest's Robe.

The Robe of the High priest cleansed the negativity caused by murder in both its literal and figurative sense. In addition to the physical killing of a person, character assassination, sabotaging a business, or damaging a relationship can also be considered forms of murder. The Ari wrote:

"You shall not murder;" (Exodus 20:13) this includes the necessity to refrain from insulting people in public, for then their blood withdraws and they become pale. Then one is considered as if he has shed blood...
— Writings of the Ari, Gate of Reincarnation, 17th Introduction: 3

וְאַבְנֵט

Exodus 28:39—The High Priest's Girdle (belt) cleansed negative thoughts.

Eventually and inevitably, negative thoughts become actions, so they need to be purged from the seed level of consciousness.

42 Make linen undergarments as a covering for the nudity of the flesh, reaching from the waist to the thigh. 43 Aaron and his sons must wear them whenever they enter the Tent of Meeting or approach the altar to minister in the sanctum, so that they will not incur sin and die. This is to be a lasting ordinance for him and his descendants.

FOURTH READING - MOSES - NETZACH

29:1 This is what you are to do to consecrate them, so they may serve Me as priests: Take a young bull and two rams without defect. 2 And make them unleavened bread, and cakes unleavened mingled with oil, and wafers unleavened spread with oil; of fine wheaten flour.

3 Put them in a basket and present them in it—along with the bull and the two rams.

4 Then bring Aaron and his sons to the entrance to the Tent of Meeting and wash them with water.

5 Take the garments and dress Aaron with the tunic, the robe of the ephod, the ephod and the breastplate. Fasten the ephod on him by its skillfully woven waistband of the ephod. 6 Put the turban on his head and attach the sacred crown to the turban.

7 Take the anointing oil and anoint him by pouring it on his head. 8 Bring his sons and dress them in tunics 9 and put headbands on them—Aaron and his sons—and tie sashes on them. The priesthood is theirs by a lasting ordinance. In this way you shall ordain Aaron and his sons.

Exodus 29:1—Offering the sacrifices.

This section contains a description of the sacrifices. The first sacrifice was for the inauguration of the *Mishkan* (the Tabernacle). This discussion of sacrifices is not merely an historic reference that allows us to feel more enlightened than our seemingly "barbaric" ancestors. In fact, it is said that the global consciousness at that time was at such a level of enlightenment that the animals themselves would recognize the merit and actually gather together and plead to be taken as a sacrifice.

They were aware that this was the purpose for which they had come to this world—to help in the process of spiritual cleansing. Today, however, our sacrifices take the form of actions that are difficult or uncomfortable for us to perform.

Exodus 29:4—Aaron and his sons.

Here we read about how, before performing the sacrifices, Aaron and his sons were immersed in water and then clothed in the holy garments. The mikveh, or spiritual cleansing bath, is used to remove negativity. After the *mikveh*, they were

43 וְהָיוּ עַל־אַהֲרֹן ע"ב ורבוע ע"ב וְעַל־בָּנָיו בְּבֹאָם | אֶל־אֹהֶל לאה מוֹעֵד אוֹ בְגִשְׁתָּם אֶל־הַמִּזְבֵּחַ ז, נגד לְשָׁרֵת בַּקֹּדֶשׁ וְלֹא־יִשְׂאוּ עָוֹן ג"פ מ"ב וָמֵתוּ חֻקַּת עוֹלָם לוֹ וּלְזַרְעוֹ אַחֲרָיו:

FOURTH READING - MOSES - NETZACH

29 1 וְזֶה הַדָּבָר ראה אֲשֶׁר־תַּעֲשֶׂה לָהֶם לְקַדֵּשׁ אֹתָם לְכַהֵן מלה לִי לְקַח פַּר מזוזר, ערי, סנדלפון אֶחָד אהבה, דאגה בֶּן־בָּקָר וְאֵילִם יהוה אדני יהוה אהיה שְׁנַיִם תְּמִימִם: 2 וְלֶחֶם ג"פ יהוה מַצּוֹת וְחַלֹּת מַצֹּת בְּלוּלֹת בַּשֶּׁמֶן וּרְקִיקֵי מַצּוֹת מְשֻׁחִים בַּשָּׁמֶן י"פ טל, י"פ כוזו; ביט סֹלֶת חִטִּים י"פ טל, י"פ כוזו; ביט תַּעֲשֶׂה אֹתָם: 3 וְנָתַתָּ אוֹתָם עַל־סַל אֶחָד אהבה, דאגה וְהִקְרַבְתָּ אֹתָם בַּסָּל וְאֶת־הַפָּר מזוזר, ערי, סנדלפון וְאֵת שְׁנֵי הָאֵילִם: 4 וְאֶת־אַהֲרֹן ע"ב ורבוע ע"ב וְאֶת־בָּנָיו תַּקְרִיב אֶל־פֶּתַח אֹהֶל לאה מוֹעֵד וְרָחַצְתָּ אֹתָם בַּמָּיִם: 5 וְלָקַחְתָּ אֶת־הַבְּגָדִים וְהִלְבַּשְׁתָּ אֶת־אַהֲרֹן ע"ב ורבוע ע"ב אֶת־הַכֻּתֹּנֶת וְאֵת מְעִיל הָאֵפֹד ע"ה קנ"א אלהים וְאֶת־הָאֵפֹד ע"ה אלהים וְאֶת־הַחֹשֶׁן וְאָפַדְתָּ לוֹ בְּחֵשֶׁב הָאֵפֹד ע"ה אלהים: 6 וְשַׂמְתָּ הַמִּצְנֶפֶת עַל־רֹאשׁוֹ וְנָתַתָּ אֶת־נֵזֶר הַקֹּדֶשׁ עַל־הַמִּצְנָפֶת: 7 וְלָקַחְתָּ אֶת־שֶׁמֶן הַמִּשְׁחָה י"פ טל, י"פ כוזו; ביט וְיָצַקְתָּ עַל־רֹאשׁוֹ וּמָשַׁחְתָּ אֹתוֹ: 8 וְאֶת־בָּנָיו תַּקְרִיב וְהִלְבַּשְׁתָּם כֻּתֳּנֹת: 9 וְחָגַרְתָּ אֹתָם אַבְנֵט אַהֲרֹן וּבָנָיו ע"ב ורבוע ע"ב וְחָבַשְׁתָּ לָהֶם מִגְבָּעֹת וְהָיְתָה לָהֶם כְּהֻנָּה לְחֻקַּת עוֹלָם וּמִלֵּאתָ יַד־

---

helped to don their vestments, then anointed to transform their clothing into a spiritual tool that would connect to the Light.

The Ari wrote:

The High Priest is in the likeness of the Supernal Man, so he used to wear the

clothes of Supernal Man.
— Writings of the Ari, Torah Compilations 5, Story of Tetzaveh: 8

¹⁰ Bring the bull to the front of the Tent of Meeting, and Aaron and his sons shall lay their hands on its head.

¹¹ Slaughter it before the Lord at the entrance to the Tent of Meeting.

¹² Take some of the bull's blood and put it on the horns of the altar with your finger, and pour out all of it at the base of the altar.

¹³ Then take all the fat around the inner parts, the covering of the liver, and both kidneys with the fat on them, and burn them on the altar.

¹⁴ But burn the bull's flesh and its hide and its offal outside the camp. It is a sin offering.

¹⁵ Take one of the rams, and Aaron and his sons shall lay their hands on its head.

¹⁶ Slaughter the ram and take the blood and sprinkle it around the altar.

¹⁷ Cut the ram into pieces and wash the inner parts and the legs, putting them with the head and the other pieces.

¹⁸ Then burn the entire ram on the altar. It is a burnt offering to the Lord, a pleasing aroma, an offering made to the Lord.

Exodus 29:10— The ox.

According to the Zohar, oxen are Left Column energy and are one of the spiritual connectors to the Upper World. Lions are Right Column, and eagles are Central Column. To control Left Column energy, which is judgment, an ox was sacrificed.

> "As for the likeness of their faces, the four had the face of a man, the face of a lion on the right...," (Ezekiel 1:10) IN WHICH the image of a man, WHICH IS MALCHUT, is included in all. And there were four faces to the four directions of the world. They are distinguished in their appearances, NAMELY A LION, AN OX, AND AN EAGLE, and all are integrated in man, THE SECRET OF MALCHUT. THE LION, OX AND EAGLE ARE CHESED, GEVURAH AND TIFERET, AND THE

FACE OF MAN IS MALCHUT, WHICH DRAWS FROM ALL, AND ALL ARE INCLUDED IN IT.
— The Zohar, Bamidbar 3:28

Exodus 29:15—The ram (goat).

As the sign of the zodiac that represents the month of Aries, the head of the year and the beginning of everything, the ram naturally also embodies the strongest Desire to Receive. Here two goats were sacrificed: one to the Creator and one to the Desire to Receive for the Self Alone. Because the goat is the essence of the Desire to Receive for the Self Alone, the sacrifice acted as an antidote, which helped to convert ego-based desire into the Desire to Receive for the Sake of Sharing.

> So did the Holy One, blessed be He, say to Israel: 'Prepare two goats, one for Me and one for that Slanderer,' NAMELY THE

אַהֲרֹן ע״ב ורבוע ע״ב וְיָדֹ־בָּנָיו׃ 10 וְהִקְרַבְתָּ֙ אֶת־הַפָּר֒ סמֶזֶּךְ, ערי, סנדלפון לִפְנֵ֣י

אֹ֣הֶל לאה בינה חכמה מוֹעֵ֔ד וְסָמַ֨ךְ אַהֲרֹ֧ן ע״ב ורבוע ע״ב וּבָנָ֛יו אֶת־יְדֵיהֶ֖ם עַל־

רֹ֥אשׁ ריבוע אלהים ואלהים דיודין ע״ה הַפָּֽר׃ סמֶזֶּךְ, ערי, סנדלפון 11 וְשָׁחַטְתָּ֥ אֶת־הַפָּ֖ר

סמֶזֶּךְ, ערי, סנדלפון לִפְנֵ֣י חכמה בינה יְהֹוָ֑הּ אדני־יאהדונהי פֶּ֖תַח אֹ֥הֶל לאה מוֹעֵֽד׃ 12 וְלָֽקַחְתָּ֙

מִדַּ֣ם רבוע אהיה הַפָּ֔ר סמֶזֶּךְ, ערי, סנדלפון וְנָֽתַתָּ֛ה עַל־קַרְנֹ֥ת הַמִּזְבֵּ֖חַ זן, נגד

בְּאֶצְבָּעֶ֑ךָ וְאֶת־כָּל־הַדָּ֣ם יֵלי־ רבוע אהיה תִּשְׁפֹּ֔ךְ אֶל־יְס֖וֹד הטל הַמִּזְבֵּֽחַ׃ זן, נגד

13 וְלָֽקַחְתָּ֗ אֶֽת־כָּל־הַחֵ֘לֶב֘ יֵלי־ הַֽמְכַסֶּ֣ה אֶת־הַקֶּ֗רֶב וְאֵ֤ת הַיֹּתֶ֨רֶת֙ עַל־

הַכָּבֵ֔ד וְאֵת֙ שְׁתֵּ֣י הַכְּלָיֹ֔ת וְאֶת־הַחֵ֖לֶב אֲשֶׁ֣ר עֲלֵיהֶ֑ן וְהִקְטַרְתָּ֖ יא אדני

הַמִּזְבֵּֽחָה׃ 14 וְאֶת־בְּשַׂ֤ר הַפָּר֙ סמֶזֶּךְ, ערי, סנדלפון וְאֶת־עֹר֣וֹ וְאֶת־פִּרְשׁ֔וֹ

תִּשְׂרֹ֣ף בָּאֵ֔שׁ אלהים דיודין ע״ה מִח֖וּץ לַֽמַּחֲנֶ֑ה חַטָּ֖את הֽוּא׃ 15 וְאֶת־הָאַ֤יִל

הָֽאֶחָ֔ד אהבה, דאגה, ואהבה תִּקָּ֑ח רבוע אהיה דאלפין וְסָ֣מְכ֡וּ אַהֲרֹ֧ן ע״ב ורבוע ע״ב וּבָנָ֛יו אֶת־

יְדֵיהֶ֖ם עַל־רֹ֥אשׁ ריבוע אלהים ואלהים דיודין ע״ה הָאָֽיִל׃ 16 וְשָׁחַטְתָּ֖ אֶת־הָאָ֑יִל

וְלָֽקַחְתָּ֙ אֶת־דָּמ֔וֹ וְזָֽרַקְתָּ֥ עַל־הַמִּזְבֵּ֖חַ זן, נגד סָבִֽיב׃ 17 וְאֶ֨ת־הָאַ֔יִל תְּנַתֵּ֖חַ

לִנְתָחָ֑יו וְרָֽחַצְתָּ֤ קִרְבּ֙וֹ וּכְרָעָ֔יו וְנָֽתַתָּ֥ עַל־נְתָחָ֖יו וְעַל־רֹאשֽׁוֹ׃ 18 וְהִקְטַרְתָּ֤

יא אדני אֶת־כָּל־הָאַ֨יִל֙ יֵלי־ הַמִּזְבֵּ֔חָה עֹלָ֥ה ה֖וּא לַֽיהֹוָ֑הּ אדני־יאהדונהי רֵ֣יחַ נִיח֗וֹחַ

אִשֶּׁ֛ה לַֽיהֹוָ֖הּ אדני־יאהדונהי הֽוּא׃

OTHER SIDE, 'so that he will think that he ate from My meal and will not know of the other, our own joyous meal. Let him take that portion and go his way and depart from My house.' Since supernal Ima, which is the World to Come, NAMELY Binah, came to dwell in the sanctuary of the Lower World, to observe it with a radiant face, it is only right that the slanderer would not be present, nor the plaintiffs, when He takes out all the blessings and illuminates everything. And all manner of freedom is available IN Malchut, and Israel receives those blessings.

— The Zohar, Tetzaveh 13:102

FIFTH READING - AARON - HOD

¹⁹ *Take the other ram, and Aaron and his sons shall lay their hands on its head.*

²⁰ *Slaughter the ram, take some of its blood and put it on the lobes of the right ears of Aaron and on the lobes of the right ears of his sons, on the thumbs of their right hands, and on the big toes of their right feet. Then sprinkle the blood around the altar.*

²¹ *And take some of the blood on the altar and some of the anointing oil and sprinkle it on Aaron and his garments and on his sons and their garments with him. Then he and his sons and their garments will be consecrated.*

²² *Take from this ram the fat, the fat tail, the fat around the inner parts, the covering of the liver, both kidneys with the fat on them, and the right thigh. This is the ram for the ordination.*

²³ *Take a loaf, and a cake made with oil, and a wafer from the basket of unleavened bread, which is before the Lord.*

²⁴ *Put all these in the hands of Aaron and his sons and wave them before the Lord as a wave offering.* ²⁵ *Then take them from their hands and burn them on the altar along with the burnt offering for a pleasing aroma to the Lord, an offering made to the Lord.*

לְחִיָּק-עוֹלָם

Exodus 29:28—The priestly succession was through Aaron.

The succession of the priesthood (the kohanim) came through the descendants of Aaron. Aaron transformed himself into a pure spiritual being and, as such, became the spiritual chariot for the *Sefira* of *Hod*. Today, for someone to be a Kohen, or priest, there must be a direct lineage from father to son, originating with Aaron. Nepotism is not the issue; this is a matter of "wiring." There needs to be an uninterrupted connection to the source, Aaron, or else the technology does not work.

"Speak to the priests the sons of Aaron." HE ASKS, what is the reason it is written here, "the sons of Aaron?" Do I not know they are the sons of Aaron? AND HE

ANSWERS, THIS TEACHES US they are "the sons of Aaron" rather than 'the sons of Levi,' because Aaron is the first of all the priests. For it is him that the Holy One, blessed be He, had chosen above everyone, so as to make peace in the world, and because Aaron's practices have brought him up to this. For Aaron strove throughout his life to increase peace in the world. Since these were his ways, the Holy One, blessed be He, raised him TO PRIESTHOOD, to introduce peace among the celestial retinue, FOR THROUGH HIS WORSHIP HE BRINGS ABOUT THE UNION OF THE HOLY ONE, BLESSED BE HE AND HIS SHECHINAH, WHICH BRINGS PEACE THROUGHOUT THE WORLDS. Hence, "Speak to the priests the sons of Aaron."
— The Zohar, Emor 1:2

FIFTH READING - AARON - HOD

19 וְלָקַחְתָּ֖ אֵ֣ת הָאַ֣יִל הַשֵּׁנִ֑י וְסָמַ֨ךְ אַהֲרֹ֧ן ע"ב ורבוע ע"ב וּבָנָ֛יו אֶת־יְדֵיהֶ֖ם

עַל־רֹ֥אשׁ ריבוע אלהים ואלהים דיודין ע"ה הָאָֽיִל׃ 20 וְשָׁחַטְתָּ֣ אֶת־הָאַ֗יִל וְלָקַחְתָּ֣

מִדָּמוֹ֮ וְנָֽתַתָּ֗ה עַל־תְּנ֨וּךְ֙ אֹ֤זֶן אַהֲרֹן֙ יוד הי ואו הה ע"ב ורבוע ע"ב וְעַל־תְּנ֜וּךְ אֹ֤זֶן

בָּנָיו֙ הַיְמָנִ֔ית וְעַל־בֹּ֤הֶן יָדָם֙ הַיְמָנִ֔ית יוד הי ואו הה וְעַל־בֹּ֥הֶן רַגְלָ֖ם הַיְמָנִ֑ית

וְזָרַקְתָּ֧ אֶת־הַדָּ֛ם ז"ן, נגד רבוע אהיה עַל־הַמִּזְבֵּ֖חַ סָבִֽיב׃ 21 וְלָקַחְתָּ֞ מִן־הַדָּ֨ם

אֲשֶׁ֥ר עַל־הַמִּזְבֵּ֘חַ֘ ז"ן, נגד רבוע אהיה וּמִשֶּׁ֣מֶן י"פ טל, י"פ כוז"ו; ביט הַמִּשְׁחָ֗ה וְהִזֵּיתָ֤

עַל־אַהֲרֹן֙ ע"ב ורבוע ע"ב וְעַל־בְּגָדָ֔יו וְעַל־בָּנָ֛יו וְעַל־בִּגְדֵ֥י בָנָ֖יו אִתּ֑וֹ וְקָ֣דַשׁ

ה֗וּא וּבְגָדָ֛יו וּבָנָ֥יו וּבִגְדֵ֥י בָנָ֖יו אִתּֽוֹ׃ 22 וְלָקַחְתָּ֣ מִן־הָ֠אַ֠יִל הַחֵ֨לֶב וְהָֽאַלְיָ֜ה

וְאֶת־הַחֵ֣לֶב ׀ הַֽמְכַסֶּ֣ה אֶת־הַקֶּ֗רֶב וְאֵ֚ת יֹתֶ֣רֶת הַכָּבֵ֔ד וְאֵ֣ת ׀ שְׁתֵּ֣י

הַכְּלָיֹ֗ת וְאֶת־הַחֵ֙לֶב֙ אֲשֶׁ֣ר עֲלֵיהֶ֔ן וְאֵ֖ת שׁ֣וֹק הַיָּמִ֑ין כִּ֛י אֵ֥יל מִלֻּאִ֖ים

הֽוּא׃ 23 וְכִכַּ֨ר ג"פ יהוה לֶ֜חֶם אַחַ֗ת וְֽחַלַּ֨ת לֶ֥חֶם ג"פ יהוה שֶׁ֛מֶן י"פ טל, י"פ כוז"ו; ביט

אַחַ֖ת וְרָקִ֣יק אֶחָ֑ד אהבה, דאגה מִסַּל֙ הַמַּצּ֔וֹת אֲשֶׁ֖ר לִפְנֵ֥י חכמה בינה

יְ֒הֹ֒וָ֒ה֒אֱלֹהִים: 24 וְשַׂמְתָּ֣ הַכֹּ֔ל ילי עַ֚ל כַּפֵּ֣י אַהֲרֹ֔ן ע"ב ורבוע ע"ב וְעַ֖ל כַּפֵּ֣י בָנָ֑יו

וְהֵנַפְתָּ֥ אֹתָ֛ם תְּנוּפָ֖ה לִפְנֵ֥י חכמה בינה יְ֒הֹ֒וָ֒ה֒אֱלֹהים: 25 וְלָקַחְתָּ֤ אֹתָם֙ מִיָּדָ֔ם

וְהִקְטַרְתָּ֥ י"א אדני הַמִּזְבֵּ֖חָה עַל־הָעֹלָ֑ה לְרֵ֤יחַ נִיח֙וֹחַ֙ לִפְנֵ֣י חכמה בינה

יְ֒הֹ֒וָ֒ה֒אֱלֹהים אִשֶּׁ֥ה ה֖וּא לַי֒הֹ֒וָ֒ה֒אֱלֹהים׃ 26 וְלָקַחְתָּ֣ אֶת־הֶֽחָזֶ֗ה מֵאֵ֤יל

הַמִּלֻּאִים֙ אֲשֶׁ֣ר לְאַֽהֲרֹ֔ן ע"ב ורבוע ע"ב וְהֵנַפְתָּ֥ אֹת֛וֹ תְּנוּפָ֖ה לִפְנֵ֣י חכמה בינה

יְ֒הֹ֒וָ֒ה֒אֱלֹהים וְהָיָ֥ה יהוה; יהה לְךָ֖ לְמָנָֽה פו"י: 27 וְקִדַּשְׁתָּ֣ ׀ אֵ֣ת יהוה, יהה חֲזֵ֣ה הַתְּנוּפָ֗ה

וְאֵת֙ שׁ֣וֹק הַתְּרוּמָ֔ה אֲשֶׁ֥ר הוּנַ֖ף וַאֲשֶׁ֣ר הוּרָ֑ם מֵאֵיל֙ הַמִּלֻּאִ֔ים מֵאֲשֶׁ֖ר

לְאַֽהֲרֹ֔ן ע"ב ורבוע ע"ב וּמֵֽאֲשֶׁ֖ר לְבָנָֽיו: 28 וְהָיָה֩ יהוה, יהה לְאַהֲרֹ֨ן ע"ב ורבוע ע"ב

וּלְבָנָ֜יו לְחָק־עוֹלָ֗ם מֵאֵת֙ בְּנֵ֣י יִשְׂרָאֵ֔ל כִּ֥י תְרוּמָ֖ה ה֑וּא וּתְרוּמָ֨ה יִֽהְיֶ֜ה

יייי מֵאֵ֤ת בְּנֵֽי־יִשְׂרָאֵל֙ מִזִּבְחֵ֣י שַׁלְמֵיהֶ֔ם תְּרֽוּמָתָ֖ם לַי֒הֹ֒וָ֒ה֒אֱלֹהים:

26 After you take the breast of the ram for Aaron's ordination, wave it before the Lord as a wave offering, and it will be your share.

27 Consecrate those parts of the ordination ram that belong to Aaron and his sons: the breast that was waved and the thigh that was presented.

28 This is always to be the regular share from the Israelites for Aaron and his sons. It is the contribution the Israelites are to make to the Lord from their fellowship offerings.

29 Aaron's sacred garments will belong to his descendants so that they can be anointed and ordained in them. 30 The son who succeeds him as priest and comes to the Tent of Meeting to minister in the sanctum is to wear these seven days.

31 Take the ram for the ordination and cook the meat in a sacred place. 32 At the entrance to the Tent of Meeting, Aaron and his sons are to eat the meat of the ram and the bread that is in the basket.

33 They are to eat these offerings by which atonement was made for their ordination and consecration. But no one else may eat them, because they are sacred.

34 And if any of the meat of the ordination ram or any bread is left over till morning, burn it up. It must not be eaten, because it is sacred.

35 Do for Aaron and his sons everything I have commanded you, taking seven days to ordain them. 36 Sacrifice a bull each day as a sin offering to make atonement. Purify the altar by making atonement for it, and anoint it to consecrate it.

37 For seven days make atonement for the altar and consecrate it. Then the altar will be most holy, and whatever touches it will be holy.

SIXTH READING - JOSEPH - YESOD

38 This is what you are to offer on the altar regularly each day: two lambs a year old.

39 Offer the one lamb in the morning and the other lamb at twilight.

40 Offer a tenth of an Ephah of fine flour mixed with a quarter of a hin of oil from pressed olives, and a quarter of a hin of wine as a drink offering with the first lamb.

41 Sacrifice the other lamb at twilight with the same grain offering and its drink offering as in the morning—a pleasing aroma, an offering made to the Lord.

29 וּבִגְדֵי הַקֹּדֶשׁ אֲשֶׁר לְאַהֲרֹן ע״ב ורבוע ע״ב יִהְיוּ אל לְבָנָיו אַחֲרָיו לְמָשְׁחָה

בָהֶם וּלְמַלֵּא־בָם מ״ב אֶת־יָדָם: 30 שִׁבְעַת יָמִים גלך יִלְבָּשָׁם הַכֹּהֵן מלה

תַּחְתָּיו מִבָּנָיו אֲשֶׁר יָבֹא אֶל־אֹהֶל לאה מוֹעֵד לְשָׁרֵת בַּקֹּדֶשׁ: 31 וְאֵת

אֵיל הַמִּלֻּאִים תִּקָּח רבוע אהיה דאלפין וּבִשַּׁלְתָּ אֶת־בְּשָׂרוֹ בְּמָקֹם קָדֹשׁ:

32 וְאָכַל אַהֲרֹן ע״ב ורבוע ע״ב וּבָנָיו אֶת־בְּשַׂר הָאַיִל וְאֶת־הַלֶּחֶם ג״פ יהוה

אֲשֶׁר בַּסָּל פֶּתַח אֹהֶל לאה מוֹעֵד: 33 וְאָכְלוּ אֹתָם אֲשֶׁר כֻּפַּר מצפץ בָּהֶם

לְמַלֵּא אֶת־יָדָם לְקַדֵּשׁ אֹתָם אור, אין סוף וְזָר לֹא־יֹאכַל כִּי־קֹדֶשׁ הֵם:

34 וְאִם יוֹדך, ע״ה מ״ב יִוָּתֵר מִבְּשַׂר הַמִּלֻּאִים וּמִן־הַלֶּחֶם ג״פ יהוה עַד־הַבֹּקֶר

וְשָׂרַפְתָּ אֶת־הַנּוֹתָר בָּאֵשׁ אלהים דיודין ע״ה לֹא יֵאָכֵל כִּי־קֹדֶשׁ הוּא:

35 וְעָשִׂיתָ לְאַהֲרֹן ע״ב ורבוע ע״ב וּלְבָנָיו כָּכָה מ״ה כְּכֹל ילי אֲשֶׁר־צִוִּיתִי

אֹתְכָה שִׁבְעַת יָמִים גלך תְּמַלֵּא יָדָם: 36 וּפַר בן/זוגך, עדי, סנדלפון וַתֹּאת

תַּעֲשֶׂה לַיּוֹם ע״ה = נגד, זן, מזבח עַל־הַכִּפֻּרִים וְחִטֵּאתָ עַל־הַמִּזְבֵּחַ זן, נגד

בְּכַפֶּרְךָ עָלָיו וּמָשַׁחְתָּ אֹתוֹ לְקַדְּשׁוֹ: 37 שִׁבְעַת יָמִים גלך תְּכַפֵּר עַל־

הַמִּזְבֵּחַ זן, נגד וְקִדַּשְׁתָּ אֹתוֹ וְהָיָה יהוה, יהה הַמִּזְבֵּחַ זן, נגד קֹדֶשׁ קָדָשִׁים כָּל

ילי הַנֹּגֵעַ מלוי אהיה דאלפין בַּמִּזְבֵּחַ זן, נגד יִקְדָּשׁ:

SIXTH READING - JOSEPH - YESOD

38 וְזֶה אֲשֶׁר תַּעֲשֶׂה עַל־הַמִּזְבֵּחַ זן, נגד כְּבָשִׂים בְּנֵי־שָׁנָה שְׁנַיִם לַיּוֹם

ע״ה = נגד, זן, מזבח נתה, ע״ה קס״א קנ״א קמ״ג תָּמִיד 39 אֶת־הַכֶּבֶשׂ ב״פ קס״א הָאֶחָד

אהבה, דאגה תַּעֲשֶׂה בַבֹּקֶר וְאֵת הַכֶּבֶשׂ ב״פ קס״א הַשֵּׁנִי תַּעֲשֶׂה בֵּין הָעַרְבָּיִם:

40 וְעִשָּׂרֹן סֹלֶת בָּלוּל בְּשֶׁמֶן י״פ טל, י״פ כוז״ו; ביט כָּתִית רֶבַע הַהִין וְנֵסֶךְ

רְבִיעִת הַהִין יַיִן מ״כ, י״פ האא לַכֶּבֶשׂ ב״פ קס״א הָאֶחָד אהבה, דאגה: 41 וְאֵת

הַכֶּבֶשׂ ב״פ קס״א הַשֵּׁנִי תַּעֲשֶׂה בֵּין הָעַרְבָּיִם כְּמִנְחַת הַבֹּקֶר וּכְנִסְכָּהּ

42 This burnt offering for generations to come is to be made regularly at the entrance to the Tent of Meeting before the Lord. There I will meet you and speak to you;

43 there also I will meet with the Israelites, and the place will be consecrated by My glory. 44 So I will consecrate the Tent of Meeting and the altar and I will consecrate Aaron and his sons to serve Me as priests.

45 Then I will dwell among the Israelites and be their God. 46 They will know that I am the Lord their God, who brought them out of Egypt so that I might dwell among them. I am the Lord their God.

SEVENTH READING - DAVID - MALCHUT

30¹ Make an altar for burning incense; of acacia wood it shall be made.

2 It is to be a cubit long and a cubit wide, square shaped, and two cubits high—its horns of one piece with it.

3 Overlay the top and all the sides and the horns with pure gold, and make a gold molding around it. 4 Make two gold rings for the altar below the molding—two on opposite sides—to house the poles used to carry it.

5 Make the poles of acacia wood and overlay them with gold. 6 Put the altar in front of the curtain that is before the Ark of the Covenant—before the atonement cover that is over the Covenant—where I will meet with you. 7 Aaron must burn fragrant incense on the altar every morning; when he tends the lamps he must burn it.

קְטֹרֶת סַמִּים

Exodus 30:7—There were two altars in the Tabernacle: one for the burnt offerings (the animal sacrifices) and one for the incense.

There were eleven spices that were burned as incense on the altar, and these cleansed the power of Satan. Ten spices represent the ten levels of Light (*Ten Sefirot*). The eleventh level, the one below *Malchut* (tenth level), is the level of Satan. We have to give proactively to Satan as we do with the piece of the challah when we bake. When he is fed, he will be happy and satisfied. If he is left hungry and we do not give him the little he requires for nourishment, then he can take what he wants, which is much more. The

incense gives Satan his piece so that he doesn't take ours. The Zohar says:

Come and see the difference between prayer and [what has been written about] incense. Prayer was composed [to take the place] of the sacrifices offered by Israel. But all those sacrifices are not as valuable as the incense. Also, the difference between them is that prayer perfects whatever needs perfection. Incense, on the other hand, does more by both perfecting and binding, THAT IS, CREATING UNITY, and brings more Light than anything else, which removes filth and cleanses the Tabernacle. And everything is shining, perfected and joined together.

--The Zohar, Vayak'hel 41:477

תַּעֲשֶׂה־לָּהּ לְרֵיחַ נִיחֹחַ אִשֶּׁה לַיהוָׁואדניאהדונהי 42 עֹלַת תָּמִיד

ע"ה קס"א קנ"א קמ"ג, ע"ה קמ"ג, ע"ה נתה לְדֹרֹתֵיכֶם פֶּתַח אֹהֶל לאה ־מוֹעֵד לִפְנֵי חכמה בינה

יְהוָׁואדניאהדונהי אֲשֶׁר אִוָּעֵד לָכֶם שָׁמָּה מהש, אל שדי, משה, מהש לְדַבֵּר ראה אֵלֶיךָ

אני, טדהד כוזו שָׁם יהוה שדי: 43 וְנֹעַדְתִּי שָׁמָּה מהש, אל שדי, משה לִבְנֵי יִשְׂרָאֵל

וְנִקְדַּשׁ בִּכְבֹדִי: 44 וְקִדַּשְׁתִּי אֶת־אֹהֶל לאה מוֹעֵד וְאֶת־הַמִּזְבֵּחַ זן, נגד

וְאֶת־אַהֲרֹן ע"ב ורבוע ע"ב וְאֶת־בָּנָיו אֲקַדֵּשׁ לְכַהֵן מלה לִי: 45 וְשָׁכַנְתִּי בְּתוֹךְ

בְּנֵי יִשְׂרָאֵל וְהָיִיתִי לָהֶם לֵאלֹהִים מום, אהיה אדני ; ילה: 46 וְיָדְעוּ כִּי אֲנִי

אני, טדהד כוזו יְהוָׁואדניאהדונהי אֱלֹהֵיהֶם ילה אֲשֶׁר הוֹצֵאתִי אֹתָם מֵאֶרֶץ

אלהים דאלפין מִצְרַיִם מצר לְשָׁכְנִי בְתוֹכָם אֲנִי אני, טדהד כוזו יְהוָׁואדניאהדונהי

אֱלֹהֵיהֶם ילה:

SEVENTH READING - DAVID - MALCHUT

30 1 וְעָשִׂיתָ מִזְבֵּחַ זן, נגד מִקְטַר קְטֹרֶת י"א אדני עֲצֵי שִׁטִּים תַּעֲשֶׂה אֹתוֹ:

2 אַמָּה דמב, מלוי ע"ב אָרְכּוֹ וְאַמָּה דמב, מלוי ע"ב רָחְבּוֹ רָבוּעַ יִהְיֶה ייי וְאַמָּתַיִם

קֹמָתוֹ מִמֶּנּוּ קַרְנֹתָיו: 3 וְצִפִּיתָ אֹתוֹ זָהָב טָהוֹר י"פ אכא אֶת־גַּגּוֹ וְאֶת־

קִירֹתָיו סָבִיב וְאֶת־קַרְנֹתָיו וְעָשִׂיתָ לּוֹ זֵר אור, אין סוף זָהָב סָבִיב: 4 וּשְׁתֵּי

טַבְּעֹת זָהָב תַּעֲשֶׂה־לּוֹ | מִתַּחַת לְזֵרוֹ עַל שְׁתֵּי צַלְעֹתָיו תַּעֲשֶׂה עַל־

שְׁנֵי צִדָּיו וְהָיָה יהוה, יהה לְבָתִּים לְבַדִּים לָשֵׂאת אֹתוֹ בָּהֵמָּה: 5 וְעָשִׂיתָ

אֶת־הַבַּדִּים עֲצֵי שִׁטִּים וְצִפִּיתָ אֹתָם זָהָב: 6 וְנָתַתָּה אֹתוֹ לִפְנֵי חכמה בינה

הַפָּרֹכֶת אֲשֶׁר עַל־אֲרֹן הָעֵדֻת לִפְנֵי חכמה בינה הַכַּפֹּרֶת אֲשֶׁר עַל־הָעֵדֻת

אֲשֶׁר אִוָּעֵד לְךָ שָׁמָּה מהש, אל שדי, משה: 7 וְהִקְטִיר עָלָיו אַהֲרֹן ע"ב ורבוע ע"ב

קְטֹרֶת י"א אדני סַמִּים ע"ה קנ"א, אלהים אדני בַּבֹּקֶר בַּבֹּקֶר בְּהֵיטִיבוֹ אֶת־

הַנֵּרֹת יַקְטִירֶנָּה:

MAFTIR

⁸ And when Aaron goes up to light the lights at twilight so he shall again burn the incense so it will burn regularly before the Lord for the generations to come.

⁹ Do not offer on this altar any other incense or any burnt offering or grain offering, and do not pour a drink offering on it.

¹⁰ Aaron shall make atonement on its horns once a year with the blood of the atoning sin offering once a year for the generations to come. It is most holy to the Lord."

HAFTARAH OF TETZAVEH

According to the sages, the Temple was destroyed because of "hatred for no reason." As long as the Temple remains "concealed," it is a sign that there is still motiveless and unresolved hatred within us.

Ezekiel 43:10-27

43:¹⁰ "Son of man, describe the Temple to the people of Israel, that they may be ashamed of their sins. Let them consider the plan,

¹¹ and if they are ashamed of all they have done, make known to them the design of the Temple—its arrangement, its exits and entrances—its whole design and all its regulations and its whole design and whole laws. Write these down before them so that they may be faithful to its design and follow all its regulations.

¹² This is the law of the Temple: All the surrounding area on top of the mountain will be most holy. Such is the law of the Temple.

¹³ These are the measurements of the altar in long cubits, that cubit being a cubit and a handbreadth: Its gutter is a cubit deep and a cubit wide, with a rim of one span around the edge. And this is the height of the altar:

¹⁴ From the gutter on the ground up to the lower ledge it is two cubits high and a cubit wide, and from the smaller ledge up to the larger ledge it is four cubits high and a cubit wide.

MAFTIR

8 וּבְהַעֲלֹת אַהֲרֹן ע״ב ורבוע ע״ב אֶת־הַנֵּרֹת בֵּין הָעַרְבַּיִם ר״ת אהבה יַקְטִירֶנָּה
קְטֹרֶת י״א אדני תָּמִיד ע״ה קס״א קנ״א קמ״ג, ע״ה נתה לִפְנֵי חכמה בינה יְהֹוָה אדני ואהדונהי
לְדֹרֹתֵיכֶם: 9 לֹא־תַעֲלוּ עָלָיו קְטֹרֶת י״א אדני זָרָה וְעֹלָה וּמִנְחָה וְנֵסֶךְ לֹא
תִסְּכוּ עָלָיו: 10 וְכִפֶּר מצפץ אַהֲרֹן ע״ב ורבוע ע״ב עַל־קַרְנֹתָיו אַחַת בַּשָּׁנָה
מִדַּם רבוע אהיה וְחַטַּאת הַכִּפֻּרִים אַחַת בַּשָּׁנָה יְכַפֵּר עָלָיו לְדֹרֹתֵיכֶם
קֹדֶשׁ־קָדָשִׁים הוּא לַיהֹוָה אדני ואהדונהי:

HAFTARAH OF TETZAVEH

The only way to conquer our hatred and reveal the Temple is through the power of unconditional love.
We must bring about this change both for ourselves and for the world.

יוֹזְקֵאל פֶּרֶק מג

43 10 אַתָּה בֶן־אָדָם מ״ה הַגֵּד ב״פ ראה אֶת־בֵּית ־יִשְׂרָאֵל אֶת־הַבַּיִת
ב״פ ראה וְיִכָּלְמוּ מֵעֲוֺנוֹתֵיהֶם וּמָדְדוּ אֶת־תָּכְנִית: 11 וְאִם יוהך, ע״ה מ״ב ־
נִכְלְמוּ מִכֹּל יל׳ אֲשֶׁר־עָשׂוּ צוּרַת הַבַּיִת ב״פ ראה וּתְכוּנָתוֹ וּמוֹצָאָיו
וּמוֹבָאָיו וְכָל ־צוּרֹתָיו יל׳ (כתיב: צורתו) וְאֵת כָּל יל׳ ־חֻקֹּתָיו יל׳ וְכָל יל׳ ־
צוּרֹתָיו (כתיב: צורתו) וְכָל יל׳ ־תּוֹרֹתָיו (כתיב: תורתו) הוֹדַע אוֹתָם וּכְתֹב
לְעֵינֵיהֶם רביע מ״ה וְיִשְׁמְרוּ אֶת־כָּל יל׳ ־צוּרָתוֹ וְאֶת־כָּל יל׳ ־חֻקֹּתָיו
וְעָשׂוּ אוֹתָם: 12 זֹאת תּוֹרַת הַבַּיִת ב״פ ראה עַל־רֹאשׁ רביע אלהים ואלהים דיודין ע״ה
הָהָר כָּל יל׳ ־גְּבֻלוֹ סָבִיב | סָבִיב קֹדֶשׁ קָדָשִׁים הִנֵּה מ״ה יה ־זֹאת
תּוֹרַת הַבָּיִת ב״פ ראה: 13 וְאֵלֶּה מ״ב מִדּוֹת הַמִּזְבֵּחַ זן, נגד בָּאַמּוֹת אַמָּה
דמב, מלוי ע״ב אַמָּה דמב, מלוי ע״ב וָטֹפַח וְחֵיק הָאַמָּה דמב, מלוי ע״ב וְאַמָּה דמב, מלוי ע״ב
־רֹחַב וּגְבוּלָהּ אֶל־שְׂפָתָהּ סָבִיב זֶרֶת הָאֶחָד אהבה, דאגה וְזֶה גַּב הַמִּזְבֵּחַ

15 The altar hearth is four cubits high, and four horns project upward from the hearth.

16 The altar hearth is square, twelve cubits long and twelve cubits wide.

17 The upper ledge also is square, fourteen cubits long and fourteen cubits wide, with a rim of half a cubit and a gutter of a cubit all around. The steps of the altar face east."

18 Then He said to me, "Son of man, this is what the Lord, God, says: "These will be the regulations for sacrificing burnt offerings and sprinkling blood upon the altar when it is built:

19 You are to give a young bull as a sin offering to the priests, who are Levites, of the family of Zadok, who come near to minister before me," declares the Lord, God.

20 You are to take some of its blood and put it on its four horns and on the four corners of the upper ledge and all around the rim, and so purify the altar and make atonement for it.

21 You are to take the bull for the sin offering and burn it in the designated part of the Temple area outside the sanctuary.

22 On the second day you are to offer a male goat without defect for a sin offering, and the altar is to be purified as it was purified with the bull.

23 When you have finished purifying it, you are to offer a young bull without defect and a ram without defect from the flock.

24 You are to offer them before the Lord, and the priests are to sprinkle salt on them and sacrifice them as a burnt offering to the Lord.

25 For seven days you are to provide a male goat daily for a sin offering; you are also to provide a young bull and a ram from the flock, both without defect.

26 For seven days they are to make atonement for the altar and cleanse it; thus they will dedicate it.

27 At the end of these days, from the eighth day on, the priests are to present your burnt offerings and fellowship offerings on the altar. Then I will accept you," declares the Lord, God.

14 וּמֵחֵיק הָאָרֶץ אלהים דההין ע"ה עַד־הָעֲזָרָה הַתַּחְתּוֹנָה שְׁתַּיִם זו, נגד
אַמּוֹת וְרֹחַב אַמָּה אֶחָת מלוי ע"ב וּמֵהָעֲזָרָה הַקְּטַנָּה עַד־הָעֲזָרָה דמב
הַגְּדוֹלָה אַרְבַּע אַמּוֹת וְרֹחַב הָאַמָּה דמב, מלוי ע"ב 15 וְהַהַרְאֵל אַרְבַּע
אַמּוֹת וּמֵהָאֲרִיאֵל (כתיב: ומהאראיל) וּלְמַעְלָה הַקְּרָנוֹת אַרְבַּע:
16 וְהָאֲרִאֵיל (כתיב: והאראיל) שְׁתַּיִם עֶשְׂרֵה אֹרֶךְ בִּשְׁתַּיִם עֶשְׂרֵה רֹחַב
רָבוּעַ אֶל אַרְבַּעַת רְבָעָיו: 17 וְהָעֲזָרָה אַרְבַּע עֶשְׂרֵה אֹרֶךְ בְּאַרְבַּע
עֶשְׂרֵה רֹחַב אֶל אַרְבַּעַת רְבָעֶיהָ וְהַגְּבוּל סָבִיב אוֹתָהּ וְחֲצִי הָאַמָּה
דמב, מלוי ע"ב וְהַחֵיק־לָהּ אַמָּה דמב, מלוי ע"ב סָבִיב וּמַעֲלֹתֵהוּ פְּנוֹת קָדִים:
18 וַיֹּאמֶר אֵלַי בֶּן־אָדָם מ"ה כֹּה הי אָמַר אֲדֹנָי יֱהֹוִה ללה אֲדֹנִיאהדונהי אֵלֶּה
חֻקּוֹת הַמִּזְבֵּחַ זו, נגד בְּיוֹם ע"ה = נגד, מזבח הֵעָשׂוֹתוֹ לְהַעֲלוֹת עָלָיו עוֹלָה
וְלִזְרֹק עָלָיו דָּם רבוע אהיה: 19 וְנָתַתָּה אֶל־הַכֹּהֲנִים מלה הַלְוִיִּם אֲשֶׁר הֵם
מִזֶּרַע צָדוֹק הַקְּרֹבִים אֵלַי נְאֻם אֲדֹנָי יֱהֹוִה ללה אֲדֹנִיאהדונהי לְשָׁרְתֵנִי
פַּר בוחור, ערי, סנדלפון בֶּן־בָּקָר לְחַטָּאת: 20 וְלָקַחְתָּ מִדָּמוֹ וְנָתַתָּה עַל־
אַרְבַּע קַרְנֹתָיו וְאֶל־אַרְבַּע פִּנּוֹת הָעֲזָרָה וְאֶל־הַגְּבוּל סָבִיב וְחִטֵּאתָ
אוֹתוֹ וְכִפַּרְתָּהוּ: 21 וְלָקַחְתָּ אֵת הַפָּר בוחור, ערי, סנדלפון הַחַטָּאת וּשְׂרָפוֹ
בְּמִפְקַד הַבַּיִת ב"פ ראה מִחוּץ לַמִּקְדָּשׁ: 22 וּבַיּוֹם ע"ה = נגד, מזבח הַשֵּׁנִי
תַּקְרִיב שְׂעִיר־עִזִּים תָּמִים לְחַטָּאת וְחִטְּאוּ אֶת־הַמִּזְבֵּחַ זו, נגד כַּאֲשֶׁר
חִטְּאוּ בַּפָּר בוחור, ערי, סנדלפון: 23 בְּכַלּוֹתְךָ מֵחַטֵּא תַּקְרִיב פַּר בוחור, ערי, סנדלפון
בֶּן־בָּקָר תָּמִים וְאַיִל מִן־הַצֹּאן מלוי אהיה דיודין ע"ה תָּמִים: 24 וְהִקְרַבְתָּם
לִפְנֵי וחכמה בינה יְהֹוָה אֲדֹנִיאהדונהי וְהִשְׁלִיכוּ הַכֹּהֲנִים מלה עֲלֵיהֶם מֶלַח ג"פ יהוה
וְהֶעֱלוּ אוֹתָם עֹלָה לַיהֹוָה אֲדֹנִיאהדונהי: 25 שִׁבְעַת יָמִים גלך תַּעֲשֶׂה שְׂעִיר־
חַטָּאת לַיּוֹם ע"ה = נגד, זו, מזבח וּפַר בוחור, ערי, סנדלפון בֶּן־בָּקָר וְאַיִל מִן־הַצֹּאן
מלוי אהיה דיודין ע"ה תְּמִימִם יַעֲשׂוּ: 26 שִׁבְעַת יָמִים גלך יְכַפְּרוּ (כתיב: וכפרו)
אֶת־הַמִּזְבֵּחַ זו, נגד וְטִהֲרוּ אֹתוֹ וּמִלְאוּ יָדָו (כתיב: ידו): 27 וִיכַלּוּ ע"ב, רבוע יהוה
אֶת־הַיָּמִים גלך וְהָיָה יהוה בַיּוֹם ע"ה = נגד, מזבח הַשְּׁמִינִי וָהָלְאָה יַעֲשׂוּ
הַכֹּהֲנִים מלה עַל־הַמִּזְבֵּחַ זו, נגד אֶת־עוֹלוֹתֵיכֶם וְאֶת־שַׁלְמֵיכֶם וְרָצִאתִי
אֶתְכֶם נְאֻם אֲדֹנָי יֱהֹוִה ללה אֲדֹנִיאהדונהי:

KI TISA

LESSON OF KI TISA
(Exodus 30:11-33:23)

Why were the adanim (the pillars of the Tabernacle) paid for with half-shekel offerings?

Money for the adanim was given by all the people of Israel. Rich or poor, every person gave the same amount: a half-shekel. People could give more, but what was important was that, at minimum, everyone participated equally.

It is said that the whole Bible is included in the description of the building of the Tabernacle found in the chapter of Ki Tisa.

> *"These are the accounts of the Tabernacle, the Tabernacle of the Testimony, as they were counted, according to the commandment of Moses." (Exodus 38:21) Rav Shimon opened the discussion with the verse: "In the beginning God created the Heavens and the Earth." (Genesis 1:1) This was already explained and expounded upon in different manners, yet the Holy One, blessed be He, created it resembling the higher one, so this world will be shaped like the higher world, WHICH IS MALCHUT. And all the supernal hues of Above were installed Below IN THIS WORLD, to join and connect world to world, THIS WORLD TO MALCHUT.*
>
> *And when the Holy One, blessed be He, wanted to create the world, He looked at the Torah and then created it. And He looked upon the Holy Name, YUD, HEI, VAV and HEI, which comprises the Torah, and gave existence to the world. The world was created by three sides—Chochmah, Tevunah, and Da'at. By Chochmah, as it is written: "God by Wisdom founded the Earth," (Proverbs 3:19) by Tevunah, as it is written: "by understanding (Heb. Tevunah) He established the heavens" (Ibid.); and by Da'at, as it is written: "by His knowledge (Heb. Da'at) the depths were broken up." (Ibid. 20) So all contribute to the existence of the world, and by these three, the Tabernacle was built, as it is written, "And I have filled him with the spirit of God, in Wisdom, and in understanding, and in knowledge." (Exodus 31:3)*
> — *The Zohar, Pekudei 4:12-13*

The pillars of the Tabernacle stand for the knowledge and certainty that are pillars of the Bible. It is both our certainty in the Light of the Creator and the reality of the spiritual system that give us the power to succeed in our physical work and our spiritual work.

The following story demonstrates the importance of knowing the spiritual system.

A child was born to a rich family in the city. Every day while he was growing up, he received freshly baked bread at his door. He never considered how the bread was made or where it came from—it was just there.

One day, the boy traveled to the countryside to visit his cousin. There he saw wheat being ground into flour, flour made into dough, and dough being fashioned into bread. Though this picture was not complete, he thought it was. Until one day he saw a farmer plowing. To the boy, it seemed that the plowing was damaging the earth. He didn't understand that this was part of the process that would culminate in the wheat that would be made into bread. After some time, however, the boy noticed the wheat growing, and now, with this new piece of the puzzle, he saw the whole picture of how the bread arrived to his home in the city.

Often, life mystifies us because we do not see the whole picture. The key is to know that a bigger picture exists, even when we don't see it. Only a half-shekel was given for the adanim to signify and make us aware that we see only half the picture.

Regarding the sin of the Golden Calf and the Red Heifer.

The creation and worship of the Golden Calf is a story of sin. Ki Tisa teaches us an important lesson about the power of Satan and the true nature of sin. In truth, we will all fall. This is not a shortcoming, nor is it a mistake. Satan is a powerful challenger because the reward is so great! What we fail to notice is how many times Babe Ruth had to come to the plate before he hit that home run. Often, our greatest triumphs come at the heels of our most painful failure.

Because we are destined to sin with the Golden Calf, the Creator, in His great love for us, also gives us the Red Heifer—the atonement for that sin. The story of the Red Heifer that we read in the biblical chapter of Chukat is the tool for this purification. The story of the Red Heifer, takes us back to the time before the sin of the Golden Calf, and by means of this connection, we become cleansed.

> *"Speak to the children of Israel, that they bring you a red heifer...." (Numbers 19:2) This cow is for the purpose of cleansing to purify the unclean, WHICH IS MALCHUT that receives from the left. Who is on that left? It is the ox THAT IS GEVURAH IN ZEIR ANPIN, as it says, "the face of the ox from the left side." (Ezekiel 1:10) Red means red as a rose, as written: "like the rose among thorns." (Song of Songs 2:2) RED MEANS a sentence of law, SINCE THE LAWS OF THE LEFT COLUMN IS CONSIDERED RED.*
> — *The Zohar, Chukat 4:18*

There is a beautiful story of the Baal Shem Tov, whose greatness was so vast and so legendary, that even with all that we know of him his concealed enlightenment was so much more. This following parable illustrates the perfection of the spiritual system as well as the importance and power of Shabbat as a tool that purifies our sins.

On one of his travels, the Baal Shem Tov and three of his students strayed into some woods and lost their way.

Finally, around noon on Friday, they saw an inn in the distance. They rejoiced that God had brought them to a place where they could rest and spend Shabbat. As they approached the inn, they saw a rough-looking innkeeper standing at the entrance. When they asked if they could stay for Shabbat, he answered, "I don't want you or your Shabbat! I can see who you are. I've always hated creatures like you, and so did my father and my grandfather. Go away!"

Unable to spend more time on the road, the students pleaded with the innkeeper to let them stay for Shabbat, even offering substantially more than the innkeeper usually charged. Finally, he agreed, albeit with conditions.

At last, they were permitted to enter. The inn was like no other that they had ever seen. The furnishings were primitive, and there were no other guests. As dusk fell, the innkeeper took a piece of black cloth and spread it on a table. He did not let them experience any joy in their Shabbat connections. He put a candle in the center of the table and one loaf of thick black bread that he cut for himself giving them each only a small piece. Then he brought a bowl of lentils, passed out spoons, and announced that everybody had to eat together from the same bowl.
He wouldn't even let them sing Shabbat songs. In short, he ruined their Shabbat.

Then, when Shabbat was over, the innkeeper cursed them almost until morning.

At last, after taking all their money, the innkeeper sent them on their way. Just as they were leaving, a beautiful woman came running out to them, calling, "Rabbi! Rabbi! Please stay in my home for a few more days and then spend a proper Shabbat with us."

The Baal Shem Tov was surprised. "How do you know I am a rabbi? And why would I stay after my last Shabbat was ruined?"

The woman answered, "Rabbi, don't you recognize me? I was a servant in your house—an orphan with no mother or father. Your wife used to scrub my head every Friday to remove the lice from my hair. Once, it was painful and I screamed and would no longer allow her to touch me. Your wife, in her frustration, hit me on my cheek, and you, sitting just next to me, didn't say a word. The Holy One Himself was very upset that you did not respect the Bible verse that says: 'A widow or an orphan should not be tortured.' Because of this, there was a decree that you should lose your place in the World to Come.

"But as it happened, I married a very righteous man. He and I saw the judgment that was hanging over you, and it hurt our hearts. We prayed to God that you be forgiven, and it was decided that you should be denied a connection for just one Shabbat. Because Shabbat is like the World to Come, by losing this one Shabbat, you made your payment and regained your place in the World to Come."

At that same moment, the Baal Shem Tov saw that everything the woman said was true, and the following week, he and his students spent a wonderful Shabbat with this holy woman and her husband, the innkeeper.

Rav Ashlag explains that "World to Come" actually refers to the Light a person can receive in the here-and-now. If we want a part of the World to Come, we have a chance every week to make this connection.

SYNOPSIS OF KI TISA

In the story of Ki Tisa, we begin at the highest point of Light—before the sin of the Golden Calf—when immortality was a reality. The message for us is that we have to keep moving forward in our spiritual work or we fall back. Our spiritual work of connecting to the Light cannot remain at one level; it requires continual movement. Like climbing a downward-motion escalator, if we don't keep moving upward, we will fall to the level below.

FIRST READING - ABRAHAM - CHESED

30:11 Then the Lord spoke to Moses, saying, 12 "When you take a census of the Israelites to count them, each one must pay the Lord a ransom for his life at the time he is counted. Then no plague will come on them when you number them.

13 Each one who passes over to those already counted is to give a half shekel, according to the holy shekel, which weighs twenty gerahs. This half shekel is a contribution to the Lord.

14 All who pass over, those twenty years old or more, are to give a contribution to the Lord. 15 The rich are not to give more than a half shekel and the poor are not to give less when you make the contribution to the Lord to atone for your lives.

16 Take the atonement money from the Israelites and use it for the service of the Tent of Meeting. It will be a memorial for the Israelites before the Lord, making atonement for your lives."

17 Then the Lord spoke to Moses, saying, 18 "Make a bronze basin, with its bronze stand, for washing. Place it between the Tent of Meeting and the altar, and put water in it.

FROM THE RAV

Since their departure from Egypt, Moses had made every attempt to bring the people to an understanding that this physical world was subject to a higher energy known as consciousness. This teaching of Moses had not been absorbed completely and therefore, it had not been finished. The people still held a fundamental belief that in this world, physicality was the most important thing. So when Moses wasn't present physically, this created a big problem in their minds: Who or what was going to replace Moses as a physical entity? Being committed to the idea of the physical realm as the only reality, they needed someone or something with a physical presence.

This is what the Golden Calf was all about. The Golden Calf was a primitive version of a computer. It spoke, it made music, it did all the things a computer does today. Did this make it a god? Do we treat a computer like a god? A computer is a tool that can assist us. But 3,400 years ago, if someone could produce a computer, it probably would indeed be seen as a god. Today, we don't think like that, but we still have that kind of consciousness, albeit in a different way and directed toward different things.

We at The Kabbalah Centre are working to change this kind of consciousness, but it's a difficult process. Many of us still worship the 1 Percent Illusionary Realm. Our physical surroundings, our entertainment, our luxuries—we still consider all these to be more significant in our lives than our spiritual work.

FIRST READING - ABRAHAM - CHESED

וַיְדַבֵּ֥ר יְהוֹוָהֵאדְנֹיֵאהדֹונַהֵי אֶל־מֹשֶׁ֖ה לֵּאמֹ֑ר: 12 כִּ֣י תִשָּׂ֞א
אֶת־רֹ֥אשׁ בְּנֵֽי־יִשְׂרָאֵ֘ל לִפְקֻֽדֵיהֶם֒ וְנָ֨תְנ֜וּ אִ֣ישׁ
כֹּ֧פֶר נַפְשׁ֛וֹ לַֽיהֹוָהֵאדְנֹיֵאהדֹונַהֵי בִּפְקֹ֥ד אֹתָ֖ם וְלֹא־
יִהְיֶ֥ה בָהֶ֛ם נֶ֖גֶף בִּפְקֹ֥ד אֹתָֽם: 13 זֶ֣ה | יִתְּנ֗וּ כָּל־הָֽעֹבֵר֙
עַל־הַפְּקֻדִ֔ים מַֽחֲצִ֥ית הַשֶּׁ֖קֶל בְּשֶׁ֣קֶל הַקֹּ֑דֶשׁ עֶשְׂרִ֤ים
גֵּרָה֙ הַשֶּׁ֔קֶל מַֽחֲצִ֣ית הַשֶּׁ֔קֶל תְּרוּמָ֖ה לַֽיהֹוָהֵאדְנֹיֵאהדֹונַהֵי: 14 כֹּ֗ל
הָֽעֹבֵר֙ עַל־הַפְּקֻדִ֔ים מִבֶּ֛ן עֶשְׂרִ֥ים שָׁנָ֖ה וָמָ֑עְלָה יִתֵּ֖ן
תְּרוּמַ֥ת יְהֹוָהֵאדְנֹיֵאהדֹונַהֵי: 15 הֶֽעָשִׁ֣יר לֹֽא־יַרְבֶּ֗ה וְהַדַּל֙ לֹ֣א יַמְעִ֔יט מִֽמַּחֲצִ֖ית
הַשָּׁ֑קֶל לָתֵת֙ אֶת־תְּרוּמַ֣ת יְהֹוָהֵאדְנֹיֵאהדֹונַהֵי לְכַפֵּ֖ר עַל־נַפְשֹֽׁתֵיכֶֽם:
16 וְלָֽקַחְתָּ֞ אֶת־כֶּ֣סֶף הַכִּפֻּרִ֗ים מֵאֵת֙ בְּנֵ֣י יִשְׂרָאֵ֔ל וְנָֽתַתָּ֤ אֹתוֹ֙ עַל־
עֲבֹדַ֖ת אֹ֣הֶל מוֹעֵ֑ד וְהָיָה֩ לִבְנֵ֨י יִשְׂרָאֵ֤ל לְזִכָּרוֹן֙
לִפְנֵ֣י יְהֹוָהֵאדְנֹיֵאהדֹונַהֵי לְכַפֵּ֖ר עַל־נַפְשֹֽׁתֵיכֶֽם: 17 וַיְדַבֵּ֥ר
יְהֹוָהֵאדְנֹיֵאהדֹונַהֵי אֶל־מֹשֶׁ֖ה לֵּאמֹֽר: 18 וְעָשִׂ֜יתָ כִּיּ֥וֹר נְחֹ֛שֶׁת וְכַנּ֥וֹ
נְחֹ֖שֶׁת לְרָחְצָ֑ה וְנָֽתַתָּ֨ אֹת֜וֹ בֵּֽין־אֹ֤הֶל מוֹעֵד֙ וּבֵ֣ין הַמִּזְבֵּ֔חַ וְנָֽתַתָּ֥
שָׁ֖מָּה מָֽיִם: 19 וְרָֽחֲצ֛וּ אַהֲרֹ֥ן וּבָנָ֖יו מִמֶּ֑נּוּ אֶת־יְדֵיהֶ֖ם

בִּפְקֹד

Exodus 30:12—Counting the Israelites.

A census was taken of all the half-shekel contributions of the Israelites as a method of counting each person. Only half a coin, not a whole one, was called for to remind us that we never know the whole picture. The more we realize that we don't see, the more we can connect to the Light of the Creator so that we can see.

כִּיּוֹר

Exodus 30:18—Washing of the hands.

A basin for washing the hands, called a laver, is discussed in this verse. This signifies the importance of washing our hands before we perform any spiritual action. As our hands are the part of our body responsible for manifestation, before participating in a spiritual connection, it is worthwhile to wash away any energy that is gathered there.

19 Aaron and his sons are to wash their hands and feet from it.

20 Whenever they enter the Tent of Meeting, they shall wash with water so that they will not die. Or when they approach the altar to minister by presenting an offering made to the Lord,

21 they shall wash their hands and feet so that they will not die. This is to be a lasting ordinance for Aaron and his descendants for the generations to come." 22 Then the Lord spoke to Moses, saying, 23 "Take the following fine spices: 500 shekels of liquid myrrh, half as much—that is, 250 shekels—of fragrant cinnamon, 250 shekels of fragrant cane,

24 500 shekels of cassia—all according to the holy shekel—and a hin of olive oil.

25 Make these into a sacred anointing oil, a fragrant blend, the work of a perfumer. It will be the sacred anointing oil.

26 Then use it to anoint the Tent of Meeting, the Ark of the Covenant, 27 the table and all its utensils, the candelabra and its utensils, the altar of incense, 28 the altar of burnt offering and all its utensils, and the basin with its stand.

29 You shall consecrate them so they will be most holy, and whatever touches them will be holy.

תִּמְשַׁח	קְטֹרֶת

Exodus 30:30—The sacred oil.

The sacred oil, used to anoint Aaron as High Priest and his sons as priests, was used to elevate a person to a higher spiritual level.

The *Zohar* says:

> "This (Heb. zot) is the anointing of Aaron, and of the anointing of his sons." (Leviticus 7:35) Rabbi Yosi said: "Zot," WHICH IS MALCHUT, is surely an anointment of Aaron. For Aaron was anointed FROM CHOCHMAH; and he brought down the supernal oil of ointment from Above, CHOCHMAH, and drew it downward TO MALCHUT. It is due to Aaron that MALCHUT was anointed and blessed with holy ointment. It therefore says, "This (Heb. zot) is the anointing of Aaron, and of the anointing of his sons," most certainly.
> —The Zohar, Tzav 23:162

Exodus 30:35—Creating the incense.

The exact mixture of the eleven herbs and spices that made up the incense of the Tabernacle was forbidden to be used as perfume anywhere other than in the Tabernacle.

The *Zohar* says:

> ... In that smoke, which is in the nose, all aspects are attached. In each individual aspect are attached many harsh antagonists of judgment, which are linked to that smoke. And all do not get incensed and scented, except by the incentive of the smoke from the altar Below. Therefore, it is written: "And God inhaled the scent of the pleasing incense smoke." (Genesis 8:21)
> —The Zohar, Ha'azinu 148a

וְאֶת־רַגְלֵיהֶם: 20 בְּבֹאָם אֶל־אֹהֶל לאה מוֹעֵד יִרְחֲצוּ־מַיִם וְלֹא יָמֻתוּ

אוֹ בְגִשְׁתָּם אֶל־הַמִּזְבֵּחַ זז, נגד לְשָׁרֵת לְהַקְטִיר אִשֶּׁה לַיהֹוָהאדנ'אהדונה':

21 וְרָחֲצוּ יְדֵיהֶם וְרַגְלֵיהֶם וְלֹא יָמֻתוּ וְהָיְתָה לָהֶם חָק־עוֹלָם

רביע ס"ג ־ י' אותיות לוֹ וּלְזַרְעוֹ לְדֹרֹתָם: 22 וַיְדַבֵּר ראה יְהֹוָהאדנ'אהדונה' אֶל־מֹשֶׁה

מהע, אל שדי לֵּאמֹר: 23 וְאַתָּה קַח־לְךָ עצ"ב = ג' מלויי אהיה בְּשָׂמִים בְּשָׂמִים רֹאשׁ

רביע אלהים ואלהים דיודין ע"ה מָר בְּפ קֹרֶן דְּרוֹר בְּפ (רבוע אלהים ־ ה) וְחֵמֵשׁ מֵאוֹת

וְקִנְּמָן־בֶּשֶׂם מַחֲצִיתוֹ חֲמִשִּׁים וּמָאתָיִם וּקְנֵה־ ע"ה יוסף, ציון, ר"פ יהוה, ה"פ אל

בֶשֶׂם חֲמִשִּׁים וּמָאתָיִם: 24 וְקִדָּה חֲמֵשׁ מֵאוֹת בְּשֶׁקֶל הַקֹּדֶשׁ וְשֶׁמֶן

י"פ טל, י"פ כוזו'; ביט זַיִת אלהים אל מצפ"צ הִין: 25 וְעָשִׂיתָ אֹתוֹ שֶׁמֶן י"פ טל, י"פ כוזו'; ביט

מִשְׁחַת־קֹדֶשׁ רֹקַח מִרְקַחַת מַעֲשֵׂה רֹקֵחַ שֶׁמֶן י"פ טל, י"פ כוזו'; ביט מִשְׁחַת־

קֹדֶשׁ יִהְיֶה זז: 26 וּמָשַׁחְתָּ בוֹ אֶת־אֹהֶל לאה מוֹעֵד וְאֵת אֲרוֹן ע"ה ג"פ אלהים

הָעֵדֻת: 27 וְאֶת־הַשֻּׁלְחָן וְאֶת־כָּל־ ילי כֵּלָיו וְאֶת־הַמְּנֹרָה וְאֶת־כֵּלֶיהָ

וְאֵת מִזְבַּח זז, נגד הַקְּטֹרֶת י"א אדנ': 28 וְאֶת־מִזְבַּח זז, נגד הָעֹלָה וְאֶת־כָּל־ ילי

כֵּלָיו וְאֶת־הַכִּיֹּר וְאֶת־כַּנּוֹ: 29 וְקִדַּשְׁתָּ אֹתָם וְהָיוּ קֹדֶשׁ קָדָשִׁים כָּל־

ילי הַנֹּגֵעַ בָּהֶם יִקְדָּשׁ: 30 וְאֶת־אַהֲרֹן ע"ב ורביע ע"ב וְאֶת־בָּנָיו תמשוח

וְקִדַּשְׁתָּ אֹתָם לְכַהֵן מלה לִי: 31 וְאֶל־בְּנֵי יִשְׂרָאֵל תְּדַבֵּר ראה לֵאמֹר

שֶׁמֶן י"פ טל, י"פ כוזו'; ביט מִשְׁחַת־קֹדֶשׁ יִהְיֶה זז זֶה לִי לְדֹרֹתֵיכֶם: 32 עַל־

בְּשַׂר אָדָם מ"ה לֹא יִיסָךְ וּבְמַתְכֻּנְתּוֹ לֹא תַעֲשׂוּ כָּמֹהוּ קֹדֶשׁ הוּא

קֹדֶשׁ יִהְיֶה זז לָכֶם: 33 אִישׁ ע"ה קנ"א קס"א אֲשֶׁר יִרְקַח כָּמֹהוּ וַאֲשֶׁר יִתֵּן

מִמֶּנּוּ עַל־זָר אור, אין סוף וְנִכְרַת מֵעַמָּיו: 34 וַיֹּאמֶר יְהֹוָהאדנ'אהדונה' אֶל־מֹשֶׁה

מהע, אל שדי קַח־לְךָ סַמִּים ע"ה קנ"א, אלהים אדני נָטָף | וּשְׁחֵלֶת וְחֶלְבְּנָה ע"ה פי

סַמִּים ע"ה קנ"א, אלהים אדני וּלְבֹנָה זַכָּה בַּד בְּבַד יִהְיֶה זז: 35 וְעָשִׂיתָ אֹתָהּ

קְטֹרֶת י"א אדני רֹקַח מַעֲשֵׂה רוֹקֵחַ שדי מְמֻלָּח י"פ אכא טָהוֹר קֹדֶשׁ ס"ת רוזאי:

36 וְשָׁחַקְתָּ מִמֶּנָּה הָדֵק וְנָתַתָּה מִמֶּנָּה לִפְנֵי וחכמה בינה הָעֵדֻת לאה בְּאֹהֶל מוֹעֵד

30 Anoint Aaron and his sons and consecrate them so they may serve Me as priests. 31 Say to the Israelites, 'This is to be my sacred anointing oil for the generations to come. 32 Do not pour it on men's bodies and do not make any oil with the same formula. It is sacred, and you are to consider it sacred.

33 Whoever makes perfume like it and whoever puts it on anyone must be cut off from his people.' " 34 Then the Lord said to Moses, "Take fragrant spices—gum resin, onycha and galbanum—and pure frankincense, all in equal amounts,

35 and make a fragrant blend of incense, the work of a perfumer. It is to be salted and pure and sacred.

36 Grind some of it to powder and place it in front of the Testimony in the Tent of Meeting, where I will meet with you. It shall be most holy to you.

37 And the incense that you will make with this formula, do not make for yourselves; consider it holy to the Lord.
38 Whoever makes any like it to enjoy its fragrance must be cut off from his people."

31:1 Then the Lord spoke to Moses, saying, 2 "See, I have chosen Betzalel son of Uri, the son of Hur, of the tribe of Judah, 3 and I will fill him with the Spirit of God, with wisdom, understanding and knowledge in all kinds of crafts

4 to make artistic designs for work in gold, silver and bronze, 5 to cut and set stones, to work in wood, and to engage in all kinds of craftsmanship. 6 Moreover, I have appointed with him Oholiab son of Achisamach, of the tribe of Dan. Also I have given skill to all the craftsmen to make everything I have commanded you:

בְּצַלְאֵל, אָהֳלִיאָב

Exodus 31:2—Bezalel and Oholiab built theTabernacle.

There were two people designated to build the Tabernacle (*Mishkan*): Bezalel and Oholiab. Bezalel was only 12 years old when he was chosen. (*Sanhedrin* 69b) This is a powerful lesson that wisdom is not dependent on how much we know or how old we are. Wisdom comes from our connection to the Light of the Creator and from the nature of our desires—that is, whether they are dominated by proactive or reactive intentions. The *Zohar* says:

It is written here, "These are the accounts of the Tabernacle,"(Exodus 38:21) and

elsewhere, "These are the generations of the Heaven and of the Earth." THIS INDICATES THAT THE ACTIONS ARE THE SAME IN BOTH CASES, for all the generations produced by the Heaven and Earth were formed and came out by the power of the stored light, and also the accounts of the Tabernacle came out by that power OF THE STORED LIGHT. From where do we know that? From the verse, "And Betzalel the son of Uri, the son of Chur, of the tribe of Judah," (Exodus 38:22) of the Right Side, WHICH IS ABRAHAM, THE STORED LIGHT AS SAID, and with him Oholiab, of the Left Side, and the Tabernacle, WHICH IS MALCHUT, was founded by Right and Left. And Moses, who was between

אֲשֶׁר אוּעֵד לְךָ שָׁמָּה מהע, משה, אל שדי קֹדֶשׁ קָדָשִׁים תִּהְיֶה לָכֶם:

37 וְהַקְטֹרֶת י"א אדני אֲשֶׁר תַּעֲשֶׂה בְּמַתְכֻּנְתָּהּ לֹא תַעֲשׂוּ לָכֶם קֹדֶשׁ

תִּהְיֶה לְךָ לַיהוה אהיהאהדונהי: 38 אִישׁ עיה קנ"א קס"א אֲשֶׁר־יַעֲשֶׂה כָמוֹהָ לְהָרִיחַ

בָּהּ וְנִכְרַת מֵעַמָּיו: 31 1 וַיְדַבֵּר ראה יהוה אהיהאהדונהי אֶל־מֹשֶׁה מהע, אל שדי

לֵּאמֹר: 2 רְאֵה ראה קָרָאתִי בְשֵׁם יהוה אל שדי בְּצַלְאֵל בֶּן־אוּרִי בֶן־חוּר

לְמַטֵּה יְהוּדָה: 3 וָאֲמַלֵּא אֹתוֹ רוּחַ מלוי אלהים דיודין אֱלֹהִים מום, אהיה אדני ; ילה

בְּחָכְמָה וּבִתְבוּנָה וּבְדַעַת וּבְכָל ב"ן, לכבד, יבמ ־מְלָאכָה אל אדני: 4 לַחְשֹׁב

מַחֲשָׁבֹת לַעֲשׂוֹת בַּזָּהָב וּבַכֶּסֶף וּבַנְּחֹשֶׁת: 5 וּבַחֲרֹשֶׁת אֶבֶן יוד הה ואו הה

לְמַלֹּאת וּבַחֲרֹשֶׁת עֵץ עיה קס"א לַעֲשׂוֹת בְּכָל ב"ן, לכבד, יבמ ־מְלָאכָה אל אדני:

6 וַאֲנִי ב"פ (אהיה יהוה) הִנֵּה מ"ה יה נָתַתִּי אִתּוֹ אֵת אָהֳלִיאָב בֶּן־אֲחִיסָמָךְ

לְמַטֵּה־דָן וּבְלֵב כָּל ילי ־חֲכַם חויים, בונה עיה ־לֵב נָתַתִּי חָכְמָה וְעָשׂוּ אֵת

כָּל ילי ־אֲשֶׁר צִוִּיתִךָ: 7 אֵת | אֹהֶל לאה מוֹעֵד וְאֶת־הָאָרֹן ע"ב ורבוע ע"ב

לָעֵדֻת וְאֶת־הַכַּפֹּרֶת אֲשֶׁר עָלָיו וְאֵת כָּל ילי ־כְּלֵי הָאֹהֶל לאה:

8 וְאֶת־הַשֻּׁלְחָן וְאֶת־כֵּלָיו וְאֶת־הַמְּנֹרָה הַטְּהֹרָה וְאֶת־כָּל ילי ־כֵּלֶיהָ

וְאֵת מִזְבַּח זן, נגד הַקְּטֹרֶת י"א אדני: 9 וְאֶת־מִזְבַּח זן, נגד הָעֹלָה וְאֶת־כָּל ילי

־כֵּלָיו וְאֶת־הַכִּיּוֹר וְאֶת־כַּנּוֹ: 10 וְאֵת בִּגְדֵי הַשְּׂרָד וְאֶת־בִּגְדֵי הַקֹּדֶשׁ

---

them, THE SECRET OF THE CENTRAL COLUMN, founded it.
-- The Zohar, Pekudei 2:8

HE ASKS: What is the meaning of "and with him?" AND HE REPLIES: We learned that Oholiab did not do the work alone but with Betzalel he did what he did. This is the meaning of "with him" and not on his own. FOR BETZALEL IS RIGHT AND OHOLIAB IS LEFT. From here we learn that the Left is always included in the Right. Therefore it is written, "I have given with him Oholiab" (Exodus 31:6). The one is Right and the other Left. AND LEFT IS INCLUDED IN THE RIGHT.
-- The Zohar, Pekudei 6:47

"And Betzalel the son of Uri, the son of Chur, of the tribe of Judah," (Exodus 38:22) of the aspect of Malchut, "made all that God commanded Moses" (Ibid.). For all the craftsmanship of the Tabernacle was prepared through them, by their hands. Betzalel performed the work and Moses after him made all ready. Moses and Betzalel were as one, Moses Above, IN TIFERET, and Betzalel Below, IN YESOD, the end of the body being also a part thereof, FOR YESOD AND TIFERET ARE ONE. Betzalel and Oholiab, it has been established, that the one is of the right, CHESED, and the other is of the left, JUDGMENT, and all is one, FOR ONE INCLUDES THE OTHER.
-- The Zohar, Pekudei 11:69

[7] the Tent of Meeting, the Ark of the Covenant with the atonement cover on it, and all the other furnishings of the tent [8] the table and its utensils, the pure candelabra and all its utensils, the altar of incense, [9] the altar of burnt offering and all its utensils, the basin with its stand [10] and also the woven garments, both the sacred garments for Aaron the priest and the garments for his sons when they serve as priests,

[11] and the anointing oil and fragrant incense for the sanctum. They are to make them just as I commanded you."

[12] Then the Lord said to Moses, saying, [13] "Speak to the Israelites, and tell them, 'You must observe My Sabbaths. This will be a sign between Me and you for the generations to come, so you may know that I am the Lord, who makes you holy.

[14] Observe the Sabbath, because it is holy to you. Anyone who desecrates it must surely be put to death; whoever does any work on that day must be cut off from his people.

[15] For six days, work is to be done, but the seventh day is a Sabbath of rest, holy to the Lord. Whoever does any work on the Sabbath day must surely be put to death.

[16] The Israelites are to observe the Sabbath, performing the Sabbath will be for generations to come as a lasting Covenant. [17] Between Me and the Israelites it will be a sign forever, for in six days the Lord made the heavens and the Earth and on the seventh day He abstained from work and rested.' "

SECOND READING - ISAAC - GEVURAH

[18] When the Lord finished speaking to Moses on Mount Sinai, He gave him the two Tablets of the Covenant, the Tablets of stone inscribed by the Finger of God.

הַשַּׁבָּת

Exodus 31:14—Shabbat.

From this section, we learn that to connect to the Light of the Creator, we must have some connection to the energy of Shabbat. We need that Light once a week. How much we choose to take in is up to us, but connection to Shabbat is necessary if we want the Light.

Therefore the Shabbat is equal in importance to the Torah, and whoever keeps the Shabbat is regarded as one who fulfills the whole Torah. It is written: "Happy is the man that does this, and the son of man that lays hold on it, that keeps the Shabbat and does not profane it, and keeps his hand from doing any evil." (Isaiah 56:2) From this we understand that for whoever keeps the Shabbat, it is as if he kept the whole Torah.
— The Zohar, Yitro 27:469

לְאַהֲרֹן ע"ב ורבוע ע"ב הַכֹּהֵן מלה וְאֶת־בִּגְדֵי בָנָיו לְכַהֵן מלה: 11 וְאֵת שֶׁמֶן

הַמִּשְׁחָה י"פ טל, י"פ כוזו; ביט וְאֶת־קְטֹרֶת י"א אדני הַסַּמִּים ע"ה קנ"א, אלהים אדני לַקֹּדֶשׁ

כְּכֹל יל אֲשֶׁר־צִוִּיתִךָ יַעֲשׂוּ: 12 וַיֹּאמֶר יְהֹוָאדֹנִיאהדונהי אֶל־מֹשֶׁה מהש, אל שדי

לֵּאמֹר: 13 וְאַתָּה דַּבֵּר ראה אֶל־בְּנֵי יִשְׂרָאֵל לֵאמֹר אַךְ אהיה אֶת־שַׁבְּתֹתַי

תִּשְׁמֹרוּ כִּי אוֹת הִוא בֵּינִי וּבֵינֵיכֶם לְדֹרֹתֵיכֶם לָדַעַת כִּי אֲנִי אני, טדהד כוזו

יְהֹוָאדֹנִיאהדונהי מְקַדִּשְׁכֶם מ"ה מ"ב: 14 וּשְׁמַרְתֶּם אֶת־ הַשַּׁבָּת כִּי קֹדֶשׁ

הִוא לָכֶם מְחַלְלֶיהָ מוֹת יוּמָת כִּי כָּל־ יל הָעֹשֶׂה בָהּ מְלָאכָה אל אדני

וְנִכְרְתָה הַנֶּפֶשׁ רמ"ח - ז הויות הַהִוא מִקֶּרֶב עַמֶּיהָ: 15 שֵׁשֶׁת יָמִים גלך י"ן יֵעָשֶׂה

מְלָאכָה אל אדני וּבַיּוֹם ע"ה = נגד, זן, מזבח הַשְּׁבִיעִי שַׁבַּת שַׁבָּתוֹן קֹדֶשׁ

לַיהֹוָאדֹנִיאהדונהי כָּל־ יל הָעֹשֶׂה מְלָאכָה אל אדני בְּיוֹם ע"ה = נגד, זן, מזבח הַשַּׁבָּת

מוֹת יוּמָת: 16 וְשָׁמְרוּ בְנֵי־יִשְׂרָאֵל אֶת־הַשַּׁבָּת לַעֲשׂוֹת אֶת־הַשַּׁבָּת

לְדֹרֹתָם ר"ת אהל בְּרִית עוֹלָם: 17 בֵּינִי וּבֵין בְּנֵי יִשְׂרָאֵל אוֹת הִוא לְעֹלָם

כִּי־שֵׁשֶׁת יָמִים גלך עָשָׂה יְהֹוָאדֹנִיאהדונהי אֶת־הַשָּׁמַיִם י"פ טל, י"פ כוזו וְאֶת־

הָאָרֶץ אלהים דההין ע"ה וּבַיּוֹם ע"ה = נגד, זן, מזבח הַשְּׁבִיעִי שָׁבַת וַיִּנָּפַשׁ:

SECOND READING - ISAAC - GEVURAH

18 וַיִּתֵּן י"פ מלוי ע"ב אֶל־מֹשֶׁה מהש, אל שדי כְּכַלֹּתוֹ לְדַבֵּר ראה אִתּוֹ בְּהַר אור, רז

סִינַי נמם, ה"פ יהוה שְׁנֵי לֻחֹת הָעֵדֻת לֻחֹת אֶבֶן יוד הה ואו הה כְּתֻבִים בְּאֶצְבַּע

שְׁנֵי לֻחֹת

Exodus 31:18—God gave Moses the Tablets.

Moses received the Tablets and the knowledge of everything: The Universal Laws that describe the nature of both the spiritual dimension and the physical realm were revealed to him. Even though the first Tablets were destroyed physically, we can still connect to them because energy never disappears,

He continued his discourse and cited: "And God said to Moses, 'Come up to Me to the mountain AND WAIT THERE; AND I WILL GIVE YOU THE TABLETS OF STONE AND THE TORAH AND THE COMMANDMENTS WHICH I HAVE WRITTEN, THAT YOU MAY TEACH THEM.'" (Exodus 24:12) "And the Torah" is the Written Law, WHICH IS ZEIR ANPIN, while "and the commandments" is the Oral Torah, WHICH IS MALCHUT.
— The Zohar, Shemini 12:93

32:¹ When the people saw that Moses was delayed in coming down from the mountain, they gathered around Aaron and said, "Get up, make us gods who will go before us, because this fellow Moses who brought us up out of Egypt—we don't know what has happened to him."

² Aaron answered them, "Take off the gold earrings that your wives, your sons and your daughters are wearing, and bring them to me."

³ So all the people took off the rings in their ears and brought them to Aaron.

⁴ He took what they handed him and made it into an idol cast in the shape of a calf, fashioning it with a tool. Then they said, "These are your gods, Israel, who brought you up out of Egypt."

⁵ When Aaron saw this, he built an altar in front of it and announced, "Tomorrow there will be a festival to the Lord."

⁶ So the next day the people arose early and sacrificed burnt offerings and presented fellowship offerings. Afterward they sat down to eat and drink and got up to indulge in revelry.

⁷ Then the Lord said to Moses, "Go down, because your people whom you brought up out of Egypt have become corrupt.

⁸ They have been quick to turn away from what I commanded them and have made themselves an idol cast in the shape of a calf. They have bowed down to it and

---

עֵגֶל מַסֵּכָה

Exodus 32:4—The sin of the Golden Calf.

The Golden Calf that the Israelites built was not just a statue of gold. It was alive—an actual moving thing, a miraculous creation.

> It is written, "And he took the gold at their hand, and fashioned it." It means that by the power of these two, YUNUS AND YAMBRUS, everything was made, AND IT WAS as though AARON himself did it. But if these two had not been present, THE CALF would not have been made, and would not have turned out with skill. But who caused it to be made? These two, while he was receiving it from their hand, performed their magic and uttered

> incantations with their mouths, and drew a spirit from the Other Side.
> — The Zohar, Ki Tisa 11:83

To manifest a miracle of transforming inanimate matter into a living thing, each Israelite had to sacrifice something of importance. How often do we sacrifice our connection to the Upper Worlds because we seek momentary pleasure (our own personal golden calf) in exchange for lasting and ultimate fulfillment.

The *Zohar* says:

> Israel, when they made the Golden Calf, separated the blessings from Mount Horeb by separating the Vav from it, and cut among the plantings of those TEN plantings. It is written, "And the children of Israel stripped themselves of

קס"ג **אֱלֹהִים** מום, אהיה אדני ; ילה: **1 וַיַּרְא** אלף למד יהוה **הָעָם כִּי־בֹשֵׁשׁ מֹשֶׁה**

מהע, אל שדי **לָרֶדֶת מִן־הָהָר וַיִּקָּהֵל הָעָם עַל־אַהֲרֹן** ע"ב ורבוע ע"ב **וַיֹּאמְרוּ**

אֵלָיו קוּם | עֲשֵׂה־לָנוּ מום, אלהים, אהיה אדני **אֱלֹהִים** מום, אהיה אדני ; ילה **אֲשֶׁר יֵלְכוּ**

לְפָנֵינוּ כִּי־זֶה | מֹשֶׁה מהע, אל שדי **הָאִישׁ** ז"פ אדם **אֲשֶׁר הֶעֱלָנוּ מֵאֶרֶץ**

אלהים דאלפין **מִצְרַיִם** מצר **לֹא יָדַעְנוּ מֶה־** מ"ה **הָיָה** יהה **לוֹ: 2 וַיֹּאמֶר אֲלֵהֶם**

אַהֲרֹן ע"ב ורבוע ע"ב **פָּרְקוּ נִזְמֵי הַזָּהָב** וזהו **אֲשֶׁר בְּאָזְנֵי נְשֵׁיכֶם בְּנֵיכֶם**

וּבְנֹתֵיכֶם וְהָבִיאוּ אֵלָי: 3 וַיִּתְפָּרְקוּ כל ילי **הָעָם אֶת־נִזְמֵי הַזָּהָב** וזהו

אֲשֶׁר בְּאָזְנֵיהֶם וַיָּבִיאוּ אֶל־אַהֲרֹן ע"ב ורבוע ע"ב **4 וַיִּקַּח** וזהם **מִיָּדָם וַיָּצַר**

אֹתוֹ בַּחֶרֶט וַיַּעֲשֵׂהוּ ‖ עֵגֶל מַסֵּכָה ‖ **וַיֹּאמְרוּ אֵלֶּה אֱלֹהֶיךָ** ילה **יִשְׂרָאֵל**

אֲשֶׁר הֶעֱלוּךָ מֵאֶרֶץ אלהים דאלפין **מִצְרָיִם** מצר **5 וַיַּרְא** אלף למד יהוה **אַהֲרֹן**

ע"ב ורבוע ע"ב **וַיִּבֶן** וזהים, בינה ע"ה **מִזְבֵּחַ** זן, נגד **לְפָנָיו וַיִּקְרָא** ב"פ קס"א + ה אותיות **אַהֲרֹן**

ע"ב ורבוע ע"ב **וַיֹּאמַר חַג לַיהֹוָה** ‖אדני‖ אהדונהי **מָחָר** רמ"ח: **6 וַיַּשְׁכִּימוּ מִמָּחֳרָת**

וַיַּעֲלוּ עֹלֹת וַיַּגִּשׁוּ שְׁלָמִים וַיֵּשֶׁב הָעָם לֶאֱכֹל וְשָׁתוֹ וַיָּקֻמוּ לְצַחֵק:

7 וַיְדַבֵּר ראה **יְהֹוָה** ‖אדני‖אהדונהי **אֶל־מֹשֶׁה** מהע, אל שדי **לֶךְ־רֵד כִּי שִׁחֵת עַמְּךָ**

ה' הויות, נגמ **אֲשֶׁר הֶעֱלֵיתָ מֵאֶרֶץ** אלהים דאלפין **מִצְרָיִם** מצר: **8 סָרוּ מַהֵר מִן־**

הַדֶּרֶךְ ב"פ יבק **אֲשֶׁר צִוִּיתִם** פוי **עָשׂוּ לָהֶם עֵגֶל מַסֵּכָה וַיִּשְׁתַּחֲווּ־לוֹ**

וַיִּזְבְּחוּ־לוֹ וַיֹּאמְרוּ אֵלֶּה אֱלֹהֶיךָ ילה **יִשְׂרָאֵל אֲשֶׁר הֶעֱלוּךָ מֵאֶרֶץ** אלהים דאלפין

מִצְרָיִם מצר: **9 וַיֹּאמֶר יְהֹוָה** ‖אדני‖אהדונהי **אֶל־מֹשֶׁה** מהע, אל שדי **רָאִיתִי אֶת־הָעָם**

הַזֶּה וזהו **וְהִנֵּה** מ"ה ה **עַם־קְשֵׁה־עֹרֶף הוּא: 10 וְעַתָּה הַנִּיחָה לִּי** ‖ וַיִּחַר־אַפִּי ‖

---

*their ornaments by the mount Horeb."
(Exodus 33:6) He removed from them
that supernal ornament, MEANING the
head Tefilin and the arm TEFILIN, that
one dons on the weaker hand. And from
which place was it given to them? From
Mount Horeb, when the Vav joined it,
MEANING ZEIR ANPIN.*
— *The Zohar, Hashmatot 33:270*

וַיִּחַר־אַפִּי

Exodus 32:10—God was angry because of the
Golden Calf. Anger does not exist in the Creator,
and God does not have emotions. What this
section reveals is the Universal Law of Cause and
Effect. God's "anger" indicates that a cleansing
process needed to take place as a result of the
previous action of the Golden Calf.

sacrificed to it and have said, 'These are your gods, Israel, who brought you up out of Egypt.' " [9] *The Lord said to Moses, "I have seen these people, and they are a stiff necked people.*

[10] *Now leave Me so that My anger may burn against them and that I may destroy them. Then I will make you into a great nation."*

[11] *But Moses sought the favor of the Lord, his God. "Lord," he said, "why should Your anger burn against Your people, whom You brought out of Egypt with great power and a mighty hand?*

[12] *Why should the Egyptians say, 'It was with evil intent that he brought them out, to kill them in the mountains and to wipe them off the face of the earth?' Turn from Your fierce anger; relent and do not bring disaster on Your people.*

[13] *Remember Your servants Abraham, Isaac and Israel, to whom You swore by Your own self: 'I will make your descendants as numerous as the stars in the sky and I will give your descendants all this land I promised them, and it will be their inheritance forever.' "* [14] *Then the Lord relented and did not bring on his people the disaster he had threatened.*

[15] *Moses turned and went down the mountain with the two Tablets of the Covenant in his hands. They were inscribed on both sides, front and back.*

וַיְחַל

Exodus 32:11—Moses prayed to God not to kill everyone.

What we learn here is not the power of Moses but rather the enormous power of our own connection to God through our prayers. Prayer activates an energy that can alter reality, enabling us to enter whole new parallel universes.

The *Midrash* says:

> *"Master of the World," said Moses, "give me permission to speak." "Say whatever you wish," said God. Moses said, "They violated the beginning of [the second] commandment: 'You shall not have any other gods before Me,' (Exodus 20:3) and You seek to violate the end of that commandment; 'Showing kindness for thousands of generations to those who*

love Me.' (Ibid. 6) You told Abraham, 'I will exercise kindness for your children.' Seven generations have passed since Abraham. If You do not show kindness to the seventh generation, how will You show kindness to the thousandth?" (Shemot Rabbah 44:9)

וַיְשַׁבֵּר

Exodus 32:19—Moses smashed the Tablets

The Zohar tells us that the Tablets, weighed down by the density of physicality, actually fell out of Moses's hands. At the moment of the sin, the Aramaic letters—the Light—engraved on the Tablets flew away, making the Tables too heavy to hold. When the Tablets lost their spiritual essence, their physicality controlled reality.

בָּהֶם וַאֲכַלֵּם וְאֶעֱשֶׂה אוֹתְךָ לְגוֹי גָּדוֹל להוי, מבה, יזל, אום: 11 וַיְחַל מֹשֶׁה

מהע, אל שדי אֶת־פְּנֵי וחכמה בינה יְהוֹוָאַדְנִיאַהֲדֹנָהי אֱלֹהָיו ילה וַיֹּאמֶר לָמָה

יְהוֹוָאַדְנִיאַהֲדֹנָהי יֶחֱרֶה אַפְּךָ בְּעַמֶּךָ ה' הויות, גמם אֲשֶׁר הוֹצֵאתָ מֵאֶרֶץ

אלהים דאלפין מִצְרַיִם מצר בְּכֹחַ גָּדוֹל להוי, מבה, יזל, אום וּבְיָד חֲזָקָה: 12 לָמָה

יֹאמְרוּ מִצְרַיִם מצר לֵאמֹר בְּרָעָה רהע הוֹצִיאָם לַהֲרֹג אֹתָם בֶּהָרִים

וּלְכַלֹּתָם מֵעַל פְּנֵי עלם הָאֲדָמָה וחכמה בינה שׁוּב מֵחֲרוֹן אַפֶּךָ וְהִנָּחֵם עַל־

הָרָעָה רהע לְעַמֶּךָ ה' הויות, גמם: 13 זְכֹר לְאַבְרָהָם וד"פ אל, רמ"ח לְיִצְחָק ד"פ ב"ן

וּלְיִשְׂרָאֵל עֲבָדֶיךָ אֲשֶׁר נִשְׁבַּעְתָּ לָהֶם בָּךְ וַתְּדַבֵּר אֲלֵהֶם אַרְבֶּה

יצחק, ד"פ ב"ן אֶת־זַרְעֲכֶם כְּכוֹכְבֵי הַשָּׁמָיִם י"פ טל, י"פ כוזו וְכָל־הָאָרֶץ ילי

אלהים דההן ע"ה הַזֹּאת אֲשֶׁר אָמַרְתִּי אֶתֵּן לְזַרְעֲכֶם וְנָחֲלוּ לְעֹלָם: 14 וַיִּנָּחֶם

יְהוֹוָאַדְנִיאַהֲדֹנָהי עַל־הָרָעָה רהע אֲשֶׁר דִּבֶּר ראה לַעֲשׂוֹת לְעַמּוֹ: 15 וַיִּפֶן

וַיֵּרֶד ריי מֹשֶׁה מהע, אל שדי מִן־הָהָר וּשְׁנֵי לֻחֹת הָעֵדֻת בְּיָדוֹ לֻחֹת כְּתֻבִים

מִשְּׁנֵי עֶבְרֵיהֶם מִזֶּה וּמִזֶּה הֵם כְּתֻבִים: 16 וְהַלֻּחֹת מַעֲשֵׂה אֱלֹהִים

מום, אהיה אדני; ילה הֵמָּה וְהַמִּכְתָּב מִכְתַּב אֱלֹהִים מום, אהיה אדני; ילה הוּא חָרוּת

עַל־הַלֻּחֹת: 17 וַיִּשְׁמַע יְהוֹשֻׁעַ אֶת־קוֹל ע"ב ס"ג ע"ה הָעָם רהע ע"ה בְּרֵעֹה וַיֹּאמֶר

אֶל־מֹשֶׁה מהע, אל שדי קוֹל ע"ב ס"ג ע"ה מִלְחָמָה בַּמַּחֲנֶה: 18 וַיֹּאמֶר אֵין קוֹל

ע"ב ס"ג ע"ה עֲנוֹת גְּבוּרָה וְאֵין קוֹל ע"ב ס"ג ע"ה עֲנוֹת חֲלוּשָׁה קוֹל ע"ב ס"ג ע"ה עַנּוֹת

אָנֹכִי איע שֹׁמֵעַ: 19 וַיְהִי אל, ייא כַּאֲשֶׁר קָרַב אֶל־הַמַּחֲנֶה וַיַּרְא אלף למד יהוה

אֶת־הָעֵגֶל וּמְחֹלֹת וַיִּחַר־אַף וַיֹּאמֶר מֹשֶׁה מהע, אל שדי וַיַּשְׁלֵךְ מִיָּדוֹ אֶת־הַלֻּחֹת

וַיְשַׁבֵּר אֹתָם תַּחַת הָהָר: 20 וַיִּקַּח וזאם אֶת־הָעֵגֶל אֲשֶׁר עָשׂוּ וַיִּשְׂרֹף

When something is void of Light, it becomes physically heavy. Consider the language we use when we experience no Light: Life can seem "heavy" or we can feel "depressed" or "down."

At that time, the first stone tablets broke. And we already explained that the stones

in the hands of Moses became heavy, fell and broke. What is the reason? The letters have flown from the stone tablets AND THE STONES REMAINED WITHOUT SPIRIT AND THEREFORE GREW HEAVY.

— The Zohar, Vayak'hel 1:11

¹⁶ *The Tablets were the work of God; the writing was the writing of God, engraved on the Tablets.* ¹⁷ *When Joshua heard the sound of the people's voice, he said to Moses, "There is the sound of war in the camp."*

¹⁸ *Moses replied: "It is not the sound of victory, it is not the sound of defeat; it is the sound of singing that I hear."*

¹⁹ *When Moses approached the camp and saw the calf and the dancing, his anger burned and he threw the Tablets out of his hands, breaking them at the foot of the mountain.*

²⁰ *And he took the calf they had made and burned it in the fire; then he ground it to powder, scattered it on the water and made the Israelites drink it.*

²¹ *Moses said to Aaron, "What did these people do to you, that you led them into such great sin?"* ²² *"Do not be angry, my lord," Aaron answered. "You know how prone these people are to evil.*

²³ *They said to me, 'Make us gods who will go before us, because this fellow Moses who brought us up out of Egypt—we don't know what has happened to him.'*

²⁴ *So I told them, 'Whoever has any gold jewelry, take it off.' Then they gave it to me, and I threw it into the fire, and out came this calf!"*

²⁵ *Moses saw that the people were wild and that Aaron had let them get out of control and so become a laughingstock to their enemies.*

²⁶ *So he stood at the entrance to the camp and said, "Whoever is for the Lord, come to me." And all the Levites rallied to him.*

²⁷ *Then he said to them, "This is what the Lord, the God of Israel, says: 'Each man strap a sword to his side. Go back and forth through the camp from one end to the other, each killing his brother and friend and neighbor.' "*

²⁸ *The Levites did as Moses said, and that day about three thousand of the people died.*

הֵבֵאתָ

Exodus 32:21—Moses explained to Aaron that despite his "good intentions," his (Aaron's) actions and energy contributed to the fashioning of the Golden Calf.

Universal Laws dictate that we are wholly responsible for all our actions, even if we are doing what we think is for the best. If our actions bring about a negative outcome, there is an effect—a payment—that must be made.

בָּאֵשׁ וַיִּטְחַן עַד אֲשֶׁר־דָּק וַיִּזֶר עַל־פְּנֵי הַמַּיִם

וַיַּשְׁקְ אֶת־בְּנֵי יִשְׂרָאֵל: 21 וַיֹּאמֶר מֹשֶׁה אֶל־אַהֲרֹן

מֶה ־עָשָׂה לְךָ הָעָם הַזֶּה כִּי־הֵבֵאתָ עָלָיו חֲטָאָה גְדֹלָה:

22 וַיֹּאמֶר אַהֲרֹן אַל־יִחַר אַף אֲדֹנִי אַתָּה יָדַעְתָּ אֶת־הָעָם

כִּי בְרָע הוּא: 23 וַיֹּאמְרוּ לִי עֲשֵׂה־לָּנוּ אֱלֹהִים

אֱלֹהִים אֲשֶׁר יֵלְכוּ לְפָנֵינוּ כִּי־זֶה | מֹשֶׁה הָאִישׁ

אֲשֶׁר הֶעֱלָנוּ מֵאֶרֶץ מִצְרַיִם לֹא יָדַעְנוּ מֶה

הָיָה לוֹ: 24 וָאֹמַר לָהֶם לְמִי זָהָב הִתְפָּרָקוּ וַיִּתְּנוּ־לִי וָאַשְׁלִכֵהוּ

בָאֵשׁ וַיֵּצֵא הָעֵגֶל הַזֶּה: 25 וַיַּרְא מֹשֶׁה

אֶת־הָעָם כִּי פָרֻעַ הוּא כִּי־פְרָעֹה אַהֲרֹן לְשִׁמְצָה בְּקָמֵיהֶם:

26 וַיַּעֲמֹד מֹשֶׁה בְּשַׁעַר הַמַּחֲנֶה וַיֹּאמֶר מִי לַיהוָה

אֵלָי וַיֵּאָסְפוּ אֵלָיו כָּל־בְּנֵי לֵוִי: 27 וַיֹּאמֶר לָהֶם כֹּה

אָמַר יְהוָה אֱלֹהֵי יִשְׂרָאֵל שִׂימוּ אִישׁ ־חַרְבּוֹ

עַל־יְרֵכוֹ עִבְרוּ וָשׁוּבוּ מִשַּׁעַר לָשַׁעַר בַּמַּחֲנֶה וְהִרְגוּ אִישׁ

־אֶת־אָחִיו וְאִישׁ אֶת־רֵעֵהוּ וְאִישׁ אֶת־

קְרֹבוֹ: 28 וַיַּעֲשׂוּ בְנֵי־לֵוִי כִּדְבַר מֹשֶׁה וַיִּפֹּל מִן־

הָעָם בַּיּוֹם הַהוּא כִּשְׁלֹשֶׁת אַלְפֵי אִישׁ 29 וַיֹּאמֶר

מֹשֶׁה מִלְאוּ יֶדְכֶם הַיּוֹם לַיהוָה כִּי אִישׁ

בִּבְנוֹ וּבְאָחִיו וְלָתֵת עֲלֵיכֶם הַיּוֹם בְּרָכָה:

30 וַיְהִי מִמָּחֳרָת וַיֹּאמֶר מֹשֶׁה אֶל־הָעָם אַתֶּם חֲטָאתֶם

The Holy One, blessed be He, said to him: Aaron, these two magicians drew you toward what they wanted. By your life, two of your sons will fall, and they will be seized for this sin. This is what is written, "And God was very angry with Aaron to have destroyed him." (Deuteronomy 9:20) This refers to his sons, as it is written, "Yet I destroyed his fruit from above," (Amos 2:9) because the fruits of a man are his children.
— The Zohar, Ki Tisa 11:92

²⁹ Then Moses said, "You have been set apart to the Lord today, for you were against your own sons and brothers, and He has blessed you this day."

³⁰ The next day Moses said to the people, "You have committed a great sin. But now I will go up to the Lord; perhaps I can make atonement for your sin."

³¹ So Moses went back to the Lord and said, "Oh, what a great sin these people have committed! They have made themselves gods of gold.

³² But now, please forgive their sin—but if not, then blot me out of the book you have written." ³³ The Lord replied to Moses, "Whoever has sinned against Me I will blot out of my book.

³⁴ Now go, lead the people to the place I spoke of, and My angel will go before you. However, when the time comes for Me to punish, I will punish them for their sin."

³⁵ And the Lord struck the people with a plague because of what they did with the calf Aaron had made.

^{33:1} Then the Lord said to Moses, "Leave this place, you and the people you brought up out of Egypt, and go up to the land I promised on oath to Abraham, Isaac and Jacob, saying, 'I will give it to your descendants.'

² I will send an angel before you and drive out the Canaanites, Amorites, Hittites, Perizzites, Hivites and Jebusites.

³ Go up to the land flowing with milk and honey. But I will not go with you, because you are a stiff-necked people and I might destroy you on the way."

⁴ When the people heard these distressing words, they began to mourn and no one put on any ornaments. ⁵ For the Lord had said to Moses, "Tell the Israelites, 'You are a stiff-necked people. If I were to go with you even for a moment, I might destroy you. Now take off your ornaments and I will decide what to do with you.' "

אוֹנָא

Exodus 32:31—Moses prayed to remove the negativity.

Prayer can change reality and remove negativity. There are certain instances where we can cleanse ourselves just by praying and invoking the Names of God.

מַלְאָךְ

Exodus 33:2—God said, "I will send an angel before you."

When the Israelites fashioned the Golden Calf, they created a system of mediation through

וְחַטָּאָ֥ה גְדֹלָ֑ה וְעַתָּה֙ אֶֽעֱלֶ֣ה אֶל־יְהֹוָ֣ה‏אהדונהי אוּלַ֛י אום אֲכַפְּרָ֖ה בְּעַ֥ד

אנא וְחַטַּאתְכֶֽם: 31 וַיָּ֥שָׁב מֹשֶׁ֖ה מהע, אל שדי אֶל־יְהֹוָ֑ה‏אהדונהי וַיֹּאמַ֑ר

ב"ן, לכב, יבם אָ֣נָּ֗א חָטָ֞א הָעָ֤ם הַזֶּה֙ והו חֲטָאָ֣ה גְדֹלָ֔ה וַיַּֽעֲשׂ֥וּ לָהֶ֖ם אֱלֹהֵ֥י דמב, ילה

זָהָֽב: 32 וְעַתָּ֖ה אִם־ תִּשָּׂ֣א חַטָּאתָ֑ם וְאִם־ יוהך ‏אַ֕יִן מְחֵ֣נִי נָ֔א

מִֽסִּפְרְךָ֖ אֲשֶׁ֥ר כָּתָֽבְתָּ: 33 וַיֹּ֥אמֶר יְהֹוָ֖ה‏אהדונהי אֶל־מֹשֶׁ֑ה מהע, אל שדי מִ֣י

ילי אֲשֶׁ֣ר חָֽטָא־לִ֔י אֶמְחֶ֖נּוּ מִסִּפְרִֽי: 34 וְעַתָּ֞ה | לֵ֣ךְ ׀ נְחֵ֣ה אֶת־הָעָ֗ם אֶ֚ל

אֲשֶׁר־ דִּבַּ֣רְתִּי לָ֔ךְ ראה הִנֵּ֥ה מלאכי מ"ה יה יֵלֵ֣ךְ לְפָנֶ֑יךָ סמ"ב וּבְי֣וֹם

ע"ה = נגד, זן, מזבח פָּקְדִ֖י וּפָֽקַדְתִּ֥י עֲלֵהֶ֖ם חַטָּאתָֽם: 35 וַיִּגֹּ֥ף יְהֹוָ֖ה‏אהדונהי אֶת־

הָעָ֑ם עַ֚ל אֲשֶׁ֣ר עָשׂ֣וּ אֶת־הָעֵ֔גֶל אֲשֶׁ֥ר עָשָׂ֖ה אַֽהֲרֹֽן ע"ב ורבוע ע"ב: 33 1 וַיְדַבֵּ֨ר

ראה יְהֹוָ֤ה‏אהדונהי אֶל־מֹשֶׁה֙ מהע, אל שדי לֵ֣ךְ עֲלֵ֣ה מִזֶּ֔ה אַתָּ֣ה וְהָעָ֔ם אֲשֶׁ֥ר

הֶֽעֱלִ֖יתָ מֵאֶ֣רֶץ אלהים דאלפין מִצְרָ֑יִם מצר אֶל־הָאָ֗רֶץ אלהים דההין ע"ה אֲשֶׁ֣ר

נִ֠שְׁבַּ֠עְתִּי לְאַבְרָהָ֨ם רמ"ח, וז"פ אל לְיִצְחָ֤ק דס"א ב"ן וּֽלְיַֽעֲקֹב֙ ז הויות, יאהדונהי אידהנויה

לֵאמֹ֔ר לְזַ֨רְעֲךָ֖ אֶתְּנֶֽנָּה: 2 וְשָׁלַחְתִּ֥י לְפָנֶ֖יךָ מלאך סמ"ב מַלְאָ֑ךְ יאהדונהי וְגֵֽרַשְׁתִּ֗י

אֶת־הַֽכְּנַעֲנִי֙ הָֽאֱמֹרִ֔י וְהַֽחִתִּי֙ וְהַפְּרִזִּ֔י הַֽחִוִּ֖י וְהַיְבוּסִֽי: 3 אֶל־אֶ֛רֶץ אלהים דאלפין

זָבַ֥ת חָלָ֖ב וּדְבָ֑שׁ כִּי֩ לֹ֨א אֶֽעֱלֶ֜ה בְּקִרְבְּךָ֗ כִּ֤י עַם־קְשֵׁה־עֹ֨רֶף֙ אַ֔תָּה פֶּן־

אֲכֶלְךָ֖ בַּדָּֽרֶךְ: ב"פ יב"ק: 4 וַיִּשְׁמַ֣ע הָעָ֗ם אֶת־הַדָּבָ֥ר ראה הָרָ֛ע רהע הַזֶּ֖ה והו

וַיִּתְאַבָּ֑לוּ וְלֹא־ שָׁ֛תוּ אִ֥ישׁ ע"ה קנ"א קס"א עֶדְי֖וֹ עָלָֽיו: 5 וַיֹּ֨אמֶר יְהֹוָ֤ה‏אהדונהי

אֶל־מֹשֶׁה֙ מהע, אל שדי אֱמֹ֣ר אֶל־בְּנֵֽי־יִשְׂרָאֵ֗ל אַתֶּ֣ם עַם־קְשֵׁה־עֹ֨רֶף֙ רֶ֣גַע

ג"פ אלהים ← ט"ו אותיות אֶחָ֤ד אהבה, דאגה אֶֽעֱלֶ֥ה בְקִרְבְּךָ֖ וְכִלִּיתִ֑יךָ וְעַתָּ֗ה הוֹרֵ֤ד

עֶדְיְךָ֙ מֵֽעָלֶ֔יךָ וְאֵֽדְעָ֖ה מ"ה מָ֥ה אֶֽעֱשֶׂה־לָּֽךְ: 6 וַיִּֽתְנַצְּל֧וּ בְנֵֽי־יִשְׂרָאֵ֛ל אֶת־

which they could connect to God. Through the worship of that idol, (the go-between) the people lost their direct connection to the Creator. God desires our connection and has given us the Zohar so that we can once again connect directly to the Creator's Light.

6 So the Israelites stripped off their ornaments at Mount Horeb.

7 Now Moses used to take a tent and pitch it outside the camp some distance away, calling it the "Tent of Meeting." Anyone inquiring of the Lord would go to the Tent of Meeting outside the camp.

8 And whenever Moses went out to the Tent, all the people rose and stood at the entrances to their tents, watching Moses until he entered the Tent.

9 As Moses went into the Tent, the pillar of cloud would come down and stay at the entrance, while It spoke with Moses.

10 Whenever the people saw the pillar of cloud standing at the entrance to the tent, they all stood and worshipped each at the entrance to his tent.

THIRD READING - JACOB - TIFERET

11 The Lord would speak to Moses face to face, as a man speaks with his friend. Then he would return to the camp, but his young aide Joshua son of Nun did not leave the Tent.

12 Moses said to the Lord, "You have been telling me, 'Lead these people,' but You have not let me know whom You will send with me. You have said, 'I know you by name and you have found favor with me.'

בַּחוּץ לְמַעְזֵנָה

Exodus 33:7—Because of his awesome spiritual energy, Moses slept apart from the people.

Moses slept in a tent away from the rest of the Israelites at Mount Sinai. He did this so that he would not connect his energy with those who built the Golden Calf. We, on the other hand, can connect to the energy of Moses every time we hear the Bible read on Shabbat. Furthermore, the sages teach that there is a Moses living in every generation. We should seek to connect with this person to receive the energy of the biblical Moses.

Exodus 33:9—Moses prayed to be connected to God at all times.

Standing in the Tabernacle and protected by a cloud that descended to cover the doorway, Moses spoke face to face with God. The people around Moses were not allowed to enter; they were so negative that Moses begged to be continually connected to God. No matter how elevated a person's spiritual level, others' can cause disturbances in his or her field of energy and bring him or her down. We must work at being connected to God at all times, as well as to people who will foster, not hinder, that Divine connection.

עֵדִים מֵהַר רבוע אלהים - ה וַוזֹרֶב רי''ו 7 וּמֹשֶׁה מהע, אל שדי יִקַּח וֹעם אֶת־הָאֹהֶל

וְנָטָה־לוֹ לאה | מִחוּץ לַמַּחֲנֶה הַרְחֵק שדי מִן־הַמַּחֲנֶה וְקָרָא לוֹ אֹהֶל לאה

מוֹעֵד וְהָיָה יהוה, יהה כָּל ילי ־מְבַקֵּשׁ יְהֹוָהאדנילאהדונהי יֵצֵא אֶל־אֹהֶל לאה

מוֹעֵד אֲשֶׁר מִחוּץ לַמַּחֲנֶה: 8 וְהָיָה יהוה, יהה כְּצֵאת מֹשֶׁה מהע, אל שדי אֶל־

הָאֹהֶל לאה יָקוּמוּ כָּל ־הָעָם וְנִצְּבוּ אִישׁ ע''ה קנ''א קס''א פֶּתַח אָהֳלוֹ

וְהִבִּיטוּ אַחֲרֵי מֹשֶׁה מהע, אל שדי עַד־בֹּאוֹ הָאֹהֱלָה: 9 וְהָיָה יהוה, יהה כְּבֹא

מֹשֶׁה מהע, אל שדי הָאֹהֱלָה יֵרֵד עַמּוּד הֶעָנָן וְעָמַד פֶּתַח הָאֹהֶל לאה

וְדִבֶּר ראה עִם־מֹשֶׁה מהע, אל שדי: 10 וְרָאָה כָּל ־הָעָם אֶת־עַמּוּד

הֶעָנָן עֹמֵד פֶּתַח הָאֹהֶל לאה וְקָם כָּל ־הָעָם ילי וְהִשְׁתַּחֲווּ אִישׁ ע''ה קנ''א קס''א

פֶּתַח אָהֳלוֹ: 11 וְדִבֶּר ראה יְהֹוָהאדנילאהדונהי אֶל־מֹשֶׁה מהע, אל שדי פָּנִים

אֶל־פָּנִים ע''ב ס''ג מ''ה כַּאֲשֶׁר יְדַבֵּר ראה אִישׁ ע''ה קנ''א קס''א אֶל־רֵעֵהוּ

וְשָׁב אֶל־הַמַּחֲנֶה וּמְשָׁרְתוֹ יְהוֹשֻׁעַ בִּן־נוּן שדי נַעַר לֹא יָמִישׁ מִתּוֹךְ הָאֹהֶל

לאה

THIRD READING - JACOB - TIFERET

12 וַיֹּאמֶר מֹשֶׁה מהע, אל שדי אֶל־יְהֹוָהאדנילאהדונהי רְאֵה ראה אַתָּה אֹמֵר אֵלַי

הַעַל אֶת־הָעָם הַזֶּה יהו וְאַתָּה לֹא הוֹדַעְתַּנִי אֵת אֲשֶׁר־תִּשְׁלַח עִמִּי

וְאַתָּה אָמַרְתָּ יְדַעְתִּיךָ בְשֵׁם יהוה שדי וְגַם ילי ־מָצָאתָ חֵן מווי בְּעֵינָי

פָּנִים אֶל־פָּנִים

Exodus 33:11—While praying, Moses saw God face to face.

This is the closest any man has ever come to the Creator. It is the ultimate connection; this world was designed so that we all can reach such a level. This is our spiritual purpose. We must strive to do in all our spiritual work—to reach God with all our heart and soul without any ego, anger, or selfishness.

13 Now, if You are pleased with me, teach me Your ways so I may know You and continue to find favor with You. Remember that this nation is Your people."

14 The Lord replied, "My Presence will go with you, and I will give you rest."

15 Then Moses said to him, "If Your Presence does not go with us, do not send us up from here.

16 How will anyone know that You are pleased with me and with Your people unless You go with us? What else will distinguish me and Your people from all the other people on the face of the earth?"

FOURTH READING - MOSES - NETZACH

17 And the Lord said to Moses, "I will do the very thing you have asked, because I am pleased with you and I know you by name."

18 Then he said, "Please show me Your glory."

19 And He said, "I will cause all My goodness to pass in front of you, and I will proclaim My Name, the Lord, in your presence. I will have mercy on whom I will have mercy, and I will have compassion on whom I will have compassion.

20 But," he said, "you cannot see My face, for no one may see Me and live."

21 Then the Lord said, "There is a place near Me where you may stand on a rock.

22 When My glory passes by, I will put you in a cleft in the rock and cover you with My hand until I have passed by.

23 Then I will remove My hand and you will see My back; but My face must not be seen."

עה קס"א 13 וְעַתָּ֡ה אִם יוהך ע"ה מ"ב עה נָ֩א מָצָ֨אתִי חֵ֜ן מוזי בְּעֵינֶ֗יךָ ע"ה קס"א הֽוֹדִעֵ֤נִי

נָ֣א אֶת־דְּרָכֶ֔ךָ וְאֵדָ֣עֲךָ֔ לְמַ֥עַן אֶמְצָא־חֵ֖ן בְּעֵינֶ֑יךָ מוזי ע"ה קס"א וּרְאֵ֕ה כִּ֥י

עַמְּךָ֖ ה הויות, נמם הַגּ֥וֹי הַזֶּֽה וה 14 וַיֹּאמַ֑ר פָּנַ֥י וחכמה בינה יֵלֵ֖כוּ וַהֲנִחֹ֥תִי לָֽךְ׃

15 וַיֹּ֖אמֶר אֵלָ֑יו יוהך ע"ה מ"ב עה אִם־אֵ֤ין פָּנֶ֨יךָ֙ סמ"ב הֹלְכִ֔ים אַֽל־תַּעֲלֵ֖נוּ מִזֶּֽה׃

16 וּבַמֶּ֣ה ׀ יִוָּדַ֣ע אֵפ֗וֹא כִּֽי־מָצָ֨אתִי חֵ֤ן מוזי בְּעֵינֶ֨יךָ֙ ע"ה קס"א אֲנִ֣י אני, טדהד כוזי

וְעַמֶּ֔ךָ ה הויות, נמם הֲל֣וֹא בְּלֶכְתְּךָ֖ עִמָּ֑נוּ וְנִפְלִ֨ינוּ֙ אֲנִ֣י אני, טדהד כוזי וְעַמְּךָ֔

ה הויות, נמם מִכָּל־הָ֣עָ֔ם יֻלֹי אֲשֶׁ֖ר עַל־פְּנֵ֥י וחכמה בינה הָאֲדָמָֽה׃

FOURTH READING - MOSES - NETZACH

17 וַיֹּ֤אמֶר יְהֹוָה֙ אדני־יאהדונהי מהמע, אל שדי אֶל־מֹשֶׁ֔ה יג"ל גַּ֣ם אֶת־הַדָּבָ֥ר ראה הַזֶּ֛ה

והו אֲשֶׁ֥ר דִּבַּ֖רְתָּ ראה אֶעֱשֶׂ֑ה כִּֽי־מָצָ֤אתָ חֵן֙ מוזי בְּעֵינַ֔י ע"ה קס"א וָאֵדָעֲךָ֖

בְּשֵֽׁם יהוה שדי ׃ 18 וַיֹּאמַ֑ר הַרְאֵ֥נִי נָ֖א אֶת־כְּבֹדֶֽךָ׃ 19 וַיֹּ֗אמֶר אֲנִ֨י אני, טדהד כוזי

אַעֲבִ֤יר כָּל־ יֻלֹי טוּבִי֙ יהוה ע"ה עַל־פָּנֶ֔יךָ סמ"ב וְקָרָ֧אתִֽי בְשֵׁ֛ם יהוה שדי

יְהֹוָ֖ה אדני־יאהדונהי לְפָנֶ֑יךָ סמ"ב וְחַנֹּתִי֙ אֶת־אֲשֶׁ֣ר אָחֹ֔ן רמזו וְרִחַמְתִּ֖י אֶת־אֲשֶׁ֥ר

אֲרַחֵֽם רמזו ׃ 20 וַיֹּ֕אמֶר לֹ֥א תוּכַ֖ל לִרְאֹ֣ת אֶת־פָּנָ֑י וחכמה בינה כִּ֛י לֹֽא־יִרְאַ֥נִי

הָאָדָ֖ם וחזי מ"ה ׃ 21 וַיֹּ֣אמֶר יְהֹוָ֔ה אדני־יאהדונהי הִנֵּ֥ה מ"ה יה מָק֖וֹם יהוה ברבוע, ר"פ אל

אִתִּ֑י וְנִצַּבְתָּ֖ עַל־הַצּֽוּר אלהים דההין ע"ה ׃ 22 וְהָיָה֙ יהוה, יהה בַּעֲבֹ֣ר כְּבֹדִ֔י

וְשַׂמְתִּ֖יךָ בְּנִקְרַ֣ת הַצּ֑וּר אלהים דההין ע"ה וְשַׂכֹּתִ֥י כַפִּ֛י עָלֶ֖יךָ עַד־עָבְרִֽי׃

23 וַהֲסִרֹתִי֙ אֶת־כַּפִּ֔י וְרָאִ֖יתָ אֶת־אֲחֹרָ֑י וּפָנַ֖י וחכמה בינה לֹ֥א יֵרָאֽוּ׃

FIFTH READING - AARON - HOD

34:1 The Lord said to Moses, "Chisel out two stone Tablets like the first ones, and I will write on the Tablets the words that were on the first Tablets, which you broke.

2 Be ready in the morning, and then come up on Mount Sinai. Present yourself to Me there on top of the mountain.

3 No one is to come with you or be seen anywhere on the mountain; not even the flocks and herds may graze in front of the mountain."

4 So Moses chiseled out two stone Tablets like the first ones and went up Mount Sinai early in the morning, as the Lord had commanded him; and he carried the two stone Tablets in his hands.

5 Then the Lord came down in the cloud and stood there with him and proclaimed His Name, the Lord.

6 And He passed in front of Moses, proclaiming, "The Lord, the Lord, the compassionate and gracious God, slow to anger, abounding in love and faithfulness,

7 maintaining love to thousands, and forgiving wickedness, rebellion and sin. Yet He does not leave the guilty unpunished; He punishes the children and their children for the sin of the fathers to the third and fourth generation."

8 Moses bowed to the ground at once and worshiped.

Exodus 34:1—The second set of Tablets.

The fashioning of the second set of Tablets is one of the most important lessons in our spiritual work: When we make mistakes in life, it is important to learn from them and to move forward.

> THEN the Holy One, blessed be He, spoke: "And they shall spread the cloth," (Deuteronomy 22:17) and the parchment of the Torah scroll unfolds, and they shall see that it is written in it, "Hew for yourself

> two tablets of stone like the first, and I will write upon these tablets the words that were on the first tablets, which you did break." (Exodus 34:1)
> — The Zohar, Ki Tetze 1:14

Exodus 34:6—The Thirteen Attributes of God.

The number thirteen represents one level above the twelve signs of the zodiac. When we rise above the controlling destiny of our astrology and of the physical world, we rise to the level of thirteen.

FIFTH READING - AARON - HOD

34 1 וַיֹּאמֶר יְהוָֹאֲדֹנָ֥יאַהדֹוּנַֿהי מהע, אל שדי אֶל־מֹשֶׁה פְּסָל־לְךָ שְׁנֵי־לֻחֹת

אֲבָנִים כָּרִאשֹׁנִים וְכָתַבְתִּי עַל־הַלֻּחֹת אֶת־הַדְּבָרִים ראה אֲשֶׁר הָי֤וּ

עַל־הַלֻּחֹת הָרִאשֹׁנִים אֲשֶׁר שִׁבַּֽרְתָּ: 2 וֶהְיֵה יהוה, יהה נָכוֹן לַבֹּקֶר וְעָלִ֤יתָ

בַבֹּקֶר אֶל־הַר רביע אלהים - ה סִינַי נמם, ה"פ יהוה וְנִצַּבְתָּ לִי שָׁם עַל־רֹאשׁ

הָהָר: 3 וְאִישׁ ע"ה קנ"א קס"א לֹא־יַעֲלֶה עִמָּךְ ה הויות, נגמם ריבוע אלהים ואלהים דיודין ע"ה

וְגַם־אִישׁ יגל ע"ה קנ"א קס"א אַל־יֵרָא אלף למד יהוה בְּכָל־ ב"ן, לכב, יבם הָהָר גַם יגל

הַצֹּאן מלוי אהיה דיודין ע"ה וְהַבָּקָר אַל־יִרְעוּ אֶל־מוּל הָהָר הַהוּא: 4 וַיִּפְסֹל

שְׁנֵי־לֻחֹת אֲבָנִים כָּרִאשֹׁנִים וַיַּשְׁכֵּם מֹשֶׁה מהע, אל שדי בַבֹּקֶר וַיַּעַל אֶל־

הָר רביע אלהים - ה סִינַי נמם, ה"פ יהוה כַּאֲשֶׁר צִוָּה פוי יְהוָֹאֲדֹנָ֥יאַהדֹוּנַֿהי אֹתוֹ וַיִּקַּח

בְּיָדוֹ שְׁנֵי לֻחֹת אֲבָנִים: 5 וַיֵּרֶד ריי יְהוָֹאֲדֹנָ֥יאַהדֹוּנַֿהי בֶּעָנָן וַיִּתְיַצֵּב עִמּוֹ

שָׁם וַיִּקְרָא ב"פ קס"א - ה אותיות בְּשֵׁם יהוה שדי יְהוָֹאֲדֹנָ֥יאַהדֹוּנַֿהי: 6 וַיַּעֲבֹר רפי"ח, ע"ב ריי"ו

יְהוָֹאֲדֹנָ֥יאַהדֹוּנַֿהי עַל־פָּנָיו וַיִּקְרָא ב"פ קס"א - ה אותיות יְהוָֹאֲדֹנָ֥יאַהדֹוּנַֿהי | יְהוָֹאֲדֹנָ֥יאַהדֹוּנַֿהי

אֵל ייאי רַחוּם וְחַנּוּן יהוה ע"ה אלהים ע"ה ר"ת אור אֶרֶךְ אַפַּיִם ע"ב ורבוע מ"ה וְרַב־

חֶסֶד ע"ב, ריבוע יהוה וֶאֱמֶת אהיה פעמים אהיה, ד"פ ס"ג: 7 נֹצֵר חֶסֶד ע"ב, ריבוע יהוה

לָאֲלָפִים קס"א ; ר"ת נֹשֵׂא עָוֹן ג"פ מ"ב וָפֶשַׁע וְחַטָּאָה וְנַקֵּה קס"א לֹא יְנַקֶּה

פֹּקֵד רבוע ע"ב עֲוֹן ג"פ מ"ב | אָבוֹת עַל־בָּנִים וְעַל־בְּנֵי בָנִים עַל־שִׁלֵּשִׁים

וְעַל־רִבֵּעִים: 8 וַיְמַהֵר מֹשֶׁה מהע, אל שדי וַיִּקֹּד אַרְצָה הההין ע"ה אלהים דההין ע"ה וַיִּשְׁתָּחוּ:

The Thirteen Attributes of God are connected to the power of miracles and wonders. There is a reality where miracles are the norm, where what we think of as the miraculous is natural.
In this reading we receive the gift of the large

Aramaic letter *Nun* found in the word *"notzer."* The large letters in the Bible carry us to the level of *Binah*, where all our spiritual energy is stored. Nun normally represents the aspect of falling (from *nefilah*, which means "to fall"). However, the large *Nun* in this case is connected to *Binah*. So this connection to *Nun* protects us from falling, and if we have already fallen, it has the power to raise up our consciousness.

⁹ *"Lord, if I have found favor in your eyes," he said, "then let the Lord go with us. Although this is a stiff-necked people, forgive our wickedness and our sin, and take us as Your inheritance."*

SIXTH READING - JOSEPH - YESOD

¹⁰ *Then the Lord said: "I am making a Covenant with you. Before all your people I will do wonders never before done in any nation in all the world. The people you live among will see how awesome is the work that I, the Lord, will do for you.*

¹¹ *Obey what I command you today. I will drive out before you the Amorites, Canaanites, Hittites, Perizzites, Hivites and Jebusites.*

¹² *Be careful not to make a treaty with those who live in the land where you are going, or they will be a snare among you.*

¹³ *Break down their altars, smash their sacred stones and cut down their Asherah trees.* ¹⁴ *Do not worship any other god, for the Lord, whose name is Jealous, is a jealous God.*

¹⁵ *Be careful not to make a treaty with those who live in the land; for when they prostitute themselves to their gods and sacrifice to them, they will invite you and you will eat their sacrifices.*

¹⁶ *And when you choose some of their daughters as wives for your sons and those daughters prostitute themselves to their gods, they will lead your sons to do the same.*

¹⁷ *Do not make cast idols.* ¹⁸ *Celebrate the Feast of Unleavened Bread. For seven days eat unleavened bread, as I commanded you. Do this at the appointed time in the month of Aviv, for in that month you came out of Egypt.*

Exodus 34:14—A large letter *Reish* is found in the word "*acher*" (other).

Reish represents the word "*rash*" (poor), signifying a lack of Light. In truth, however, a lack of Light is really an opportunity to get more Light. By hearing this section read on Shabbat, we are empowered with the strength to overcome obstacles and to take advantage that this "lack" of Light affords us.

9 וַיֹּאמֶר אִם ־נָא מָצָאתִי חֵן בְּעֵינֶיךָ אֲדֹנָי יֵלֶךְ ־נָא אֲדֹנָי בְּקִרְבֵּנוּ כִּי עַם ־קְשֵׁה ־עֹרֶף הוּא וְסָלַחְתָּ לַעֲוֺנֵנוּ וּלְחַטָּאתֵנוּ וּנְחַלְתָּנוּ׃

SIXTH READING - JOSEPH - YESOD

10 וַיֹּאמֶר הִנֵּה אָנֹכִי כֹּרֵת בְּרִית נֶגֶד כָּל ־עַמְּךָ אֶעֱשֶׂה נִפְלָאֹת אֲשֶׁר לֹא ־נִבְרְאוּ בְכָל ־הָאָרֶץ וּבְכָל ־הַגּוֹיִם וְרָאָה כָל ־הָעָם אֲשֶׁר ־אַתָּה בְקִרְבּוֹ אֶת ־מַעֲשֵׂה יְהוָה כִּי ־נוֹרָא הוּא אֲשֶׁר אֲנִי עֹשֶׂה עִמָּךְ׃ 11 שְׁמָר ־לְךָ אֵת אֲשֶׁר אָנֹכִי מְצַוְּךָ הַיּוֹם הִנְנִי גֹרֵשׁ מִפָּנֶיךָ אֶת ־הָאֱמֹרִי וְהַכְּנַעֲנִי וְהַחִתִּי וְהַפְּרִזִּי וְהַחִוִּי וְהַיְבוּסִי׃ 12 הִשָּׁמֶר לְךָ פֶּן ־תִּכְרֹת בְּרִית לְיוֹשֵׁב הָאָרֶץ אֲשֶׁר אַתָּה בָּא עָלֶיהָ פֶּן ־יִהְיֶה לְמוֹקֵשׁ בְּקִרְבֶּךָ׃ 13 כִּי אֶת ־מִזְבְּחֹתָם תִּתֹּצוּן וְאֶת ־מַצֵּבֹתָם תְּשַׁבֵּרוּן וְאֶת ־אֲשֵׁרָיו תִּכְרֹתוּן׃ 14 כִּי לֹא תִשְׁתַּחֲוֶה לְאֵל אַחֵר כִּי יְהוָה קַנָּא שְׁמוֹ אֵל קַנָּא הוּא׃ 15 פֶּן ־תִּכְרֹת בְּרִית לְיוֹשֵׁב הָאָרֶץ וְזָנוּ | אַחֲרֵי אֱלֹהֵיהֶם וְזָבְחוּ לֵאלֹהֵיהֶם וְקָרָא לְךָ וְאָכַלְתָּ מִזִּבְחוֹ׃ 16 וְלָקַחְתָּ מִבְּנֹתָיו לְבָנֶיךָ וְזָנוּ בְנֹתָיו אַחֲרֵי אֱלֹהֵיהֶן וְהִזְנוּ אֶת ־בָּנֶיךָ אַחֲרֵי אֱלֹהֵיהֶן׃ 17 אֱלֹהֵי מַסֵּכָה לֹא תַעֲשֶׂה ־לָּךְ׃ 18 אֶת ־חַג הַמַּצּוֹת תִּשְׁמֹר שִׁבְעַת יָמִים תֹּאכַל מַצּוֹת אֲשֶׁר צִוִּיתִךָ לְמוֹעֵד חֹדֶשׁ הָאָבִיב כִּי בְּחֹדֶשׁ הָאָבִיב יָצָאתָ מִמִּצְרָיִם׃ 19 כָּל ־פֶּטֶר רֶחֶם לִי וְכָל ־מִקְנְךָ תִּזָּכָר פֶּטֶר שׁוֹר

19 The first offspring of every womb belongs to Me, including all the firstborn males of your livestock, whether from herd or flock. 20 Redeem the firstborn donkey with a lamb, but if you do not redeem it, break its neck. Redeem all your firstborn sons. No one is to appear before Me empty-handed.

21 Six days you shall labor, but on the seventh day you shall rest; even during the plowing season and harvest you must rest.

22 Celebrate the Feast of Weeks with the first fruits of the wheat harvest, and the Feast of Ingathering at the turn of the year.

23 Three times a year all your men are to appear before the Sovereign Lord, the God of Israel.

24 I will drive out nations before you and enlarge your territory, and no one will covet your land when you go up three times each year to appear before the Lord your God.

25 Do not offer the blood of a sacrifice to Me along with anything containing yeast, and do not let any of the sacrifice from the Passover Feast remain until morning.

26 Bring the best of the first fruits of your soil to the house of the Lord your God. Do not cook a young goat in its mother's milk."

SEVENTH READING - DAVID - MALCHUT

27 Then the Lord said to Moses, "Write down these words, for in accordance with these words I have made a Covenant with you and with Israel."

28 He was there with the Lord forty days and forty nights without eating bread or drinking water. And he wrote on the Tablets the words of the Covenant—the Ten Utterances.

שָׁלֹשׁ פְּעָמִים

Exodus 34:23—*Pesach, Shavuot*, and *Sukkot*.

The holidays of *Pesach, Shavuot*, and *Sukkot* are referred to in this reading. Throughout the year, there are cosmic windows that connect us to different energies: We connect to freedom on Pesach, to immortality on Shavuot, and to mercy and achieving our potential on Sukkot. By reading about these holidays on this Shabbat, we are fortified with the particular Light of these holidays without having to wait until they come around again.

וְשֵׂה: 20 וּפֶטֶר רפ״ח ע״ה חֲמוֹר תִּפְדֶּה בְשֶׂה וְאִם יוהך ־לֹא תִפְדֶּה וַעֲרַפְתּוֹ

כֹּל יל בְּכוֹר בָּנֶיךָ תִּפְדֶּה וְלֹא־יֵרָאוּ פָנַי וחכמה בינה רֵיקָם: 21 שֵׁשֶׁת יָמִים

גלך תַּעֲבֹד וּבַיּוֹם ע״ה = נגד, זן, מזבח הַשְּׁבִיעִי תִּשְׁבֹּת בֶּחָרִישׁ וּבַקָּצִיר

תִּשְׁבֹּת: 22 וְחַג שָׁבֻעֹת תַּעֲשֶׂה לְךָ בִּכּוּרֵי קְצִיר חִטִּים וְחַג הָאָסִיף

תְּקוּפַת הַשָּׁנָה: 23 ‏⎡שָׁלֹשׁ פְּעָמִים⎤ בַּשָּׁנָה יֵרָאֶה רי״ו, גבורה כָּל יל ־זְכוּרְךָ

אֶת־פְּנֵי וחכמה בינה הָאָדֹן ע״ה אני | יְהוָֹאֲדֹנָֿיֶאֱהֹדוֹנָֿהי ע״ה אני אֱלֹהֵי דמב, ילה יִשְׂרָאֵל: 24 כִּי־

אוֹרִישׁ גּוֹיִם מִפָּנֶיךָ סמ״ב וְהִרְחַבְתִּי אֶת־גְּבֻלֶךָ וְלֹא־יַחְמֹד אִישׁ ע״ה קנ״א קס״א

אֶת־אַרְצְךָ בַּעֲלֹתְךָ לֵרָאוֹת אֶת־פְּנֵי וחכמה בינה יְהוָֹאֲדֹנָֿיֶאֱהֹדוֹנָֿהי אֱלֹהֶיךָ ילה

שָׁלֹשׁ פְּעָמִים בַּשָּׁנָה: 25 לֹא־תִשְׁחַט עַל־חָמֵץ רבוע אהיה דַּם ־זִבְחִי וְלֹא־

יָלִין לַבֹּקֶר זֶבַח חַג הַפָּסַח: 26 רֵאשִׁית בִּכּוּרֵי אַדְמָתְךָ תָּבִיא בֵּית

ב״פ ראה יְהוָֹאֲדֹנָֿיֶאֱהֹדוֹנָֿהי אֱלֹהֶיךָ ילה לֹא־תְבַשֵּׁל גְּדִי והו בַּחֲלֵב אִמּוֹ:

SEVENTH READING - DAVID - MALCHUT

27 וַיֹּאמֶר יְהוָֹאֲדֹנָֿיֶאֱהֹדוֹנָֿהי אֶל־מֹשֶׁה מהע, אל שדי כְּתָב־לְךָ אֶת־הַדְּבָרִים ראה

הָאֵלֶּה כִּי עַל־פִּי הַדְּבָרִים ראה הָאֵלֶּה כָּרַתִּי אִתְּךָ בְּרִית וְאֶת־

יִשְׂרָאֵל: 28 וַיְהִי אל, ייא ־שָׁם יהוה שדי עִם־יְהוָֹאֲדֹנָֿיֶאֱהֹדוֹנָֿהי אַרְבָּעִים יוֹם

ע״ה = נגד, זן, מזבח וְאַרְבָּעִים לַיְלָה מלה לֶחֶם גי׳ פ יהוה לֹא אָכַל וּמַיִם לֹא שָׁתָה

וַיִּכְתֹּב עַל־הַלֻּחֹת אֵת דִּבְרֵי ראה הַבְּרִית עֲשֶׂרֶת הַדְּבָרִים ראה: 29 וַיְהִי

אל, ייא ‏⎡בְּרֶדֶת⎤ מֹשֶׁה מהע, אל שדי מֵהַר מִדְהַר רבוע אלהים ＝ ה סִינַי נגמב, ה״פ יהוה וּשְׁנֵי לֻחֹת

הָעֵדֻת בְּיַד־מֹשֶׁה מהע, אל שדי בְּרִדְתּוֹ מִן־הָהָר וּמֹשֶׁה מהע, אל שדי לֹא־

בְּרֶדֶת

Exodus 34:29—Moses came down from the mountain with the second set of Tablets. He had been on the mountain for forty days and forty nights, during which time he neither ate nor slept. He was not operating under the laws of physicality, but instead was lifted to another dimension.

29 *When Moses came down from Mount Sinai with the two Tablets of the Covenant in Moses' hands, he was not aware that his face was radiant because he had spoken with the Lord.*

30 *When Aaron and all the Israelites saw Moses, his face was radiant, and they were afraid to come near him.* 31 *But Moses called to them; so Aaron and all the leaders of the community came back to him, and Moses spoke to them.*

32 *Afterward all the Israelites came near him, and he commanded them with all that the Lord had told him on Mount Sinai.*

MAFTIR

33 *When Moses finished speaking to them, he put a veil over his face.*

34 *But whenever he entered the Lord's presence to speak with him, he removed the veil until he came out. And when he came out and told the Israelites what he had been commanded,*

35 *they saw that his face was radiant. Then Moses would put the veil back over his face until he went in to speak with Him.*

No human had ever reached this spiritual level before. Moses achieved the impossible. For us to make miracles happen, we have to do what we think is impossible for us. Attempting to do whatever we think impossible is precisely how the Light can be found. Doing the "impossible" is the only way we can reveal Light and find fulfillment.

In the *Zohar*, Rav Shimon speaks to his friends, saying:

> *I now see what no human has seen from the day that Moses ascended Mount Sinai for the second time, since I perceive my face to be illuminating like the powerful sun that is destined to heal the world in the future. It is written: "But to you who fear My Name the sun of righteousness shall arise with healing in its wings."*

> *(Malachi 3:20) Moreover, I am aware that my face is illuminating, but Moses was not aware that the skin on his face was aglow, as it is written: "Moses knew not that the skin of his face shone."'* *(Exodus 34:29)*
> — *The Zohar, Naso, 12:120*

Exodus 34:33—Moses came down from the mountain.

When Moses descended, he had to conceal his face. Moses was on a higher plane and did not connect to the energy of death, as did the people below. In fact, Moses did not die; he left this world by elevating to a higher dimension. If we're on a

יָדַע ב"פ מ"ב כִּי קָרַן עוֹר פָּנָיו בְּדַבְּרוֹ אִתּוֹ: רֹאה 30 וַיַּרְא אלף למד יהוה אַהֲרֹן

ע"ב ורבוע ע"ב יְלִי ־בְּנֵי יִשְׂרָאֵל אֶת־מֹשֶׁה מהע, אל שדי וְהִנֵּה מ"ה יה קָרַן עוֹר

פָּנָיו וַיִּירְאוּ מִגֶּשֶׁת אֵלָיו: 31 וַיִּקְרָא ב"פ קס"א ־ ה אותיות אֲלֵהֶם מֹשֶׁה מהע, אל שדי

וַיָּשֻׁבוּ אֵלָיו אַהֲרֹן ע"ב ורבוע ע"ב יְלִי ־הַנְּשִׂאִים בָּעֵדָה וַיְדַבֵּר רֹאה מֹשֶׁה

מהע, אל שדי אֲלֵהֶם: 32 וְאַחֲרֵי־כֵן נִגְּשׁוּ כָל יְלִי ־בְּנֵי יִשְׂרָאֵל וַיְצַוֵּם אֵת כָּל

־אֲשֶׁר דִּבֶּר רֹאה יְהוָֹוה‎יאהדונהי אִתּוֹ בְּהַר אור, רז סִינָי נמם, ה"פ יהוה:

MAFTIR

33 וַיְכַל מֹשֶׁה מהע, אל שדי מִדַּבֵּר רֹאה אִתָּם וַיִּתֵּן י"פ מלוי ע"ב עַל־פָּנָיו   מַסְוֶה

מ"ה אדני ע"ה 34 וּבְבֹא מֹשֶׁה מהע, אל שדי לִפְנֵי וֹחכמה בינה יְהוָֹוה‎יאהדונהי לְדַבֵּר רֹאה

אִתּוֹ יָסִיר אֶת־הַמַּסְוֶה מ"ה אדני ע"ה עַד־צֵאתוֹ וְיָצָא וְדִבֶּר רֹאה אֶל־בְּנֵי

יִשְׂרָאֵל אֵת אֲשֶׁר יְצֻוֶּה: 35 וְרָאוּ בְנֵי־יִשְׂרָאֵל אֶת־פְּנֵי מֹשֶׁה

מהע, אל שדי כִּי קָרַן עוֹר פְּנֵי מהע, אל שדי חכמה בינה מֹשֶׁה מהע, אל שדי וְהֵשִׁיב מֹשֶׁה

מהע, אל שדי אֶת־הַמַּסְוֶה מ"ה אדני ע"ה עַל־פָּנָיו עַד־בֹּאוֹ לְדַבֵּר רֹאה אִתּוֹ:

---

higher level of consciousness than those around us, we have to conceal ourselves by veiling our knowledge. People don't necessarily want the best from us or for us. We should choose to be with people who are going to help us in this life and who can see through the veil.

The Ari wrote:

When Moses was talking with God and then with Israel, Yesod would have been cleft and the Light revealed. Because [the people of] Israel were ready, he removed the veil and the Light remained exposed, because the Light of Mem-Hei and Samech-Hei was covered with Yesod of Tevunah. So that the Light would not

be seen when [Moses] spoke only to the people, he covered the Light with the two Names Mem-Hei and Samech-Hei, and the Light did not show much. But the cover was not from the Vessel, like Tevunah that covers the two Upper Levels; instead it is a much thicker cover, for Mem-Hei and Samech-Hei are to Aba and Ima as the body to the soul—for that, there was a veil. And after all, the veil (cover) is the body for the Light, so he made it into a veil only, although the illumination of his face shone through the veil.

— Writings of the Ari, Torah Compilations 5, Ki Tisa 36

HAFTARAH OF KI TISA

The Haftarah tells of the duel between Elijah the Prophet and the false prophets of Baal to prove whose God was the real God. The false prophets prayed for their god to create fire on their altar and burn their sacrifice. But nothing happened. Elijah prayed and poured water on his sacrifice to make it even more challenging for the miraculous fire to burn.

I Kings 18:20-39

18:20 So Ahab sent word throughout all Israel and assembled the prophets on Mount Carmel.

21 Elijah went before the people and said, "How long will you waver between two opinions? If the Lord is God, follow him; but if Baal is god, follow him." But the people said nothing.

22 Then Elijah said to them, "I am the only one of the Lord's prophets left, but Baal has four hundred and fifty prophets.

23 Get two bulls for us. Let them choose one for themselves, and let them cut it into pieces and put it on the wood but not set fire to it. I will prepare the other bull and put it on the wood but not set fire to it.

24 Then you call on the name of your god, and I will call on the Name of the Lord. The god who answers by fire—he is God." Then all the people said, "What you say is good."

25 Elijah said to the prophets of Baal, "Choose one of the bulls and prepare it first, since there are so many of you. Call on the name of your god, but do not light the fire."

26 So they took the bull given them and prepared it. Then they called on the name of Baal from morning till noon. "Baal, answer us!" they shouted. But there was no response; no one answered. And they danced around the altar they had made.

27 At noon Elijah began to taunt them. "Shout louder!" he said. "Surely he is a god! Perhaps he is deep in thought, or busy, or traveling. Maybe he is sleeping and must be awakened."

28 So they shouted louder and slashed themselves with swords and spears, as was their custom, until their blood flowed.

HAFTARAH OF KI TISA

Yet, miraculously, fire came from God and consumed the sacrifice in response to Elijah's prayers. We learn from Elijah that when a person is connected to the Light of the Creator, everything is in the realm of possibility. There is nothing that cannot be done.

מלכים א פרק יח

18 20 וַיִּשְׁלַח אַחְאָב בְּכָל בְּנֵי יִשְׂרָאֵל וַיִּקְבֹּץ אֶת־
הַנְּבִיאִים אֶל־הַר הַכַּרְמֶל: 21 וַיִּגַּשׁ אֵלִיָּהוּ אֶל־
כָּל־הָעָם וַיֹּאמֶר עַד־מָתַי אַתֶּם פֹּסְחִים עַל־שְׁתֵּי הַסְּעִפִּים אִם
יְהֹוָה הָאֱלֹהִים לְכוּ אַחֲרָיו וְאִם־
הַבַּעַל לְכוּ אַחֲרָיו וְלֹא־עָנוּ הָעָם אֹתוֹ דָּבָר: 22 וַיֹּאמֶר
אֵלִיָּהוּ אֶל־הָעָם אֲנִי נוֹתַרְתִּי נָבִיא לַיהֹוָה
לְבַדִּי וּנְבִיאֵי הַבַּעַל אַרְבַּע־מֵאוֹת וַחֲמִשִּׁים אִישׁ: 23 וְיִתְּנוּ
לָנוּ שְׁנַיִם פָּרִים וְיִבְחֲרוּ לָהֶם הַפָּר
הָאֶחָד וִינַתְּחֻהוּ וְיָשִׂימוּ עַל־הָעֵצִים וְאֵשׁ לֹא
יָשִׂימוּ וַאֲנִי אֶעֱשֶׂה | אֶת־הַפָּר הָאֶחָד
וְנָתַתִּי עַל־הָעֵצִים וְאֵשׁ לֹא אָשִׂים: 24 וּקְרָאתֶם
בְּשֵׁם אֱלֹהֵיכֶם וַאֲנִי אֶקְרָא בְשֵׁם
יְהֹוָה וְהָיָה הָאֱלֹהִים אֲשֶׁר־יַעֲנֶה בָאֵשׁ
הוּא הָאֱלֹהִים וַיַּעַן כָּל־הָעָם וַיֹּאמְרוּ
טוֹב הַדָּבָר: 25 וַיֹּאמֶר אֵלִיָּהוּ לִנְבִיאֵי הַבַּעַל בַּחֲרוּ
לָכֶם הַפָּר הָאֶחָד וַעֲשׂוּ רִאשֹׁנָה כִּי אַתֶּם
הָרַבִּים וְקִרְאוּ בְּשֵׁם אֱלֹהֵיכֶם וְאֵשׁ לֹא
תָשִׂימוּ: 26 וַיִּקְחוּ אֶת־הַפָּר אֲשֶׁר־נָתַן לָהֶם וַיַּעֲשׂוּ
וַיִּקְרְאוּ בְשֵׁם־הַבַּעַל מֵהַבֹּקֶר וְעַד־הַצָּהֳרַיִם לֵאמֹר הַבַּעַל

29 Midday passed, and they continued their frantic prophesying until the time for the evening sacrifice. But there was no response, no one answered, no one paid attention.

30 Then Elijah said to all the people, "Come here to me." They came to him, and he repaired the altar of the Lord, which was in ruins.

31 Elijah took twelve stones, one for each of the tribes descended from Jacob, to whom the word of the Lord had come, saying, "Your name shall be Israel."

32 With the stones he built an altar in the Name of the Lord, and he dug a trench around it large enough to hold two se'ahs of seed.

33 He arranged the wood, cut the bull into pieces and laid it on the wood.

34 Then he said to them, "Fill four large jars with water and pour it on the offering and on the wood. Do it again," he said, and they did it again. "Do it a third time," he ordered, and they did it the third time.

35 The water ran down around the altar and even filled the trench.

36 At the time of sacrifice, the prophet Elijah stepped forward and prayed: "Lord, God of Abraham, Isaac and Israel, let it be known today that You are God in Israel and that I am Your servant and have done all these things at your command.

37 Answer me, Lord, answer me, so these people will know that You, Lord, are God, and that You are turning their hearts back again."

38 Then the fire of the Lord fell and burned up the sacrifice, the wood, the stones and the soil, and also licked up the water in the trench.

39 When all the people saw this, they fell prostrate, and cried, "The Lord - He is God! The Lord - He is God!"

עֲנוּ וְאֵין קוֹל וְאֵין עֹנֶה וַיְפַסְּחוּ עַל־הַמִּזְבֵּחַ אֲשֶׁר
עָשָׂה: 27 וַיְהִי בַצָּהֳרַיִם וַיְהַתֵּל בָּהֶם אֵלִיָּהוּ וַיֹּאמֶר
קִרְאוּ בְקוֹל־גָּדוֹל כִּי־אֱלֹהִים
הוּא כִּי שִׂיחַ וְכִי־שִׂיג לוֹ וְכִי־דֶרֶךְ לוֹ אוּלַי יָשֵׁן הוּא וְיִקָץ:
28 וַיִּקְרְאוּ בְּקוֹל גָּדוֹל וַיִּתְגֹּדְדוּ כְּמִשְׁפָּטָם
בַּחֲרָבוֹת וּבָרְמָחִים עַד־שְׁפָךְ־דָּם עֲלֵיהֶם: 29 וַיְהִי כַּעֲבֹר
הַצָּהֳרַיִם וַיִּתְנַבְּאוּ עַד לַעֲלוֹת הַמִּנְחָה וְאֵין־קוֹל
וְאֵין־עֹנֶה וְאֵין קָשֶׁב: 30 וַיֹּאמֶר אֵלִיָּהוּ לְכָל־הָעָם
גְּשׁוּ אֵלַי וַיִּגְּשׁוּ כָל־הָעָם אֵלָיו וַיְרַפֵּא אֶת־מִזְבַּח
יְהוָה הֶהָרוּס: 31 וַיִּקַּח אֵלִיָּהוּ שְׁתֵּים עֶשְׂרֵה
אֲבָנִים כְּמִסְפַּר שִׁבְטֵי בְנֵי־יַעֲקֹב אֲשֶׁר הָיָה
דְבַר־יְהוָה אֵלָיו לֵאמֹר יִשְׂרָאֵל יִהְיֶה שְׁמֶךָ: 32 וַיִּבְנֶה
אֶת־הָאֲבָנִים מִזְבֵּחַ בְּשֵׁם יְהוָה וַיַּעַשׂ תְּעָלָה
כְּבֵית סָאתַיִם זֶרַע סָבִיב לַמִּזְבֵּחַ: 33 וַיַּעֲרֹךְ אֶת־הָעֵצִים
וַיְנַתַּח אֶת־הַפָּר וַיָּשֶׂם עַל־הָעֵצִים: 34 וַיֹּאמֶר מִלְאוּ
אַרְבָּעָה כַדִּים מַיִם וְיִצְקוּ עַל־הָעֹלָה וְעַל־הָעֵצִים וַיֹּאמֶר שְׁנוּ
וַיִּשְׁנוּ וַיֹּאמֶר שַׁלֵּשׁוּ וַיְשַׁלֵּשׁוּ: 35 וַיֵּלְכוּ הַמַּיִם סָבִיב
לַמִּזְבֵּחַ וְגַם אֶת־הַתְּעָלָה מִלֵּא־מָיִם: 36 וַיְהִי | בַּעֲלוֹת
הַמִּנְחָה וַיִּגַּשׁ אֵלִיָּהוּ הַנָּבִיא וַיֹּאמַר יְהוָה
אֱלֹהֵי אַבְרָהָם יִצְחָק וְיִשְׂרָאֵל הַיּוֹם
יִוָּדַע כִּי־אַתָּה אֱלֹהִים בְּיִשְׂרָאֵל וַאֲנִי עַבְדֶּךָ
וּבִדְבָרְךָ (כתיב: ובדבריך) עָשִׂיתִי אֵת כָּל־הַדְּבָרִים הָאֵלֶּה:
37 עֲנֵנִי יְהוָה עֲנֵנִי וְיֵדְעוּ הָעָם הַזֶּה כִּי־אַתָּה יְהוָה
הָאֱלֹהִים וְאַתָּה הֲסִבֹּתָ אֶת־לִבָּם אֲחֹרַנִּית: 38 וַתִּפֹּל אֵשׁ־
יְהוָה וַתֹּאכַל אֶת־הָעֹלָה וְאֶת־הָעֵצִים וְאֶת־
הָאֲבָנִים וְאֶת־הֶעָפָר וְאֶת־הַמַּיִם אֲשֶׁר־בַּתְּעָלָה לִחֵכָה: 39 וַיַּרְא
כָּל־הָעָם וַיִּפְּלוּ עַל־פְּנֵיהֶם וַיֹּאמְרוּ יְהוָה הוּא
הָאֱלֹהִים יְהוָה הוּא הָאֱלֹהִים:

VAYAK'HEL

LESSON OF VAYAK'HEL
(Exodus 35:1-38:20)

"And all the congregation, the children of Israel departed from the presence of Moses." (*Exodus 35:20*)

Why is it written that "...the children of Israel departed?" In truth, it was their physical selves that "departed," but their souls turned inward. There is a very important lesson about those who seek to go within for the purpose of growing spiritually. They will receive wisdom, a connection to a righteous person, the totality of the Bible, and the Light of the Creator.

On the other hand, Rav Menachem Mendel of Kotzk (1787–1859) wrote that if we pray and yet remain unchanged internally, it is worse than if we hadn't prayed at all—in truth, we are actually considered wicked people. The reason why some people remain unchanged by their prayers is that they do not extend themselves; they do not go inward, nor do they open themselves to the Light of the Creator.

The chapter of Vayak'hel offers us another opportunity to connect to the power of renewal—to become transformed, newly open to receive the Creator's Light.

The goal of spiritual work is not just to show up to "worship" on Shabbat. The real purpose for participating in a Shabbat is to make a connection to the Light so that we can use it throughout the week. And what is even more important than simply making the connection with the Light of the Creator is that we make use of this Light and that it remains with us in the days that follow.

There is a story of poor man named Josef who lived long ago in Jerusalem. He desperately needed to find work to support himself and his family. One night, Josef had a dream about a treasure buried under the palace in the city of Vilna in Lithuania. Although Vilna was in northern Europe, thousands of miles from Jerusalem, Josef resolved to go there to find the treasure.

The journey took four months. When Josef arrived at the palace, he was immediately confronted by the king's guards. Josef was tempted to lie about the reason for his long journey. But he decided that telling the truth was a better course of action, since he hadn't done anything wrong. So Josef told the captain about his dream.

As the captain listened to Josef, he laughed. "If I listened to all my dreams, I'd be in Jerusalem right now. You see, just last night I had a dream about a man who has a treasure buried under his house!"

At the instant the words left the captain's mouth, Josef understood the real reason for his journey: It was to learn that the treasure was, after all, under his own home.

The lesson in this familiar story is that the treasure we seek is right in our own backyard. But for me, the deeper lesson is in the understanding that when we make our connections on Shabbat or holidays, "going to the service" is not the end goal but rather, the means to an end goal. We have not finished the job just by making the journey, that is, by saying the prayers and listening to the Bible story. It is what happens afterwards that is the key: We must return to our lives, to our homes, and take action there with the Light we have received.

The secret of the truth

Although the chapter this week refers to the Tabernacle and to our connection to it, we must understand that, as in all things Kabbalah, preparation is the real work, the real connection, the real fulfillment. The work to be done in this instance involves two principles. One is truth—what is true and what is not true, both globally and in our personal lives. The second is ownership— what truly belongs to us and what only seems to belong to us. Many of us think that we are the true "owners" of our money and our physical possessions. But in truth, those possessions are temporary—here one day and gone the next—because they do not really belong to us. Only our spiritual actions belong to us, and they belong to us forever.

Our sages explain this with a story that is a metaphor for our lives.

A man named Jacob had three friends: Reuben, Simon, and Levi. Jacob loved Reuben very much and always wanted to spend time with him, and he thought that Reuben loved him in return. He did not like Simon as much as he did Reuben, but he still spent a good deal of time with Simon. Jacob didn't see Levi very often, as he considered Levi to be only an acquaintance.

It came to pass that Jacob received an order to appear before the king. Jacob reasoned that one of his enemies must have said something disparaging about him. He decided, therefore, to take one of his friends with him so that the friend could speak on his behalf.

Jacob asked his good friend, Reuben, if he would appear with him before the king. But Reuben was afraid to associate himself with Jacob in this uncomfortable situation.

Jacob was terribly hurt when Reuben refused him, but he continued and asked Simon. Simon, too, refused to put himself in jeopardy.

Having no choice, Jacob approached Levi. This seemed hopeless, as Levi was just an acquaintance. Surprisingly, however, Levi answered that he would of course appear before the king with his good friend, Jacob. "This is exactly what friends are for, is it not?" Levi asked. "When a friend needs you, you have to help, no matter what."

If we have a true desire to reveal the Light, we will find a way to do it—and sometimes, that way appears before us quite unexpectedly. This is the message of the story. The truth is, there is always a way. Even when the friends whom we thought were dependable and trustworthy prove not to be, we can turn this disappointment to our blessing by discovering new friends of great value who were previously unknown to us. In this story, Jacob's first two friends symbolize the material possessions and relationships to which we attach such importance. But Levi, the third friend, symbolizes the Light that is always there for us, if only we choose to trust and reveal it.

Rav Berg explains that the biblical chapter of Vayak'hel is the same as Terumah—except for the lack of the offerings from the *erev rav* (the mixed multitude, or wicked people). In Vayak'hel the Tabernacle is built without their contributions—and therefore, without the consciousness of evil people. Any negative consciousness involved in the process of building the Tabernacle would have prevented the Tabernacle from removing chaos from the world. Even today, money should never be accepted from the *erev rav*.

The Rav teaches that the Tabernacle itself was a representation of physical man, so that the skins and the boards are the physical structure of a human being. The items in the Tabernacle were tools to tap into the Lightforce. The *Kohen HaGadol* (High Priest) wore his special garments to elevate his consciousness.

The Rav says that even with all these tools to help us make our connection, there is still, unfortunately, no school that teaches human dignity; that teaches how to live by the precept of "Love your neighbor." This precept is of supreme importance because it is only when we treat others with tolerance and acceptance that we remove our *Desire to Receive for the Self Alone*. The *Desire to Receive* doesn't exist within God. And only when we eliminate this desire from ourselves that we become like God, which means that we don't need to turn to the Creator to remove chaos from our lives: We can do it ourselves.

SYNOPSIS OF VAYAK'HEL

Much of Vayak'hel repeats the preceding chapters of Terumah and Tetzaveh. The story is told again here because following the incident of the Golden Calf, the *erev rav* injected the energy of hatred. Before the Golden Calf, there was no energy of death and everyone was invited into the Tabernacle. But after the Golden Calf, the erev rav embodied the energy of hatred and death and were therefore, banned from the Tabernacle, preventing the energy of death from entering. Likewise, our hatred can cause us to disconnect from the Light and connect to death.

FIRST READING - ABRAHAM - CHESED

35:1 **M**oses assembled the whole Israelite community and said to them, "These are the things the Lord has commanded to do:

2 For six days, work is to be done, but the seventh day shall be your holy day, a Sabbath of rest to the Lord. Whoever does any work on it will die.

3 Do not light a fire in any of your dwellings on the Sabbath day."

4 Moses said to the whole Israelite community, "This is what the Lord has commanded:

5 Take from what you have a contribution for the Lord. Everyone who is willing is to bring to the Lord an offering of gold, silver and bronze;

FROM THE RAV

Human Dignity
The previous chapter of Terumah is duplicated here in the chapter of Vayak'hel because the earlier chapter included the consciousness of evil people known as the *erev rav* (the mixed multitude). The repetition stresses how much our consciousness weighs and influences this physical reality. And therefore if we think we can removechaos by physical methodologies, we're still going along the path of the erev rav, the anti-kabbalists. We're still hovering around this expectation and hope for a better world, based on the superiority of physicality. And my friends, it hasn't worked for three thousand four hundred years, and there is no question that it will never achieve the removal of chaos.

The chaos that exists today comes and goes—seemingly by some new physical development, or some new physical advancement. Only again to crumble and again thrust the entire world back into a chaotic condition.

Vayak'hel concerns the environment and how we deal with everything and everyone around us. Are we respectful? Do we treat others with dignity? Or is it just our personal domain that we take care of, dismissing everything and everyone else?

By participating in this reading, we strengthen our consciousness to treat everything and everyone in all areas outside of ourselves with human dignity. It is not an easy task to constantly be in a consciousness of human dignity. And this task is made even more difficult by Satan who is so old and so experienced at manipulating us and maneuvering us away from having respect for and treating others with dignity.

שַׁבָּת

Exodus 35:2—**The power of Shabbat**
The power of Shabbat is one of the strongest ways to connect to God. This connection can be made by anyone of any faith. Shabbat is not a religious experience meant for Jewish people only; it is a technology meant for all. If we commit even five minutes on Shabbat toward a connection to the Light, it will be easier to

FIRST READING - ABRAHAM - CHESED

35 1 וַיַּקְהֵל קְנ"א, מקוה מֹשֶׁה מהוע, אל עדי אֶת־כָּל יוי ־עֲדַת בְּנֵי יִשְׂרָאֵל

וַיֹּאמֶר אֲלֵהֶם אֵלֶּה הַדְּבָרִים ראה אֲשֶׁר ־צִוָּה פוי יְהוָֹאדניליאהדונהי לַעֲשֹׂת

אֹתָם: 2 שֵׁשֶׁת יָמִים נכך תֵּעָשֶׂה מְלָאכָה אל ארני ובֵיּוֹם ע"ה = נגד, זן, מזבח

הַשְּׁבִיעִי יִהְיֶה ... לָכֶם קֹדֶשׁ שַׁבַּת שַׁבָּתוֹן לַיהוָֹאדניליאהדונהי כֹּל יוי ־

הָעֹשֶׂה בוֹ מְלָאכָה אל ארני יוּמָת: 3 לֹא־תְבַעֲרוּ אֵשׁ אלהים דיורין ע"ה בְּכֹל

בּ"ן, לכב, יבם מֹשְׁבֹתֵיכֶם בְּיוֹם ע"ה = נגד, זן, מזבח הַשַּׁבָּת מהוע, מזבח: 4 וַיֹּאמֶר מֹשֶׁה מהוע, אל עדי

אֶל־כָּל יוי ־עֲדַת בְּנֵי־יִשְׂרָאֵל לֵאמֹר זֶה הַדָּבָר ראה אֲשֶׁר־צִוָּה פוי

יְהוָֹאדניליאהדונהי לֵאמֹר: 5 קְחוּ מֵאִתְּכֶם תְּרוּמָה לַיהוָֹאדניליאהדונהי כֹּל יוי

נְדִיב לִבּוֹ יְבִיאֶהָ אֵת תְּרוּמַת יְהוָֹאדניליאהדונהי זָהָב וָכֶסֶף וּנְחֹשֶׁת:

---

connect to the energy of the Creator at any other time during the week. Rav Isaac Luria (the Ari), explains:

> "During the weekdays, the lines between good and evil are somewhat blurred. This makes it very easy to slip into the trap of materialism and egocentricity, so one must be constantly on guard, as opposed to Shabbat, when Satan is held at a distance. Since Malchut ascends by itself on Shabbat, it is not necessary for us to engage actively in the process of elevating sparks of Light on the Sabbath as we do during the work week. Instead, our spiritual work is to leave aside certain types of physical work that could create separation from this higher level of Light (Binah)."
> —Writings of the Ari, Torah Compilations

תְּרוּמָה

Exodus 35:5—Contributions to the Tabernacle.

When Moses was directing the construction of the Tabernacle, anyone whose heart moved them to charity was asked to bring donations for the new building.

He opened and said, "Take from among you an offering to God: whoever is of a willing heart, let him bring it...." (Exodus 35:5) Come and see, when a man wills himself to worship his Master, the will first reaches the heart, which is the basis and foundation of the entire body. Then that goodwill is diffused in all the members of the body; and the will of the members of the body and the will of the heart combine, and draw to themselves the splendor of the Shechinah to rest on them. Such a man becomes the portion of the Holy One, blessed be He. This is implied in "Take from among you an offering," that is, drawing to receive upon you that offering, WHICH IS THE SHECHINAH, so that THIS MAN would be a portion to God.
— The Zohar, Vayak'hel 5:71

When we tithe or give charity, it is vital do so with a pure and generous heart; otherwise, the act of giving won't impart any spiritual benefit. When our heart is glad and when we are conscious that the act of sharing brings more into both our own lives and the world by revealing Light, then the power of our donation becomes activated.

6 blue, purple and scarlet yarn and fine linen; goat hair; 7 ram skins dyed red and seal skins, acacia wood;

8 olive oil for the light; spices for the anointing oil and for the fragrant incense; 9 and onyx stones and other gems for the ephod and breastplate.

10 All who are skilled among you are to come and make everything the Lord has commanded: 11 the Tabernacle with its tent and its covering, clasps, frames, crossbars, pillars and sockets;

12 the Ark with its poles and the atonement cover and the curtain that shields it;

13 the table with its poles and all its articles and the bread of the Presence;

14 the candelabra that is for light with its accessories, lamps and oil for the light;

15 the altar of incense with its poles, the anointing oil and the fragrant incense; the curtain for the doorway at the entrance to the Tabernacle;

16 the altar of burnt offering with its bronze grating, its poles and all its utensils; the bronze basin with its stand;

17 the curtains of the courtyard with its pillars and sockets, and the curtain for the entrance to the courtyard;

18 the tent pegs for the Tabernacle and the tent pegs for the courtyard, and their ropes; 19 the woven garments worn for ministering in the sanctuary—both the sacred garments for Aaron the priest and the garments for his sons when they serve as priests." 20 Then the whole Israelite community withdrew from Moses' presence,

---

...Anybody who desires to endeavor for Torah merits it. The striving after the Holy One, blessed be He, is to know Him; for anyone who desires it will merit it without any payment whatsoever. But if the striving after the Holy One, blessed be He, is in the form of an action, it is prohibited to perform that action empty-handed and in vain, because one will not merit the drawing down of a spirit of holiness unless he pays in full.
— The Zohar, Terumah 6:35

פָּרֹכֶת הַמָּסָךְ

Exodus 35:12—The Holy of Holies was separated from the rest of the Tabernacle.

There was a division between the Holy of Holies and the rest of the Tabernacle. This teaches us that there are distinctions in life between what is ordinary and what is very special. The opportunities that Shabbat, Rosh Chodesh, and the holidays give us, in particular, are unique. It is valuable to know about these windows of time so that we can make a special effort and focus all of our energy on our connection.

For that reason, none is allowed into the Holy of Holies IN THIS WORLD except for the High Priest that comes from the aspect of Chesed, since no one enters that place above, THAT IS, YESOD OF MALCHUT CALLED ZION except that which is called Chesed OF ZEIR ANPIN, THE ASPECT OF THE HIGH PRIEST that enters the Holy of Holies. Malchut

6 וּתְכֵלֶת וְאַרְגָּמָן קנ״א קמ״ג וְתוֹלַעַת שקוצי״ת שָׁנִי וְשֵׁשׁ וְעִזִּים: 7 וְעֹרֹת אֵילִם

מְאָדָּמִים וְעֹרֹת תְּחָשִׁים וַעֲצֵי שִׁטִּים: 8 וְשֶׁמֶן י״פ טל, י״פ כוזו; ביט לַמָּאוֹר

וּבְשָׂמִים עצ״ב = ג׳ מלוי אהיה לְשֶׁמֶן י״פ טל, י״פ כוזו; ביט הַמִּשְׁחָה וְלִקְטֹרֶת י״א אדני

הַסַּמִּים ע״ה קנ״א, אלהים אדני: 9 וְאַבְנֵי־שֹׁהַם מהש, אל שדי וְאַבְנֵי מִלֻּאִים לָאֵפוֹד

יהוה אדני וְלַחֹשֶׁן: 10 וְכָל־חֲכַם־לֵב יל״י חוזכם בינה ע״ה בָּכֶם יָבֹאוּ וְיַעֲשׂוּ אֵת

כָּל־אֲשֶׁר צִוָּה יל״י פוי יְהוָֹאהדונה״י ב״פ (רבוע אלהים ‒ ה) 11 אֶת־הַמִּשְׁכָּן אֶת־

אָהֳלוֹ וְאֶת־מִכְסֵהוּ אֶת־קְרָסָיו וְאֶת־קְרָשָׁיו אֶת־בְּרִיחָו אֶת־עַמֻּדָיו

וְאֶת־אֲדָנָיו: 12 אֶת־הָאָרֹן ע״ב ורבוע ע״ב וְאֶת־בַּדָּיו אֶת־הַכַּפֹּרֶת וְאֵת

13 אֶת־הַשֻּׁלְחָן וְאֶת־בַּדָּיו וְאֶת־כָּל־ יל״י כֵּלָיו וְאֵת

לֶחֶם ג״פ יהוה הַפָּנִים ע״ב ס״ג מ״ה: 14 וְאֶת־מְנֹרַת הַמָּאוֹר וְאֶת־כֵּלֶיהָ וְאֶת־

נֵרֹתֶיהָ וְאֵת שֶׁמֶן הַמָּאוֹר י״פ טל, ביט י״פ כוזו; הַ וְאֶת־מִזְבַּח זן, נגד הַקְּטֹרֶת

י״א אדני וְאֶת־בַּדָּיו וְאֵת שֶׁמֶן הַמִּשְׁחָה י״פ טל, י״פ כוזו; ביט וְאֵת קְטֹרֶת י״א אדני

הַסַּמִּים ע״ה קנ״א, אלהים אדני וְאֶת־מָסַךְ הַפֶּתַח לְפֶתַח הַמִּשְׁכָּן ב״פ (רבוע אלהים ‒ ה)⸪

16 אֵת | מִזְבַּח זן, נגד הָעֹלָה וְאֶת־מִכְבַּר הַנְּחֹשֶׁת אֲשֶׁר־לוֹ אֶת־בַּדָּיו

וְאֶת־כָּל־ יל״י כֵּלָיו אֶת־הַכִּיֹּר וְאֶת־כַּנּוֹ: 17 אֵת קַלְעֵי הֶחָצֵר אֶת־

עַמֻּדָיו וְאֶת־אֲדָנֶיהָ וְאֵת מָסַךְ שַׁעַר הֶחָצֵר: 18 אֶת־יִתְדֹת הַמִּשְׁכָּן

ב״פ (רבוע אלהים ‒ ה) וְאֶת־יִתְדֹת הֶחָצֵר וְאֶת־מֵיתְרֵיהֶם: 19 אֶת־בִּגְדֵי הַשְּׂרָד

לְשָׁרֵת בַּקֹּדֶשׁ אֶת־בִּגְדֵי הַקֹּדֶשׁ לְאַהֲרֹן ע״ב ורבוע ע״ב הַכֹּהֵן מלה וְאֶת־

בִּגְדֵי בָנָיו לְכַהֵן מלה: 20 וַיֵּצְאוּ כָּל־ יל״י עֲדַת בְּנֵי־יִשְׂרָאֵל מִלִּפְנֵי חכמה

בינה מֹשֶׁה מהש, אל שדי:⸪

---

is mitigated and the Holy of Holies is blessed to its innermost, WHICH IS the place called Zion. Zion and Jerusalem are two grades—one Mercy and the other Judgment. Zion IS MERCY, as written, "Zion shall be redeemed with justice,"

(Isaiah 1:27) JUSTICE BEING MERCY; Jerusalem IS JUDGMENT as written, "righteousness lodged in it," (Ibid. 21) RIGHTEOUSNESS BEING JUDGMENT as we explained.

— The Zohar, Ha'azinu 47:194

ON A LEAP YEAR: SECOND READING - ISAAC - GEVURAH

[21] *and everyone who was willing and whose heart moved him came and brought an offering to the Lord for the work on the Tent of Meeting, for all its service, and for the sacred garments.*

[22] *All who were willing, men and women, came and brought gold jewelry of all kinds: brooches, earrings, rings and ornaments. They all presented their gold as a wave offering to the Lord.*

[23] *Everyone who had blue, purple or scarlet yarn or fine linen, or goat hair, ram skins dyed red or seal skins brought them.* [24] *Those presenting an offering of silver or bronze brought it as an offering to the Lord, and everyone who had acacia wood for any part of the work brought it.*

[25] *Every skilled woman spun with her hands and brought what she had spun—blue, purple or scarlet yarn or fine linen.*

[26] *And all the women who were willing and had the skill spun the goat hair.* [27] *The leaders brought onyx stones and other gems for the ephod and breastplate.*

[28] *They also brought spices and olive oil for the light and for the anointing oil and for the fragrant incense.* [29] *All the Israelite men and women who were willing brought to the Lord freewill offerings for all the work the Lord through Moses had commanded them to do.*

WHEN CONNECTED: SECOND READING - ISAAC - GEVURAH
ON A LEAP YEAR: THIRD READING - JACOB - TIFERET

[30] *Then Moses said to the Israelites, "See, the Lord has chosen Betzalel son of Uri, the son of Hur, of the tribe of Judah,*

בְּצַלְאֵל

Exodus 35:30—The builders of the Tabernacle.

Moses said there would be two people who would help to build the Tabernacle: Oholiab and Betzalel. Although Bezalel was only 12 years of age, he was already a pure channel. The Zohar speaks about the roles of Moses, Betzalel, and Oholiab in this way:

...Moses withdrew FROM THE CONSTRUCTION OF THE TABERNACLE, and gave his place to another, BECAUSE HE WANTED OTHERS TO HAVE THE MERIT. So God told him, "See, I have called by name Bezalel...and with him Oholiab." (Exodus 31:2) And it is written, "And Betzalel and Oholiab, and every wisehearted man." (Exodus 36:1) And if that honor was reserved for Moses,

ON A LEAP YEAR: SECOND READING - ISAAC - GEVURAH

21 וַיָּבֹאוּ כָּל־אִישׁ עה קנ"א קס"א אֲשֶׁר־נְשָׂאוֹ לִבּוֹ וְכֹל יֹלי אֲשֶׁר נָדְבָה
רוּחוֹ אֹתוֹ הֵבִיאוּ אֶת־תְּרוּמַת יְהֹוָה אהדונהי לִמְלֶאכֶת אֹהֶל מוֹעֵד
וּלְכָל־עֲבֹדָתוֹ וּלְבִגְדֵי הַקֹּדֶשׁ: 22 וַיָּבֹאוּ הָאֲנָשִׁים עַל־הַנָּשִׁים
כֹּל נְדִיב לֵב הֵבִיאוּ חָח וָנֶזֶם וְטַבַּעַת וְכוּמָז כָּל־כְּלִי זָהָב
וְכָל־אִישׁ עה קנ"א קס"א אֲשֶׁר הֵנִיף תְּנוּפַת זָהָב לַיהֹוָה אהדונהי: 23 וְכָל־
אִישׁ יֹלי קנ"א קס"א אֲשֶׁר־נִמְצָא אִתּוֹ תְּכֵלֶת וְאַרְגָּמָן קנ"א קמ"ג וְתוֹלַעַת
שָׁנִי וְשֵׁשׁ וְעִזִּים וְעֹרֹת אֵילִם מְאָדָּמִים וְעֹרֹת תְּחָשִׁים הֵבִיאוּ:
24 כָּל־מֵרִים תְּרוּמַת כֶּסֶף וּנְחֹשֶׁת הֵבִיאוּ אֵת תְּרוּמַת יְהֹוָה אהדונהי
וְכֹל אֲשֶׁר נִמְצָא אִתּוֹ עֲצֵי שִׁטִּים לְכָל־מְלֶאכֶת הָעֲבֹדָה
הֵבִיאוּ: 25 וְכָל־אִשָּׁה חַכְמַת־לֵב בְּיָדֶיהָ טָווּ וַיָּבִיאוּ מַטְוֶה אֶת־
הַתְּכֵלֶת וְאֶת־הָאַרְגָּמָן קנ"א קמ"ג אֶת־תּוֹלַעַת הַשָּׁנִי וְאֶת־הַשֵּׁשׁ:
26 וְכָל־הַנָּשִׁים אֲשֶׁר נָשָׂא לִבָּן אֹתָנָה בְּחָכְמָה טָווּ אֶת־הָעִזִּים:
27 וְהַנְּשִׂאִם הֵבִיאוּ אֵת אַבְנֵי הַשֹּׁהַם וְאֵת אַבְנֵי הַמִּלֻּאִים
לָאֵפוֹד וְלַחֹשֶׁן: 28 וְאֶת־הַבֹּשֶׂם וְאֶת־הַשָּׁמֶן לַמָּאוֹר
וּלְשֶׁמֶן הַמִּשְׁחָה וְלִקְטֹרֶת הַסַּמִּים: 29 כָּל־אִישׁ עה קנ"א קס"א וְאִשָּׁה אֲשֶׁר נָדַב לִבָּם אֹתָם לְהָבִיא לְכָל־
הַמְּלָאכָה אֲשֶׁר צִוָּה יְהֹוָה אהדונהי לַעֲשׂוֹת בְּיַד־מֹשֶׁה
הֵבִיאוּ בְנֵי־יִשְׂרָאֵל נְדָבָה לַיהֹוָה אהדונהי:

WHEN CONNECTED: SECOND READING - ISAAC - GEVURAH
ON A LEAP YEAR: THIRD READING - JACOB - TIFERET

30 וַיֹּאמֶר מֹשֶׁה אֶל־בְּנֵי יִשְׂרָאֵל רְאוּ קָרָא יְהֹוָה אהדונהי
בְּשֵׁם בְּצַלְאֵל בֶּן־אוּרִי בֶן־חוּר לְמַטֵּה יְהוּדָה: 31 וַיְמַלֵּא אֹתוֹ

31 and he has filled him with the Spirit of God, with skill, ability and knowledge in all kinds of crafts, 32 to make designs for work in gold, silver and bronze, 33 to cut and set stones, to work in wood and to engage in all kinds of artistic craftsmanship.

34 And he has given both him and Oholiab son of Achisamach, of the tribe of Dan, the ability to teach others.

35 He has filled them with skill to do all kinds of work as craftsmen, designers, embroiderers in blue, purple and scarlet yarn and fine linen, and weavers—all of them master craftsmen and designers.

36:1 So Betzalel, Oholiab and every skilled person to whom the Lord has given skill and ability to know how to carry out all the work of constructing the sanctuary are to do the work just as the Lord has commanded."

2 Then Moses summoned Betzalel and Oholiab and every skilled person to whom the Lord had given ability and who was willing to come and do the work.

3 They took from Moses all the offerings the Israelites had brought to carry out the work of constructing the sanctuary. And the people continued to bring freewill offerings morning after morning.

4 So all the skilled craftsmen who were doing all the work on the sanctuary left their work

5 and said to Moses, "The people are bringing more than enough for doing the work the Lord commanded to be done."

6 Then Moses gave an order and they sent this word throughout the camp: "No man or woman is to make anything else as an offering for the sanctuary." And so the people were restrained from bringing more,

7 because what they already had was more than enough to do all the work.

---

that he would [be the one to] make THE TABERNACLE, AS IT IS WRITTEN, "AND SEE THAT YOU MAKE," it would have been forever his. WHY THEN DID GOD ORDER, "AND BEZALEL AND OHOLIAB...DID?" BECAUSE FROM THIS WE UNDERSTAND, THAT MOSES HIMSELF WITHDREW FROM THE WORK TO GIVE MERIT TO OTHERS.
— The Zohar, Pekudei 40:400

Part of our spiritual work is to constantly seek out our mission in life. The promptings of our soul—often initiated by feelings of discontent and unhappiness—tell us that we should be channeling our energy toward an altogether different purpose. We must listen to these promptings, even if we can only move one small step at a time. If, on the other hand, we are blessed to be doing what we are called to do, we need to ask ourselves whether we are giving 100 percent of our energy to the task. It is important to be aware of our own agendas regarding our reputation or our need for approval. Far too often, we fail to give others their due credit.

The contents of the Tabernacle are described once again, as they were in Terumah.

רוּחַ מלוי אלהים דיודין אֱלֹהִים מום, אהיה אדני ; ילה בְּחָכְמָה בִּתְבוּנָה וּבְדַעַת

וּבְכָל בן, לכב, יבם ־מְלָאכָה אל אדני 32 וְלַחְשֹׁב מַחֲשָׁבֹת לַעֲשֹׂת בַּזָּהָב

וּבַכֶּסֶף וּבַנְּחֹשֶׁת: 33 וּבַחֲרֹשֶׁת אֶבֶן יוד הה ואו הה לְמַלֹּאת וּבַחֲרֹשֶׁת עֵץ

עה קסא לַעֲשׂוֹת בְּכָל בן, לכב, יבם ־מְלֶאכֶת מַחֲשָׁבֶת: 34 וּלְהוֹרֹת נָתַן

בְּלִבּוֹ הוּא וְאָהֳלִיאָב בֶּן־אֲחִיסָמָךְ לְמַטֵּה־דָן: 35 מִלֵּא אֹתָם חָכְמַת־

לֵב לַעֲשׂוֹת כָּל יִלי ־מְלֶאכֶת חָרָשׁ | וְחֹשֵׁב וְרֹקֵם בַּתְּכֵלֶת וּבָאַרְגָּמָן

קנא קמג בְּתוֹלַעַת שקרציה הַשָּׁנִי וּבַשֵּׁשׁ וְאֹרֵג עֹשֵׂי כָּל יִלי ־מְלָאכָה אל אדני

וְחֹשְׁבֵי מַחֲשָׁבֹת: 36 1 וְעָשָׂה בְצַלְאֵל וְאָהֳלִיאָב וְכֹל יִלי ־אִישׁ עה קנא קסא

וְחַכַם־ ווייס, בינה עה ־לֵב אֲשֶׁר נָתַן יְהוָֹהאהדיאהרונהי חָכְמָה וּתְבוּנָה בָּהֵמָּה

לָדַעַת לַעֲשֹׂת אֶת־כָּל יִלי ־מְלֶאכֶת עֲבֹדַת הַקֹּדֶשׁ לְכֹל יה אדני אֲשֶׁר־

צִוָּה פוי יְהוָֹהאהדיאהרונהי: 2 וַיִּקְרָא בפ קסא א ־ ה אותיות מֹשֶׁה מהש, אל שדי אֶל־

בְּצַלְאֵל וְאֶל־אָהֳלִיאָב וְאֶל כָּל יִלי ־אִישׁ עה קנא קסא ־חֲכַם־ ווייס, בינה עה ־לֵב אֲשֶׁר נָתַן יְהוָֹהאהדיאהרונהי חָכְמָה בְּלִבּוֹ כֹּל יִלי אֲשֶׁר נְשָׂאוֹ לִבּוֹ

לְקָרְבָה אֶל־הַמְּלָאכָה אל אדני לַעֲשֹׂת אֹתָהּ: 3 וַיִּקְחוּ וועם מִלִּפְנֵי וחכמה בינה

מֹשֶׁה מהש, אל שדי אֵת כָּל יִלי ־הַתְּרוּמָה אֲשֶׁר הֵבִיאוּ בְּנֵי יִשְׂרָאֵל

לִמְלֶאכֶת עֲבֹדַת הַקֹּדֶשׁ לַעֲשֹׂת אֹתָהּ וְהֵם הֵבִיאוּ אֵלָיו עוֹד נְדָבָה

וויים בַּבֹּקֶר בַּבֹּקֶר: 4 וַיָּבֹאוּ כָּל יִלי ־הַחֲכָמִים הָעֹשִׂים אֶת כָּל יִלי

מְלֶאכֶת הַקֹּדֶשׁ אִישׁ עה קנא קסא ־אִישׁ עה קנא קסא ־מִמְּלַאכְתּוֹ אֲשֶׁר־

הֵמָּה עֹשִׂים: 5 וַיֹּאמְרוּ אֶל־מֹשֶׁה מהש, אל שדי לֵאמֹר מַרְבִּים הָעָם

לְהָבִיא מִדֵּי הָעֲבֹדָה לַמְּלָאכָה אל אדני אֲשֶׁר־צִוָּה פוי יְהוָֹהאהדיאהרונהי

לַעֲשֹׂת אֹתָהּ: 6 וַיְצַו מֹשֶׁה מהש, אל שדי וַיַּעֲבִירוּ קוֹל עב סג עה בַּמַּחֲנֶה

לֵאמֹר אִישׁ עה קנא קסא ־וְאִשָּׁה אַל־יַעֲשׂוּ־עוֹד מְלָאכָה אל אדני לִתְרוּמַת

הַקֹּדֶשׁ וַיִּכָּלֵא הָעָם מֵהָבִיא: 7 וְהַמְּלָאכָה אל אדני הָיְתָה דַיָּם לְכָל יה אדני

־הַמְּלָאכָה אל אדני לַעֲשׂוֹת אֹתָהּ וְהוֹתֵר:

ON A LEAP YEAR: FOURTH READING - MOSES - NETZACH

8 All the skilled men among the workmen made the Tabernacle with ten curtains of finely twisted linen and blue, purple and scarlet yarn, with cherubim worked into them by a skilled craftsman.

9 The length of one curtain was twenty-eight cubits long and four cubits wide—all the curtains were the same size.

10 He joined five of the curtains together and did the same with the other five.

11 Then he made loops of blue material along the edge of the end curtain in one set, and the same was done with the end curtain in the other set.

12 He also made fifty loops on one curtain and fifty loops on the end curtain of the other set, with the loops opposite each other.

13 Then he made fifty gold clasps and used them to fasten the two sets of curtains together so that the Tabernacle was one.

14 He made curtains of goat hair for the tent over the Tabernacle—eleven altogether.

15 The length of one curtain was thirty cubits long and four cubits wide—all eleven curtains were the same size.

יְרִיעֹת

Exodus 36:8—The ten inner curtains of the Tabernacle. The *Zohar* says:

There are curtains and curtains. The curtains of the Tabernacle are called the firmaments of the beasts of the Holy Tabernacle. The curtains of goats' hair [on the other hand], are different firmaments, of the Other Side. These firmaments OF THE TABERNACLE [carry] the secret of the Chariots of the Holy Spirits, and these firmaments without, THE CURTAINS OF GOATS HAIR, shine with worldly matters, and are considered aspects of repentance and bodily worship FROM BY THE INHABITANTS OF THE WORLD. And they cover the firmaments inside as a skull covers the brain. The firmaments inside are like a thin MEMBRANE around the brain, and are called "the heavens of God," NAMELY the one name

YUD, HEI, VAV AND HEI, down below IN MALCHUT.
— The Zohar, Vayak'hel 25:360

The curtains of the Tabernacle are symbolic of the things that remain veiled from us in our own lives. They remind us of the importance of our spiritual work in discovering those things about ourselves that we need to transform.

עַשְׁתֵּי־עֶשְׂרֵה

Exodus 36:14—This section describes the eleven outer coverings of the Tabernacle.

There are ten dimensions in this universe, corresponding to the *Ten Sefirot*, the Tree of Life. The eleventh level, represented by the eleventh covering, is the dimension where Satan lives. It reminds us that we need to give to Satan the food he requires. In doing so, Satan is distracted with his "light" that he has been given and will not interfere in our own connection with the Light. In other words, we have re-directed Satan's radar away from us.

ON A LEAP YEAR: FOURTH READING - MOSES - NETZACH

8 וַיַּעֲשׂוּ כָל יכי חֲכַם לֵב בְּעֹשֵׂי הַמְּלָאכָה אל אדני אֶת הַמִּשְׁכָּן ב"פ (רבוע אלהים - ה) עֶשֶׂר יְרִיעֹת שֵׁשׁ מָשְׁזָר וּתְכֵלֶת וְאַרְגָּמָן וְתוֹלַעַת שני כְּרֻבִים מַעֲשֵׂה חֹשֵׁב עָשָׂה אֹתָם: 9 אֹרֶךְ הַיְרִיעָה הָאַחַת שְׁמֹנֶה וְעֶשְׂרִים בָּאַמָּה וְרֹחַב אַרְבַּע בָּאַמָּה הַיְרִיעָה הָאֶחָת מִדָּה אַחַת לְכָל הַיְרִיעֹת: 10 וַיְחַבֵּר אֶת חֲמֵשׁ הַיְרִיעֹת אַחַת אֶל אֶחָת וְחָמֵשׁ יְרִיעֹת חִבַּר אַחַת אֶל אֶחָת: 11 וַיַּעַשׂ לֻלְאֹת תְּכֵלֶת עַל שְׂפַת הַיְרִיעָה הָאֶחָת מִקָּצָה בַּמַּחְבֶּרֶת כֵּן עָשָׂה בִּשְׂפַת הַיְרִיעָה הַקִּיצוֹנָה בַּמַּחְבֶּרֶת הַשֵּׁנִית: 12 וַחֲמִשִּׁים לֻלָאֹת עָשָׂה בַּיְרִיעָה הָאֶחָת וַחֲמִשִּׁים לֻלָאֹת עָשָׂה בִּקְצֵה הַיְרִיעָה אֲשֶׁר בַּמַּחְבֶּרֶת הַשֵּׁנִית מַקְבִּילֹת הַלֻּלָאֹת אַחַת אֶל אֶחָת: 13 וַיַּעַשׂ חֲמִשִּׁים קַרְסֵי זָהָב וַיְחַבֵּר אֶת הַיְרִיעֹת אַחַת אֶל אֶחָת בַּקְּרָסִים וַיְהִי הַמִּשְׁכָּן אֶחָד: 14 וַיַּעַשׂ יְרִיעֹת עִזִּים לְאֹהֶל עַל הַמִּשְׁכָּן עַשְׁתֵּי עֶשְׂרֵה יְרִיעֹת עָשָׂה אֹתָם: 15 אֹרֶךְ הַיְרִיעָה הָאַחַת שְׁלֹשִׁים בָּאַמָּה וְאַרְבַּע אַמּוֹת רֹחַב הַיְרִיעָה

On the outside, THE CURTAINS OF GOATS' HAIR, whatever is added, lessens, an example of which are the bulls on Sukkot that diminish SINCE THEY ARE SACRIFICED ON BEHALF OF THE NATIONS, WHICH ARE EXTERNAL FORCES. Also, here it is written about the inside, "and you shall make the Tabernacle with ten curtains." (Exodus 26:1) Of the outside, "eleven (Aramaic ashtei esreh) curtains," (Ibid. 7) is spelled with an additional letter. THE LETTER AYIN IS ADDED TO THE WORD SHTEI ESREH (LIT. 'TWELVE'), reducing the number. THE NUMBER TWELVE IS REDUCED BY ONE, DUE TO THE ADDED AYIN TO SHTEI ESREH (TO ASHTEI). Thus adding to reckoning is [actually] lessening. There is addition in number in the words: "the length of one curtain shall be thirty cubits, and the breadth of one curtain four cubits," (Ibid. 8) WHILE THE INNER CURTAINS WERE ONLY TWENTY EIGHT CUBITS LONG. Adding in number is lessening, for it amounts to 34 (Dalet-Lamed), the most severe connotation of poverty being poor (Heb. dal). And that is why, what is added, lessens.

— The Zohar, Pekudei 26:249

16 *He joined five of the curtains into one set and the other six into another set.*

17 *Then they made fifty loops along the edge of the end curtain in one set and also fifty loops along the edge of the end curtain in the other set.*

18 *He made fifty bronze clasps to fasten the tent together as one.*

19 *Then he made for the tent a covering of ram skins dyed red, and over that a covering of seal skins.*

ON A LEAP YEAR: FIFTH READING - AARON - HOD

20 *He made upright frames of acacia wood for the Tabernacle.* *21* *Each frame was ten cubits long and a cubit and a half wide,* *22* *with two projections set parallel to each other. He made all the frames of the Tabernacle in this way.*

23 *He made twenty frames for the south side of the Tabernacle* *24* *and he made forty silver bases to go under the twenty frames—two bases for one frame, one under each projection, and two bases for the other frame, one under each projection.*

25 *For the other side, the north side of the Tabernacle, he made twenty frames* *26* *and forty silver bases—two under one frame and two under the other frame.*

וַיַּעַשׂ

Exodus 36:20—The Tabernacle walls.

The wooden boards used to build the Tabernacle had sockets of silver and were ringed and plated with gold.

> *"And Moses erected the Tabernacle." HE ASKS: With what did he erect it? AND HE ANSWERS: It is written, "...and fastened its sockets." (Exodus 40:18) He laid the sockets underneath the boards, so that the hinges of the doors will revolve upon them, because the hinges underneath give support and firmness upon which they can revolve. Why is it WRITTEN "fastened?" Because he fixed and strengthened them with all his might. At that time the other sockets of the Other Side were removed.*
> *— The Zohar, Pekudei 40:379*

> *"Moses erected" (Exodus 40:18) the side of Holiness, and the Other Side of defilement sank, "and fastened ITS SOCKETS" of the side of Holiness, and that side of defilement was enfeebled. He "set up ITS BOARDS" (Ibid.) of the side of holiness, and the Other Side of defilement was subjugated. Then he "put up its bars." (Ibid.)*
> *— The Zohar, Pekudei 43:422*

In life, there is no clear divide between black and white; life generally reveals itself in shades of gray. Most of us, when we are unsure about something, fail to act; we make no decision either way. The walls of the Tabernacle remind us that there is no gray. Our spiritual work is to develop the clarity to choose between black and white. We may not always make the right decision, but at least in making a choice, we can learn from our mistake and correct it. The important thing is to understand that no Light is revealed in shades of gray.

16 וַיְחַבֵּר֙ אַחַ֔ת לְעַשְׁתֵּ֥י עֶשְׂרֵ֖ה יְרִיעֹ֑ת אהיה ע״ה יהוה ע״ה הָאֹחָ֖ת מִדָּֽה

אֶת־חֲמֵ֥שׁ הַיְרִיעֹ֖ת לְבָ֑ד וְאֶת־שֵׁ֥שׁ הַיְרִיעֹ֖ת לְבָֽד: 17 וַיַּ֣עַשׂ לֻֽלָאֹ֣ת

חֲמִשִּׁ֗ים עַ֣ל שְׂפַ֤ת הַיְרִיעָה֙ הַקִּ֣יצֹנָ֔ה בַּמַּחְבָּ֑רֶת וַחֲמִשִּׁ֣ים לֻֽלָאֹ֗ת

עָשָׂה֙ עַל־שְׂפַ֣ת הַיְרִיעָ֔ה הַחֹבֶ֖רֶת הַשֵּׁנִֽית: 18 וַיַּ֛עַשׂ קַרְסֵ֥י נְחֹ֖שֶׁת

חֲמִשִּׁ֖ים לְחַבֵּ֣ר רבוע ס״ג ורבוע אהיה אֶת־הָאֹ֑הֶל לאה לִהְיֹ֖ת אֶחָֽד: אהבה, דאגה

19 וַיַּ֤עַשׂ מִכְסֶה֙ לָאֹ֔הֶל לאה עֹרֹ֥ת אֵילִ֖ם מְאָדָּמִ֑ים וּמִכְסֵ֛ה עֹרֹ֥ת

תְּחָשִׁ֖ים מִלְמָֽעְלָה:

ON A LEAP YEAR: FIFTH READING - AARON - HOD

20 וַיַּ֥עַשׂ אֶת־הַקְּרָשִׁ֖ים לַמִּשְׁכָּ֑ן ב״פ (רבוע אלהים ∸ ה) עֲצֵ֥י שִׁטִּ֖ים עֹמְדִֽים:

21 עֶ֥שֶׂר אַמֹּ֖ת אֹ֣רֶךְ הַקָּ֑רֶשׁ וְאַמָּה֙ דמב, מלוי ע״ב וַחֲצִ֣י הָֽאַמָּ֔ה דמב, מלוי ע״ב

רֹ֖חַב הַקֶּ֥רֶשׁ הָאֶחָֽד: אהבה, דאגה 22 שְׁתֵּ֣י יָד֗וֹת לַקֶּ֙רֶשׁ֙ הָֽאֶחָ֔ד אהבה, דאגה

מְשֻׁלָּבֹ֔ת אַחַ֖ת אֶל־אֶחָ֑ת יה אדני כֵּ֣ן עָשָׂ֔ה לְכֹ֖ל קַרְשֵׁ֥י הַמִּשְׁכָּֽן

ב״פ (רבוע אלהים ∸ ה) 23 וַיַּ֥עַשׂ אֶת־הַקְּרָשִׁ֖ים לַמִּשְׁכָּ֑ן ב״פ (רבוע אלהים ∸ ה) עֶשְׂרִ֣ים

קְרָשִׁ֔ים לִפְאַ֖ת נֶ֥גֶב תֵּימָֽנָה: 24 וְאַרְבָּעִ֞ים אַדְנֵי־כֶ֣סֶף עָשָׂ֔ה תַּ֚חַת

עֶשְׂרִ֣ים הַקְּרָשִׁ֔ים שְׁנֵ֣י אֲדָנִ֗ים תַּֽחַת־הַקֶּ֤רֶשׁ הָֽאֶחָד֙ אהבה, דאגה לִשְׁתֵּ֣י

יְדֹתָ֔יו וּשְׁנֵ֣י אֲדָנִ֗ים תַּֽחַת־הַקֶּ֥רֶשׁ הָאֶחָ֖ד אהבה, דאגה לִשְׁתֵּ֥י יְדֹתָֽיו:

25 וּלְצֶ֥לַע הַמִּשְׁכָּ֛ן ב״פ (רבוע אלהים ∸ ה) הַשֵּׁנִ֖ית לִפְאַ֣ת צָפ֑וֹן עָשָׂ֖ה עֶשְׂרִ֥ים

קְרָשִֽׁים: 26 וְאַרְבָּעִ֥ים אַדְנֵיהֶ֖ם כָּ֑סֶף שְׁנֵ֣י אֲדָנִ֗ים תַּ֚חַת הַקֶּ֣רֶשׁ הָֽאֶחָ֔ד

אהבה, דאגה וּשְׁנֵ֣י אֲדָנִ֔ים תַּ֖חַת הַקֶּ֥רֶשׁ הָאֶחָֽד: אהבה, דאגה 27 וּֽלְיַרְכְּתֵ֥י

הַמִּשְׁכָּ֖ן ב״פ (רבוע אלהים ∸ ה) יָ֑מָּה עָשָׂ֖ה שִׁשָּׁ֥ה קְרָשִֽׁים: 28 וּשְׁנֵ֣י קְרָשִׁ֔ים

עָשָׂ֖ה לִמְקֻצְעֹ֣ת הַמִּשְׁכָּ֑ן ב״פ (רבוע אלהים ∸ ה) בַּיַּרְכָתָֽיִם: 29 וְהָי֣וּ תוֹאֲמִם֮

מִלְּמַטָּה֒ וְיַחְדָּ֗ו יִהְי֤וּ אל תַמִּים֙ עַל־רֹאשׁ֔וֹ אֶל־הַטַּבַּ֖עַת הָאֶחָ֑ת כֵּ֚ן עָשָׂ֣ה

²⁷ He made six frames for the far end, that is, the west end of the Tabernacle, ²⁸ and two frames were made for the corners of the Tabernacle at the far end. ²⁹ At these two corners the frames were double from the bottom all the way to the top and fitted into a single ring; both were made alike. ³⁰ So there were eight frames and sixteen silver bases—two bases under each frame.

³¹ He also made crossbars of acacia wood: five for the frames on one side of the Tabernacle, ³² five crossbars for those on the second side, and five crossbars for the frames on the west, at the far end of the Tabernacle.

³³ He made the center crossbar so that it extended from end to end at the middle of the frames. ³⁴ He overlaid the frames with gold and made gold rings to hold the crossbars. He also overlaid the crossbars with gold.

³⁵ He made the curtain of blue, purple and scarlet yarn and finely twisted linen, with cherubim worked into it by a skilled craftsman. ³⁶ He made four pillars of acacia wood for it and overlaid them with gold. He made gold hooks for them and cast their four silver bases. ³⁷ For the entrance to the tent he made a curtain of blue, purple and scarlet yarn and finely twisted linen—the work of an embroiderer; ³⁸ and he made five pillars with hooks for them. He overlaid the tops of the pillars and their bands with gold and made their five bases of bronze. 37:¹ Betzalel made the Ark of acacia wood—two and a half cubits long, a cubit and a half wide, and a cubit and a half high.

הָאָרֹן

Exodus 37:1—The Ark of the Covenant.

Only the High Priest was given access to the Holy of Holies—the Inner Sanctum—once a year on *Yom Kippur.* The Ark contained all the answers to all questions—including everything—all there is to know about the past, present, and future. The source of wisdom that was once available in the Ark is still available for all of us today in the *Zohar.*

This is the secret of the Ark: which is reckoned whence it takes, whence it receives and what it possesses. HE EXPLAINS: It takes from the two sides, RIGHT AND LEFT. ALSO, WHATEVER it receives IS from the same two sides. Therefore, there is one cubit on this side, RIGHT, and one cubit on that side, LEFT, and a half cubit it has on its own. Hence it is written, "two cubits and a half was the length of it," (Exodus 37:1) two cubits from the two sides, RIGHT AND

LEFT, and a half of its own, regarding length. It is one cubit and a half wide and high; one CUBIT from the side which takes more, the same as it took from right and left, and a half of its own, for a thing dwells but upon some substance, hence there is a half in each and every reckoning. And that is why the Ark, WHICH IS MALCHUT, receives from all, and is found to contain the secret of the reckoning of them all.
— *The Zohar, Pekudei 26:256*

מִבַּיִת וּמִחוּץ

Exodus 37:2—The Ark is described as being covered inside and out with gold.

This verse reminds us that we must be the same both inside and out. It also points out the importance of our internal work.

It was explained why THE ARK was inlaid with gold inside and outside, WHICH IS THE SECRET OF THE INCLUSION OF

לִשְׁנֵיהֶם לִשְׁנֵי הַמִּקְצֹעֹת: 30 וְהָיוּ שְׁמֹנָה קְרָשִׁים וְאַדְנֵיהֶם כֶּסֶף

שִׁשָּׁה עָשָׂר אֲדָנִים שְׁנֵי אֲדָנִים שְׁנֵי אֲדָנִים תַּחַת הַקֶּרֶשׁ הָאֶחָד

אהבה, דאגה 31 וַיַּעַשׂ בְּרִיחֵי עֲצֵי שִׁטִּים חֲמִשָּׁה לְקַרְשֵׁי צֶלַע־הַמִּשְׁכָּן

ב"פ (רבוע אלהים ־ ה) הָאֶחָת: 32 וַחֲמִשָּׁה בְרִיחִם לְקַרְשֵׁי צֶלַע־הַמִּשְׁכָּן

ב"פ (רבוע אלהים ־ ה) הַשֵּׁנִית וַחֲמִשָּׁה בְרִיחִם לְקַרְשֵׁי הַמִּשְׁכָּן ב"פ (רבוע אלהים ־ ה)

לַיַּרְכָתַיִם יָמָּה: 33 וַיַּעַשׂ אֶת־הַבְּרִיחַ הַתִּיכֹן לִבְרֹחַ בְּתוֹךְ הַקְּרָשִׁים

מִן־הַקָּצֶה הי"פ טל, ג"פ אדני אֶל־הַקָּצֶה הי"פ טל, ג"פ אדני 34 וְאֶת־הַקְּרָשִׁים צִפָּה

זָהָב וְאֶת־טַבְּעֹתָם עָשָׂה זָהָב בָּתִּים לַבְּרִיחִם וַיְצַף אֶת־הַבְּרִיחִם

זָהָב: 35 וַיַּעַשׂ אֶת־הַפָּרֹכֶת תְּכֵלֶת קנ"א קמ"ג וְאַרְגָּמָן וְתוֹלַעַת שקוצי"ת שָׁנִי

וְשֵׁשׁ מָשְׁזָר מַעֲשֵׂה חֹשֵׁב עָשָׂה אֹתָהּ כְּרֻבִים: 36 וַיַּעַשׂ לָהּ אַרְבָּעָה

עַמּוּדֵי שִׁטִּים וַיְצַפֵּם זָהָב וָוֵיהֶם זָהָב וַיִּצֹק לָהֶם אַרְבָּעָה אַדְנֵי־כָסֶף:

37 וַיַּעַשׂ מָסָךְ לְפֶתַח הָאֹהֶל לאה תְּכֵלֶת וְאַרְגָּמָן קנ"א קמ"ג וְתוֹלַעַת שקוצי"ת

שָׁנִי וְשֵׁשׁ מָשְׁזָר מַעֲשֵׂה רֹקֵם: 38 וְאֶת־עַמּוּדָיו חֲמִשָּׁה וְאֶת־וָוֵיהֶם

וְצִפָּה רָאשֵׁיהֶם וַחֲשֻׁקֵיהֶם זָהָב וְאַדְנֵיהֶם חֲמִשָּׁה נְחֹשֶׁת: 37 1 וַיַּעַשׂ

בְּצַלְאֵל אֶת־הָאָרֹן ע"ב ורבוע ע"ב עֲצֵי שִׁטִּים אַמָּתַיִם וָחֵצִי אָרְכּוֹ וְאַמָּה

דמב, מלוי ע"ב וָחֵצִי רָחְבּוֹ וְאַמָּה דמב, מלוי ע"ב וָחֵצִי קֹמָתוֹ: 2 וַיְצַפֵּהוּ זָהָב טָהוֹר

י"פ אכא מִבַּיִת בי"פ ראה וּמִחוּץ אור וַיַּעַשׂ לוֹ זֵר זָהָב סָבִיב: 3 וַיִּצֹק לוֹ

THE ILLUMINATION OF CHOCHMAH
THAT IS CALLED 'GOLD.'
    — *The Zohar, Pekudei 26:257*

The *Zohar* discusses the differences and similarities of both the Ark and the Torah that was contained within it. In essence, man is like both the Ark and the Torah. Our purpose is to ignite the Light that exists within us so that we can connect to the Light of the Creator. Then, based on the Kabbalistic law of similarity of form—when our essence matches the essence of the Creator—our nature becomes one with the nature of the Creator.

He opened the discussion with the verse: "And they shall make an Ark of Acacia wood." (Exodus 25:10) The Book of Torah is the Central Pillar, NAMELY ZEIR ANPIN. Its Ark is the Shechinah and "inside and outside shall he overlay it;" (Ibid. 11) namely the Holy One, blessed be He, with His Shechinah THAT COVERS HIM from "outside and inside." THE HOLY ONE, BLESSED BE HE, AND HIS SHECHINAH are all one. This is not so with the Ark in this world, for the Torah which is inside is one kind and the Ark is another kind. The one is written with ink

2 He overlaid it with pure gold, both inside and out, and made a gold molding around it.

3 He cast four gold rings for it and fastened them to its four feet, with two rings on one side and two rings on the other.

4 Then he made poles of acacia wood and overlaid them with gold.

5 And he inserted the poles into the rings on the sides of the Ark to carry the Ark.

6 He made the atonement cover of pure gold—two and a half cubits long and a cubit and a half wide.

7 Then he made two cherubim out of hammered gold at the ends of the cover.

8 He made one cherub on one end and the second cherub on the other; at the two ends he made them of one piece with the cover.

9 The cherubim had their wings spread upward, overshadowing the cover with their wings. The cherubim faced each other, looking toward the cover.

10 He made the table of acacia wood—two cubits long, a cubit wide, and a cubit and a half high.

---

and the other is wood overlaid with gold. Certainly the Torah is more beloved than everything, as it is written: "Gold and glass cannot equal it." (Job 28:17) From a different view even, THE TORAH AND THE ARK THAT ARE in this world show that it is all one, ink and wood, LIKE THE HOLY ONE, BLESSED BE HE, AND HIS SHECHINAH, because ink is made of apples, which are of wood, NAMELY OF GALLNUTS. SO WE FIND THAT A TORAH SCROLL THAT IS WRITTEN WITH INK IS OF ONE KIND WITH THE ARK THAT IS MADE OF WOOD, FOR THIS IS THE SECRET OF THE HOLY ONE, BLESSED BE HE, AND HIS SHECHINAH. Moreover, ink, NAMELY THE LETTERS, is black on the outside and white on the inside, as are the Torah scholars and sages black in this world, which is outside. They are beautiful in the World to Come, which is in the inside. Therefore, ink (Heb. dyo) is the same expression as 'Dayo (Eng. 'sufficient') for a servant to be like his master.' Dyo CONTAINS THE LETTERS IN YUD OR THE LETTERS OF 'yado'

(Eng. 'his hand') THAT ALLUDE TO Chochmah, Binah and Da'at, WHICH IS THE SECRET OF YUD, for a man writes with his hand.
— *The Zohar, Terumah, The Faithful Shepherd 55:594-595*

Exodus 37:7—Two cherubs

Two cherubs were formed from the same piece of gold that the cover of the Ark was made from (Rashi). Between the cherubs, the voice of God would emanate.

When the priest heard their voices in the Temple, he placed the incense in its right place and meditated on something, in order that the blessing should flow to all. The wings of the Cherubs were moving up and down, singing and covering the ark. Then they would raise them. This is the meaning of "overspreading." "Overspreading" is precise. From where do we derive that their voices were

אַרְבַּע טַבְּעֹת זָהָב עַל אַרְבַּע פַּעֲמֹתָיו וּשְׁתֵּי טַבָּעֹת עַל־צַלְעוֹ הָאֶחָת

וּשְׁתֵּי טַבָּעֹת עַל־צַלְעוֹ הַשֵּׁנִית: 4 וַיַּעַשׂ בַּדֵּי עֲצֵי שִׁטִּים וַיְצַף אֹתָם

זָהָב: 5 וַיָּבֵא אֶת־הַבַּדִּים בַּטַּבָּעֹת עַל צַלְעֹת הָאָרֹן עב ורבוע עב לָשֵׂאת

אֶת־הָאָרֹן עב ורבוע עב: 6 וַיַּעַשׂ כַּפֹּרֶת זָהָב טָהוֹר יפ אכא אַמָּתַיִם וָחֵצִי

אָרְכָּהּ וְאַמָּה דמב, מלוי עב רָחְבָּהּ: 7 וַיַּעַשׂ שְׁנֵי [כְרֻבִים] זָהָב

מִקְשָׁה עָשָׂה אֹתָם מִשְּׁנֵי קְצוֹת הַכַּפֹּרֶת: 8 כְּרוּב־אֶחָד אהבה, דאגה

מִקָּצָה היפ טל, גיפ אדני מִזֶּה וּכְרוּב־אֶחָד אהבה, דאגה מִקָּצָה היפ טל, גיפ אדני מִזֶּה

מִן־הַכַּפֹּרֶת עָשָׂה אֶת־הַכְּרֻבִים מִשְּׁנֵי קְצוֹתָיו (כתיב: קצוותו): 9 וַיִּהְיוּ

מלוי סג הַכְּרֻבִים פֹּרְשֵׂי כְנָפַיִם לְמַעְלָה סֹכְכִים בְּכַנְפֵיהֶם עַל־הַכַּפֹּרֶת

וּפְנֵיהֶם אִישׁ עה קנא קסא אֶל־אָחִיו אֶל־הַכַּפֹּרֶת הָיוּ פְּנֵי וחכמה בינה הַכְּרֻבִים:

10 וַיַּעַשׂ אֶת־ [הַשֻּׁלְחָן] עֲצֵי שִׁטִּים אַמָּתַיִם אָרְכּוֹ וְאַמָּה דמב, מלוי עב

רָחְבּוֹ וְאַמָּה דמב, מלוי עב וָחֵצִי קֹמָתוֹ: 11 וַיְצַף אֹתוֹ זָהָב טָהוֹר יפ אכא

---

heard? NAMELY from the verse, "I heard the noise of their wings." (Ezekiel 1:24)
— The Zohar, Acherei Mot, 8:55

This reinforces our awareness of the spiritual system that exists in the universe. Angels are the link between our world and the Upper World, and we activate both positive and negative angels by our thoughts and actions. Having this awareness of the system of angels empowers us to be conscious of our thoughts and actions so that we can attract the positive angels to carry our prayers.

The Cherubs were of gold, as we have established, because they are from the side of gold, WHICH IS THE SECRET OF FEAR THAT CHANGED INTO GLORY. Neither silver nor any other color is mixed in with them. This is greenish gold, NAMELY THE GOLD THAT IS AT THE HEAD OF MALCHUT THAT IS CALLED THUS.
— The Zohar, Terumah 36:408

הַשֻּׁלְחָן

Exodus 37:10—The twelve loaves of bread.

Inside the Tabernacle was a table on which twelve loaves of bread for Shabbat were placed.

There are twelve loaves of bread that are on the table of the Holy One, blessed be He, WHICH IS MALCHUT. We have established the secret of the bread, which is the secret of the face, MEANING THE TWELVE FACES THAT ARE IN ZEIR ANPIN, WHICH ARE CHESED AND GEVURAH, TIFERET AND MALCHUT, WHICH ARE THE FOUR FACES OF THE LIVING CREATURES, THE FACE OF THE LION, THE FACE OF THE OX, THE FACE OF THE EAGLE, THE FACE OF MAN. EACH ONE OF THEM IS COMBINED OF THREE FACES, NAMELY LION, OX, AND EAGLE, AND THEY ARE TWELVE FACES. Therefore, they are called 'the Shew (lit. 'face') Bread,' because the food and sustenance of the world, WHICH IS

¹¹ Then he overlaid it with pure gold and made a gold molding around it.

¹² He also made around it a rim a handbreadth wide and put a gold molding on the rim.

¹³ He cast four gold rings for the table and fastened them to the four corners, where the four legs were.

¹⁴ The rings were put close to the rim to house the poles used in carrying the table.

¹⁵ The poles were made of acacia wood and were overlaid with gold, to carry the table.

¹⁶ And he made from pure gold the articles for the table—its plates and dishes and bowls and its pitchers for the pouring out of drink offerings.

WHEN CONNECTED: THIRD READING - JACOB - TIFERET ON A LEAP YEAR: SIXTH READING - JOSEPH - YESOD

¹⁷ He made the candelabra of pure gold and hammered it out, base and shaft; its flowerlike cups, buds and blossoms were of one piece with it.

¹⁸ Six branches extended from its sides—three branches of the candelabra on one side and three branches of the candelabra on the other.

¹⁹ Three cups shaped like almond flowers with buds and blossoms were on one branch, three cups shaped like almond flowers with buds and blossoms on the next branch, and the same for all six branches extending from the candelabra.

²⁰ And on the candelabra were four cups shaped like almond flowers with buds and blossoms. ²¹ One bud was under the first pair of branches extending from it, a

---

MALCHUT, comes from these supernal faces OF ZEIR ANPIN. Therefore, this bread is the inner part of everything, WHICH IS THE FOOD OF MALCHUT, AND IT is in the supernal secret OF ZEIR ANPIN, as is proper.
—The Zohar, Terumah 47:526

In describing the loaves of bread, the *Zohar* reveals that Supernal blessings come to the tables of all mankind and that it is our responsibility to share with those less fortunate than ourselves. The more we share, the closer our connection with the Light of the Creator.

הַמְּנֹרָה

Exodus 37:17—The table also held a Menorah—a candelabrum with three branches on either side and another candleholder in the center— made out of beaten gold and richly decorated with the symbols of the almond tree. Reading about the Menorah is a reminder that the Light of the Creator wants to give us more than we could ever hope for, but we have to expand our Vessel to contain this Light. The technology to expand our Vessel teaches us to ignite the Light within us by sharing and caring for others and by transforming our reactive nature.

וַיַּעַשׂ לוֹ זֵר בֵּ"פ אוֹר זָהָב סָבִיב: 12 וַיַּעַשׂ לוֹ מִסְגֶּרֶת טֹפַח סָבִיב וַיַּעַשׂ

זֵר אוֹר זָהָב לְמִסְגַּרְתּוֹ סָבִיב: 13 וַיִּצֹק לוֹ אַרְבַּע טַבְּעֹת זָהָב וַיִּתֵּן

אֶת־הַטַּבָּעֹת עַל אַרְבַּע הַפֵּאֹת אֲשֶׁר לְאַרְבַּע רַגְלָיו: 14 לְעֻמַּת יֵ"פ מְלֵאוּ עֵ"ב

הַמִּסְגֶּרֶת הָיוּ הַטַּבָּעֹת בָּתִּים לַבַּדִּים לָשֵׂאת אֶת־הַשֻּׁלְחָן: 15 וַיַּעַשׂ

אֶת־הַבַּדִּים עֲצֵי שִׁטִּים וַיְצַף אֹתָם זָהָב לָשֵׂאת אֶת־הַשֻּׁלְחָן: 16 וַיַּעַשׂ

אֶת־הַכֵּלִים | אֲשֶׁר עַל־הַשֻּׁלְחָן אֶת־קְעָרֹתָיו וְאֶת־כַּפֹּתָיו וְאֵת

מְנַקִּיֹּתָיו וְאֶת־הַקְּשָׂוֹת אֲשֶׁר יֻסַּךְ בָּהֵן זָהָב טָהוֹר: יֵ"פ אכא

WHEN CONNECTED: THIRD READING - JACOB - TIFERET
ON A LEAP YEAR: SIXTH READING - JOSEPH - YESOD

17 וַיַּעַשׂ אֶת־הַמְּנֹרָה זָהָב טָהוֹר יֵ"פ אכא מִקְשָׁה עָשָׂה אֶת־הַמְּנֹרָה

יְרֵכָהּ וְקָנָהּ עֵ"ה = יוסף, ציון, רֵ"פ יהו"ה, הֵ"פ אל גְּבִיעֶיהָ כַּפְתֹּרֶיהָ וּפְרָחֶיהָ מִמֶּנָּה הָיוּ:

18 וְשִׁשָּׁה קָנִים יֹצְאִים מִצִּדֶּיהָ שְׁלֹשָׁה | קְנֵי מְנֹרָה מִצִּדָּהּ הָאֶחָד

אהבה, דאגה וּשְׁלֹשָׁה קְנֵי מְנֹרָה מִצִּדָּהּ הַשֵּׁנִי: 19 שְׁלֹשָׁה גְבִעִים מְשֻׁקָּדִים

בַּקָּנֶה עֵ"ה = יוסף, ציון, רֵ"פ יהו"ה, הֵ"פ אל הָאֶחָד אהבה, דאגה כַּפְתֹּר וָפֶרַח רֵפ"ח וּשְׁלֹשָׁה

גְבִעִים מְשֻׁקָּדִים בַּקָּנֶה עֵ"ה = יוסף, ציון, רֵ"פ יהו"ה, הֵ"פ אל אֶחָד אהבה, דאגה כַּפְתֹּר

וָפֶרַח רֵפ"ח כֵּן לְשֵׁשֶׁת הַקָּנִים הַיֹּצְאִים מִן־הַמְּנֹרָה: 20 וּבַמְּנֹרָה אַרְבָּעָה

גְבִעִים מְשֻׁקָּדִים כַּפְתֹּרֶיהָ וּפְרָחֶיהָ: 21 וְכַפְתֹּר תַּחַת שְׁנֵי הַקָּנִים

מִמֶּנָּה וְכַפְתֹּר תַּחַת שְׁנֵי הַקָּנִים מִמֶּנָּה וְכַפְתֹּר תַּחַת־שְׁנֵי הַקָּנִים

מִמֶּנָּה לְשֵׁשֶׁת הַקָּנִים הַיֹּצְאִים מִמֶּנָּה: 22 כַּפְתֹּרֵיהֶם וּקְנֹתָם מִמֶּנָּה

...Because everything above rises in one manner, it neither changes nor will it change, as it is written: "For I am God, I do not change." (Malachi 3:6) Rav Yehuda said: All the candles illuminate from one, FROM THE BLESSED ENDLESS LIGHT, and they depend upon one. All the candles are one, and one must not distinguish BETWEEN THEM, for one who separates between them is separated from eternal life.

— The Zohar, Terumah 96:921

second bud under the second pair of branches extending from it, and a third bud under the third pair of branches extending from it —six branches in all.

[22] The buds and the branches were all of one piece with it, hammered out of pure gold.

[23] He made its seven lamps, as well as its wick trimmers and trays, of pure gold. [24] He made the candelabra and all its accessories from one talent of pure gold.

[25] He made the altar of incense out of acacia wood. It was square, a cubit long and a cubit wide, and two cubits high—its horns of one piece with it.

[26] He overlaid it with pure gold—the top and all the sides and the horns—and made a gold molding around it.

[27] He made two gold rings below the molding on its two sides—two on opposite sides—to house the poles used to carry it.

[28] He made the poles of acacia wood and overlaid them with gold. [29] He also made the sacred anointing oil and the pure, fragrant incense—the work of a perfumer.

WHEN CONNECTED: FOURTH READING - MOSES - NETZACH
ON A LEAP YEAR: SEVENTH READING - DAVID - MALCHUT

38:[1] He built the altar of burnt offering of acacia wood, five cubits long and five cubits wide; it was square, three cubits high. [2] He made a horn at each of the four corners, so that the horns and the altar were of one piece, and they overlaid the altar with bronze.

הַקְּטֹרֶת

Exodus 37:25—The construction of the altar upon which incense was to be burned is described.

> Come and look at the verse, "an altar for the burning of incense." (Exodus 30:1) HE ASKS: Why is it called an altar, if it is meant for burning incense? HE ANSWERS: this is because FIRE is taken from that place to burn incense, like Aaron did, AS IS WRITTEN: "TAKE A CENSER, AND PUT FIRE IN IT FROM OFF THE ALTAR." (NUMBERS 17:11) Moreover, since it is an altar, it must be sanctified by that incense, therefore it is

for the burning of incense. ANOTHER SENSE is that 'the burning of incense' literally means that incense must be burnt only in a censer.
> — The Zohar, Vayak'hel 41:474

This altar was gilded and crowned, and ringed so that it could be carried on two staves, the same way the Ark was carried. When the incense was lit on the incense altar, the perfume filled the entire Tabernacle, sweetening judgment with mercy. As the Zohar says:

> And when the smoke has arisen to the nostrils, it is called "incense," as it is written: "They shall put incense in your nostrils." (Deuteronomy 33:10) And nothing is as effective as incense for

הָיוּ כֻלָּהּ מִקְשָׁה אַחַת זָהָב טָהוֹר יפּ אכא: 23 וַיַּעַשׂ אֶת־נֵרֹתֶיהָ שִׁבְעָה

וּמַלְקָחֶיהָ וּמַחְתֹּתֶיהָ זָהָב טָהוֹר יפּ אכא: 24 כִּכָּר זָהָב טָהוֹר יפּ אכא עָשָׂה

אֹתָהּ וְאֵת כָּל־כֵּלֶיהָ: יל 25 וַיַּעַשׂ אֶת־מִזְבַּח זח, נגד [הַקְּטֹרֶת] יא אדני עֲצֵי

שִׁטִּים אַמָּה דמב, מלוי ע״ב אָרְכּוֹ וְאַמָּה דמב, מלוי ע״ב רָחְבּוֹ רָבוּעַ וְאַמָּתַיִם

קֹמָתוֹ מִמֶּנּוּ הָיוּ קַרְנֹתָיו: 26 וַיְצַף אֹתוֹ זָהָב טָהוֹר יפּ אכא אֶת־גַּגּוֹ וְאֶת־

קִירֹתָיו סָבִיב וְאֶת־קַרְנֹתָיו וַיַּעַשׂ לוֹ זֵר אור זָהָב סָבִיב: 27 וּשְׁתֵּי

טַבְּעֹת זָהָב עָשָׂה־לוֹ | מִתַּחַת לְזֵרוֹ עַל שְׁתֵּי צַלְעֹתָיו עַל שְׁנֵי צִדָּיו

לְבָתִּים לְבַדִּים לָשֵׂאת אֹתוֹ בָּהֶם: 28 וַיַּעַשׂ אֶת־הַבַּדִּים עֲצֵי שִׁטִּים

וַיְצַף אֹתָם זָהָב: 29 וַיַּעַשׂ אֶת־שֶׁמֶן יפּ טל, יפּ כוזו, ביט הַמִּשְׁחָה קֹדֶשׁ וְאֶת־

קְטֹרֶת הַסַּמִּים יא אדני טָהוֹר עה קנ״א, אלהים אדני יפּ אכא מַעֲשֵׂה רֹקֵחַ:

WHEN CONNECTED: FOURTH READING - MOSES - NETZACH
ON A LEAP YEAR: SEVENTH READING - DAVID - MALCHUT

38 1 וַיַּעַשׂ אֶת־[מִזְבַּח] זח, נגד הָעֹלָה עֲצֵי שִׁטִּים חָמֵשׁ אַמּוֹת אָרְכּוֹ

וְחָמֵשׁ־אַמּוֹת רָחְבּוֹ רָבוּעַ וְשָׁלֹשׁ אַמּוֹת קֹמָתוֹ: 2 וַיַּעַשׂ קַרְנֹתָיו עַל

---

doing away with death in the world, for incense is the connecting of Judgment with Mercy with the sweet savor in the nostrils. For the Hebrew for 'connect' is ktiru in Aramaic, AND HENCE INCENSE (HEB. KETORET) MEANS CONNECTION.
— The Zohar, Pinchas 38:206

Come and see, the incense always comes first and precedes everything. For this reason the section of the incense comes before prayer, hymns and praises. For nothing rises, is perfected or connected, before filth is removed BY INCENSE. It is written: "and he shall make atonement for the holy place" first, and then "because of their transgressions in all their sins" (Leviticus 16:16). Therefore, one should atone for the holy place, and remove filth, and purify the holiness BY USE OF INCENSE, and then sing hymns and pray, as we already said.
— The Zohar, Vayak'hel 41:438

מִזְבֵּחַ

Exodus 38:1—The burnt-offering altar is described here.

This is where sacrifices were performed in the Tabernacle, but this reading is not about animal sacrifice. It's about sacrifices we must make in our own lives. When we do things that are hard for us to do, our actions bring us Light. Sacrificing

3 He made all its utensils—its pots, shovels, sprinkling bowls, meat forks and firepans—of bronze.

4 He made a grating for the altar, a bronze network, to be under its ledge, halfway up the altar. 5 He cast four bronze rings to hold the poles for the four corners of the bronze grating.

6 He made the poles of acacia wood and overlaid them with bronze. 7 He inserted the poles into the rings so they would be on the sides of the altar for carrying it. He made it hollow, out of boards.

8 They made the basin out of bronze and its stand out of bronze from the mirrors of the women who served at the entrance to the Tent of Meeting.

9 He made the courtyard. The south side had curtains of finely twisted linen and was a hundred cubits long and, 10 had twenty pillars and twenty bronze sockets, and with silver hooks and bands on the posts.

11 The north side was a hundred cubits long and had twenty pillars and twenty bronze sockets, with silver hooks and bands on the pillars. 12 The west end was fifty cubits wide and had curtains, with ten pillars and ten sockets, with silver hooks and sockets on the pillars.

---

our *Desire to Receive for the Self Alone* alters our path and provides us with a better one. It erases the potential for chaos. If we're destined to get sick, for example, we can change our fate through sacrifice.

> *Another explanation: "This is the Torah" refers to the Congregation of Israel, WHICH IS MALCHUT. "The burnt offering" is an evil thought, taking over the desire of man to lead him astray from the way of truth. "The burnt offering" rises and denounces man. It should be burnt by fire, so it will not increase.*
> *— The Zohar, Pikudei 39:367*

הַכִּיּוֹר

Exodus 38:8—A laver, or basin, used for washing the hands is discussed in this section.

We always wash our hands before we perform any spiritual action. Everything we do is manifested by our hands, so all positive and negative energies have to be cleansed before we make any further connection on either a physical or spiritual level.

We have learned that when a man wakes up in the morning, he should wash his hands with a laver, and he SHOULD BE WASHED by someone who has already washed, as has been explained. Come and behold: We have learned all this for the sake of the laver. THIS EXPOSITION WAS MEANT TO TEACH US THAT WE NEED A LAVER TO WASH OUR HANDS IN THE MORNING.
— The Zohar, Miketz 8:117

The Holy One, blessed be He, said to him: "Evil man, My children preceded you. They have something among themselves for which no Evil Sides, no wicked species, nor any magic in the world can approach them; all flee them. What is this? It is the Tent of Meeting, with its vessels of Holiness and articles of service of the Temple: incense of spices that annuls any wrath and fury in the world both above and below, the daily offerings and the burnt offerings, two altars upon which to perform the service of the altar, a table and its showbread, the

אַרְבַּע פִּנֹּתָיו מִמֶּנּוּ הָיוּ קַרְנֹתָיו וַיְצַף אֹתוֹ נְחֹשֶׁת: 3 וַיַּעַשׂ אֶת־כָּל־ יּלי

כְּלֵי כּלּי הַמִּזְבֵּחַ ‏ יּ‎, נגד אֶת־הַסִּירֹת וְאֶת־הַיָּעִים וְאֶת־הַמִּזְרָקֹת אֶת־

הַמִּזְלָגֹת וְאֶת־הַמַּחְתֹּת כָּל־ יּלי כֵּלָיו עָשָׂה נְחֹשֶׁת: 4 וַיַּעַשׂ לַמִּזְבֵּחַ ‏ יּ‎, נגד

מִכְבָּר מַעֲשֵׂה רֶשֶׁת נְחֹשֶׁת תַּחַת כַּרְכֻּבּוֹ מִלְּמַטָּה עַד־חֶצְיוֹ: 5 וַיִּצֹק

אַרְבַּע טַבָּעֹת בְּאַרְבַּע הַקְּצָוֹת לְמִכְבַּר הַנְּחֹשֶׁת בָּתִּים לַבַּדִּים:

6 וַיַּעַשׂ אֶת־הַבַּדִּים עֲצֵי שִׁטִּים וַיְצַף אֹתָם נְחֹשֶׁת: 7 וַיָּבֵא אֶת־

הַבַּדִּים בַּטַּבָּעֹת עַל צַלְעֹת הַמִּזְבֵּחַ ‏ יּ‎, נגד לָשֵׂאת אֹתוֹ בָּהֶם נְבוּב לֻחֹת

עָשָׂה אֹתוֹ: 8 וַיַּעַשׂ אֵת הַכִּיּוֹר נְחֹשֶׁת וְאֵת כַּנּוֹ נְחֹשֶׁת בְּמַרְאֹת

הַצֹּבְאֹת אֲשֶׁר צָבְאוּ פֶּתַח אֹהֶל לאה מוֹעֵד: 9 וַיַּעַשׂ אֶת־הֶחָצֵר

לִפְאַת | נֶגֶב תֵּימָנָה קַלְעֵי הֶחָצֵר שֵׁשׁ מָשְׁזָר מֵאָה דמב, מלוי ע״ב בָּאַמָּה

דמב, מלוי ע״ב 10 עַמּוּדֵיהֶם עֶשְׂרִים וְאַדְנֵיהֶם עֶשְׂרִים נְחֹשֶׁת וָוֵי הָעַמֻּדִים

וַחֲשֻׁקֵיהֶם כָּסֶף: 11 וְלִפְאַת צָפוֹן מֵאָה דמב, מלוי ע״ב בָּאַמָּה

עַמּוּדֵיהֶם עֶשְׂרִים וְאַדְנֵיהֶם עֶשְׂרִים נְחֹשֶׁת וָוֵי הָעַמּוּדִים וַחֲשֻׁקֵיהֶם

כָּסֶף: 12 וְלִפְאַת־יָם קְלָעִים יּלי חֲמִשִּׁים בָּאַמָּה דמב, מלוי ע״ב עַמּוּדֵיהֶם

עֲשָׂרָה וְאַדְנֵיהֶם עֲשָׂרָה וָוֵי הָעַמֻּדִים וַחֲשׁוּקֵיהֶם כָּסֶף: 13 וְלִפְאַת

---

laver and its pedestal. There are also its articles of service RELATED TO speech: the Ark, the two Tablets of the Torah and Aaron who daily atones for the people in prayer." When that wicked man saw this, he said: *"Surely there is no enchantment in Jacob, nor is there any divination in Israel."* Why? BECAUSE *"God his Elohim is with him, and the trumpet blast of a king is in him."* (Numbers 23:21)
     — The Zohar, Bechokutai 1:9

הֶחָצֵר

Exodus 38:9—The courtyard of the Tabernacle. The perimeter of the Tabernacle was delineated by pillars hung with lace-work curtains made of linen. Within this courtyard—or energy field—the spiritual and holy work of prayer and sacrifice was performed. Outside of this energy field, beyond the pillars, the work of the world went on.

Every person is surrounded by an energy field about eight feet in diameter. This energy can be transferred to other people when we interact with them, so we must make certain the people in our energy field are positive. At the same time, we need to make sure people aren't giving us the evil eye. Negative people can detract from our positive energy field, and their negativity can affect us.

13 *The east end, toward the sunrise, was fifty cubits wide.*

14 *Curtains fifteen cubits long were on one side of the entrance, with three pillars and three sockets,*

15 *and curtains fifteen cubits long were on the other side of the entrance to the courtyard, with three pillars and three sockets.*

16 *All the curtains around the courtyard were of finely twisted linen.*

17 *The bases for the pillars were bronze. The hooks and bands on the pillars were silver, and their tops were overlaid with silver; so all the pillars of the courtyard had silver bands.*

ON A LEAP YEAR: MAFTIR

18 *The curtain for the entrance to the courtyard was the work of an embroiderer,*

made of blue, purple and scarlet yarn and finely twisted linen. It was twenty cubits long and, like the curtains of the courtyard, five cubits high,

19 *with four pillars and four bronze sockets. Their hooks and bands were silver, and their tops were overlaid with silver.*

20 *All the tent pegs of the Tabernacle and of the surrounding courtyard were bronze.*

14 קְלָעִים וַחֲמֵשׁ־עֶשְׂרֵה אַמָּה דמב, מלוי ע"ב קֵדְמָה מִזְרָחָה וַחֲמִשִּׁים אַמָּה

אֶל־הַכָּתֵף דמב, מלוי ע"ב עַמֻּדֵיהֶם שְׁלֹשָׁה וְאַדְנֵיהֶם שְׁלֹשָׁה: אַמָּה

15 וְלַכָּתֵף הַשֵּׁנִית מִזֶּה וּמִזֶּה לְשַׁעַר הֶחָצֵר קְלָעִים חֲמֵשׁ עֶשְׂרֵה

כָּל יל׳ ־קַלְעֵי 16 אַמָּה דמב, מלוי ע"ב עַמֻּדֵיהֶם שְׁלֹשָׁה וְאַדְנֵיהֶם שְׁלֹשָׁה:

הֶחָצֵר סָבִיב שֵׁשׁ מָשְׁזָר: 17 וְהָאֲדָנִים לָעַמֻּדִים נְחֹשֶׁת וָוֵי הָעַמּוּדִים

כֶּסֶף וְצִפּוּי רָאשֵׁיהֶם כֶּסֶף וְהֵם מְחֻשָּׁקִים כֶּסֶף כֹּל יל׳ כֹּל וַחֲשׁוּקֵיהֶם

עַמֻּדֵי הֶחָצֵר:

ON A LEAP YEAR: MAFTIR

18 וּמָסַךְ שַׁעַר יל׳ ז״ר הֶחָצֵר מַעֲשֵׂה רֹקֵם תְּכֵלֶת וְאַרְגָּמָן קנ"א קמ"ג

וְתוֹלַעַת שָׁקוּצ"ת שָׁנִי וְשֵׁשׁ מָשְׁזָר וְעֶשְׂרִים אַמָּה דמב, מלוי ע"ב אֹרֶךְ וְקוֹמָה

בְרֹחַב וְחָמֵשׁ אַמּוֹת לְעֻמַּת קַלְעֵי הֶחָצֵר: 19 וְעַמֻּדֵיהֶם אַרְבָּעָה

וְאַדְנֵיהֶם אַרְבָּעָה נְחֹשֶׁת וָוֵיהֶם כֶּסֶף וְצִפּוּי רָאשֵׁיהֶם וַחֲשֻׁקֵיהֶם

כָּסֶף: 20 וְכָל יל׳ ־הַיְתֵדֹת לַמִּשְׁכָּן ב"פ (רבוע אלהים ÷ ה) וְלֶחָצֵר סָבִיב

נְחֹשֶׁת:

ON A LEAP YEAR: HAFTARAH OF VAYAK'HEL

This Haftarah is about King Solomon building the Temple. Many years before that, Moses had built the Tabernacle, which was as movable as we are. But the Temple is always in Jerusalem, and it

1 Kings 7:13 - 26

7:13 King Solomon sent and brought Hiram from Tyre.

14 His mother was a widow from the tribe of Naphtali and his father was a man of Tyre and a craftsman in bronze. He was highly skilled and experienced in all kinds of bronze work. He came to King Solomon and did all the work assigned to him.

15 He cast two bronze pillars, each eighteen cubits high and twelve cubits around, by line.

16 He also made two capitals of cast bronze to set on the tops of the pillars; the first capital was five cubits high, and the second capital was five cubits high.

17 A network of interwoven chains festooned the capitals on top of the pillars, seven for the first capital and seven for the second capital.

18 He made the pillars with two rows surrounding one network to decorate the capitals on top of the pomegranates. He did the same for the second capital.

19 The capitals on top of the pillars in the portico were in the shape of lilies, four cubits high.

20 On the capitals of both pillars, above the bowl-shaped part next to the network, were the two hundred pomegranates in rows all around.

21 He erected the pillars at the portico of the Temple. He erected the pillar to the right and named it Jakin and erected the pillar to the left and named it Boaz.

22 The capitals on top were in the shape of lilies. And so the work on the pillars was completed.

23 He made the sea of cast metal, circular in shape, measuring ten cubits from rim to rim and five cubits high. It took a line of thirty cubits to measure around it.

ON A LEAP YEAR: HAFTARAH OF VAYAK'HEL

cannot be moved—it is our anchor. This teaches us that no matter where we may roam, we have to be anchored somewhere spiritually, whether through a teacher or a place of learning.

מלכים א פרק ז

7 13 וַיִּשְׁלַח הַמֶּלֶךְ שְׁלֹמֹה וַיִּקַּח אֶת־חִירָם עיה גיפ אלהים מֵצֹר־ 14 בֶּן־
אִשָּׁה אַלְמָנָה כוק, רבוע אדני הוּא מִמַּטֵּה נַפְתָּלִי וְאָבִיו אִישׁ־ עיה קניא קסיא
צֹרִי מצפצ, ייפ יייי, אלהים דיודין וֹחֹרֵשׁ נְחֹשֶׁת וַיִּמָּלֵא אֶת־הַחָכְמָה וְאֶת־הַתְּבוּנָה
וְאֶת־הַדַּעַת לַעֲשׂוֹת כָּל יבי ־מְלָאכָה אל אדני בַּנְּחֹשֶׁת וַיָּבוֹא אֶל־הַמֶּלֶךְ
שְׁלֹמֹה וַיַּעַשׂ אֶת־כָּל יבי ־מְלַאכְתּוֹ זדעד 15 וַיָּצַר אֶת־שְׁנֵי הָעַמּוּדִים נְחֹשֶׁת
שְׁמֹנֶה עֶשְׂרֵה אַמָּה דמב, מלוי עיב קוֹמַת הָעַמּוּד הָאֶחָד אהבה, דאגה וְחוּט
שְׁתֵּים־עֶשְׂרֵה אַמָּה דמב, מלוי עיב יָסֹב אֶת־הָעַמּוּד הַשֵּׁנִי: 16 וּשְׁתֵּי כֹתָרֹת
עָשָׂה לָתֵת עַל־רָאשֵׁי הָעַמּוּדִים מֻצַק נְחֹשֶׁת וְחָמֵשׁ אַמּוֹת קוֹמַת
הַכֹּתֶרֶת הָאֶחָת וְחָמֵשׁ אַמּוֹת קוֹמַת הַכֹּתֶרֶת הַשֵּׁנִית: 17 שְׂבָכִים
מַעֲשֵׂה שְׂבָכָה גְּדִלִים מַעֲשֵׂה שַׁרְשְׁרוֹת לַכֹּתָרֹת אֲשֶׁר עַל־רֹאשׁ
הָעַמּוּדִים רבוע אלהים ואלהים דיודין עיה שִׁבְעָה לַכֹּתֶרֶת הָאֶחָת וְשִׁבְעָה
לַכֹּתֶרֶת הַשֵּׁנִית: 18 וַיַּעַשׂ אֶת־הָעַמּוּדִים וּשְׁנֵי טוּרִים סָבִיב עַל־
הַשְּׂבָכָה הָאֶחָת לְכַסּוֹת אֶת־הַכֹּתָרֹת אֲשֶׁר עַל־רֹאשׁ
הָרִמֹּנִים רבוע אלהים ואלהים דיודין עיה וְכֵן עָשָׂה לַכֹּתֶרֶת הַשֵּׁנִית: 19 וְכֹתָרֹת
אֲשֶׁר עַל־רֹאשׁ רבוע אלהים ואלהים דיודין עיה הָעַמּוּדִים מַעֲשֵׂה שׁוּשַׁן בָּאוּלָם
אַרְבַּע אַמּוֹת: 20 וְכֹתָרֹת עַל־שְׁנֵי הָעַמּוּדִים גַּם יגל ־מִמַּעַל עלם
מִלְּעֻמַּת הַבֶּטֶן אֲשֶׁר לְעֵבֶר רבוע יהוה ורבוע אלהים הַשְּׂבָכָה (כתיב: שבכה)
וְהָרִמּוֹנִים מָאתַיִם טֻרִים סָבִיב עַל הַכֹּתֶרֶת הַשֵּׁנִית: 21 וַיָּקֶם אֶת־

[24] *Below the rim, gourds encircled it—ten to a cubit, surrounding the sea. The gourds were cast in two rows in one piece with it.*

[25] *It stood on twelve bulls, three facing north, three facing west, three facing south and three facing east. The sea rested on top of them, and their hindquarters were toward the center.*

[26] *It was a handbreadth in thickness, and its rim was like the rim of a cup, like a lily blossom. It held two thousand baths.*

הָעֹמְדִים לְאֻלָם הַהֵיכָל אדני, ללה וַיָּקֶם אֶת־הָעַמּוּד הַיְמָנִי וַיִּקְרָא

אֶת־שְׁמוֹ ב״פ קס״א ‑ ה אותיות מהשע ע״ה, אל שדי ע״ה יָכִין וַיָּקֶם אֶת־הָעַמּוּד הַשְּׂמָאלִי

וַיִּקְרָא ב״פ קס״א ‑ ה אותיות אֶת־שְׁמוֹ מהשע ע״ה, אל שדי ע״ה בֹּעַז: 22 וְעַל רֹאשׁ

הָעַמּוּדִים ריבוע אלהים ואלהים דיודין ע״ה מַעֲשֵׂה שׁוֹשָׁן וַתִּתֹּם מְלֶאכֶת הָעַמּוּדִים:

23 וַיַּעַשׂ אֶת־הַיָּם ילי מוּצָק עֶשֶׂר בָּאַמָּה דמב, מלוי ע״ב מִשְּׂפָתוֹ עַד־שְׂפָתוֹ

עָגֹל | סָבִיב וְחָמֵשׁ בָּאַמָּה קוֹמָתוֹ וְקָו (כתיב: וקוה) שְׁלֹשִׁים

בָּאַמָּה דמב, מלוי ע״ב יָסֹב אֹתוֹ סָבִיב: 24 וּפְקָעִים מִתַּחַת לִשְׂפָתוֹ | סָבִיב

סֹבְבִים אֹתוֹ עֶשֶׂר בָּאַמָּה דמב, מלוי ע״ב מַקִּפִים אֶת־הַיָּם ילי סָבִיב שְׁנֵי

טוּרִים הַפְּקָעִים יְצֻקִים בִּיצֻקָתוֹ: 25 עֹמֵד עַל־שְׁנֵי עָשָׂר בָּקָר שְׁלֹשָׁה

פֹנִים | צָפוֹנָה ע״ה עסמ״ב וּשְׁלֹשָׁה פֹנִים | יָמָּה וּשְׁלֹשָׁה | פֹנִים נֶגְבָּה

וּשְׁלֹשָׁה פֹנִים מִזְרָחָה וְהַיָּם ילי עֲלֵיהֶם מִלְמָעְלָה וְכָל ילי ־אֲחֹרֵיהֶם

בָּיְתָה: 26 וְעָבְיוֹ טֶפַח וּשְׂפָתוֹ כְּמַעֲשֵׂה שְׂפַת־כּוֹס מום, אלהים, אהיה אדני פֶּרַח

רפ״ח שׁוֹשָׁן אַלְפַּיִם קס״א בַּת יָכִיל:

PEKUDEI

LESSON OF PEKUDEI
(Exodus 38:21-40:38)

In this last story of the Book of Exodus, the people brought to Moses all the finished materials he needed to erect the Tabernacle and to fill it with—the completed furnishings, decorations, altars, and vestments. Every single item was ready. An exact accounting of these items was done because Moses was afraid the people might accuse him of stealing; they might question where all of their donations went. With the negativity that had been generated during the incident of the Golden Calf, it was possible that the people might accuse even Moses of stealing. Once the energy of death or negativity enters, there's no limit to the harm it can do.

Yet even though all the contents of the Tabernacle were present and all the work already completed—including the fashioning of the vestments of the *Kohen haGadol*, the High Priest— nothing could be manifested without the energy of Moses, who had to bring it all together. He was the channel, the highest soul that ever lived. We may begin our spiritual work alone, but we need our teachers and God to reach the next level. We cannot do it alone.

The spiritual law of similarity of form reveals a contradiction. To connect with the Light, we must be in affinity with the Light, meaning that our essence is the same as the essence of the Creator— the Desire to Share. Yet we cannot complete the work of transforming our Desire to Receive for the Self Alone without the help of the Light. This is a complex paradox. By connecting with righteous people like Moses, we can use their corrected Vessels to connect with the Creator, a feat we would be incapable of achieving on our own. We borrow their Vessels every time we study from their works, read about the lessons of their lives, visit their gravesites, emulate their actions, and follow their example.

Every *tzadik* had (or has) a unique gift that he or she came to share with the world. For example, through the unconditional love in his heart, Rav Yehuda Tzvi Brandwein, the Rav's teacher, had a special ability for drawing people closer to God—people who had been very far away from the Creator. Rav Brandwein did not use words, only love.

There is a telling story that the Rav shares about his teacher:

Not long after my introduction to my teacher and The Kabbalah Centre, I saw a dramatic instance of Rav Brandwein's power to touch people on a spiritual level. It was in Haifa on a Shabbat morning in early spring. The weather was very clear with hardly a cloud in the sky. We were approaching the main square of the city when we saw a tall, well-dressed man walking toward us. He was smiling and smoking a cigarette.

"That is Mr. Aba Chushi," Rav Brandwein said to me. "He's the mayor of Haifa."

As Aba Chushi greeted us, he and Rav Brandwein had a brief, pleasant conversation. Then they wished each other Shabbat Shalom, and we continued on our way.

A month later when we returned to Haifa, I accompanied my teacher on a visit to the mayor, who set a gracious meal for us to enjoy. At one point, Mr. Chushi set down his fork.

"I must tell you, Rav. You have been a profound influence on my life."

This seemed surprising to me since I knew that Rav Brandwein did not know the mayor particularly well.

"Do you remember when we met last month on Shabbat?" Mr. Chushi asked.

My teacher smiled, "Of course."

"If you recall, I was smoking, and now I have given it up."

My teacher did not say, "Good!" He only asked why.

"Frankly, it was because I saw the pain on your face that I was smoking. I immediately felt your deep concern for me. And do you know, since I stopped, I have gone to my doctor, and he has told me it was a very lucky thing that I did."

"I am happy for you," Rav Brandwein said. "Your doctor was right. You are a very lucky man."

Beyond doubt, something in the tone of his voice showed that this was a wise and learned man speaking. More important, however, this was a kabbalist talking, and the purpose of this story is to make clear exactly what that means. The purpose is not just to tell an anecdote about Rav Brandwein, but to show how he conducted himself day by day in the real world. A kabbalist practices Kabbalah, not only during prayers in the sanctuary but in literally everything he or she does.

Therefore, just as important as the time we spend reading the Zohar is the time we spend thinking about and emulating Rav Shimon and his actions.

When Moses prepared the Tabernacle on the first day of the first month, Nissan (Aries), everything was anointed so that its molecular structure could be converted from a physical to a spiritual level. This conversion takes place in our own lives, as well. A dollar is merely a piece of paper, but when given to someone in need, that dollar becomes the manifestation of a spiritual action. Even sexual relations can and should be transformed from an action of the body into an action of the soul.

The first day of *Nissan*, when the Tabernacle was finally completed, is one of the most powerful days of the year. It is the seed that enables us to control the external influences on our lives, as on Rosh Hashanah. On this day, Moses put everything in its proper place. Without order, there is no completion. We, too, need to put order into our lives. We may have all the pieces of the puzzle, but if we don't put them in their proper place, we can't see the complete picture.

Once everything was in its place and the Vessel (the Tabernacle itself) was prepared, the Light of the Creator entered the Tabernacle. This was the first time there had ever been a physical location for the Light of the Creator to enter and dwell. The building of the Tabernacle for the Creator symbolizes how each of us builds and prepares our personal Vessel so that the Light can fulfill it.

SYNOPSIS OF PEKUDEI

Pekudei is the last chapter of the Book of Shemot (Book of Names)—more commonly known as the Book of Exodus. In this chapter, we learn the value of the tools that have been given to us: the 72 Names of God and the 42-Letter Name of God (the *Ana Beko'ach*). When we experience chaos in our lives, it is often because we have forgotten or neglected to make use of the tools available to us.

> *Come and see: The world, MALCHUT, had been engraved with and exists by 42 letters. They are all a crown for the Holy Names…. These 42 letters are a high mystery, with which were created the Upper World, ZEIR ANPIN, and the Lower World, MALCHUT…. It is written, "and you shall put in the Breastplate of judgment the Urim and the Tumim." (Exodus 28:30). It was explained that the MEANING OF Urim (Eng. 'lights') is that they illuminate, in the secret of the shining mirror, NAMELY, ZEIR ANPIN, and this is the engravings of the letters of the Holy Name in the secret of 42, with which the worlds were created. The letters were sunken into it. "The Tumim" refer to the secret of the letters contained in the mirror which does not shine, WHICH IS MALCHUT, shining with the 72 engraved letters, in the secret of the Holy Name. THE NAME OF 72 IS THE SECRET OF REVEALING THE LIGHT OF CHOCHMAH THAT IS WITHIN MALCHUT. Together they are called 'Urim and Tumim' … This is the secret of "and Moses erected the Tabernacle," (Exodus 40:18) erecting it by these letters with which heaven and earth were created, REFERRING TO THE NAME OF 42.*
> — The Zohar, Pekudei 27:264, 267, 268,

God frequently directs us to act in a certain way, and yet we all too often don't heed His direction. We all have a part of God within us, and yet we don't act as if we do. Every time we treat someone unkindly, we are not reflecting the God inside of us or the God inside of them. This is an indication that we don't always value what God tells us. It's important to remember that God exists in every one of us and that negativity has an effect on the entire world.

ON A LEAP YEAR: FIRST READING - ABRAHAM - CHESED

²¹ These are the amounts of the materials used for the Tabernacle, the Tabernacle of the Covenant, which were recorded at Moses' command by the Levites under the direction of Itamar son of Aaron, the priest.

²² Betzalel son of Uri, the son of Hur, of the tribe of Judah, made everything the Lord commanded Moses;

²³ with him was Oholiab son of Achisamach, of the tribe of Dan—a craftsman and designer, and an embroiderer in blue, purple and scarlet yarn and fine linen.

²⁴ The total amount of the gold from the wave offering used for all the work on the sanctuary was 29 talents and 730 shekels, according to the holy shekel.

FROM THE RAV

A "Good Clerk"

"*Eile pekudei*," loosely translated, means "These are the accounts." This is not a good translation, however, as English doesn't have words that are equivalent to the Hebrew. *Pakid* in English really means "clerk." So these are the clerks of the Temple and of the Tabernacle. What the Torah is trying to teach us here is that whatever is transmitted needs to be done through a "good clerk."

Language is our biggest barrier. This is the whole idea of what happened in the story of the Tower of Babel, where God, to disarm evil, created seventy languages. "Babel" is *bilbul* in Hebrew, which is translated as "confusion." The *Zohar* says that the only way Satan can create confusion—or the only way sometimes we can—is through the fostering of multiple languages instead of having one universal language. I know you have heard this all before, but who of us truly applies this information that we have in our daily lives? Most of us are too busy trying to figure it out.

We don't have a proper language. Every language, in fact, is bilbul. But because language is such a powerful tool of connection, the concept of a "good clerk" is vital for effective communication and connection.

So, you may ask, what a "good clerk" is. A good clerk doesn't try to figure things out; a good clerk follows the instructions of his or her employer. The employer doesn't want clerks to make decisions on their own without consulting him or her. Clerks have to be a channel, nothing more.

We've got to communicate through the universal language of Hebrew. It's got to be. We can't decide on our own. The chapter of Pekudei provides us with a channel to receive and transmit undistorted information.

Exodus 38:24—Moses was given all the materials he needed to erect and furnish the Tabernacle.

Moses rendered an exact accounting of these items so that he would not be accused of

ON A LEAP YEAR: FIRST READING - ABRAHAM - CHESED

אֵלֶּה פְקוּדֵי הַמִּשְׁכָּן ב"פ (רבוע אלהים + ה) מִשְׁכַּן ב"פ (רבוע אלהים + ה) הָעֵדֻת 21

אֲשֶׁר פֻּקַּד רבוע ע"ב עַל-פִּי מֹשֶׁה מהש, אל שדי עֲבֹדַת הַלְוִיִּם בְּיַד אִיתָמָר

בֶּן-אַהֲרֹן ע"ב ורבוע ע"ב הַכֹּהֵן מלה: 22 וּבְצַלְאֵל בֶּן-אוּרִי בֶן-חוּר לְמַטֵּה

יְהוּדָה עָשָׂה אֵת כָּל-אֲשֶׁר-צִוָּה יְהֹוָאדנילאהדונהי פוי אֶת-מֹשֶׁה

מהש, אל שדי: 23 וְאִתּוֹ אָהֳלִיאָב בֶּן-אֲחִיסָמָךְ לְמַטֵּה-דָן חָרָשׁ וְחֹשֵׁב

וְרֹקֵם בַּתְּכֵלֶת וּבָאַרְגָּמָן קנ"א קמ"ג וּבְתוֹלַעַת הַשָּׁנִי שקוצי"ת וּבַשֵּׁשׁ: 24 כָּל-

הַזָּהָב וזה יְהֹוָה יכי הֶעָשׂוּי לַמְּלָאכָה בְּכֹל ב"ן, לכב, יבמ מְלֶאכֶת הַקֹּדֶשׁ וַיְהִי

אל, יאי | זְהַב הַתְּנוּפָה תֵּשַׁע וְעֶשְׂרִים כִּכָּר וּשְׁבַע מֵאוֹת וּשְׁלֹשִׁים

---

stealing or questioned as to the whereabouts of the contributions. Many of the great spiritual teachers throughout history were challenged or ostracized, maligned or tortured, and their authenticity and honesty questioned. There is a great lesson here. Wherever there is Light to be revealed, Satan must take his share. He initiates doubt so that we will not have the certainty to finish the job. If we experience formidable obstacles in our spiritual work, it is a sign of certainty that we are on the right path. But once the energy of doubt and negativity enters, there's no limit to the harm it can do, as we can see in this reading where, after all that they had seen Moses do for them, the people still believed it possible that Moses could steal.

And when all the work was completed, Moses had to count everything, so Israel would not say that some gold and silver was left, and that he was planning to take it. Therefore, he counted before Israel, as it is written, "and be guiltless before God and before Israel." (Numbers 32:22)

"These are the accounts of the Tabernacle." Come and see: At the time when the construction of the Tabernacle took place, the Other Side roamed about, to bring accusations. He found no flaw in the faithfulness of the craftsmen, so

the Holy One, blessed be He, caused him to yield before Moses. And he, THE OTHER SIDE, had to check their worthiness in spite of himself and to acknowledge it before all. This is the mystery of the verse, "These are the accounts of the Tabernacle." And we explained that "These" is the same as in "even these may forget," (Isaiah 49:15) REFERRING TO THE OTHER SIDE, FOR BOTH CASES ALLUDE TO THE OTHER SIDE. It is also written, "as they were counted according to the commandment of Moses." For there, ACCORDING TO MOSES, all was counted and numbered, until the accounting of the Tabernacle was complete before Moses and all of Israel.
— The Zohar, Pekudei 4:18, 20

But Moses did not build the *Mishkan* (Tabernacle) —Betzalel and Oholiab did.

So Betzalel carried out all the work of the Tabernacle using the secret of the engraved letters, with which Heaven and Earth were created, NAMELY, THE NAME OF 42. He was therefore called 'Betzalel', since he knew the engraving of these letters, with which Heaven and Earth were created. Unless he knew

25 *The silver obtained from the community who were counted in the census was 100 talents and 1,775 shekels, according to the holy shekel.*

26 *One beka per person, that is, half a shekel, according to the holy shekel, from everyone who had crossed over to those counted, twenty years old or more, a total of 603,550 men.*

27 *The 100 talents of silver were used to cast the sockets for the sanctuary and for the curtain—100 sockets from the 100 talents, one talent for each socket.*

28 *They used the 1,775 shekels to make the hooks for the pillars, to overlay the tops of the pillars, and to make their sockets.*

29 *The bronze from the wave offering was 70 talents and 2,400 shekels.*

30 *He used it to make the bases for the entrance to the Tent of Meeting, the bronze altar with its bronze grating and all its utensils,*

31 *the sockets for the surrounding courtyard and those for the courtyard's entrance and all the tent pegs for the Tabernacle and those for the surrounding courtyard.*

39:1 *From the blue, purple and scarlet yarn they made woven garments for ministering in the sanctuary. They also made sacred garments for Aaron, as the Lord commanded Moses.*

---

them, he could not have done the work in the Tabernacle. The sense thereof is that as the Upper Tabernacle was built, and all its actions done, only by the secret of these letters, OF THE NAME 42, so here in the Tabernacle Below, nothing was built save by the secrets of these letters. Betzalel was combining the letters, OF THE NAME 42, and did the various works with different combinations thereof. He used each combination to do one task, and all that pertains to it. And so with all the works in the Tabernacle, together with its parts and amendments, he used combinations of the letters of the Holy Name 42.
— The Zohar, Pekudei 27:272-274

THE TABERNACLE BELOW was built in the same manner. Betzalel and Oholiab worked one on the Right Side,
CHASSADIM, and the other on the Left Side, CHOCHMAH. Betzalel was of the Right and Oholiab of the Left, this one of the tribe of Judah, THE RIGHT SIDE OF MALCHUT, and that one of the tribe of Dan, OF THE LEFT. THEY CORRESPOND TO THE RIGHT AND LEFT SIDES OF ZEIR ANPIN. After them, "every wise hearted man," (Exodus 36:1) "and all the wise men, that carried out," CORRESPONDING TO THE OTHER SIDES OF ZEIR ANPIN. And we explained that all IN THE TABERNACLE BELOW was like THE TABERNACLE above.
— The Zohar, Pekudei 32:298

Nothing was complete without the energy of Moses.

HE ASKS: Why did they bring the Tabernacle? AND HE ANSWERS: It was

שֶׁקֶל בְּשֶׁקֶל הַקֹּדֶשׁ: 25 וְכֶסֶף פְּקוּדֵי הָעֵדָה מְאַת כִּכָּר וְאֶלֶף

אלף למד - עין דלת יוד ע"ה וּשְׁבַע מֵאוֹת וַחֲמִשָּׁה וְשִׁבְעִים שֶׁקֶל בְּשֶׁקֶל

הַקֹּדֶשׁ: 26 בֶּקַע לַגֻּלְגֹּלֶת מַחֲצִית הַשֶּׁקֶל בְּשֶׁקֶל הַקֹּדֶשׁ לְכֹל יה אדני

הָעֹבֵר רבוע יהוה ורבוע אלהים עַל־הַפְּקֻדִים מִבֶּן עֶשְׂרִים שָׁנָה וָמַעְלָה לְשֵׁשׁ־

מֵאוֹת אֶלֶף אלף למד עין דלת יוד ע"ה וּשְׁלֹשֶׁת אֲלָפִים קס"א וַחֲמֵשׁ מֵאוֹת

וַחֲמִשִּׁים: 27 וַיְהִי אל מְאַת כִּכַּר הַכֶּסֶף לָצֶקֶת אֵת אַדְנֵי הַקֹּדֶשׁ וְאֵת

אַדְנֵי הַפָּרֹכֶת מְאַת אֲדָנִים לִמְאַת הַכִּכָּר כִּכָּר לָאָדֶן: 28 וְאֶת־

הָאֶלֶף אלף למד עין דלת יוד ע"ה וּשְׁבַע הַמֵּאוֹת וַחֲמִשָּׁה וְשִׁבְעִים עָשָׂה וָוִים

לָעַמּוּדִים וְצִפָּה רָאשֵׁיהֶם וְחִשַּׁק אֹתָם: 29 וּנְחֹשֶׁת הַתְּנוּפָה שִׁבְעִים

כִּכָּר וְאַלְפַּיִם קס"א וְאַרְבַּע־מֵאוֹת שָׁקֶל: 30 וַיַּעַשׂ בָּהּ אֶת־אַדְנֵי פֶּתַח

אֹהֶל לאה מוֹעֵד וְאֵת מִזְבַּח זן, נגד הַנְּחֹשֶׁת וְאֶת־מִכְבַּר הַנְּחֹשֶׁת אֲשֶׁר־

לוֹ וְאֵת כָּל־כְּלֵי יל"י הַמִּזְבֵּחַ כלי זן, נגד: 31 וְאֶת־אַדְנֵי הֶחָצֵר סָבִיב וְאֶת־

אַדְנֵי שַׁעַר הֶחָצֵר וְאֵת כָּל־יִתְדֹת יל"י הַמִּשְׁכָּן ב"פ (רבוע אלהים - ה) וְאֶת־

כָּל־יִתְדֹת יל"י הֶחָצֵר סָבִיב: 39 1 וּמִן־הַתְּכֵלֶת וְהָאַרְגָּמָן קנ"א קמ"ג וְתוֹלַעַת

שקוצי"ת הַשָּׁנִי עָשׂוּ בִגְדֵי והו ־שְׂרָד לְשָׁרֵת בַּקֹּדֶשׁ וַיַּעֲשׂוּ אֶת־בִּגְדֵי והו

הַקֹּדֶשׁ אֲשֶׁר לְאַהֲרֹן ע"ב ורבוע ע"ב כַּאֲשֶׁר צִוָּה פוי יהו אהדונהיאהדונהי אֶת־מֹשֶׁה

מהש, אל עדי:

---

then the time of espousals of Moses,
ZEIR ANPIN, and therefore, they brought
the Tabernacle, MALCHUT, to Moses,
like a bride coming to the house of the
groom. For first the bride should be
brought to the groom, as it is written, "I
gave my daughter to this man to wed."

(Deuteronomy 22:16) Then he comes
to her, as said, "and went in to her,"
(Genesis 38:2) and "Moses went into
the Tent of Testimony," (Numbers 17:23)
WHICH IS MALCHUT.
— The Zohar, Pekudei 29:284

WHEN CONNECTED: FIFTH READING - AARON - HOD
ON A LEAP YEAR: SECOND READING - ISAAC - GEVURAH

² He made the ephod of gold, and of blue, purple and scarlet yarn, and of finely twisted linen.

³ They hammered out thin sheets of gold and cut strands to be worked into the blue, purple and scarlet yarn and fine linen—the work of a skilled craftsman.

⁴ They made shoulder pieces for it, which were attached to two of its corners, so it could be fastened.

⁵ Its skillfully woven waistband was like it—of one piece with the ephod and made with gold, and with blue, purple and scarlet yarn, and with finely twisted linen, as the Lord commanded Moses.

⁶ They mounted the onyx stones in gold filigree settings and engraved them like a seal with the names of the sons of Israel.

⁷ Then he fastened them on the shoulder pieces of the ephod as memorial stones for the sons of Israel, as the Lord commanded Moses.

⁸ He fashioned the breastplate—the work of a skilled craftsman. They made it like the ephod: of gold, and of blue, purple and scarlet yarn, and of finely twisted linen.

⁹ It was square—a span long and a span wide—and folded double.

¹⁰ Then they mounted four rows of precious stones on it. In the first row there was a ruby, a topaz and a beryl; ¹¹ in the second row a turquoise, a sapphire and an emerald;

¹² in the third row a jacinth, an agate and an amethyst;

¹³ in the fourth row a chrysolite, an onyx and a jasper. They were mounted in gold settings.

¹⁴ There were twelve stones, one for each of the names of the sons of Israel, each engraved like a seal with the name of one of the twelve tribes.

¹⁵ For the breastplate they made thickly braided chains of pure gold.

WHEN CONNECTED: FIFTH READING - AARON - HOD
ON A LEAP YEAR: SECOND READING - ISAAC - GEVURAH

2 וַיַּעַשׂ אֶת־הָאֵפֹד ע״ה אלהים זָהָב תְּכֵלֶת וְאַרְגָּמָן קנ״א קמ״ג וְתוֹלַעַת שקוצית

שָׁנִי וְשֵׁשׁ מָשְׁזָר: 3 וַיְרַקְּעוּ אֶת־פַּחֵי הַזָּהָב וחותי וְקִצֵּץ פְּתִילִם יפ בן

לַעֲשׂוֹת בְּתוֹךְ הַתְּכֵלֶת וּבְתוֹךְ הָאַרְגָּמָן קנ״א קמ״ג וּבְתוֹךְ תּוֹלַעַת שקוצית

הַשָּׁנִי וּבְתוֹךְ הַשֵּׁשׁ מַעֲשֵׂה חֹשֵׁב: 4 כְּתֵפֹת עָשׂוּ־לוֹ חֹבְרֹת עַל־שְׁנֵי

קְצוֹתָיו (כתיב: קצוותו) וְחֻבָּר רבוע ס״ג ורבוע אהיה: 5 וְחֵשֶׁב אֲפֻדָּתוֹ אֲשֶׁר עָלָיו

מִמֶּנּוּ הוּא כְּמַעֲשֵׂהוּ זָהָב תְּכֵלֶת וְאַרְגָּמָן קנ״א קמ״ג וְתוֹלַעַת שקוצית שָׁנִי

וְשֵׁשׁ מָשְׁזָר כַּאֲשֶׁר צִוָּה פוי יְהֹוָ֔ה/אֲדֹנָי/אהיה אֶת־מֹשֶׁה מהש, אל שדי: 6 וַיַּעֲשׂוּ

אֶת־אַבְנֵי הַשֹּׁהַם מהש, אל שדי מֻסַבֹּת מִשְׁבְּצֹת זָהָב מְפֻתָּחֹת פִּתּוּחֵי

חוֹתָם ע״ה נתה, ע״ה קס״א קמ״ג עַל־שְׁמוֹת בְּנֵי יִשְׂרָאֵל: 7 וַיָּשֶׂם אֹתָם עַל

כִּתְפֹת הָאֵפֹד ע״ה אלהים אַבְנֵי זִכָּרֹן ע״ב קס״א נע״ו לִבְנֵי יִשְׂרָאֵל כַּאֲשֶׁר צִוָּה

פוי יְהֹוָ֔ה/אֲדֹנָי/אהיה אֶת־מֹשֶׁה מהש, אל שדי: 8 וַיַּעַשׂ אֶת־הַחֹשֶׁן שדי ורבוע אהיה

מַעֲשֵׂה חֹשֵׁב כְּמַעֲשֵׂה אֵפֹד ע״ה אלהים זָהָב תְּכֵלֶת וְאַרְגָּמָן קנ״א קמ״ג

וְתוֹלַעַת שקוצית שָׁנִי וְשֵׁשׁ מָשְׁזָר: 9 רָבוּעַ הָיָה יהה כָּפוּל עָשׂוּ אֶת־הַחֹשֶׁן

שדי ורבוע אהיה זֶרֶת אָרְכּוֹ וְזֶרֶת רָחְבּוֹ כָּפוּל: 10 וַיְמַלְאוּ־בוֹ אַרְבָּעָה טוּרֵי

אָבֶן יוד הה ואו הה טוּר אֹדֶם מ״ה פִּטְדָה וּבָרֶקֶת הַטּוּר הָאֶחָד אהבה, דאגה:

11 וְהַטּוּר הַשֵּׁנִי נֹפֶךְ סַפִּיר וְיָהֲלֹם: 12 וְהַטּוּר הַשְּׁלִישִׁי לֶשֶׁם שְׁבוֹ

וְאַחְלָמָה: 13 וְהַטּוּר הָרְבִיעִי תַּרְשִׁישׁ שֹׁהַם מהש, אל שדי וְיָשְׁפֵה מוּסַבֹּת

מִשְׁבְּצוֹת זָהָב בְּמִלֻּאֹתָם: 14 וְהָאֲבָנִים עַל־שְׁמֹת בְּנֵי־יִשְׂרָאֵל הֵנָּה

מ״ה יה שְׁתֵּים עֶשְׂרֵה עַל־שְׁמֹתָם פִּתּוּחֵי חֹתָם אִישׁ ע״ה קנ״א קס״א עַל־שְׁמוֹ

מהש ע״ה, אל שדי ע״ה לִשְׁנֵים עָשָׂר שָׁבֶט: 15 וַיַּעֲשׂוּ עַל־הַחֹשֶׁן שדי ורבוע אהיה

שַׁרְשְׁרֹת גַּבְלֻת מַעֲשֵׂה עֲבֹת זָהָב טָהוֹר יפ אכא: 16 וַיַּעֲשׂוּ שְׁתֵּי מִשְׁבְּצֹת

16 They made two gold settings and two gold rings, and fastened the rings to two of the corners of the breastplate.

17 They fastened the two gold chains to the rings at the corners of the breastplate,

18 and the other ends of the chains to the two settings, attaching them to the shoulder pieces of the ephod at the front.

19 They made two gold rings and attached them to the other two corners of the breastplate on the inside edge next to the ephod.

20 Then they made two gold rings and attached them to the bottom of the shoulder pieces on the front of the ephod, close to the seam just above the waistband of the ephod.

21 They tied the rings of the breastplate to the rings of the ephod with blue cord, connecting it to the waistband so that the breastplate would not swing out from the ephod—as the Lord commanded Moses.

WHEN CONNECTED: SIXTH READING - JOSEPH - YESOD
ON A LEAP YEAR: THIRD READING - JACOB - TIFERET

22 He made the robe of the ephod entirely of blue cloth - the work of a weaver.

23 The opening in the center of the robe was like the opening of a collar, and a band around this opening, so that it would not tear.

24 They made pomegranates of blue, purple and scarlet yarn and finely twisted linen around the hem of the robe.

25 And they made bells of pure gold between the pomegranates and attached them around the hem between the pomegranates.

26 A bell and a pomegranate, a bell and a pomegranate, around the hem of the robe to be worn for ministering, as the Lord commanded Moses.

27 They made tunics of fine linen—the work of a weaver—for Aaron and his sons,

28 and the turban of fine linen, the linen headbands and the undergarments of finely twisted linen.

זָהָב וּשְׁתֵּי טַבְּעֹת זָהָב וַיִּתְּנוּ אֶת־שְׁתֵּי הַטַּבָּעֹת עַל־שְׁנֵי קְצוֹת הַחֹשֶׁן

שדי ורבוע אהיה: 17 וַיִּתְּנוּ שְׁתֵּי הָעֲבֹתֹת הַזָּהָב ווה עַל־שְׁתֵּי הַטַּבָּעֹת עַל־

קְצוֹת הַחֹשֶׁן שדי ורבוע אהיה: 18 וְאֵת שְׁתֵּי קְצוֹת שְׁתֵּי הָעֲבֹתֹת נָתְנוּ עַל־

שְׁתֵּי הַמִּשְׁבְּצֹת וַיִּתְּנֻם עַל־כִּתְפֹת הָאֵפֹד ע"ה אלהים אֶל־מוּל פָּנָיו:

19 וַיַּעֲשׂוּ שְׁתֵּי טַבְּעֹת זָהָב וַיָּשִׂימוּ עַל־שְׁנֵי קְצוֹת הַחֹשֶׁן שדי ורבוע אהיה

עַל־שְׂפָתוֹ אֲשֶׁר אֶל־עֵבֶר רבוע יהוה אלהים ורבוע אלהים הָאֵפֹד ע"ה אלהים בָּיְתָה:

20 וַיַּעֲשׂוּ שְׁתֵּי טַבְּעֹת זָהָב וַיִּתְּנֻם עַל־שְׁתֵּי כִתְפֹת הָאֵפֹד ע"ה אלהים

מִלְּמַטָּה מִמּוּל פָּנָיו לְעֻמַּת מֶחְבַּרְתּוֹ מִמַּעַל עלם לְחֵשֶׁב הָאֵפֹד ע"ה אלהים:

21 וַיִּרְכְּסוּ אֶת־הַחֹשֶׁן שדי ורבוע אהיה מִטַּבְּעֹתָיו אֶל־טַבְּעֹת הָאֵפֹד ע"ה אלהים

בִּפְתִיל יפ בן תְּכֵלֶת לִהְיֹת עַל־חֵשֶׁב הָאֵפֹד ע"ה אלהים וְלֹא־יִזַּח הַחֹשֶׁן

שדי ורבוע אהיה מֵעַל עלם הָאֵפֹד ע"ה אלהים כַּאֲשֶׁר צִוָּה פוי יהואהדונהי אֶת־

מֹשֶׁה מהש, אל שדי:

WHEN CONNECTED: SIXTH READING - JOSEPH - YESOD
ON A LEAP YEAR: THIRD READING - JACOB - TIFERET

22 וַיַּעַשׂ אֶת־מְעִיל ע"ה קנ"א הָאֵפֹד ע"ה אלהים מַעֲשֵׂה אֹרֵג כְּלִיל תְּכֵלֶת:

23 וּפִי־הַמְּעִיל ע"ה קנ"א בְּתוֹכוֹ כְּפִי תַחְרָא שָׂפָה ע"ה אלהים פשוט וורדין לְפִיו

סָבִיב לֹא יִקָּרֵעַ: 24 וַיַּעֲשׂוּ עַל־שׁוּלֵי הַמְּעִיל ע"ה קנ"א רִמּוֹנֵי תְּכֵלֶת

וְאַרְגָּמָן קנ"א קמ"ג וְתוֹלַעַת שקוצית שָׁנִי מָשְׁזָר: 25 וַיַּעֲשׂוּ פַעֲמֹנֵי זָהָב טָהוֹר

יפ אכא וַיִּתְּנוּ אֶת־הַפַּעֲמֹנִים בְּתוֹךְ הָרִמֹּנִים עַל־שׁוּלֵי הַמְּעִיל ע"ה קנ"א

סָבִיב בְּתוֹךְ הָרִמֹּנִים: 26 פַּעֲמֹן וְרִמֹּן פַּעֲמֹן וְרִמֹּן עַל־שׁוּלֵי הַמְּעִיל

ע"ה קנ"א סָבִיב לְשָׁרֵת כַּאֲשֶׁר צִוָּה פוי יהואהדונהי אֶת־מֹשֶׁה מהש, אל שדי:

27 וַיַּעֲשׂוּ אֶת־הַכָּתְנֹת שֵׁשׁ מַעֲשֵׂה אֹרֵג ע"ב ורבוע ע"ב לְאַהֲרֹן וּלְבָנָיו:

28 וְאֵת הַמִּצְנֶפֶת שֵׁשׁ וְאֶת־פַּאֲרֵי הַמִּגְבָּעֹת שֵׁשׁ וְאֶת־מִכְנְסֵי הַבָּד

29 The sash was of finely twisted linen and blue, purple and scarlet yarn—the work of an embroiderer—as the Lord commanded Moses.

30 They made the plate, the sacred diadem, out of pure gold and engraved on it, like an inscription on a seal: HOLY TO THE LORD.

31 Then they fastened a blue cord to it to attach it to the turban, as the Lord commanded Moses.

32 So all the work on the Tabernacle, the Tent of Meeting, was completed. The Israel-.ites did everything just as the Lord commanded Moses.

ON A LEAP YEAR: FOURTH READING - MOSES - NETZACH

33 Then they brought the Tabernacle to Moses: the tent and all its furnishings, its clasps, frames, crossbars, posts and bases;

34 the covering of ram skins dyed red, the covering of seal skins and the shielding curtain; 35 the Ark of the Covenant with its poles and the atonement cover;

36 the table with all its articles and the bread of the Presence; 37 the pure gold cande-labra with its row of lamps and all its accessories, and the oil for the light;

38 the gold altar, the anointing oil, the fragrant incense, and the curtain for the en-trance to the tent;

39 the bronze altar with its bronze grating, its pillars and all its utensils; the basin with its stand;

40 the curtains of the courtyard with its pillars and sockets, and the curtain for the entrance to the courtyard; the ropes and tent pegs for the courtyard; all the furnish-ings for the Tabernacle, the Tent of Meeting;

41 and the woven garments worn for ministering in the sanctuary, both the sacred garments for Aaron the priest and the garments for his sons when serving as priests.

עֵשׂ מָשְׁזָר: 29 וְאֶת־הָאַבְנֵט שֵׁשׁ מָשְׁזָר וּתְכֵלֶת וְאַרְגָּמָן קנ״א קמ״ג

וְתוֹלַעַת שקוצי״ת שָׁנִי מַעֲשֵׂה רֹקֵם כַּאֲשֶׁר צִוָּה פי׳ יְהֹוָאֲדֹנִיאהדונהי אֶת־

מֹשֶׁה מהע, אל שדי: 30 וַיַּעֲשׂוּ אֶת־צִיץ נֵזֶר־הַקֹּדֶשׁ זָהָב טָהוֹר י״פ אכא

וַיִּכְתְּבוּ עָלָיו מִכְתַּב פִּתּוּחֵי חוֹתָם ע״ה נתה, ע״ה קס״א קנ״א קמ״ג קֹדֶשׁ

לַיהֹוָאֲדֹנִיאהדונהי: 31 וַיִּתְּנוּ עָלָיו פְּתִיל י״פ בן תְּכֵלֶת לָתֵת עַל־הַמִּצְנֶפֶת

מִלְמָעְלָה כַּאֲשֶׁר צִוָּה פי׳ יְהֹוָאֲדֹנִיאהדונהי אֶת־מֹשֶׁה מהע, אל שדי: 32 וַתֵּכֶל

כָּל־ ילי עֲבֹדַת מִשְׁכַּן ב״פ (רבוע אלהים - ה) אֹהֶל לאה מוֹעֵד וַיַּעֲשׂוּ בְּנֵי יִשְׂרָאֵל

כְּכֹל ילי אֲשֶׁר צִוָּה פי׳ יְהֹוָאֲדֹנִיאהדונהי אֶת־מֹשֶׁה מהע, אל שדי כֵּן עָשׂוּ:

ON A LEAP YEAR: FOURTH READING - MOSES - NETZACH

33 וַיָּבִיאוּ אֶת־הַמִּשְׁכָּן ב״פ (רבוע אלהים - ה) אֶל־מֹשֶׁה מהע, אל שדי אֶת־הָאֹהֶל

לאה וְאֶת־כָּל־ ילי ־כֵּלָיו קְרָסָיו קְרָשָׁיו בְּרִיחָו וְעַמֻּדָיו וַאֲדָנָיו: 34 וְאֶת־

מִכְסֵה עוֹרֹת הָאֵילִם הַמְאָדָּמִים וְאֶת־מִכְסֵה עֹרֹת הַתְּחָשִׁים וְאֵת

פָּרֹכֶת הַמָּסָךְ: 35 אֶת־אֲרוֹן ע״ה ג״פ אלהים הָעֵדֻת וְאֶת־בַּדָּיו וְאֵת הַכַּפֹּרֶת:

36 אֶת־הַשֻּׁלְחָן אֶת־כָּל־ ילי ־כֵּלָיו וְאֵת לֶחֶם ג״פ יהוה הַפָּנִים ע״ב ס״ג מ״ה:

37 אֶת־הַמְּנֹרָה הַטְּהֹרָה אֶת־נֵרֹתֶיהָ נֵרֹת הַמַּעֲרָכָה וְאֶת־כָּל־ ילי ־

כֵּלֶיהָ וְאֵת שֶׁמֶן י״פ טל, י״פ כוזו, ביט הַמָּאוֹר: 38 וְאֵת מִזְבַּח זן, נגד הַזָּהָב חזו

וְאֵת שֶׁמֶן י״פ טל, י״פ כוזו, ביט הַמִּשְׁחָה וְאֵת קְטֹרֶת י״א אדני הַסַּמִּים ע״ה קנ״א, אלהים אדני

וְאֵת מָסַךְ פֶּתַח הָאֹהֶל לאה: 39 אֵת | מִזְבַּח זן, נגד הַנְּחֹשֶׁת וְאֶת־מִכְבַּר

לב הַנְּחֹשֶׁת אֲשֶׁר־לוֹ אֶת־בַּדָּיו וְאֶת־כָּל־ ילי ־כֵּלָיו אֶת־הַכִּיֹּר וְאֶת־כַּנּוֹ:

40 אֵת קַלְעֵי הֶחָצֵר אֶת־עַמֻּדֶיהָ וְאֶת־אֲדָנֶיהָ וְאֶת־הַמָּסָךְ לְשַׁעַר

הֶחָצֵר אֶת־מֵיתָרָיו וִיתֵדֹתֶיהָ וְאֵת כָּל־ ילי ־כֵּלֵי כלי עֲבֹדַת הַמִּשְׁכָּן

ב״פ (רבוע אלהים - ה) לְאֹהֶל לאה מוֹעֵד: 41 אֶת־בִּגְדֵי הַשְּׂרָד לְשָׁרֵת בַּקֹּדֶשׁ

42 As the Lord had commanded Moses—so, too, the Israelites did all the work.

43 Moses inspected the work and saw that they had done it just as the Lord had commanded. So Moses blessed them.

WHEN CONNECTED: SEVENTH READING - DAVID - MALCHUT
ON A LEAP YEAR: FIFTH READING - AARON - HOD

40:1 Then the Lord said to Moses:

2 "On the first day of the first month, set up the Tabernacle, the Tent of Meeting.

3 Place the Ark of the Covenant in it and shield the Ark with the curtain.

4 Bring in the table and set out what belongs on it. Then bring in the candelabra and set up its lamps.

5 Place the gold altar of incense in front of the Ark of the Covenant and put the curtain at the entrance to the Tabernacle.

6 Place the altar of burnt offering in front of the entrance to the Tabernacle, the Tent of Meeting;

7 place the basin between the Tent of Meeting and the altar and put water in it.

8 Set up the courtyard around it and put the curtain at the entrance to the courtyard.

9 Take the anointing oil and anoint the Tabernacle and everything in it; consecrate it and all its furnishings, and it will be holy.

10 Then anoint the altar of burnt offering and all its utensils; consecrate the altar, and it will be most holy.

11 Anoint the basin and its stand and consecrate them.

12 Bring Aaron and his sons to the entrance of the Tent of Meeting and wash them with water.

אֶת־בִּגְדֵי הַקֹּדֶשׁ לְאַהֲרֹן ע״ב ורבוע ע״ב הַכֹּהֵן מלה וְאֶת־בִּגְדֵי בָנָיו לְכַהֵן

מלה: 42 כְּכֹל ילי אֲשֶׁר־צִוָּה פוי יְהוָֹאהדונהי אֶת־מֹשֶׁה מהש, אל שדי כֵּן עָשׂוּ

בְּנֵי יִשְׂרָאֵל אֵת כָּל ילי הָעֲבֹדָה: 43 וַיַּרְא אלף למד יהוה מֹשֶׁה מהש, אל שדי

אֶת־כָּל הַמְּלָאכָה ילי וְהִנֵּה אל אדני עָשׂוּ אֹתָהּ כַּאֲשֶׁר צִוָּה פוי

יְהוָֹאהדונהי כֵּן עָשׂוּ וַיְבָרֶךְ עסמ״ב אֹתָם מֹשֶׁה מהש, אל שדי:

WHEN CONNECTED: SEVENTH READING - DAVID - MALCHUT
ON A LEAP YEAR: FIFTH READING - AARON - HOD

40 1 וַיְדַבֵּר ראה יְהוָֹאהדונהי מהש, אל שדי אֶל־מֹשֶׁה לֵּאמֹר: 2 בְּיוֹם

נגד, זן, מזבח הַחֹדֶשׁ הָרִאשׁוֹן י״ב הויות בְּאֶחָד אהבה, דאגה לַחֹדֶשׁ י״ב הויות תָּקִים

אֶת־מִשְׁכַּן ב״פ (רבוע אלהים - ה) אֹהֶל לאה מוֹעֵד: 3 וְשַׂמְתָּ שָׁם יהוה שדי אֵת

אֲרוֹן ע״ה ג״פ אלהים הָעֵדוּת וְסַכֹּתָ עַל־הָאָרֹן ע״ב ורבוע ע״ב אֶת־הַפָּרֹכֶת:

4 וְהֵבֵאתָ אֶת־הַשֻּׁלְחָן וְעָרַכְתָּ אֶת־עֶרְכּוֹ וְהֵבֵאתָ אֶת־הַמְּנֹרָה וְהַעֲלֵיתָ

אֶת־נֵרֹתֶיהָ: 5 וְנָתַתָּה אֶת־מִזְבַּח זן, נגד הַזָּהָב וחהו לִקְטֹרֶת י״א אדני לִפְנֵי

אֲרוֹן ע״ה ג״פ אלהים הָעֵדֻת וְשַׂמְתָּ אֶת־מָסַךְ הַפֶּתַח לַמִּשְׁכָּן

ב״פ (רבוע אלהים - ה) 6 וְנָתַתָּה אֵת מִזְבַּח זן, נגד הָעֹלָה לִפְנֵי וחכמה בינה פֶּתַח

מִשְׁכַּן ב״פ (רבוע אלהים - ה) אֹהֶל לאה ־מוֹעֵד: 7 וְנָתַתָּ אֶת־הַכִּיֹּר בֵּין־אֹהֶל

לאה מוֹעֵד וּבֵין הַמִּזְבֵּחַ זן, נגד וְנָתַתָּ שָׁם יהוה שדי מָיִם: 8 וְשַׂמְתָּ אֶת־הֶחָצֵר

סָבִיב וְנָתַתָּ אֶת־מָסַךְ שַׁעַר י״פ זין הֶחָצֵר: 9 וְלָקַחְתָּ אֶת־שֶׁמֶן י״פ טל, י״פ כוזו, ביט

הַמִּשְׁחָה וּמָשַׁחְתָּ אֶת־הַמִּשְׁכָּן ב״פ (רבוע אלהים - ה) וְאֶת־כָּל ילי ־אֲשֶׁר־בּוֹ

וְקִדַּשְׁתָּ אֹתוֹ וְאֶת־כָּל ילי ־כֵּלָיו יהוה, יהה וְהָיָה קֹדֶשׁ: 10 וּמָשַׁחְתָּ אֶת־

מִזְבַּח זן, נגד הָעֹלָה וְאֶת־כָּל ילי ־כֵּלָיו וְקִדַּשְׁתָּ אֶת־הַמִּזְבֵּחַ זן, נגד וְהָיָה

13 Then dress Aaron in the sacred garments, anoint him and consecrate him so he may serve Me as priest.

14 Bring his sons and dress them in tunics.

15 Anoint them just as you anointed their father, so they may serve Me as priests. Their anointing will be to a priesthood that will continue for all generations to come."

16 Moses did so; everything the Lord commanded him, he did.

ON A LEAP YEAR: SIXTH READING - JOSEPH - YESOD

17 On the first day of the first month in the second year, the Tabernacle was erected.

18 When Moses set up the Tabernacle, he put the sockets in place, erected the frames, inserted the crossbars and set up the pillars. *19* Then he spread the tent over the Tabernacle and put the covering over the tent, as the Lord commanded Moses.

Exodus 40:17—Moses set up the Tabernacle on the first day of the first month, *Nissan* (Aries).

Therefore, "they brought the Tabernacle to Moses, the tent, and all its furniture." (Exodus 39:33) When they brought it all to Moses, they brought all its parts, so each may be joined one to the other. When they wanted to insert them one within the other THEMSELVES, they could not do it; only when they brought it to Moses, he straight away succeeded. Each part advanced and fit into its place. This is the mystery of "and Moses erected the Tabernacle," (Exodus 40:18) and "the Tabernacle was reared up" (Ibid. 17) which we already explained. Come and see: When Moses started to construct the Tabernacle, he started by fixing the parts and putting them together. Then all the parts and constructions of the Other Side became enfeebled. Once the holy side strengthens, the Other Side

became weak. One gets stronger and the other gets weaker. We already explained that while HOLINESS is strong, all the members of the Other Side become enfeebled; the one becomes full, and the other dry. This is the secret of Jerusalem and the evil Tyre, when one is full the other is ruined. Therefore, when HOLINESS gets stronger, THE OTHER SIDE becomes weak.
          — The Zohar, Pekudei 38:346-347

Moses then created order and put everything in its place. He connected all the boards and sockets; erected the pillars; spread the tenting over the top; placed the Tablets in the Ark and moved the Ark into place with its cover; and placed the table and the Menorah, the altars, the curtains, and the laver. Through his care and love for every detail, Moses changed the molecular structure of the physical reality to a spiritual reality. In our own lives, many things are physical, but we can transform them into spiritual realities with our consciousness.

יהוה, יהה ‎_זו, נגד הַמִּזְבֵּחַ 11 וּמָשַׁחְתָּ אֶת־הַכִּיֹּר וְאֶת־כַּנּוֹ

וְקִדַּשְׁתָּ אֹתוֹ: 12 וְהִקְרַבְתָּ אֶת־אַהֲרֹן ‎ע״ב ורבוע ע״ב וְאֶת־בָּנָיו אֶל־פֶּתַח

אֹהֶל לאה מוֹעֵד וְרָחַצְתָּ אֹתָם בַּמָּיִם: 13 וְהִלְבַּשְׁתָּ אֶת־אַהֲרֹן ‎ע״ב ורבוע ע״ב

אֵת בִּגְדֵי הַקֹּדֶשׁ וּמָשַׁחְתָּ אֹתוֹ וְקִדַּשְׁתָּ אֹתוֹ וְכִהֵן ‎מלה לִי: 14 וְאֶת־

בָּנָיו תַּקְרִיב וְהִלְבַּשְׁתָּ אֹתָם כֻּתֳּנֹת: 15 וּמָשַׁחְתָּ אֹתָם כַּאֲשֶׁר מָשַׁחְתָּ

אֶת־אֲבִיהֶם וְכִהֲנוּ לִי וְהָיְתָה לִהְיֹת לָהֶם מָשְׁחָתָם לִכְהֻנַּת עוֹלָם

לְדֹרֹתָם: 16 וַיַּעַשׂ מֹשֶׁה ‎מהש, אל שדי כְּכֹל ‎ילי אֲשֶׁר צִוָּה ‎פוי יְהֹוֹאדניאהדונהי

אֹתוֹ כֵּן עָשָׂה:

ON A LEAP YEAR: SIXTH READING - JOSEPH - YESOD

אל, ייא״י בַּחֹדֶשׁ ‎י״ב הוויות הָרִאשׁוֹן בַּשָּׁנָה הַשֵּׁנִית בְּאֶחָד ‎אהבה, דאגה ‎「וַיְהִי」 17

לַחֹדֶשׁ ‎י״ב הוויות הוּקַם הַמִּשְׁכָּן ‎ב״פ (רבוע אלהים ‎- ה) 18 וַיָּקֶם מֹשֶׁה ‎מהש, אל שדי

אֶת־הַמִּשְׁכָּן ‎ב״פ (רבוע אלהים ‎- ה) וַיִּתֵּן ‎י״פ מלוי ע״ב אֶת־אֲדָנָיו וַיָּשֶׂם אֶת־קְרָשָׁיו

וַיִּתֵּן ‎י״פ מלוי ע״ב אֶת־בְּרִיחָיו וַיָּקֶם אֶת־עַמּוּדָיו: 19 וַיִּפְרֹשׂ אֶת־הָאֹהֶל לאה

עַל־הַמִּשְׁכָּן ‎ב״פ (רבוע אלהים ‎- ה) וַיָּשֶׂם אֶת־מִכְסֵה הָאֹהֶל ‎לאה עָלָיו מִלְמָעְלָה

כַּאֲשֶׁר צִוָּה ‎פוי יְהֹוֹאדניאהדונהי אֶת־מֹשֶׁה ‎מהש, אל שדי: 20 וַיִּקַּח וחעם וַיִּתֵּן

---

*Come and see: "Moses erected,"
(Exodus 40:18) the side of holiness,
and the Other Side of defilement sank,
"and fastened ITS SOCKETS" of the side
of holiness, and that side of defilement
was enfeebled. He "set up ITS BOARDS"
(Ibid.) of the side of holiness, and the
Other Side of defilement was subjugated.
Then he "put up its bars" (Ibid.).*
— *The Zohar, Pekudei 43:422*

Once the Vessel—the Tabernacle itself—was
prepared, the Light of the Creator was able to
enter and fill it. This was the first time such a
place existed in the physical world. Every time

we create a space for the Creator to enter our
life, we rebuild the Tabernacle in our own lives.
We create a space for the Creator to dwell in our
business, in our relationships, in everything we
do.

Moses anointed Aaron and his sons as priests,
bringing them to wash their hands and feet
before they approached the Altar. Our hands
and feet are tools for the manifestation of
spiritual actions. Before we perform a spiritual
action, it is important to cleanse ourselves of any
negativity.

20 *He took the Covenant and placed it in the Ark, attached the poles to the Ark and put the atonement cover over the Ark, on top of it.*

21 *Then he brought the Ark into the Tabernacle and hung the shielding curtain and shielded the Ark of the Covenant, as the Lord commanded Moses.*

22 *Moses placed the table in the Tent of Meeting on the north side of the Tabernacle outside the curtain*

23 *and set out the bread on it before the Lord, as the Lord commanded Moses.*

24 *He placed the candelabra in the Tent of Meeting opposite the table on the south side of the Tabernacle*

25 *and set up the lamps before the Lord, as the Lord commanded Moses.*

26 *Moses placed the gold altar in the Tent of Meeting in front of the curtain*

27 *and burned fragrant incense on it, as the Lord commanded Moses.*

ON A LEAP YEAR: SEVENTH READING - DAVID - MALCHUT

28 *Then he put up the curtain at the entrance to the Tabernacle.*

29 *He set the altar of burnt offering near the entrance to the Tabernacle, the Tent of Meeting, and offered on it burnt offerings and grain offerings, as the Lord commanded Moses.*

30 *He placed the basin between the Tent of Meeting and the altar and put water in it for washing,*

31 *and Moses and Aaron and his sons used it to wash their hands and feet.*

32 *They washed whenever they entered the Tent of Meeting or approached the altar, as the Lord commanded Moses.*

33 *Then Moses set up the courtyard around the Tabernacle and altar and put up the curtain at the entrance to the courtyard. And so Moses finished the work.*

יֵ"פ מלוי ע"ב אֶת־הָעֵדֻת אֶל־הָאָרֹן ע"ב ורבוע ע"ב וַיָּשֶׂם אֶת־הַבַּדִּים עַל־הָאָרֹן

ע"ב ורבוע ע"ב וַיִּתֵּן יֵ"פ מלוי ע"ב אֶת־הַכַּפֹּרֶת עַל־הָאָרֹן ע"ב ורבוע ע"ב מִלְמָעְלָה:

21 וַיָּבֵא אֶת־הָאָרֹן ע"ב ורבוע ע"ב אֶל־הַמִּשְׁכָּן ב"פ (רבוע אלהים ־ ה) וַיָּשֶׂם אֶת

פָּרֹכֶת הַמָּסָךְ וַיָּסֶךְ עַל אֲרוֹן ע"ה ג"פ אלהים הָעֵדֻות כַּאֲשֶׁר מלוי אהיה דיודין צִוָּה

פוי יְהֹוָ‏‏ַאהדונהי אֶת־מֹשֶׁה מהע, אל שדי: 22 וַיִּתֵּן יֵ"פ מלוי ע"ב אֶת־הַשֻּׁלְחָן

בְּאֹהֶל לאה מוֹעֵד עַל יֶרֶךְ הַמִּשְׁכָּן ב"פ (רבוע אלהים ־ ה) צָפֹנָה ע"ה עסמ"ב מִחוּץ

לַפָּרֹכֶת: 23 וַיַּעֲרֹךְ עָלָיו עֵרֶךְ לֶחֶם ג"פ יהוה לִפְנֵי וחכמה בינה יְהֹוָ‏‏ַאהדונהי

כַּאֲשֶׁר צִוָּה פוי יְהֹוָ‏‏ַאהדונהי אֶת־מֹשֶׁה מהע, אל שדי: 24 וַיָּשֶׂם אֶת־הַמְּנֹרָה

בְּאֹהֶל לאה מוֹעֵד נֹכַח ג"פ יהוה הַשֻּׁלְחָן עַל יֶרֶךְ הַמִּשְׁכָּן ב"פ (רבוע אלהים ־ ה)

נֶגְבָּה: 25 וַיַּעַל הַנֵּרֹת לִפְנֵי וחכמה בינה יְהֹוָ‏‏ַאהדונהי כַּאֲשֶׁר צִוָּה פוי

יְהֹוָ‏‏ַאהדונהי אֶת־מֹשֶׁה מהע, אל שדי: 26 וַיָּשֶׂם אֶת־מִזְבַּח זַ, נגד הַזָּהָב וחהו

בְּאֹהֶל לאה מוֹעֵד לִפְנֵי וחכמה בינה הַפָּרֹכֶת: 27 וַיַּקְטֵר עָלָיו קְטֹרֶת י"א אדני

סַמִּים ע"ה קנ"א, אלהים אדני כֵּן אדני כַּאֲשֶׁר צִוָּה פוי יְהֹוָ‏‏ַאהדונהי אֶת־מֹשֶׁה

מהע, אל שדי:

ON A LEAP YEAR: SEVENTH READING - DAVID - MALCHUT

28 וַיָּשֶׂם אֶת־מָסַךְ הַפֶּתַח לַמִּשְׁכָּן ב"פ (רבוע אלהים ־ ה): 29 וְאֵת מִזְבַּח זַ, נגד

הָעֹלָה שָׂם פֶּתַח מִשְׁכַּן ב"פ (רבוע אלהים ־ ה) אֹהֶל לאה ־מוֹעֵד וַיַּעַל עָלָיו

אֶת־הָעֹלָה וְאֶת־הַמִּנְחָה כַּאֲשֶׁר צִוָּה פוי יְהֹוָ‏‏ַאהדונהי אֶת־מֹשֶׁה

מהע, אל שדי: 30 וַיָּשֶׂם אֶת־הַכִּיֹּר בֵּין־אֹהֶל לאה מוֹעֵד וּבֵין הַמִּזְבֵּחַ זַ, נגד

וַיִּתֵּן יֵ"פ מלוי ע"ב שָׁמָּה מהע, משה, אל שדי בַּיִם לְרָחְצָה: 31 וְרָחֲצוּ מִמֶּנּוּ מֹשֶׁה

מהע, אל שדי וְאַהֲרֹן ע"ב ורבוע ע"ב וּבָנָיו אֶת־יְדֵיהֶם וְאֶת־רַגְלֵיהֶם: 32 בְּבֹאָם

אֶל־אֹהֶל לאה מוֹעֵד וּבְקָרְבָתָם אֶל־הַמִּזְבֵּחַ זַ, נגד יִרְחָצוּ כֵּן כַּאֲשֶׁר צִוָּה

MAFTIR

[34] *Then the cloud covered the Tent of Meeting, and the glory of the Lord filled the Tabernacle.* [35] *Moses could not enter the Tent of Meeting because the cloud had settled upon it, and the glory of the Lord filled the Tabernacle.*

[36] *In all the travels of the Israelites, whenever the cloud lifted from above the Tabernacle, they would set out;* [37] *but if the cloud did not lift, they did not set out—until the day it lifted.*

[38] *So the cloud of the Lord was over the Tabernacle by day, and fire was in the cloud by night, in the sight of all the house of Israel during all their travels.*

וַיְכַס

Exodus 40:34—A cloud covered the Tabernacle, which was also known as the Tent of Meeting.

When the cloud rested on it, the glory of God filled the entire Tabernacle. Rashi tells us that the glory of God was so intense that Moses could not enter the Tabernacle when the cloud was resting there. And according to the Ramban, when God wished to speak to Moses, He summoned him and Moses stood outside the Tent, not entering the place that was filled with God's glory.

It is written, "...and Moses was not able to enter into the Tent of Testimony, because the cloud rested on it..." (Exodus 40:35). The sense is that it adorned itself as a woman prepares and adorns herself for her husband. And when she does so, it is not fit that her husband should enter to her. Therefore, "Moses was not able to enter into the Tent of Testimony because the cloud rested on it." For this reason "they brought the Tabernacle to Moses." Also, "Moses saw all the work...." (Exodus 39:43)
— *The Zohar, Pekudei 29:285*

It is written, "And Moses was not able to enter the Tent of Meeting, because the cloud rested on it" (Exodus 40:35), as the Holy Spirit dwelt upon the world, and the defiled spirit vanished, except when the wicked draw it again upon the world. If they do not, it is not there.
— *The Zohar, Pekudei 63:958*

הֶעָנָן מֵעַל

Exodus 40:36—When the cloud rose up from the Tabernacle, the children of Israel would embark on their journey, and when it did not rise up, they stayed where they were.

The people were thus guided by the cloud in the daytime and the fire at night; one or the other was always before their eyes. To this day, that guidance is always before us; however, we don't always choose to follow. It is hard work to awake from our slumber when the fire begins to move; or to move our home when the cloud travels. Guidance from the Creator is often uncomfortable in the short term, but the chaos that we experience when we refuse to listen is painful in the long term

When we conclude our reading of a Book of the Torah, we say chazak (meaning "strength") three times. The numerical value of repeating chazak three times is Mem, Hei, Shin, which gives us healing. We also use one of the 72 Names—Pei, Hei, Lamed—to activate our strength. The spiritual path is not easy, and we require strength and certainty to take advantage of all that is put before us. The 72 Names of God connects us to the source of Light that we need to gain the power of mind over matter. And when we use the tools of the 72 Names, we tap into the dimension where consciousness controls reality.

פְּי יְהֹוָה אֶת־מֹשֶׁה מהע, אל שׁדי 33 וַיָּקֶם אֶת־הֶחָצֵר סָבִיב לַמִּשְׁכָּן

ב"פ (רבוע אלהים - ה) וְלַמִּזְבֵּחַ זן, נגד וַיִּתֵּן יפ מלוי ע"ב אֶת־מָסַךְ שַׁעַר הֶחָצֵר וַיְכַל

מֹשֶׁה מהע, אל שׁדי אֶת־הַמְּלָאכָה אל אדני׃

MAFTIR

34 וַיְכַס הֶעָנָן אֶת־אֹהֶל לאה מוֹעֵד וּכְבוֹד ל"ב יְהֹוָה בָּלֵא אֶת־

הַמִּשְׁכָּן ב"פ (רבוע אלהים - ה)׃ 35 וְלֹא־יָכֹל מֹשֶׁה מהע, אל שׁדי לָבוֹא אֶל־אֹהֶל לאה

מוֹעֵד כִּי־שָׁכַן ש"ע עָלָיו הֶעָנָן וּכְבוֹד ל"ב יְהֹוָה בָּלֵא אֶת־הַמִּשְׁכָּן

ב"פ (רבוע אלהים - ה)׃ 36 וּבְהֵעָלוֹת הֶעָנָן מֵעַל עלם הַמִּשְׁכָּן ב"פ (רבוע אלהים - ה) יִסְעוּ

בְּנֵי יִשְׂרָאֵל בְּכֹל ב"ן, לכב, יבם מַסְעֵיהֶם׃ 37 וְאִם יוהך ־לֹא יֵעָלֶה הֶעָנָן וְלֹא

יִסְעוּ עַד־יוֹם גגד, זן, מזבח הֵעָלֹתוֹ׃ 38 כִּי עֲנַן יְהֹוָה עַל־הַמִּשְׁכָּן

ב"פ (רבוע אלהים - ה) יוֹמָם וְאֵשׁ אלהים דיודין ע"ה תִּהְיֶה לַיְלָה מלה בּוֹ לְעֵינֵי ריבוע מ"ה

כָל ילי ־בֵּית ב"פ ראה יִשְׂרָאֵל בְּכֹל ב"ן, לכב, יבם ־מַסְעֵיהֶם׃

חֲזַק (יסוד־ימין) פהל   (גבורה־שמאל) חֲזַק פהל   (תפארת־אמצע) חֲזַק פהל; מהע

וְנִתְחַזֵּק (מלכות)

HAFTARAH OF PEKUDEI

In this Haftarah, we read about the completion of the Temple by King Solomon and we learn that the location of the Temple had been intended since Creation. It is the same location where Abraham offered his son, Isaac, up to God and where Jacob had his dream. However, it was not until King Solomon completed the Temple that the Light could be revealed.

Kings 1 7:40-50

7:40 Hiram made the basins and shovels and sprinkling bowls. So Huram finished all the work he had undertaken for King Solomon in the Temple of the Lord:

41 The two pillars; the two bowl-shaped capitals on top of the pillars; the two sets of network decorating the two bowl-shaped capitals on top of the pillars;

42 the four hundred pomegranates for the two sets of network (two rows of pomegranates for each network, decorating the bowl-shaped capitals on top of the pillars);

43 the ten stands with the ten basins on top of the stands;

44 the sea and the twelve bulls under the sea;

45 the pots, shovels and sprinkling bowls. All these objects that Hiram made for King Solomon for the Temple of the Lord were of burnished bronze.

46 The king had them cast in clay molds in the plain of the Jordan between Succoth and Zarethan.

47 Solomon left all these things unweighed, because there were so many; the weight of the bronze was not determined.

48 Solomon also made all the furnishings that were in the Lord's Temple: the golden altar; the golden table on which was the golden bread of the Presence;

49 the candelabras of pure gold (five on the right and five on the left, in front of the inner sanctuary) the gold floral work and lamps and tongs;

50 the pure gold basins, wick trimmers, sprinkling bowls, dishes and censers; and the gold sockets for the doors of the innermost room, the Holy of Holies, and also for the doors of the main hall of the Temple.

HAFTARAH OF PEKUDEI

The lesson here is that each and every one of us is born with tremendous potential, but we often fail to manifest it. The connection we make to the Light by hearing this Haftarah gives us the energy we need to manifest the potential that has been ours since the beginning of time.

מלכים א פרק ז

7 40 וַיַּעַשׂ חִירוֹם אֶת־הַכִּיֹרוֹת וְאֶת־הַיָּעִים וְאֶת־הַמִּזְרָקוֹת וַיְכַל
חִירָם עֹ"ה גֵּ"פ אלהים לַעֲשׂוֹת אֶת־כָּל־הַמְּלָאכָה אֲשֶׁר עָשָׂה לַמֶּלֶךְ
שְׁלֹמֹה בֵּית יְהֹוָה: 41 עַמֻּדִים שְׁנַיִם וְגֻלֹּת הַכֹּתָרֹת
אֲשֶׁר־עַל־רֹאשׁ הָעַמּוּדִים שְׁתַּיִם וְהַשְּׂבָכוֹת שְׁתַּיִם
לְכַסּוֹת אֶת־שְׁתֵּי גֻּלֹּת הַכֹּתָרֹת אֲשֶׁר עַל־רֹאשׁ
הָעַמּוּדִים: 42 וְאֶת־הָרִמֹּנִים אַרְבַּע מֵאוֹת לִשְׁתֵּי הַשְּׂבָכוֹת שְׁנֵי־
טוּרִים רִמֹּנִים לַשְּׂבָכָה הָאֶחָת לְכַסּוֹת אֶת־שְׁתֵּי גֻּלֹּת הַכֹּתָרֹת אֲשֶׁר
עַל־פְּנֵי הָעַמּוּדִים: 43 וְאֶת־הַמְּכֹנוֹת עָשֶׂר וְאֶת־הַכִּיֹרֹת עֲשָׂרָה
עַל־הַמְּכֹנוֹת: 44 וְאֶת־הַיָּם הָאֶחָד וְאֶת־הַבָּקָר שְׁנֵים־עָשָׂר
תַּחַת הַיָּם: 45 וְאֶת־הַסִּירוֹת וְאֶת־הַיָּעִים וְאֶת־הַמִּזְרָקוֹת וְאֵת כָּל
הַכֵּלִים הָאֵלֶּה (כתיב: הָאֹהֶל) אֲשֶׁר עָשָׂה חִירָם לַמֶּלֶךְ שְׁלֹמֹה בֵּית
יְהֹוָה נְחֹשֶׁת מְמֹרָט: 46 בְּכִכַּר הַיַּרְדֵּן יְצָקָם
הַמֶּלֶךְ בְּמַעֲבֵה הָאֲדָמָה בֵּין סֻכּוֹת וּבֵין צָרְתָן: 47 וַיַּנַּח שְׁלֹמֹה אֶת־
כָּל־הַכֵּלִים מֵרֹב מְאֹד מְאֹד לֹא נֶחְקַר מִשְׁקַל
הַנְּחֹשֶׁת: 48 וַיַּעַשׂ שְׁלֹמֹה אֵת כָּל־הַכֵּלִים אֲשֶׁר בֵּית
יְהֹוָה אֵת מִזְבַּח הַזָּהָב וְאֶת־הַשֻּׁלְחָן אֲשֶׁר עָלָיו לֶחֶם
הַפָּנִים זָהָב: 49 וְאֶת־הַמְּנֹרוֹת חָמֵשׁ מִיָּמִין וְחָמֵשׁ
מִשְּׂמֹאול לִפְנֵי הַדְּבִיר זָהָב סָגוּר וְהַפֶּרַח וְהַנֵּרֹת וְהַמֶּלְקַחַיִם
זָהָב: 50 וְהַסִּפּוֹת וְהַמְזַמְּרוֹת וְהַמִּזְרָקוֹת וְהַכַּפּוֹת וְהַמַּחְתּוֹת זָהָב סָגוּר
וְהַפֹּתוֹת לְדַלְתוֹת הַבַּיִת הַפְּנִימִי לְקֹדֶשׁ הַקֳּדָשִׁים לְדַלְתֵי הַבַּיִת
לַהֵיכָל זָהָב:

SPECIAL READINGS

MAFTIR OF SHABBAT SHEKALIM

Shekalim is the plural form of the word *shekel*, an ancient currency still used in Israel today. During the month of *Adar* (Pisces), each person paid half a shekel to the Temple. The half-shekel offering teaches us a lesson in consciousness: No matter how smart we think we are, no matter how much we think we see, we only perceive half of the total picture. Knowing that what we see is limited creates a humility that allows the Light to direct and support us. When we think we see everything, we give in to judgment and negativity, and the Creator says, "If you know everything, why do you

Exodus 30:11-16

30:11 Then the Lord spoke to Moses, saying,

12 "When you take a census of the Israelites to count them, each one must pay the Lord a ransom for his life at the time he is counted. Then no plague will come on them when you number them.

13 Each one who passes over to those already counted is to give a half shekel, according to the holy shekel, which weighs twenty gerahs. This half shekel is a contribution to the Lord.

14 All who pass over, those twenty years old or more, are to give a contribution to the Lord.

15 The rich are not to give more than a half shekel and the poor are not to give less when you make the contribution to the Lord to atone for your lives.

16 Take the atonement money from the Israelites and use it for the service of the Tent of Meeting. It will be a memorial for the Israelites before the Lord, making atonement for your lives."

MAFTIR OF SHABBAT SHEKALIM

need Me?" The Maftir of Shabbat Shekalim gives us the ability to see beyond the boundaries that ordinarily limit us.

Scripture says that only people who were at least twenty years old gave the offering. "The rich shall not give more, and the poor shall not give less than half a *shekel*, when they give an offering unto the Lord, to make atonement for your souls." (*Exodus 30:15*)

שמות פרק ל

30 11 וַיְדַבֵּר ראה יְהֹוָאהּדִּיאָהּהֹוּנֵי אֶל־מֹשֶׁה מהע, אל שדי לֵאמֹר: 12 כִּי תִשָּׂא

אֶת־רֹאשׁ ריבוע אלהים ואלהים דיודין ע״ה בְּנֵי־יִשְׂרָאֵל לִפְקֻדֵיהֶם וְנָתְנוּ

אבגית״ץ, ושר, אהבת חנם אִישׁ ע״ה קנ״א קס״א כֹּפֶר מצפ״ץ נַפְשׁוֹ לַיהֹוָאהּדּיּאהּהֹוּנֵי בִּפְקֹד

רבוע ע״ב אֹתָם וְלֹא־יִהְיֶה ... בָהֶם נֶגֶף בִּפְקֹד רבוע ע״ב אֹתָם: 13 זֶה | יִתְּנוּ

כָּל יִלי הָעֹבֵר רבוע יהוה ורבוע אלהים עַל־הַפְּקֻדִים מַחֲצִית הַשֶּׁקֶל בְּשֶׁקֶל

הַקֹּדֶשׁ עֶשְׂרִים גֵּרָה דֵּ׳פ בן הַשֶּׁקֶל מַחֲצִית הַשֶּׁקֶל תְּרוּמָה לַיהֹוָאהּדּיּאהּהֹוּנֵי:

14 כֹּל יִלי הָעֹבֵר רבוע יהוה ורבוע אלהים עַל־הַפְּקֻדִים מִבֶּן עֶשְׂרִים שָׁנָה

וָמָעְלָה יִתֵּן תְּרוּמַת יְהֹוָאהּדּיּאהּהֹוּנֵי: 15 הֶעָשִׁיר לֹא־יַרְבֶּה וְהַדַּל לֹא

יַמְעִיט מִמַּחֲצִית הַשֶּׁקֶל לָתֵת אֶת־תְּרוּמַת יְהֹוָאהּדּיּאהּהֹוּנֵי לְכַפֵּר מצפ״ץ

עַל־נַפְשֹׁתֵיכֶם: 16 וְלָקַחְתָּ אֶת־כֶּסֶף הַכִּפֻּרִים מֵאֵת בְּנֵי יִשְׂרָאֵל וְנָתַתָּ

אֹתוֹ עַל־עֲבֹדַת אֹהֶל לאה מוֹעֵד יהוה, יהה וְהָיָה לִבְנֵי יִשְׂרָאֵל לְזִכָּרוֹן

ע״ב קס״א נ״א״ב לִפְנֵי וחכמה בינה יְהֹוָאהּדּיּאהּהֹוּנֵי לְכַפֵּר מצפ״ץ עַל־נַפְשֹׁתֵיכֶם:

HAFTARAH OF SHABBAT SHEKALIM

This Haftarah describes the period when Joash became king of Jerusalem at the age of seven and went on to reign for forty years. Once again, we are reminded that to be a pure channel, like Betzalel, the twelve year old builder of the Tabernacle, one does not need to have lived many

2 Kings 11:17-12:17

11: [17] Jehoiada then made a covenant between the Lord and the king and people that they would be the Lord's people. He also made a covenant between the king and the people.

[18] All the people of the land went to the temple of Baal and tore it down. They smashed the altars and idols to pieces and killed Mattan the priest of Baal in front of the altars. Then the priest posted guards at the temple of the Lord.

[19] He took with him the commanders of hundreds, the Carites, the guards and all the people of the land, and together they brought the king down from the Temple of the Lord and went into the palace, entering by way of the gate of the guards. The king then took his place on the royal throne,

[20] and all the people of the land rejoiced. And the city was quiet, because Athaliah had been slain with the sword at the palace.

[21] Joash was seven years old when he began to reign.

12:[1] In the seventh year of Jehu, Joash became king, and he reigned in Jerusalem forty years. His mother's name was Zibiah; she was from Beersheba.

[2] Joash did what was right in the eyes of the Lord all his years, in the way Jehoiada, the priest, instructed him.

[3] The high places, however, were not removed; the people continued to offer sacrifices and burn incense there.

[4] Joash said to the priests, "Collect all the money that is brought as sacred offerings to the Temple of the Lord - the money collected in the census, the money received from personal vows and the money brought voluntarily to the temple.

[5] Let every priest receive the money from one of the treasurers, and let it be used to repair whatever damage is found in the Temple."

HAFTARAH OF SHABBAT SHEKALIM

years or studied a great deal. Wisdom does not depend on how much we know or how old we are, but on how connected we are to the Light.

מלכים ב פרק יא

17 וַיִּכְרֹת יְהוֹיָדָע אֶת־הַבְּרִית בֵּין יְהֹוָֹאהדנהי וּבֵין הַמֶּלֶךְ וּבֵין 11
הָעָם לִהְיוֹת לְעָם ליהֹוָֹאהדנהי וּבֵין הַמֶּלֶךְ וּבֵין הָעָם: 18 וַיָּבֹאוּ
כָל־עַם הָאָרֶץ בֵּית־הַבַּעַל וַיִּתְּצֻהוּ אֶת־מִזְבְּחֹתָו
וְאֶת־צְלָמָיו שִׁבְּרוּ הֵיטֵב וְאֵת מַתָּן כֹּהֵן הַבַּעַל הָרְגוּ לִפְנֵי
הַמִּזְבְּחוֹת וַיָּשֶׂם הַכֹּהֵן פְּקֻדֹּת עַל־בֵּית יְהֹוָֹאהדנהי: 19 וַיִּקַּח
אֶת־שָׂרֵי הַמֵּאוֹת וְאֶת־הַכָּרִי וְאֶת־הָרָצִים וְאֵת | כָּל־עַם
הָאָרֶץ וַיֹּרִידוּ אֶת־הַמֶּלֶךְ מִבֵּית יְהֹוָֹאהדנהי וַיָּבוֹאוּ
דֶרֶךְ־שַׁעַר הָרָצִים בֵּית הַמֶּלֶךְ וַיֵּשֶׁב עַל־כִּסֵּא
הַמְּלָכִים: 20 וַיִּשְׂמַח כָּל־עַם־הָאָרֶץ וְהָעִיר
שָׁקָטָה וְאֶת־עֲתַלְיָהוּ הֵמִיתוּ בַחֶרֶב בֵּית
הַמֶּלֶךְ (כתיב: מלך): 12 1 בֶּן־שֶׁבַע שָׁנִים יְהוֹאָשׁ
בְמָלְכוֹ: 2 בִּשְׁנַת־שֶׁבַע לְיֵהוּא מָלַךְ יְהוֹאָשׁ וְאַרְבָּעִים
שָׁנָה מָלַךְ בִּירוּשָׁלָ͏ִם וְשֵׁם אִמּוֹ צִבְיָה מִבְּאֵר שָׁבַע
3 וַיַּעַשׂ יְהוֹאָשׁ הַיָּשָׁר בְּעֵינֵי יְהֹוָֹאהדנהי כָּל־
יָמָיו אֲשֶׁר הוֹרָהוּ יְהוֹיָדָע הַכֹּהֵן: 4 רַק הַבָּמוֹת לֹא־סָרוּ עוֹד הָעָם
מְזַבְּחִים וּמְקַטְּרִים בַּבָּמוֹת: 5 וַיֹּאמֶר יְהוֹאָשׁ אֶל־הַכֹּהֲנִים כָּל
כֶּסֶף הַקֳּדָשִׁים אֲשֶׁר־יוּבָא בֵית־יְהֹוָֹאהדנהי כֶּסֶף עוֹבֵר אִישׁ
כֶּסֶף נַפְשׁוֹת עֶרְכּוֹ כָּל־כֶּסֶף אֲשֶׁר יַעֲלֶה עַל לֶב־אִישׁ
לְהָבִיא בֵּית יְהֹוָֹאהדנהי: 6 יִקְחוּ לָהֶם הַכֹּהֲנִים

[6] *But by the twenty-third year of King Joash the priests still had not repaired the Temple.*

[7] *King Joash summoned Jehoiada, the priest, and the other priests and asked them, "Why aren't you repairing the damage done to the Temple? Take no more money from your treasurers, but hand it over for repairing the Temple."*

[8] *The priests agreed that they would not collect any more money from the people and that they would not repair the Temple themselves.*

[9] *Jehoiada, the priest, took a chest and bored a hole in its lid. He placed it beside the altar, on the right side as one enters the Temple of the Lord. The priests who guarded the entrance put into the chest all the money that was brought to the Temple of the Lord.*

[10] *Whenever they saw that there was a large amount of money in the chest, the royal secretary and the High Priest came, counted the money that had been brought into the temple of the Lord and put it into bags.*

[11] *When the amount had been determined, they gave the money to the men appointed to supervise the work on the Temple. With it they paid those who worked on the Temple of the Lord - the carpenters and builders,*

[12] *the masons and stonecutters. They purchased timber and dressed stone for the repair of the Temple of the Lord, and met all the other expenses of restoring the temple.*

[13] *The money brought into the Temple was not spent for making silver basins, wick trimmers, sprinkling bowls, trumpets or any other articles of gold or silver for the Temple of the Lord;*

[14] *it was paid to the workmen, who used it to repair the Temple.*

[15] *They did not require an accounting from those to whom they gave the money to pay the workers, because they acted with complete honesty.*

[16] *The money from the guilt offerings and sin offerings was not brought into the Temple of the Lord; it belonged to the priests.*

[17] *About this time Hazael, king of Aram, went up and attacked Gath and captured it. Then he turned to attack Jerusalem.*

אִישׁ מֵאֵת מַכָּרוֹ וְהֵם יְחַזְּקוּ אֶת־בֶּדֶק הַבַּיִת לְכֹל

אֲשֶׁר־יִמָּצֵא שָׁם בָּדֶק: 7 וַיְהִי בִּשְׁנַת עֶשְׂרִים וְשָׁלֹשׁ

שָׁנָה לַמֶּלֶךְ יְהוֹאָשׁ לֹא־חִזְּקוּ הַכֹּהֲנִים אֶת־בֶּדֶק הַבָּיִת:

8 וַיִּקְרָא הַמֶּלֶךְ יְהוֹאָשׁ לִיהוֹיָדָע הַכֹּהֵן וְלַכֹּהֲנִים

וַיֹּאמֶר אֲלֵהֶם מַדּוּעַ אֵינְכֶם מְחַזְּקִים אֶת־בֶּדֶק הַבָּיִת וְעַתָּה

אַל־תִּקְחוּ־כֶסֶף מֵאֵת מַכָּרֵיכֶם כִּי־לְבֶדֶק הַבַּיִת תִּתְּנֻהוּ:

9 וַיֵּאֹתוּ הַכֹּהֲנִים לְבִלְתִּי קְחַת־כֶּסֶף מֵאֵת הָעָם וּלְבִלְתִּי חַזֵּק

אֶת־בֶּדֶק הַבָּיִת: 10 וַיִּקַּח יְהוֹיָדָע הַכֹּהֵן אֲרוֹן

אֶחָד וַיִּקֹּב חֹר בְּדַלְתּוֹ וַיִּתֵּן אֹתוֹ אֵצֶל הַמִּזְבֵּחַ

מִיָּמִין (כתיב: בימין) בְּבוֹא־אִישׁ בֵּית יְהוָה וְנָתְנוּ

שָׁמָּה הַכֹּהֲנִים שֹׁמְרֵי הַסַּף אֶת־כָּל־הַכֶּסֶף

הַמּוּבָא בֵית יְהוָה: 11 וַיְהִי כִּרְאוֹתָם כִּי־רַב

הַכֶּסֶף בָּאָרוֹן וַיַּעַל סֹפֵר הַמֶּלֶךְ וְהַכֹּהֵן הַגָּדוֹל

וַיָּצֻרוּ וַיִּמְנוּ אֶת־הַכֶּסֶף הַנִּמְצָא בֵית יְהוָה:

12 וְנָתְנוּ אֶת־הַכֶּסֶף הַמְתֻכָּן עַל־יְדֵי (כתיב: יד) עֹשֵׂי הַמְּלָאכָה

הַמֻּפְקָדִים (כתיב: הפקדים) בֵּית יְהוָה וַיּוֹצִיאֻהוּ לְחָרָשֵׁי הָעֵץ

וְלַבֹּנִים הָעֹשִׂים בֵּית יְהוָה: 13 וְלַגֹּדְרִים וּלְחֹצְבֵי

הָאֶבֶן וְלִקְנוֹת עֵצִים וְאַבְנֵי מַחְצֵב לְחַזֵּק אֶת־בֶּדֶק בֵּית

יְהוָה וּלְכֹל אֲשֶׁר־יֵצֵא עַל־הַבַּיִת לְחָזְקָה:

14 אַךְ לֹא יֵעָשֶׂה בֵּית יְהוָה סִפּוֹת כֶּסֶף מְזַמְּרוֹת מִזְרָקוֹת

חֲצֹצְרוֹת כָּל־כְּלִי־זָהָב וּכְלִי־כָסֶף מִן־הַכֶּסֶף הַמּוּבָא בֵית

יְהוָה: 15 כִּי־לְעֹשֵׂי הַמְּלָאכָה יִתְּנֻהוּ וְחִזְּקוּ־בוֹ

אֶת־בֵּית יְהוָה: 16 וְלֹא יְחַשְּׁבוּ אֶת־הָאֲנָשִׁים אֲשֶׁר יִתְּנוּ

אֶת־הַכֶּסֶף עַל־יָדָם לָתֵת לְעֹשֵׂי הַמְּלָאכָה כִּי בֶאֱמֻנָה הֵם עֹשִׂים:

17 כֶּסֶף אָשָׁם וְכֶסֶף חַטָּאוֹת לֹא יוּבָא בֵּית יְהוָה לַכֹּהֲנִים

יִהְיוּ {פ}

MAFTIR OF SHABBAT ZACHOR

Uncertainty is our greatest opportunity for positive change because it gives us a chance to confront and overcome the negative power of doubt. When we overcome doubt, we overcome all our fears at the seed level—which is the source of unhappiness in our lives. This reading deals with the war against the nation of Amalek. The *Zohar* tells us that Amalek is not a nation, but a concealed

Deuteronomy 25:17-19

25:17 "Remember what Amalek did to you along the way, when you came out from Egypt,

18 how he met you along the way and attacked among you all the stragglers at your rear when you were faint and weary; and he did not fear God.

19 It shall come about when the Lord, your God has given you rest from all your surrounding enemies, in the land which the Lord, your God gives you as an inheritance to possess, you shall blot out the memory of Amalek from under heaven. You must not forget.

HAFTARAH OF SHABBAT ZACHOR

This Haftarah recounts the war against Amalek. The Talmud says that King David sinned twice and King Saul only once, yet King David was forgiven and King Saul was killed and his kingdom taken away. When God came to King Saul and said, "Go and kill Amalek," King Saul thought to

1 Samuel 15:1-34

15:1 Samuel said to Saul, "I am the one the Lord sent to anoint you king over His people Israel; so listen now to the message from the Lord.

2 This is what the Lord of Hosts says: 'I will punish the Amalekites for what they did to Israel when they waylaid them as they came up from Egypt.

MAFTIR OF SHABBAT ZACHOR

truth about life. The word *amalek* has the same numerical value as the Aramaic word *safek*, which means "doubt." According to Kabbalah, words of equivalent numerical value share the same meaning. With this reading, we receive the power of certainty to overcome our own Amalek (doubt).

דברים פרק כה

25 17 זָכֹור עֽ״ב קס״א אֵת אֲשֶׁר־עָשָׂה לְךָ עֲמָלֵק בֽ״פ ק׽׳ר בַּדֶּרֶךְ בֽ״פ יבֽ״ק

בְּצֵאתְכֶם מִמִּצְרָיִם מצֽ״ר: 18 אֲשֶׁר קָרְךָ בַּדֶּרֶךְ בֽ״פ יבֽ״ק וַיְזַנֵּב בְּךָ כָּל־ ילֽי

הַנֶּחֱשָׁלִים אַחֲרֶיךָ וְאַתָּה עָיֵף וְיָגֵעַ וְלֹא יָרֵא אלף למד יהוה אֱלֹהִים

מום, אהיה אדני ; ילֽה: 19 וְהָיָה יהוה, יהה בְּהָנִיחַ יְהֹוָאֳדׁנִיאהדונהי אֱלֹהֶיךָ ילֽה | לְךָ

מִכָּל־ ילֽי ־אֹיְבֶיךָ מִסָּבִיב בָּאָרֶץ אלהים דאלפין אֲשֶׁר יְהֹוָאֳדׁנִיאהדונהי אֱלֹהֶיךָ

ילֽה נֹתֵן אבגית״ץ, ושר, אהבת חנם לְךָ נַחֲלָה לְרִשְׁתָּהּ תִּמְחֶה אֶת־זֵכֶר עֲמָלֵק

בֽ״פ ק׽׳ר מִתַּחַת הַשָּׁמָיִם אֽ״ת בֽ״ש יֽ״פ טל, יֽ״פ כוזו עֽ״ה קרעשטן לֹא תִּשְׁכָּח:

HAFTARAH OF SHABBAT ZACHOR

himself that maybe God wanted him to kill all the people but not the animals. The problem for King Saul was not that he was wrong, but that he made a calculation.

שמואל א פרק טו

15 1 וַיֹּאמֶר שְׁמוּאֵל אֶל־שָׁאוּל אֹתִי שָׁלַח יְהֹוָאֳדׁנִיאהדונהי לִמְשָׁחֳךָ

לְמֶלֶךְ עַל־עַמּוֹ עַל־יִשְׂרָאֵל וְעַתָּה שְׁמַע לְקוֹל עֽ״ב סֽ״ג עֽ״ה דִּבְרֵי ראה

יְהֹוָאֳדׁנִיאהדונהי: 2 כֹּה הֽי אָמַר יְהֹוָאֳדׁנִיאהדונהי צְבָאוֹת נתה ורבוע אהיה; פני שכינה

3 Now go, attack the Amalekites and totally destroy everything that belongs to them. Do not spare them; put to death men and women, children and infants, cattle and sheep, camels and donkeys.' "

4 So Saul summoned the men and mustered them at Telaim—two hundred thousand foot soldiers and ten thousand men from Judah.

5 Saul went to the city of Amalek and set an ambush in the ravine.

6 Then he said to the Kenites, "Go away, leave, go down from the Amalekites so that I do not destroy you along with them; for you showed kindness to all the Israelites when they came up out of Egypt." So the Kenites moved away from the Amalekites.

7 Then Saul attacked the Amalekites all the way from Havilah to Shur, to the east of Egypt.

8 He captured Agag, king of the Amalekites, alive and all his people he totally destroyed with the sword.

9 But Saul and the army spared Agag and the best of the sheep and cattle, the fat calves and lambs—everything that was good. These they were unwilling to destroy completely, but everything that was despised and weak they totally destroyed.

10 Then the word of the Lord came to Samuel:

11 "I am grieved that I have made Saul king, because he has turned away from Me and has not carried out my instructions." Samuel was troubled, and he cried out to the Lord all that night.

12 Early in the morning Samuel got up and went to meet Saul, but Samuel was told, "Saul has gone to Carmel. There he has set up a monument in his own honor and has turned and gone on down to Gilgal."

13 When Samuel reached Saul, Saul said, "The Lord bless you! I have carried out the Lord's instructions."

14 But Samuel said, "What then is this bleating of sheep in my ears? What is this lowing of cattle that I hear?"

15 Saul answered, "They brought them from the Amalekites; they spared the best of the sheep and cattle to sacrifice to the Lord your God, but we totally destroyed the rest." 16 "Stop!" Samuel said to Saul. "Let me tell you what the Lord said to me last night." "Speak," Saul replied.

פָּקַדְתִּי אֵת אֲשֶׁר־עָשָׂה עֲמָלֵק ב"פ ק"ר לְיִשְׂרָאֵל אֲשֶׁר־שָׂם יהוה שדי לוֹ

בַּדֶּרֶךְ ב"פ יב"ק בַּעֲלֹתוֹ מִמִּצְרָיִם מצר 3 עַתָּה לֵךְ וְהִכִּיתָה אֶת־עֲמָלֵק

ב"פ ק"ר וְהַחֲרַמְתֶּם אֶת־כָּל־ ילי אֲשֶׁר־לוֹ וְלֹא תַחְמֹל עָלָיו וְהֵמַתָּה מֵאִישׁ

ע"ה קנ"א קס"א עַד־אִשָּׁה מֵעֹלֵל וְעַד־יוֹנֵק מִשּׁוֹר אבגיתץ, ושר, אהבת חנם וְעַד־שֶׂה

מִגָּמָל וְעַד־חֲמוֹר: 4 וַיְשַׁמַּע שָׁאוּל אֶת־הָעָם וַיִּפְקְדֵם בַּטְּלָאִים

אלף למד עין דלת יוד ע"ה מָאתַיִם אֶלֶף רַגְלִי וַעֲשֶׂרֶת אֲלָפִים קס"א אֶת־אִישׁ

ע"ה קנ"א קס"א יְהוּדָה: 5 וַיָּבֹא שָׁאוּל עַד־עִיר סוחור, ערי, סנדלפון עֲמָלֵק ב"פ ק"ר

וַיָּרֶב בַּנָּחַל: 6 וַיֹּאמֶר שָׁאוּל אֶל־הַקֵּינִי לְכוּ סֻּרוּ רְדוּ יפ אהיה מִתּוֹךְ

עֲמָלֵקִי פֶּן־אֹסִפְךָ עִמּוֹ וְאַתָּה עָשִׂיתָה חֶסֶד ע"ב, ריבוע יהוה עִם־כָּל־ ילי בְּנֵי

יִשְׂרָאֵל בַּעֲלוֹתָם מִמִּצְרָיִם מצר וַיָּסַר קֵינִי מִתּוֹךְ עֲמָלֵק ב"פ ק"ר 7 וַיַּךְ

שָׁאוּל אֶת־עֲמָלֵק ב"פ ק"ר מֵחֲוִילָה בּוֹאֲךָ שׁוּר אבגיתץ, ושר, אהבת חנם אֲשֶׁר

עַל־פְּנֵי חכמה בינה מִצְרָיִם מצר: 8 וַיִּתְפֹּשׂ אֶת־אֲגַג מֶלֶךְ־עֲמָלֵק ב"פ ק"ר חָי

וְאֶת־כָּל־ ילי הָעָם הֶחֱרִים לְפִי־חָרֶב רבוע ס"ג ורבוע אהיה: 9 וַיַּחְמֹל שָׁאוּל

וְהָעָם עַל־אֲגָג וְעַל־מֵיטַב הַצֹּאן מלוי אהיה דיודין ע"ה וְהַבָּקָר וְהַמִּשְׁנִים וְעַל־

הַכָּרִים וְעַל־כָּל־ ילי עמם הַטּוֹב והו וְלֹא אָבוּ הַחֲרִימָם וְכָל־ ילי הַמְּלָאכָה

אל אדני נְמִבְזָה וְנָמֵס אֹתָהּ הֶחֱרִימוּ: 10 וַיְהִי אל, ייא"י דְּבַר־ ראה יְהוָֹה אדני...אהדונהי אֶל־

שְׁמוּאֵל לֵאמֹר: 11 נִחַמְתִּי כִּי־הִמְלַכְתִּי אֶת־שָׁאוּל לְמֶלֶךְ כִּי־שָׁב

מֵאַחֲרַי וְאֶת־דְּבָרַי ראה לֹא הֵקִים וַיִּחַר לִשְׁמוּאֵל וַיִּזְעַק אֶל־

יְהוָֹה אדני...אהדונהי כָּל־ ילי הַלָּיְלָה: 12 וַיַּשְׁכֵּם שְׁמוּאֵל לִקְרַאת שָׁאוּל

בַּבֹּקֶר וַיֻּגַּד לִשְׁמוּאֵל לֵאמֹר בָּא־שָׁאוּל הַכַּרְמֶלָה וְהִנֵּה מ"ה יה מַצִּיב

לוֹ יָד וַיִּסֹּב וַיַּעֲבֹר רפ"ח, ע"ב רי"ו וַיֵּרֶד רי הַגִּלְגָּל: 13 וַיָּבֹא שְׁמוּאֵל אֶל־

שָׁאוּל וַיֹּאמֶר לוֹ שָׁאוּל בָּרוּךְ יהוה ע"ב ורבוע מ"ה אַתָּה לַיהוָֹה אדני...אהדונהי

הֲקִימֹתִי אֶת־דְּבַר ראה יְהוָֹה אדני...אהדונהי: 14 וַיֹּאמֶר שְׁמוּאֵל וּמֶה מ"ה קוֹל

ע"ב ס"ג ע"ה הַצֹּאן מלוי אהיה דיודין ע"ה הַזֶּה מ"ה בְּאָזְנָי והו וְקוֹל ע"ב ס"ג ע"ה הַבָּקָר אֲשֶׁר

¹⁷ Samuel said, "Although you were once small in your own eyes, did you not become the head of the tribes of Israel? The Lord anointed you king over Israel.

¹⁸ And He sent you on a mission, saying, 'Go and completely destroy those wicked people, the Amalekites; make war on them until you have wiped them out.'

¹⁹ Why did you not obey the Lord's voice? Why did you pounce on the plunder and do evil in the eyes of the Lord?"

²⁰ "But I did obey the Lord," Saul said to Samuel. "I went on the mission the Lord assigned me. I completely destroyed the Amalekites and brought back Agag their king.

²¹ The soldiers took sheep and cattle from the plunder, the best of what was devoted to God, in order to sacrifice them to the Lord, your God at Gilgal."

²² But Samuel replied: "Does the Lord delight in burnt offerings and sacrifices as much as in obeying the voice of the Lord? To obey is better than sacrifice, and to heed is better than the fat of rams.

²³ For rebellion is like the sin of divination, and arrogance like the evil of idolatry. Because you have rejected the word of the Lord, he has rejected you as king."

²⁴ Then Saul said to Samuel, "I have sinned. I violated the Lord's command and your instructions. I was afraid of the people and so I gave in to them.

²⁵ Now I beg you, forgive my sin and come back with me, so that I may worship the Lord."

²⁶ But Samuel said to Saul, "I will not go back with you. You have rejected the word of the Lord, and the Lord has rejected you as king over Israel!"

²⁷ As Samuel turned to leave, he caught hold of the hem of his robe, and it tore.

²⁸ Samuel said to him, "The Lord has torn the kingdom of Israel from you today and has given it to one of your neighbors—to one better than you.

²⁹ He who is the Glory of Israel does not lie or change his mind; for he is not a man, that he should change his mind."

אָנֹכִי אִיע שֹׁמֵעַ: 15 וַיֹּאמֶר שָׁאוּל מֵעֲמָלֵקִי הֱבִיאוּם אֲשֶׁר חָמַל הָעָם

עַל־מֵיטַב הַצֹּאן מלוי אהיה דיודין ע״ה וְהַבָּקָר לְמַעַן זְבֹחַ לַיהֹוָהאהדנהי

אֱלֹהֶיךָ ילה וְאֶת־הַיּוֹתֵר הֶחֱרַמְנוּ: 16 וַיֹּאמֶר שְׁמוּאֵל אֶל־שָׁאוּל הֶרֶף

וְאַגִּידָה לְּךָ אֵת אֲשֶׁר דִּבֶּר ראה יְהֹוָהאהדנהי אֵלַי הַלָּיְלָה מלה וַיֹּאמֶר

(כתיב: ויאמרו) לוֹ דַבֵּר ראה: 17 וַיֹּאמֶר שְׁמוּאֵל הֲלוֹא אִם יוהך, ע״ה מ״ב קָטֹן

אַתָּה בְּעֵינֶיךָ ע״ה קס״א רֵאשׁ ריבוע אלהים ואלהים דיודין ע״ה שִׁבְטֵי ש״ך ע״ה יִשְׂרָאֵל

אָתָּה וַיִּמְשָׁחֲךָ יְהֹוָהאהדנהי לְמֶלֶךְ עַל־יִשְׂרָאֵל: 18 וַיִּשְׁלָחֲךָ

יְהֹוָהאהדנהי ב״פ יב״ק בְּדָרֶךְ וַיֹּאמֶר לֵךְ וְהַחֲרַמְתָּה אֶת־הַחַטָּאִים אֶת־

עֲמָלֵק ב״פ קי״ך וְנִלְחַמְתָּ בּוֹ עַד כַּלּוֹתָם אֹתָם: 19 וְלָמָּה לֹא־שָׁמַעְתָּ

בְּקוֹל ע״ב ס״ג ע״ה יְהֹוָהאהדנהי וַתַּעַט אֶל־הַשָּׁלָל ב״פ עס״מ וַתַּעַשׂ הָרַע ילפ ז״ן

בְּעֵינֵי ריבוע מ״ה יְהֹוָהאהדנהי: 20 וַיֹּאמֶר שָׁאוּל אֶל־שְׁמוּאֵל אֲשֶׁר שָׁמַעְתִּי

בְּקוֹל ע״ב ס״ג ע״ה יְהֹוָהאהדנהי וָאֵלֵךְ בַּדֶּרֶךְ ב״פ יב״ק אֲשֶׁר־שְׁלָחַנִי

יְהֹוָהאהדנהי וָאָבִיא אֶת־אֲגַג מֶלֶךְ עֲמָלֵק ב״פ קי״ך וְאֶת־עֲמָלֵק ב״פ קי״ך

הֶחֱרַמְתִּי: 21 וַיִּקַּח וֹאם הָעָם מֵהַשָּׁלָל צֹאן מלוי אהיה דיודין ע״ה וּבָקָר רֵאשִׁית

הַחֵרֶם לִזְבֹּחַ לַיהֹוָהאהדנהי אֱלֹהֶיךָ ילה בַּגִּלְגָּל: 22 וַיֹּאמֶר שְׁמוּאֵל

הַחֵפֶץ לַיהֹוָהאהדנהי בְּעֹלוֹת וּזְבָחִים כִּשְׁמֹעַ בְּקוֹל ע״ב ס״ג ע״ה יְהֹוָהאהדנהי

הִנֵּה מ״ה יה שְׁמֹעַ מִזֶּבַח טוֹב והו לְהַקְשִׁיב מֵחֵלֶב אֵילִים: 23 כִּי חַטַּאת־

קֶסֶם רבוע אלהים מֶרִי וְאָוֶן וּתְרָפִים הַפְצַר יַעַן מָאַסְתָּ אֶת־דְּבַר ראה

יְהֹוָהאהדנהי וַיִּמְאָסְךָ מִמֶּלֶךְ: 24 וַיֹּאמֶר שָׁאוּל אֶל־שְׁמוּאֵל חָטָאתִי

כִּי־עָבַרְתִּי אֶת־פִּי־יְהֹוָהאהדנהי וְאֶת־דְּבָרֶיךָ ראה כִּי יָרֵאתִי אֶת־הָעָם

וָאֶשְׁמַע בְּקוֹלָם: 25 וְעַתָּה שָׂא נָא אֶת־חַטָּאתִי וְשׁוּב עִמִּי וְאֶשְׁתַּחֲוֶה

לַיהֹוָהאהדנהי ילפ ע״ב: 26 וַיֹּאמֶר שְׁמוּאֵל אֶל־שָׁאוּל לֹא אָשׁוּב עִמָּךְ

ה הוויות, נמם כִּי מָאַסְתָּה אֶת־דְּבַר ראה יְהֹוָהאהדנהי וַיִּמְאָסְךָ יְהֹוָהאהדנהי

מִהְיוֹת מֶלֶךְ עַל־יִשְׂרָאֵל: 27 וַיִּסֹּב שְׁמוּאֵל לָלֶכֶת וַיַּחֲזֵק בִּכְנַף

[30] He replied, "I have sinned. But please honor me before the elders of my people and before Israel; come back with me, so that I may worship the Lord, your God."

[31] So Samuel went back with Saul, and Saul worshiped the Lord.

[32] Then Samuel said, "Bring me Agag king of the Amalekites." Agag came to him confidently, thinking, "Surely the bitterness of death is past."

[33] But Samuel said, "As your sword has made women childless, so will your mother be childless among women." And Samuel put Agag to death before the Lord at Gilgal.

[34] Then Samuel left for Ramah, but Saul went up to his home in Gibeah-Saul.

עֹ״ה קנ״א, אלהים אדני ־מְעִילֹוֹ וַיִּקָּרֵעַ: 28 וַיֹּאמֶר אֵלָיו שְׁמוּאֵל קָרַע ב״פ אלף למד, ע״ע

יְהֹוָהאהדונהי אֶת־מַמְלְכוּת יִשְׂרָאֵל מֵעָלֶיךָ הַיֹּום ע״ה = נגד, מזבח, זן וּנְתָנָהּ

לְרֵעֲךָ הַטֹּוב והו מִמֶּךָּ: 29 וְגַם יכ״ל נֵצַח יִשְׂרָאֵל לֹא יְשַׁקֵּר וְלֹא יִנָּחֵם

כִּי לֹא אָדָם מ״ה הוּא לְהִנָּחֵם: 30 וַיֹּאמֶר חָטָאתִי עַתָּה כַּבְּדֵנִי נָא נֶגֶד

זן נגד, מזבח וְזִקְנֵי־עַמִּי וְנֶגֶד יִשְׂרָאֵל וְשׁוּב עִמִּי וְהִשְׁתַּחֲוֵיתִי זן נגד, מזבח

לַיהֹוָהאהדונהי אֱלֹהֶיךָ יכה: 31 וַיָּשָׁב שְׁמוּאֵל אַחֲרֵי שָׁאוּל וַיִּשְׁתַּחוּ

שָׁאוּל לַיהֹוָהאהדונהי: 32 וַיֹּאמֶר שְׁמוּאֵל הַגִּישׁוּ אֵלַי אֶת־אֲגַג מֶלֶךְ

עֲמָלֵק ב״פ ק״ך וַיֵּלֶךְ כ״ל אֵלָיו אֲגַג מַעֲדַנֹּת וַיֹּאמֶר אֲגַג אָכֵן יהוה מ״ה סָר

י הויות מַר ב״פ ק״ך דְּ הַבֹּוֶת: 33 וַיֹּאמֶר שְׁמוּאֵל כַּאֲשֶׁר שִׁכְּלָה נָשִׁים חַרְבֶּךָ

כֵּן־תִּשְׁכַּל מִנָּשִׁים אִמֶּךָ וַיְשַׁסֵּף שְׁמוּאֵל אֶת־אֲגַג לִפְנֵי וחכמה בינה

יְהֹוָהאהדונהי בַּגִּלְגָּל: 34 וַיֵּלֶךְ כ״ל שְׁמוּאֵל הָרָמָתָה וְשָׁאוּל עָלָה אֶל־

בֵּיתֹו ב״פ ראה גִּבְעַת שָׁאוּל:

MAFTIR OF SHABBAT PARAH

This reading connects us with the power to cleanse our negativity. According to the *Zohar*, the Red Heifer is the mother of the Golden Calf. Therefore, by sacrificing the Red Heifer, we correct the sin of worshipping the Golden Calf. The *Zohar* tells us that before the creation of Golden Calf, we achieved the consciousness where immortality was a reality. Through reading this Bible passage, we can connect with the taste of immortality once again, reminding us that it is in our destiny.

…after the giving of Torah, the Shechinah was a mere Tent, as it is written: "A Tabernacle that shall not be taken down, not one of the stakes thereof shall ever be removed," (Isaiah 33:20)

Numbers 19:1-22

19:1 Then the Lord spoke to Moses and Aaron, saying,

2 "This is the statute of the law which the Lord has commanded, saying, 'Speak to the sons of Israel and they will bring you an unblemished red heifer in which there is no defect and on which a yoke has never been placed.

3 You shall give it to Eleazar, the priest, and it shall be brought outside the camp and be slaughtered in his presence.

4 Next, Eleazar, the priest, shall take some of its blood with his finger and sprinkle some of its blood toward the front of the tent of meeting seven times.

5 Then the heifer shall be burnt in his sight; its hide and its flesh and its blood, with its refuse, shall be burned.

6 The priest shall take cedar wood and hyssop and scarlet material and cast it into the midst of the burning heifer.

7 The priest shall then wash his clothes and bathe his body in water, and afterward come into the camp, but the priest shall be unclean until evening.

8 The one who burns it shall also wash his clothes in water and bathe his body in water, and shall be unclean until evening.

9 Now a man who is clean shall gather up the ashes of the heifer and deposit them outside the camp in a clean place, and the congregation of the sons of Israel shall keep it as water to remove impurity; it is purification from sin.

MAFTIR OF SHABBAT PARAH

and it was continuously illuminated. But now, after the sin of the Calf, it was called the Tabernacle of Appointment [or the Tent of Meeting], because it was only illuminated periodically. Before, it had given long life to the world, and death was powerless. After the giving of the Torah, there was freedom from the Angel of Death. But, after the sin of the Calf, the Shechinah became the Tabernacle of Periodic Congregation, as it is written: "the house of appointment to all the living." (Job 30:33) Now it is governed by time, and life is limited in the world.

— The Zohar, Beresheet B 57:297

בְּמִדְבַּר פֶּרֶק יט

19 1 וַיְדַבֵּר ראה יְהֹוָה⟨אדניאהדונהי⟩ אֶל־מֹשֶׁה מהש, אל שדי וְאֶל־אַהֲרֹן ע"ב ורבוע ע"ב

לֵאמֹר: 2 זֹאת חֻקַּת הַתּוֹרָה אֲשֶׁר־צִוָּה פוי יְהֹוָה⟨אדניאהדונהי⟩ לֵאמֹר

דַּבֵּר ראה | אֶל־בְּנֵי יִשְׂרָאֵל וְיִקְחוּ וזעם אֵלֶיךָ אני פָרָה אֲדֻמָּה עסמ"ב ורבוע עסמ"ב

תְּמִימָה אֲשֶׁר אֵין־בָּהּ מוּם מום, אלהים, אהיה אדני אֲשֶׁר לֹא־עָלָה עָלֶיהָ פהל

עֹל: 3 וּנְתַתֶּם אֹתָהּ אֶל־אֶלְעָזָר הַכֹּהֵן מלה וְהוֹצִיא אֹתָהּ אֶל־מִחוּץ

לַמַּחֲנֶה וְשָׁחַט אֹתָהּ לְפָנָיו: 4 וְלָקַח ב"פ יהוה אדני אהיה אֶלְעָזָר הַכֹּהֵן מלה

מִדָּמָהּ בְּאֶצְבָּעוֹ וְהִזָּה אֶל־נֹכַח ג"פ יהוה פְּנֵי חכמה בינה אֹהֶל לאה ־מוֹעֵד

מִדָּמָהּ שֶׁבַע ע"ב ואלהים דיודין פְּעָמִים: 5 וְשָׂרַף אֶת־הַפָּרָה לְעֵינָיו ריבוע מ"ה

אֶת־עֹרָהּ וְאֶת־בְּשָׂרָהּ וְאֶת־דָּמָהּ עַל־פִּרְשָׁהּ יִשְׂרֹף: 6 וְלָקַח

ב"פ יהוה אדני אהיה הַכֹּהֵן מלה עֵץ ע"ה קס"א אֶרֶז ד"פ בן וְאֵזוֹב וּשְׁנִי תוֹלַעַת עקוצי"ת

וְהִשְׁלִיךְ אֶל־תּוֹךְ שְׂרֵפַת הַפָּרָה: 7 וְכִבֶּס בְּגָדָיו הַכֹּהֵן מלה וְרָחַץ

בְּשָׂרוֹ בַּמַּיִם וְאַחַר יָבֹא אֶל־הַמַּחֲנֶה וְטָמֵא הַכֹּהֵן מלה עַד־הָעָרֶב

רבוע יהוה ורבוע אלהים: 8 וְהַשֹּׂרֵף אֹתָהּ יְכַבֵּס בְּגָדָיו בַּמַּיִם וְרָחַץ בְּשָׂרוֹ

בַּמָּיִם וְטָמֵא עַד־הָעָרֶב רבוע יהוה ורבוע אלהים: 9 וְאָסַף | אִישׁ ע"ה קנ"א קס"א

טָהוֹר י"פ אכא אֵת אֵפֶר מזח"פ ע"ה הַפָּרָה וְהִנִּיחַ מִחוּץ לַמַּחֲנֶה בְּמָקוֹם

¹⁰ The one who gathers the ashes of the heifer shall wash his clothes and be unclean until evening; and it shall be a perpetual statute to the sons of Israel and to the alien who sojourns among them.

¹¹ The one who touches the corpse of any person will be unclean for seven days,

¹² that one shall purify himself from uncleanness with it on the third day and on the seventh day, and then he will be clean; but if he does not purify himself on the third day and on the seventh day, he will not be clean.

¹³ Anyone who touches a corpse, the body of a man who has died, and does not purify himself, defiles the Tabernacle of the Lord; and that person shall be cut off from Israel. Because the water for impurity was not sprinkled on him, he shall be unclean; his uncleanness is still on him.

¹⁴ This is the law when a man dies in a tent: everyone who comes into the tent and everyone who is in the tent shall be unclean for seven days.

¹⁵ Every open vessel, which has no covering tied down on it, shall be unclean.

¹⁶ Also, anyone who in the open field touches one who has been slain with a sword or who has died naturally, or a human bone or a grave, shall be unclean for seven days.

¹⁷ Then for the unclean person they shall take some of the ashes of the burnt purification from sin and flowing water shall be added to them in a vessel.

¹⁸ A clean person shall take hyssop and dip it in the water, and sprinkle it on the tent and on all the furnishings and on the souls who were there, and on the one who touched the bone, or the one slain or the one dying naturally, or on the grave.

¹⁹ Then the clean person shall sprinkle on the unclean on the third day and on the seventh day; and on the seventh day he shall purify him, and he shall wash his clothes and bathe himself in water and shall be clean by evening.

²⁰ But the man who is unclean and does not purify himself, that person shall be cut off from the midst of the assembly, because he has defiled the Sanctuary of the Lord; the water for impurity has not been sprinkled on him; he is unclean.

טָהוֹר וְהָיְתָה לַעֲדַת בְּנֵי־יִשְׂרָאֵל לְמִשְׁמֶרֶת לְמֵי

נִדָּה חַטָּאת הִוא: 10 וְכִבֶּס הָאֹסֵף אֶת־אֵפֶר הַפָּרָה אֶת־בְּגָדָיו

וְטָמֵא עַד־הָעָרֶב וְהָיְתָה לִבְנֵי יִשְׂרָאֵל וְלַגֵּר הַגָּר

בְּתוֹכָם לְחֻקַּת עוֹלָם: 11 הַנֹּגֵעַ בְּמֵת לְכָל

נֶפֶשׁ אָדָם וְטָמֵא שִׁבְעַת יָמִים: 12 הוּא יִתְחַטָּא־

בוֹ בַיּוֹם הַשְּׁלִישִׁי וּבַיּוֹם הַשְּׁבִיעִי יִטְהָר וְאִם

לֹא יִתְחַטָּא בַּיּוֹם הַשְּׁלִישִׁי וּבַיּוֹם

הַשְּׁבִיעִי לֹא יִטְהָר: 13 כָּל־הַנֹּגֵעַ בְּמֵת בְּנֶפֶשׁ

הָאָדָם אֲשֶׁר־יָמוּת וְלֹא יִתְחַטָּא אֶת־מִשְׁכַּן

יְהוָה טִמֵּא וְנִכְרְתָה הַנֶּפֶשׁ הַהִוא מִיִּשְׂרָאֵל כִּי מֵי

נִדָּה לֹא־זֹרַק עָלָיו טָמֵא יִהְיֶה עוֹד טֻמְאָתוֹ בוֹ: 14 זֹאת הַתּוֹרָה

אָדָם כִּי־יָמוּת בְּאֹהֶל כָּל־הַבָּא אֶל־הָאֹהֶל וְכָל־

אֲשֶׁר בָּאֹהֶל יִטְמָא שִׁבְעַת יָמִים: 15 וְכֹל כְּלִי פָתוּחַ אֲשֶׁר

אֵין־צָמִיד פָּתִיל עָלָיו טָמֵא הוּא: 16 וְכֹל אֲשֶׁר־יִגַּע עַל־פְּנֵי

הַשָּׂדֶה בַּחֲלַל־חֶרֶב אוֹ בְמֵת

אוֹ־בְעֶצֶם אָדָם אוֹ בְקָבֶר יִטְמָא שִׁבְעַת יָמִים:

17 וְלָקְחוּ לַטָּמֵא מֵעֲפַר שְׂרֵפַת הַחַטָּאת וְנָתַן עָלָיו

מַיִם חַיִּים אֶל־כֶּלִי: 18 וְלָקַח אֵזוֹב וְטָבַל בַּמַּיִם

אִישׁ טָהוֹר וְהִזָּה עַל־הָאֹהֶל וְעַל־כָּל־הַכֵּלִים

וְעַל־הַנְּפָשׁוֹת אֲשֶׁר הָיוּ־שָׁם וְעַל־הַנֹּגֵעַ בַּעֶצֶם אוֹ

בֶחָלָל אוֹ בַמֵּת אוֹ בַקָּבֶר: 19 וְהִזָּה הַטָּהֹר

עַל־הַטָּמֵא בַּיּוֹם הַשְּׁלִישִׁי וּבַיּוֹם הַשְּׁבִיעִי

וְחִטְּאוֹ בַּיּוֹם הַשְּׁבִיעִי וְכִבֶּס בְּגָדָיו וְרָחַץ בַּמַּיִם וְטָהֵר

בָּעֶרֶב: 20 וְאִישׁ אֲשֶׁר־יִטְמָא וְלֹא

21 So it shall be a perpetual statute for them. And he who sprinkles the water for impurity shall wash his clothes, and he who touches the water for impurity shall be unclean until evening.

22 Furthermore, anything that the unclean person touches shall be unclean; and the person who touches it shall be unclean until evening.' "

HAFTARAH OF SHABBAT PARAH

Ezekiel tells the people that God will gather them from their exile and cleanse them of their iniquities so that they may once again dwell in the Land of Israel. This was not because the people had transformed, but rather because God wanted it so. We have an opportunity during this reading to

Ezekiel 36:16-36

36:16 The word of the Lord was to me:

17 "Son of man, when the people of Israel were living in their own land, they defiled it by their conduct and their actions. Their conduct was like a woman's monthly uncleanness in My sight.

18 So I poured out My wrath on them because they had shed blood in the land and because they had defiled it with their idols.

19 I dispersed them among the nations, and they were scattered through the countries; I judged them according to their conduct and their actions.

20 And wherever they went among the nations they profaned My Holy Name, for it was said of them, 'These are the Lord's people, and yet they had to leave his land.'

21 I had concern for My Holy Name, which the house of Israel profaned among the nations where they had gone.

יִתְחַטָּא וְנִכְרְתָה הַנֶּפֶשׁ רמ"ח - ז הויות הַהִוא מִתּוֹךְ הַקָּהָל ע"ב ס"ג כִּי אֶת־
מִקְדַּשׁ יְהֹוָאדִניאהדונהי טִמֵּא מֵי יל נִדָּה לֹא־זֹרַק עָלָיו טָמֵא הוּא:
21 וְהָיְתָה לָהֶם לְחֻקַּת עוֹלָם וּמַזֵּה מֵי ־הַנִּדָּה יְכַבֵּס בְּגָדָיו וְהַנֹּגֵעַ
בְּמֵי יל הַנִּדָּה יִטְמָא עַד־הָעָרֶב רבוע יהוה ורבוע אלהים: 22 וְכֹל יל אֲשֶׁר־יִגַּע־
בּוֹ הַטָּמֵא יִטְמָא וְהַנֶּפֶשׁ רמ"ח - ז הויות הַנֹּגַעַת תִּטְמָא עַד־הָעָרֶב
רבוע יהוה ורבוע אלהים:

HAFTARAH OF SHABBAT PARAH

search within and identify those areas where we worship idols—addictions, our need for approval, the voyeurism of our society—and ask for the Creator's help to cleanse them. Only then can we transform and connect more closely to the true source of fulfillment—the Light of the Creator.

יוֹזְקֵאל פרק לו

36 16 וַיְהִי אל, יא"י אֶל ־יְהֹוָאדִניאהדונהי דְּבַר רָאה אֵלַי לֵאמֹר: 17 בֶּן־אָדָם מ"ה
בֵּית ב"פ ראה יִשְׂרָאֵל יֹשְׁבִים עַל־אַדְמָתָם וַיְטַמְּאוּ אוֹתָהּ בְּדַרְכָּם
וּבַעֲלִילוֹתָם כְּטֻמְאַת הַנִּדָּה הָיְתָה דַרְכָּם לְפָנָי וחכמה בינה: 18 וָאֶשְׁפֹּךְ
חֲמָתִי עֲלֵיהֶם עַל־הַדָּם רבוע אהיה אֲשֶׁר־שָׁפְכוּ עַל־הָאָרֶץ אלהים דההין ע"ה
וּבְגִלּוּלֵיהֶם טִמְּאוּהָ: 19 וָאָפִיץ אֹתָם בַּגּוֹיִם וַיִּזָּרוּ בָּאֲרָצוֹת כְּדַרְכָּם
וְכַעֲלִילוֹתָם שְׁפַטְתִּים: 20 וַיָּבוֹא אֶל־הַגּוֹיִם אֲשֶׁר־בָּאוּ שָׁם וַיְחַלְּלוּ
אֶת־שֵׁם יהוה שדי קָדְשִׁי בֶּאֱמֹר לָהֶם עַם־יְהֹוָאדִניאהדונהי אֵלֶּה וּמֵאַרְצוֹ
יָצָאוּ: 21 וָאֶחְמֹל עַל־שֵׁם יהוה שדי קָדְשִׁי אֲשֶׁר חִלְּלֻהוּ בֵּית ב"פ ראה
יִשְׂרָאֵל בַּגּוֹיִם אֲשֶׁר־בָּאוּ שָׁמָּה מהע, משה, אל שדי: 22 לָכֵן אֱמֹר לְבֵית
ב"פ ראה ־יִשְׂרָאֵל כֹּה הי אָמַר אֲדֹנָי יְהֹוִואדניאהדונהי ללה לֹא לְמַעַנְכֶם אֲנִי

²² Therefore say to the house of Israel, this is what the Lord, God, says: 'It is not for your sake, house of Israel, that I am going to do these things, but for the sake of My Holy Name, which you have profaned among the nations where you have gone.

²³ I will show the holiness of My great Name, which has been profaned among the nations, the Name you have profaned among them. Then the nations will know that I am the Lord,' declares the Lord, God, 'when I show Myself holy through you before their eyes.

²⁴ For I will take you out of the nations; I will gather you from all the countries and bring you into your own land.

²⁵ I will sprinkle pure water on you, and you will be pure; I will purify you from all your impurities and from all your idols.

²⁶ I will give you a new heart and put a new spirit in you; I will remove from you your heart of stone and give you a heart of flesh.

²⁷ And I will put My spirit in you and move you to follow My decrees and be careful to keep My laws.

²⁸ You will live in the land I gave your forefathers; you will be My people, and I will be your God.

²⁹ I will save you from all your uncleanness. I will call for the grain and make it plentiful and will not bring famine upon you.

³⁰ I will increase the fruit of the trees and the crops of the field, so that you will no longer suffer disgrace among the nations because of famine.

³¹ Then you will remember your evil ways and wicked deeds, and you will loathe yourselves for your sins and detestable practices.

³² I want you to know that I am not doing this for your sake,' declares the Lord, God. 'Be ashamed and disgraced for your conduct, house of Israel!'

³³ This is what the Lord, God, says: 'On the day I purify you from all your sins, I will resettle your towns, and the ruins will be rebuilt.

³⁴ The desolate land will be cultivated instead of lying desolate in the sight of all who pass through it.

עֲשֶׂה בֵּית בּ"פ ראה יִשְׂרָאֵל כִּי אִם ע"הך, ע"ה מ"ב יהוה, יהוה עדי ־לָשֵׁם אני, טדהה"ד כוזו

קָדְשִׁי אֲשֶׁר חִלַּלְתֶּם בַּגּוֹיִם אֲשֶׁר־בָּאתֶם שָׁם יהוה עדי 23 וְקִדַּשְׁתִּי

אֶת־שְׁמִי רבוע ע"ב ורבוע ס"ג הַגָּדוֹל להה, מבה, יזל, אום הַמְחֻלָּל בַּגּוֹיִם אֲשֶׁר

חִלַּלְתֶּם בְּתוֹכָם וְיָדְעוּ הַגּוֹיִם כִּי־אֲנִי אני, טדהה"ד כוזו יְהֹוָהאדניאהדונהי נְאֻם

אֲדֹנָי יְהֹוִהאהדונהי ללה בְּהִקָּדְשִׁי בָכֶם לְעֵינֵיהֶם רבוע מ"ה: 24 וְלָקַחְתִּי

אֶתְכֶם מִן־הַגּוֹיִם וְקִבַּצְתִּי אֶתְכֶם מִכָּל ־הָאֲרָצוֹת וְהֵבֵאתִי אֶתְכֶם ילי

אֶל־אַדְמַתְכֶם: 25 וְזָרַקְתִּי עֲלֵיכֶם מַיִם טְהוֹרִים וּטְהַרְתֶּם מִכֹּל ילי

טֻמְאוֹתֵיכֶם וּמִכָּל־גִּלּוּלֵיכֶם אֲטַהֵר אֶתְכֶם: 26 וְנָתַתִּי לָכֶם לֵב חָדָשׁ

וְרוּחַ י"ב הוויות מלוי אלהים דיודין חֲדָשָׁה אֶתֵּן בְּקִרְבְּכֶם וַהֲסִרֹתִי אֶת־לֵב

הָאֶבֶן יוד הה ואו הה מִבְּשַׂרְכֶם וְנָתַתִּי לָכֶם לֵב בָּשָׂר: 27 וְאֶת־רוּחִי אֶתֵּן

בְּקִרְבְּכֶם וְעָשִׂיתִי אֵת אֲשֶׁר־בְּחֻקַּי תֵּלֵכוּ וּמִשְׁפָּטַי תִּשְׁמְרוּ וַעֲשִׂיתֶם:

28 וִישַׁבְתֶּם בָּאָרֶץ אלהים דאלפין אֲשֶׁר נָתַתִּי לַאֲבֹתֵיכֶם וִהְיִיתֶם לִי לְעָם

וְאָנֹכִי איע אֶהְיֶה בי"ט לָכֶם לֵאלֹהִים מום, אהיה אדני; ילה 29 וְהוֹשַׁעְתִּי אֶתְכֶם

מִכֹּל ילי טֻמְאוֹתֵיכֶם וְקָרָאתִי אֶל־הַדָּגָן גגד, זן, מזבח וְהִרְבֵּיתִי אֹתוֹ וְלֹא־

אֶתֵּן עֲלֵיכֶם רָעָב בַּגּוֹיִם: 30 וְהִרְבֵּיתִי אֶת־פְּרִי ע"ה אלהים דאלפין הָעֵץ ע"ב ורבוע אלהים

וּתְנוּבַת הַשָּׂדֶה ע"ה קס"א לְמַעַן אֲשֶׁר עדי לֹא תִקְחוּ עוֹד חֶרְפַּת רָעָב

בַּגּוֹיִם: 31 וּזְכַרְתֶּם אֶת־דַּרְכֵיכֶם הָרָעִים ע"ב ורבוע אלהים ה"פ אדני, שכ"ה

וּמַעַלְלֵיכֶם אֲשֶׁר לֹא־טוֹבִים וּנְקֹטֹתֶם בִּפְנֵיכֶם עַל עֲוֹנֹתֵיכֶם וְעַל

תּוֹעֲבוֹתֵיכֶם: 32 לֹא לְמַעַנְכֶם אֲנִי אני, טדהה"ד כוזו ־עֹשֶׂה נְאֻם אֲדֹנָי ללה

יְהֹוִהאדניאהדונהי יִוָּדַע לָכֶם בּוֹשׁוּ וְהִכָּלְמוּ מִדַּרְכֵיכֶם בֵּית בּ"פ ראה יִשְׂרָאֵל:

33 כֹּה הי אָמַר אֲדֹנָי ללה יְהֹוִהאדניאהדונהי בְּיוֹם ע"ה = גגד, זן, מזבח טַהֲרִי אֶתְכֶם

מִכֹּל ילי עֲוֹנוֹתֵיכֶם וְהוֹשַׁבְתִּי אֶת־הֶעָרִים שכ"ה, ה"פ אדני וְנִבְנוּ הֶחֳרָבוֹת:

34 וְהָאָרֶץ אלהים דההין ע"ה הַנְּשַׁמָּה תֵּעָבֵד תַּחַת אֲשֶׁר הָיְתָה שְׁמָמָה לְעֵינֵי

כָּל ילי ־עוֹבֵר רבוע מ"ה: 35 וְאָמְרוּ הָאָרֶץ אלהים דההין ע"ה הַלֵּזוּ הַנְּשַׁמָּה הָיְתָה

[35]{.superscript} They will say, "This land that was laid waste has become like the Garden of Eden; the cities that were lying in ruins, desolate and destroyed, are now fortified and inhabited."

[36]{.superscript} Then the nations around you that remain will know that I, the Lord, have rebuilt what was destroyed and have replanted what was desolate. I, the Lord, have spoken, and I will do it.' "

MAFTIR OF SHABBAT HACHODESH

The first month of the year from an astrological point of view is the month of Aries (*Nissan*). As the first month, Aries is also the seed of the year. This means that the whole year is contained within it. The first twelve days of Aries control all the other months and all zodiac signs of the

Exodus 12:1-20

12:[1]{.superscript} The Lord said to Moses and Aaron in Egypt,

[2]{.superscript} "This month is to be for you the first month, the first of the months of the year.

[3]{.superscript} Speak to the entire Congregation of Israel, saying that on the tenth day of this month each man is to take a lamb for his family, one for each household.

[4]{.superscript} If any household is too small for a whole lamb, they must share one with their nearest neighbor, accounting for each person according to how much of the lamb he would consume.

[5]{.superscript} The lamb must be a pure, year-old male lamb, from the lambs and the goats you shall take.

[6]{.superscript} You will guard them until the fourteenth day of the month, and slaughter it – the entire assembly of the Congregation of Israel – at twilight.

[7]{.superscript} And you shall take from the blood and put it on the two doorposts and on the frame of the houses where the lambs are eaten.

כְּגַן־עֵ֫דֶן יהוה אלהים אדני הַּעָרִ֗ים עכ״ה, ה״פ אדני, ה״פ אדני הַחֳרֵב֗וֹת וְהַנְשַׁמּ֛וֹת וְהַנֶּהֱרָס֖וֹת

בְּצוּר֣וֹת יֵשֵׁ֑בוּ: 36 וְיָדְע֣וּ הַגּוֹיִ֗ם אֲשֶׁ֤ר יִֽשָּׁאֲרוּ֙ סְבִיבֽוֹתֵיכֶ֔ם כִּ֣י | אֲנִ֣י

אֲנִי, טדהד כולו יְהֹוָ֣האדניאהדונהי בָּנִ֙יתִי֙ הַנֶּ֣הֱרָס֔וֹת נָטַ֖עְתִּי הַנְּשַׁמָּ֑ה אֲנִ֥י, טדהד כולו

יְהֹוָ֖האדניאהדונהי דִּבַּ֥רְתִּי רַאה וְעָשִֽׂיתִי:

MAFTIR OF SHABBAT HACHODESH

year: The first day controls Aries, the second controls Taurus, the third controls Gemini, and so on. By connecting to this Maftir we connect to and control the month of Aries, and thus, we control the whole year.

שמות פרק יב

12 1 וַיֹּ֤אמֶר יְהֹוָה֙אדניאהדונהי אֶל־מֹשֶׁ֣ה מהצע, אל שדי וְאֶֽל־אַהֲרֹ֔ן ע״ב רבוע ע״ב

בְּאֶ֥רֶץ אלהים דאלפין מִצְרַ֖יִם מצר לֵאמֹֽר: 2 הַחֹ֧דֶשׁ י״ב הוויות הַזֶּ֛ה והו לָכֶ֖ם

רֹ֣אשׁ רבוע אלהים ואלהים דיודין ע״ה חֳדָשִׁ֑ים רִאשׁ֥וֹן הוּא֙ לָכֶ֔ם לְחָדְשֵׁ֖י הַשָּׁנָֽה:

3 דַּבְּר֗וּ ראה אֶֽל־כׇּל־עֲדַ֤ת יִשְׂרָאֵל֙ לֵאמֹ֔ר בֶּעָשֹׂ֖ר לַחֹ֣דֶשׁ י״ב הוויות

הַזֶּ֑ה והו וְיִקְח֣וּ וֹאם לָהֶ֗ם אִ֛ישׁ ע״ה קנ״א קס״א שֶׂ֥ה לְבֵית־אָבֹ֖ת ב״פ ראה שֶׂ֥ה

לַבָּֽיִת ב״פ ראה: 4 וְאִם־יִמְעַ֣ט ע״ה, מ״ב יוהך, הַבַּ֘יִת֮ ב״פ ראה מִהְיֹ֣ת מִשֶּׂה֒ וְלָקַ֣ח

ב״פ יהוה אדני אהיה ה֗וּא וּשְׁכֵנ֛וֹ הַקָּרֹ֥ב אֶל־בֵּית֖וֹ ב״פ ראה בְּמִכְסַ֣ת נְפָשֹׁ֑ת

איע ע״ה קנ״א קס״א אִ֚ישׁ לְפִ֣י אׇכְל֔וֹ תָּכֹ֖סּוּ עַל־הַשֶּֽׂה: 5 שֶׂ֧ה תָמִ֛ים זָכָ֥ר בֶּן־שָׁנָ֖ה

יִהְיֶ֣ה יהי לָכֶ֑ם מִן־הַכְּבָשִׂ֥ים וּמִן־הָעִזִּ֖ים תִּקָּֽחוּ: 6 וְהָיָ֤ה יהוה, יהה לָכֶם֙

לְמִשְׁמֶ֔רֶת עַ֣ד אַרְבָּעָ֥ה עָשָׂ֛ר י֖וֹם ע״ה = נגד, זן, מזבח לַחֹ֣דֶשׁ י״ב הוויות הַזֶּ֑ה והו

וְשָׁחֲט֣וּ אֹת֗וֹ כֹּ֛ל יל קְהַ֥ל ע״ב ס״ג עֲדַֽת־יִשְׂרָאֵ֖ל בֵּ֥ין הָעַרְבָּֽיִם: 7 וְלָֽקְחוּ֙

מִן־הַדָּ֔ם רבוע אהיה וְנָ֥תְנ֛וּ עַל־שְׁתֵּ֥י הַמְּזוּזֹ֖ת וְעַל־הַמַּשְׁק֑וֹף עַ֚ל הַבָּ֣תִּ֔ים

8 And you shall eat the meat on that night roasted over fire, and unleavened bread with bitter herbs you shall eat.

9 Do not eat the meat raw or cooked in water, but roast it over the fire—head, legs and inner parts.

10 Do not leave any of it till morning; if some is left till morning, you must burn it.

11 This is how you are to eat it: with your cloak tucked into your belt, your sandals on your feet and your staff in your hand. Eat it in haste; it is the Lord's Passover.

12 I will pass through Egypt on that same night and strike every firstborn in Egypt—both men and animals—and I will bring judgment on all the gods of Egypt. I am the Lord.

13 The blood will be a sign for you on the houses where you are; and when I see the blood, I will pass over you. No deadly plague will touch you when I strike Egypt.

14 This is a day you are to commemorate; for the generations to come you shall celebrate it as a festival to the Lord—a lasting ordinance.

15 For seven days you are to eat unleavened bread, but on the first day you shall remove grain from your houses, for whoever eats anything leavened must be cut off from Israel, from the first day through the seventh day.

16 On the first day hold a sacred assembly, and another one on the seventh day. You shall do no work at all on these days, except to prepare food for everyone to eat—that is all you may do.

17 And you shall guard the unleavened bread, because it was on this very day that I brought your legions out of Egypt. You shall keep this day as a lasting ordinance for the generations to come.

18 From the beginning of the fourteenth day, in the evening, you shall eat unleavened bread until the twenty-first day of the month in the evening.

אֲשֶׁר־יֹאכְלוּ אֹתוֹ בָּהֶם: 8 וְאָכְלוּ אֶת־הַבָּשָׂר בַּלַּיְלָה מלה הַזֶּה והו צְלִי־

אֵשׁ אלהים דיודין ע״ה וּמַצּוֹת עַל־מְרֹרִים יֹאכְלֻהוּ: 9 אַל־תֹּאכְלוּ מִמֶּנּוּ נָא

וּבָשֵׁל מְבֻשָּׁל בַּמָּיִם כִּי אִם יוהך, ע״ה מ״ב ־צְלִי־אֵשׁ אלהים דיודין ע״ה רֹאשׁוֹ

עַל־כְּרָעָיו וְעַל־קִרְבּוֹ: 10 וְלֹא־תוֹתִירוּ מִמֶּנּוּ עַד־בֹּקֶר וְהַנֹּתָר מִמֶּנּוּ

עַד־בֹּקֶר בָּאֵשׁ אלהים דיודין ע״ה תִּשְׂרֹפוּ: 11 וְכָכָה תֹּאכְלוּ אֹתוֹ מָתְנֵיכֶם

חֲגֻרִים נַעֲלֵיכֶם בְּרַגְלֵיכֶם וּמַקֶּלְכֶם בְּיֶדְכֶם וַאֲכַלְתֶּם אֹתוֹ בְּחִפָּזוֹן

פֶּסַח הוּא לַיהֹוָה: 12 וְעָבַרְתִּי בְאֶרֶץ ־מִצְרַיִם מצר

בַּלַּיְלָה מלה הַזֶּה והו וְהִכֵּיתִי כָל ־בְּכוֹר בְּאֶרֶץ מִצְרַיִם מצר

מֵאָדָם מ״ה וְעַד־בְּהֵמָה וּבְכָל ־אֱלֹהֵי מִצְרַיִם

מצר אֶעֱשֶׂה שְׁפָטִים אֲנִי יְהֹוָה: 13 וְהָיָה הַדָּם

לָכֶם לְאֹת עַל הַבָּתִּים אֲשֶׁר אַתֶּם שָׁם וְרָאִיתִי אֶת־

הַדָּם וּפָסַחְתִּי עֲלֵכֶם וְלֹא־יִהְיֶה בָכֶם נֶגֶף לְמַשְׁחִית

בְּהַכֹּתִי בְּאֶרֶץ מִצְרָיִם: 14 וְהָיָה הַיּוֹם

הַזֶּה והו לָכֶם לְזִכָּרוֹן וְחַגֹּתֶם אֹתוֹ חַג לַיהֹוָה לְדֹרֹתֵיכֶם

חֻקַּת עוֹלָם תְּחָגֻּהוּ: 15 שִׁבְעַת יָמִים מַצּוֹת תֹּאכֵלוּ אַךְ בַּיּוֹם

הָרִאשׁוֹן תַּשְׁבִּיתוּ שְּׂאֹר מִבָּתֵּיכֶם כִּי |

כָּל ־אֹכֵל חָמֵץ וְנִכְרְתָה הַנֶּפֶשׁ הַהִוא מִיִּשְׂרָאֵל מִיּוֹם

הָרִאשֹׁן עַד־יוֹם הַשְּׁבִעִי: 16 וּבַיּוֹם

הָרִאשׁוֹן מִקְרָא ־קֹדֶשׁ וּבַיּוֹם הַשְּׁבִיעִי

מִקְרָא ־קֹדֶשׁ יִהְיֶה לָכֶם כָּל ־מְלָאכָה לֹא ־

יֵעָשֶׂה בָהֶם אַךְ אֲשֶׁר יֵאָכֵל לְכָל ־נֶפֶשׁ הוּא

לְבַדּוֹ יֵעָשֶׂה לָכֶם: 17 וּשְׁמַרְתֶּם אֶת־הַמַּצּוֹת כִּי בְּעֶצֶם הַיּוֹם

הַזֶּה והו הוֹצֵאתִי אֶת־צִבְאוֹתֵיכֶם מֵאֶרֶץ מִצְרָיִם

מצר וּשְׁמַרְתֶּם אֶת־הַיּוֹם הַזֶּה והו לְדֹרֹתֵיכֶם חֻקַּת עוֹלָם:

18 בָּרִאשֹׁן בְּאַרְבָּעָה עָשָׂר יוֹם לַחֹדֶשׁ בָּעֶרֶב

¹⁹ For seven days no grain shall be found in your houses, because anyone who eats that which is leavened shall be cut off from the Congregation of Israel, whether he is a stranger or native-born.

²⁰ Eat nothing that is leavened; in all of your habitations, you shall eat unleavened bread."

HAFTARAH OF SHABBAT HACHODESH

This Haftarah is read the Shabbat before or on Rosh Chodesh *Nissan* (Aries). *Nissan* is the first month of the year, and is also known as the *Rosh Hashanah* for Kings. Not that we are kings, but this tells us that we can connect to the power of renewal, to become a new person, open to receive the Light of the Creator.

Reb Menachem Mendel of Kotzk said: "If you pray and nothing changes and you are the same person as you were before you prayed, it is not only as if you had not prayed, but you are called evil." Evil in this case does not mean getting into evil affairs; it's about being given an opportunity to change and not doing so. For example each Shabbat we have an opportunity to connect to and receive Light of the Torah so that every one of us can find the Light of Creator that lies within. But if we do not open ourselves to receive the Light of Shabbat, nothing will come in.

Ezekiel 45:18-46:15

45:¹⁸ This is what the Lord, God says: "In the first month on the first day you are to take a young bull without defect and purify the sanctuary.

¹⁹ The priest is to take some of the blood of the sin offering and put it on the doorposts of the Temple, on the four corners of the upper ledge of the altar and on the gateposts of the inner court.

²⁰ You are to do the same on the seventh day of the month for anyone who sins unintentionally or through ignorance; so you are to make atonement for the temple.

רבוע יהוה ורבוע אלהים תֹּאכְלוּ מַצֹּת עַד יוֹם ע"ה = נגד, זן, מזבח הָאֶחָד אהבה, דאגה

וְעֶשְׂרִים לַחֹדֶשׁ י"ב הוייות בָּעָרֶב רבוע יהוה ורבוע אלהים 19 שִׁבְעַת יָמִים נלך

שְׂאֹר ג' מוזין דאלהים דקטנות לֹא יִמָּצֵא בְּבָתֵּיכֶם כִּי | כָּל ילי ־אֹכֵל מַחְמֶצֶת

וְנִכְרְתָה הַנֶּפֶשׁ רמ"ח ־ ז' הוייות הַהִוא מֵעֲדַת יִשְׂרָאֵל בַּגֵּר בין קס"א וּבְאֶזְרַח

הָאָרֶץ אלהים דההין ע"ה: 20 כָּל ילי ־מַחְמֶצֶת לֹא תֹאכֵלוּ בְּכֹל בין, לכב, יבמ

מוֹשְׁבֹתֵיכֶם תֹּאכְלוּ מַצּוֹת:

HAFTARAH OF SHABBAT HACHODESH

As the Rav says, the month of *Nissan* is the best concealed secret in the world—it is about eliminating chaos from our lives at the seed level. It is an opportunity to change our destiny; everything of a physical nature is in the palm of your hands. However, Satan's most potent weapon is that he has us convinced that we can not extricate ourselves from chaos; he makes us think that we can not do it alone.

The Haftarah of Shabbat haChodesh, gives us this opening and makes it possible for us to transform and be different on a seed level, and when our consciousness is different create a new destiny for the coming year, for ourselves and the world.

יוזקאל פרק מה

45 18 כֹּה הֵי ־אָמַר אֲדֹנָי ללה יְהֹוָאֵדָנִיל אהדונהי דן, ואדני בָּרִאשׁוֹן בְּאֶחָד אהבה, דאגה

לַחֹדֶשׁ י"ב הוייות תִּקַּח רבוע אהיה דאלפין פַּר בן זוהר, ערי, סנדלפון ־בֶּן־בָּקָר תָּמִים

וְחִטֵּאתָ אֶת־הַמִּקְדָּשׁ: 19 וְלָקַח יהוה אהיה אהיה אדני רבוע אהיה הַכֹּהֵן מלה מִדַּם

הַחַטָּאת וְנָתַן אבגית"ץ, ועדר, אהבת חנם אֶל־מְזוּזַת נית, זו מות הַבַּיִת ב"פ ראה וְאֶל־

אַרְבַּע פִּנּוֹת הָעֲזָרָה דן, נגד לַמִּזְבֵּחַ זן, נגד וְעַל־מְזוּזַת נית, זו מות שַׁעַר הֶחָצֵר

הַפְּנִימִית: 20 וְכֵן תַּעֲשֶׂה בְּשִׁבְעָה בַחֹדֶשׁ י"ב הוייות מֵאִישׁ ע"ה קנ"א קס"א שֹׁגֶה

וּמִפֶּתִי וְכִפַּרְתֶּם אֶת־הַבָּיִת ב"פ ראה: 21 בָּרִאשׁוֹן בְּאַרְבָּעָה עָשָׂר יוֹם

²¹ *In the first month on the fourteenth day will be to you the Passover, a feast lasting seven days, during which you shall eat unleavened bread.*

²² *On that day the prince is to provide a bull as a sin offering for himself and for all the people of the land.*

²³ *Every day during the seven days of the Feast he is to provide seven bulls and seven rams without defect as a burnt offering to the Lord, and a male goat for a sin offering.*

²⁴ *He is to provide as a grain offering an ephah for each bull and an ephah for each ram, along with a hin of oil for each ephah.*

²⁵ *During the seven days of the Feast, which begins in the seventh month on the fifteenth day, he is to make the same provision for sin offerings, burnt offerings, grain offerings and oil."*

46:¹ This is what the Lord, God says: "The gate of the inner court facing east is to be shut on the six working days, but on the Sabbath day and on the day of the New Moon it is to be opened.

² *The prince is to enter from the outside through the portico of the gateway and stand by the gatepost. The priests are to sacrifice his burnt offering and his fellowship offerings. He is to worship at the threshold of the gateway and then go out, but the gate will not be shut until evening.*

³ *On the Sabbaths and New Moons the people of the land are to worship in the presence of the Lord at the entrance to that gateway.*

⁴ *The burnt offering the prince brings to the Lord on the Sabbath day is to be six male lambs without defect and a ram without defect.*

⁵ *The grain offering given with the ram is to be an ephah, and the grain offering with the lambs is to be as much as he pleases, along with a hin of oil for each ephah.*

⁶ *On the day of the New Moon he is to offer a young bull, six lambs and a ram, all without defect.*

⁷ *He is to provide as a grain offering one ephah with the bull, one ephah with the ram, and with the lambs as much as his hand can reach, along with a hin of oil with each ephah.*

⁸ *When the prince enters, he is to go in through the portico of the gateway, and he is to come out the same way.*

לַחֹדֶשׁ יְהְיֶה לָכֶם הַפֶּסַח וְחַג שְׁבֻעוֹת יָמִים

מַצּוֹת יֵאָכֵל: 22 וְעָשָׂה הַנָּשִׂיא בַּיּוֹם הַהוּא בַּעֲדוֹ וּבְעַד

כָּל־עַם הָאָרֶץ פַּר וְחַטָּאת: 23 וְשִׁבְעַת

יְמֵי־הֶחָג יַעֲשֶׂה עוֹלָה לַיהוה שִׁבְעַת פָּרִים וְשִׁבְעַת אֵילִים

תְּמִימִם לַיּוֹם וְחַטָּאת שְׂעִיר עִזִּים לַיּוֹם

24 וּמִנְחָה אֵיפָה לַפָּר וְאֵיפָה לָאַיִל

יַעֲשֶׂה וְשֶׁמֶן הִין לָאֵיפָה: 25 בַּשְּׁבִיעִי בַּחֲמִשָּׁה עָשָׂר יוֹם

לַחֹדֶשׁ בֶּחָג יַעֲשֶׂה כָּאֵלֶּה שִׁבְעַת הַיָּמִים

כַּחַטָּאת כָּעֹלָה וְכַמִּנְחָה וְכַשָּׁמֶן 46 1 כֹּה אָמַר

אֲדֹנָי יְהוה שַׁעַר הֶחָצֵר הַפְּנִימִית הַפֹּנֶה קָדִים יִהְיֶה

סָגוּר שֵׁשֶׁת יְמֵי הַמַּעֲשֶׂה וּבְיוֹם הַשַּׁבָּת יִפָּתֵחַ וּבְיוֹם

הַחֹדֶשׁ יִפָּתֵחַ: 2 וּבָא הַנָּשִׂיא דֶּרֶךְ אוּלָם

הַשַּׁעַר מִחוּץ וְעָמַד עַל־מְזוּזַת הַשַּׁעַר וְעָשׂוּ הַכֹּהֲנִים אֶת־

עוֹלָתוֹ וְאֶת־שְׁלָמָיו וְהִשְׁתַּחֲוָה עַל־מִפְתַּן הַשַּׁעַר וְיָצָא וְהַשַּׁעַר לֹא־

יִסָּגֵר עַד־הָעָרֶב: 3 וְהִשְׁתַּחֲווּ עַם־הָאָרֶץ

פֶּתַח הַשַּׁעַר הַהוּא בַּשַּׁבָּתוֹת וּבֶחֳדָשִׁים לִפְנֵי יְהוה: 4 וְהָעֹלָה

אֲשֶׁר־יַקְרִב הַנָּשִׂיא לַיהוה בְּיוֹם הַשַּׁבָּת שִׁשָּׁה

כְבָשִׂים תְּמִימִם וְאַיִל תָּמִים: 5 וּמִנְחָה אֵיפָה לָאַיִל וְלַכְּבָשִׂים

מִנְחָה מַתַּת יָדוֹ וְשֶׁמֶן הִין לָאֵיפָה: 6 וּבְיוֹם

הַחֹדֶשׁ פַּר בֶּן־בָּקָר תְּמִימִם וְעֵשֶׂת

כְבָשִׂים וְאַיִל תְּמִימִם יִהְיוּ: 7 וְאֵיפָה לַפָּר וְאֵיפָה

לָאַיִל יַעֲשֶׂה מִנְחָה וְלַכְּבָשִׂים כַּאֲשֶׁר תַּשִּׂיג יָדוֹ וְשֶׁמֶן

הִין לָאֵיפָה: 8 וּבְבוֹא הַנָּשִׂיא דֶּרֶךְ אוּלָם הַשַּׁעַר

יָבוֹא וּבְדַרְכּוֹ יֵצֵא: 9 וּבְבוֹא עַם־הָאָרֶץ לִפְנֵי

⁹ *When the people of the land come before the Lord at the appointed feasts, whoever enters by the north gate to worship is to go out the south gate; and whoever enters by the south gate is to go out the north gate. No one is to return through the gate by which he entered, but each is to go out the opposite gate.*

¹⁰ *The prince is to be among them, going in when they go in and going out when they go out.*

¹¹ *At the festivals and the appointed feasts, the grain offering is to be an ephah with a bull, an ephah with a ram, and with the lambs as much as one pleases, along with a hin of oil for each ephah.*

¹² *When the prince provides a freewill offering to the Lord - whether a burnt offering or fellowship offerings—the gate facing east is to be opened for him. He shall offer his burnt offering or his fellowship offerings as he does on the Sabbath day. Then he shall go out, and after he has gone out, the gate will be shut.*

¹³ *Every day you are to provide a year-old lamb without defect for a burnt offering to the Lord; morning by morning you shall provide it.*

¹⁴ *You are also to provide with it morning by morning a grain offering, consisting of a sixth of an ephah with a third of a hin of oil to moisten the flour. The presenting of this grain offering to the Lord is a lasting ordinance.*

¹⁵ *So the lamb and the grain offering and the oil shall be provided morning by morning for a regular burnt offering."*

יְהֹוָ֣ה֩אֲדֹנָי בַּמּֽוֹעֲדִים֮ הַבָּא֒ בְּדֶ֣רֶךְ ב"פ יב"ק ־שַׁ֣עַר צָפ֗וֹן לְהִשְׁתַּחֲוֺת֙ יֵצֵ֔א

דֶּ֜רֶךְ ב"פ יב"ק ־שַׁ֣עַר נֶ֙גֶב֙ וְהַבָּא֙ דֶּ֣רֶךְ ב"פ יב"ק ־שַׁ֣עַר נֶ֗גֶב יֵצֵא֙ דֶּ֣רֶךְ ב"פ יב"ק

־שַׁ֣עַר צָפ֔וֹנָה עֵ"ה עסמ"ב לֹ֣א יָשׁ֔וּב דֶּ֣רֶךְ ב"פ יב"ק הַשַּׁ֔עַר אֲשֶׁר־בָּ֣א ב֔וֹ כִּ֥י

נִכְח֖וֹ יֵצֵֽא (כתיב: יצאו): 10 וְהַנָּשִׂ֕יא בְּתוֹכָ֖ם בְּבוֹאָ֣ם יָב֑וֹא וּבְצֵאתָ֖ם

יֵצֵֽאוּ: 11 וּבַחַגִּ֣ים וּבַמּֽוֹעֲדִ֗ים תִּהְיֶ֣ה הַמִּנְחָה֮ עֵ"ה ב"פ ב"ן אֵיפָ֣ה לַפָּ֗ר

סֵ֣זֹהַר, ערי, סנדלפון וְאֵיפָ֣ה לָאַ֔יִל וְלַכְּבָשִׂ֛ים מַתַּ֥ת יָד֖וֹ וְשֶׁ֑מֶן י"פ טל, י"פ כוז"ו; ביט הִ֖ין

לָאֵיפָֽה: 12 וְכִֽי־יַעֲשֶׂה֩ הַנָּשִׂ֨יא נְדָבָ֜ה וזיים, בינה עֵ"ה עוֹלָ֣ה אֽוֹ־שְׁלָמִים֮ נְדָבָה֮

וזיים, בינה עֵ"ה לַֽיהֹוָ֣ה֩אֲדֹנָי וּפָ֣תַֽח ל֗וֹ אֶת־הַשַּׁ֙עַר֙ הַפֹּנֶ֣ה קָדִ֔ים וְעָשָׂ֣ה אֶת־

עֹֽלָת֗וֹ וְאֶת־שְׁלָמָיו֙ כַּאֲשֶׁ֣ר יַעֲשֶׂ֣ה בְּי֣וֹם עֵ"ה = נגד, זן, מזבח הַשַּׁבָּ֔ת וְיָצָ֕א וְסָגַ֖ר

אֶת־הַשַּׁ֑עַר אַחֲרֵ֖י צֵאתֽוֹ: 13 וְכֶ֨בֶשׂ ב"פ קס"א בֶּן־שְׁנָת֜וֹ תָּמִ֗ים תַּעֲשֶׂ֥ה

עוֹלָ֛ה לַיּ֖וֹם עֵ"ה = נגד, זן, מזבח לַיהֹוָ֑ה֩אֲדֹנָי בַּבֹּ֥קֶר בַּבֹּ֖קֶר תַּעֲשֶׂ֥ה אֹתֽוֹ:

14 וּמִנְחָה֩ עֵ"ה ב"פ ב"ן תַעֲשֶׂ֨ה עָלָ֜יו בַּבֹּ֤קֶר בַּבֹּ֙קֶר֙ שִׁשִּׁ֣ית הָֽאֵיפָ֔ה וְשֶׁ֗מֶן

י"פ טל, י"פ כוז"ו, ביט שְׁלִישִׁ֤ית הַהִין֙ לָרֹ֣ס אֶת־הַסֹּ֔לֶת מִנְחָה֙ עֵ"ה ב"פ ב"ן לַֽיהֹוָ֣ה֩אֲדֹנָי

חֻקּ֥וֹת עוֹלָ֖ם תָּמִֽיד עֵ"ה נתה, עֵ"ה קס"א קנ"א קמ"ג: 15 יַעֲשׂ֨וּ (כתיב: ועשו) אֶת־הַכֶּ֧בֶשׂ

ב"פ קס"א וְאֶת־הַמִּנְחָ֛ה עֵ"ה ב"פ ב"ן וְאֶת־הַשֶּׁ֖מֶן י"פ טל, י"פ כוז"ו; ביט בַּבֹּ֣קֶר בַּבֹּ֑קֶר

עוֹלַ֖ת אבגיתצ, ועיר, אהבת וזזם תָּמִֽיד עֵ"ה נתה, עֵ"ה קס"א קנ"א קמ"ג:

HAFTARAH OF SHABBAT HAGADOL

This is the Shabbat before *Pesach* (Passover), the most powerful Shabbat of the whole year. Passover gives us freedom from all the forces that enslave us, from all of the beliefs that keep us in bondage and limit our potential. The energy of this particular Shabbat empowers us and fortifies

Malachi 3:4-24

3:4 "Then the offering of Judah and Jerusalem will be pleasant to the Lord as in the days of old; as in former years.

5 And I will come near you for judgment; I will be a swift witness against sorcerers, against adulterers, against perjurers, against those who exploit wage earners and widows and orphans, and against those who turn away an alien—because they do not fear Me," says the Lord of Hosts.

6 "For I am the Lord, I do not change; you are not consumed, sons of Jacob.

7 Yet from the days of your fathers you have gone away from My ordinances and have not kept them. Return to Me, and I will return to you," says the Lord of Hosts. But you said, 'In what way shall we return?'

8 Will a man rob God? Yet you have robbed Me! But you say, 'In what way have we robbed You?' In tithes and offerings.

9 You are cursed with a curse, for you have robbed Me, even this whole nation.

10 Bring all the tithes into the storehouse, that there may be food in My house, and try Me now in this," says the Lord of Hosts, "If I will not open for you the windows of heaven and pour out for you such blessing that there will not be room enough to receive it.

11 And I will rebuke the devourer for your sakes, so that he will not destroy the fruit of your ground, nor shall the vine fail to bear fruit for you in the field," says the Lord of Hosts;

12 and all nations will call you blessed, for you will be a delightful land," says the Lord of Hosts.

HAFTARAH OF SHABBAT HAGADOL

our Passover connection so that we can more powerfully connect to the week that can remove the chains of our bondage. Without connecting to this Shabbat, it is very difficult to really receive all the benefit of Passover and the freedom that it offers.

מלאכי פרק ג

4 וְעָרְבָה לַיהוָֹה מִנְחַת יְהוּדָה וִירוּשָׁלָ͏ִם כִּימֵי עוֹלָם וּכְשָׁנִים קַדְמֹנִיֹּת: 5 וְקָרַבְתִּי אֲלֵיכֶם לַמִּשְׁפָּט וְהָיִיתִי | עֵד מְמַהֵר בַּמְכַשְּׁפִים וּבַמְנָאֲפִים וּבַנִּשְׁבָּעִים לַשָּׁקֶר וּבְעשְׁקֵי שְׂכַר שָׂכִיר אַלְמָנָה וְיָתוֹם וּמַטֵּי־גֵר וְלֹא יְרֵאוּנִי אָמַר יְהוָֹה צְבָאוֹת: 6 כִּי אֲנִי יְהוָֹה לֹא שָׁנִיתִי וְאַתֶּם בְּנֵי־יַעֲקֹב לֹא כְלִיתֶם: 7 לְמִימֵי אֲבֹתֵיכֶם סַרְתֶּם מֵחֻקַּי וְלֹא שְׁמַרְתֶּם שׁוּבוּ אֵלַי וְאָשׁוּבָה אֲלֵיכֶם אָמַר יְהוָֹה צְבָאוֹת וַאֲמַרְתֶּם בַּמֶּה נָשׁוּב: 8 הֲיִקְבַּע אָדָם אֱלֹהִים כִּי אַתֶּם קֹבְעִים אֹתִי וַאֲמַרְתֶּם בַּמֶּה קְבַעֲנוּךָ הַמַּעֲשֵׂר וְהַתְּרוּמָה: 9 בַּמְּאֵרָה אַתֶּם נֵאָרִים וְאֹתִי אַתֶּם קֹבְעִים הַגּוֹי כֻּלּוֹ: 10 הָבִיאוּ אֶת־כָּל־הַמַּעֲשֵׂר אֶל־בֵּית הָאוֹצָר וִיהִי טֶרֶף בְּבֵיתִי וּבְחָנוּנִי נָא בָּזֹאת אָמַר יְהוָֹה צְבָאוֹת אִם־לֹא אֶפְתַּח לָכֶם אֵת אֲרֻבּוֹת הַשָּׁמַיִם וַהֲרִיקֹתִי לָכֶם בְּרָכָה עַד־בְּלִי־דָי: 11 וְגָעַרְתִּי לָכֶם בָּאֹכֵל וְלֹא־יַשְׁחִת לָכֶם אֶת־פְּרִי הָאֲדָמָה וְלֹא־תְשַׁכֵּל לָכֶם הַגֶּפֶן בַּשָּׂדֶה אָמַר יְהוָֹה צְבָאוֹת: 12 וְאִשְּׁרוּ אֶתְכֶם כָּל־הַגּוֹיִם כִּי־תִהְיוּ אַתֶּם אֶרֶץ חֵפֶץ אָמַר יְהוָֹה צְבָאוֹת: 13 חָזְקוּ עָלַי דִּבְרֵיכֶם אָמַר יְהוָֹה וַאֲמַרְתֶּם מַה־נִּדְבַּרְנוּ

[13] *"Your words have been harsh against Me," says the Lord, "yet you say, 'What have we spoken against You?'*

[14] *You have said, 'It is useless to serve God; what profit is it that we have kept His ordinance, and that we have walked as mourners before the Lord of Hosts?*

[15] *So now we call the proud blessed, for those who do wickedness are raised up; they even tempt God and go free.'"*

[16] *Then those who feared the Lord spoke to one another, and the Lord listened and heard them; so a book of remembrance was written before Him for those who fear the Lord and who meditate on His name.*

[17] *"They shall be Mine," says the Lord of Hosts, "on the day that I make them My jewels. And I will spare them as a man spares his own son who serves him."*

[18] *Then you shall again discern between the righteous and the wicked, between one who serves God and one who does not serve Him.*

[19] *For, behold, the day comes, it burns as a furnace; and all the proud, and all that work wickedness, shall be stubble; and the day that cometh shall set them ablaze," said the Lord of Hosts, "that it shall leave them neither root nor branch.*

[20] *But unto you that fear My name shall the sun of righteousness arise with healing in its wings; and you shall go forth, and gambol as calves of the stall.*

[21] *And you shall tread down the wicked; for they shall be ashes under the soles of your feet in the day that I do make," said the Lord of Hosts.*

[22] *"Remember you the law of Moses My servant, which I commanded unto him in Horeb for all Israel, even statutes and ordinances.*

[23] *Behold, I will send you Elijah the prophet before the coming of the great and terrible day of the Lord. [24] And he shall turn the heart of the fathers to the children, and the heart of the children to their fathers; lest I come and smite the land with utter destruction.*

ראה עֲלֵיךָ רבוע מ״ה: 14 אֲמַרְתֶּם שָׁוְא עֲבֹד אֱלֹהִים מום, אהיה אדני ; ילה וּמַה מ״ה ־בֶּצַע כִּי שָׁמַרְנוּ מִשְׁמַרְתּוֹ וְכִי הָלַכְנוּ קְדֹרַנִּית מִפְּנֵי וחכמה בינה יְהוָֹואהדונהי צְבָאוֹת נתה ורבוע אהיה; פני שכינה: 15 וְעַתָּה אֲנַחְנוּ מְאַשְּׁרִים זֵדִים גַּם יכל ־נִבְנוּ עֹשֵׂי רִשְׁעָה גַּם יכל בָּחֲנוּ אֱלֹהִים מום, אהיה אדני ; ילה וַיִּמָּלֵטוּ: 16 אָז נִדְבְּרוּ ראה יִרְאֵי יְהוָֹואהדונהי ע״ה קנ״א קס״א אִישׁ אֶל־רֵעֵהוּ וַיַּקְשֵׁב יְהוָֹואהדונהי וַיִּשְׁמָע וַיִּכָּתֵב סֵפֶר זִכָּרוֹן ע״ב קס״א נע״ב לְפָנָיו לְיִרְאֵי יְהוָֹואהדונהי וּלְחֹשְׁבֵי שְׁמוֹ מהש ע״ה, אל שדי ע״ה: 17 וְהָיוּ לִי אָמַר יְהוָֹואהדונהי צְבָאוֹת נתה ורבוע אהיה; פני שכינה לַיּוֹם ע״ה = נגד, זן, מזבח אֲשֶׁר אֲנִי אנ״י, טדהד״ר כוזו עֹשֶׂה סְגֻלָּה וְחָמַלְתִּי עֲלֵיהֶם כַּאֲשֶׁר יַחְמֹל אִישׁ ע״ה קנ״א קס״א עַל־בְּנוֹ הָעֹבֵד אֹתוֹ: 18 וְשַׁבְתֶּם וּרְאִיתֶם בֵּין צַדִּיק לְרָשָׁע בֵּין עֹבֵד אֱלֹהִים מום, אהיה אדני ; ילה לַאֲשֶׁר לֹא עֲבָדוֹ: 19 כִּי־הִנֵּה מ״ה יה הַיּוֹם ע״ה = נגד, זן, מזבח בָּא בֹּעֵר כַּתַּנּוּר וְהָיוּ כָל יכל ־זֵדִים וְכָל יכל ־עֹשֵׂה רִשְׁעָה קַשׁ וְלִהַט אֹתָם הַיּוֹם ע״ה = נגד, זן, מזבח רבוע אהיה הַבָּא אָמַר יְהוָֹואהדונהי צְבָאוֹת נתה ורבוע אהיה; פני שכינה אֲשֶׁר לֹא־יַעֲזֹב לָהֶם שֹׁרֶשׁ וְעָנָף רבוע אלהים: 20 וְזָרְחָה לָכֶם יִרְאֵי שְׁמִי רבוע ע״ב ורבוע ס״ג שֶׁמֶשׁ ב״פ ש״ך צְדָקָה ע״ה ריבוע אלהים וּמַרְפֵּא בִּכְנָפֶיהָ וִיצָאתֶם וּפִשְׁתֶּם כְּעֶגְלֵי מַרְבֵּק: 21 וְעַסּוֹתֶם רְשָׁעִים כִּי־יִהְיוּ אֵל, יא״י אֵפֶר סזוזהד״ך ע״ה תַּחַת כַּפּוֹת רַגְלֵיכֶם בַּיּוֹם ע״ה = נגד, זן, מזבח אֲשֶׁר אֲנִי אנ״י, טדהד״ר כוזו עֹשֶׂה אָמַר יְהוָֹואהדונהי צְבָאוֹת נתה ורבוע אהיה; פני שכינה: 22 זִכְרוּ תּוֹרַת מֹשֶׁה מהש, אל שדי עַבְדִּי אֲשֶׁר צִוִּיתִי אוֹתוֹ בְחֹרֵב רבוע ס״ג ורבוע אהיה עַל־כָּל יכל, עמם ־יִשְׂרָאֵל חֻקִּים וּמִשְׁפָּטִים: 23 הִנֵּה מ״ה יה אָנֹכִי איע שֹׁלֵחַ לָכֶם אֵת אֵלִיָּה הַנָּבִיא לִפְנֵי וחכמה בינה בּוֹא יוֹם ע״ה = נגד, זן, מזבח יְהוָֹואהדונהי הַגָּדוֹל להוו, מבה, יזל, אום וְהַנּוֹרָא ע״ה ג״פ אלהים: 24 וְהֵשִׁיב לֵב־אָבוֹת עַל־בָּנִים וְלֵב בָּנִים עַל־אֲבוֹתָם פֶּן־אָבוֹא וְהִכֵּיתִי אֶת־הָאָרֶץ אלהים דההין ע״ה חֵרֶם: הִנֵּה מ״ה יה אָנֹכִי איע שֹׁלֵחַ לָכֶם אֵת אֵלִיָּה הַנָּבִיא לִפְנֵי וחכמה בינה בּוֹא יוֹם ע״ה = נגד, זן, מזבח יְהוָֹואהדונהי הַגָּדוֹל להוו, מבה, יזל, אום וְהַנּוֹרָא ע״ה ג״פ אלהים:

HAFTARAH OF THE EVE OF ROSH CHODESH

On one level, this Haftarah concerns the eve of Rosh Chodesh, the eve of a new lunar (astrological) month. In a deeper sense, it speaks of the love between David and Jonathan. Although Jonathan was heir to the throne, he knew that David might become king. Yet Jonathan loved David and felt

1 Samuel 20:18-42

20:[18] *Then Jonathan said to him, "Tomorrow is the New Moon, and you will be missed because your seat will be empty.*

[19] *When you have stayed for three days, you shall go down quickly and come to the place where you hid yourself on that eventful day, and you shall remain by the stone Ezel.*

[20] *I will shoot three arrows to the side, as though I shot at a target.*

[21] *And behold, I will send the lad, saying, 'Go, find the arrows.' If I specifically say to the lad, 'Behold, the arrows are on this side of you, get them,' then come; for there is safety for you and no harm, as the Lord lives.*

[22] *"But if I say to the youth, 'Behold, the arrows are beyond you,' go, for the Lord has sent you away.*

[23] *As for the agreement of which you and I have spoken, behold, the Lord is between you and me forever."*

[24] *So David hid in the field; and when the New Moon came, the king sat down to eat food.*

[25] *The king sat on his seat as usual, the seat by the wall; then Jonathan rose up and Abner sat down by Saul's side, but David's place was empty.*

[26] *Nevertheless Saul did not speak anything that day, for he thought, "It is an accident, he is not clean, surely he is not clean."*

[27] *It came about the next day, the second day of the New Moon, that David's place was empty; so Saul said to Jonathan his son, "Why has the son of Jesse not come to the meal, either yesterday or today?"*

[28] *Jonathan then answered Saul, "David earnestly asked leave of me to go to Bethlehem,* [29] *for he said, 'Please let me go, since our family has a sacrifice in the*

HAFTARAH OF THE EVE OF ROSH CHODESH

no jealousy. To truly feel love for another person, we must give up our own selfish desires. To have a successful relationship of any kind, we must be willing to sacrifice something.

שמואל 1 פרק 20

20 18 וַיֹּאמֶר־לוֹ יְהוֹנָתָן מָחָר רמ״ח חֹדֶשׁ י״ב הויות וְנִפְקַדְתָּ כִּי יִפָּקֵד

מוֹשָׁבֶךָ: 19 וְשִׁלַּשְׁתָּ תֵּרֵד מְאֹד מ״ה וּבָאתָ אֶל־הַמָּקוֹם יהוה ברבוע אֲשֶׁר־

נִסְתַּרְתָּ שָּׁם בְּיוֹם נגד, זן, מזבח הַמַּעֲשֶׂה וְיָשַׁבְתָּ אֵצֶל הָאֶבֶן יוד הה וֵאו הה הָאָזֶל: 20 וַאֲנִי ב״פ אהיה יהוה שְׁלֹשֶׁת הַחִצִּים צִדָּה אוֹרֶה לְשַׁלַּח־לִי

לְמַטָּרָה: 21 וְהִנֵּה מ״ה יה אֶשְׁלַח אֶת־הַנַּעַר ש״ך לֵךְ מְצָא אֶת־הַחִצִּים

אִם־אָמֹר אֹמַר יוהך לַנַּעַר הִנֵּה מ״ה יה הַחִצִּים ש״ך | מִמְּךָ וָהֵנָּה מ״ה יה

קָחֶנּוּ | וָבֹאָה כִּי־שָׁלוֹם לְךָ וְאֵין דָּבָר ראה וַחַי־יְהֹוָאַדְנִיליאהדונהי: 22 וְאִם וׁהך

כֹּה הי אֹמַר לָעֶלֶם הִנֵּה מ״ה יה הַחִצִּים מִמְּךָ וָהָלְאָה לֵךְ כִּי שִׁלַּחֲךָ

יְהֹוָאַדְנִיליאהדונהי: 23 וְהַדָּבָר ראה אֲשֶׁר דִּבַּרְנוּ ראה אֲנִי אני וָאָתָּה הִנֵּה מ״ה יה

יְהֹוָאַדְנִיליאהדונהי בֵּינִי וּבֵינְךָ עַד־עוֹלָם: [ס] 24 וַיִּסָּתֵר ב״פ מצר דָּוִד בַּשָּׂדֶה

וַיְהִי הַחֹדֶשׁ י״ב הויות וַיֵּשֶׁב הַמֶּלֶךְ אֶל־ (כתיב: על-) הַלֶּחֶם ג״פ יהוה לֶאֱכוֹל:

25 וַיֵּשֶׁב הַמֶּלֶךְ עַל־מוֹשָׁבוֹ כְּפַעַם | בְּפַעַם אֶל־מוֹשַׁב הַקִּיר וַיָּקָם

יְהוֹנָתָן וַיֵּשֶׁב אַבְנֵר מִצַּד שָׁאוּל וַיִּפָּקֵד מְקוֹם יהוה ברבוע דָּוִד: 26 וְלֹא־

דִבֶּר ראה שָׁאוּל מְאוּמָה בַּיּוֹם נגד, זן, מזבח הַהוּא כִּי אָמַר מִקְרֶה הוּא

בִּלְתִּי טָהוֹר הוּא כִּי־לֹא טָהוֹר י״פ אכא: [ס] 27 וַיְהִי אל מִמָּחֳרַת

הַחֹדֶשׁ י״ב הויות הַשֵּׁנִי וַיִּפָּקֵד מְקוֹם יהוה ברבוע דָּוִד [פ] וַיֹּאמֶר שָׁאוּל אֶל־

יְהוֹנָתָן בְּנוֹ מַדּוּעַ לֹא־בָא בֶן־יִשַׁי גם תְּמוֹל גַּם יגל הַיּוֹם נגד, זן, מזבח

אֶל־הַלָּחֶם ג״פ יהוה: 28 וַיַּעַן יְהוֹנָתָן אֶת־שָׁאוּל נִשְׁאֹל נִשְׁאַל דָּוִד מֵעִמָּדִי

עַד־בֵּית ב״פ ראה לָחֶם: 29 וַיֹּאמֶר שְׁלָחֵנִי נָא כִּי זֶבַח מִשְׁפָּחָה לָנוּ

city, and my brother has commanded me to attend. And now, if I have found favor in your sight, please let me get away that I may see my brothers.' For this reason he has not come to the king's table."

³⁰ *Then Saul's anger burned against Jonathan and he said to him, "You son of a perverse, rebellious woman! Do I not know that you are choosing the son of Jesse to your own shame and to the shame of your mother's nakedness?*

³¹ *For as long as the son of Jesse lives on the Earth, neither you nor your kingdom will be established. Now, send and bring him to me, for he must surely die."*

³² *But Jonathan answered Saul, his father, and said to him, "Why should he be put to death? What has he done?"*

³³ *Then Saul hurled his spear at him to strike him down; so Jonathan knew that his father had decided to put David to death.*

³⁴ *Then Jonathan arose from the table in fierce anger, and did not eat food on the second day of the New Moon, for he was grieved over David because his father had dishonored him.*

³⁵ *Now it came about in the morning that Jonathan went out into the field for the appointment with David, and a little lad was with him.*

³⁶ *He said to his lad, "Run, find now the arrows which I am about to shoot." As the lad was running, he shot an arrow past him.*

³⁷ *When the lad reached the place of the arrow which Jonathan had shot, Jonathan called after the lad and said, "Is not the arrow beyond you?"*

³⁸ *And Jonathan called after the lad, "Hurry, be quick, do not stay!" And Jonathan's lad picked up the arrow and came to his master.*

³⁹ *The lad was not aware of anything; only Jonathan and David knew about the matter.*

⁴⁰ *Then Jonathan gave his weapons to his lad and said to him, "Go; bring them to the city."*

⁴¹ *When the lad was gone, David rose from the south side and fell on his face to the ground and bowed three times, and they kissed each other and wept together, but David wept more.*

⁴² *Jonathan said to David, "Go in safety, inasmuch as we have sworn to each other in the Name of the Lord, saying, 'The Lord will be between me and you, and between my descendants and your descendants forever.' "*

בְּעִיר סוֹזוֹרְךָ, עֲרִי, סְנַדְלְפוֹן וְהוּא צִוָּה פֵּי ־לִי אוֹרֵי וְעַתָּה אִם יוֹהִרְ אֱלֹהִים, מוּם

מְצָאתִי חֵן בְּעֵינֶיךָ מוּוֹי ע״ה קס״א אֲמַלְּטָה נָּא וְאֶרְאֶה אֶת־אֶחַי עַל־כֵּן

לֹא־בָא אֶל־שֻׁלְחַן הַמֶּלֶךְ: [ס] 30 וַיִּחַר־אַף שָׁאוּל בִּיהוֹנָתָן וַיֹּאמֶר לוֹ

בֶּן־נַעֲוַת הַמַּרְדּוּת הֲלוֹא יָדַעְתִּי כִּי־בֹחֵר אַתָּה לְבֶן־יִשַׁי לְבָשְׁתְּךָ

וּלְבֹשֶׁת עֶרְוַת אִמֶּךָ: 31 כִּי כָל־הַיָּמִים יִלִי אֲשֶׁר בֶּן־יִשַׁי חַי עַל־ גֹּלֶךְ

הָאֲדָמָה לֹא תִכּוֹן אַתָּה וּמַלְכוּתֶךָ וְעַתָּה שְׁלַח וְקַח אֹתוֹ אֵלַי כִּי בֶן־

מָוֶת הוּא: [ס] 32 וַיַּעַן יְהוֹנָתָן אֶת־שָׁאוּל אָבִיו וַיֹּאמֶר אֵלָיו לָמָּה יוּמַת

מֶה מ״ה עָשָׂה: 33 וַיָּטֶל שָׁאוּל אֶת־הַחֲנִית עָלָיו לְהַכֹּתוֹ וַיֵּדַע יְהוֹנָתָן

כִּי־כָלָה הִיא מֵעִם עמם אָבִיו לְהָמִית אֶת־דָּוִד: [ס] 34 וַיָּקָם יְהוֹנָתָן

מֵעִם עמם הַשֻּׁלְחָן בָּחֳרִי־אָף וְלֹא־אָכַל בְּיוֹם נֵגֶד, זֶן, מזבח הַחֹדֶשׁ ־הַשֵּׁנִי יֹ״ב הַוויות

הַשֵּׁנִי לֶחֶם גֹּ״ס יהוה כִּי נֶעֱצַב אֶל־דָּוִד כִּי הִכְלִמוֹ אָבִיו: [ס] 35 וַיְהִי אֵל

בַּבֹּקֶר וַיֵּצֵא יְהוֹנָתָן הַשָּׂדֶה שׁ״ד לְמוֹעֵד דָּוִד וְנַעַר שׁ״ר קָטֹן עִמּוֹ:

36 וַיֹּאמֶר לְנַעֲרוֹ רֻץ מְצָא נָא אֶת־הַחִצִּים אֲשֶׁר אָנֹכִי אים מוֹרֶה

הַנַּעַר שׁ״ר רָץ וְהוּא־יָרָה הַחֵצִי לְהַעֲבִרוֹ: 37 וַיָּבֹא הַנַּעַר שׁ״ר עַד־מְקוֹם

יהוה ברבוע הַחֵצִי אֲשֶׁר יָרָה יְהוֹנָתָן וַיִּקְרָא עם ה׳ אותיות = ב״פ קס״א יְהוֹנָתָן אַחֲרֵי

הַנַּעַר שׁ״ר וַיֹּאמֶר הֲלוֹא הַחֵצִי מִמְּךָ וָהָלְאָה: 38 וַיִּקְרָא עם ה׳ אותיות = ב״פ קס״א

יְהוֹנָתָן אַחֲרֵי הַנַּעַר שׁ״ר מְהֵרָה חוּשָׁה אַל־תַּעֲמֹד וַיְלַקֵּט נַעַר שׁ״ר

יְהוֹנָתָן אֶת־הַחִצִּים (כתיב: הַחִצִי) וַיָּבֹא אֶל־אֲדֹנָיו: 39 וְהַנַּעַר שׁ״ר לֹא־יָדַע

מְאוּמָה אַךְ אהיה יְהוֹנָתָן וְדָוִד יָדְעוּ אֶת־הַדָּבָר ראה: [ס] 40 וַיִּתֵּן יֹ״פ מלוי ע״ב

יְהוֹנָתָן אֶת־כֵּלָיו כלי אֶל־הַנַּעַר שׁ״ר אֲשֶׁר־לוֹ וַיֹּאמֶר לוֹ לֵךְ הָבֵיא הָעִיר:

סוֹזוֹרְךָ, עֲרִי, סְנַדְלְפוֹן 41 הַנַּעַר שׁ״ר בָּא וְדָוִד קָם מֵאֵצֶל הַנֶּגֶב וַיִּפֹּל לְאַפָּיו

אַרְצָה אֱלֹהִים דההין ע״ה וַיִּשְׁתַּחוּ שָׁלֹשׁ פְּעָמִים וַיִּשְּׁקוּ | אִישׁ ע״ה קנ״א קס״א אֶת־

רֵעֵהוּ וַיִּבְכּוּ אִישׁ ע״ה קנ״א קס״א אֶת־רֵעֵהוּ עַד־דָּוִד הִגְדִּיל: 42 וַיֹּאמֶר

יְהוֹנָתָן לְדָוִד לֵךְ לְשָׁלוֹם אֲשֶׁר נִשְׁבַּעְנוּ שְׁנֵינוּ אֲנַחְנוּ בְּשֵׁם שׁ״ד יהוה

יהוה אדני אהדונהי לֵאמֹר יְהוָה אדני אהדונהי יְהוָה יי׳ | בֵּינִי וּבֵינֶךָ וּבֵין זַרְעִי וּבֵין

זַרְעֲךָ עַד־עוֹלָם: [פ]

MAFTIR OF SHABBAT ROSH CHODESH

In this Maftir, we read about the tribes of Reuben, Shimon and Gad, which were stationed in the south. The *Zohar* in Terumah130 says that the south signifies *Chesed*, or love and mercy, and is a place of quiet that is protected by the angel Michael. And that the south is where everything is

Numbers 28:9-15

28:9 *"On the Sabbath day, make an offering of two lambs a year old without defect, together with its drink offering and a grain offering of two-tenths of an ephah of fine flour mixed with oil.*

[10] *This is the burnt offering for every Sabbath, in addition to the regular burnt offering and its drink offering.*

[11] *On the first of every month, present to the Lord a burnt offering of two young bulls, one ram and seven male lambs a year old, all without defect.*

[12] *With each bull there is to be a grain offering of three-tenths of an ephah of fine flour mixed with oil; with the ram, a grain offering of two-tenths of an ephah of fine flour mixed with oil;*

[13] *and with each lamb, a grain offering of a tenth of an ephah of fine flour mixed with oil. This is for a burnt offering, a pleasing aroma, an offering made to the Lord by fire.*

[14] *With each bull there is to be a drink offering of half a hin of wine; with the ram, a third of a hin; and with each lamb, a quarter of a hin. This is the monthly burnt offering to be made at each new moon during the year.*

[15] *Besides the regular burnt offering with its drink offering, one male goat is to be presented to the Lord as a sin offering."*

MAFTIR OF SHABBAT ROSH CHODESH

manifested once we've completed our spiritual connections. By listening to this reading, we have an opportunity to go within ourselves, finding the clarity to manifest all our spiritual connections and imbuing the coming month with Light.

במדבר פרק 28

9 וּבְיוֹם נגד, זן, מזבח הַשַּׁבָּת שְׁנֵי־כְבָשִׂים בְּנֵי־שָׁנָה תְּמִימִם וּשְׁנֵי עֶשְׂרֹנִים סֹלֶת מִנְחָה עֹה ב״פ בן בְּלוּלָה בַשֶּׁמֶן יֹ״פ טל, יֹ״פ כוזו, ביט וְנִסְכּוֹ: 10 עֹלַת שַׁבַּת בְּשַׁבַּתּוֹ עַל־עֹלַת הַתָּמִיד נתה, קס״א + קנ״א + קמ״ג אבגיתצ, ושר, אהבת חנם וְנִסְכָּהּ: [פ] 11 וּבְרָאשֵׁי ריבוע אלהים + אלהים דיודין עה חָדְשֵׁיכֶם י״ב הויות תַּקְרִיבוּ עֹלָה לַיהֹוָאֲדֹנָיאהדונהי פָּרִים בְּנֵי־בָקָר שְׁנַיִם וְאַיִל אֶחָד אהבה, דאגה כְּבָשִׂים בְּנֵי־שָׁנָה שִׁבְעָה תְּמִימִם: 12 וּשְׁלֹשָׁה עֶשְׂרֹנִים סֹלֶת מִנְחָה עה ב״פ בן בְּלוּלָה בַשֶּׁמֶן יֹ״פ טל, יֹ״פ כוזו, ביט לַפָּר ⁎מוֹחִין, ערי הָאֶחָד אהבה, דאגה וּשְׁנֵי עֶשְׂרֹנִים סֹלֶת מִנְחָה עה ב״פ בן בְּלוּלָה בַשֶּׁמֶן יֹ״פ טל, יֹ״פ כוזו, ביט לָאַיִל הָאֶחָד אהבה, דאגה: 13 וְעִשָּׂרֹן עִשָּׂרוֹן סֹלֶת מִנְחָה עה ב״פ בן בְּלוּלָה בַשֶּׁמֶן יֹ״פ טל, יֹ״פ כוזו, ביט לַכֶּבֶשׂ ב״פ קס״א הָאֶחָד אהבה, דאגה עֹלָה רֵיחַ נִיחֹחַ אִשֶּׁה לַיהֹוָאֲדֹנָיאהדונהי: 14 וְנִסְכֵּיהֶם חֲצִי הַהִין יִהְיֶה יְיָ לַפָּר ⁎מוֹחִין, ערי וּשְׁלִישִׁת הַהִין לָאַיִל וּרְבִיעִת הַהִין לַכֶּבֶשׂ ב״פ קס״א יָיִן קס״א מיכ, י״פ האא אבגיתצ, ושר, אהבת חנם זֹאת עֹלַת חֹדֶשׁ י״ב הויות בְּחָדְשׁוֹ י״ב הויות לְחָדְשֵׁי י״ב הויות הַשָּׁנָה: 15 וּשְׂעִיר עִזִּים אֶחָד אהבה, דאגה לְחַטָּאת לַיהֹוָאֲדֹנָיאהדונהי עַל־עֹלַת אבגיתצ, ושר, אהבת חנם הַתָּמִיד יֵעָשֶׂה יְיָ וְנִסְכּוֹ: [ס] נתה, קס״א + קנ״א + קמ״ג

HAFTARAH OF SHABBAT ROSH CHODESH

Just as Shabbat cools the fires of Hell, these same fires are shut down on Rosh Chodesh giving us the power to deflect and avoid judgment.

Isaiah 66:1-24

66:¹ This is what the Lord says: "Heaven is My Throne, and the Earth is My Footstool. Where is the House you will build for Me? Where will My Resting Place be?

² Has not My hand made all these things, and so they came into being?" declares the Lord. "This is the one I esteem: he who is humble and contrite in spirit, and trembles at My Word.

³ But whoever sacrifices a bull is like one who kills a man, and whoever offers a lamb, like one who breaks a dog's neck; whoever makes a grain offering is like one who presents pig's blood, and whoever burns memorial incense, like one who worships an idol. They have chosen their own ways, and their souls delight in their abominations;

⁴ so I also will choose harsh treatment for them and will bring upon them what they dread. For when I called, no one answered, when I spoke, no one listened. They did evil in My sight and chose what displeases Me."

⁵ Hear the Word of the Lord, you who tremble at His Word: "Your brothers who hate you, and exclude you because of My Name, have said, 'Let the Lord be glorified, that we may see your joy!' Yet they will be put to shame.

⁶ Hear that uproar from the city, hear that noise from the temple! It is the sound of the Lord repaying His enemies all they deserve.

⁷ Before she goes into labor, she gives birth; before the pains come upon her, she delivers a son.

⁸ Who has ever heard of such a thing? Who has ever seen such things? Can a country be born in a day or a nation be brought forth in a moment? Yet no sooner is Zion in labor than she gives birth to her children.

HAFTARAH OF SHABBAT ROSH CHODESH

ישעיהו פרק 66

‎66 1 כֹּה אָמַר יְהֹוָה הַשָּׁמַיִם כִּסְאִי וְהָאָרֶץ הֲדֹם רַגְלָי אֵי־זֶה בַיִת אֲשֶׁר תִּבְנוּ־לִי וְאֵי־זֶה מָקוֹם מְנוּחָתִי: 2 וְאֶת־כָּל־אֵלֶּה יָדִי עָשָׂתָה וַיִּהְיוּ כָל־אֵלֶּה נְאֻם־יְהֹוָה וְאֶל־זֶה אַבִּיט אֶל־עָנִי וּנְכֵה־רוּחַ וְחָרֵד עַל־דְּבָרִי: 3 שׁוֹחֵט הַשּׁוֹר מַכֵּה־אִישׁ זוֹבֵחַ הַשֶּׂה עֹרֵף כֶּלֶב מַעֲלֵה מִנְחָה דַּם־חֲזִיר מַזְכִּיר לְבֹנָה מְבָרֵךְ אָוֶן גַּם־הֵמָּה בָּחֲרוּ בְּדַרְכֵיהֶם וּבְשִׁקּוּצֵיהֶם נַפְשָׁם חָפֵצָה: 4 גַּם־אֲנִי אֶבְחַר בְּתַעֲלֻלֵיהֶם וּמְגוּרֹתָם אָבִיא לָהֶם יַעַן קָרָאתִי וְאֵין עוֹנֶה דִּבַּרְתִּי וְלֹא שָׁמֵעוּ וַיַּעֲשׂוּ הָרַע בְּעֵינַי וּבַאֲשֶׁר לֹא־חָפַצְתִּי בָּחָרוּ: [ס] 5 שִׁמְעוּ דְּבַר־יְהֹוָה הַחֲרֵדִים אֶל־דְּבָרוֹ אָמְרוּ אֲחֵיכֶם שֹׂנְאֵיכֶם מְנַדֵּיכֶם לְמַעַן שְׁמִי יִכְבַּד יְהֹוָה וְנִרְאֶה בְשִׂמְחַתְכֶם וְהֵם יֵבֹשׁוּ: 6 קוֹל שָׁאוֹן מֵעִיר קוֹל מֵהֵיכָל קוֹל יְהֹוָה מְשַׁלֵּם גְּמוּל לְאֹיְבָיו: 7 בְּטֶרֶם תָּחִיל יָלָדָה בְּטֶרֶם יָבוֹא חֵבֶל לָהּ וְהִמְלִיטָה זָכָר: 8 מִי־שָׁמַע כָּזֹאת מִי רָאָה כָּאֵלֶּה הֲיוּחַל אֶרֶץ בְּיוֹם אֶחָד אִם־יִוָּלֵד גּוֹי פַּעַם אֶחָת כִּי־חָלָה גַּם־יָלְדָה צִיּוֹן אֶת־בָּנֶיהָ: 9 הַאֲנִי אַשְׁבִּיר וְלֹא אוֹלִיד יֹאמַר

⁹ Do I bring to the moment of birth and not give delivery?" says the Lord. "Do I close up the womb when I bring to delivery?" says your God.

¹⁰ "Rejoice with Jerusalem and be glad for her, all you who love her; rejoice greatly with her, all you who mourn over her.

¹¹ For you will nurse and be satisfied at her comforting breasts; you will drink deeply and delight in her overflowing abundance."

¹² For this is what the Lord says: "I will extend peace to her like a river, and the wealth of nations like a flooding stream; you will nurse and be carried on her arm and dandled on her knees.

¹³ As a mother comforts her child, so will I comfort you; and you will be comforted over Jerusalem."

¹⁴ When you see this, your heart will rejoice and you will flourish like grass; the hand of the Lord will be made known to His servants, but his fury will be shown to His foes.
¹⁵ See, the Lord is coming with fire, and His chariots are like a whirlwind; He will bring down His anger with fury, and His rebuke with flames of fire.

¹⁶ For with fire and with his sword the Lord will execute judgment upon all men, and many will be those slain by the Lord.

¹⁷ "Those who consecrate and purify themselves to go into the gardens, following the one in the midst of those who eat the flesh of pigs and rats and other abominable things—they will meet their end together," declares the Lord.

¹⁸ "And I, because of their actions and their imaginations, am about to come and gather all nations and tongues, and they will come and see My glory.

¹⁹ I will set a sign among them, and I will send some of those who survive to the nations—to Tarshish, to the Libyans and Lydians (famous as archers), to Tubal and Greece, and to the distant islands that have not heard of My fame or seen My glory. They will proclaim My glory among the nations.

²⁰ And they will bring all your brothers, from all the nations, to My Holy Mountain in Jerusalem as an offering to the Lord—on horses, in chariots and wagons, and on mules and camels," says the Lord. "They will bring them, as the Israelites bring their grain offerings, to the Temple of the Lord in ceremonially clean vessels.

[ס] ילה: אָם הַמּוֹלִיד וְעָצַרְתִּי אָמַר אֱלֹהָיִךְ יְהֹוָה אֲנִי אֲנִי

10 שִׂמְחוּ אֶת־יְרוּשָׁלַ͏ִם וְגִילוּ בָהּ כָּל־אֹהֲבֶיהָ שִׂישׂוּ אִתָּהּ

מָשׂוֹשׂ כָּל־הַמִּתְאַבְּלִים עָלֶיהָ: 11 לְמַעַן תִּינְקוּ וּשְׂבַעְתֶּם מִשֹּׁד

תַּנְחֻמֶיהָ לְמַעַן תָּמֹצּוּ וְהִתְעַנַּגְתֶּם מִזִּיז כְּבוֹדָהּ: [ס] 12 כִּי־כֹה אָמַר

יְהֹוָה הִנְנִי נֹטֶה־אֵלֶיהָ כְּנָהָר שָׁלוֹם וּכְנַחַל שׁוֹטֵף כְּבוֹד

גּוֹיִם וִינַקְתֶּם עַל־צַד תִּנָּשֵׂאוּ וְעַל־בִּרְכַּיִם תְּשָׁעֳשָׁעוּ: 13 כְּאִישׁ

אֲשֶׁר אִמּוֹ תְּנַחֲמֶנּוּ כֵּן אָנֹכִי אֲנַחֶמְכֶם וּבִירוּשָׁלַ͏ִם תְּנֻחָמוּ:

14 וּרְאִיתֶם וְשָׂשׂ לִבְּכֶם וְעַצְמוֹתֵיכֶם כַּדֶּשֶׁא תִפְרַחְנָה וְנוֹדְעָה יַד־

יְהֹוָה אֶת־עֲבָדָיו וְזָעַם אֶת־אֹיְבָיו: [ס] 15 כִּי־הִנֵּה יְהֹוָה

בָּאֵשׁ יָבוֹא וְכַסּוּפָה מַרְכְּבֹתָיו לְהָשִׁיב בְּחֵמָה אַפּוֹ וְגַעֲרָתוֹ

בְּלַהֲבֵי־אֵשׁ: 16 כִּי בָאֵשׁ יְהֹוָה נִשְׁפָּט

וּבְחַרְבּוֹ אֶת־כָּל־בָּשָׂר וְרַבּוּ חַלְלֵי יְהֹוָה:

17 הַמִּתְקַדְּשִׁים וְהַמִּטַּהֲרִים אֶל־הַגַּנּוֹת אַחַר אַחַת (כתיב: אוֹד) בַּתָּוֶךְ

אֹכְלֵי בְּשַׂר הַחֲזִיר וְהַשֶּׁקֶץ וְהָעַכְבָּר יַחְדָּו יָסֻפוּ נְאֻם־יְהֹוָה:

18 וְאָנֹכִי מַעֲשֵׂיהֶם וּמַחְשְׁבֹתֵיהֶם בָּאָה לְקַבֵּץ אֶת־כָּל־הַגּוֹיִם

וְהַלְּשֹׁנוֹת וּבָאוּ וְרָאוּ אֶת־כְּבוֹדִי: 19 וְשַׂמְתִּי בָהֶם אוֹת וְשִׁלַּחְתִּי

מֵהֶם פְּלֵיטִים אֶל־הַגּוֹיִם תַּרְשִׁישׁ פּוּל וְלוּד מֹשְׁכֵי קֶשֶׁת תֻּבַל

וְיָוָן הָאִיִּים הָרְחֹקִים אֲשֶׁר לֹא־שָׁמְעוּ אֶת־שִׁמְעִי וְלֹא־

רָאוּ אֶת־כְּבוֹדִי וְהִגִּידוּ אֶת־כְּבוֹדִי בַּגּוֹיִם: 20 וְהֵבִיאוּ אֶת־כָּל־

אֲחֵיכֶם מִכָּל־הַגּוֹיִם מִנְחָה לַיהֹוָה בַּסּוּסִים

וּבָרֶכֶב וּבַצַּבִּים וּבַפְּרָדִים וּבַכִּרְכָּרוֹת עַל הַר

קָדְשִׁי יְרוּשָׁלַ͏ִם אָמַר יְהֹוָה כַּאֲשֶׁר יָבִיאוּ בְנֵי יִשְׂרָאֵל

אֶת־הַמִּנְחָה בִּכְלִי טָהוֹר בֵּית יְהֹוָה:

21 וְגַם־מֵהֶם אֶקַּח לַכֹּהֲנִים לַלְוִיִּם אָמַר יְהֹוָה:

²¹ And I will select some of them also to be priests and Levites," says the Lord.

²² "As the New Heavens and the New Earth that I make will endure before Me," declares the Lord, "so will your name and descendants endure.

²³ From one New Moon to another and from one Sabbath to another, all mankind will come and bow down before Me," says the Lord.

²⁴ "And they will go out and look upon the dead bodies of those who rebelled against Me; their worm will not die, nor will their fire be quenched, and they will be loathsome to all mankind."

22 כִּי כַאֲשֶׁר הַשָּׁמַיִם י"פ טל, י"פ כחו הַחֲדָשִׁים וְהָאָרֶץ אלהים דאלפין הַחֲדָשָׁה
אֲשֶׁר אֲנִי אני עֹשֶׂה עֹמְדִים לְפָנַי נְאֻם־יְהֹוָהאדני־יאהדונהי כֵּן יַעֲמֹד זַרְעֲכֶם
וְשִׁמְכֶם: 23 וְהָיָה מִדֵּי־חֹדֶשׁ י"ב הוויות בְּחָדְשׁוֹ י"ב הוויות וּמִדֵּי שַׁבָּת בְּשַׁבַּתּוֹ
יָבוֹא כָל יל' ־בָּשָׂר לְהִשְׁתַּחֲוֺת לְפָנַי אָמַר יְהֹוָהאדני־יאהדונהי: 24 וְיָצְאוּ וְרָאוּ
בְּפִגְרֵי הָאֲנָשִׁים הַפֹּשְׁעִים בִּי כִּי תוֹלַעְתָּם לֹא תָמוּת וְאִשָּׁם לֹא
תִכְבֶּה וְהָיוּ דֵרָאוֹן לְכָל יה ∽ אדני ־בָּשָׂר: וְהָיָה מִדֵּי־חֹדֶשׁ י"ב הוויות בְּחָדְשׁוֹ
י"ב הוויות וּמִדֵּי שַׁבָּת בְּשַׁבַּתּוֹ יָבוֹא כָל יל' ־בָּשָׂר לְהִשְׁתַּחֲוֺת לְפָנַי אָמַר
יְהֹוָהאדני־יאהדונהי:

In loving memory of my mother Janet; my father Frank; and my sister Denise.

May the Light of the Creator bring peace, prosperity and enlightenment to the entire world.

May the Light of God bless us all with loving soul mates and families.

Paula Porcaro